Linguistic Anthropology

Blackwell Anthologies in Social and Cultural Anthropology

Series Editor: Parker Shipton, Boston University

Drawing from some of the most significant scholarly work of the 19th and 20th centuries, the *Blackwell Anthologies in Social and Cultural Anthropology* series offers a comprehensive and unique perspective on the ever-changing field of anthropology. It represents both a collection of classic readers and an exciting challenge to the norms that have shaped this discipline over the past century.

Each edited volume is devoted to a traditional subdiscipline of the field such as the anthropology of religion, linguistic anthropology, or medical anthropology; and provides a foundation in the canonical readings of the selected area. Aware that such subdisciplinary definitions are still widely recognized and useful – but increasingly problematic – these volumes are crafted to include a rare and invaluable perspective on social and cultural anthropology at the onset of the 21st century. Each text provides a selection of classic readings together with contemporary works that underscore the artificiality of subdisciplinary definitions and point students, researchers, and general readers in the new directions in which anthropology is moving.

1   *Linguistic Anthropology*: *A Reader*
    edited by Alessandro Duranti

In preparation

Anthropology of Religion
edited by Michael Lambek

Political Anthropology
edited by Joan Vincent

Historical Anthropology
edited by Nicholas Dirks

The Anthropology of Development: Classical Political Economy to Contemporary Globalization
edited by Marc Edelman and Angelique Haugerud

Linguistic Anthropology

A Reader

Edited by

Alessandro Duranti

BLACKWELL
Publishers

Copyright © Blackwell Publishers Ltd 2001

First published 2001

2 4 6 8 10 9 7 5 3 1

Blackwell Publishers Inc.
350 Main Street
Malden, Massachusetts 02148
USA

Blackwell Publishers Ltd
108 Cowley Road
Oxford OX4 1JF
UK

Library of Congress Cataloging-in-Publication Data is available for this book.

ISBN 0-631-22110-7 (hardback); 0-631-22111-5 (paperback)

British Library Cataloguing in Publication Data
A CIP catalogue record for this book is available from the British Library.

Typeset in 10 on 12pt Sabon
by Kolam Information Services Pvt. Ltd, Pondicherry, India

Printed in Great Britain by MPG Books Ltd, Bodmin, Cornwall

This book is printed on acid-free paper.

Contents

Acknowledgments

Special thanks to my editor at Blackwell, Jane Huber, for her vision, wit, and endless enthusiasm and to Tracy Rone for being such a great research assistant. I am also grateful to Parker Shipton, who first approached me with the idea of doing a Reader for Blackwell, and to Richard Bauman, Jane Hill, Judith Irvine, Elinor Ochs, and Bambi Schieffelin for their advice. Responsibility for the final selection is, of course, solely mine.

For permission to publish copyright material in this book grateful acknowledgment is made to the following:

Gumperz, J. J. (1968). The Speech Community. *International Encyclopedia of the Social Sciences* (pp. 381–6). New York: Macmillan. Reprinted by Permission of The Gale Group.

Hymes, D. (1972). On Communicative Competence. In J. B. Pride and J. Holmes (eds.), *Sociolinguistics* (pp. 269–93). Harmondsworth: Penguin.

Morgan, M. (1994). The African-American Speech Community: Reality and Sociolinguists. In M. Morgan (ed.), *Language and the Social Construction of Identity in Creole Situations* (pp. 121–48). Los Angeles: The Center for Afro-American Studies, UCLA. Reprinted by permission of the author.

Spitulnik, D. (1996). The Social Circulation of Media Discourse and the Mediation of Communities. *Journal of Linguistic Anthropology*, 6(2), 161–87. © 1997 American Anthropological Association.

Bailey, B. (1997). Communication of Respect in Interethnic Service Encounters. *Language in Society*, 26(3), 327–56. © Cambridge University Press. Reprinted with permission of Cambridge University Press.

Mitchell-Kernan, C. (1972). Signifying and Marking: Two Afro-American Speech Acts. In J. J. Gumperz and D. Hymes (eds.), *Directions in Sociolinguistics: The Ethnography of*

Communication (pp. 161–79). New York: Holt, Rinehart & Winston. Used with permission of the author.

Bauman, R. (1975). Verbal Art as Performance. *American Anthropologist*, 77, 290–311. Published by American Anthropological Association.

Irvine, J. T. (1979). Formality and Informality in Communicative Events. *American Anthropologist*, 81(4), 773–90. Published by American Anthropological Association.

Duranti, A. (1997). Universal and Culture-Specific Properties of Greetings. *Journal of Linguistic Anthropology*, 7(1), 63–97. © 1997 American Anthropological Association.

Goodwin, M. H., and Goodwin, C. (2000). Emotion within Situated Activity. In N. Budwig, I. C. Uzgiris, and J. V. Wertsch (eds.), *Communication: An Arena of Development* (pp. 33–53). Published by Greenwood Publishing Group Inc.

Ochs, E., and Schieffelin, B. B. (1984). Language Acquisition and Socialization: Three Developmental Stories and Their Implications. In R. A. Shweder and R. A. LeVine (eds.), *Culture Theory: Essays on Mind, Self, and Emotion* (pp. 276–320). Cambridge: Cambridge University Press. Reprinted with permission of Cambridge University Press.

Philips, S. U. (1970). Participant Structures and Communicative Competence: Warm Springs Children in Community and Classroom. In J. E. Alatis (ed.) *Bilingualism and Language Contact: Anthropological, Linguistic, Psychological, and Social Aspects – Acquisition of Rules for Appropriate Speech Usage*. Washington D.C.: Georgetown University Press. Reprinted with permission of Georgetown University Press.

Heath, S. B. (1982). What No Bedtime Story Means: Narrative Skills at Home and School. *Language in Society*, 11(1), 49–76. Published by Cambridge University Press. Reprinted with permission of Cambridge University Press.

Baquedano-López, P. (1997). Creating Social Identities Through *Doctrina* Narratives. *Issues in Applied Linguistics*, 8(1), 27–45. © Regents of the University of California. Reprinted with permission of Issues in Applied Linguistics.

Whorf, B. L. (1956). The Relation of Habitual Thought and Behavior to Language. In J. B. Carroll (ed.), *Language, Thought, and Reality: Selected Writings of Benjamin Lee Whorf* (pp. 134–59). Cambridge, MA: MIT Press.

Silverstein, M. (1981). *The Limits of Awareness. Sociolinguistic Working Paper No. 84.* Austin: Southwest Educational Development Laboratory.

Kroskrity, P. V. (1998). Arizona Tewa Kiva Speech as a Manifestation of a Dominant Language Ideology. In B. B. Schieffelin, K. Woolard, and P. V. Kroskrity (eds.), *Language Ideologies: Practice and Theory* (pp. 103–22). New York: Oxford University Press. Copyright © 1998 by Oxford University Press Inc. Used with permission of Oxford University Press Inc.

Gal, S. (1991). Language, Gender, and Power: An Anthropological Review. In M. di Leonardo (ed.) *Gender at the Crossroads of Knowledge: Feminist Anthropology in the Postmodern Era* (pp. 175–203). Reprinted with permission of University of California Press.

Ochs, E., and Taylor, C. (1995). The "Father Knows Best" Dynamic in Dinnertime Narratives. In K. Hall and M. Bucholtz (eds.), *Gender Articulated: Language and the Socially Constructed Self* (pp. 97–120). New York: Routledge. Reprinted by permission of Routledge Inc., a Taylor & Francis Company, New York.

Hill, J. H. (1998). Language, Race, and White Public Space. *American Anthropologist*, 100(3), 680–9. Copyright © 1999 American Anthropological Association.

Every effort has been made to trace copyright holders, but in some cases this has proved impossible. The publishers would be happy to hear from any copyright holder that has not been acknowledged.

Linguistic Anthropology: History, Ideas, and Issues

Alessandro Duranti

1 Introduction[1]

We are born with the ability to learn languages. However, the contexts in which we learn them, the manner in which we use them, and the extent to which they help or hinder us in achieving our goals is culturally mediated. If we want to understand the role of languages in people's lives, we must go beyond the study of their grammar and venture into the world of social action, where words are embedded in and constitutive of specific cultural activities such as telling a story, asking for a favor, greeting, showing respect, praying, giving directions, reading, insulting, praising, arguing in court, making a toast, or explaining a political agenda.

Linguistic anthropology is one of many disciplines dedicated to the study of the role of languages (and the language faculty) in these and the many other activities that make up the social life of individuals and communities. To pursue such an agenda, researchers have had to master the intricate logic of linguistic systems – e.g. their grammars – and document the activities in which those systems are used and reproduced through routine and yet highly creative acts. The articles collected in this Reader are a representative sample of the best scholarship in this tradition. They should give readers a clear sense of what it means to study language in a way that often starts from utterances but always looks for the cultural fabric within which such utterances are shaped and meanings are produced.

When Dell Hymes put together what could be easily recognized as the first comprehensive Reader in linguistic anthropology (Hymes 1964d), he included writings whose authors would not have defined themselves as linguistic anthropologists (e.g. Marcel Mauss, Antoine Meillet, Claude Lévi-Strauss, Roger Brown, Leonard Bloomfield). Such an editorial decision was not just a declaration of interdisciplinarity; it was also the reconstitution of a field (or subfield) relying on any solid piece of work that could give a sense of (i) the importance of language(s) for an understanding of culture and society and (ii) the relevance of cultural and social phenomena for an understanding of language(s). Looking for articles to include in this Reader, I found myself in a very different situation. Since Hymes' 1964 collection there has been such a wealth of research and writing in linguistic anthropology that, although I would have liked to include articles by authors from other fields whose work has been influential to our discipline – the linguist Roman Jakobson and the sociologist Erving Goffman are the first two names that come to mind – it became very difficult to include such authors without excluding an even greater number that have recently helped to define linguistic anthropology as a discipline with its own unique vision of language structures and language practices. What is this unique vision? In what follows I will try to provide a brief overview of the field beginning with a discussion of two names that are often used as synonyms for linguistic anthropology, namely, anthropological linguistics and sociolinguistics. I will suggest that the difference between the names "linguistic anthropology" and "anthropological linguistics" has to do with different histories, professional identities, and theoretical interests. In the case of linguistic anthropology vs. sociolinguistics, I will argue that, although in the 1960s and 1970s they were thought of as one field, they have moved further apart since that time. Despite continuous cross-fertilization and sharing of topics (especially "gender and language"), sociolinguistics and linguistic anthropology constitute at the moment two related but separate research enterprises. The rest of this introductory chapter provides a brief overview of the history of linguistic anthropology in the United States (section 3); a discussion of linguistic relativity (section 4), which was until the 1960s the major theoretical issue in the discipline; a discussion of the four areas of research represented in this Reader (sections 5, 6, 7, and 8); and some final comments that connect the past with the foreseeable future (section 9).

2   What's in a Name? Linguistic Anthropology, Anthropological Linguistics, and Sociolinguistics

In contemporary academic and scientific discourse, the name "linguistic anthropology" coexists with a number of other names that are often understood to be synonyms for the same intellectual enterprise. The two most common variants are "anthropological linguistics" and "sociolinguistics"[2] (with "ethnolinguistics" being a distant third within the United States[3]). Although it could be argued that this semantic ambiguity has helped construct a loosely tied community of scholars – many of whom might have been intellectually isolated within the boundaries of larger disciplines such as linguistics and anthropology – there are some differences that have emerged over the years. An understanding of such differences will help us further define the discipline represented by the articles included in this Reader.

2.1   *Anthropological linguistics and linguistic anthropology*

There is linguistics, there is linguistics in anthropology, and there is linguistic anthropology, but if we wish our terms to have unambiguous and pertinent reference, there is no anthropological linguistics.

(Teeter 1964:878)

Whether or not there is in fact a field called "anthropological linguistics," there is no question that the term often functions as a synonym for linguistic anthropology, both within and outside the United States. This is, for example, the way it is used in William Bright's series *Oxford Studies in Anthropological Linguistics*, which includes books that cover classic topics in the study of language and culture such as sound symbolism (Nuckolls 1996) and new theoretical perspectives such as language ideologies (Schieffelin, Woolard, & Kroskrity 1998). From the point of view of its scope, the series could have been called "Oxford Studies in Linguistic Anthropology." The same could be said about William Foley's *Anthropological Linguistics: An Introduction*, which has chapters on many of the topics and approaches represented in this Reader. Foley's (1997:3) definition of anthropological linguistics ("that sub-field of linguistics which is concerned with the place of language in its wider social and cultural context, its role in forging and sustaining cultural practices and social structures") is close to the one given in this introduction (see above) and even closer to the one given in my *Linguistic Anthropology*,[4] with one exception. Foley sees the field he is describing as a subfield of linguistics, whereas I see it as a subfield of anthropology. This difference can be explained at least in part by the different intellectual climates in which we work – Foley teaches in a linguistics department in Australia and I teach in an anthropology department in the United States. Australian linguistics was strongly influenced in the 1970s and 1980s by (mostly British) scholars who were committed to a view of language as a social tool (e.g. Halliday 1973, 1978) and to fieldwork among Australian Aborigines with the goal of producing comprehensive and sophisticated reference grammars (e.g. Dixon 1972, 1977). This intellectual heritage has meant that linguistics in Australia has been less directly affected than linguistics in the USA by the so-called "Chomskian revolution," whose followers since the 1960s have pursued and encouraged "autonomous" models of grammar and discouraged the study of cultural or sociological dimensions of language (Chomsky 1965, 1986, 1995; Newmeyer 1980, 1986).

The linguists in Australia who are still concerned with the documentation and preservation of Australian aboriginal languages live in an academic climate that is, at least in some respects, similar to the one found in the USA (and Canada) at the end of the nineteenth century and the beginning of the twentieth century, when the documentation of American Indian languages and cultures was the intellectual project through which anthropology – with material support from a very interested party, the US government – became a profession (Darnell 1998a; Stocking 1974; Voegelin 1952) (see section 3).[5] It was in that intellectual climate that Alfred Kroeber and Edward Sapir matured and, through them, that an entire new generation of scholars was formed, including Harry Hoijer, Carl Voegelin, Benjamin Lee Whorf, Mary Haas, and Morris Swadesh. These researchers – like Bright and Foley today – thought of themselves primarily as linguists and thus it is not surprising to know that in the 1950s several of them chose the name "anthropological linguistics" for their work (Haas 1953, 1977; Hoijer 1961; Voegelin & Harris 1952).[6] Their main concerns were (i) the documentation of grammatical structures of American Indian languages and other indigenous languages without writing,[7] (ii) language as the medium through which myths and historical narratives could take form,[8] and (iii) the use of language as a window on culture (understood as worldview or

Weltanschauung). These goals were pursued by studying nomenclatures and taxonomies (of animals, plants, types of disease, kinship terms, color terms) – an area
that eventually developed into ethnoscience (e.g. Conklin 1962; Frake 1969; Goodenough 1956, 1965; Lounsbury 1969) – genetic relations among languages (e.g.
through the comparative method), the impact of culture on language (e.g. euphemisms, taboo words, sacred or respectful terms) or of language on culture, in various
versions of linguistic relativity (see section 4). Overall, from the point of view of
teaching, linguists working within anthropology departments in the first half of the
twentieth century saw themselves as in charge of training graduate students from
other subfields (cultural anthropology in particular) to use linguistic data for their
research. It was this goal that justified what Voegelin and Harris called "technical
linguistics":

> The importance of relating anthropological training to technical linguistics is that the latter
> brings to the former a few necessary but not too difficult techniques for exploring culture.
> Cultural studies without linguistic consideration tend to be narrowly sociological rather than
> broadly anthropological. On the other hand, ethnolinguistic studies essayed by anthropolo-
> gists innocent of technical linguistic training tend to be amateurish. (Voegelin & Harris
> 1952:326)

It was only in the 1960s that this view was revised and the subfield moved from a
position of "service" to the rest of anthropology to one of independence. Two
projects that instigated this new professional identity were Charles Ferguson and
John Gumperz's (1960) investigation of dialect variation and language contact in
South Asia[9] (see section 2.2) and Dell Hymes' call for an "ethnography of speaking"
(Hymes 1962), soon renamed "ethnography of communication" (Hymes 1964c).[10]
It was in those years that Hymes proposed to use the name "linguistic anthropology"
– which had been first introduced in the late 1870s (see section 3) but not quite
adopted by the practitioners – to designate a distinctly anthropological approach to
the study of language:

> Put in terms of history and practice, the thesis is that there is a distinctive field, linguistic
> anthropology, conditioned, like other subfields of linguistics and anthropology, by certain
> bodies of data, national background, leading figures, and favorite problems. In one sense, it
> is a characteristic activity, the activity of those whose questions about language are shaped by
> anthropology. Its scope is not defined by logic or nature, but by the range of active anthro-
> pological interest in linguistic phenomena. Its scope may include problems that fall outside
> the active concern of linguistics, and *always it uniquely includes the problem of integration
> with the rest of anthropology*. In sum, linguistic anthropology can be defined as *the study of
> language within the context of anthropology*. (Hymes 1964a:xxiii) (emphasis in the original)

This programmatic statement had at least two concerns: (i) to keep the study of
language as a central part of the discipline of anthropology (instead of letting it "slip
away" to the numerous linguistics departments that were being established in the
1960s); and (ii) to broaden the concept of language beyond the narrow interest in
grammatical structures. However, despite the birth of sociolinguistics in the 1960s
(see section 2.2) and discourse analysis in the 1970s (Brown & Yule 1983; Givón
1979; Schiffrin 1994; Stubbs 1983), the situation has not changed much since
Hymes' statement. In the USA and elsewhere, many anthropologists still take lan-

guage for granted, as if it were a transparent medium for culture, relegating it to the role of what Tedlock (1983) called "a postcard from the field," and mainstream linguistics continues to be fundamentally concerned with grammars rather than with speakers, with *forms in isolation* rather than *forms in relation* to the context of their use. Of course, as Hymes himself noted, "[o]n general intellectual principle, of course, nothing linguistic is alien to anthropology" (Hymes 1964a:xxiii). For one thing, the description of previously undocumented languages is still relevant to the anthropological enterprise because, as Franz Boas and Bronislaw Malinowski reminded us, it is impossible to understand a community without an understanding of the language(s) used by its members.[11] It is also true that linguistic reconstruction, for example through the comparative method, can be a useful tool for archaeology and historical anthropology (e.g. Kirch 1984; McConvell & Evans 1997). It is only in this broad sense of linguistics as always relevant to the general anthropological enterprise (because language *is* culture) that we can make sense of the title of Joseph Greenberg's (1968) *Anthropological Linguistics: An Introduction.*[12] The book introduces the study of phonology, morphology, language change, and potential synchronic and diachronic universals. But linguistic anthropology as practiced today and represented in this Reader is more than grammatical description and historical reconstruction, and it is also more than collection of texts, regardless of whether those texts were collected in one's office or under a tent. It is the understanding of the crucial role played by language (and other semiotic resources) in the constitution of society and its cultural representations. To pursue this goal, linguistic anthropologists have ventured into the study of everyday encounters, language socialization, ritual and political events, scientific discourse, verbal art, language contact and language shift, literacy events, and media. To the extent to which anthropology can offer the intellectual and institutional support for such a broad research program, it makes sense to use, as Hymes proposed, the name "linguistic anthropology" for such an enterprise. A great part of the research discussed by Foley (1997) was in fact done by scholars who see themselves as working within an anthropological paradigm rather than within a linguistic one and for this reason tend to call themselves linguistic anthropologists.[13] On the other hand, should linguistics revise its theoretical and analytical horizon to include in the center a notion of language that is more than grammar and an interest in speakers as more than producers of linguistic forms, scholars like Bright and Foley might see their dream of a truly *anthropological* linguistics realized.

2.2 Sociolinguistics and linguistic anthropology

Sociolinguistics was born in the early 1960s as the study of linguistic forms in relation to the social context of their use. Both the types of phenomena studied and the methods used for their study varied, depending on the researchers involved. For example, Charles Ferguson and John Gumperz (1960) were interested in understanding language contact through qualitative methods involving work with informants, informal observations, and (sometimes) questionnaires (e.g. Blom & Gumperz 1972). Starting a few years later, William Labov was interested in providing an empirical basis for the study of language change that could start from actual language use in urban communities. He pursued this goal by developing a method for the study of speech in social context based on statistical analysis of a large corpus of data extracted from recorded interviews.[14] In collaboration with Joshua Waletzky, Labov also developed an analysis of the syntax and structural organization of elicited narratives (Labov & Waletzky 1966) that became very influential in a number of fields (see the contributions in Bamberg 1997).

The different methodological orientation and theoretical goals produced distinct schools of research on language use, but the term "sociolinguistics" has survived, with various qualifiers doing the work of acknowledging some differences among approaches. Thus, Labov-style sociolinguistics has been known as "quantitative," "macro," or "urban," whereas Gumperz-style sociolinguistics has been called "qualitative," "micro," or "interactional."[15] In part due to the collaboration between Gumperz and Hymes in the 1960s (while Hymes was at the University of California at Berkeley[16]), the term "sociolinguistics" was used to cover a wide range of approaches, including some distinctively anthropological and sociological perspectives. For example, such collections as Bright's (1966) *Sociolinguistics: Proceedings of the UCLA Sociolinguistics Conference, 1964* and Gumperz and Hymes' (1972) *Directions in Sociolinguistics: The Ethnography of Communication* include quantitatively oriented studies of language variation and language change in urban settings (e.g. Labov 1966a, 1972b), correlational studies between language forms and speakers' social status (e.g. Ervin-Tripp 1972a, 1972b; Friedrich 1966), specific guidelines for the ethnographic descriptions of language use within a community (e.g. Hymes 1966, 1972a), componential analysis (e.g. Tyler 1972), ethnoscience (e.g. Frake 1972), ethnomethodology (e.g. Garfinkel 1972), and conversation analysis (Schegloff 1972). Until the 1970s, ethnographic studies of language were considered part of sociolinguistics, as implied in Dell Hymes' *Foundations in Sociolinguistics: An Ethnographic Approach* (1974a).[17] Since then, however, the situation has changed considerably.

Despite Hymes' renewed attempt, especially through his long tenure as the founding editor of the journal *Language in Society*, to keep sociolinguistics and linguistic anthropology under the same umbrella, or at least not to draw any sharp boundaries, since the mid-1980s there has been an increasing separation between the two subdisciplines. Except for the occasional chapter on "Language and Culture" or on "The Ethnography of Communication,"[18] textbooks and edited books in sociolinguistics tend to focus almost exclusively on either quantitatively oriented studies of mostly urban speech communities or studies of patterns of language use and language change that are attentive to sociological variables (especially social status and gender) and pragmatic dimensions (e.g. politeness), but are not informed by anthropological theory or methods (e.g. ethnography). In parallel sign of incipient separatism, recently published textbooks in linguistic anthropology and anthropological linguistics dedicate very little or no space at all to sociolinguistic theories and methods (e.g. Duranti 1997b; Foley 1997; Hanks 1996; Palmer 1996; Salzmann 1993).

The roots of this separation are both methodological and theoretical. Most sociolinguists – especially quantitatively oriented ones – continue to use today the same methodology introduced by Labov in the 1960s, that is, they typically rely on statistical analysis of data collected through interviews. There is no question that through these methods sociolinguists have produced an impressive body of work which can tell us a great deal about the internal dynamics of speech communities and the relevance of social class, sex, and age for a number of linguistic phenomena, most typically (and most effectively) dialect variation and sound change in progress. At the same time, these methods and some of the theoretical implications of socio-linguistic research are problematic for many linguistic anthropologists. First, the treatment of sociological concepts such as social class, sex, gender, race, and gen-eration as independent variables is not universally accepted in the social sciences, anthropology in particular. From the 1980s there has been a considerable amount of writing devoted to the cultural construction of these sociological categories (Gal 1992, 1995). This literature is ignored by most quantitative sociolinguists. Second, the definition of context as a constantly changing frame that needs reference to speech itself as one of its constitutive elements (e.g. Duranti & Goodwin 1992) is usually absent from quantitative sociolinguistic studies. Third, the exclusive reliance on the interview as the only reliable method for recording spontaneous speech is viewed with suspicion by most linguistic anthropologists, who see speaking as an interactional achievement. Over thirty years of research on conversational exchanges[19] and on the speech patterns that ensue from those exchanges have taught us that speakers are constantly engaged in the business of fashioning their speech for their interlocutors and that stories rarely have only one author in conversation.[20] The texts collected by sociolinguists tend to be (or be presented as) monologic. Questions and feedback channel responses by fieldworkers are often left out of transcripts together with other features of the interaction (e.g. pauses, false starts) that do not seem relevant to the study of phonological features (e.g. deletion of final consonant). And yet, some of these features are considered important by linguistic anthropologists and other researchers who believe in the co-construction of narrat-ive accounts and the importance of the mutual monitoring that goes on in any encounter.

On the other hand, it would be naïve not to recognize that, in turn, many studies within linguistic anthropology do not match the kind of scientific standards aimed at by sociolinguists, not simply because of linguistic anthropologists' tendency toward qualitative as opposed to quantitative analysis – with the common strategy of discussing only a few examples and then generalizing from them – but because many of the studies within linguistic anthropology, as most of those within its closest sibling, cultural anthropology, are based on data that are not easily accessible for counter-arguments or independent testing. This lack of accessibility is due to a number of factors, including (i) the anthropological tradition of working in isolated small communities or in communities that require considerable time and financial investment for anyone else to go and collect additional data, and (ii) the lack of shared corpora, in part due to ethical considerations (see Duranti 1997b:119–21) and in part to the unwillingness of researchers to expose their data to the scrutiny of others without the proper contextualization, which would be very difficult to provide without knowing how the data might be used by others. If one rejects the idea that talk alone (whether in a recording or in a transcript) constitutes "the data," the entire idea of sharing "a corpus" becomes problematic.

These methodological, analytical, and theoretical differences are reinforced by the institutional separation due to the tendency for sociolinguists to work in depart-ments of linguistics or foreign language and for linguistic anthropologists to work in

departments of anthropology. The result is a separation that is by no means beneficial to either one of the two fields, especially for training new scholars. Linguistic
anthropologists could certainly benefit from the systematic attention to broad
patterns of variation in linguistic forms and social networks that characterizes
contemporary sociolinguistic research. Sociolinguists, in turn, could take more
advantage of ethnographic methods and the theoretical concerns regarding the
cultural construction of social categories of participants (e.g. ethnicity, race, gender).
One domain of inquiry where there has been some exchange between sociolinguists
and linguistic anthropologists is the study of gender differences (see section 8).
Although it is difficult to say whether this convergence will provide a model to be
emulated in other research areas, it does show that a concentration on issues (e.g. is
men's and women's language different and if so why? how is gender made to count
in an interaction?) can draw together researchers who are usually kept apart by
methodological and epistemological differences.[21]

3   The Birth of Linguistic Anthropology in the United States

If one were asked to name the one work which has been of greatest importance and influence
in the development of American anthropology, it could scarcely be any other than Powell's
"Indian Linguistic Families of America North of Mexico," published in the Seventh Annual
Report of the Bureau of Ethnology fourteen years ago.

(Kroeber 1905:579)

The inclusion of linguistic anthropology as an integral part of mainstream anthropology – the "four field approach"[22] – is a phenomenon that is unique to the USA –
as opposed to European countries like Great Britain for example[23] – and must be
understood within the context of the research program under which anthropology
became a profession in the USA, namely, the documentation of North American
aboriginal cultures. In this (largely government-sponsored) project, the study of
American Indian languages played a major role. Under the auspices first of the
Smithsonian Institution (founded in 1846) and later of the Bureau of Ethnology
(founded in 1879 and later renamed Bureau of American Ethnology [BAE]), the
documentation of aboriginal languages spoken north of Mexico became an important part of the work pursued by anthropologists in private and public institutions.
   The person who more than anyone else helped organize, direct, and find funds for
the survey of American Indian languages in North America in the second part of the
nineteenth century was the founder of the BAE, John Wesley Powell (1834–1902). A
natural scientist who retrained as a geologist and saw an obvious connection
between the study of the land and the cultural tradition of its inhabitants (Darnell
1998a:25), Powell believed that languages could be an excellent instrument for
classifying cultures and he employed linguists and other scholars to collect as
much material as possible on American Indian languages (e.g. word lists, myths,
descriptions of ritual life). On the basis of this material, those employed by the BAE
worked on linguistic classifications and tried to organize the surveyed languages in
families (Powell 1880). It is then not surprising that what is perhaps the oldest use of
the term "linguistic anthropology" is found in the 1st Annual Report of the Bureau

for 1879–1880 (published in 1881), in a section prepared by Otis T. Mason (1838–1908), a curator of artifacts at the Bureau who also became fascinated by linguistic classifications (Darnell 1998a:38–9; Mason 1900). With the establishment of the American Anthropological Association (see note 25), there began a period of intense interest in linguistic matters in American anthropology, as shown by the numerous articles that provide grammatical descriptions, classifications, texts, and notes on nomenclatures (almost exclusively on American Indian languages[24]) in the first issues of the official organ of the Association, the *American Anthropologist*.[25] For example, in Volume 2 (1900), we find John R. Swanton's "Morphology of the Chinook Verb," Albert S. Gatschet's "Grammatical Sketch of the Catawba Language," and Franz Boas' "Sketch of the Kwakiutl Language." By Volume 7 (1905), the articles on linguistic topics and issues had risen to ten.

Despite the importance of Powell and the BAE, however, it is Franz Boas who is credited with transforming what was originally an almost exclusive interest in classification of American Indian languages (largely based on word lists) into a systematic study of their grammatical structures. Boas, who taught himself linguistic analysis, set the standards that were to be followed by subsequent generations of scholars through his own grammatical descriptions and his editorial work on the *Handbook of American Indian Languages* published in 1911 (Jakobson 1944; Stocking 1974; Voegelin 1952).[26] His "Introduction" to that volume was a major departure from the perspective on non-Indo-European languages that was popular at the time.

Boas argued that there was no necessary correlation between a given language and a given race or between a given language and a given culture. This claim constituted an implicit rejection of Powell's goal of using Native American languages for ethnic classification (Boas was also skeptical of genetic classification of considerable time depth and more inclined toward acculturation as an explanation for linguistic and cultural change[27]). At the same time, Boas, certainly influenced by eighteenth- and nineteenth-century German philosophical tradition, agreed with Powell that language plays a crucial role in culture and should be studied by ethnologists: "If ethnology is understood as the science dealing with the mental phenomena of the life of the peoples of the world, human language, one of the most important manifestations of mental life, would seem to belong naturally to the field of work of ethnology..." (Boas 1911:63). This perspective had methodological implications, one of the most important of which was that ethnographic fieldwork should be done using the native language of the people one wanted to study instead of speaking through an interpreter or using a lingua franca (e.g. a pidgin). Since he saw the categories formed in or through language as unconscious, Boas believed that languages provided excellent material for the study of cultural phenomena (Hymes 1964b:7–9; Stocking 1974).[28]

In addition to being interested in language as a window on the human mind, Boas was also committed to a theoretical understanding of grammatical systems, their differences and similarities. He identified the sentence (as opposed to the word) as the fundamental unit for expressing ideas in any language[29] and listed a number of grammatical categories that are likely to be found in all languages. His criticism of some common prejudices about American Indian languages (and implicitly of other languages of the people who were then called "primitive") helped to establish scientific standards for linguistic investigation. He stressed the importance of making orthographic conventions and analytical categories appropriate for the languages under investigation instead of uncritically extending categories originally developed for the study of ancient European languages. Boas argued against the then commonly held idea that speakers of American Indian languages are less accurate in their pronunciation than speakers of Indo-European languages. Repeating an argument first made in his 1889 article "On Alternating Sounds," Boas argued that this is a false perception due to the difficulty that linguistically unsophisticated listeners had in making the phonetic distinctions that are relevant in these languages. While stressing that different languages may classify the world differently, Boas also cautioned against interpreting the lack of certain linguistic forms as evidence of the lack of abstract thought or ability to generalize (Boas 1911; Lévi-Strauss 1966).

Thus the Indian will not speak of goodness as such, although he may very well speak of the goodness of a person...It is, however, perfectly conceivable that an Indian trained in philosophic thought would proceed to free the underlying nominal forms from the possessive elements, and thus reach abstract forms strictly corresponding to the abstract forms of our modern languages. (Boas 1911:65)

Thus, while continuing to use the term "primitive languages," as in vogue at the time,[30] Boas in fact showed that such languages were by no means primitive.[31]

Unlike Powell (1880), Boas did not see the different types of morphological patterns (e.g. word formation) in the world languages along an evolutionary scale, especially not one that ended with English at the top. Instead, in his investigation of grammatical structure, vocabulary, and poetry in American Indian languages, Boas found support for an underlying unity of the human mind (Boas 1911, 1925; Hymes 1999:87; Lucy 1992a:11–17).

This general stance toward aboriginal languages was restated by his students. For example, Edward Sapir started his 1933 entry "Language" for the *Encyclopedia of the Social Sciences* with a statement that echoes the Boasian view of human languages:

The gift of speech and a well ordered language are characteristic of every known group of human beings. No tribe has ever been found which is without language, and all statements to the contrary may be dismissed as mere folklore. There seems to be no warrant whatever for the statement which is sometimes made that there are certain people whose vocabulary is so limited that they cannot get on without the supplementary use of gesture so that intelligible communication between members of such a group becomes impossible in the dark. The truth of the matter is that language is an essentially perfect means of expression and communication among every known people. Of all aspects of culture, it is a fair guess that language was the first to receive a highly developed form and that its essential perfection is a prerequisite to the development of culture as a whole. (Sapir [1933] 1949a:7)

The obvious implication is that language is the most sophisticated cultural system available to human societies and to their members, and, therefore, there can be no anthropology without the study of language.

4 Linguistic Relativity

The first major theoretical issue that occupied linguistic anthropologists was linguistic relativity. The interest in this issue was born out of a marriage between an idea and an encounter. The idea is the nineteenth-century Romantic association between a language and the "spirit" (German *Geist*) of a nation or the language and the worldview (*Weltanschauung*) of its speakers. The encounter was with the languages of the indigenous peoples of the Americas and the other continents (re)discovered or conquered by Europeans. The subsequent attempt by missionaries, travelers, and linguists to describe those languages (Salmon 1986) highlighted the difficulty in translating and in adapting grammatical categories originally developed for Indo-European languages (Cardona 1976; Haas 1977). Boas' cultural relativism was extended to (or perhaps inspired by) his linguistic relativism:

As is well known, Boas's most important theoretical contribution to the study of linguistics was his promulgation of the concept of linguistic relativism, that is, that each language had to be studied in and for itself. It was not to be forced into a mold that was more appropriate to some other language. Side by side with this was his insistence on seeing the language as a whole. (Haas 1978b:195)

The efforts to find analytical categories that could adequately describe the grammatical structures of non-Indo-European languages resulted in the realization that languages have quite different ways of encoding information about the world and our experience of it. One possible inference from these observations on linguistic diversity was that languages are arbitrary systems and one cannot predict how they will classify the world (linguistic relativism). Another inference was that languages would develop distinctions and categories that are needed to deal with the reality surrounding the people who speak them (linguistic functionalism). A third inference was that the different conceptual systems represented in different languages would direct their speakers to pay attention to different aspects of reality, hence, language could condition thinking (linguistic relativity). An earlier version of this last view is found in the posthumous *Linguistic Variability and Intellectual Development* by the German diplomat and linguist Wilhelm von Humboldt (1767–1835):

Each tongue draws a circle about the people to whom it belongs, and it is possible to leave this circle only by simultaneously entering that of another people. Learning a foreign language ought hence to be the conquest of a new standpoint in the previously prevailing cosmic attitude of the individual. In fact, it is so to a certain extent, inasmuch as every language contains the entire fabric of concepts and the conceptual approach of a portion of humanity. But this achievement is not complete, because one always carries over into a foreign tongue to a greater or lesser degree one's own cosmic viewpoint – indeed one's personal linguistic pattern. (von Humboldt [1836]1971:39–40)

As shown in this passage, von Humboldt's view was that the conceptual world represented in each language is *sui generis* and as such incommensurable with the worlds represented in other languages. This makes the perfect acquisition of a foreign language impossible unless speakers are willing and able to leave behind the ways of thinking acquired through their first language (competent multilingual speakers – of which there are millions in the world – would then be people who can successfully switch from one worldview to another). About a hundred years later, Edward Sapir expressed a very similar view:[32]

Language is not merely a more or less systematic inventory of the various items of experience which seem relevant to the individual, as is so often naïvely assumed, but is also a self-contained, creative symbolic organization, which not only refers to experience largely acquired without its help but actually defines experience for us by reason of its formal completeness and because of our unconscious projection of its implicit expectations into the field of experience. [. . .] Such categories as number, gender, case, tense, mode, voice, "aspect" and a host of others, many of which are not recognized systematically in our Indo-European languages, are, of course, derivative of experience at last analysis, but, once abstracted from experience, they are systematically elaborated in language and are not so much discovered in experience as imposed upon it because of the tyrannical hold that linguistic form has upon our orientation in the world. (Sapir [1931]1964:128)

Sapir's ideas had a profound impact on Benjamin Lee Whorf (1897–1941), a chemical engineer who worked as an insurance inspector while pursuing a number of intellectual quests, including linguistics (see Carroll 1956; Lucy 1992a:24). After Sapir moved to Yale from Chicago in the Fall of 1931, Whorf attended Sapir's courses and became part of the cohort of Sapir's students (Carroll 1956; Darnell 1990). Soon after, he started to study Hopi, the language through which he was able to best articulate his views on the relation between linguistic patterns and thinking (Whorf 1938, 1941, 1956a). The frequent use of the term "Sapir–Whorf Hypothesis," as a synonym for linguistic relativity comes from the intellectual association between Sapir's and Whorf's ideas on the role of linguistic patterns on thinking and acting in the world (see Koerner 1992 for a review of the literature generated by this "hypothesis"). The term "Sapir–Whorf Hypothesis," however, is misleading.[33] The two scholars never worked out a joint statement about the relation between language and thought, and a close analysis of their writings shows some important differences, including the different conceptual level reached by the two scholars (Lucy 1992a). Furthermore, for some time Whorf's name was more closely associated with that of Dorothy Lee than with that of Sapir (e.g. Lee 1944).[34]

The "tyrannical hold" of linguistic forms, as expressed in the passage quoted above, was perhaps for Sapir a way of articulating a number of insights he had developed on the relation between language, culture, and personality. Two of them in particular are recurrent in his writing and his teaching (as reconstructed by Judith Irvine in Sapir 1994). One was the realization of what he saw as a fundamental paradox of human life, namely, the need that each individual has to use a shared and predefined (we could say "public") code in expressing what are subjectively different experiences. The other was the arbitrary (i.e. non-natural) character of linguistic structures, which makes them the most advanced type of cultural forms – a basic theme of Sapir's 1927 article "The Unconscious Patterning of Behavior in Society." The two insights inform the idea expressed in his lectures that language "is one of the most patterned, one of the most culturalized, of habits, yet that one, above all others, which is supposed capable of articulating our inmost feelings" (Sapir 1994:55).

The comparative study of typologically different languages (e.g. English and Chinese) shows that the specific properties of linguistic systems cannot be explained functionally given that what is obligatory in one language (e.g. the distinction between singular and plural nouns) may be optional in another. In order to make sense of the way in which each language has its own (arbitrary) logic, Sapir compared the logic of grammars to the logic of artistic codes: "Every language is itself a collective art of expression. There is concealed in it a particular set of esthetic factors – phonetic, rhythmic, symbolic, morphological – which it does not completely share with any other language" (Sapir 1921:225). For Sapir, then, just as we cannot easily give functional explanations of aesthetic forms and aesthetic taste, we cannot easily give a functional explanation (e.g. in terms of communicative needs) for why languages behave the way they do.[35] Linguistic rules are usually unconscious but with an internal coherence (Lucy 1992a:23). It is this coherence that makes it difficult for individual speakers to enter the logic of the linguistic system and alter it to their liking. Sapir ([1927] 1949a) illustrates this point with the marking of plural in English. There seem to be no functional reasons for the use of plural with nouns that are accompanied by numerals. Hence, why do English speakers need to say *five men* instead of **five man*? For Sapir, it is a question of aesthetic taste (or, as he says in the following quote, "feeling"): "English, like all of the other Indo-European languages, has developed a feeling for the classification of all expressions which have a nominal form into singulars and plurals" (Sapir 1949b:550). On the other hand, in languages like Chinese, where nouns are not marked for number, if there is a need for being specific, numerals (e.g. words for "five," "ten") and quantifiers (e.g. "all," "several") can be added.

Cross-linguistic comparison then reveals the arbitrary nature of the grammatical distinction between singular and plural and its taken-for-granted necessity in the minds of those speakers of languages that do have such an obligatory feature. Sapir, however, never developed a conceptual apparatus for testing the implications of these observations.

Whorf started out sharing several of the basic positions held by Sapir on the nature of linguistic classification, but he went on to develop his own conceptual apparatus and his own version of linguistic relativity. This apparatus included the important distinction between *overt* and *covert* grammatical categories (Whorf 1956b; Duranti 1997b:58–9; Lucy 1992a:26–31). Overt categories are marked in the morphology of the word or in accompanying words. For example, in Spanish, gender is an overt category because it is usually given by the ending of the noun (e.g. *-o* vs. *-a*) or by a number of accompanying elements, e.g. the article (*el* vs. *la*). In English, instead, gender tends to be a covert category that is made explicit only under particular circumstances. When someone says, "I met a neighbor at the store," we don't have a way of inferring the gender of the neighbor. But if a personal pronoun is used next, we will know, without asking, whether the friend in question is a man or a woman ("I met a neighbor at the store. **She** was buying French wine"). The distinction between overt and covert was a precursor of Chomsky's (1965) distinction between "surface" and "deep" structure[36] and it carried an important implication for cultural analysis because it underscored that conceptual distinctions are made in languages even when no overt signs of them can be recognized. What is overt, explicit in one language may not be in another. The analyst's task is to uncover the hidden cultural logic of the linguistic system and ascertain whether this logic has implications for thinking or acting in the world.

The statement that comes the closest to being a hypothesis about the relationship between language and thought is Whorf's "linguistic relativity principle," according to which "... users of markedly different grammars are pointed by their grammars toward different types of observations and different evaluations of extremely similar acts of observation, and hence are not equivalent as observers but must arrive at somewhat different views of the world" (Whorf 1956b:221). The same essay in which this principle is stated contains the much quoted – and later criticized – comparison of the conceptualization of time in Hopi and SAE (Standard Average European) and the English example of the wrong inference produced by the use of the word *empty* in describing drums that had previously contained gasoline. Whorf explains that the lack of contents described by *empty* is interpreted by English speakers as implying that the drum is no longer dangerous, whereas in effect it is more dangerous than when full because it contains explosive vapor (see Lucy 1992a: 50 for a clear diagram that illustrates the inference process).

Whorf's "linguistic relativity principle" generated a considerable amount of research mostly by linguistic anthropologists and psycholinguists from the 1940s to the 1960s (see Lucy 1992a). In the 1960s, in conjunction with the rise of cognitive science and other research paradigms aimed at linguistic and cognitive universals, Whorf's claims underwent a period of harsh criticism, which culminated on the one hand with Brent Berlin and Paul Kay's (1969) claim that there are cross-linguistic universals in the elaboration of color coding across a large number of languages[37] and on the other with the reanalysis of Hopi tense and aspect and the correction of some of Whorf's original claims, including the one that Hopi does not have a future tense (Malotki 1983; P. Lee 1991, 1996). During the same period, there arose a misguided view of linguistic relativity, which continues into the present, as pertaining to differences among languages in number of words for the "same" concept. Thus, the (questionable) claim that Eskimo dialects have more words for *snow* than English dialects (see Martin 1986 for a criticism of this claim) was believed to be evidence of different thinking patterns between Eskimo and English speakers. Rather than talking about "habitual thought" being directly influenced by lexical choices or grammatical patterns, Whorf was focusing on how a way of thinking may arise *by analogy* with "fashions of speaking" (a term later echoed by Hymes' [1974b] "ways of speaking").

Among the new efforts to test, reframe, and extend Whorf's original intuitions, John Lucy's (1992b) comparison of the performance of speakers of Yucatec and speakers of English in a series of cognitive tasks has been so far the most successful within an experimental paradigm. Starting from the observation that English marks plural overtly and obligatorily on a wide range of noun phrases, whereas Yucatec usually does not mark plural and when it does, it is optional, Lucy hypothesizes that English speakers should habitually attend to the number of various objects more than Yucatec speakers do, and for more types of referents. The results of his experiments support his hypothesis. Another hypothesis was built on the use and distribution of classifiers (these are nouns or particles that many languages employ to encode information on the type of category represented by a given noun). Yucatec nouns that take a plural marker need to be accompanied by a classifier. Thus, whereas in English one can say *three men* (numeral + noun), in Yucatec, one must say "numeral (*óos*) + human classifier (*túul*) + man (*máak*)." This constraint is similar to the one for so-called mass nouns in English (e.g. *sugar, cotton, zinc*), which also need classifiers to be modified by a numeral. One cannot say *two cottons, but must say *two balls of cotton* (Lucy 1992b:73). From these observations Lucy inferred that many English lexical items presuppose a unit as part of their meaning and for this reason no classifier is needed, whereas Yucatec lexical items do not presuppose a unit. The unit presupposed by English lexical nouns referring to inanimate objects tends to be the form or shape of the object (Lucy 1992b:89). Yucatec nouns, instead, have no such presupposed unit and their meaning implies types of substance or material composition. For example, in Yucatec the same word *che'* "wood" is used to form words referring to objects like trees, sticks, and boards, which are of different shapes but are made out of wood substance. This is a different lexical strategy from the one adopted in English, where objects of the same substance (wood) but different shapes are referred to with different lexical items, e.g. *tree, stick, board, table, shelf*.[38] From these considerations, Lucy (1992b:89) hypothesized that "*English speakers should attend relatively more to the shape of objects* and *Yucatec speakers should attend relatively more to the material composition of objects* in other cognitive activities" (emphasis in the original). This hypothesis was tested with a series of tasks involving recognition and recollection of pictures where the number of items (people, animals, tools) and various substances (corn, firewood, rock) varied. The results demonstrated that indeed English speakers and Yucatec speakers differ in how they categorize and recall different types of referents. For example, English speakers tend to group objects in terms of common shape whereas Yucatec speakers tend to group them in terms of common substance (e.g. wood, water). "These patterns suggest that the underlying lexical structures associated with the number marking in the two languages have an influence on the nonverbal interpretation of objects" (Lucy 1992b:157).[39]

4.1 Extensions of linguistic relativity

Over the years, the original conceptualization of linguistic relativity has often been reformulated or extended to new research questions. For example, Hymes (1966) expanded the notion of linguistic relativity to include not only the ways in which linguistic structure may influence our experience of the world but also the ways in which cultural patterns, for example, specific cultural activities, can influence language use and determine the functions of language in social life. This second type of linguistic relativity draws attention to the uses of language and the cultural values associated with such uses. Communities can be shown to differ in the ways in which they use and value names, silence, or the telling of traditional stories and myths.

Another line of research that expands on the notion of linguistic relativity is represented by Michael Silverstein's notion of **metapragmatic awareness**, that is, the ability that speakers have to talk about the pragmatics of their language use. This concept draws from and extends the discussion of the unconscious nature of linguistic knowledge found in the writings of Boas, Sapir, and Whorf. Silverstein formulated a hypothesis about three specific features of language structure, which, depending on their value, can either favor or hinder native speakers' ability to interpret the pragmatic force of specific linguistic forms (Silverstein 1981) [this volume] – hence, they are indicators of metapragmatic awareness. The three features are: (i) unavoidable referentiality (i.e. whether the linguistic expression unambiguously identifies one and only one referent); (ii) continuous segmentability (i.e. whether the pragmatic meaning is expressed by a discrete and continuous linguistic segment, e.g. a word, a single suffix, an entire phrase), and (iii) relative presupposing vs. creative quality (e.g. the extent to which the linguistic expression in question presupposes the existence of a given relation, status, act or instead helps constitute that relation, status, act by being used).[40]

In addition to being used to talk about the limits of native speakers' intuitions on the force of their utterances, the same categories can also provide the foundations for a cultural critique of the ways in which certain language philosophers described and classified the social acts performed by speech. In his article "Cultural Prerequisites to Grammatical Analysis," Silverstein (1977) argues that even philosophers are not immune to the limits of metapragmatic awareness and have tended to focus on those effects of language that can be explicitly represented by linguistic expressions. For example, the "things done by language" – or speech acts – identified by the philosopher J. L. Austin (1962, 1975) are the acts that can be described by (referential) expressions such as *I promise that, I declare that, I order you to . . .* etc. In other words, Silverstein argues that "promising" is recognized as a possible speech act because it is lexicalized (through the word *promise*) and can be articulated in a sentence that involves the speaker as the agent of the act and an embedded clause. But there are plenty of social acts done through language that cannot be easily named by such referential expressions and therefore may not be as easily accessible to native speakers' consciousness. These phenomena have consequences for social scientists' ability to use members' intuitions in their research, and therefore they should be taken into consideration by social and cultural anthropologists who rely on the natives' intuitions in their interpretations of interactions or texts (see also B. Lee 1997; Silverstein, this volume, p. 400; Silverstein & Urban 1996).

Another extension of this work is found in the burgeoning field of **language ideologies**, which investigates the impact of speakers' beliefs about their language (and other languages) on language structure and language use (Kroskrity 2000b; Schieffelin, Woolard, & Kroskrity 1998; Woolard & Schieffelin 1994). In this perspective, speakers' search for an ideal common language (e.g. "the Standard") that can unite a nation or any other aggregate is viewed as a phenomenon quite similar to the working hypothesis of those linguists who want to limit their study of language to an ideal homogeneous speech community, ignoring the variation found at all levels of language use (see section 5).

In most of the earlier studies on linguistic relativity – at least up to the 1960s – language was fundamentally taken as a taxonomic system whereby speakers classify the experiential world (the objects and people around us, our actions and emotions) into distinct (and arbitrary) units. In testing whether language "guides" speakers' understanding of the world, researchers assumed that linguistic expressions (i) can be easily identified and isolated from the stream of behaviors within which they are routinely embedded in social action, and (ii) constitute an autonomous system that can be studied on its own, without regard for the other semiotic resources that typically coexist with them, and contribute to their meaning. A different approach is pursued by those researchers who have recently stressed the importance of looking at how speaking is part of a broader array of activities. These include at a micro-interactional level the semiotic exploitation of the human body, e.g. through gestures (Haviland 1996; Levinson 1996, 1997), and of the material artifacts with which humans surround themselves (C. Goodwin 1996a, 1997).

5 Communicative Competence and the Speech Community

While Hymes (1962, 1964c) was launching his call for an ethnographic study of language use across speech communities, a new theoretical paradigm was being established in linguistics: generative grammar. This was primarily due to the writing of Zellig Harris' student Noam Chomsky, who, after attacking behaviorist conceptions of language (Chomsky 1959) and American structuralism (Chomsky, Halle, & Lukoff 1956),[41] went on to propose a mentalistic model of grammar, to be understood as "concerned with discovering a mental reality underlying actual behavior" (Chomsky 1965:4). This mentalistic perspective was foremost expressed by Chomsky's distinction between **competence** (knowledge of language) and **performance** (use of language) and his research strategy to focus exclusively on the study of competence, conceived of as an idealized system:

Linguistic theory is concerned primarily with an ideal speaker-listener, in a completely homogeneous speech-community, who knows its language perfectly and is unaffected by such grammatically irrelevant conditions as memory limitations, distractions, shifts of attention and interest, and errors (random or characteristic) in applying his knowledge of the language in actual performance. This seems to me to have been the position of the founders of modern general linguistics, and no cogent reason for modifying it has been offered. (Chomsky 1965:3–4)

Furthermore, for Chomsky, the focus on competence meant that the study of performance had to be postponed, until a full description of competence could be available.[42]

After praising Chomsky's approach for shifting the conceptualization of language from an independent object to a human capacity, Hymes argued that the distinction between competence and performance presented a number of problems: "The term 'competence' promises more than it in fact contains. Restricted to the purely grammatical, it leaves other aspects of speakers' tacit knowledge and ability in confusion, thrown together under a largely unexamined concept of 'performance'" (Hymes 1971a:55). Starting from a commonsense notion of competence, Hymes held that speakers are "competent" not only when they have the knowledge of grammatical rules but also when they have the knowledge of how to use them appropriately. Furthermore, language acquisition could not be restricted to the process of acquiring knowledge of grammatical rules given that in acquiring a language, "a child becomes able to accomplish a repertoire of speech acts, to take part in speech events, and to evaluate their accomplishment by others" (Hymes 1972b:277) [this volume]. To be a member of a particular community, one must know when to speak and when not to speak, how to be polite, how to request or offer collaboration, how to sound calm, surprised, interested, concerned, and so forth. Finally, not all members of the speech community have access to the same knowledge or to the same repertoire (Gumperz 1964). Not everyone knows how to deliver a lecture or how to understand a clinician's diagnosis. Rather than focus on the innate aspects of linguistic compet- ence – the phylogenetic correlate of the observed human universal capacity for language acquisition – Hymes shifted the focus to the diversity that is apparent when we study how language is used in social life. Instead of ignoring differences for the sake of creating a homogeneity that can be more easily accessed through a scientific method, Hymes assumed that an anthropological program for the study of language must start from the assumption of heterogeneity (Duranti 1997b:chap- ter 3). He defined "an ethnography of speaking" as "a theory of speech as a system of cultural behaviour; a system not necessarily exotic, but necessarily concerned with the organization of diversity" (Hymes 1971b:51).

By proposing an alternative research paradigm, Hymes replaced Chomsky's notion of competence as tacit (typically unconscious) knowledge of grammatical rules with the notion of **communicative competence**, which includes both tacit knowledge and ability to use language (Hymes 1972b:282). This new notion of competence is analytically tied to new units of analysis. Instead of sentences, researchers are required to look at acts, situations, events (Hymes 1972a). This change for Hymes "entails social description (ethnography)" (Hymes 1971b:52). In philosophy and cognitive science, it is perfectly acceptable to talk about acts (Searle 1965, 1969) or situations (Barwise & Perry 1983) without having to engage in the systematic observation and documentation of actual behavior (ethnography). In contrast, for Hymes the study of language as social action commits the researcher to ethnography. This commitment locates the notion of communicative competence within the field of anthropology at large. The revision of the notion of competence also implies a new way of thinking about performance, first of all giving it a positive rather than a negative definition (anything left after competence) and, second, tying it to aesthetic dimensions of speaking (see section 6).

In his criticism of Chomsky's "ideal speaker-hearer" and of the assumption of homogeneity as a necessary precondition for linguistic analysis, Hymes was by no means alone. Starting in the 1960s, sociolinguists like Labov demonstrated again and again that even within monolingual communities, there is a considerable amount of linguistic variation and that such variation correlates with social strati- fication (Labov 1966a, 1966b, 1972b, 1972c). The notion of "ideal speaker" is then questionable on empirical and theoretical grounds (Labov 1972c). While Labov stressed the importance of thinking of a large metropolitan area like New York City as a single speech community – based on speakers' shared norms for evaluating variation – Gumperz was motivated by his own work on multilingualism to look for analytical concepts that could help him make sense of the ability that speakers have to shift from one language, dialect, or style to another and the variation found in the access speakers have to various linguistic resources. The notion of **repertoire** (Gum- perz 1964) was meant to account for the range of varieties speakers had access to, and the notion of **linguistic community** (Gumperz [1962] 1968b), later renamed **speech community** (Gumperz 1968a [this volume]), was meant to account for the boundaries of what should be studied as a unit.[43] People routinely switch within a predictable range of linguistic **varieties**, a general term that covers language, dialect, style, and register:[44]

A variety is any body of human speech patterns which is sufficiently homogeneous to be analyzed by available techniques of synchronic description and which has a sufficiently large repertory of elements and their arrangements or processes with broad enough semantic scope to function in all normal contexts of communication. (Ferguson & Gumperz 1960:3)

At the same time, variation is not simply determined by the situation and there are limits to what the analyst can predict (Blom & Gumperz 1972). A series of studies addressed the issue of language choice in multilingual communities. In looking at which language was spoken by whom to whom and when, researchers were trying to come up with hypotheses about language choice that could give us hints about the causes of language change (Romaine 1995; Sankoff 1980). Gal's study of declining bilingualism in a small Austrian town connects the abandonment of Hungarian and the resulting German monolingualism of young women to their rejection of peasant life and values and their embracing of an industrial economy (Gal 1978, 1979).

Within the United States, the study of language variation and of the differences between standard and non-standard dialects carried out by urban sociolinguists gave educators the tools to avoid racial stereotypes based on prejudice and ignorance of linguistic matters. The work of Labov on the logic of Non-Standard English was particularly influential in helping define Black English Vernacular (BEV) as a dialect of English with its own distinct phonological and syntactic rules (some of which are in fact similar to other non-standard dialects of English) (Labov 1969, 1972a). The attitudes toward BEV (or AAVE, that is, African American Vernacular English) by members of the black community were then left unanalyzed. Marcyliena Morgan's discussion of the views expressed within the African American speech community was at the same time an attempt to encourage sociolinguists to face the consequences of their own scientific efforts and an occasion to look at the language ideology of African Americans, tying it to the history of race relations within the United States (Morgan 1994a [this volume], 1994b; Rickford 1997, 1999).

The attention paid to different types of variation within multilingual communities eventually led Gumperz to concentrate on the mechanisms through which speakers signal to each other how to interpret what they are saying (e.g. what the hearer should pay attention to, how the speaker feels about something). He referred to these mechanisms as **contextualization cues**. They are linguistic features that can operate at different levels of the linguistic system involving intonation, rhythm, lexical selection, organization of information in an utterance or in a stretch of discourse, or language or dialect selection (Gumperz 1977, 1982a, 1992). When contextualization cues are missed or misread, communication is in trouble. Since the early 1980s, miscommunication based on different ways of communicating has been known among linguistic anthropologists as **crosstalk**, a term originally invented by T. C. Jupp and used as a title for a well-known BBC program centered around Gumperz's work on miscommunication between British speakers and South Asian immigrants (Jupp, Roberts, & Cook-Gumperz 1982). Gumperz's work has been extended to a number of areas, including miscommunication between genders (Maltz & Borker 1982; Tannen 1990).

Despite the fact that scholars like John Gumperz had been working on language contact since the late 1950s, it was not until the 1980s that linguistic anthropologists became intellectually engaged with the issue of heterogeneity. This shift was partly due to the difficulty in ignoring the linguistic effects of new and massive immigration and the globalization of economic markets. At the same time, there were new intellectual sources that allowed a reconceptualization of "language"; among them the writings of Mikhael Bakhtin were particularly influential (Bakhtin 1981, 1984, 1986; Vološinov 1973). In his analysis of the novel, Bakhtin (1981:261) argued that investigators are confronted with a variety of coexisting styles, which represent different "voices" (the author's, the characters'). It is through these voices that language as a fundamentally stratified and differentiated code, what he called **heteroglossia** (Russian *raznorecie*), can enter the novel – as well as everyday talk (Lucy 1993). In this perspective the notion of a unitary language is not just a working hypothesis, as proposed by Chomsky, but an ideological stance. Rather than homogeneity, we find differentiation, which on the one side creates . . . inequality among speakers and on the other it allows for subtle aesthetic effects (through the juxtaposition of multiple voices and coexisting varieties). This work inspired a number of linguistic anthropologists including Jane and Kenneth Hill (1986), whose notion of **syncretic language** to describe language use and language ideology among Mexicano (Nahuatl) speakers is informed by some of Bakhtin's writings. Along similar lines, Duranti and Ochs (1997) coined the term **syncretic literacy** for activities that are informed by teaching and learning strategies that draw from different cultural traditions. The main idea behind this notion is the belief that when different cultural systems meet, it is rarely the case that one simply replaces the other. As pointed out by Hanks (1986, 1987) for the Maya, as soon as contact takes place, any pre-existing indigenous tradition is bound to be affected by the new tradition proposed (or imposed) by the newcomers.

Until recently, linguistic anthropologists thought of communities as entities constituted by daily face-to-face interaction. This is in part due to the fact that most anthropologists worked in small rural communities. Even those who worked in the city tended to concentrate on a relatively small territory, such as a neighborhood or a block. Some even worked with isolated individuals or families who did not know each other. These fieldworkers often acted as if their subjects were isolated from the rest of the world, that is, as if there were no connection or communication with parties who were not physically present or as if such parties were not important or relevant. The situation has started to change in recent years, as some researchers have become interested in the role played by media and new technologies in the daily life of speakers all over the world and the impact of media on everyday communication. For example, Debra Spitulnik (1998a, 1998b, 1999) has analyzed the role of the audience in recontextualizing the messages produced by national and local radio in Zambia, providing a rich documentation of linguistic transfer and transformation from media discourse to popular (and everyday) discourse. Equally important has been the work on the use (and abuse) of new technologies for guiding interpretation of reality through what Charles Goodwin (1994) calls "professional vision" (see section 8).

6   A Focus on Performance

The reframing of the notion of competence came with a rethinking of the notion of performance. Chomsky's view of performance was guided by two assumptions. The first was that to speak of performance meant to speak of perception and production. The second was that the scientific method requires us to ignore performance because it is subject to "memory limitations, distractions, shifts of attention and interest, and errors (random or characteristic)" (Chomsky 1965:3). Hymes revised and extended Chomsky's notion of performance to include something more than the behavioral record of what speakers do when they talk. For Hymes, as for folklorists and aesthetic anthropologists, performance is a realm of social action, which emerges out of interaction with other speakers, and as such it cannot be described in terms of individual knowledge (Hymes 1972b:283 [this volume]). Rather than thinking about performance as a residual category – that is, whatever is left after having defined what constitutes competence – Hymes (1981:81–2) underscored the positive and creative nature of performance (see also Duranti 1997b:14–17). Instead of reducing our ability to generalize about language, the view of speakers as performers allows us to broaden the analytical horizon of language use in a number of ways.

First, it recognizes a different notion of creativity from the one emphasized by Chomsky's notion of grammar, which must be able to produce a potentially infinite set of sentences on the basis of a finite set of rules. The creativity of performance refers to the ability (and sometimes necessity) to adapt speech to the situation or the situation to speech, as well as the ability to extend, manipulate, and reframe meanings in ways that are related to or identical to what we call poetic language. Metaphors abound in all kinds of speech situations – much of what we say cannot be taken to be "literal" – and both child and adult conversation is full of parallelism and other poetic devices.[45] If it is true, as argued by Friedrich (1986), that there is a poet in each of us, one of the goals of any serious study of language use implies not only the identification of the special features that go into great verbal art and performance but also the discovery of the creative aspects of language in everyday talk. Contrary to popular belief, even scientists are not immune to the creative power of linguistic metaphors and other poetic devices; in fact they routinely rely on them in their problem-solving activities. In their study of a physics laboratory in the USA, Ochs, Gonzales, and Jacoby (1996) found that physicists discussing experiments involving changes in temperature that bring about changes of "states" (e.g. from "paramagnetic" to "domain") attribute human qualities to physical entities, for example, producing utterances like "this system has no knowledge of that system." At other times the physicists' language suggests a blend of different identities: the researchers use personal pronouns (*I, you*) with predicates that refer to change of states undergone by particles: "When I come down I'm in the domain state." In this construction, the speaker (the physicist) appears to assume the identity of a physical entity, producing a semantically ungrammatical sentence. And yet, it is through the use of such supposedly impossible sentences that scientists are able to think creatively.

Second, the view of speakers as performers also recognizes individuals' unique contribution to any given situation and to the evolution of any linguistic tradition. This has been difficult to do within formal linguistics because the emphasis (from Saussure to Chomsky) has been on the linguistic system – often described in terms of context-independent rules – rather than on what specific speakers do with language in specific situations. Both the structuralist linguistics of the first half of the twentieth century and the rationalist (mostly synchronic) paradigm of formal linguistics, which started in the 1960s, favored linguistic forms over their users because of the fear that a focus on individual performance detracts from the ability to generalize. This has allowed researchers to improve their descriptions of the formal properties of languages but has revealed very little about individual differences and the role of individuals in linguistic change. As pointed out by Barbara Johnstone (1996:19), "[t]hinking about language from the perspective of the individual requires a pragmatics that deals centrally with newness and idiosyncrasy rather than a pragmatics in which conventionality is the focus."

Third, the focus on performance singles out those situations in which speakers are accountable not only for *what* they say but also, and sometimes predominantly, for *the way* in which they say it (Bauman 1975 [this volume], 1977; Hymes 1975, 1981). This perspective unites a concern with the aesthetic dimensions of speaking with their social and political implications.[46] The identification of a good leader with a good orator is common enough around the world to suggest that evaluation of the way in which a message is delivered enters into and informs political judgment. Furthermore, the speaker's commitment to an audience is only one side of a complex relationship that must be understood as crucial for the shaping of messages and meanings (Duranti 1993; Hill & Irvine 1993; Streeck 1980, 1994).

Fourth, the focus on performance recognizes the role of the audience in the construction of messages and their meanings (Duranti & Brenneis 1986; Graham 1995) and the complexity underlying the apparent simplicity of the distinction between speaker and hearer (Goffman 1981; Hymes 1972a). This is a point that has been at the center of a number of recent and not-so-recent enterprises, including hermeneutics (e.g. Gadamer 1976), Bakhtin's dialogism (see above), Goffman's strategic interactionism (Goffman 1959, 1963, 1971), and conversation analysis (Goodwin & Heritage 1990). The challenge for contemporary researchers is to provide sound empirical results that can test, inform, and refine abstract theoretical positions. Despite the recurrent emphasis on dialogue and intertextuality, relatively few researchers have actually looked at spontaneous verbal interaction in everyday life, where most of the "text" of our social life is constructed. For example, Marjorie H. Goodwin's (1990b) study of teenage boys' and girls' talk in a Philadelphia neighborhood in the early 1970s remains unsurpassed for empirical rigor, depth of documentation, and ability to provide us with solid generalizations about narrative structure and argumentation in natural settings.

The role of the audience is but one of the aspects of context that linguistic anthropologists have been eager to capture (Goodwin & Duranti 1992). As demonstrated by the work of Gumperz, Labov, and others, at any given time, speakers may have at their disposal not just one or more codes (for example, English as opposed to English and Korean) but a vast range of registers, genres, routines, activities, expressions, accents, prosodic and paralinguistic features (e.g. volume, tempo, rhythm, voice quality). The choices available to speakers are a repertoire acquired through life experiences and subject to change through the life cycle, and partly due to one's social network (L. Milroy 1987; Milroy & Milroy 1992), including the effects of schooling, profession, and a person's special interests. The concern for the role of the audience and for the construction of messages across speakers, turns, and channels makes us question the view of speaking as merely the expression of an individual's intentions (Du Bois 1993; Duranti 1988, 1993; Moerman 1988; Rosen 1995). If we take a socio-historical approach, we must agree with Bakhtin (1981:294) that "[l]anguage is not a neutral medium that passes freely and easily into the private property of the speaker's intentions; it is populated – overpopulated – with the intentions of others. Expropriating it, forcing it to submit to one's own intentions and accents, is a difficult and complicated process." Furthermore, our original intentions must be constantly updated by the effect we produce on our interlocutors, the knowledge we have of their background knowledge (C. Goodwin 1979, 1981; Heritage 1990/91), and their willingness or ability to go down the interpretive path we have sketched up thus far. For example, when an audience treats as humorous something that was meant to be serious, the speaker must confront a difficult choice: whether to reclaim his original interpretive key ("this is meant to be serious") or adapt ("this is meant to be funny"). A focus on performance makes us particularly aware of the relative control that we as speakers have on what Hymes (1972a) (borrowing the term from Birdwhistell) called the "key" of our messages. By moving into the realm of performance, we must face the fact that interpretation of what we say is always a joint production.

7   Language Acquisition and Language Socialization

Chomsky's hypothesis that the language faculty is innate and that the universal properties of languages can be studied and described in terms of grammatical rules (to be written using the formalism of generative grammar) inspired a new generation of psychologists to venture into the study of language acquisition. One way to test Chomsky's hypothesis about the innate quality of Universal Grammar (UG) was to go into great depth in the analysis of one language and find out what information is lacking in the linguistic input but necessary for a child to make generalizations and thus formulate rules for interpreting and producing speech. This was the strategy first followed by Chomsky himself, who, throughout the 1960s and 1970s, felt fully entitled to talk about language universals by working exclusively on English.[47] Another approach was to study the acquisition of as many languages as possible to see what common patterns (e.g. in the order of what is acquired, in the mistakes that children make, in their successes) they display. One of the first and most ambitious projects in this direction was the collaborative effort by psychologists, linguists, and anthropologists at the University of California at Berkeley in the mid- to late 1960s that produced *A Field Manual for Cross-Cultural Study of the Acquisition of Communicative Competence* (Slobin 1967).[48] Dan Slobin had studied at Harvard and MIT with a number of prominent linguists and psychologists, including Noam Chomsky, Roman Jakobson, Jerome Bruner, and Roger Brown. Soon after he was hired at Berkeley, he became part of a reading and discussion group that first included Susan Ervin-Tripp, John Gumperz, Erving Goffman, John Searle, and Dell Hymes, and by 1966 had also expanded to their graduate students. Prompted by Slobin's talk about language universals and his review of the existing literature on child language acquisition across languages, the group adopted Hymes' notion of communicative competence and mapped out an ambitious plan for the cross-cultural study of language acquisition. It was an attempt to merge experimental methods (from psychology) and ethnographic methods (from anthropology) and thus bring together Chomsky's cognitivism with the ethnographic approach promoted by Gumperz and Hymes.

Armed with the Field Manual, students took off for their field sites and came back after a year with lots of data and lots of questions. These early attempts at the cross-cultural study of language acquisition encountered a considerable number of problems, mostly due to the fact that it was difficult, if not impossible, to carry out the planned experiments in the field. Even the mere observation of adult–child interactions was at times highly problematic due to local expectations about how children should behave when a stranger enters the domestic space (Schieffelin 1979a:75; Ochs 1988:1–2). The discussion of these problems at Berkeley produced a new awareness of the issues involved in the extension of a paradigm developed to work with white middle-class families (where one caretaker, usually the mother, attends one or two children) to speech communities with a different social organization (sibling caregiving, extended family) and different beliefs about children and their relationship with adults. Taking into consideration these limitations, Slobin decided to reframe the enterprise in terms of cross-*linguistic* rather than cross-*cultural* comparison and organized a collaborative effort with colleagues in other countries to study language acquisition of English, Italian, Serbo-Croatian, and Turkish. Concentrating on linguistic dimensions that seemed to be fruitful for developmental psycholinguistic analysis, Slobin and his colleagues avoided the issue of the impact of culture on language acquisition by homogenizing the sample, that is, by working only with children of literate, professional, and urban parents (Slobin, personal communication).[49]

Two studies that more fully realized the goal of studying the acquisition of communicative competence in non-Western communities were done by Bambi B. Schieffelin and Elinor Ochs, who were aware of the work done in Berkeley but had received their training at different universities.[50] In both cases, the task was approached with a different and, in some respects, richer set of intellectual and human resources than those of the earlier fieldworkers who had tried to implement the model of the Field Manual.

Both Schieffelin and Ochs had previous fieldwork experience (in Papua New Guinea and in Madagascar respectively), had already collected child language data, and were not isolated from other researchers during their fieldwork. In 1975, Schieffelin returned to Mount Bosavi, Papua New Guinea, where she had been in 1967–8 with Edward L. Schieffelin (he was also with her in 1975–7 working on spirit mediums). In 1976, they were joined by ethnomusicologist Steven Feld who carried out a dissertation project on music and emotions (Feld 1982). As Schieffelin acknowledged in her dissertation (1979b) and in her 1990 book *The Give and Take of Everyday Life: Language Socialization of Kaluli Children*, the interaction with the other two anthropologists played an important role in her study of Kaluli culture. Equally important was the training she had previously received from Lois Bloom at Columbia University. By the time she went to Bosavi, Schieffelin knew how to carry out a longitudinal study and was familiar with the existing literature on child language acquisition.

Elinor Ochs had written a dissertation on oratory in Madagascar (Keenan 1974) and had been teaching in the linguistics department at the University of Southern California since 1974. Her earlier work based on the video recording of the interaction between her own twins encouraged her to venture into the study of child language.[51] In the summer of 1978, Ochs went to a (Western) Samoan village to carry out a longitudinal study of children's acquisition of Samoan. With her were two graduate students, Martha Platt and myself. Platt followed and documented the acquisition of three of the six children in the acquisition and socialization study (Platt 1982). I concentrated on adult grammar and language use across contexts (Duranti 1981, 1994).

Ochs and Schieffelin, who had met in 1974 and collaborated on a number of articles together, went to the field with very similar goals:

The goal of my research in Papua New Guinea was the description of the development of communicative competence in a small-scale, nonliterate society. . . . The first endeavor . . . was to determine and describe the significant, recurring situations and interactions in the everyday life of Kaluli children. I needed to know the pattern of their daily activities, how and by whom they were organized (or not organized), who was responsible for feeding them, settling disputes between them, and where, when, and how these children regularly interacted with adults and other children. Initially these questions were partially answered through extensive observations of children over entire days and by interviewing adults for their views on what was going on and why. Both my actual observations and what the Kaluli themselves said about things helped formulate the first ethnographic accounts of what Kaluli children do all day and with whom they do it. (Schieffelin 1979a:78)

In making sense out of what people are saying and in speaking in a sensible fashion themselves, children relate linguistic forms to social situations. Part of their acquired knowledge of a linguistic form is the set of relations that obtain between that form and social situations, just as part of their acquired knowledge of a social situation includes the linguistic forms that define or characterize it. (Ochs 1988:2)

As discussed earlier (see section 5), the acquisition of communicative competence was always meant to be a crucial area of study in the type of linguistic anthropology proposed by Gumperz and Hymes in the 1960s (see Sherzer & Darnell 1972). However, the two longitudinal studies by Ochs and Schieffelin were the first to fully integrate an interest in the acquisition of grammar and the acquisition of other cultural patterns. The publication of their joint article "Language Acquisition and Socialization: Three Developmental Stories and Their Implications" (Ochs & Schieffelin 1984 [this volume]) – written in 1981, during a period spent at the Research School of Pacific Studies at the Australian National University[52] – set up the basic theoretical framework for what then became the field of language socialization. Starting from a definition of language socialization as (i) the process of getting socialized *through* language and (ii) the process of getting socialized *to* language, Ochs and Schieffelin re-examined prior work on language acquisition as embedded in culturally specific expectations about the role of children and adults in society. For example, they used their discovery that neither the Kaluli nor the Samoans have a register corresponding to what linguists call **baby talk** (Ferguson 1964) and psycholinguists call **Motherese** (Newport 1976) not only to argue that (*pace* Ferguson 1978) baby talk is *not* universal,[53] but also that its presence or absence is tied to the presence or absence of other forms of accommodation to children and to local conceptualizations of children and their place in society.

Their work inspired others to look at the cultural implications of talk to children and by children in other societies. For example, Don Kulick adopted a language socialization perspective in his study of language shift in the village of Gapun in

Papua New Guinea, where children are growing up speaking Tok Pisin instead of their parents' first language, Taiap, the local vernacular. Kulick argued that macro-sociological factors such as migration, assimilation, and the formation of a nation-state are not sufficient to explain the abandonment of the vernacular by these children and that we need to look at the daily practices of language use to understand "the conceptions that people have about language, children, the self" (Kulick 1992:17; see also Ochs & Schieffelin 1995).

Ochs and Schieffelin assumed that socialization is a never-ending process that starts at birth (or even earlier) and continues throughout the life span. This perspective extends the notion of language socialization to language-mediated peer-interaction, apprenticeship and everyday cognition, literacy activities, language contact, and cross-cultural encounters.[54] Elizabeth Mertz's study of the ways in which Law School students are taught how to read a text and argue its potential interpretations is a good example of how institutions and professional organizations socialize adults into **entextualization** – the process of transforming experience into text – and **recontextualization** – the process of making texts relevant to the ongoing situation[55] (Mertz 1996).

8   The Power of Language

There are two main strategies for analyzing the relationship between language and culture. One is to start from linguistic forms (e.g. words or parts of words, intonational contours, syntactic constructions, conversational routines) and then try to discover what those forms accomplish in social interaction or, more generally, in the construction of everyday life. This strategy has often been used to discuss the expression of respect or politeness (Agha 1994; Brown & Levinson 1978, 1987). The other strategy is to start from a particular cultural construct (e.g. gender, power, race, ethnicity, disability, conflict, emotions) or social process (e.g. socialization, marginalization, conflict, healing, advertising, play, verbal performance) and then try to find out how specific linguistic forms participate in (or constitute) such constructs or processes.

Much of the work on linguistic relativity (see section 4) can be thought of as part of the first method. Linguistic forms, either because of their arbitrary nature (for Sapir) or because of their implicit worldview (for Whorf), arc seen as constraints on the ways in which individual speakers as members of speech communities perceive reality or are able to represent it. Silverstein's work on metalinguistic and metapragmatic awareness (see section 4.1) can be seen as an extension of this tradition in that it provides a framework for thinking about the power of specific linguistic forms to reveal or to hide (from speakers' consciousness) their indexical value, that is, their dependence or ability to impact upon reality.

Maurice Bloch's (1975a) "Introduction" to *Political Language and Oratory in Traditional Society* represents another trend within this tradition. Bloch argued that the very form of traditional political oratory, especially the routinized formulae used to express respect toward tradition and politeness toward leaders, provides a framework for the unconscious acceptance of authority and the status quo. For Bloch, formalized speech – as opposed to conversation – restricts the range of possible questions and possible answers and therefore limits freedom of expression and any real challenge of authority. Although the category of formalization he used was later criticized (Irvine 1979 [this volume]; Brenneis & Myers 1984), Bloch's ideas made it possible to rethink the power of language on human action and strengthen the ties between political anthropology and linguistic anthropology.[56]

The argument of the power of language over mind and society was also present in the discussion of the impact of the invention of literacy. Jack Goody and Ian Watt (1962) argued that alphabetic writing had a crucial role in the development of Western civilization. This role was accomplished by transforming oral messages into a permanent record and thus introducing the practice of "history" (as opposed to "myths" or "legends") and by helping the "change from mythical to logico-empirical modes of thought" (Goody & Watt [1962] 1968:43). A number of empirical studies were designed to test Goody and Watt's hypotheses about the impact of alphabetic writing on cognitive abilities and social change (Kingten, Kroll, & Rose 1988; Olson & Torrance 1991; Street & Besnier 1994). Eventually, most linguistic anthropologists have come to share Scribner and Cole's (1981) view that there are different types of literacy and that many of the earlier generalizations were conflating differences, including the difference between literacy as an isolated, autonomous activity and literacy as embedded in other activities and in institutions, for example, schools or state bureaucracies.[57] Goody's "autonomous model" of literacy was also criticized by Brian Street (1984) who proposed an "ideological model" of literacy, that is, a perspective that links writing practices to power structures in a society (e.g. establishment of authority, access to institutional resources, wealth). He also stressed the importance for ethnographic studies of literacy, based on "detailed, in-depth accounts of actual practice in different cultural settings" (Street 1993:1).

Within linguistic anthropology, the interest in literacy revived an earlier interest in schooling and classroom interaction (Cazden, John, & Hymes 1972) and Shirley Brice Heath's (1983) groundbreaking study of home literacy activities in three communities in the United States had a tremendous influence on future research. On the basis of extensive observation and documentation of the various ways in which children from different communities were engaged with written texts, Heath argued that earlier experiences within the family and the community have an impact on a child's ability to succeed in a school system whose model of literacy events is based on the same principles that guide reading and writing in white middle- (and upper-middle) class families. The study of literacy merged with language socialization and has since been an important part of linguistic anthropology, with an ever-expanding set of issues and dimensions, including the relation between literacy and the formation of class, gender, racial, and ethnic identities (Collins 1995).

The technological revolution of the 1980s and 1990s extended the notion of literacy so that now we easily talk about "video literacy" or "computer literacy." Within linguistic anthropology, a growing number of researchers have been using these new technologies for documenting and analyzing social interaction (Duranti 1997b:chapter 5). It is now common practice to use the latest audio-visual technology to store, retrieve, and code verbal behavior. Just as the invention of the portable audio tape recorder revolutionized the study of talk – it is difficult to imagine the birth of sociolinguistics without the portable tape recorder – the more recent digital innovations have opened up the possibility of a different type of linguistic anthropology. Analysts can now study in great detail the simultaneous operations that produce and make possible any stretch of talk.[58] Through new kinds of **inscription** (Ricoeur 1981:198) these tools allow us to see (as opposed to only hear) talk as collaboratively produced by participants with the help of a number of semiotic resources, including the human body, the built environment, and a variety of material artifacts and tools. These technological innovations also came with a rethinking of the notion of "context," which is no longer understood as an independent variable (e.g. a speaker's social status) or a given backdrop against which to analyze linguistic forms, but as the product of specific ways of behaving. Participants in an interaction are constantly and mostly implicitly preoccupied with defining the context against which their actions should be interpreted. The analyst's job is to reconstruct such a process of contextualization (Goodwin & Duranti 1992:3–4) while being conscious of the fact that analysis itself is a form of contextualization. The power to frame events and provide a preferred interpretation is both within the interaction (as negotiated by the participants) and outside of it, as researchers (and other "experts") frame the event in order to produce an analysis of it.

In this, the work of Michel Foucault on the institutionalization of madness and other forms of social control over deviance and transgression was very important in alerting social scientists to the power of observation, documentation, and classification, as well as to their participation in social control and surveillance (e.g. Foucault 1979, 1980, 1984). Albeit coming from a different tradition (the study of face-to-face interaction), Charles Goodwin's notion of **professional vision** is a recent contribution to a related issue: the power that certain interpretive procedures have to convince an audience. Goodwin analyzes three practices used by experts: "(1) *coding*, which transforms phenomena observed in a specific setting into the objects of knowledge that animate the discourse of a profession; (2) *highlighting*, which makes specific phenomena in a complex perceptual field salient by marking them in some fashion; and (3) *producing and articulating material representations*" (C. Goodwin 1994:607, emphasis in the original). One of the events analyzed by Goodwin was the televised proceedings of one of the most widely watched criminal trials of the twentieth century, in which four police officers from the Los Angeles Police Department were accused of using excessive force against an African American motorist, Mr Rodney King. Goodwin argues that the prosecutors lost the case[59] because they treated the video of the beating (which had originally caused public outrage when broadcast on television) as a *natural* object, whose content would be self-explanatory. The defense, instead, treated the video tape as a document in need of interpretation and employed experts who used the three practices mentioned above to socialize the jury to see the actions recorded as justifiable.

One of the ways in which a community dominates another, or some members of a community dominate other members, is by determining the acceptable ways of speaking. For this reason linguists have long been interested in the process that defines a variety as the Standard and in its use by the dominant class to maintain control (Bloomfield 1935; Labov 1970; Baugh 1999; Rickford 1999). Standardization is common in the formation of a nation-state and is a weapon by the central government against linguistic minorities. A classic study of this process is Bruce Mannheim's (1991) reconstruction of the rise of Quechua to the status of the standard language of the Inka Empire (in Southern Peru) after the Spanish invasion, in the sixteenth century. Minority languages, however, are not always dominated by the majority language as shown by Kathryn Woolard's (1989) research in Barcelona, where a national minority language (Catalan), spoken by the ethnic group that has economic control in the region, is the "high prestige" language and the nation's Standard (Castilian) is the "low prestige" language.

In their efforts to connect the details of language use in everyday life with the political and economic institutions and processes that allow for those details to be interpreted and be either effective or futile, linguistic anthropologists have relied on a number of theorists and concepts from other fields. I will mention two theorists here: Antonio Gramsci and Pierre Bourdieu. For Gramsci, as he wrote in his "Prison Notebooks" (*Quaderni del carcere*), it is not sufficient for a dominant class to rule through state institutions such as the legal system, the police, and the military. It must also succeed at imposing its own intellectual and moral standards, possibly and more effectively through persuasion. Gramsci's notion of **hegemony** was meant to capture the ability that a ruling class has to build consensus through the work of all kinds of intellectuals (e.g. managers in industrial societies, priests in feudal societies) who give the rest of the population a political, intellectual, and moral direction (Gramsci 1971, 1975; Williams 1977). These ideas have been adopted – sometimes critically, other times not – by linguistic anthropologists and other students of language use to illuminate the processes through which a group or class manages to impose its own view of what constitutes the prestige dialect (Standard English vs. African American English), the prestige language (e.g. English vs. Spanish, Spanish vs. Mexicano), or even the prestige accent (Philips 1998:215–16; Woolard 1985). By being interested in language use and more generally communication, of course, linguistic anthropologists cannot but be interested in the inequality that characterizes speakers' ability to control different linguistic varieties, whether they are recognized "languages" or registers (e.g. the way in which doctors or lawyers talk) (Hymes 1996). The focus on inequality, however, has been only recently conceptualized through a direct concern with the relationship between language and political economy (Gal 1989). In this endeavor, the work of French sociologist Pierre Bourdieu has been influential, especially his notions of **habitus** and **cultural capital**. Bourdieu's notion of habitus is related to Gramsci's notion of hegemony in that it is an unconscious set of dispositions that are connected to and recursively activated by participation in specific activities or practices. But the concept of habitus also has the meaning of "regulated improvisations" (only apparently an oxymoron) and is more easily related to socialization and the study of language as a practice that draws from and maintains traces of a variety of social sources and "voices" (Bakhtin 1981). Bourdieu's notion of cultural capital – which includes not only aesthetic taste but also linguistic skills – allows us to think of linguistic varieties as having a "value" within a "market" (Bourdieu 1982, 1985; Gal 1989; Woolard 1985). William Hanks' study of sixteenth-century texts produced by native Maya officials takes advantage of these insights in making sense of how both old and new conventions were drawn upon in the production of "boundary genres," that is, ways of organizing texts and expressing ideas that "derived from a fusion of Spanish and Maya frameworks" (Hanks 1987:677).

It is this interest in the heterogeneity of texts and their political implications that characterizes some of the most recent contributions in linguistic anthropology. Jane

Hill's (1998 [this volume]) study of Mock Spanish by government officials and the media is an example of this trend, which combines a long-standing interest in language contact (e.g. borrowings, code-switching) and linguistic creativity with a more recent interest in the use of language in the construction, maintenance, and challenging of racial stereotypes and ethnic division within a society (see also Baugh 1999; Mendoza-Denton 1999; Rampton 1995a, 1995b; Spears 1999; Urciuoli 1991; Wodak & Reisigl 1999; Zentella 1997).

After a pre-feminist era in which scholars were mostly interested in uncovering the logic of the encoding of sex differences in languages (e.g. Sapir 1929), the first generation of feminist linguists – as pointed out by Bucholtz (1999) – concentrated on the oppressive implications of ordinary speech (e.g. R. Lakoff 1973) and on the differences between men's speech and women's speech (e.g. West & Zimmerman 1983), whereas the second generation became preoccupied with trying to explain why there were communication problems between men and women. Borrowing from Gumperz's concept of interethnic miscommunication, some researchers suggested that miscommunication between men and women was due to the fact that the two groups belong to different cultures (Maltz & Borker 1982; Tannen 1990). A more recent trend of studies has adopted the view that gender is constructed and interacts with other identities (Anzaldúa 1987, 1990; Bucholtz, Liang, & Sutton 1999; Eckert & McConnell-Ginet 1992a, 1992b; Hall & Bucholtz 1995; Mendoza-Denton 1996). The role of language in helping establish gender identity is part of a broader range of processes through which membership in particular groups is activated, imposed, and sometimes contested through the use of linguistic forms that do not simply index "woman" vs. "man" or "feminine" vs. "masculine," but activate stances or perform speech acts that are associated with a particular gender (Ochs 1992, 1996). This constructivist and interactional view of gender (and more generally identity) has been more open to the integration of verbal communication with other semiotic practices within the lived space of human interaction (M. H. Goodwin 1999; Goodwin & Goodwin 2000 [this volume]; Sidnell 1997).

9 Conclusions

What needs to be clearly seen by anthropologists, who to a large extent may have gotten the idea that linguistics is merely a highly specialized and tediously technical pigeonhole in a far corner of the anthropological workshop, is that linguistics is essentially the quest of MEANING.

(Whorf 1956a:73)

In order to have a better sense of the future of a discipline, we need to have a better sense of its past. When we look back at our history, we learn a number of important lessons, including the following.

1 The basic assumption of linguistic anthropology is that to understand the meaning of linguistic messages one must study them within the contexts in which they are produced and interpreted. This commitment to contextualized language is

supported by a number of units of analysis that go beyond the word, the sentence, and the notion of language as an ideal system to include speech communities, speech events, activities, and acts as well as the notions of register and variety.

2 The different names used for referring to the study of language in/and/as culture (e.g. linguistic anthropology, anthropological linguistics, sociolinguistics) can be made sense of by a historical overview of the methods, goals, and academic affiliation of the researchers involved (section 2). The term "anthropological linguistics" reveals a strong identification with the discipline of linguistics as opposed to anthropology and a "service" mentality, that is, a view of linguistics as a tool for training social or cultural anthropologists to do fieldwork. The term "linguistic anthropology" – used as early as 1880 but more widely adopted only in the 1960s – places the enterprise squarely within the field of anthropology and starts from an understanding of speaking as an activity that has its own cultural organization, to be studied by means of a combination of linguistic (read "structuralist") analysis and ethnographic methods. As discussed in section 2.2, in the 1960s and 1970s the term "sociolinguistics" served as a cover term for a variety of approaches to the study of language in context which included quantitative studies of variation within and across communities and ethnographic studies of verbal genres and speech events (e.g. the ethnography of communication). However, contemporary sociolinguistics and linguistic anthropology seem directed toward separate paths (with the possible exception of the study of gender, where there is more communication across methodological and theoretical boundaries). Despite an earlier convergence of interests (language variation, the role of context), most contemporary linguistic anthropologists subscribe to a constructivist view of social categories (e.g. gender, status) and thus reject the sharp separation between dependent and independent variables found in sociolinguistics, especially in its quantitatively oriented research. The reliance on interviews as the primary source for data collection is still a defining feature of sociolinguistic surveys whereas linguistic anthropologists tend to record spontaneous verbal interaction across a range of situations.

3 What we presently call linguistic anthropology started out in the 1880s as an attempt to document and describe aboriginal North American languages and as such it coincided for about seventy years with descriptive, historical, and (to a lesser extent) theoretical linguistics (section 3). That tradition continues through those linguists who carry out fieldwork in geographical areas (e.g. Australia, Papua New Guinea, the Amazon) where there are still languages that have not been properly described (e.g. Foley 1986; Dixon & Aikhenvald 1999) or who try to document and help revive languages that are considered endangered (Dorian 1993, 1994; Grenoble & Whaley 1998; Hale et al. 1992). Theoretically, there is also continuity between Boas' original plan (and his diffusionism) and some of the more recent work on linguistic diversity and the relationship between the spread of languages and the spread of populations (e.g. Nichols 1992, 1995a, 1995b; Nichols & Peterson 1996).

4 The earlier encounters with American Indian languages sparked an interest in what a language could reveal about a people's view of the world, while an increased understanding of the complexities of linguistic forms and their organization in systems (e.g. grammars) suggested the possibility of constraints on speakers' ability to see the world "with the naked eye." Since to be a full participant in a community, a person needs to be a speaker of the language(s) spoken in that community, in some

way our interaction with the animate and inanimate world around us is always mediated through language(s). Sapir's and Whorf's ideas on these issues inspired a series of empirical and theoretical studies around the issue of "linguistic relativity" (section 4). Some of the themes found in Sapir's and Whorf's work have been recently reframed within a number of new enterprises, including the work on metapragmatics and language ideology (section 4.1).

5 The study of language as a cultural resource has motivated the extension of Chomsky's cognitive notion of "competence" to include socio-cultural knowledge, i.e. Hymes' notion of communicative competence. The interest in language contact and language variation produced an awareness of the role played by the community in providing guidance and meaning for language use and language choice. In the future, the notion of community is likely to expand to include aggregates that are not defined by face-to-face communication and take into consideration the impact of old (print) and new media (radio, television, computers) on language use and linguistic standards.

6 Since the 1960s there has been a shift from an interest in what language encodes (reference, denotation) to what language does (performance) (see section 6). This shift has fostered an interest in the social and cultural organization of linguistic activities (e.g. speech acts, speech events) and the subtle ways in which linguistic forms are existentially connected with the situations in which they are used and the people who use them (indexicality). Verbal performance has been shown to have a cultural organization of its own, which needs to be studied by researchers who are able to combine the ethnographic methods practiced by socio-cultural anthropologists with the structuralist methods practiced by linguists (based on the documentation of actual language use).

7 The developmental dimension of the study of competence and communities has been developed in the field of language socialization (see section 7), which looks at the impact of cultural expectations and social interaction on the acquisition of language and at the role of language in creating competent and productive members of society.

8 As the most complex symbolic system developed by the species *Homo sapiens*, language has the power to convince, seduce, obscure, highlight, frame, and reframe social reality. Contemporary linguistic anthropology uses a variety of analytical tools and concepts to examine the power of language in a wide range of social situations. Social categories that used to be studied separately, e.g. race, class, and gender, are now analyzed as interdependent. While paying attention to the local and global context of communication, it is the moment-by-moment construction of "texts" – broadly defined – that is emphasized in the effort to uncover the mechanisms and resources that make the meaning of human action, words included, possible, interpretable, and consequential.

NOTES

1   Special thanks to the people who helped me become a better historian of my discipline by providing invaluable recollections, references, clarifications, and corrections: Regna Darnell,

John Gumperz, Dell Hymes, Paul Kroskrity, Dan Slobin, William Foley, Mary Bucholtz, Elinor Ochs, Bambi B. Schieffelin, and Laura Nader. I would also like to thank Vincent Barletta and Sarah Meacham for detailed comments on the first draft of this chapter and Tracy Rone for her suggestions and editorial advice. My second draft benefited from very detailed comments by Dell Hymes, who was particularly generous with factual and theoretical corrections to my representation of the history of the field. I remain, of course, solely responsible for any remaining errors, misrepresentations, or omissions.

2   A good example of apparent free variation among the different terms is Stephen Murray's *American Sociolinguistics: Theorists and Theory Groups* (1998), which alternates from one term to the other usually without warning. For example, although the title of the book promises a study of "sociolinguistics," its first sentence reads: "This study of postwar anthropological linguistics in North America..." (p. 1). Particularly puzzling is the choice of the term "ethno-linguistics" for describing the work by John Gumperz and his students at the University of California at Berkeley in the 1980s (Murray:chapter 9), given Gumperz's preference for either "the ethnography of communication" (in his collaboration with Hymes) or "sociolinguistics" (see n. 15).

3   Except for a brief period in the 1940s and 1950s (e.g. Garvin & Riesenberg 1952; Voegelin & Harris 1945), the terms "ethnolinguistic" and "ethnolinguistics" have been more popular in European circles than in the USA (see Duranti 1997b:2; Hymes 1971a:48). A notable exception in recent years is Paul Kroskrity's monograph on the Arizona Tewa speech community where the term "ethnolinguistics" is used in the more restricted sense of "native metalinguistics" (Kroskrity 1993:34). This perspective was later developed in the study of language ideologies (see Woolard & Schieffelin 1994; Schieffelin, Woolard, & Kroskrity 1998; Kroskrity 2000a, 2000b).

4   "Simply stated, in this book linguistic anthropology will be presented as *the study of language as a cultural resource and speaking as a cultural practice*. As an inherently interdisciplinary field, it relies on and expands existing methods in other disciplines, linguistics and anthropology in particular, with the general goal of providing an understanding of the multifarious aspects of language as a set of cultural practices, that is, as a system of communication that allows for interpsychological (between individuals) and intrapsychological (in the same individual) representations of the social order and helps people use such representations for constitutive social acts" (Duranti 1997b:2–3).

5   My interpretation of the situation in Australia was largely confirmed by Foley during a recent exchange over electronic mail. On December 21, 1999, he wrote: "I think you're right about my being influenced by the Australian situation in which in most universities there are close connections between linguistics and anthropology. Due to the fieldwork emphasis, most departments of linguistics here regard some anthro expertise as essential. Fieldwork is greatly devalued in linguistics in the US, that's true, but to the extent that it is important in some departments, e.g. Berkeley [where Foley received his Ph.D. in linguistics], there is a niche for anthropological linguistics, albeit often unrealized. I suppose my own ideological position is that yes, anthropological linguistics is an integral part of linguistics, however how much hegemonic forces at work in the discipline have worked to and largely have sidelined it. That is the current situation, I agree, but things change, hegemonies don't last forever, and I would deplore any redefinition of linguistics which would actually help to institutionalize the current situation."

6   A thorough reconstruction of the history of the relationship between linguistics and anthropology in the first half of the twentieth century is well beyond the scope of this chapter. Valuable information regarding Edward Sapir's relationship with anthropology and linguistics and the impact that this relationship had on his students is provided by Regna Darnell's historical reconstructions (1990, 1998b). Regarding Sapir's association with the Yale linguistics department while chairing the anthropology department, Darnell (1998b:362) wrote: "Sapir encouraged his linguistic students to take their degrees in linguistics rather than anthropology. This was in line with the increasing autonomy of linguistics from anthropology signaled by the establishment of the Linguistic Society of America and its journal *Language* after 1925. At Chicago, Sapir's failure to establish flexible working relations with Carl Buck in classical philology effectively restricted anthropological linguists to working in anthropology.

Moreover, the linguistics that Sapir wanted his students to learn was not anthropological in the sense proselytized by Boas. The "first Yale school" in linguistics developed around Sapir and the advanced graduate students he brought with him from Chicago, with Morris Swadesh, Stanley Newman, and Mary Haas as the core, later joined by Charles Hockett, George Trager, Benjamin Whorf, Charles Voegelin, Zellig Harris, George Herzog, and others..."

Darnell's reconstruction is supported by David Sapir (1985), who suggested that his father had a much stronger identification with linguistics than with anthropology: "Sapir considered himself a linguist. He thought of himself as only accidentally an anthropologist" (D. Sapir 1985:291).

7 For example, Harry Hoijer (1961:10) defined anthropological linguistics as "...an area of research which is devoted in the main to studies, synchronic and diachronic, of the languages of the people who have no writing."

8 I owe the articulation of this second goal to Dell Hymes' comments on an earlier draft of this chapter.

9 Ferguson and Gumperz originally approached their research as part of linguistics, as shown by the following quote: "No great effort is made to carry the interpretation far afield from linguistics, but each of the studies contains suggestive material for the approaches of other disciplines in the study of contemporary South Asia" (Ferguson & Gumperz 1960:1).

10 See Murray (1998:96–8, 101–3, and passim) for a useful historical reconstruction of this period, but beware of his occasionally inaccurate terminology. For example, Murray (1998:98) refers to Ferguson and Gumperz (1960) as "the first exemplar of what would be dubbed 'the ethnography of speech.'" But "the ethnography of speech" is not the name of a school or paradigm and Gumperz has never used it (John Gumperz, personal communication). The terms that are found in the literature are "the ethnography of speaking" (Hymes 1971b; Bauman & Sherzer 1975) and "the ethnography of communication" (Gumperz and Hymes 1964).

11 "Linguistics without ethnography would fare as badly as ethnography would without the light thrown on it by language" (Malinowski 1920:78). For Boas' position, see section 3.

12 Greenberg's vision of linguistics was also important to anthropological linguists because it was comparative-typological and provided an alternative to the Chomskian paradigm, as made evident in the following statement by Mary Haas (1978a:121–2): "Concentration on one's own language somehow seems to lead to the conclusion that there is a universal grammar that can be deduced from one's own language. Now this is certainly not a new idea but the very one that Boas and his followers had been at such pains to dispel. Fortunately it has not become for us necessary to fall back into the beliefs of the pre-Boasian period. Instead in recent years there has been another kind of linguistic activity, standing somewhat aside from both the Bloomfieldian and the Chomskian paradigms, which has come to the rescue in this impasse. The activity referred to has been the work of Joseph H. Greenberg and his staff at Stanford University on language typology and language universals. Clearly such a project cannot be pursued by limiting it to the perusal of grammars of languages written by authors who are native speakers thereof. Indeed for the purposes of a universal project, the more languages for which information can be obtained the better. Happily, then, there is now a renewed interest in all kinds of languages spoken near and far and it is by necessity accepted that information on most of them may have to be supplied through field work done by nonnative speakers. Consequently, there has been a renewal of interest in field work."

13 This is particularly true of Foley's (1997) Part V "The Ethnography of Speaking" (chapters 13–18). The one topic treated by Foley that does not include research by linguistic anthropologists is chapter 2, "The Evolution of Language." This topic has not been a subject of interest within linguistic anthropology in recent years. Agha (1997) is a rare exception.

14 "The most detailed contributions [on the relation between language and society] have come from the anthropologists working in Southeast Asia. However, for the study of the complex communities of the United States and Western Europe, it appears that quantitative methods are required" (Labov 1966b:23). The implicit reference here is to Ferguson and Gumperz (1960) and Gumperz (1958), both of which are mentioned by Labov earlier (Labov 1966b:21).

15 "Interactional sociolinguistics" is the title of Gumperz's Cambridge University Press series, which includes contributions by Gumperz himself (Gumperz 1982a), Jenny Cook-Gumperz

(1986), some of his former students (Brown & Levinson 1987; Gumperz 1982b; Tannen 1989), discourse analysts (Schiffrin 1987), and conversation analysts (Drew & Heritage 1992).

16   See Murray (1998:100–3).

17   This view is confirmed in an earlier publication, where Hymes defines the ethnography of speaking as "a particular approach" within sociolinguistics, understood as "an area of research that links linguistics with anthropology and sociology" (Hymes 1971b:47).

18   For example, Wardhaugh (1986), out of 16 chapters, dedicates one (chapter 16) to "Language and Culture" and another to "Ethnography and Ethnomethodology." Ralph Fasold, in the second volume of his *Introduction to Sociolinguistics*, includes one chapter on "The Ethnography of Communication" (1990:chapter 2).

19   The work on conversation was pioneered by sociologists Harvey Sacks, Emanuel A. Schegloff and Gail Jefferson in the 1960s and has since expanded its influence on a number of disciplines, among them pragmatics (e.g. Levinson 1983), child language studies (e.g. McTear 1985; Ochs & Schieffelin 1983), and grammatical analysis (e.g. Ford 1993; Ochs, Schegloff, & Thompson 1996). For a discussion of conversation analysis from the point of view of linguistic anthropology, see Duranti (1997b:chapter 8).

20   The literature on this subject is vast. It includes methodologically oriented studies such as Briggs (1986) and a voluminous body of empirical research on conversation that shows how speakers are constantly monitoring and adapting their speech according to the type of recipients they are interacting with (e.g. Duranti & Brenneis 1986; C. Goodwin 1981; Schegloff 1972, 1986), detailed discussion of how stories in conversation are typically co-authored (e.g. Capps & Ochs 1995; Goodwin 1986; Mandelbaum 1987a, 1987b, 1989; Ochs 1997; Ochs & Capps 1996), and the role of interaction in the shaping of grammar itself (Ochs, Schegloff, & Thompson 1996; Silverstein 1997).

21   As often in history, the efforts of a few individuals who manage to win a minimal institutional support can make a difference. A good example is the interdisciplinary enterprise known as the Berkeley Women and Language Group, which started in 1985 with a small conference organized by Sue Bremner, Noelle Caskey, Elisabeth Kuhn, and Birch Moonwomon. In 1992, a second conference was held with about 80 papers and over 300 participants (Hall, Bucholtz, & Moonwomon 1992). The group held three other large conferences (every other year) with a rotating group of facilitators, until the fall of 1999 when it was disbanded. Its legacy is expected to be continued at Stanford University as the International Gender and Language Association (IGALA).

22   The four fields are archaeology, biological anthropology (formerly "physical"), linguistic anthropology (formerly "linguistics" or "philology"), and sociocultural anthropology (formerly "ethnology"). The Boasian conceptualization of anthropology as a four field discipline is often contested today given the recent multiplication of subdisciplines and the internal debate regarding the goals of anthropological research and the limit of the Boasian, holistic approach.

23   Hillary Henson convincingly argued that, despite the influence of Bronislaw Malinowski's work on British anthropology, "[i]n the period from about 1920 until 1960, British social anthropologists paid no serious attention to language" (Henson 1974:119). For a review of anthropology departments in Canada, with some data on linguistic anthropology in that country, see Darnell (1998c).

24   A notable exception is a series of articles by William Edwin Safford on Chamorro, one of the two major languages spoken in the Philippines.

25   The *American Anthropologist* was started in 1888 as the organ of the Anthropological Society of Washington, which relinquished it in 1899 when the founders of the American Anthropological Association (AAA) asked to use the same name for the AAA journal. Since the AAA did not officially start until 1902, the journal predates the Association (the first meeting was held in 1901).

26   "Bureau members did *collect* considerable bodies of linguistic material, but prior to Boas' time they *published* relatively little in the way of extended grammatical analysis. And despite all this material, despite decades of speculation on the "incorporating" or "polysynthetic" character of American Indian languages, the amount of detailed and systematic study of specific Indian

languages which would stand professional scrutiny – at least as far as Franz Boas and Edward Sapir were concerned – was virtually nil" (Stocking 1974:458–9) (emphasis in the original). Although Stocking gives Boas credit for his important role in the planning and editing of the *Handbook*, he rejects Voegelin's (1952) claim that Boas should be considered the author or co-author of most of the grammatical sketches contained in it.

27   Boas was a strong believer in the power of acculturation and some of the articles collected in Boas (1940) contain statements that reveal his aversion to hasty genetic classification for American Indian languages. For example, in an article originally published in 1920, he wrote: "In other words, the whole theory of an 'Ursprache' for every group of modern languages must be held in abeyance until we can prove that these languages go back to a single stock and that they have not originated, to a large extent, by the process of acculturation" (1940:217).

28   "The great advantage that linguistics offer in this respect is the fact that, on the whole, the categories which are formed always remain unconscious, and that for this reason the processes which lead to their formation can be followed without the misleading and disturbing factors of secondary explanations, which are so common in ethnology, so much so that they generally obscure the real history of the development of ideas entirely" (Boas 1911:70–1).

29   This idea is the linguistic equivalent of the position held in logic by Gottlob Frege, Ludwig Wittgenstein, and others that meaning is not to be found in words but in propositions (the distinction made by English-speaking philosophers between "sentence" and "proposition" is vacuous in German, where the term *Satz* has been used to mean "proposition" or "sentence").

30   This practice continued for several decades, in concomitance with the reference to "primitive society" and "primitive culture." For example, the 1931–32 catalog for the graduate program in anthropology at Yale, which is very likely to have been written by Sapir (Darnell 1998b:363), mentions "primitive linguistics" (which could not possibly mean "a primitive form of linguistics" but "a linguistic study of primitive languages"). The belief that anthropological linguists study "primitive communities" is unfortunately still found in some circles, as shown by the following definition of anthropological linguistics in David Crystal's *Dictionary of Linguistics*: "A branch of LINGUISTICS which studies language variation and use in relation to human cultural patterns and beliefs, as investigated using the theories and methods of anthropology. For example, it studies the way in which linguistic features may identify a member of *a (usually primitive) community* with a social, religious, occupational or kinship group. . . ." (Crystal 1997:20) (emphasis mine).

31   See also Hill (1964) and the Editor's "General comments and references" after Hill's article (Hymes 1964d:89).

32   It is not clear whether Sapir actually read von Humboldt, although there were several ways for him to be exposed to von Humboldt's ideas, for example, through Boas (see Drechsel 1988).

33   For example, Hill and Mannheim (1992:383) argue that the term "hypothesis" is not appropriate in this case: "We maintain that 'linguistic relativity' as proposed by Boas, Sapir, and Whorf is not a hypothesis in the traditional sense, but an axiom, a part of the initial epistemology and methodology of the linguistic anthropologist. Boas, Sapir, and Whorf were not relativists in the extreme sense often suggested by modern critics . . ."

34   Dell Hymes, personal communication.

35   The second part of the twentieth century saw the establishment of a strong functional tradition in linguistics that tries to explain grammatical forms in terms of communicative needs or discourse functions (e.g. Hopper & Thompson 1980; Givón 1989; Hopper & Traugott 1993). Somewhat paradoxically, the argument in favor of the non-functional, autonomous nature of linguistic forms has been pursued not by linguistic anthropologists but by formal grammarians who have shown little or no interest in the relationship between language and culture.

36   This connection is not acknowledged by Chomsky, who prefers to trace ancestry within the French rationalist tradition (Chomsky 1966) rather than admitting any link to Whorf, whose basic approach he harshly criticized in the context of an unflattering introduction to Adam Schaff's (1973) *Language and Cognition*: "My impression is that Schaff vastly over-estimates the quality of the material that ethnolinguistics can provide. It sheds no discredit on the anthropological linguist, who is faced with problems of vast complexity and scope, to point

out that the evidence that he can provide is of an altogether superficial sort" (Chomsky 1973:ix).

37   For a revision of the original theory of "basic color terms," see Kay and Maffi (2000). For a criticism of the model, see Lucy and Shweder (1979) and Levinson (2000).

38   This is the same phenomenon illustrated by Boas' (1911:25) example of the distinct lexical items through which English expresses the shapes of WATER: *lake, river, brook, rain, dew, wave, foam.*

39   A similar line of work on linguistic relativity has been pursued since the early 1990s by researchers at the Max Planck Institute for Psycholinguistics under the direction of Stephen Levinson, who launched a comparative study of the ways in which space is conceptualized across typologically different languages (Levinson 1992). A programmatic paper by Gumperz and Levinson (1991) was followed by a conference where a number of linguists, anthropologists, and psychologists reopened the discussion of linguistic relativity that had been almost forgotten (Gumperz & Levinson 1996).

40   For an interesting use of this classification, see Merlan & Rumsay (1991:97–8).

41   For an appraisal of Chomsky's ability to redirect American linguistics, see Murray (1993:chapter 9) and Newmeyer (1980, 1986).

42   "There seems to be little reason to question the traditional view that investigation of performance will proceed only so far as understanding of underlying competence permits" (Chomsky 1965:10). Despite the considerable amount of research on language use within quantitative sociolinguistics, linguistic anthropology, discourse analysis, and conversation analysis, Chomsky's position has not changed on this issue over the years, as shown by the following statement: "it would be unreasonable to pose the problem of how Jones [a typical speaker of English] decides what he does, or how he interprets what he hears in particular circumstances. But highly idealized aspects of the problem are amenable to study" (Chomsky 1995:18).

43   "We will define [linguistic community] as a social group which may be either monolingual or multilingual, held together by frequency of social interaction patterns and set off from the surrounding areas by weaknesses in the lines of communication. Linguistic communities may consist of small groups bound together by face-to-face contact or may cover large regions, depending on the level of abstraction we wish to achieve" (Gumperz 1968b:463). For a recent critique of the notion of "speech community," see Silverstein (1996a).

44   On the term "variety," see Hudson (1980); on dialect and contact among dialects, see Trudgill (1986); on register, see the essays in Biber & Finegan (1994); on speech communities, see Romaine (1982).

45   See Goodwin & Goodwin (1987), G. Lakoff (1987), Lakoff & Johnson (1980), Ochs & Schieffelin (1983), Sapir & Crocker (1977), Silverstein (1984, 1997), Wilce (1998).

46   See Briggs & Bauman (1992), Beeman (1993), Caton (1990), Du Bois (1986), Keane (1997), Keating (1998), Keil & Feld (1994), Kuipers (1990), Palmer & Jankowiak (1996), Sherzer (1983, 1990), Yankah (1995).

47   "A valid observation that has frequently been made (and often, irrationally denied) is that a great deal can be learned about U[niversal]G[rammar] from the study of a single language, if such study achieves sufficient depth to put forth rules or principles that have explanatory force but are underdetermined by evidence available to the language learner. Then it is reasonable to attribute to UG those aspects of these rules or principles that are uniformly attained but underdetermined by evidence" (Chomsky 1982:6).

48   The following recounting of the Berkeley project owes a great deal to personal correspondence with Dan Slobin, who generously provided me with a historical account of his involvement in the design of a cross-cultural/cross-linguistic study of language acquisition.

49   These efforts culminated in a number of articles on universals of language acquisition (Slobin 1973, 1982, 1985a, 1985b) and a series of edited volumes that included acquisition studies by linguists, psycholinguists, and linguistic anthropologists.

50   In 1975 Bambi Schieffelin was a Ph.D. student in anthropology at Columbia University, where she had received an M.A. in developmental psychology under the direction of Lois Bloom. Before and after her fieldwork, Schieffelin spent time at Berkeley, first preparing for fieldwork and then writing her dissertation on Kaluli language acquisition (Schieffelin 1979b). In 1979–80, after completing her dissertation under Bloom's supervision, she had a postdoctoral

fellowship in developmental psychology at the University of California at Berkeley, taught a course with Dan Slobin, and participated in the group he led on the cross-linguistic study of language acquisition. Elinor Ochs (formerly Elinor O. Keenan) received her Ph.D. in anthropology in 1974 from the University of Pennsylvania, where she studied with Dell Hymes (her primary advisor), Ward Goodenough, and David Sapir.

51 The reader for her first seminars at USC on children's discourse became the basis for *Developmental Pragmatics*, the first collection of essays Ochs edited with Schieffelin (Ochs & Schieffelin 1979). Ochs and Schieffelin's earlier joint papers were later collected in Ochs & Schieffelin (1983).

52 They were part of a Working Group on Language and Cultural Context organized by Roger Keesing that included Penelope Brown, Alessandro Duranti, John B. Haviland, Stephen Levinson, Judith Irvine, Edward Schieffelin, Michael Silverstein, and Robert Van Valin.

53 This discovery is still ignored by psychologists who continue to write as if baby talk and Motherese are universals (e.g. Gopnik, Meltzoff, & Kuhl 1999) and it is even difficult to accept for linguistic anthropologists who worked in societies where adults do modify their speech to infants. Blount (1995), for example, first concludes that one cannot take Ochs' findings as conclusive because the youngest child in her corpus was 19 months old (Blount 1995:560) and then tries to explain the Samoan data (which he had previously dismissed) and some of his own findings on the Luo by extending the notion of accommodation to include accommodation to the local cultural model, suggesting that even when parents do not accommodate to children, they are in fact accommodating, because they are adapting to their own cultural model: "In one sense, the form of Samoan and Luo parental speech behavior could also be viewed as accommodative, since it was selected to be consistent with and thus to model the appropriate language interaction with children, appropriate according to cultural expectations. In other words, the absence of salient linguistic markers in Samoan parental speech does not mean that no accommodation is made to the child's linguistic interactive capacity. To the contrary, the speech appears, in fact, to be tailored to the cultural definition of the child and thus consistent with the broader cultural parameters" (Blount 1995:561). This position stretches the notion of accommodation to such an extent that it becomes difficult to see its value.

54 On peer-interaction, see M. H. Goodwin (1990b, 1999), Goodwin & Goodwin (1987), Schlegel (1998); on apprenticeship and everyday cognition, see Lave (1988, 1990), Lave & Wenger (1991), Rogoff (1990), Rogoff & Lave (1984), Scribner (1984); on literacy activities, see Besnier (1995), Heath (1983), Kuipers (1998:chapter 6), Scribner & Cole (1981), Street (1984); on language contact and linguistic syncretism, see Errington (1998), Hill & Hill (1986), Kulick (1992), Zentella (1997).

55 There is now a considerable amount of work on the transformation of experience in text or entextualization; see for example Briggs & Bauman (1992), Capps & Ochs (1995), Ochs & Capps (1996), Silverstein & Urban (1996).

56 Some scholars independently argued that the use of formal language can be used to restrict the choices that a person of higher rank has (e.g. Duranti 1992b; E. Goody 1972; Irvine 1974).

57 There is also a considerable amount of published research on the differences between spoken and written language, e.g. Tannen (1982), Biber (1988).

58 See Duranti (1992a), C. Goodwin (1981), Goodwin & Goodwin (1992, 2000), M. H. Goodwin (1990a, 1995), Woolard (1998).

59 Two of the police officers were convicted of violating Mr King's civil rights at a second, federal, trial.

Part I

Speech Community and Communicative Competence

Introduction

Any effort to study such a complex phenomenon as language must start from a shared understanding among researchers of the units of analysis that are needed for collecting information and identifying interesting phenomena. *Speech community* and *competence* are two such units. They help us think about a language not simply in terms of a grammatical system but also in terms of the people who use it as a powerful intellectual tool in their daily life. Linguistic anthropologists start from the assumption that for speakers to be able to acquire and use language skills, they must be members of a community within which those skills are transmitted and valued (Gumperz). Furthermore, to understand what a language is, what its boundaries are, and how communication is made possible or difficult, we need to pay attention to the relation between utterances and their contexts of use. "Communicative competence" is the ability to make language relevant to the context and, in turn, sustain the context through language (Hymes). For a truly anthropological understanding of a speech community and its members' communicative competence, we not only need to describe language use, we also need to gain an understanding of how speakers value their own language and see it connected to their history (Morgan). Recent work on discourse generated through the media extends the notion of speech community and reveals the subtle recontextualization of media discourse in everyday life (Spitulnik). Finally, the observation and recording of service encounters between members of two groups who have blamed each other for lack of "respect" allows us to examine the role of divergent verbal strategies in the production of conflict (Bailey).

Questions about Speech Community and Communicative Competence

1 What is a speech community? Why is the notion of speech community important in the study of language use?
2 Which speech community or communities do you belong to? How do you know (i.e. what are the criteria you used in your assessment)?
3 Why is the type of competence discussed by Hymes called *communicative*? What is the type of distinction that is being implied? On which grounds?
4 Morgan questions some of the assumptions held by linguists describing language use in the African American speech community. What are they? Could you extend some of her points to the study of other communities?
5 How could you design a study of communicative competence that would satisfy current scientific standards and community members' expectations?
6 Thinking about your own experience, can you think of examples of transfer from media discourse into everyday discourse? What do those examples tell you about your peer-group and your beliefs and values?
7 Does the language used by/in the media make you feel part of a larger community or does it make you feel disconnected from the rest of the world? Can you use Spitulnik's analysis to make sense of the analysis of your situation?
8 What are the differences in the interactional styles described by Bailey as characteristic of the encounters he recorded and analyzed? How can you use the notions of speech community and communicative competence to explain those differences?
9 Does Bailey's analysis help you understand other cases of miscommunication between groups? What would you do to extend his analysis to cases you are familiar with?

Suggestions for Further Reading

For a general introduction to contemporary theories, concepts, and issues in the study of language: Crystal, D. (1987). *The Cambridge Encyclopedia of Language*. Cambridge: Cambridge University Press (an excellent resource for non-specialists); and Duranti, A. (ed.) (1999). *Language Matters in Anthropology: A Lexicon for the New Millennium*. Special Issue of the *Journal of Linguistic Anthropology*, 9 (a collection of 75 entries on linguistic concepts, issues, and theories, written by leading experts, with recommended readings for each entry), reprinted as A. Duranti (ed.) (2001). *Key Terms in Language and Culture*. Malden, MA: Blackwell.

For Chomsky's ideas on language, the most accessible text is one based on interviews: Chomsky, N. (1977). *Language and Responsibility*. Based on conversations with Mitsou Ronat. New York: Pantheon Books.

A readable introduction to the study of language that highlights its innate properties and downplays its cultural prerequisites is: Pinker, S. (1994). *The Language Instinct: How the Mind Creates Language*. New York: William Morrow and Company.

Hymes' writings are collected in: Hymes, D. (1974). *Foundations in Sociolinguistics: An Ethnographic Approach*. Philadelphia: University of Pennsylvania Press;

Hymes, D. (1981). *"In Vain I Tried to Tell You": Essays in Native American Ethnopoetics*. Philadelphia: University of Pennsylvania Press; and Hymes, D. (1996). *Ethnography, Linguistics, Narrative Inequality*. Bristol, PA: Taylor & Francis.

A good synthesis of Gumperz's work on multilingualism is: Gumperz, J. J. (1982). *Discourse Strategies*. Cambridge: Cambridge University Press. See also Gumperz, J. J. (ed.) (1982). *Language and Social Identity*. Cambridge: Cambridge University Press.

An ethnography of language use that puts into practice Hymes' approach is: Sherzer, J. (1983). *Kuna Ways of Speaking: An Ethnographic Perspective*. Austin: University of Texas Press; see also the articles in Bauman, R., and Sherzer, J. (eds.) (1989). *Explorations in the Ethnography of Speaking* (2nd edn.). Cambridge: Cambridge University Press.

Important methodological considerations on how to conduct interviews that take into consideration the points made by the chapters in Part I can be found in: Briggs, C. L. (1986). *Learning How to Ask: A Sociolinguistic Appraisal of the Role of the Interview in Social Science Research*. Cambridge: Cambridge University Press.

A useful review of the work on bilingual communities, code-switching, and the communicative competence of bilingual children is: Romaine, S. (1995). *Bilingualism* (2nd edn.). Oxford: Blackwell.

1

The Speech Community

John J. Gumperz

Although not all communication is linguistic, language is by far the most powerful and versatile medium of communication; all known human groups possess language. Unlike other sign systems, the verbal system can, through the minute refinement of its grammatical and semantic structure, be made to refer to a wide variety of objects and concepts. At the same time, verbal interaction is a social process in which utterances are selected in accordance with socially recognized norms and expectations. It follows that linguistic phenomena are analyzable both within the context of language itself and within the broader context of social behavior. In the formal analysis of language the object of attention is a particular body of linguistic data abstracted from the settings in which it occurs and studied primarily from the point of view of its referential function. In analyzing linguistic phenomena within a socially defined universe, however, the study is of language usage as it reflects more general behavior norms. This universe is the speech community: any human aggregate characterized by regular and frequent interaction by means of a shared body of verbal signs and set off from similar aggregates by significant differences in language usage.

Most groups of any permanence, be they small bands bounded by face-to-face contact, modern nations divisible into smaller subregions, or even occupational associations or neighborhood gangs, may be treated as speech communities, provided they show linguistic peculiarities that warrant special study. The verbal behavior of such groups always constitutes a system. It must be based on finite sets of grammatical rules that underlie the production of well-formed sentences, or else messages will not be intelligible. The description of such rules is a precondition for the study of all types of linguistic phenomena. But it is only the starting point in the sociolinguistic analysis of language behavior.

Grammatical rules define the bounds of the linguistically acceptable. For example, they enable us to identify "How do you do?" "How are you?" and "Hi" as proper American English sentences and to reject others like "How do you?" and "How you are?" Yet speech is not constrained by grammatical rules alone. An individual's choice from among permissible alternates in a particular speech event may reveal his family background and his social intent, may identify him as a Southerner, a Northerner, an urbanite, a rustic, a member of the educated or uneducated classes, and may even indicate whether he wishes to appear friendly or distant, familiar or deferential, superior or inferior.

Just as intelligibility presupposes underlying grammatical rules, the communication of social information presupposes the existence of regular relationships between language usage and social structure. Before we can judge a speaker's social intent, we must know something about the norms defining the appropriateness of linguistically acceptable alternates for particular types of speakers; these norms vary among subgroups and among social settings. Wherever the relationships between language choice and rules of social appropriateness can be formalized, they allow us to group relevant linguistic forms into distinct dialects, styles, and occupational or other special parlances. The sociolinguistic study of speech communities deals with the linguistic similarities and differences among these speech varieties.

In linguistically homogeneous societies the verbal markers of social distinctions tend to be confined to structurally marginal features of phonology, syntax, and lexicon. Elsewhere they may include both standard literary languages, and grammatically divergent local dialects. In many multilingual societies the choice of one language over another has the same signification as the selection among lexical alternates in linguistically homogeneous societies. In such cases, two or more grammars may be required to cover the entire scope of linguistically acceptable expressions that serve to convey social meanings.

Regardless of the linguistic differences among them, the speech varieties employed within a speech community form a system because they are related to a shared set of social norms. Hence, they can be classified according to their usage, their origins, and the relationship between speech and social action that they reflect. They become indices of social patterns of interaction in the speech community.

Historical Orientation in Early Studies

Systematic linguistic field work began in the middle of the nineteenth century. Prior to 1940 the best-known studies were concerned with dialects, special parlances, national languages, and linguistic acculturation and diffusion.

Dialectology

Among the first students of speech communities were the dialectologists, who charted the distribution of colloquial speech forms in societies dominated by German, French, English, Polish, and other major standard literary tongues. Mapping relevant features of pronunciation, grammar, and lexicon in the form of *isoglosses*, they traced in detail the range and spread of historically documented changes in language habits. Isoglosses were grouped into bundles of two or more and then mapped; from the geographical shape of such isogloss bundles, it was possible to distinguish the *focal areas*, centers from which innovations radiate into the surrounding regions; *relic zones*, districts where forms previously known only from old texts were still current; and *transition zones*, areas of internal diversity marked by the coexistence of linguistic forms identified with competing centers of innovation.

Analysis along these lines clearly established the importance of social factors in language change. The distribution of rural speech patterns was found to be directly related to such factors as political boundaries during the preceding centuries, traditional market networks, the spread of important religious movements, etc. In this fashion dialectology became an important source of evidence for social history.

Special parlances, classical languages

Other scholars dealt with the languages of occupationally specialized minority groups, craft jargons, secret argots, and the like. In some cases, such as the Romany of the gypsies and the Yiddish of Jews, these parlances derive from foreign importations which survive as linguistic islands surrounded by other tongues. Their speakers tend to be bilinguals, using their own idiom for in-group communication and the majority language for interaction with outsiders.

Linguistic distinctness may also result from seemingly intentional processes of distortion. One very common form of secret language, found in a variety of tribal and complex societies, achieves unintelligibility by a process of verbal play with majority speech, in which phonetic or grammatical elements are systematically reordered. The pig Latin of English-speaking schoolchildren, in which initial consonants are transferred to the end of the word and followed by "-ay," is a relatively simple example of this process. Thieves' argots, the slang of youth gangs, and the jargon of traveling performers and other occupational groups obtain similar results by assigning special meanings to common nouns, verbs, and adjectives.

Despite their similarities, the classical administrative and liturgical languages – such as the Latin of medieval Europe, the Sanskrit of south Asia, and the Arabic of the Near East – are not ordinarily grouped with special parlances because of the prestige of the cultural traditions associated with them. They are quite distinct from and often unrelated to popular speech, and the elaborate ritual and etiquette that surround their use can be learned only through many years of special training. Instruction is available only through private tutors and is limited to a privileged few who command the necessary social status or financial resources. As a result, knowledge of these languages in the traditional societies where they are used is limited to relatively small elites, who tend to maintain control of their linguistic skills in somewhat the same way that craft guilds strive for exclusive control of their craft skills.

The standard literary languages of modern nation-states, on the other hand, tend to be representative of majority speech. As a rule they originated in rising urban centers, as a result of the free interaction of speakers of a variety of local dialects, became identified with new urban elites, and in time replaced older administrative languages. Codification of spelling and grammar by means of dictionaries and dissemination of this information through public school systems are characteristic of standard-language societies. Use of mass media and the prestige of their speakers tend to carry idioms far from their sources; such idioms eventually replace many preexisting local dialects and special parlances.

Linguistic acculturation, language shift

Wherever two or more speech communities maintain prolonged contact within a broad field of communication, there are crosscurrents of diffusion. The result is the formation of a *Sprachbund*, comprising a group of varieties which coexist in social space as dialects, distinct neighboring languages, or special parlances. Persistent borrowing over long periods creates within such groups similarities in linguistic structure, which tend to obscure pre-existing genetic distinctions; a commonly cited example is the south Asian subcontinent, where speakers of Indo-Aryan, Dravidian, and Munda languages all show significant overlap in their linguistic habits.

It appears that single nouns, verbs, and adjectives are most readily diffused, often in response to a variety of technological innovations and cultural or religious trends. Pronunciation and word order are also frequently affected. The level of phonological and grammatical pattern (i.e., the structural core of a language), however, is more resistant to change, and loanwords tend to be adapted to the patterns of the recipient language. But linguistic barriers to diffusion are never absolute, and in situations of extensive bilingualism – two or more languages being regularly used in the course of the daily routine – even the grammatical cores may be affected.

Cross-cultural influence reaches a maximum in the cases of pidgins and creoles, idioms combining elements of several distinct languages. These hybrids typically arise in colonial societies or in large trading centers where laborers torn out of their native language environments are forced to work in close cooperation with speakers of different tongues. Cross-cultural influence may also give rise to language shift, the abandonment of one native tongue in favor of another. This phenomenon most frequently occurs when two groups merge, as in tribal absorption, or when minority groups take on the culture of the surrounding majority.

Although the bulk of the research on speech communities that was conducted prior to 1940 is historically oriented, students of speech communities differ markedly from their colleagues who concentrate upon textual analysis. The latter tend to treat languages as independent wholes that branch off from uniform protolanguages in accordance with regular sound laws. The former, on the other hand, regard themselves primarily as students of behavior, interested in linguistic phenomena for their broader sociohistorical significance. By relating dialect boundaries to settlement history, to political and administrative boundaries, and to culture areas and by charting the itineraries of loanwords in relation to technical innovations or cultural movements, they established the primacy of social factors in language change, disproving earlier theories of environmental or biological determinism.

The study of language usage in social communities, furthermore, revealed little of the uniformity ordinarily ascribed to protolanguages and their descendants; many exceptions to the regularity of sound laws were found wherever speakers of genetically related languages were in regular contact. This led students of speech communities to challenge the "family-tree theory," associated with the neogrammarians of nineteenth-century Europe, who were concerned primarily with the genetic reconstruction of language history. Instead, they favored a theory of diffusion which postulates the spread of linguistic change in intersecting "waves" that emanate from different centers of innovation with an intensity proportionate to the prestige of their human carriers.

Thus, while geneticists regarded modern language distribution as the result of the segmentation of older entities into newer and smaller subgroups, diffusionists viewed the speech community as a dynamic field of action where phonetic change, borrowing, language mixture, and language shift all occur because of social forces, and where genetic origin is secondary to these forces. In recent years linguists have begun to see the two theories as complementary. The assumption of uniformity among protolanguages is regarded as an abstraction necessary to explain existing regularities of sound change and is considered extremely useful for the elucidation of long-term prehistoric relationships, especially since conflicting short-term diffusion currents tend to cancel each other. Speech-community studies, on the other hand, appear better adapted to the explanation of relatively recent changes.

Language Behavior and Social Communication

The shift of emphasis from historical to synchronic problems during the last three decades has brought about some fundamental changes in our theories of language, resulting in the creation of a body of entirely new analytical techniques. Viewed in the light of these fresh insights, the earlier speech-community studies are subject to serious criticism on grounds of both linguistic and sociological methodology. For some time, therefore, linguists oriented toward formal analysis showed very little interest. More recent structural studies, however, show that this criticism does not affect the basic concept of the speech community as a field of action where the distribution of linguistic variants is a reflection of social facts. The relationship between such variants when they are classified in terms of usage rather than of their purely linguistic characteristics can be examined along two dimensions: the *dialectal* and the *superposed*.

Dialectal relationships are those in which differences set off the vernaculars of local groups (for example, the language of home and family) from those of other groups within the same, broader culture. Since this classification refers to usage rather than to inherent linguistic traits, relationships between minority languages and majority speech (e.g., between Welsh and English in Britain or French and English in Canada) and between distinct languages found in zones of intensive intertribal contact (e.g., in modern Africa) can also be considered dialectal, because they show characteristics similar to the relationship existing between dialects of the same language.

Whereas dialect variation relates to distinctions in geographical origin and social background, superposed variation refers to distinctions between different types of activities carried on within the same group. The special parlances described above form a linguistic extreme, but similar distinctions in usage are found in all speech communities. The language of formal speechmaking, religious ritual, or technical discussion, for example, is never the same as that employed in informal talk among friends, because each is a style fulfilling particular communicative needs. To some extent the linguistic markers of such activities are directly related to their different technical requirements. Scientific discussion, for instance, requires precisely defined terms and strict limitation on their usage. But in other cases, as in greetings, forms of address, or choosing between "isn't" and "ain't," the primary determinant is the social relationship between speakers rather than communicative necessity. Language choice in these cases is limited by social barriers; the existence of such barriers lends significance to the sociolinguistic study of superposed variation.

This distinction between dialectal and superposed varieties obviates the usual linguistic distinction between geographically and socially distributed varieties, since the evidence indicates that actual residence patterns are less important as determinants of distribution than social interaction patterns and usage. Thus, there seems to be little need to draw conceptual distinctions upon this basis.

Descriptions of dialectal and superposed variation relate primarily to social groups. Not all individuals within a speech community have equal control of the entire set of superposed variants current there. Control of communicative resources varies sharply with the individual's position within the social system. The more narrowly confined his sphere of activities, the more homogeneous the social environment within which he interacts, and the less his need for verbal facility. Thus, housewives, farmers, and laborers, who rarely meet outsiders, often make do with only a narrow range of speech styles, while actors, public speakers, and businessmen command the greatest range of styles. The fact that such individual distinctions are found in multilingual as well as in linguistically homogeneous societies suggests that the common assertion which identifies bilingualism with poor scores in intelligence testing is in urgent need of re-examination, based, as it is, primarily on work with underprivileged groups. Recent work, in fact, indicates that the failure of some self-contained groups to inculcate facility in verbal manipulation is a major factor in failures in their children's performances in public school systems.

Attitudes to language choice

Social norms of language choice vary from situation to situation and from community to community. Regularities in attitudes to particular speech varieties, however, recur in a number of societies and deserve special comment here. Thieves' argots, gang jargons, and the like serve typically as group boundary maintaining mechanisms, whose linguistic characteristics are the result of informal group consensus and are subject to continual change in response to changing attitudes. Individuals are accepted as members of the group to the extent that their usage conforms to the practices of the day. Similar attitudes of exclusiveness prevail in the case of many tribal languages spoken in areas of culture contact where other superposed idioms serve as media of public communication. The tribal language here is somewhat akin to a secret ritual, in that it is private knowledge to be kept from outsiders, an attitude which often makes it difficult for casual investigators to collect reliable information about language distribution in such areas.

Because of the elaborate linguistic etiquette and stylistic conventions that surround them, classical, liturgical, and administrative languages function somewhat like secret languages. Mastery of the conventions may be more important in gaining social success than substantive knowledge of the information dispensed through these languages. But unlike the varieties mentioned above, norms of appropriateness are explicit in classical languages; this permits them to remain unchanged over many generations.

In contrast, the attitude to pidgins, trade languages, and similar intergroup media of communication tends to be one of toleration. Here little attention is paid to linguistic markers of social appropriateness. It is the function of such languages to facilitate contact between groups without constituting their respective social cohesiveness; and, as a result, communication in these languages tends to be severely restricted to specific topics or types of interaction. They do not, as a rule, serve as vehicles for personal friendships.

We speak of *language loyalty* when a literary variety acquires prestige as a symbol of a particular nationality group or social movement. Language loyalty tends to unite diverse local groups and social classes, whose members may continue to speak their own vernaculars within the family circle. The literary idiom serves for reading and for public interaction and embodies the cultural tradition of a nation or a sector thereof. Individuals choose to employ it as a symbol of their allegiance to a broader set of political ideals than that embodied in the family or kin group.

Language loyalty may become a political issue in a modernizing society when hitherto socially isolated minority groups become mobilized. Their demands for closer participation in political affairs are often accompanied by demands for language reform or for the rewriting of the older, official code in their own literary idiom. Such demands often represent political and socioeconomic threats to the established elite, which may control the distribution of administrative positions through examination systems based upon the official code. The replacement of an older official code by another literary idiom in modernizing societies may thus represent the displacement of an established elite by a rising group.

The situation becomes still more complex when socioeconomic competition between several minority groups gives rise to several competing new literary standards, as in many parts of Asia and Africa, where language conflicts have led to civil disturbances and political instability. Although demands for language reform are usually verbalized in terms of communicative needs, it is interesting to observe that such demands do not necessarily reflect important linguistic differences between the idioms in question. Hindi and Urdu, the competing literary standards of north India, or Serbian and Croatian, in Yugoslavia, are grammatically almost identical. They differ in their writing systems, in their lexicons, and in minor aspects of syntax. Nevertheless, their proponents treat them as separate languages. The conflict in language loyalty may even affect mutual intelligibility, as when speakers' claims that they do not understand each other reflect primarily social attitudes rather than linguistic fact. In other cases serious linguistic differences may be disregarded when minority speakers pay language loyalty to a standard markedly different from their own vernacular. In many parts of Alsace-Lorraine, for example, speakers of German dialects seem to disregard linguistic fact and pay language loyalty to French rather than to German.

Varietal distribution

Superposed and dialectal varieties rarely coincide in their geographical extent. We find the greatest amount of linguistic diversity at the level of local, tribal, peasant, or lower-class urban populations. Tribal areas typically constitute a patchwork of distinct languages, while local speech distribution in many modern nations takes the form of a dialect chain in which the speech of each locality is similar to that of adjoining settlements and in which speech differences increase in proportion to geographical distance. Variety at the local level is bridged by the considerably broader spread of superposed varieties, serving as media of supralocal communication. The Latin of medieval Europe and the Arabic of the Near East form extreme examples of supralocal spread. Uniformity at the superposed level in their case, however, is achieved at the expense of large gaps in internal communication channels. Standard languages tend to be somewhat more restricted in geographical spread than classical languages, because of their relationship to local dialects. In contrast to a society in which classical languages are used as superposed varieties, however, a standard-language society possesses better developed channels of internal communication, partly because of its greater linguistic homogeneity and partly because of the internal language loyalty that it evokes.

In fact, wherever standard languages are well-established they act as the ultimate referent that determines the association of a given local dialect with one language or another. This may result in the anomalous situation in which two linguistically similar dialects spoken on different sides of a political boundary are regarded as belonging to different languages, not because of any inherent linguistic differences but because their speakers pay language loyalty to different standards. Language boundaries in such cases are defined partly by social and partly by linguistic criteria.

Verbal repertoires

The totality of dialectal and superposed variants regularly employed within a community make up the *verbal repertoire* of that community. Whereas the bounds of a language, as this term is ordinarily understood, may or may not coincide with that of a social group, verbal repertoires are always specific to particular populations. As an analytical concept the verbal repertoire allows us to establish direct relationships between its constituents and the socioeconomic complexity of the community.

We measure this relationship in terms of two concepts: *linguistic range* and *degree of compartmentalization*. Linguistic range refers to internal language distance between constituent varieties, that is, the total amount of purely linguistic differentiation that exists in a community, thus distinguishing among multilingual, multidialectal, and homogeneous communities. Compartmentalization refers to the sharpness with which varieties are set off from each other, either along the superposed or the dialectal dimension. We speak of compartmentalized repertoires, therefore, when several languages are spoken without their mixing, when dialects are set off from each other by sharp isogloss bundles, or when special parlances are sharply distinct from other forms of speech. We speak of fluid repertoires, on the other hand, when transitions between adjoining vernaculars are gradual or when one speech style merges into another in such a way that it is difficult to draw clear borderlines.

Initially, the linguistic range of a repertoire is a function of the languages and special parlances employed before contact. But given a certain period of contact, linguistic range becomes dependent upon the amount of internal interaction. The greater the frequency of internal interaction, the greater the tendency for innovations arising in one part of the speech community to diffuse throughout it. Thus, where the flow of communication is dominated by a single all-important center – for example, as Paris dominates central France – linguistic range is relatively small. Political fragmentation, on the other hand, is associated with diversity of languages or of dialects, as in southern Germany, long dominated by many small, semi-independent principalities.

Over-all frequency in interaction is not, however, the only determinant of uniformity. In highly stratified societies speakers of minority languages or dialects typically live side by side, trading, exchanging services, and often maintaining regular social contact as employer and employee or master and servant. Yet despite this contact, they tend to preserve their own languages, suggesting the existence of social norms that set limits to freedom of intercommunication. Compartmentalization reflects such social norms. The exact nature of these sociolinguistic barriers is not yet clearly understood, although some recent literature suggests new avenues for investigation.

We find, for example, that separate languages maintain themselves most readily in closed tribal systems, in which kinship dominates all activities. Linguistically distinct special parlances, on the other hand, appear most fully developed in highly stratified societies, where the division of labor is maintained by rigidly defined barriers of ascribed status. When social change causes the breakdown of traditional social structures and the formation of new ties, as in urbanization and colonialization, linguistic barriers between varieties also break down. Rapidly changing societies typically show either gradual transition between speech styles or, if the community is bilingual, a range of intermediate varieties bridging the transitions between extremes.

BIBLIOGRAPHY

Barth, Frederik (1964). Ethnic Processes on the Pathan-Baluch Boundary. Pages 13–20 in *Indo-Iranica: Mélanges présentés à Georg Morgenstierne, à l'occasion de son soixante-dixième anniversaire*. Wiesbaden (Germany): Harrassowitz.

Bernstein, Basil ([1958] 1961). Social Class and Linguistic Development: A Theory of Social Learning. Pages 288–314 in A. H. Halsey et al. (eds.), *Education, Economy, and Society*. New York: Free Press. → First published in Volume 9 of the *British Journal of Sociology*.

Bloomfield, Leonard ([1933] 1951). *Language*. Rev. edn. New York: Holt.

Brown, Roger W. (1965). *Social Psychology*. New York: Free Press.

Gumperz, John J., and Hymes, Dell H. (eds.) (1964). The Ethnography of Communication. *American Anthropologist* New Series 66, no. 6, part 2.

Halliday, Michael A. K., McIntosh, Angus, and Strevens, Peter ([1964] 1965). *The Linguistic Sciences and Language Teaching*. Bloomington: Indiana University Press.

Haugen, Einar I. (1956). *Bilingualism in the Americas: A Bibliography and Research Guide*. University, Ala.: American Dialect Society.

Haugen, Einar I. (1966). *Language Conflict and Language Planning*. Cambridge, Mass.: Harvard University Press.

Hertzler, Joyce O. (1965). *A Sociology of Language*. New York: Random House.

Hymes, Dell H. (ed.) (1964). *Language in Culture and Society: A Reader in Linguistics and Anthropology*. New York: Harper.

Jespersen, Otto ([1925] 1964). *Mankind, Nation and the Individual, From a Linguistic Point of View*. Bloomington: Indiana University Press. → First published as *Menneskehed, nasjon og individ i sproget*.

Kurath, Hans (ed.) (1939–1943). *Linguistic Atlas of New England*. 3 vols. and a handbook. Providence, R.I.: Brown University Press.

Labov, William (1966). *The Social Stratification of English in New York City*. Arlington: Center for Applied Linguistics.

Passin, Herbert (1963). Writer and Journalist in the Transitional Society. Pages 82–123 in Conference on Communication and Political Development, Dobbs Ferry, N.Y., 1961, *Communications and Political Development*. Edited by Lucian W. Pye. Princeton University Press. → Contains a discussion of the relationship of national languages to political development.

Weinreich, Uriel (1953). *Languages in Contact: Findings and Problems*. New York: Linguistic Circle of New York.

2

On Communicative Competence

Dell Hymes

I

This paper is theoretical. One connotation of "theoretical" is "programatic"; a related connotation is that one knows too little about the subject to say something practical. Both connotations apply to this attempt to contribute to the study of the "language problems of disadvantaged children". Practical work, however, must have an eye on the current state of theory, for it can be guided or misguided, encouraged or discouraged, by what it takes that state to be. Moreover, the language development of children has particular pertinence just now for theory. The fundamental theme of this paper is that the theoretical and the practical problems converge.

It is not that there exists a body of linguistic theory that practical research can turn to and has only to apply. It is rather that work motivated by practical needs may help build the theory that we need. To a great extent programs to change the language situation of children are an attempt to apply a basic science that does not yet exist. Let me review the present stage of linguistic theory to show why this is so.

Consider a recent statement, one that makes explicit and precise an assumption that has underlain much of modern linguistics (Chomsky, 1965, p. 3):

Linguistic theory is concerned primarily with an ideal speaker-listener, in a completely homogeneous speech community, who knows its language perfectly and is unaffected by such grammatically irrelevant conditions as memory limitations, distractions, shifts of attention and interest, and errors (random or characteristic) in applying his knowledge of the language in actual performance.

From the standpoint of the children we seek to understand and help, such a statement may seem almost a declaration of irrelevance. All the difficulties that confront the children and ourselves seem swept from view.

One's response to such an indication of the state of linguistic theory might be to ignore fundamental theory and to pick and choose among its products. Models of language structure, after all, can be useful in ways not envisioned in the statements of their authors. Some linguists (e.g., Labov, Rosenbaum, Gleitman) use transformational generative grammar to study some of the ways in which a speech community is not homogeneous and in which speaker-listeners clearly have differential knowledge of a language. Perhaps, then, one ought simply to disregard how linguists define the scope of "linguistic" theory. One could point to several available models of language – Trager-Smith-Joos, tagnemic, stratificational, transformational-generative (in its MIT, Pennsylvania, Harvard and other variants), and, in England, "system-structure" (Halliday and others); remark that there are distinguished scholars using each to analyse English; regret that linguists are unable to agree on the analysis of English; and pick and choose, according to one's problem and local situation, leaving grammarians otherwise to their own devices.

To do so would be a mistake for two reasons: on the one hand, the sort of theoretical perspective quoted above *is* relevant in ways that it is important always to have in mind; on the other hand, there is a body of linguistic data and problems that would be left without theoretical insight, if such a limited conception of linguistic theory were to remain unchallenged.

The special relevance of the theoretical perspective is expressed in its representative anecdote (to use Kenneth Burke's term), the image it puts before our eyes. The image is that of a child, born with the ability to master any language with almost miraculous ease and speed; a child who is not merely molded by conditioning and reinforcement, but who actively proceeds with the unconscious theoretical interpretation of the speech that comes its way, so that in a few years and with a finite experience, it is master of an infinite ability, that of producing and understanding in principle any and all grammatical sentences of language. The image (or theoretical perspective) expresses the essential equality in children just as human beings. It is noble in that it can inspire one with the belief that even the most dispiriting conditions can be transformed; it is an indispensable weapon against views that would explain the communicative differences among groups of children as inherent, perhaps racial.

The limitations of the perspective appear when the image of the unfolding, mastering, fluent child is set beside the real children in our schools. The theory must seem, if not irrelevant, then at best a doctrine of poignancy: poignant, because of the difference between what one imagines and what one sees; poignant too, because the theory, so powerful in its own realm, cannot on its terms cope with the difference. To cope with the realities of children as communicating beings requires a theory within which sociocultural factors have an explicit and constitutive role; and neither is the case.

For the perspective associated with transformational generative grammar, the world of linguistic theory has two parts: linguistic *competence* and linguistic *performance*. Linguistic competence is understood as concerned with the tacit knowledge of language structure, that is, knowledge that is commonly not conscious or available for spontaneous report, but necessarily implicit in what the (ideal) speaker-listener can say. The primary task of theory is to provide for an explicit account of such knowledge, especially in relation to the innate structure on which it must depend. It is in terms of such knowledge that one can produce and understand an infinite set of sentences, and that language can be spoke of as "creative", as *energeia*. Linguistic performance is most explicitly understood as concerned with the processes often termed encoding and decoding.

Such a theory of competence posits ideal objects in abstraction from sociocultural features that might enter into their description. Acquisition of competence is also seen as essentially independent of sociocultural features, requiring only suitable speech in the environment of the child to develop. The theory of performance is the one sector that might have a specific sociocultural content; but while equated with a theory of language use, it is essentially concerned with psychological by-products of the analysis of grammar, not, say, with social interaction. As to a constitutive role for sociocultural features in the acquisition or conduct of perform-ance, the attitude would seem quite negative. Little or nothing is said, and if some-thing were said, one would expect it to be depreciatory. Some aspects of performance are, it is true, seen as having a constructive role (e.g., the cycling rules that help assign stress properly to sentences), but if the passage quoted at the outset is recalled, however, and if the illustrations of performance phenomena in the chapter from which the passage comes are reviewed, it will be seen that the note struck is persistently one of limitation, if not disability. When the notion of performance is introduced as "the actual use of language in concrete situations", it is immediately stated that only under the idealization quoted could performance directly reflect competence, and that in actual fact it obviously could not. "A record of natural speech will show numerous false starts, deviations from rules, changes of plan in mid-course, and so on." One speaks of primary linguistic data as "fairly degenerate in quality" (Chomsky, 1965, p. 31), or even of linguistic performance as "adulteration" of ideal competence (Katz, 1967, p. 144). While "performance" is something of a residual category for the theory, clearly its most salient connotation is that of imperfect manifestation of underlying system.

I do not think the failure to provide an explicit place for sociocultural features to be accidental. The restriction of competence to the notions of a homogeneous community, perfect knowledge, and independence of sociocultural factors does not seem just a simplifying assumption, the sort that any scientific theory must make. If that were so, then some remark to that effect might be made; the need to include a sociocultural dimension might be mentioned; the nature of such inclusion might even be suggested. Nor does the predominant association of performance with imperfection seem accidental. Certainly, any stretch of speech is an imperfect indica-tion of the knowledge that underlies it. For users that share the knowledge, the arrangement might be thought of as efficient. And if one uses one's intuitions as to speech, as well as to grammar, one can see that what to grammar is imperfect, or unaccounted for, may be the artful accomplishment of a social act (Garfinkel, 1972), or the patterned, spontaneous evidence of problem solving and conceptual thought (John, 1967, p. 5). These things might be acknowledged, even if not taken up.

It takes the absence of a place for sociocultural factors, and the linking of performance to imperfection, to disclose an ideological aspect to the theoretical standpoint. It is, if I may say so, rather a Garden of Eden view. Human life seems divided between grammatical competence, an ideal innately-derived sort of power, and performance, an exigency rather like the eating of the apple, thrusting the perfect speaker-hearer out into a fallen world. Of this world, where meanings may be won by the sweat of the brow, and communication achieved in labor (cf. Bonhoffer, 1965, p. 365), little is said. The controlling image is of an abstract, isolated individual, almost an unmotivated cognitive mechanism, not, except incidentally, a person in a social world.

Any theoretical stance of course has an ideological aspect, and that aspect of present linguistic theory is not its invention. A major characteristic of modern linguistics has been that it takes structure as primary end in itself, and tends to depreciate use, while not relinquishing any of its claim to the great significance that is attached to language. (Contrast classical antiquity, where structure was a means to use, and the grammarian subordinate to the rhetor.) The result can sometimes seem a very happy one. On the one hand, by narrowing concern to independently and readily structurable data, one can enjoy the prestige of an advanced science; on the other hand, despite ignoring the social dimensions of use, one retains the prestige of dealing with something fundamental to human life.

In this light, Chomsky is quite correct when he writes that his conception of the concern of linguistic theory seems to have been also the position of the founders of modern general linguistics. Certainly if modern structural linguistics is meant, then a major thrust of it has been to define the subject matter of linguistic theory in terms of what it is not. In de Saussure's linguistics, as generally interpreted, *la langue* was the privileged ground of structure, and *la parole* the residual realm of variation (among other things). Chomsky associates his views of competence and performance with the Saussurian conceptions of langue and parole, but sees his own conceptions as superior, going beyond the conception of language as a systematic inventory of items to renewal of the Humboldtian conception of underlying processes. The Chomsky conception is superior, not only in this respect, but also in the very terminology it introduces to mark the difference. "Competence" and "performance" much more readily suggest concrete persons, situations, and actions. Indeed, from the standpoint of the classical tradition in structural linguistics, Chomsky's theoretical standpoint is at once its revitalization and its culmination. It carries to its perfection the desire to deal in practice only with what is internal to language, yet to find in that internality that in theory is of the widest or deepest human significance. No modern linguistic theory has spoken more profoundly of either the internal structure or the intrinsic human significance.

This revitalization flowers while around it emerge the sprouts of a conception that before the end of the century may succeed it. If such a succession occurs, it will be because, just as the transformational theory could absorb its predecessors and handle structural relationships beyond their grasp, so new relationships, relationships with an ineradicable social component, will become salient that will require a broader theory to absorb and handle them. I shall return to this historical conjecture at the end of this paper. Let me now sketch considerations that motivate a broader theory. And let me do this by first putting forward an additional representative anecdote.

II

As against the ideal speaker-listener, here is Bloomfield's account of one young Menomini he knew (1927, p. 437):

White Thunder, a man around forty, speaks less English than Menomini, and that is a strong indictment, for his Menomini is atrocious. His vocabulary is small; his inflections are often barbarous; he constructs sentences of a few threadbare models. He may be said to speak no language tolerably. His case is not uncommon among younger men, even when they speak but little English.

Bloomfield goes on to suggest that the commonness of the case is due, in some indirect way, to the impact of the conquering language. In short, there is here *differential competence* within a *heterogeneous speech community*, both undoubtedly shaped by acculturation. (The alternative to a constitutive role for the novel sociocultural factor is to assume that atrocious Menomini was common also before contact. If taken seriously, the assumption would still implicate sociocultural factors.) Social life has affected not merely outward performance, but inner competence itself.

Let me now review some other indications of the need to transcend the notions of perfect competence, homogeneous speech community, and independence of sociocultural features.

In her excellent article reviewing recent studies of subcultural differences in language development in the United States, Cazden (1966, p. 190) writes that one thing is clear:

The findings can be quickly summarized: on all the measures, in all the studies, the upper socio-economic status children, however defined, are more advanced than the lower socio-economic status children.

The differences reviewed by Cazden involve enabling effects for the upper status children just as much as disabling effects for the lower status children. Moreover, given subcultural differences in the patterns and purposes of language use, children of the lower status may actually excel in aspects of communicative competence not observed or measured in the tests summarized. And among the Menomini there were not only young men like White Thunder, but also those like Red Cloud Woman, who

speaks a beautiful and highly idiomatic Menomini ... (and) speaks Ojibwa and Potawatomi fluently. ... Linguistically, she would correspond to a highly educated American woman who spoke, say, French and Italian in addition to the very best type of cultivated, idiomatic English. (Bloomfield, 1927, p. 437)

There are tribes of the northeast Amazon among whom the normal scope of linguistic competence is a control of at least four languages, a spurt in active command coming during adolescence, with repertoire and perfection of competence continuing to be augmented throughout life. Here, as in much of our world, the ideally fluent speaker-listener is multilingual. (Even an ideally fluent monolingual of course is master of functional varieties within the one language.)

In this connection it should be noted that fluent members of communities often regard their languages, or functional varieties, as not identical in communicative adequacy. It is not only that one variety is obligatory or preferred for some uses, another for others (as is often the case, say, as between public occasions and personal relationships). Such intuitions reflect experience and self-evaluation as to what one can in fact do with a given variety. This sort of differential competence has nothing to do with "disadvantage" or deficiency relative to other normal members of the community. All of them may find Kurdish, say, the medium in which most things can best be expressed, but Arabic the better medium for religious truth; users of Berber may find Arabic superior to Berber for all purposes except intimate domestic conversation (Ferguson, 1966).

The combination of community diversity and differential competence makes it necessary not to take the presence in a community of a widespread language, say, Spanish or English, at face value. Just as one puts the gloss of a native word in quotation marks, so as not to imply that the meaning of the word is thereby accurately identified, so one should put the name of a language in quotation marks, until its true status in terms of competence has been determined. (Clearly there is need for a theoretically motivated and empirically tested set of terms by which to characterize the different kinds of competence that may be found.) In an extreme case what counts as "English" in the code repertoire of a community may be but a few phonologically marked forms (the Iwam of New Guinea). The cases in general constitute a continuum, perhaps a scale, from more restricted to less restricted varieties, somewhat crosscut by adaptation of the same inherited "English" materials to different purposes and needs. A linguist analysing data from a community on the assumption "once English, always English" might miss and sadly misrepresent the actual competence supposedly expressed by his grammar.

There is no way within the present view of linguistic competence to distinguish between the abilities of one of the pure speakers of Menomini noted by Bloomfield and those of whom White Thunder was typical. Menomini sentences from either would be referred to a common grammar. Perhaps it can be said that the competence is shared with regard to the recognition and comprehension of speech. While that would be an important (and probably true) fact, it has not been the intention of the theory to distinguish between models of competence for reception and models of competence for production. And insofar as the theory intends to deal with the "creative" aspect of language, that is, with the ability of a user to devise novel sentences appropriate to situations, it would seem to be a retrenchment, if not more, to claim only to account for a shared ability to *understand* novel sentences produced by others. In some fundamental sense, the competence of the two groups of speakers, in terms of ability to make "creative" use of Menomini, is clearly distinct. Difference in judgement of acceptability is not in question. There is simply a basic sense in which users of Menomini of the more versatile type have a knowledge (syntactic as well as lexical) that users of White Thunder's type do not. [. . .]

Labov has documented cases of dual competence in reception, but single competence in production, with regard to the ability of lower-class Negro children to interpret sentences in either standard or substandard phonology, while consistently using only substandard phonology in speaking themselves. An interesting converse kind of case is that in which there is a dual competence for production, a sort of "competence for incompetence" as it were. Thus among the Burundi of East Africa (Albert, 1964) a peasant may command the verbal abilities stressed and valued in the culture but cannot display it in the presence of a herder or other superior. In such cases appropriate behavior is that in which "their words are haltingly delivered, or run on uncontrolled, their voices are loud, their gestures wild, their figures of speech ungainly, their emotions freely displayed, their words and sentences clumsy." Clearly the behavior is general to all codes of communication, but it attaches to the grammatical among them.

Such work as Labov's in New York City, and examples such as the Burundi, in which evidence for linguistic competence co-varies with interlocutor, point to the necessity of a social approach even if the goal of description is a single homogeneous code. Indeed, much of the difficulty in determining what is acceptable and intuitively correct in grammatical description arises because social and contextual determinants are not controlled. By making explicit the reference of a description to a single use in a single context, and by testing discrepancies and variations against differences of use and context, the very goal of not dealing with diversity can be achieved – in the limited, and only possible, sense in which it can be achieved. The linguist's own intuitions of underlying knowledge prove difficult to catch and to stabilize for use (and of course are not available for languages or varieties he does not himself know). If analysis is not to be reduced to explication of a corpus, or debauch into sub- jectivity, then the responses and judgements of members of the community whose language is analysed must be utilized – and not merely informally or *ad hoc*, but in some explicit, systematic way. In particular, since every response is made in some context, control of the dependence of judgements and abilities on context must be gained. It may well be that the two dimensions found by Labov to clarify phonolo- gical diversity – social hierarchy of varieties of usage, and range (formal to informal) of "contextual styles", together with marking for special functions (expressivity, clarity, etc.) will serve for syntactic diversity as well. Certainly some understanding of local criteria of fluency, and conditions affecting it, is needed just insofar as the goal is to approximate an account of ideal fluency in the language in question. In sum, if one analyses the language of a community as if it should be homogeneous, its diversity trips one up around the edges. If one starts with analysis of the diversity, one can isolate the homogeneity that is truly there.

Clearly work with children, and with the place of language in education, requires a theory that can deal with a heterogeneous speech community, differential compet- ence, the constitutive role of sociocultural features – that can take into account such phenomena as White Thunder, socioeconomic differences, multilingual mastery, relativity of competence in "Arabic", "English", etc., expressive values, socially determined perception, contextual styles and shared norms for the evaluation of variables. Those whose work requires such a theory know best how little of its content can now be specified. Two things can be said. First, linguistics needs such a theory too. Concepts that are unquestioningly postulated as basic to linguistics (speaker-listener, speech community, speech act, acceptability, etc.) are, as we see, in fact sociocultural variables, and only when one has moved from their postulation to their analysis can one secure the foundations of linguistic theory itself. Second, the notion of competence may itself provide the key. Such comparative study of the role of language as has been undertaken shows the nature and evaluation of linguistic ability to vary cross-culturally; even what is to count as the same language, or variety, to which competence might be related, depends in part upon social factors (cf. Gumperz, 1964; Hymes, 1968a; Labov, 1966). Given, then, the assumption that the competency of users of language entails abilities and judgements relative to, and interdependent with, sociocultural features, one can see how to extend the notion to allow for this. I shall undertake this, by recasting first the representative

anecdote of the child, and then the notions of competence and performance themselves.

III

Recall that one is concerned to explain how a child comes rapidly to be able to
produce and understand (in principle) any and all of the grammatical sentences of a
language. Consider now a child with just that ability. A child who might produce
any sentence whatever – such a child would be likely to be institutionalized: even
more so if not only sentences, but also speech or silence was random, unpredictable.
For that matter, a person who chooses occasions and sentences suitably, but is
master only of fully grammatical sentences, is at best a bit odd. Some occasions
call for being appropriately ungrammatical.

We have then to account for the fact that a normal child acquires knowledge of
sentences, not only as grammatical, but also as appropriate. He or she acquires
competence as to when to speak, when not, and as to what to talk about with whom,
when, where, in what manner. In short, a child becomes able to accomplish a
repertoire of speech acts, to take part in speech events, and to evaluate their
accomplishment by others. This competence, moreover, is integral with attitudes,
values, and motivations concerning language, its features and uses, and integral with
competence for, and attitudes toward, the interrelation of language with the other
codes of communicative conduct (cf. Goffman, 1956, p. 477; 1963, p. 335; 1964).
The internalization of attitudes towards a language and its uses is particularly
important (cf. Labov, 1965, pp. 84–5, on priority of subjective evaluation in social
dialect and processes of change), as is internalization of attitudes toward use of
language itself (e.g. attentiveness to it) and the relative place that language comes to
play in a pattern of mental abilities (cf. Cazden, 1966), and in strategies – what
language is considered available, reliable, suitable for, *vis-à-vis* other kinds of code.

The acquisition of such competency is of course fed by social experience, needs,
and motives, and issues in action that is itself a renewed source of motives, needs,
experience. We break irrevocably with the model that restricts the design of language to one face toward referential meaning, one toward sound, and that defines the
organization of language as solely consisting of rules for linking the two. Such a
model implies naming to be the sole use of speech, as if languages were never
organized to lament, rejoice, beseech, admonish, aphorize, inveigh (Burke, 1966,
p. 13), for the many varied forms of persuasion, direction, expression and symbolic
play. A model of language must design it with a face toward communicative conduct
and social life.

Attention to the social dimension is thus not restricted to occasions on which
social factors seem to interfere with or restrict the grammatical. The engagement of
language in social life has a positive, productive aspect. There are rules of use
without which the rules of grammar would be useless. Just as rules of syntax can
control aspects of phonology, and just as semantic rules perhaps control aspects of
syntax, so rules of speech acts enter as a controlling factor for linguistic form as a
whole. Linguists generally have developed a theory of levels by showing that what is
the same on one level of representation has in fact two different statuses, for which a
further level must be posited. The seminal example is in Sapir (1925) on phonology,

while the major recent examples are in the work of Chomsky and Lamb. A second aspect is that what is different at one level may have in fact the same status at the further level. (Thus the two interpretations of "He decided on the floor" – the floor as what he decided on/as where he decided – point to a further level at which the sameness of structure is shown.) Just this reasoning requires a level of speech acts. What is grammatically the same sentence may be a statement, a command, or a request; what are grammatically two different sentences may as acts both be requests. One can study the level of speech acts in terms of the conditions under which sentences can be taken as alternative types of act, and in terms of the conditions under which types of act can be realized as alternative types of sentence. And only from the further level of acts can some of the relations among communicative means be seen, e.g. the mutual substitutability of a word and a nod to realize an act of assent, the necessary co-occurrence of words and the raising of a hand to realize an oath.

The parallel interpretations of "he decided on the floor" and "she gave up on the floor" point to a further level at which the sameness in structure is shown.

Rules of use are not a late grafting. Data from the first years of acquisition of English grammar show children to develop rules for the use of different forms in different situations and an awareness of different acts of speech (Ervin-Tripp, personal communication). Allocation of whole languages to different uses is common for children in multilingual households from the beginning of their acquisition. Competency for use is part of the same developmental matrix as competence for grammar.

The acquisition of competence for use, indeed, can be stated in the same terms as acquisition of competence for grammar. Within the developmental matrix in which knowledge of the sentences of a language is acquired, children also acquire knowledge of a set of ways in which sentences are used. From a finite experience of speech acts and their interdependence with sociocultural features, they develop a general theory of the speaking appropriate in their community, which they employ, like other forms of tacit cultural knowledge (competence) in conducting and interpreting social life (cf. Goodenough, 1957; Searle, 1967). They come to be able to recognize, for example, appropriate and inappropriate interrogative behavior (e.g. among the Araucanians of Chile, that to repeat a question is to insult; among the Tzeltal of Chiapas, Mexico, that a direct question is not properly asked (and to be answered "nothing"); among the Cahinahua of Brazil, that a direct answer to a first question implies that the answerer has no time to talk, a vague answer that the question will be answered directly the second time, and that talk can continue).

The existence of competency for use may seem obvious, but if its study is to be established, and conducted in relation to current linguistics, then the notions of competence and performance must themselves be critically analysed, and a revised formulation provided.

The chief difficulty of present linguistic theory is that it would seem to require one to identify the study of the phenomena of concern to us here with its category of performance. The theory's category of competence, identified with the criterion of grammaticality, provides no place. Only performance is left, and its associated criterion of acceptability. Indeed, language use is equated with performance: "the theory of language use – the theory of performance" (Chomsky, 1965, p. 9).

The difficulty with this equation, and the reasons for the making of it, can be explained as follows. First, the clarification of the concept of performance offered by Chomsky (1965, pp. 10–15), as we have seen, omits almost everything of socio-cultural significance. The focus of attention is upon questions such as which among grammatical sentences are most likely to be produced, easily understood, less clumsy, in some sense more natural; and such questions are studied initially in relation to formal tree-structures, and properties of these such as nesting, self-embedding, multiple-branching, left-branching, and right-branching. The study of such questions is of interest, but the results are results of the psychology of perception, memory, and the like, not of the domain of cultural patterning and social action. Thus, when one considers what the sociocultural analogues of performance in this sense might be, one sees that these analogues would not include major kinds of judgement and ability with which one must deal in studying the use of language (see below under appropriateness).

Second, the notion of performance, as used in discussion, seems confused between different meanings. In one sense, performance is observable behavior, as when one speaks of determining from the data of performance the underlying system of rules (Chomsky, 1965, p. 4), and of mentalistic linguistics as that linguistics that uses performance as data, along with other data, e.g. those of introspection, for determination of competence (p. 193). The recurrent use of "actual" implies as much, as when the term is first introduced in the book in question, "actual perform-ance", and first characterized: "performance (the actual use of language in concrete situations)" (pp. 3–4). In this sense performance is "actual", competence underlying. In another sense, performance itself also underlies data, as when one constructs a performance model, or infers a performative device (e.g. a perceptual one) that is to explain data and be tested against them (p. 15); or as when, in a related sense, one even envisages the possibility of stylistic "rules of performance" to account for occurring word orders not accounted for by grammatical theory (p. 127).

When one speaks of performance, then, does one mean the behavioral data of speech? or all that underlies speech beyond the grammatical? or both? If the ambiguity is intentional, it is not fruitful; it smacks more of the residual category and marginal interest.

The difficulty can be put in terms of the two contrasts that usage manifests:

1   (underlying) competence v. (actual) performance;
2   (underlying) grammatical competence v. (underlying) models/rules of perform-ance.

The first contrast is so salient that the status of the second is left obscure. In point of fact, I find it impossible to understand what stylistic "rules of performance" could be, except a further kind of underlying competence, but the term is withheld. [. . .]

It remains that the present vision of generative grammar extends only a little way into the realm of the use of language. To grasp the intuitions and data pertinent to underlying competence for use requires a sociocultural standpoint. To develop that standpoint adequately, one must transcend the present formulation of the dichotomy of competence:performance, as we have seen, and the associated formulation of the judgements and abilities of the users of a language as well. To this I now turn.

IV

There are several sectors of communicative competence, of which the grammatical is one. Put otherwise, there is behavior, and, underlying it, there are several systems of rules reflected in the judgements and abilities of those whose messages the behavior manifests. (The question of how the interrelationships among sectors might be conceived is touched upon below.) In the linguistic theory under discussion, judgements are said to be of two kinds: of *grammaticality*, with respect to competence, and of *acceptability*, with respect to performance. Each pair of terms is strictly matched; the critical analysis just given requires analysis of the other. In particular, the analysis just given requires that explicit distinctions be made within the notion of "acceptability" to match the distinctions of kinds of "performance", and at the same time, the entire set of terms must be examined and recast with respect to the communicative as a whole.

If an adequate theory of language users and language use is to be developed, it seems that judgements must be recognized to be in fact not of two kinds but of four. And if linguistic theory is to be integrated with theory of communication and culture, this fourfold distinction must be stated in a sufficiently generalized way. I would suggest, then, that for language and for other forms of communication (culture), four questions arise:

1   Whether (and to what degree) something is formally *possible*;
2   Whether (and to what degree) something is *feasible* in virtue of the means of implementation available;
3   Whether (and to what degree) something is *appropriate* (adequate, happy, successful) in relation to a context in which it is used and evaluated;
4   Whether (and to what degree) something is in fact done, actually *performed*, and what its doing entails.

A linguistic illustration: a sentence may be grammatical, awkward, tactful and rare. (One might think of the four as successive subsets; more likely they should be pictured as overlapping circles.)

These questions may be asked from the standpoint of a system *per se*, or from the standpoint of persons. An interest in competence dictates the latter standpoint here. Several observations can be made. There is an important sense in which a normal member of a community has knowledge with respect to all these aspects of the communicative systems available to him. He will interpret or assess the conduct of others and himself in ways that reflect a knowledge of each (possible, feasible, appropriate), done (if so, how often). There is an important sense in which he would be said to have a capability with regard to each. This latter sense, indeed, is one many would understand as included in what would be meant by his competence. Finally, it cannot be assumed that the formal possibilities of a system and individual knowledge are identical; a system may contain possibilities not part of the present knowledge of a user (cf. Wallace, 1961b). Nor can it be assumed that the knowledge acquired by different individuals is identical, despite identity of manifestation and apparent system.

Given these considerations, I think there is not sufficient reason to maintain a terminology at variance with more general usage of "competence" and "performance" in the sciences of man, as is the case with the present equations of competence, knowledge, systemic possibility, on the one hand, and of performance, behavior, implementational constraints, appropriateness, on the other. It seems necessary to distinguish these things and to reconsider their relationship, if their investigation is to be insightful and adequate.

I should take *competence* as the most general term for the capabilities of a person. (This choice is in the spirit, if at present against the letter, of the concern in linguistic theory for underlying capability.) Competence is dependent upon both (tacit) *knowledge* and (ability for) *use*. *Knowledge* is distinct, then, both from competence (as its part) and from systemic possibility (to which its relation is an empirical matter). Notice that Cazden (1967), by utilizing what is in effect systemic possibility as a definition of competence is forced to separate it from what persons can do. The "competence" underlying a person's behavior is identified as one kind of "performance" (performance A, actual behavior being performance B). The logic may be inherent in the linguistic theory from which Cazden starts, once one tries to adapt its notion of competence to recognized facts of personal knowledge. The strangely misleading result shows that the original notion cannot be left unchanged.

Knowledge also is to be understood as subtending all four parameters of communication just noted. There is knowledge of each. *Ability for use* also may relate to all four parameters. Certainly it may be the case that individuals differ with regard to ability to use knowledge of each: to interpret, differentiate, etc. The specification of *ability for use* as part of competence allows for the role of non-cognitive factors, such as motivation, as partly determining competence. In speaking of competence, it is especially important not to separate cognitive from affective and volitive factors, so far as the impact of theory on educational practice is concerned; but also with regard to research design and explanation (as the work of Labov indicates). Within a comprehensive view of competence, considerations of the sort identified by Goffman (1967, pp. 218–26) must be reckoned with – capacities in interaction such as courage, gameness, gallantry, composure, presence of mind, dignity, stage confidence, capacities which are discussed in some detail by him and, explicitly in at least one case, as kinds of competency (p. 224).

Turning to judgements and intuitions of persons, the most general term for the criterion of such judgements would be acceptable. Quirk (1966) so uses it, and Chomsky himself at one point remarks that "grammaticalness is only one of the many factors that interact to determine acceptability" (1965, p. 11). (The term is thus freed from its strict pairing with "performance".) The sources of acceptability are to be found in the four parameters just noted, and in interrelations among them that are not well understood.

Turning to actual use and actual events, the term *performance* is now free for this meaning, but with several important reminders and provisos. The "performance models" studied in psycholinguistics are to be taken as models of aspects of ability for use, relative to means of implementation in the brain, although they could now be seen as a distinct, contributory factor in general competence. There seems, indeed, to have been some unconscious shifting between the sense in which one would speak of the performance of a motor, and that in which one would speak of the performance of a person or actor (cf. Goffman, 1959, pp. 17–76, "Perform-ances") or of a cultural tradition (Singer, 1955; Wolf, 1964, pp. 75–6). Here the performance of a person is not identical with a behavioral record, or with the imperfect or partial realization of individual competence. It takes into account the interaction between competence (knowledge, ability for use), the competence of others, and the cybernetic and emergent properties of events themselves. A perform-ance, as an event, may have properties (patterns and dynamics) not reducible to terms of individual or standardized competence. Sometimes, indeed, these properties are the point (a concert, play, party).

The concept of "performance" will take on great importance, insofar as the study of communicative competence is seen as an aspect of what from another angle may be called the ethnography of symbolic forms – the study of the variety of genres, narration, dance, drama, song, instrumental music, visual art, that interrelate with speech in the communicative life of a society, and in terms of which the relative importance and meaning of speech and language must be assessed. The recent shift in folklore studies and much of anthropology to the study of these genres in terms of performances with underlying rules (e.g. Abrahams, 1967) can be seen as a recon-struction on an ethnographic basis of the vision expressed in Cassirer's philosophy of symbolic forms. (This reconstruction has a direct application to the communicative competence of children in American cities, where identification and understanding of differences in kinds of forms, abilities, and their evaluation is essential.)

The concept of "performance" will be important also in the light of sociological work such as that of Goffman (cited above), as its concern with general interactional competence helps make precise the particular role of linguistic competence.

In both respects the interrelation of knowledge of distinct codes (verbal:non-verbal) is crucial. In some cases these interrelations will bespeak an additional level of competence (cf., e.g., Sebeok, 1959, pp. 141–2): "Performance constitutes a concurrently ordered selection from two sets of acoustic signals – in brief, codes – language and music.... These are integrated by special rules...."). In others, per-haps not, as when the separate cries of vendors and the call to prayer of a muezzin are perceived to fit by an observer of an Arabic city, but with indication of intent or plan.

The nature of research into symbolic forms and interactional competence is already influenced in important part by linguistic study of competence (for some discussion see Hymes, 1968b). Within the view of communicative competence taken here, the influence can be expected to be reciprocal.

Having stated these general recommendations, let me now review relations between the linguistic and other communicative systems, especially in terms of cultural anthropology. I shall consider both terminology and content, using the four questions as a framework.

1 Whether (and to what degree) something is formally possible

This formulation seems to express an essential concern of present linguistic theory for the openness, potentiality, of language, and to generalize it for cultural systems. When systemic possibility is a matter of language, the corresponding term is of course *grammaticality*. Indeed, language is so much the paradigmatic example that one uses "grammar" and "grammaticality" by extension for other systems of formal possibility (recurrent references to a cultural grammar, Kenneth Burke's *A Grammar of Motives*, etc.). For particular systems, such extension may well be the easiest course; it is much easier to say that something is "grammatical" with respect to the underlying structure of a body of myth, than to say in a new sense that it is "mythical". As a general term, one does readily enough speak of "cultural" in a way analogous to grammatical (Sapir once wrote of "culturalized behavior", and it is clear that not all behavior is cultural). We may say, then, that something possible within a formal system is grammatical, cultural, or, on occasion, communicative (cf. Hymes, 1967b). Perhaps one can also say uncultural or uncommunicative, as well as ungrammatical, for the opposite.

2   Whether (and to what degree) something is feasible

The predominant concern here, it will be recalled, has been for psycholinguistic factors such as memory limitation, perceptual device, effects of properties such as nesting, embedding, branching, and the like. Such considerations are not limited to linguistics. A parallel in cultural anthropology is Wallace's hypothesis (1961a, p. 462) that the brain is such that culturally institutionalized folk taxonomies will not contain more than twenty-six entities and consequently will not require more than six orthogonally related binary dimensions for the definitions of all terms. With regard to the cultural, one would take into account other features of the body and features of the material environment as well. With regard to the communicative, the general importance of the notion of means of implementation available is clear.

As we have seen, question 2 defines one portion of what is lumped together in linguistic theory under the heading of performance, and, correspondingly, acceptability. Clearly a more specific term is needed for what is in question here. No general term has been proposed for this property with regard to cultural behavior as a whole, so far as I know, and *feasible* seems suitable and best for both. Notice, moreover, that the implementational constraints affecting grammar may be largely those that affect the culture as a whole. Certainly with regard to the brain there would seem to be substantial identity.

3   Whether (and to what degree) something is appropriate

As we have seen, appropriateness is hardly brought into view in the linguistic theory under discussion, and is lumped under the heading of performance, and, correspondingly, acceptability. With regard to cultural anthropology, the term *appropriate* has been used (Conklin, Frake, etc.), and has been extended to language (Hymes, 1964, pp. 39–41). "Appropriateness" seems to suggest readily the required sense of relation to contextual features. Since any judgement is made in some defining context, it may always involve a factor of appropriateness, so that this dimension must be controlled even in study of purely grammatical competence (cf. Labov, 1966). From a communicative standpoint, judgements of appropriateness may not be assignable to different spheres, as between the linguistic and the cultural; certainly, the spheres of the two will intersect. (One might think of appropriateness with regard to grammar as the context-sensitive rules of sub-categorization and selection to which the base component is subject; there would still be intersection with the cultural.)

Judgement of appropriateness employs a tacit knowledge. Chomsky himself discusses the need to specify situations in mentalistic terms, and refers to proper notions of "what might be expected from anthropological research" (1965, p. 195, n. 5). Here there would seem to be recognition that an adequate approach to the relation between sentences and situations must be "mentalistic", entailing a tacit knowledge, and, hence, competence (in the usage of both Chomsky and this paper). But the restriction of competence (knowledge) to the grammatical prevails, so far as explicit development of theory is concerned. By implication, only "performance" is left. There is no mention of what might contribute to judgement of sentences in relation to situations, nor how such judgements might be analysed. The lack of explicitness here, and the implicit contradiction of a "mentalistic" account of what must in terms of the theory be a part of "performance" show again the need to place linguistic theory within a more general sociocultural theory.

4 Whether (and to what degree) something is done

The study of communicative competence cannot restrict itself to occurrences, but it cannot ignore them. Structure cannot be reduced to probabilities of occurrence, but structural change is not independent of them. The capabilities of language users do include some (perhaps unconscious) knowledge of probabilities and shifts in them as indicators of style, response, etc. Something may be possible, feasible, and appropriate and not occur. No general term is perhaps needed here, but the point is needed, especially for work that seeks to change what is done. This category is necessary also to allow for what Harold Garfinkel (in discussion in Bright, 1966, p. 323) explicates as application of the medieval principle, *factum valet*: "an action otherwise prohibited by rule is to be treated as correct if it happens nevertheless".

In sum, the goal of a broad theory of competence can be said to be to show the ways in which the systemically possible, the feasible, and the appropriate are linked to produce and interpret actually occurring cultural behavior. [...]

V

We spoke first of a child's competence as "in principle". Of course no child has perfect knowledge or mastery of the communicative means of his community. In particular, differential competence has itself a developmental history in one's life. The matrix formed in childhood continues to develop and change throughout life with respect both to sentence structures and their uses (cf. Labov, 1965, pp. 77, 91–2; Chomsky, 1965, p. 202) and recall the northeast Amazon situation mentioned earlier. Tanner (1967, p. 21) reports for a group of Indonesians: "Although the childhood speech patterns...foreshadowed those of the adult, they did not determine them.... For these informants it is the principle of code specialization that is the important characteristic of childhood linguistic experience, not the pattern of code specialization itself. (All are multilingual from childhood.) Not one person interviewed reported a static linguistic history in this respect." (See now also Carroll, 1968.)

Perhaps one should contrast a "long" and a "short" range view of competency, the short range view being interested primarily in understanding innate capacities as unfolded during the first years of life, and the long range view in understanding the continuing socialization and change of competence through life. In any case, here is one major respect in which a theory of competence must go beyond the notion of ideal fluency in a homogeneous community, if it is to be applicable to work with disadvantaged children and with children whose primary language or language variety is different from that of their school; with intent to change or add, one is presupposing the possibility that competence that has unfolded in the natural way can be altered, perhaps drastically so, by new social factors. One is assuming from the outset a confrontation of different systems of competency within the school and community, and focusing on the way in which one affects or can be made to affect the other. One encounters phenomena that pertain not only to the separate structures of languages, but also to what has come to be called *interference* (Weinreich, 1953) between them: problems of the interpretation of manifestations of one system in terms of another.

Since the interference involves features of language and features of use together, one might adopt the phrase suggested by Hayes, and speak of *sociolinguistic interference*. (More generally, one would speak of *communicative interference* to allow for the role of modes of communication other than language; in this section, however, I shall focus on phenomena of language and language *per se*.)

When a child from one developmental matrix enters a situation in which the communicative expectations are defined in terms of another, misperception and misanalysis may occur at every level. As is well known, words may be misunderstood because of differences in phonological systems; sentences may be misunderstood because of differences in grammatical systems; intents, too, and innate abilities, may be misevaluated because of differences of systems for the use of language and for the import of its use (as against other modalities).

With regard to education, I put the matter some years ago in these words (Hymes, 1961, pp. 65–6):

...new speech habits and verbal training must be introduced, necessarily by particular sources to particular receivers, using a particular code with messages of particular forms via particular channels, about particular topics and in particular settings – and all this from and to people for whom there already exist definite patternings of linguistic routines, of personality expression via speech, of uses of speech in social situations, of attitudes and conceptions toward speech. It seems reasonable that success in such an educational venture will be enhanced by an understanding of this existing structure, because the innovators' efforts will be perceived and judged in terms of it, and innovations which mesh with it will have greater success than those which cross its grain.

The notion of sociolinguistic interference is of the greatest importance for the relationship between theory and practice. First of all, notice that a theory of sociolinguistic interference must begin with heterogeneous situations, whose dimensions are social as well as linguistic. (While a narrow theory seems to cut itself off from such situations, it must of course be utilized in dealing with them. See, for example,

Labov and Cohen (1967) on relations between standard and non-standard phonological and syntactic rules in Harlem, and between receptive and productive competence of users of the non-standard vernacular.)

Second, notice that the notion of sociolinguistic interference presupposes the
notion of sociolinguistic systems between which interference occurs, and thus
helps one see how to draw on a variety of researches that might be overlooked or
set aside. (I have in mind for example obstacles to use of research on "second-
language learning" in programs for Negro students because of the offensiveness of
the term.) The notions of sociolinguistic interference and system require a conception of an *integrated theory of sociolinguistic description*. Such work as has been
done to contribute to such a theory has found it necessary to start, not from the
notion of a language, but from the notion of a *variety* or *code*. In particular, such a
descriptive theory is forced to recognize that the historically derived status of
linguistic resources as related or unrelated languages and dialects, is entirely secondary to their status in actual social relationships. Firstly, recall the need to put
language names in quotes (section II). Secondly, the degree of linguistic similarity
and distance cannot predict mutual intelligibility, let alone use. Thirdly, from the
functional standpoint of a sociolinguistic description, means of quite different scope
can be employed in equivalent roles. A striking example is that the marking of
intimacy and respect served by shift of second person pronoun in French (*tu:vous*)
may be served by shift of entire language in Paraguay (Guarani:Spanish). Conversely, what seem equivalent means from the standpoint of languages may have quite
different roles, e.g., the elaborated and restricted codes of English studied by
Bernstein (1965). In short, we have to break with the tradition of thought which
simply equates one language, one culture, and takes a set of functions for granted. In
order to deal with the problems faced by disadvantaged children, and with education in much of the world, we have to begin with the conception of the speech habits,
or competencies, of a community or population, and regard the place among them of
the resources of historically-derived languages as an empirical question. As functioning codes, one may find one language, three languages; dialects widely divergent or
divergent by a hair; styles almost mutually incomprehensible, or barely detectable as
different by the outsider; the objective linguistic differences are secondary, and do
not tell the story. What must be known is the attitude toward the differences, the
functional role assigned to them, the use made of them. Only on the basis of such a
functionally motivated description can comparable cases be established and valid
theory developed.

Now with regard to sociolinguistic interference among school children, much
relevant information and theoretical insight can come from the sorts of cases
variously labelled "bilingualism", "linguistic acculturation", "dialectology", "creolization", whatever. The value of an integrated theory of sociolinguistic description to
the practical work would be that

1   it would attempt to place studies, diversely labelled, within a common analytical
    framework; and
2   by placing such information within a common framework, where one can talk
    about relations among codes, and types of code-switching, and types of inter-
    ference as between codes, one can make use of the theory while perhaps avoiding

connotations that attach to such labels as "second-language learning". (I say perhaps because of course it is very difficult to avoid unpleasant connotations for any terms used to designate situations that are themselves intrinsically sensitive and objectionable.)

William Stewart's (1965, p. 11, n. 2) suggestion that some code relationships in the United States might be better understood if seen as part of a continuum of cases ranging to the Caribbean and Africa, for example, seems to me from a theoretical standpoint very promising. It is not that most code relationships in the United States are to be taken as involving different languages, but that they do involve relationships among different codes, and that the fuller series illuminates the part. Stewart has seen through the different labels of dialect, creole, pidgin, language, bilingualism, to a common sociolinguistic dimension. Getting through different labels to the underlying sociolinguistic dimensions is a task in which theory and practice meet.

Let me now single out three interrelated concepts, important to a theory of sociolinguistic description, which have the same property of enabling us to cut across diverse cases and modes of reporting, and to get to basic relationships. One such concept is that of *verbal repertoire*, which Gumperz (1964) has done much to develop. The heterogeneity of speech communities, and the priority of social relationships, is assumed, and the question to be investigated is that of the set of varieties, codes, or subcodes, commanded by an individual, together with the types of switching that occur among them. (More generally, one would assess communicative repertoire.)

A second concept is that of *linguistic routines*, sequential organizations beyond the sentence, either as activities of one person, or as the interaction of two or more. Literary genres provide obvious examples; the organization of other kinds of texts, and of conversation, is getting fresh attention by sociologists, such as Sacks, and sociologically oriented linguists, such as Labov. One special importance of linguistic routines is that they may have the property that the late English philosopher Austin dubbed *performative* (Searle, 1967). That is, the saying does not simply stand for, refer to, some other thing; it is itself the thing in question. To say "I solemnly vow" is to solemnly vow; it does not name something else that is the act of vowing solemnly. Indeed, in the circumstances no other way to vow solemnly is provided other than to do so by saying that one does so. From this standpoint, then, disability and ability with regard to language involve questions that are not about the relation between language and something else that language might stand for or influence; sometimes such questions are about things that are done linguistically or not at all. (More generally, one would analyse linguistic routines, comprising gesture, paralinguistics, etc. as well.)

A third concept is that of *domains of language behavior*, which Fishman has dealt with insightfully in his impressive work on *Language Loyalty in the United States* (1966, pp. 424–39). Again, the complexity and patterning of use is assumed, and the focus is upon "the most parsimonious and fruitful designation of the occasions on which one language (variant, dialect, style, etc.) is habitually employed rather than (or in addition to) another" (p. 428). (More generally, one would define domains of communicative behavior.)

Too often, to be sure, the significance of a sociolinguistic feature, such as a code, routine, or term or level of address, is sought by purely distributional means. The feature is traced through the set of contexts in which it can be used without regard to an intervening semantic structure. Such an approach neglects the fact that sociolinguistic features, like linguistic features, are "signs" in the classical Saussurean sense, comprising both a form and a meaning (*signifiant* and *signifié*). The difference is that one thinks of a typical linguistic sign as comprising a phonological form and a referential meaning (*chien* and the corresponding animal), whereas a sociolinguistic sign may comprise with respect to form an entire language, or some organized part of one, while meaning may have to do with an attitude, norm of interaction, or the like. (Recall the Paraguayan case of Spanish/distance:Guarani/ closeness (among other dimensions).) Thus the relation between feature and context is mediated by a semantic paradigm. There is an analogue here to the representation of a lexical element in a language in terms of form (phonological features), meaning (semantic features), and context (features of syntactic selection), or, indeed, to the tripartite semiotic formula of Morris, syntactics, semantics, pragmatics, if these three can be interpreted here as analogous of form, meaning and context.

If the distributional approach neglects semantic structure, there is a common semantic approach that neglects context. It analyses the structure of a set of elements (say, codes, or terms of personal reference) by assuming one normal context. This approach (typical of much componential analysis) is equally unable to account for the range of functions a fluent user of language is able to accomplish (cf. Tyler, 1966). It is true that the value of a feature is defined first of all in relation to a set of normal contexts (settings, participants, personal relationships, topics, or whatever). But given this "unmarked" (presupposed) usage, an actor is able to insult, flatter, color discourse as comic or elevated, etc., by "marked" use of the feature (code, routine, level of address, whatever) in other contexts. Given their tacit knowledge of the normal values, hearers can interpret the nature and degree of markedness of the use.

Thus the differences that one may encounter within a community may have to do with:

1 Presence or absence of a feature (code, routine, etc.).
2 The semantic value assigned a feature (e.g., English as having the value of distance and hostility among some American Indians).
3 The distribution of the feature among contexts, and
4 The interrelations of these with each other in unmarked and marked usages.

This discussion does not exhaust the concepts and modes of analysis relevant to the sort of theory that is needed. A number of scholars are developing relevant conceptual approaches, notably Bernstein, Fishman, Gumperz, Labov (my own present formulation is indicated in Hymes, 1967a). The three concepts singled out do point up major dimensions: the capacities of persons, the organization of verbal means for socially defined purposes, and the sensitivity of rules to situations. And it is possible to use the three concepts to suggest one practical framework for use in sociolinguistic description. [...]

NOTE

This paper is revised from one presented at the Research Planning Conference on Language Development Among Disadvantaged Children, held under the sponsorship of the Department of Educational Psychology and Guidance, Ferkauf Graduate School, Yeshiva University, June 7–8, 1966. The original paper is included in the report of that conference, issued by the Department of Educational Psychology and Guidance (pp. 1–16). I wish to thank Dr Beryl Bailey and Dr Edmund Gordon of Yeshiva University for inviting me to participate and Dr Courtney Cazden, Dr John Gumperz, Dr Wayne O'Neill and Dr Vera John for their comments at that time.

REFERENCES

Abrahams, R. D. (1967). "Patterns of Performance in the British West Indies", Mimeographed working paper.

Albert, E. M. (1964). "Rhetoric, Logic and Poetics in Burundi: Culture Patterning of Speech Behaviour". In J. J. Gumperz and D. Hymes (eds.), *The Ethnography of Communication. American Anthropologist*, vol. 66, no. 6, part 2.

Bernstein, B. (1965). "A Sociolinguistic Approach to Social Learning". In J. Gould (ed.), *Social Science Survey*. Penguin.

Bloomfield, L. (1927). "Literate and Illiterate Speech". *American Speech*, vol. 2, pp. 432–9.

Bonhoffer, D. (1965). "What is Meant by 'Telling the Truth'?" *Ethics*, pp. 363–72.

Bright, W. (1966). *Sociolinguistics*. Mouton.

Burke, K. (1966). *Towards a Better Life. Being a Series of Epistles, or Declamations*. University of California Press (first published 1932).

Carroll, J. B. (1968). "Development of Native Language Skills beyond the Early Years". In C. E. Reed and J. B. Carroll (eds.), *Language Learning*. National Council of Teachers of English.

Cazden, C. B. (1966). "Subcultural Differences in Child Language: An Interdisciplinary Review". *Merrill-Palmer Q.*, vol. 12, pp. 185–218.

Cazden, C. B. (1967). "On Individual Differences in Language Competence and Performance". *Journal of Special Education*, vol. 1, pp. 135–50.

Chomsky, N. (1965). *Aspects of the Theory of Syntax*. MIT Press.

Ferguson, C. A. (1966). "On Sociolinguistically Oriented Surveys". *Linguistic Reporter*, vol. 8, no. 4, pp. 1–3.

Fishman, J. A. (1966). *Language Loyalty in the United States*. Mouton.

Garfinkel, H. (1972). "Remarks on Ethnomethodology". In J. J. Gumperz and D. Hymes (eds.), *Directions in Sociolinguistics*. Holt, Rinehart, & Winston.

Goffman, E. (1956). "The Nature of Deference and Demeanor". *American Anthropologist*, vol. 58, pp. 473–502.

Goffman, E. (1959). *The Presentation of Self in Everyday Life*. Doubleday; Allen Lane The Penguin Press.

Goffman, E. (1963). *Behavior in Public Places*. Free Press.

Goffman, E. (1964). "The Neglected Situation". In J. J. Gumperz and D. Hymes (eds.), *The Ethnography of Communication, American Anthropologist*, vol. 66, no. 6, part 2.

Goffman, E. (1967). *Interaction Ritual*. Doubleday.

Goodenough, W. H. (1957). "Cultural Anthropology and Linguistics". In P. Garvin (ed.), *Report of the Seventh Annual Round Table Meeting on Languages and Linguistics*. Georgetown University Press.

Gumperz, J. J. (1964). "Linguistic and Social Interaction in Two Communities". In J. J. Gumperz and D. Hymes (eds.), *The Ethnography of Communication. American Anthropologist*, vol. 66, no. 6, part 2.

Hymes, D. (1961). "Functions of Speech: An Evolutionary Approach". In F. Gruber (ed.), *Anthropology and Education*. University of Pennsylvania.

Hymes, D. (1964). "Directions in (Ethno-) Linguistic Theory". In A. K. Romney and R. G. D'Andrade (eds.), *Transcultural Studies of Cognition*. American Anthropological Association.

Hymes, D. (1967a). "Models of the Interaction of Language and Social Setting". *Journal of Social Issues*, vol. 23, pp. 8–28.

Hymes, D. (1967b). "The Anthropology of Communication". In F. Dance (ed.), *Human Communication Theory: Original Essays*. Holt, Rinehart, & Winston.

Hymes, D. (1968a). "Linguistic Problems in Defining the Concept of the Tribe". In J. Helm (ed.), *Proceedings of the 1967 Spring Meeting of the American Ethnological Society*. University of Washington Press.

Hymes, D. (1968b). "Linguistics – the Field". *International Encyclopedia of the Social Sciences*. Macmillan Co.

Hymes, D. (in press). Review of Kenneth Burke, *Language as Symbolic Action. Language*.

John, V. (1967). "Communicative Competence of Low-income Children: Assumptions and Programs". *Report of Language Development Study Group*, Ford Foundation.

Katz, J. J. (1967). "Recent Issues in Semantic Theory". *Foundations of Language*, vol. 3, pp. 124–94.

Labov, W. (1965). "Stages in the Acquisition of Standard English". In R. Shuy (ed.), *Social Dialects and Language Learning*. National Council of Teachers of English.

Labov, W. (1966). *The Social Stratification of English in New York City*. Center for Applied Linguistics.

Labov, W., and Cohen, P. (1967). "Systematic Relations of Standard and Non-standard Rules in the Grammar of Negro Speakers". Paper for Seventh Project Literacy Conference, Cambridge, Mass.

Quirk, R. (1966). "Acceptability in Language". *Proceedings of the University of Newcastle-upon-Tyne Philosophical Society*, vol. 1, no. 7, pp. 79–92.

Sapir, E. (1925). "Sound Patterns in Language". *Language*, vol. 1, pp. 37–51.

Searle, J. (1967). "Human Communication Theory and the Philosophy of Language: Some Remarks". In F. Dance (ed.), *Human Communication Theory*. Holt, Rinehart, & Winston.

Sebeok, T. (1959). "Folksong Viewed as Code and Message". *Anthropos*, vol. 54, pp. 141–53.

Singer, M. (1955). "The Cultural Pattern of Indian Civilization: A Preliminary Report of a Methodological Field Study". *Far East. Q.*, vol. 15, pp. 223–36.

Stewart, W. (1965). "Urban Negro Speech: Sociolinguistic Factors Affecting English Teaching". In R. Shuy (ed.), *Social Dialects and Language Learning*. National Council of Teachers of English.

Tanner, N. (1967). "Speech and Society among the Indonesian Élite: A Case Study of a Multilingual Community". *Anthropological Linguistics*, vol. 9, no. 3, pp. 15–40.

Tyler, S. (1966). "Context and Variation in Koya Kinship Terminology". *American Anthropologist*, vol. 68, pp. 693–707.

Wallace, A. F. C. (1961a). "On Being Just Complicated Enough". *Proceedings of the National Academy of Sciences*, vol. 47, pp. 438–64.

Wallace, A. F. C. (1961b). *Culture and Personality*. Random House.

Weinreich, U. (1953). *Languages in Contact*. Linguistic Circle of New York.

Wolf, E. (1964). *Anthropology*. Prentice-Hall.

3

The African-American Speech Community: Reality and Sociolinguists[1]

Marcyliena M. Morgan

One of the more persistent challenges in creole language studies and sociolinguistics in general is to determine the extent and ways in which information or linguistic facts gathered from a particular speech community can, in some way, benefit that community. This challenge is directly related to what Labov (1982) identifies as the two questions most frequently put to linguists by the public: "What is linguistics about?" and "What is it good for?" How linguists address these questions is often more important to the speech community under study than the linguistic information that has been assembled. For the most part, sociolinguistic training focuses on the identification and analysis of linguistic variation compared to sociological variables such as ethnicity, class, age, and gender. Training does not stress the identification and incorporation of intragroup language norms and values – and often considers these subjects as falling outside the realm of sociolinguistics.[2] Consequently, language plans and policies that may be theoretically sound from a linguistic perspective do not necessarily address the speech community's notion of language as a reflection of social reality, especially theories concerning language and identity, power and loyalty. Such shortcomings often lead to the reconstitution of hegemonic theories that marginalize culturally different speech communities. Once sociolinguistic theories privilege the standard variety as the "norm" in relation to competing varieties, the intent of both language plans and planners becomes suspect, and speakers sense that linguistics may be dangerous to the health of their speech community. One of the clearest examples of the conflict that can result from excluding a community's language ideology (cf. Schieffelin et al. 1998) from language planning and policy comes from African-American English (AAE), a variety often characterized as surrounded by a history of controversy.[3]

Sociolinguistics and Language Planning and Policy in the African-American Speech Community

Beginning in the mid-1960s and for a decade thereafter, many dialectologists and creolists devoted considerable attention to the historical development and linguistic description of AAE.[4] These linguists, most notably, Bailey (1969, 1971), Dillard (1968, 1972), Stewart (1968), Labov (1972), Wolfram (1969), and Fasold (1969, 1972), presented their research in a political climate that included, on the one hand, the expression of African-American pride and identity and, on the other, reactions to the charge that African-American culture and language is deviant and deficient.[5] Few linguists of the day could remain silent when asked: "What is Black English? What is it good for?" Their nearly unanimous response to attacks from educational and psychological quarters was that AAE, while different from American English (AE), is as logical and as capable of representing intelligent ideas as any other language or dialect.[6] Linguists addressed the misinformed and often racist arguments by educating students of linguistics as well as members of the educational establishment on the system and structure of AAE. Their opinions and research results appeared in introductory language and linguistics texts under the heading of "cultural difference" or "cultural diversity."[7]

A decade later, texts on the language education of African-American children appeared again. The contributors to these anthologies, many of whom are members of the African-American community, presented arguments, plans, and proposals that they believed represented their community's language, educational, and cultural interests. In contrast to earlier arguments for the legitimacy of AAE within the national landscape, publications such as Smitherman (1981a) and Brooks (1985) focused on the educational system's continuing failure to incorporate knowledge of AAE into curriculum in ways that benefit the education of African-American children. This state of affairs provoked Smitherman (1981b) to conclude that the bottom line in language-policy debates about AAE is the fate of Black children as victims of miseducation.

The volumes written on the language and education of African Americans reflect the tremendous effort expended over the past 20 years in proving that society in general, and the educational system in particular, should respect AAE and its speakers. Yet, the most dissident and serious obstacle to the implementation of these efforts has been the African-American community itself (Baugh 1983b). Although their rejection has been characterized as self-hate by Stewart (1975), it is partly due to the failure of sociolinguists to incorporate the language and educational values and beliefs of the African-American community within language and education plans. While examples of conflicts between the community and linguists have existed since the 1970s,[8] the following discussion will focus on two specific proposals that resulted in conflict: the King case, which ended in 1979, and a study conducted by William Labov (1985) on the divergence of African-American and white dialects. These two highly publicized events are of great interest for three reasons. First, they were discussed extensively within both the linguistic and African-American communities. Second, the proposals were popularly interpreted as representing two opposite views on the significance of AAE. Finally, despite the fact that each proposal incorporated different views on the function of AAE in education, both plans were rejected by significant segments of the African-American community.

Martin Luther King Junior Elementary School versus the Ann Arbor School District Board

In 1977, the legal case filed on behalf of the children of the Martin Luther King Junior Elementary School against the Ann Arbor School District Board (USDC Eastern District of Michigan Southern Division Civil Action No. 7–71861) charged that school officials had placed African-American children in learning-disabled and speech-pathology classes and held them at low grade levels because of language, cultural, and class differences. Geneva Smitherman (1981a, 1981b), the linguist most centrally involved in the case, described the Martin Luther King School as an institution that subscribed to liberal goals and philosophies but was unable to reconcile either its practice regarding cultural and class biases or its ignorance of cultural differences and values. Though the suit's initial legal arguments considered the problem of cultural and class bias on the part of the school, the presiding judge determined that children are not protected from that particular form of prejudice in education under the U.S. Constitution. Instead, citing section 1703(f) of the 1974 Equal Education Opportunity Act, which guarantees that race, color, sex, national origin, or language barrier cannot impede equal education, the judge decided that the case would focus on the question of the children's language. The expert witnesses on AAE included J. L. Dillard and William Labov (both of whom participated in the defense of Black English in the early 1970s), as well as other linguists and scholars from psychology and education.[9] On 12 July 1979, two years after the initial lawsuit was filed, presiding Judge Charles W. Joiner ruled that there is a substantial difference between AAE and AE and that to ignore the existence of AAE in the education of African-American youth constituted failure on the part of the school district to provide equal education under the law. In his written opinion on the 1979 King case, Judge Joiner described AAE as a language variety spoken by 80 percent of the African-American community, which is part of, but different from, the English used in schools. Labov (1982) describes the consensus reached by linguists on the nature and origin of AAE as follows:

a.   The Black English vernacular is a subsystem of English with a distinct set of phonological and syntactic rules that are now aligned in many ways with the rules of other dialects.

b.   It incorporates many features of Southern phonology, morphology and syntax; Blacks in turn have exerted influence on the dialects of the South where they have lived.

c.   It shows evidence of derivation from an earlier Creole that was closer to the present-day Creoles of the Caribbean.

d.   It has a highly developed aspect system, quite different from other dialects of English, which shows a continuing development of its semantic structure. (192)

Judge Joiner then ruled that the Ann Arbor school district must help its teachers recognize the home language (AAE) of the students and to use that knowledge in their attempts to teach reading skills in Standard English (41).

As mentioned earlier, Smitherman (1981a, 1981b) was critically aware that the issues concerning the King case were not only about the language variety spoken by the children. Rather, the intolerance toward AAE also embodies a bias against the cultural, political, and social reality it represents. Along with having to contend with the justice system's refusal to recognize the connection between language, culture, and class, Smitherman was also confronted with the "broad misinterpretations and gross distortions" that surrounded the press reporting of the case. Headlines from the African-American press included: "Judge to Hear the 'Black Slang' Case," "Black English Must Go!," "Black English Would Doom Blacks to Fail," "Black English Is Silly."

The perversive manner in which the press reported the case was partly responsible for the community's suspicious reaction to the final verdict. In particular, the African-American middle class considered the King case a threat to freedom and believed it would encourage segregation. June Brown (1979), a popular African-American columnist for the *Detroit News*, reduced the issues and intent of the actual ruling on the case to insipid self-interest on the part of scholars and teaching professionals. Though Brown acknowledged in her series of articles on the case that ineffective reading and teaching methods were important issues, she concluded:

The court should not order Black children into a separate program because the facts do not support the need for one...As for whites understanding Blacks, many white teachers in inner city schools understand "Black English" clearly and do outstanding jobs in teaching Black kids...Whites can understand just as much "Black English" as they want to.

Though representing a different constituency, Samuel 17X (1975), writing in the *Bilalian News*, the newspaper of the Nation of Islam, supported Brown's suspicions. He refers to AAE as "slave speech" and quotes a Chicago Southside street observer: "That old Black English thing is just a shrewd Black...hustler's game to make a job for himself as a counselor or teacher in some slick educational program."

The Divergence of Black and White Dialects

Considering the misrepresentation and misinterpretations surrounding the King case, it is not surprising that vocal and influential members of the African-American community suspected that the ruling was a trick to continue oppression through miseducation by teaching AAE in the schools. Yet, some ten years later, when Labov (1985) argued for the importance of Standard English in the education of African-American children, the community showed little support for either his theories or his concern that continued language divergence leads to educational failure.

In 1985, the results of the National Science Foundation (NSF) project conducted by William Labov on "The Influence of Urban Minorities on Linguistic Change" were widely reported by the international and national print and electronic media.[10] According to Vaughn-Cooke (1987), at least 157 domestic and foreign newspapers reported on the findings of the study and their implications. News items appeared in the *New York Times*, and all the major news programs and talk shows described the study's findings. The NSF project maintained that African Americans in Philadelphia are not participating in the vernacular changes that are going on in other dialect varieties of the city. Instead, Labov and Harris (1986) discovered that in Philadelphia and other Northern cities, the speech pattern of African Americans was developing in its own direction and was becoming increasingly more different from the speech of whites in the same communities.[11] The reason for divergence from white social dialect varieties, according to Labov and Harris (1983, 2), is that "there is a close parallel between residential segregation and linguistic segregation, and between residential segregation and educational failure." Labov proposed to address the problem of increasing language divergence by developing a program for language arts in the integrated classroom.

The results of Labov's (1985) study, as well as his intent to put sociolinguists' understanding of language difference to use, were not unanimously embraced by linguists. A special issue of the *Journal of American Speech* (Butters 1987), which was devoted to the controversy, reveals considerable disagreement over the claims made by Labov (1987), Bailey and Maynor (1987), and others on the divergence of AAE from AE. Vaughn-Cooke (1987), perhaps the most outspoken of the African-American linguists, assailed Labov and referred to his study as poorly investigated, "flawed and misguided," and ultimately detrimental to the education of African-American children.[12]

In the same publication, Arthur Spears (1987) questioned another aspect of Labov's findings as reported in a news release from the University of Pennsylvania, dated 15 March 1985. The release in part read:

These language differences have contributed to widespread educational failure in the inner-city schools.... And the problem seems to be getting worse over time rather than better. Labov believes that language division has been caused by decreasing personal contact between Blacks and whites. The most effective way for Black children to learn other dialects of English in addition to their own dialects is through greater interaction with whites.... The mass media, including television and radio, have had little influence on the speech patterns of Blacks or any other group.

Spears (1987) considered the above release enigmatic because it linked the acquisition of AE to racial integration. He reasoned that linguistic divergence could not result from the lack of integration, as the 1985 study argues, since AE is spoken by middle-class African Americans who mainly live and socialize among mixed classes of African Americans. Spears concluded that lack of opportunity for African-American youth is the likely cause of Labov's (1985) findings.

As some linguists found exceptions to various aspects of Labov's (1985) results and educational proposals, the speech community concurred. Considering the position taken by the middle class on the King case, perhaps the most surprising reaction to the divergence controversy appeared in Kenneth M. Jones's September 1986 article in *EM: Ebony Man*, a middle-class publication devoted to African-American men. In this article, Jones maintained that many sociolinguists simply did not understand the community's notion of pride or power. He argued that AAE is the language variety of choice throughout the African-American community and cites language use in rap and hip-hop music as an example of the expressive character and "African beat" inherent in African-American speech styles. In the Jones article Spears explains, "Generally everybody thought that all Black people wanted to do was assimilate. So when we found divergence, the reason had to be social isolation... we hadn't had the chance to be around whites, so we haven't learned their ways."

Though *EM* exalts AAE, it does not argue for its exclusive use within or outside of the community, but rather for verbal dexterity or code switching. Kenneth Jones (1986) qualifies his position with quotes from several African-American artists and linguists.

"The requirement that you be verbally dexterous is one of your admission fees to Black culture," Redmond adds. For this very reason, certain elements of the Black community lash out against "talking proper." "If your language shifts are extreme," observes Dr. Scott, "the Black community interprets that as your being pretentious or unnatural. In other words, you are trying to be something you are not." (69)

EM's final appraisal of the speech community's notion of AAE is enmeshed in a sense of African identity: "Former President of Senegal Leopold Senghor once said that Africans abhor the straight line. We speak in rhythms and blues. Our speech is African and our speech is American. Our speech is inevitable" (K. Jones 1986, 69).

In the King case, the African-American middle class responded with hostility to the proposal that AAE should be considered a valid language alternative in education settings. In fact, Carl Rowan, a radio personality and newspaper columnist, referred to AAE as "ghetto language" in his syndicated column ("Rowan Report," RR 12 and 13, 14 and 15 August 1979), while some African-American newspapers like the *Chicago Defender* called the whole case "phony." Yet, *EM* (K. Jones 1986) bristles at the notion that AE is as essential as Labov (1985) suggests or that integration with whites is important in order to speak AE. Instead, Jones invokes an African continuum and then focuses on the beauty of African-American language. These two perspectives, while opposing, reflect how language, identity, culture, and social reality interact and are reflected within the African-American community. The dialogue on AAE has and continues to focus on two fundamental issues that constitute the symbolic and ideological context in which it is used: the history and function of AAE within the speech community and its function in relation to AE.

Perspectives of African-American English

The African-American speech community operates according to an intricate integration of language norms and values associated with the symbolic and practical functions of AAE and AE. The complexities of this system are aptly illustrated by the author Langston Hughes (Smitherman, 1977) in his use of "the voice of the community," Jesse B. Simple.[13]

Simple: Do you want me to talk like Edward R. Murrow?

Joyce: No! But when we go to formals I hate to hear you saying, for example, "I taken" instead of "I took." Why do colored people say, "I taken" so much?

Simple: Because we are taken – taken until we are undertaken, and, Joyce, baby, funerals is high!

Simple's explanation of *taken*, which is neither questioned nor disputed by Joyce, represents the speech community's view of the nature of AAE (cf. Smitherman 1977). It historicizes an African-American linguistic reality that was framed by the public use of language, a use that accommodated dominant racist and class ideology and discourse concerning African Americans while indirectly resisting it. Thus, for Simple, *taken* can refer to being taken from Africa and cheated in life and death through social injustice. Though Simple's expression of the community's social and historical reality is accepted without question, his grammar, as Joyce attests, is not. It is in this sense that AAE reflects language as a symbol of "actual social life...a multitude of concrete worlds...of bounded verbal-ideological and social belief systems" (Bakhtin 1981, 288).

Until the 1970s, the African-American community was composed of different social classes that lived and interacted within racially segregated institutions and geographical areas (Drake and Cayton 1945; Wilson 1978; Dillingham 1981). As a speech community, it has been characterized by anthropologists, folklorists, and literary critics as an oral culture (Kochman 1972; Abrahams 1976) with a tradition of "talk" (discourse) about language use (Morrison 1981; Gates 1988). Because of the community's social-class mixing, this "talk" has included both formal and informal uses and understanding of language and its importance in representing social reality, history, and identity.

As the language and education debates discussed above raged in academic institutions, their implications were extensively examined among African-American scholars and community activists in popular, theoretical, and research journals.[14] Poets, writers, and musicians all contributed to the developing positions that were often framed by a particular understanding of Africans before U.S. slavery. AAE was discussed from three related perspectives: (1) in terms of its "expressive" African character, (2) as a symbol of resistance to slavery and oppression and, the opposite view, (3) as an indicator of a slave "mentality" or consciousness.

In the first conception of AAE, the indigenous languages of Africa are considered to be symbolic of African culture, identity, and power. Africans of the diaspora, who speak their native languages, are described in terms of their enslavement and forced learning of English, which represents the language of oppression and domination and thus a symbol of their loss of power and identity. In an earlier work, Harrison (1972, 53) described the situation: "After a lifetime of speaking their own native tongues they [Africans in slavery] were forced to learn English so that they would be able to communicate, not *among* themselves but *with* their masters." Yet, both community and institutional scholars argue that the essence of the language and therefore the culture survived. For instance, K. Jones (1986, 69) cites writer Halima Toure, who notes: "We were together in the slave quarters and in the fields. Communication between Blacks and the overseer was usually conducted by one person. It wasn't necessary for all the slaves to deal with the slave master." Harrison (1972) lambastes linguists' tendency to ignore the African ancestry of AAE and the multiple realities of the African-American experience.

Until recently, linguists had placed the colloquial expressions used on the block, without properly being advised by their African roots, into a category of non-language, a form of speech given toward immature usages. There had been a consensus of opinion that the common language of Black people was static, since to those unattuned to the communicative context, the words seemed never to develop or advance in meaning. Black language is anything but static; it receives its dynamism from the constant change of a context which influences the spoken word, giving it new meaning and a wide latitude of expression. (52)

Some, like Burgest (1973, 14), attach metaphysical significance to African continuity and suggest that "many Africans have a psyche . . . which prevents the admission of the foreign racist destructive language from entering into their system. . . . " Writer Eugene Redmond, as reported in *EM* (K. Jones 1986, 69), concludes: "We talk in English but think in African. We actually speak English with an African accent."

Thus the African identity, whether idealized or historically situated, is firmly established in this argument as the foundation of AAE. As Langston Hughes (1957) might have argued, African language style was the thing not "taken" but transformed. While community discussions of the existence of AAE are often explained in terms of an African continuity, proof of a linguistic genealogy is not a requisite. Rather, the discussion recognizes that the language behavior of African Americans is different from that of whites and similar to that of Africans in Africa and the diaspora. This attention to African identity and AAE has been addressed by African-American linguists such as Taylor (1975) and Smitherman (1977), as well as writers such as Baldwin (1979), Morrison (1981), and Redmond (1986). Rather than focus on the details or particulars of the historical origins of AAE, they attend to the ways in which the social and political conditions of slavery and Jim Crow laws affected the language and identity of a people.[15] This issue is represented by the commonly asked question: Does AAE represent resistance to slavery or a slave mentality?

The resistance theory of AAE is based on the function, nature, and importance of indirect speech and ambiguity in African-American speech. Morgan (1989, 1991, 1993a) argues that a counterlanguage emerged during slavery that was based on African systems of communication. Smitherman (1977) describes the context that necessitated this language strategy.

The condition of servitude and oppression contributed to the necessity for coding or disguising English from the white man. Since slaves were forced to communicate in the white man's tongue, they had to devise ways of running it down that would be powerful and meaningful to the Black listener, but harmless and meaningless to any whites who might overhear their rap. (47)

This counterlanguage was a conscious attempt on the part of U.S. slaves and their descendants to represent an alternative reality through a communication style based on ambiguity, irony, and satire.[16]

Indeed counterlanguage, as a language choice, is at the heart of "talk" surrounding African-American speech. Its existence is apparent in lexical usage throughout the community (cf. Holt 1972; Levine 1977; Smitherman 1977), and it is the basis of much of the lexical creativity found in hip-hop and rap as well as the source of indirection used in socially conscious hip-hop and rap styles (Morgan 1993b). In addition to support for counterlanguage styles, when the syntactic and phonological characteristics of African-American speech – for example, camou-flaged forms like *come* (Spears 1982) and stressed *been* as an anterior marker (Rickford 1973) – are discussed in terms of norms, function, or meaning, there is little or no dispute in terms of AAE's importance or significance as an intragroup communication system. In contrast, when AAE is discussed in reference to contexts or domains identified with AE usage, serious disagreement can develop.

Both addressing and redressing issues associated with slavery are the purview of many African-American nationalist groups. While all of these groups consider African heritage incontrovertible, they do not support the notion that AAE sustains an African origin. In 1975, the article by Samuel 17X became the source of heated debate in the African-American community. Because he insisted that during slavery English functioned to maintain a subservient relationship between master and slave, Samuel 17X maintained that AAE is a symbol of that oppressive relationship and therefore argued against its use.

One fact is that "Black English" is a language which emanates from slavery. It is a slave mentality and a slave's way of thinking. If we spoke a certain type language during slavery, then by continuing to speak that language we are transmitting the legacy of slavery, its culture, thinking, and reality on which that language is based.

In a dialogue with the *Bilalian News* about their position on AAE (or Bilalian English), Ernie Smith (1976) argued against Samuel 17X's interpretation.

Now what can be more indicative of a "slave mentality" and a "slave's way of thinking" than a Bilalian [African American] who is sycophant and so obsequiously enamored with the language of his Euro-American slave masters that he publicly reveres their language, and finds it necessary to denigrate the Bilalian language as a "sloppy lan-guage" which reflects "sloppy thinking"? (6)

The tension that emerges from AAE as a complex sign of both resistance and oppression problematizes Bakhtin's (1981) notion of language use reflecting multi-ple concrete worlds. Indeed, the discussion historicizes AAE as a dual sign and mediates discourse concerning which position best reflects the essence of the African-American experience (cf. Vološinov 1973). Yet, it is only within the context of African-American language norms and values that AAE is a cultural sign repre-senting the experiences, norms, and values of the community. For AAE speakers outside the community and in contact with dominant discourse that attempts to control and marginalize their existence, AAE becomes a political sign of solidarity and resistance. This rise to counterhegemonic sign occurs when confronted with the "ideal" language variety and "citizenship standard": AE.

American English

The language "legitimacy" of African Americans who seek citizenship rights has been a recurring issue in American society (Frazier 1968; Mitchell-Kernan 1972; Winfrey 1987). Yet, as Mitchell-Kernan (1972) demonstrates in her classic study of African-American attitudes toward AAE and AE, the interplay between "good" English and AAE is extremely complex because both are considered crucial to improve life chances. Those who choose to accommodate the demands of non-African-American society and use AE exclusively risk losing community membership and, as Mitchell-Kernan (1972) warns, earning a pariah status that can lead to abuse. Indeed, there is a pejorative variety of English referred to as "talking white."[17]

Speaking good and proper English becomes equivalent to "light skinned," and "good (straight like whites') hair." It is not foreign for Blacks to have suffered condescension from other Blacks for not being able to master the "King's English." By the same token, it is in the experiences of the "good (white) English user" to have received "compliments" from whites like, "you don't talk like the rest of them," insinuating that you are different and "better" because you speak more like whites. The inability to master the language becomes equated with being "uneducated," "deprived," "disadvantaged." In other words, Black is defined from its racist perspective. (Burgest 1973, 41)

The above depiction focuses on AE as a racially identified variety and as symbolic of a culture that considers its norms and values a model for all others and exercises power and control over life chances. Consequently, through language, mono-AE speakers constitute a reality that excludes the language and cultural values of the wider African-American community. As a result, AE can be symbolic of historical oppression and the annihilation of African consciousness and resistance when it is used in contexts where AAE is normally spoken. Because AE plays a political role in African-American life, only those who celebrate African heritage and identity have the authority to talk about the politics of its use without being castigated for trading identities. The *Bilalian News* (1975), though severely criticized, could launch a provocative discussion about AAE without fear of censure because the Nation of Islam's ideological foundation was based on an African heritage and the necessity of competing for and achieving power within and in spite of dominant ideology. Likewise, the "Graffiti" column of the January 1990 issue of *Essence* magazine (a publication that celebrates African-American culture) stressed the importance of achieving success in both school and the "white working world" by reminding its readers to say *ask* instead of *ax* and *specific* instead of *pacific*.[18] In contrast, *Newsweek* magazine's "My Turn" column chronicled Rachel Jones's experience as a mono-AE speaker in the African-American community. Jones (1986) describes her childhood as difficult because of hounding by other children with questions like "Why do you talk like you're white?" In defending her pariah status, Jones insists "I don't think I talk white, I think I talk right."

As discussed above, in the African-American speech community, disputes regarding language choice revolve around how those living under slavery and later social and economic discrimination viewed their reality. Since social reality is constructed via language here, two questions emerge (Berger and Luckman 1966; Smitherman 1991). The first question is whether AAE signifies the resistance to an imposed definition of personhood that constructs African Americans as dependent "others" who rely on those of European ancestry for recognition and existence. The second is whether AAE represents acquiescence and participation in the imposed definition. These questions are essential to understand attitudes toward both AAE and AE. The first question focuses on the ways in which Africans sought to forge an identity within slavery by employing generalized African norms of communication to establish an antisociety with AAE as counterlanguage. The second question accepts the designation of "Other" and AE as the vehicle with which one can transcend the noncitizenship status of "different" and become the model of good and humanity and, therefore, citizen. Within this framework, monolingual AE in intragroup interaction symbolizes self-hate regarding an African-American identity and an exaltation of European values. Thus, in terms of language choice, AE is the only variety that one can choose to speak, while AAE is a variety that one may *choose not* to speak. Consequently, AE is a symbol of both the speaker's desire to be accepted by whites as well as a symbol of accomplishment toward life goals. This problematic is played out on many levels.

It is into this complicated and often volatile debate that sociolinguists have entered. In an attempt to right perceived wrongs that have been inflicted on the African-American community by educational policies and psychological theories of deficit, sociolinguists have inadvertently focused on the very aspects of AAE that are most symbolic and significant to the community itself. To fully comprehend the motivations and ideology that influence sociolinguistic theories about the function of AAE, it is useful to further explore three general methodological and theoretical issues: (1) how speech community membership is determined, (2) the symbolic function of education, and (3) the role of speech styles and events.

The African-American Speech Community: Race Consciousness, Class Consciousness, and Education

It is impossible to provide a simple definition of the African-American speech community, or any urban speech community. This is true not only because of its complicated history and countless attacks designed to elicit compliance within a hegemonic system based on race, class, and gender hierarchies, but also because the community expands and contracts across class and geographic lines. Considering its complexity, it is not surprising that one source of criticism of linguistic plans and proposals can be traced to early descriptions of the African-American speech community and what constitutes membership. Confusion regarding who speaks AAE began in the late 1960s with the pronouncement from creolists and dialectologists that "eighty percent of all Black people speak Black English" (Dillard 1972, 229). In rendering his legal decision in the King case, Judge Joiner referred to 80 percent of African-American speakers of AAE. The 80 percent theory emerged during the deficit/difference debates in an attempt to identify African Americans in terms of culture, history, and language, and to decide whose rights, therefore, must be protected. It is based on the notion that AAE is spoken by the working class and at least 80 percent of all African Americans are working class.

Unfortunately, this theory does not attach cultural significance to AAE and excludes age differences, context, group, individual variation, and African-American systems of class and status distinctions. To further complicate matters, because vernacular AAE has been defined as hip, male, adolescent, street, or gang-related speech, nonvernacular speech is described as weak, lame, or white (Labov 1972). Those who do not fit the model of the vernacular-idealized speaker (the 20 percent) are therefore, according to this sociolinguistic paradigm, not African American or, to put it in modern terms, not the "authentic Other." Gilyard (1991) provides a particularly critical portrayal of the issues in relation to Labov's (1972) chapter, "The Linguistic Consequences of Being a Lame." As the above discussion of the cultural and political significance of AAE and AE reveals, sociolinguists have constituted speech community membership and style in ways that reinscribe the dominant society's interpretation of AAE as a sign of poverty and oppression. The apparent confusion over what constitutes speech community membership is analogous to the difficulty that sociologists have in describing the relationship between class and racial consciousness in the African-American community.

Because the community has historically been denied access to traditional indicators of the dominant social class – housing, employment, occupation – how the community assigns class and status remains open to question. An analytical problem emerges because in order for class differences to exist, "a population must differentiate to a minimum extent with respect to an attribute before that attribute can serve as a basis for invidious distinction" (Glenn 1963, 665). In his analysis of the basis of social prestige found in 16 studies of the African-American community between 1899 and 1960, Glenn (1963) found that in all but one case, African Americans considered education more important in determining class and status than income and occupation. These findings corroborated Drake and Cayton's (1945) earlier classic study of Chicago's African-American community, in which they found that during the 1940s, advanced education virtually secured membership at the top of the Black social hierarchy of Chicago.[19] Though the community was composed of members who earned large incomes, the exclusion from typical middle-class occupations meant that earned income did not play a significant role as a class indicator since it was secured through nontraditional means.

In 1978 and later in 1987, Wilson argued that in the African-American community, class consciousness is becoming more important than race in determining life chances. One consequence of the change is that African-American middle and working classes are becoming more stratified. If Wilson is correct, it would explain Labov's (1985) contention that racial integration is necessary since, following Wilson's theory, middle-class African Americans lose their racial identity and take on the characteristics of middle-class whites. However, Dillingham (1981, 432) argues that in an ethnically stratified society it is more feasible that subjective feelings of ethnic group or racial identification become more powerful determinants of behavior than objective assessments of socioeconomic status. In a study of three hundred African Americans, Dillingham (1981) found that contrary to Wilson's (1978) analysis, the higher the class of the respondent, the higher the racial consciousness. Other studies (Ginzberg 1967; Kronus 1970; Sampson and Milam 1975) also report that middle-class African Americans have a positive attitude toward the lower class and continue to feel an obligation to their race due to their more privileged position.

In fact, during my research (Morgan 1989, 1991, 1993b) I have had numerous discussions about class and race with middle-class African Americans. None of them equate being middle-class with an absence of African-American culture and values. They argue that the street culture (as defined by sociologists) is integral to the community, and they object to any attempt to identify it as either representative or separate. Thus, though the representation of class may be changing in the African-American community – and quite likely the significance of education as an indicator of social class – racial consciousness continues to be an important indicator of community membership.

Recent studies on language in context have revealed the extent to which AAE functions to signal community membership and solidarity across class lines. The importance of functioning within multiple contexts is accentuated by the use of AAE among those middle-class African Americans who were not socialized in the speech community, as well as by the use of AE by rap and hip-hop artists who were (Morgan 1993b). In the first instance, there is a developing trend among upper middle-class African-American students attending elite college campuses to use lexical, phonological, and grammatical features of AAE in both formal and informal contexts (cf. Baugh 1987). DeBose (1992) and Spears (1988) report that in their research on language use among working- and middle-class African-American adults, both AAE and AE are used in informal mixed-class conversations, regardless of the class of the speaker. In addition, Morgan (1993b) reports that the hip-hop community, whose membership is based on the ability to represent the truth about life in the city by using "real" street AAE (reflecting current usage), relies on both AE and AAE grammar and phonology, and AAE lexical and morphological style (dope rhymes).

The tendency of sociolinguists to include some segments of the African-American community and exclude others extends beyond class to gender. With few exceptions (Mitchell-Kernan 1971; Goodwin 1990; Morgan 1989, 1991) research on discourse and verbal genres has highlighted male-centered activities and male sexual exploits. As a consequence, African-American women are either erased from the urban landscape because of their purported linguistic conservatism or portrayed as willing interlocutors and audiences for the plethora of street hustler raps and misogynistic boasting reported by researchers. Since the speech community, in this case, is viewed as a monistic entity, a specific speech event is often presented as a generalized norm rather than characteristic of a particular style or genre.[20] Kochman (1981, 75) is emblematic of this problem with his statement, "In Black culture it is customary for Black men to approach Black women in a manner that openly expresses a sexual interest, while in white culture it is equally customary for 'respectable' women to be offended by an approach that presumes sexual interest and availability." Kochman contends that this form of "rapping" is a norm, though his assumptions are mainly based on male self-reporting of street culture and street observations.[21]

The fallout that results from this rendering is, once again, both the African-American community's rejection of research on AAE and accusations from linguists of community self-hate. The extent of this problem was revealed in a conflict at the University of Wisconsin's (Beloit) Rock County Center regarding an assigned reading by Kochman (1981, 1990) in an introductory anthropology text.[22] The dispute began when, after reading the chapter entitled "Race, Culture and Misunderstanding," an African-American woman taking the course called her mother at work and asked "Mom, what's a pimp eye?" (Ostrander 1990). Following is one of the many examples of African-American male and female interactions included in the reading.

In one street rap a young man says to a woman of about 20, who is walking by in tight shorts:

Male: What's happenin', fox?
Female: Nothing.
Male: You mean with all that you got ain't nothin' happenin'?
Female: Get lost nigger.
Male: Come here you funky bitch.
Female: What the hell do you want?
Male: I want some leg baby.

Ostrander (1990) reported the mother's outrage: "The reading portrays us like a bunch of animals.... It takes the very worst things about a Black person – or any person – and makes it out like all Blacks act that way." The Reverend Floyd Prude added, "You can use all sorts of adjectives – disgusting, appalling, derogatory, demeaning – they all apply. I wouldn't want that kind of thing to be taught in school. What if this is a person's only contact with Afro-Americans?"

The *Beloit* dispute resulted in the university's removal of the text (Kochman 1990) and a promise from the publisher to reevaluate the chapter's inclusion in the text's next edition. While these actions may have placated the community in this particular instance, the dispute also proved provocative because it elicited an argument from both the mother and minister that was not disguised as a subjective plea for self-representation but rather a demand that the language styles purported to describe the African-American community represent the entire social field. The examples favored by Kochman (1981) denoted African-American verbal genres as "others" because they were evaluated according to white middle-class cultural norms. They imply that street behavior is typical (normal) and the African-American community is sexually charged, with women "ready" for sex and not worthy of respect and men, at least when they talk to women, in constant pursuit of it. Women, from the linguists' perspective, can be either wild (because they speak like men) or frigid (because they don't).

Conclusion

Members of society construct and communicate meanings through language. In this sense, language does not use its users but is employed by active agents to represent, invoke, symbolize, and even embellish concrete situations that arise from multiple realities (Vološinov 1973; Bakhtin 1981). For the African-American community, AAE is multiply constructed as a variety and in relation to AE.

The preceding discussion argues that choosing AAE or AE invokes alternative cultural, social, and linguistic home environments (Duranti and Goodwin 1992) and therefore ideologies. For African-American speech community members, AAE is a language choice that (1) is influenced by African culture, (2) is a symbol of African-American identity, and (3) may function as a counterlanguage. There is disagreement over whether syntactic and phonological features of AAE represent resistance to oppression or the proof of domination. Correspondingly, there is dispute over whether exclusive use of AE represents a break with slave mentality and movement toward empowerment or a break with African tradition and identity. Because of the many-faceted ways in which speech situations are constituted, on the one hand, the community fully supports AE in schools since it is both an alternative choice within the speech community and the language of education and formal settings. On the other hand, it also considers AAE a variety that should not be denigrated since it too is a grammatical and communicative alternative, though not the language of education.

Once the King case was reduced to proving AAE was sufficiently different from AE to impede learning, the concern of the community was that the children needed AE, "the language of education," in order to receive an education. Likewise, once Labov (1985) seemed to question socializing tendencies among African Americans with his argument for social and language integration, the community became concerned that his position did not value the multisituated nature of African-American life.

When linguistic facts or descriptions are gathered without acknowledging the ideological precepts inherent in both the disciplinary activity and the attempt to assign significance through plans and policies, linguistics as a science perpetuates the prevailing dominant ideology that language study is objective and neutral (cf. Joseph and Taylor 1990). Under these circumstances, linguistics cannot "do good" for any subordinated group. AAE is a resilient language variety whose emergence flourished under historical conditions that required concealment of the belief that African-American self-identity included a sense of history, pride, emotion, and intelligence as complex as that experienced by other human beings. As the modern urban landscape continues its drift away from cultural enactments, which marginalize those who do not embody dominant cultural practices, AAE's dual value and use as both a cultural and counterhegemonic sign within the African-American community in particular and urban society in general may actually increase.

NOTES

1   This paper was completed while I was a fellow at the University of California's Humanities Research Institute at Irvine. I am especially appreciative of the discussions I've had with Valerie Smith, Kobena Mercer, Anthony Brown, Jon Cruz, Raul Fernandez, Lindon Barrett, Marta Sanchez, Jeffrey Belnap, Sarah Banet-Weiser, Karen Christian, and Heartha Wong. Earlier versions of this paper benefited from the input of Alessandro Duranti, Salikoko Mufwene, Bambi Schieffelin, two anonymous reviewers, and students in my African-American-English class at UCLA.

2   This essay recognizes the distinction between the definition of the speech community used by quantitative sociolinguists and that used by those also involved in the ethnography of speaking (Gumperz and Hymes 1972). Sankoff (1974, 45) has argued that it is possible to combine the two methodologies and writes of "the desire of sociolinguists for their results to have some sociocultural validity." In fact, as this essay demonstrates, sociolinguists have had a profound influence on movements for the educational equality of African Americans. However, until recently, it was Sankoff's (1974, 45) second observation that sociolinguists should "attempt to define categories that are socially meaningful to the people whose linguistic behavior is being investigated" that was left wanting. Rickford (1985, 1986) provides a detailed analysis of the problem, as well as an example of how other theoretical models can be employed.

3   Some linguists (eg., Bailey and Maynor 1989) actually continue the controversy when they
    reintroduce categorical stereotypes by assigning equal historical value to racist phenotype
    arguments (thick lips) and linguistic arguments.

4   Except for direct quotes, or to remain consistent with the publications under discussion, the
    name African-American English will be used instead of Black English or Black vernacular
    English. American English (AE) will be used except in those cases where class, ethnicity,
    region, gender, or age are considered constitutive of the language variety.

5   Earlier, one widely popularized educational theory promoted by Bereiter and Engleman
    (1966), Jensen (1969), and others was that AAE itself was deficient and produced deficient
    thinking. The work of William Labov (1972) and others effectively argued that AAE was not
    deficient but different from AE in systematic ways.

6   The history of sociolinguists' association with the education of African-American children has
    been discussed in detail in Baratz (1973) and Baugh (1983a, 1983b).

7   These include the edited collections: Johanna DeStephano (1973), *Language, Society and
    Education: A Profile of Black English*, Ralph Fasold and Roger Shuy (1970), *Teaching
    Standard English in the Inner City*, and Joan Baratz and Roger W. Shuy (1969), *Teaching
    Black Children to Read*.

8   The Standard English as a Second Dialect (SESD) teaching method (Stewart 1964, 1965; Allen
    1967; Lin 1965, etc.) was not warmly accepted. Nor were dialect readers such as those of the
    Board of Education, City of Chicago (1966, 1968). When Stewart (1975, 117) introduced AAE
    dialect reading material into the language arts curriculum of the Florida school system, the
    response of the community was "These were bad language, bad materials. This bad language
    shouldn't be put in the schools."

9   The list of King case witnesses is as follows: Geneva Smitherman, professor of speech com-
    munication and director of the Center for Black Studies, Wayne State University; Daniel N.
    Fader, professor of English language and literature, University of Michigan; Jerrie Scott,
    assistant professor of English and linguistics, University of Florida; William Labov, professor
    of linguistics, University of Pennsylvania, with a secondary appointment in psychology and
    education; J. L. Dillard, assistant professor of languages, Northwestern State University,
    Natchitoches, Louisiana; Gary Simpkins, director of social health services and chief of mental
    health, Watts Health Foundation; Richard Bailey, professor of English, University of Michigan;
    Ronald Edmonds, member of faculty, Harvard Graduate School of Education; Kenneth
    Haskins, president, Roxbury Community College.

10 For example, see: *The New York Times* article by Williams Stevens (14 March 1985, A14),
    "Black and Standard English Held Diverging More"; the "CBS Evening News"; *The Baltimore
    Sun* (18 March 1985); and 157 domestic and foreign newspapers (as reported by Vaughn-
    Cooke 1987, 13).

11 While the linguistic details of the study from which his argument is based are not the subject of
    this chapter, it is important to note that Labov's current evidence appears in four studies
    (Sankoff, D. 1986) that examine specific phonological and morphological features. In addi-
    tion, a separate study by Bailey and Maynor (1987) supports Labov's claim that AAE is
    becoming less like white speech. Bailey and Maynor examine the use of invariant *be* in the
    speech of older adults and young children in east-central Texas and conclude that the younger
    generation uses this form more frequently in specific environments than the older generation.
    They go even further than Labov and consider the younger generation's use an "innovation"
    since they believe it is not prevalent in the speech of older speakers. They argue not only that
    Black and white speech forms are diverging, but also that older and younger AAE speakers
    actually represent two separate speech communities.

12 Both Rickford (1987) and Wolfram (1987), in the same volume, support most of Vaughn-
    Cooke's claims.

13 This particular excerpt is cited by Smitherman (1977, 167–9). Hughes was a popular African-
    American newspaper columnist who wrote for the *Chicago Defender* in the 1950s. The
    Defender was widely read by all segments of the community, and it was often referred to as
    "the Black Bible" since it played a significant role in encouraging Northern migration, civil
    rights, and racial pride. Hughes's character, Jesse B. Simple, was developed shortly after World
    War II. The philosophy and exploits of Simple, who was based in Harlem, were

hotly contested by all segments of the community because of the character's working-class values.

14   An entire issue of the *Journal of Black Studies* (1979) was devoted to AAE. In addition, African-American linguists have debated which name (e.g., Ebonics) best reflects both its African origin and development in the United States (cf. Mufwene 1992).

15   There is some discussion that the destruction of AAE will aid those who are intent on destroying African-American people and culture because it will destroy the African character as well as the ability to surreptitiously communicate.

16   For detailed discussion on the similarities see Levine (1977). Even the literary critic Joyce (1987) refers to the need to "speak in such a way that the master does not grasp their meaning" while writing in scholarly journals.

17   The terms "good English," "talking white," "talking proper," and "talking good" are widely reported in literature on the African-American speech community (Mitchell-Kernan 1972; Spears 1988). More recently, these terms were used interchangeably during a lively talk show discussion/debate under the topic of Black English (Winfrey 1987).

18   The inclusion of these words in *Essence* magazine identifies them as marked by AAE speakers and the object of discussion in the speech community irrespective of social class and region.

19   Gregory (1992) also reveals the importance of education in distinguishing class in the late 1970s in an African-American community in Queens. Landry (1987, 104) assigns even more significance to education but for different reasons. By the mid-1970s, he says, a college education could mean securing middle-class occupations: "Eighty percent of Black males and 60 percent of Black females from middle-class families who remained in the middle-class had attended college. . . . Education was at last beginning to pay off for Blacks – if it could be acquired."

20   Henley (1995) provides a detailed critique of the problem of ethnicity and gender issues in sociolinguistic inquiry.

21   *Rapping* means many things including talk. This complicates the problem, since male–female talk can include a rap. But rap is also associated with asking for a date, which, at least at the time of this publication, does not necessarily include sex. See Smitherman (1977) for a fuller discussion of the uses of rap.

22   The reading by Thomas Kochman appeared in the seventh edition of an anthropology text entitled *Conformity and Conflict*, edited by Spradley and McCurdy (Kochman 1990). It was taken from his 1981 text, *Black and White Styles in Conflict*.

REFERENCES

Abrahams, Roger (1976). *Talking Black*. Rowley, MA: Newbury.

Abrahams, Roger, and John Szwed (1983). *After Africa: Extracts from the British Travel Accounts and Journals of the Seventeenth, Eighteenth and Nineteenth Centuries Concerning the Slaves, Their Manners and Customs in the British West Indies*. New Haven, CT: Yale University Press.

Allen, Virginia (1967). Teaching standard English as a second dialect. *Teachers College Record*. Reprint. In *Linguistic-cultural Differences and American Education* (special anthology issue), *The Florida FL Reporter* 7:1.

Ash, Sharon, and John Myhill (1983). Linguistic Correlates of Inter-ethnic Contact. Manuscript, Department of Linguistics, University of Pennsylvania.

Bailey, Beryl Loftman (1969). Language and communication styles of Afro-American children in the United States. The *Florida FL Reporter* 7:46, 153.

Bailey, Beryl (1971). Towards a new perspective in Negro English dialectology. In *Readings in American Dialectology*, ed. Harold B. Allen and Gary N. Underwood. New York: Appleton-Century-Crofts.

Bailey, Guy, and Natalie Maynor (1987). Decreolization? *Language in Society* 16:449–73.

Bailey, Guy, and Natalie Maynor (1989). The divergence controversy. *American Speech* 64(1): 12–39.

Bakhtin, M. M. (1981). *The Dialogic Imagination*. Austin: University of Texas Press.

Baldwin, James (29 July 1979). If Black English isn't a language, then tell me, what is? *New York Times*.

Baratz, Joan (1973). Language abilities of Black Americans. In *Comparative Studies of Blacks and Whites in the United States*, ed. Kent S. Miller and Ralph Mason Dreger. New York: Seminar Press.

Baratz, Joan, and Roger W. Shuy (eds.) (1969). *Teaching Black Children to Read*. Washington, DC: Center for Applied Linguistics.

Baugh, John (1983a). A survey of Afro-American English. *Annual Review of Anthropology* 12:335–54.

Baugh, John (1983b). *Black Street Speech: Its History, Structure and Survival*. Austin: University of Texas Press.

Baugh, John (1987). The situational dimension of linguistic power. *Language Arts* 64:234–40.

Bereiter, Carl, and Seigfried Engelman (1966). *Teaching Disadvantaged Children in the Pre-school*. Englewood Cliffs, NJ: Prentice-Hall.

Berger, Peter, and Thomas Luckman (1966). *The Social Construction of Reality*. Middlesex, England: Penguin.

Brooks, Charlotte K. (ed.) (1985). *Tapping Potential: English and Language Arts for the Black Learner*. Urbana, IL: National Council of Teachers of English.

Brown, June (1 July 1979). Black English – Poor excuse for incorrect use of language. *Detroit News*, pp. 1B, 4B.

Burgest, David R. (1973). The racist use of the English language. *Black Scholar* (September): 37–45.

Butters, Ronald R. (ed.) (1987). Are Black and white vernaculars diverging? Papers from the NWAVE XIV panel discussion. *American Speech* 62:3–80.

Dandy, Evelyn (1991). *Black Communications: Breaking Down the Barriers*. Chicago: African American Images.

DeBose, Charles (1992). Codeswitching: Black English and standard English in the African-American linguistic repertoire. *Journal of Multilingual and Multicultural Development*, 131 (1–2):157–67.

DeStephano, Johanna (ed.) (1973). *Language, Society and Education: A Profile of Black English*. Worthington, OH: Charles A. Jones.

Dillard, J. L. (1968). Non-standard dialects – Convergence or divergence? *The Florida FL Reporter* 6:9–10, 12.

Dillard, J. L. (1972). *Black English*. New York: Random House.

Dillingham, Gerald (1981). The emerging Black middle class: Class conscious or race conscious? *Ethnic and Racial Studies* 4(4):432–51.

Drake, St. Clair, and Horace Cayton (1945). *Black Metropolis*. New York: Harcourt, Brace.

Duranti, Alessandro, and Charles Goodwin (1992). *Rethinking Context: Language as an Interactive Phenomenon*. Cambridge: Cambridge University Press.

Fasold, Ralph (1969). Tense and the form *be* in Black English. *Language* 45:763–76.

Fasold, Ralph (1972). *Tense-marking in Black English*. Washington, DC: Center for Applied Linguistics.

Fasold, Ralph, and Roger Shuy (eds.) (1970). *Teaching Standard English in the Inner City*. Washington, DC: Center for Applied Linguistics.

Frazier, E. Franklin (1968). *On Race Relations*. Chicago: University of Chicago Press.

Gates, Jr., Henry Louis (1988). *The Signifying Monkey: A Theory of African-American Literary Criticism*. Oxford: Oxford University Press.

Gilyard, Keith (1991). *Voices of the Self: A Study of Language Competence*. Detroit: Wayne State University Press.

Ginzberg, Eli (1967). *The Middle Class Negro in a White Man's World*. New York: Columbia University Press.

Glenn, Norval (1963). Negro prestige criteria: A case study in the bases of prestige. *American Journal of Sociology* 68(6):645–57.

Goodwin, Marjorie (1990). *He-Said-She-Said: Talk as Social Organization among Black Children*. Bloomington: Indiana University Press.

Graff, David, William Labov, and Wendell Harris (1983). Testing Listeners' Reactions to Phonological Markers of Ethnic Identity: A New Method for Sociolinguistic Research. Manuscript.

Graffiti. *Essence*, January 1990.

Gregory, Steven (1992). The changing significance of race and class in an African American community. *American Ethnologist* 19(2):255–74.

Gumperz, John, and Dell Hymes (1972). *Directions in Sociolinguistics: The Ethnography of Communication*. New York: Holt, Rinehart, and Winston.

Harrison, Paul Carter (1972). *The Drama of Nommo*. New York: Grove Press.

Henley, Nancy (1995). Ethnicity and gender issues in language. In *Bringing Cultural Diversity to Feminist Psychology*, ed. H. Landrine. Washington, DC: American Psychological Association.

Holt, Grace (1972). Inversion in Black Communication. In *Rappin' and Stylin' Out*, ed. Thomas Kochman. Urbana: University of Illinois Press.

Hughes, Langston (1957). *Simple Stakes a Claim*. New York: Rinehart.

Hymes, Dell (1974). *Foundations in Sociolinguistics – An Ethnographic Approach*. Philadelphia: University of Pennsylvania.

Jensen, Arthur (1969). How much can we boost IQ and scholastic achievement? *Harvard Educational Review* 39(1):1–123.

Jones, Kenneth (1986). Blacktalk: The controversy and color of Black speech. *Ebony Man* 9:68–9.

Jones, Rachel (27 December 1986). My Turn. *Newsweek*.

Joseph, John, and Talbot J. Taylor (1990). *Ideologies of Language*. London: Routledge.

Joyce, Joyce (1987). The Black canon: Reconstructing Black American literary criticism. *New Literary History* 18(2):335–44.

Kochman, Thomas (ed.) (1972). *Rappin' and Stylin' Out: Communication in Urban Black America*. Urbana: University of Illinois Press.

Kochman, Thomas (1981). *Black and White Styles in Conflict*. Chicago: University of Chicago Press.

Kochman, Thomas (1990). Race, culture and misunderstanding. In *Conformity and Conflict – Readings in Cultural Anthropology*, ed. David W. Spradley and James P. McCurdy. Glenview, IL: Scott, Foresman.

Kronus, Sidney (1970). Some neglected aspects of Negro class comparisons. *Phylon* 31(4):359–71.

Labov, William (1972). *Language in the Inner City: Studies in the Black English Vernacular*. Philadelphia: University of Pennsylvania Press.

Labov, William (1982). Objectivity and commitment in linguistic science: The case of the Black English trial in Ann Arbor. *Language in Society* 11:165–202.

Labov, William (1985). The Increasing Divergence of Black and White Vernaculars: Introduction to the Research Reports. Typescript, Department of Linguistics, University of Pennsylvania.

Labov, William (1987). Are Black and white vernaculars diverging? Papers from the NWAVE XIV panel discussion, ed. Ronald R. Butters. *American Speech* 62:5–12, 62–74.

Labov, William, and Wendell Harris (1986). Defacto Segregation of Black and White Vernaculars. In *Diversity and Diachrony*, ed. D. Sankoff. Amsterdam: John Benjamins.

Landry, Bart (1987). The *New Black Middle Class*. Berkeley: University of California Press.

Levine, Lawrence (1977). *Black Culture and Black Consciousness*. Oxford: Oxford University Press.

Lin, San-Su C. (1965). *Pattern Practice in the Teaching of Standard English to Students with a Nonstandard Dialect*. New York: Teachers College, Columbia University.

Mitchell-Kernan, Claudia (1971). *Language Behavior in a Black Urban Community* (Working Paper 23). Berkeley, CA: Language Behavior Research Laboratory.

Mitchell-Kernan, Claudia (1972). On the status of Black English for native speakers: An assessment of attitudes and values. In *Functions of Language in the Classroom*, ed. Courtney Cazden, Vera P. John, and Dell Hymes. New York: Teachers College Press.

Morgan, Marcyliena (1989). From Down South to Up South: The Language Behavior of Three Generations of Black Women Residing in Chicago. Ph.D. diss., University of Pennsylvania.

Morgan, Marcyliena (1991). Indirectness and interpretation in African American women's discourse. *Pragmatics* 1(4):421–51.

Morgan, Marcyliena (1993a). The Africanness of counterlanguage among Afro-Americans. In *Africanisms in Afro-American Language Varieties*, ed. Salikoko Mufwene. Athens: University of Georgia Press.

Morgan, Marcyliena (1993b). In Search of the Hip Hop Nation: Language and Social Identity. Paper read at the Humanities Research Institute, University of California, Irvine.

Morrison, Toni (1981). "The language must not sweat": A conversation with Toni Morrison. By Thomas LeClair. *New Republic*, 21 March 1981.

Mufwene, Salikoko (1992). Ideology and facts on African American English. *Pragmatics* 2(2):141–68.

Mufwene, Salikoko (n.d.). African-American English. In *The Cambridge History of the English Language*. Vol. 6, *History of American English*, ed. John Algeo. Forthcoming.

Myhill, John, and Wendell Harris (1983). The Use of the Verbal -*s* Inflection in BEV. Manuscript.

Ostrander, Kathleen (12 February 1990). Text called demeaning to Blacks. *Beloit Daily News*.

Pickford, Ruth (1956). American linguistic geography: A sociological appraisal. *Word* 12:211–33.

Redmond, Eugene (1986[1973]). *In a Time of Rain and Desire: New Love Poems*. East St. Louis, IL: Black River Writers.

Rickford, John (1975). Carrying the new wave into syntax: The case of Black English BIN. In *Analyzing Variation in Language*, ed. R. Fasold and R. Shuy. Washington, DC: Georgetown University Press.

Rickford, John (1985). Ethnicity as a sociolinguistic boundary. *American Speech* 60:99–125.

Rickford, John (1986). The need for new approaches to social class analysis in sociolinguistics. *Language and Communication* 6(3):215–21.

Rickford, John (1987). Are Black and white vernaculars diverging? Papers from the NWAVE XIV panel discussion, ed. Ronald R. Butters. *American Speech* 62:55–62, 73.

Samuel 17X (22 October 1975). Analysts warn about pitfalls of "Black" English. *Bilalian News*.

Sampson, William, and Vera Milam (1975). The intraracial attitudes of the Black middle-class: Have they changed? *Social Problems* 23(2):151–65.

Sankoff, David (ed.) (1986). Defacto segregation of Black and white vernaculars. In *Diversity and Diachrony*. Amsterdam: John Benjamins Publishing Co., 1–24.

Sankoff, Gillian (1974). A quantitative paradigm for the study of communicative competence. In *Explorations in the Ethnography of Speaking*, ed. R. Bauman and J. Sherzer. Cambridge: Cambridge University Press, 18–49.

Schieffelin, B. B., K. A. Woolard, and P. V. Kroskrity (eds.) (1998). *Language Ideologies: Practice and Theory*. New York: Oxford University Press.

Smith, Ernie (1976). Personal correspondence to Brother Lawrence X.

Smitherman, Geneva (1977). *Talkin and Testifyin: The Language of Black America*. Boston: Houghton Mifflin.

Smitherman, Geneva (ed.) (1981a). *Black English and the Education of Black Children and Youth – Proceedings of the National Invitational Symposium on the King Decision*. Detroit: Harpo Press.

Smitherman, Geneva (1981b). What go round come round: King in perspective. *Harvard Educational Review* 1:40–56.

Smitherman, Geneva (1991). What is Africa to me? Language, ideology and African American. *American Speech* 66:115–32.

Spears, A. (1982). The Black English semi-auxiliary auxiliary *Come*. *Language* 58:850–72.

Spears, Arthur (1987). Are Black and white vernaculars diverging? Papers from the NWAVE XIV panel discussion, ed. Ronald R. Butters. *American Speech* 62:48–55, 71–2.

Spears, Arthur (1988). Black American English. In *Anthropology for the Nineties: Introductory Readings*, ed. Johnetta Cole. New York: The Free Press.

Spradley, James P., and David W. McCurdy (eds.) (1990). *Conformity and Conflict: Readings in Cultural Anthropology*. Glenview, IL: Scott, Foresman/Little, Brown Higher Education.

Stewart, William (1964). Urban Negro speech: Sociolinguistic factors affecting English teaching. In *Social Dialects and Language Learning*, ed. Roger Shuy. Urbana, IL: National Council of Teachers of English.

Stewart, William (1965). Foreign language teaching methods. In *Quasi-foreign Language Situations in Non-standard Speech and the Teaching of English*, ed. W. A. Stewart. Washington, DC: Center for Applied Linguistics.

Stewart, William (1968). Continuity and change in American Negro dialects. *The Florida FL Reporter* 6:3–4, 14–16, 18.

Stewart, William (1975). Teaching Blacks to read against their will. In *Linguistic Perspectives on Black English*, ed. Philip A. Luelsdorff, 107–32. Germany: Verlag Hans Carl Regensburg.

Taylor, Orlando (1975). Black language and what to do about it. *Ebonics: The True Language of Black Folks*, ed. R. Williams. St. Louis: Institute of Black Studies.

Vaughn-Cooke, Fay (1987). Are Black and white vernaculars diverging? Papers from the NWAVE XIV panel discussion, ed. Ronald R. Butters. *American Speech* 62:12–32, 67–70.

Vološinov, V. N. (1973). *Marxism and the Philosophy of Language*, translated by Ladislav Matejka and I. R. Titunik. New York: Seminar Press (original work published 1929, 1930).

Williams, R. (ed.) (1975). *Ebonics: The True Language of Black Folks*. St. Louis: Institute of Black Studies.

Willie, Charles (1989). *Caste and Class Controversy on Race and Poverty: Round Two on the Wilson/Willie Debate*. New York: General Hall.

Wilson, Julius (1978). *The Declining Significance of Race*. Chicago: University of Chicago Press.

Wilson, Julius (1987). *The Truly Disadvantaged*. Chicago: University of Chicago Press.

Winfrey, Oprah (19 November 1987). Standard and "Black" English. "The Oprah Winfrey Show." New York: Journal Graphics, Inc.

Wolfram, Walter (1969). *A Sociolinguistic Description of Detroit Negro Speech*. Washington, DC: Center for Applied Linguistics.

Wolfram, Walter (1987). Are Black and white vernaculars diverging? Papers from the NWAVE XIV panel discussion, ed. Ronald R. Butters. *American Speech* 62:40–8, 73–4.

4

The Social Circulation of Media Discourse and the Mediation of Communities

Debra Spitulnik

Nothing begins from zero, and this is especially true when it comes to the mass mediation of communities that are large, shifting, and somewhat intangible, like those that extend across cities, regions, and nations. When we look at the communications that emanate from mass media, we see that, like most other forms of speaking, they are preceded and succeeded by numerous other dialogues and pieces of language that both implicate them and render them interpretable. Such is the social life of language – as an abundance of scholars have repeatedly argued – to be imbricated in innumerable webs of connection with other utterances (Bakhtin 1981, 1986; Foucault 1972), indexically linked to past and future speech events (Bauman and Briggs 1990:64; Irvine 1996; Silverstein 1976), and vitally entangled with the ongoing practices of everyday life (Hanks 1996).

In this article, I would like to explore how such cross-linkages of language in use – what have come to be called relations of intertextuality (following Bakhtin; cf. Briggs and Bauman 1992) – factor into the mediation of communities. Undertaking this task requires a return to the older and very complex question of what constitutes a speech community. It also leads us into the relatively new terrain of investigating the actual processes of intertextuality, for example, questions about the transportability of speech forms from one context to another and the conditions that enable their decontextualization and recontextualization (Bauman and Briggs 1990; Briggs and Bauman 1992; Lucy 1993; Silverstein and Urban 1996).

The specific problem to be examined here concerns the social circulation of media discourse in Zambian popular culture. We will consider several cases in which phrases and discourse styles are extracted from radio broadcasting and then recycled and reanimated in everyday usage, outside of the contexts of radio listening. As Urban has argued, such social circulation of discourse is essential for the existence of every society or culture because it creates a kind of "public accessibility" that is vital for the production of shared meaning (Urban 1991:10, also 27, 191). Relations of intertextuality are elemental in this process, according to Urban (1991:20), because shared meanings result from the construing of interconnections across different instances of publicly accessible discourse. While Urban focuses on how social circulation leads to public accessibility, much of the material considered here exhibits somewhat of a reverse direction – where the widespread availability of the communication form itself creates possibilities for social circulation.[1]

The discussion below demonstrates that, because of their extensive accessibility and scope, mass media can serve as both reservoirs and reference points for the circulation of words, phrases, and discourse styles in popular culture.[2] In addition, it explores how mass media – as ongoing, high-status, public communication forms – have the potential to magnify and even create the "socially charged life" of certain linguistic forms (Bakhtin 1981:293). Thus as confirmation of Gumperz's early insight that "mass media and the prestige of their speakers tend to carry idioms far from their sources" (1971:223), we will see how radio's impact on everyday language extends from the introduction of single lexical items and catchphrases to the shifting of semantic fields and the modeling of discourse styles. And finally, the analysis below makes some broader linguistic and cultural generalizations about both the kinds of media discourse that circulate and the kinds of conditions that enable this circulation.

The implications of the social circulation of media discourse for questions about speech communities are far-reaching and go beyond Gumperz's (1971) important points about their impact on language change. First, it provides evidence that particular kinds of social situations and social institutions have greater weight than others in establishing the sociolinguistic significance of certain linguistic forms (Bourdieu 1991; Gal 1989; Gumperz 1971; Irvine 1987; Kroskrity 1992). For example, in some societies, the dominant site for producing normative standards for linguistic usage might be political oratory, while in other societies it might be television newscasting. This has relevance for thinking about the constitution of speech communities, because it suggests that there is a correlation between social scale and the type of communication modality that dominates the mediation of community. Along these lines, one question that definitely merits much more exploration is whether *mass* communication itself is a necessary precondition for the construction of community in large-scale societies (Anderson 1983; Habermas 1989). This seems inherently to be the case, since public accessibility means something quite different in large-scale societies than in small-scale societies.

Second, it leads to a series of questions concerning the definition of the speech community and its applicability to large-scale societies. For example, does it even make sense to speak of a speech community across the nation-state when there is no one common language? When we are talking about millions of people who may never know or interact with one another, how do we handle questions about density of communication, frequency of interaction, and shared linguistic knowledge – three key features that figure prominently in various definitions of the speech community and that seem to be a prerequisite for the kind of discursive mediation of society described by Urban? While these three criteria have been challenged (or just abandoned) in recent work, along with the general utility of the speech community concept itself, I believe that they are relevant in important and interesting ways for thinking about the social and linguistic effects of mass mediated communication and that they merit another look.[3] For example, in large-scale societies, a high frequency of interaction and density of communication do occur in a vertical sense – that is, the dominant directionality of mass media – even if they do not occur in a lateral sense – that is, the typical (or idealized) directionality of face-to-face communication. Thus people have frequent interactions or *frequent acts of consumption* with certain media forms, even if they do not directly interact with other users of the same media. Similarly, there is a density of communication in the sense that there is *large-scale exposure* to a common communication form, such as simultaneous listening to a radio drama or a newscast. And finally, as suggested earlier, questions concerning the production of shared linguistic knowledge, while greatly vexed, can be productively reworked to include analysis of how certain institutions provide *common linguistic reference points*.

Mediating Communities

These various features – common reference points, frequency of consumption, common exposure, simultaneity – are not adequate, however, to ensure that mass media will contribute to the formation of a community (speech or otherwise) in large-scale societies. The mass mediation of large-scale societies requires that some *experience* of belonging and mutuality be generated as well. Anderson's notion of the imagined community is useful in this regard, because it provides a model of a community where members may not all know one another but all share an idea of belonging to a collectivity, that is, "in the minds of each lives the image of their communion" (1983:15). While Anderson's work has been criticized for its idealized model of a fairly homogeneous, egalitarian, and equally believed in community (Bhabha 1994; Gal 1995; Spitulnik 1994a), it is still extremely valuable because it demonstrates how linguistic practices create possibilities for shared identities to be imagined.

For example, Anderson (1983:33–6) discusses how, through both definite description and generic reference (naming *familiar* places and invoking *types* of places and *types* of persons), the 18th-century novel constructed a sense of a shared world, a common social and cultural milieu that belonged to both author and reader and to a collective readership. In contrast to the book, the newspaper enabled such simultaneous mass consumption of an identical communication form to occur on a daily basis, as modern man's "substitute for morning prayers" (Anderson 1983:39). Anderson argues that these new communication forms helped to create the feeling of belonging to a shared but anonymous community of fellow readers.

These insights into the mass mediation of communal identity are important because they point out how community and belonging are indexically constructed in texts. The major drawback of Anderson's work, however, is that it overemphasizes the power of vertical modes of communication at the expense of *lateral* communication. For example, we learn little about the practices of consumption and even less about what people are saying to each other about their experiences of consumption. Instead, reminiscent of the earlier "hypodermic" models of media effects and media power (see Spitulnik 1993), there is a privileging of a one-way directionality from a mass communication form to the masses, who supposedly receive it and consume it. The implicit assumption is that, as soon as this mass-produced communication form (e.g., a novel or a newspaper) is distributed, it is simultaneously participated in and almost *automatically* produces a feeling of a shared collectivity because of specific textual features.

While textual acts of asserting or indexing collective identity are important, they do not guarantee that this identity actually corresponds to anything at the experiential level. Production is only half of the picture. We need also to factor in what is happening at the levels of reception and lateral communication, such as the social circulation of media discourse outside of contexts of direct media consumption. I suggest in the following that the repeating, recycling, and recontextualizing of media discourse is an important component in the formation of community in a kind of subterranean way, because it establishes an indirect connectivity or intertextuality across media consumers and across instances of media consumption. Returning to the earlier discussion about speech communities, then, this indicates that even for large-scale societies, it is possible to speak of a density of communication and frequency of interaction in a lateral sense. That is, there can be a density and frequency of common communications and cross-linkages, mediated in a *transitive* fashion by mass media, without a high density or frequency of direct communication between all members of a society.

Public Words and the Semiotics of Circulation

The social circulation of media discourse provides a clear and forceful demonstration of how media audiences play an *active* role in the interpretation and appropriation of media texts and messages. It is possible to investigate these processes in semiotic terms, and recent work on genre and performance theory offers a very valuable starting point. For example, of the many important semiotic questions that Bauman and Briggs (1990; Briggs and Bauman 1992) raise in their discussions of decontextualized (decentered) and recontextualized (recentered) discourse, three are particularly pertinent for studying the circulation of media discourse: How are decontextualization and recontextualization possible? What does the recontextualized text bring with it from its earlier context(s) (e.g., what kind of history does it carry with it)? What formal, functional, and semantic changes does it undergo as it is recentered? (Bauman and Briggs 1990:72–5; Briggs and Bauman 1992:141 ff.).

The following analysis of how media language is recontextualized, reinterpreted, and played with in everyday discourse, focuses specifically on the recycling of radio expressions such as program titles, broadcasters' trademark phrases, and broadcasters' turn-taking routines. These phrases are in English and ChiBemba, two of the country's most widely spoken lingua francas and two of the eight languages that are sanctioned for use on national radio (Spitulnik 1992).[4] The data on recycled media discourse considered here stem from dialogue that I either participated in or overheard during ethnographic research in the capital city of Lusaka and in the semiurban/semirural provincial capital of Kasama; it was not elicited and was not studied systematically across a structured sample population. The data on media discourse stem from listening notes on and recordings of radio broadcasts from the three channels of Radio Zambia – Radio 1, Radio 2, Radio 4 – which are part of the Zambia National Broadcasting Corporation (ZNBC). The linguistic significance of radio in Zambia is substantial because it is the most widely consumed medium in the country, it is a primary site for exposure to English, and it is the only widespread mass communication form that uses Zambian languages.[5] Furthermore, given the fact that Radio Zambia is a centralized state-run monopoly with simultaneous national transmission (i.e., there is no regional broadcasting), the same broadcasts are accessible to the entire national population at the same time and, thus, allow for the possibility of producing a degree of shared linguistic knowledge across a population of roughly 9.1 million.

As we investigate the semiotics of how this radio discourse circulates, four basic issues will concern us: (1) the inherent reproducibility and transportability of radio phrases; (2) the "dialogic [or intertextual] overtones" (Bakhtin 1986:92) that are carried over into the new context of use; (3) the formal, functional, and semantic alterations that occur in the recontextualization; and (4) the degree to which knowledge of the original radio source is relevant for understanding the recycled phrase. We will see, for example, that many recycled radio phrases have a formal "prepared-for detachability" (Bauman and Briggs 1990:74), which enables them to be circulated in particular ways in everyday discourse. We will also see that there is a degree of semantic open-endedness and flexibility that fosters an ease of recontextualization and that people actively exploit this semantic flexibility to create their own meanings for radio-derived discourse.

Overall, the cases considered here exemplify how radio is a source and reference point for phrases and tropes which circulate across communities. Many of these are so well-known and standardized that knowledge of them is virtually essential for one to be considered a communicatively competent member of a particular society or subculture. As such, they are part of what can be termed a society's (or a subculture's) "public words." Public words, understood in this sense, are nothing particularly new to the world or to linguistic anthropologists, and they exist in societies of all scales and scopes. They are standard phrases such as proverbs, slogans, clichés, and idiomatic expressions that are remembered, repeated, and quoted long after their first utterance. Some public words are anonymous and unattributable, for others the sources may be well or vaguely known and perhaps even invoked. Often, these public words are condensations or extracts from much longer speech events, and when used, they may function metonymically to index the entire frame or meaning of the earlier speech situation (Basso 1990a, 1990b; Urban 1991). In the United States such words are the stuff of popular culture, endlessly recycled and renewed by mass media, politicians, culture critics, bumper stickers, and the young and trendy. Examples include: "Make my day," "Been there," "Big brother (is watching)," "The buck stops here," "Beam me up (Scotty)," "Play it again, Sam," and "Hasta la vista, baby."[6]

While linguistic anthropology has tended to focus on the analysis of narrative, oratory, ritual speech, and other very well bounded and easily identifiable speech genres, little has been said about the smaller, scattered pieces of formulaic language, for example, the public words of street signs, graffiti, and political parties, or the popular extracts from radio, film, and the world of advertising. I argue here that tuning into these smaller genres or "minor media" (Fischer and Abedi 1990:335 ff.) is one productive avenue for beginning an analysis of the linguistic intertextuality of contemporary societies. Further, I suggest that for large-scale societies from the city to the nation and even the global village, the pervasive connections among these smaller genres (and between them and the larger genres) is actually a key constitutive and integrating feature of what can be called a community.

Recycling Metapragmatic Discourse

Many of the public words inspired by Zambian broadcasters are actually more than just single expressions; they are interactional routines and, in particular, dyadic exchanges that are about the communication event itself. Radio broadcasters are faced with the fairly unique condition of having to generate and maintain an ongoing flow of communication in the absence of a face-to-face context and within the constraints of an entirely aural medium. As with telephone communication or other modes of radio use (e.g., in the taxi-driving profession), cues such as gaze and gesture are simply not available for assessing whether the channel is open and working or whether one's intended interlocutor is listening. Because of these parti-cular contextual constraints, several types of metapragmatic discourse are extremely pervasive in radio broadcasting.[7] Many of these expressions constitute broadcasters' channel-monitoring and turn-taking routines. Other types are designed explicitly to build audience expectations and involvement. For example, broadcasting requires title announcements and other framing devices to demarcate what would otherwise be a continuous flow of voices and sound. The frequent practices of entitling and announcing function as important contextualization cues about what listeners should expect; they also serve as key signposts for listeners who have fluctuating attention or who enter into a speech event that is already underway.

Metapragmatic discourse is not the only kind of discourse which is recycled from the realm of radio into contexts of face-to-face communication, but it is readily seized upon. Why is this so? This is an open question and certainly one that requires more extensive research. Three explanations are proposed here as the most likely candidates. First, as Silverstein (1992:67 ff.) has argued, metapragmatic discourse has a particular kind of *transparency of both form and function*. Because it explicitly serves to frame and orchestrate communication, it tends to be more subject to awareness and segmentation than other linguistic forms (Silverstein 1976:49 f., 1992, 1993). Second, since metapragmatic discourse is speech about speaking, it is easily transferable to other speech contexts. For example, in many of the cases considered below, the significant feature that enables the decontextualization and recontextualization of metapragmatic discourse is its *general applicability* to vir-tually any kind of dyadic exchange. And third, I suggest that the detachability and the repeatability of a given radio expression can be fueled by the medium itself, as it lends *prominence* to the phrase, for example, through frequent occurrence or through association with colorful personalities, heightened drama, or humorous moments. It is especially in these latter cases that the transportability of a radio phrase is driven by the specific connotations that it has in the original context. This is illustrated in our first example.

Checking the Channel

Nearly all national broadcasting in Zambia emanates from the capital city of Lusaka, but every Monday through Friday four hours of broadcasting on Radio 2 (one of the English-language channels) are handled by the Kitwe studios in the Zambian Copperbelt region. When the Lusaka broadcaster is getting ready to "cross over to the Kitwe studios," that is, hand over operations to the Kitwe-based broadcaster, he or she may say: "Kitwe, are you there?," "Kitwe, can you hear me?," or "Hello, Kitwe?" If all goes smoothly, the Kitwe-based broadcaster responds affirmatively, with greetings, thanks, and good-byes to the Lusaka broadcaster. If the connection is not good, however, several awkward seconds of airtime may be spent checking the channel, with the Lusaka-based broadcaster repeating the meta-pragmatic phrases: "Hello, hello?," "Kitwe, are you there?," "Kitwe, can you hear me?," or "Hello, Kitwe?" This scenario is rather common at ZNBC (temporary linkup failures occur almost weekly), and thus it is no surprise that the Kitwe crossover itself can serve as an analogy for temporarily failed communication, as illustrated in the following vignette.

One day I was shopping in a very large and crowded Lusaka store, and I noticed a woman trying to get the attention of a friend standing in the next aisle. She was whispering loudly in the friend's direction, "Hello, hello? Hello?" The friend didn't respond, and the woman, a bit embarrassed over drawing attention to herself while still not able to attract the friend, laughed and shouted, "Hello, Kitwe?" This definitely got the attention of the friend, as well as several other customers, who were clearly amused by this clever allusion to the bungled ZNBC communication link.[8]

How is the recontextualization of a radio phrase made possible in this comic scene? Primarily, the successful recycling of "Hello Kitwe?" rests on the transposition of two basic components of the original radio event: (1) the existence of two interlocutors at different locales (Lusaka : Kitwe :: aisle 1 : aisle 2), and (2) uncertainty about the existence of a shared channel. Furthermore, knowledge of the original radio source is essential for understanding the recycled expression. "Kitwe" is not a personal name; it is the place-name for a city on the Zambian Copperbelt. On radio, "Kitwe" metonymically functions as the proper name of the broadcaster and/or studio based in the city of Kitwe. In the context of a Lusaka store, however, there is no obvious link between an individual shopper and the name "Kitwe." Unless, of course, one understands it, within the vocative construction, as an echoing of the well-known radio scenario. "Kitwe" then becomes a name for a person who is hard of hearing.[9] The remarkable humor here is further enhanced by the fact that the sequence "Hello, hello? Hello, Kitwe? Kitwe, can you hear me?" *has no other context* besides the famous radio interaction. The entire expression is uniquely identified with its context of occurrence, and this identification is what triggers the parodic mood that results from the expression's unusual displacement.

Turn-Taking Routines

While the previous example represents what may be a single, idiosyncratic, instance of radio-discourse recycling – and one that I just happened to overhear in an urban store – there are numerous cases of recycled radio phrases that have become fairly ordinary and that occur in a wide range of social contexts. One of these is the title of the popular radio program *Over to You*, which runs in six different languages and which has been running in English for over 30 years.[10] In this program a team of two broadcasters alternate as disc jockeys and signal the handing over of speaker role by uttering the phrase "Over to you." One broadcaster is based in the Lusaka studios, and the other is in the Kitwe studios. The program features musical selections, many of which are listeners' requests accompanied by their dedications and greetings, and the witty exchange between the two broadcasters. In the show, uttering "Over to you" creates an opening for the transfer of speaker role, in which the co-DJ will select a song or read a listener's letter.

In the Zambian-language programs, the title and turn-taking phrase is phonologically assimilated from English: *Ovata yu* (ChiNyanja) and *Ofata yu* (Chi-Bemba).[11] The phrase's assimilation into Zambian culture is also evidenced by the completeness of its linguistic assimilation. In many usages, especially among speakers who do not know English, the phrase functions as a Zambian-language expression with no connotations of foreign origin.

As with the successful recycling of "Hello, Kitwe?," the use of "Over to you" outside the context of radio requires that certain components of the original radio event also be in place. There must be another person to assume the speaker role, and there must be an expectation that the other speaker perform in some way. Four brief ethnographic examples illustrate this usage.

In a ChiBemba speaking context during a traditional Bemba marriage preparation ceremony, one of the prominent elder women who had been leading a series of songs in ChiBemba addressed a group of women sitting on the opposite side of the room: "Ofata yu," she said, expecting that the addressees would select and lead the next song. In an analogous, but more "modern" and urban setting in Lusaka, I witnessed the use of the idiom again in the context of song turn-taking among women instructors/advisors. This was at a prewedding "kitchen party," an event that merges the traditional wedding preparations with the European-derived bridal shower. In this case, the family and the elder women were upper-class and highly fluent speakers of English. The ceremonial songs were in ChiBemba, but the turns were signaled with the English "Over to you." I came across yet another example of the phrase's use in the context of women singing during a practice session of a Seventh-Day Adventist choral group. After finishing an English-language song that she had selected and led, the leader of the singing group handed the hymn book to one of her colleagues and said, "Over to you."

A final instance of the use of this expression occurred on a letter that I received from a neighbor in Kasama. Written along the bottom of an envelope addressed to me and handed to me by the writer, a 14-year-old girl, was the phrase "Over '2' you, D.S." The young girl, whom I had just met a few days earlier, was very interested in becoming my pen pal and was hoping that she might be able to visit me in the United States. Her written recontextualization of the radio idiom added a special flair to the hand-delivered envelope, as it both foregrounded and played with the form of the phrase. The symbol 2 took the place of its homonym *to*, and this deviation was acknowledged with quotation marks. In addition, my personal initials were appended to the construction in a form analogous to the way that radio disc jockeys identify themselves and each other. This cleverly elaborated on the transposition of the radio speech event to the context of personal letter writing, and further indexed the young girl's conversancy with the latest trends in popular expressions.

Returning to our questions about the semiotics of circulation, what is transported in the recentering of "Over to you" (and its variants) is the basic discourse format of turn exchange *combined with* a performance format in which the animation of a different genre is embedded. The data here suggest that the phrase is primarily tied to the turn-taking contexts of song choice and letter-reading/writing, both of which are elemental in the radio program. But to what degree is knowledge of the radio source crucial for understanding "Ofata you" and "Over to you" in these contexts? For the most part, these phrases have filtered into popular usage, and attributability to a radio source is not as necessary for interpretability as it is with the phrase "Hello, Kitwe." It is only in the final example that knowledge of the radio program really enhances the interpretation of the utterance. Here, the radio context is invoked with special written flourishes such as abbreviations and quotation marks. The message on the envelope is interpretable without knowledge of its intertextuality with the radio program and disc-jockey nicknames, but awareness of these links is crucial for a full appreciation of the form and its potential currency for a young girl writing to acquire an American pen pal.

"Getting It" from Radio

Many of the popular phrases inspired by radio broadcasting have a distinctive kind of symbolic value because of their association with the medium, which itself is a site of innovation, word play, and colorful drama. Young Zambians, in particular, closely attend to the linguistic nuances of radio and creatively poach from radio discourse to make their own trendy formulations. The following example of recontextualized metapragmatic discourse illustrates how such processes work and raises larger questions about the media-external forces that propel the recycling of media language.

When a ChiBemba broadcaster is handing over operations to another broadcaster or when a live reporter is linked in from an outside location, the following exchange may occur on air:[12]

(1) *Mwaikata* line? "Do you have the line?"
     Ninjikata   "I've got (it)."

The verb root *-ikata* means "hold," "grasp," or "catch"; thus this interchange refers to the grasping of a transmission link. Among young Zambians, however, the radio-derived phrase "*Mwaikata* line?" has been transformed into a popular slang expression that focuses on the successful relay of the *message* rather than the successful link up of the physical *channel*:

(2) *Waikata* line?   "Do you understand?" "Do you get me?"

In addition to this semantic shift, the original radio phrase also undergoes a formal change as it is recontextualized. The expressions in (1) and (2) differ in the second-person form. The radio utterance in (1) utilizes the second-person plural form (*mu-*, assimilated as *mw-*) in reference to single addressees. This polite usage (V of T/V) is mandatory for radio announcers in such contexts. In the slang usage in (2), however, the second-person singular form (*u*-, assimilated as *w*-) is more appropriate for single addressees as it connotes familiarity and informality.

Linguistic evidence suggests that the recyclability of the radio expression "*Mwaikata* line?" as "*Waikata* line?" is supplemented, or even motivated, by two other key factors that are external to the original radio context: (1) other usages of the verb -*ikata* within Zambian popular culture and (2) the existence of a more general paradigmatic set of slang expressions for "getting it." Regarding the first factor, the verb -*ikata* features prominently in idioms of relay (both channel relay and message relay) during musical performances, for example, in the imperative phrase "ikata, ikata" "grab, grab". This phrase occurs as part of a chorus or transition point where one musician is inviting another musician to come in, that is, to seize the beat or to take the opportunity to do a special solo. Such musical relays are analogous to the announcer relay in (1), where one performer hands over the stage to another. During a performance, "ikata, ikata" "grab, grab" can also be an exhortation to the listeners to "get it" or "dig it." Here, the meaning is more analogous to that of the slang usage (2), which focuses on addressee's comprehension or engagement.

The second motivating factor outside of the realm of radio – the existence of other related slang expressions for "getting it" – also raises an important question about the cosmopolitan connotations of recontextualized radio phrases. Significantly, the slang phrase "Waikata line?" joins a host of other nearly synonymous code-mixed expressions within Zambian youth culture such as:

(3) *Naugeta?*   "Do you[sg] get (me/it)?"
     Namugeta?   "Do you[pl] get (me/it)?"
     Naudiga?   "Do you[sg] dig (me/it)?"
     Namudiga?   "Do you[pl] dig (me/it)?"

In these popular phrases, the English verbs *get* and *dig* have been morphologically incorporated as ChiBemba verb roots. They are inflected with the present perfect tense (*na*-), the second-person singular or plural subject markers (*u*-, *mu*-), and the indicative suffix (-*a*). But they are not phonologically assimilated (the consonants *g* and *d* would undergo devoicing), and thus they retain the indexical link with their fashionable English counterparts "Do ya get me?" and "Do you dig it?" The recontextualized radio phrase is not therefore an isolated linguistic innovation; it participates in a more general pattern of similar expressions for interpersonal rapport within Zambian youth culture.

These two motivating factors highlight the critical fact that radio is not the be-all and end-all for putting a phrase into motion. Indeed, they generate a crucial modification of Gumperz's important observation that "mass media and the prestige of their speakers tend to carry idioms far from their sources" (1971:223), one that is consistent with other principles of diachronic linguistics. Specifically, we see here that the social circulation of media discourse is often propelled by other (media-external) linguistic lines of influence of many different orders (e.g., structural, pragmatic, sociolinguistic, paradigmatic, analogic, ideological, etc.) that must be accounted for as well.

This point then leads us to a final question, about the sociolinguistic significance of the codeswitching in the expressions "Mwaikata line?" and "Waikata line?". How does this factor into the processes of recycling media discourse? In Zambia, as well as in many parts of the world, the strategic use of codeswitching has the potential to function as "a sign of social distinction or urbanity" (Kashoki 1978b:94; also see Gumperz 1982 and Myers-Scotton 1993). It is important to note, however, that not all codeswitching is necessarily trendy or exceptional. It may be a relatively normal and unmarked feature of urban speech (Swigart 1994), or it may be fairly ordinary as in utterance (1): "Mwaikata line?" Here, in the context of a ChiBemba broadcast, the usage of *line* is motivated by a lexical gap and is thus more a case of borrowing than of codeswitching. *Line* is simply a technical word imported from the realm of modern utilities, for example, electricity, telephone, water, sanitation, and broadcasting. By contrast, the blend of ChiBemba and English in (2) is more marked and unusual. Indeed, it is the basic index of the expression's trendiness. This sociolinguistic difference between (1) and (2) thus demonstrates how recentered radio phrases may also undergo subtle functional changes in addition to semantic and formal ones.

Entitling and Naming

Radio program titles constitute another form of metapragmatic discourse which – comparable to the various interpersonal expressions discussed above – has a high degree of transparency of form and function. Titles also have a certain prominence derived from frequent repetition and their placement within the flow of broadcasting. As stated earlier, titles function as announcing, captioning, or (re)framing devices. They are designed for reproducibility and recognizability, and these factors render them particularly available for recontextualization in popular usage.

Even *within* broadcasting, program titles are recycled from other sources. For example, nearly all English-language program titles on Radio Zambia (as well as most program formats) derive from Western sources such as the BBC and the VOA: for example *Main News Bulletin, The Breakfast Show, Up-to-Date, The World of Sport*, and *Sports Roundup*.[13] Most Zambian language program titles are also indebted to other external sources, and many are strikingly intertextual. For example, the ChiBemba advice program *Kabuusha Taakolelwe Boowa* takes its name from a well-known Bemba proverb meaning "the asker was not poisoned by a mushroom." The program has, in turn, become the source of coinage for the occupational title *kabuusha* "advisor". Another advice program, *Baanacimbuusa* "Women Advisors," has as its source the name for the ritual leaders of the Bemba girls' initiation ceremony. And in an interesting twist on origins, the title of the comic drama series *Ifyabukaaya* ("Things That Are Familiar" or "Things from Around Here") derives its name from a ChiBemba reader constructed for basic literacy during the colonial period by the White Fathers missionaries.

In short, virtually all radio titles represent a reanimation or invocation of another source or another genre. The larger point, then, is that radio programs themselves represent a range of recyclings, transpositions, and cannibalizations of other discourse genres. Moreover, this inherent intertextuality of radio itself seems to be a dynamic contributing factor in the recycling of radio words outside of broadcasting and the ease with which they circulate and become recontextualized. In popular usage, radio titles are transported to everyday situations as labels for speech events, experiences, and even personality types. As we saw in the case of "Over to you," a radio program title is used to caption a component of a speech event, namely, the handing over of a turn. The following example illustrates how a program title can also become the title of a personal experience.

One evening about 7 o'clock, my neighbor returned home from selling buns at the market, and I asked her how her day went. Using the title of a ChiBemba radio program, she sighed, "Ah mayo, 'Imbila ya Bulanda'" [Oh dear, "News of Suffering"]. One of the most popular programs on Radio Zambia, *Imbila ya Bulanda* airs virtually every day and serves as a primary vehicle for individuals to send messages announcing illnesses, deaths, and funerals. Here, my neighbor was using the radio program title to entitle the events of her day. She went on to explain how all the places at the market were filled when she went there at 5:30 a.m., and how she unsuccessfully tried to maneuver for a spot. She was forced to return later in the afternoon and finally did manage to find a place to sell her baked goods, but the day had been very long and exhausting.

Analogous to the Kitwe example above, this recycling injects a bit of humor into the situation through a marked contrast with the expression's original context. The phrase "imbila ya bulanda" is unmistakably welded to the popular program that features news of death and illness; so virtually any utterance of it outside this context intertextually invokes the program. By recontextualizing the phrase as a caption for her day, my neighbor did indeed exploit the functional force of the phrase to announce that a tale of woe was forthcoming. But since these events were far less serious than those announced on radio, her entitling was hyperbolic and lent an ironic humor to the tale, which after all, had a happy ending.

In addition to providing a common public source for ways of entitling situations and experiences, media can also be a source for proper names and names of types of people (table 4.1). These humorous modes of naming and labeling exhibit elements of what is a very pervasive kind of playful, ironic kind of public verbal culture in Zambia which is not limited to any particular age, locale, or language (Spitulnik 1994b). They also illustrate how active audience interpretations enter into the mediated construction of a world of familiar people, social types, and locales, as described by Anderson (1983). Some of the particular examples shown here are urban and youth based, and others are ones that originated in urban-youth slang but are now more widely used.[14] The meaning and derivation of most items in table 4.1 are self-evident, but the first two need some explanation.[15]

The labeling of party vigilantes as "By Air Boys" in the late 1980s essentially began with a television advertisement for Zambian Airways. The ad pictures a smiling customer sitting in a disembodied plane seat floating across the sky, while the announcer talks about the pleasure of traveling "by air" with Zambia Airways. This striking image of the floating customer was then applied to the way that the party vigilantes remove illegal traders from local marketplaces.[16] Once discovered without the proper papers, the marketeer is lifted on both sides and is suddenly whisked away by the vigilantes while still in a sitting position, much like the man in the ad who somehow floats across the screen while seated in a chair.

The story of *chongololo* also illustrates the creative reworking of a media name that imports distinctive imagery from the original source. The Wildlife Conservation Society of Zambia and Bata Shoe Company sponsor a children's program entitled

Table 4.1   Innovative names derived from media sources

Name	Meaning	Media source
By Air Boys	political-party vigilantes	TV commercial
Chongololo	pretentious, European-like Zambian	radio program
BaSix Koloko	people from the Northwestern Province (the ones whose newscasts start at 6 a.m.)	radio newscasts
Dallas City	the Lusaka neighborhood of Kabwata (an upper-middle-class residential area)	TV show *Dallas*
Hawaii	women's dorms at Copperbelt University ("because the ladies there live like they are at a resort")	TV show *Hawaii Five-O*
Ninja	50-kwacha bill (the highest currency denomination in the late 1980s)	foreign movies

Chongololo ("centipede" in ChiNyanja), which is produced in ChiNyanja, ChiBemba, and English. This educational program features two or three adult hosts who discuss the habits and habitats of Zambian wildlife. Interspersed with their comments, fictional outings, and the sound effects of wild animals are songs about animals sung by a chorus of children. Listeners can become members of the Chongololo Radio Club of the Air by submitting their answers to the question "Why is it so important for us to conserve nature?" In all three languages, the program opens and closes with the children's chorus singing their theme song in English:

Chongololo, it's our favorite club.
Chongololo, it's the club we love.
Come and join us on this show, and you'll have lots of fun.
Learn about the living things [*clap*] under the sun.[17]

In popular Zambian slang, *chongololo* has become a term for Zambians who try to speak like Europeans. The English-language program is hosted by a British male who is typically joined by two Zambian females, all of whom speak with a slow and deliberate British Received Pronunciation (RP) accent. The Zambian children on the program also speak this form of English very well for their ages (roughly 8 to 12 years old) and thus sound particularly precocious and privileged. Even in the ChiBemba and ChiNyanja programs, this is reflected in the English theme song. One young Zambian explained to me:

Chongololo is a word for Zambians who try to adopt a foreign accent so that to a Zambian they sound like they are Europeans, while Europeans on the other hand fail to understand what they say.... [University of Zambia] students say, "They speak in tongues."

A less affected form of Zambian English (with a phonology closer to that of Zambian languages) is preferred by most Zambians, even by those who are highly educated and frequently exposed to the English of Europeans and Americans. For example, a 20-year-old student at a technical training college walked into the dormitory common room to watch the television news (which is always in English) and declared in ChiNyanja:

Ah, lelo niza nvelako news *cifukwa si achongololo amene azabelenga.* [Oh, today I'm going to listen to the news because it's not the chongololos reading it.]

The young man clearly approved of the pronunciation of the two newscasters; presumably if they had spoken like chongololos, he would have walked out.

Not only is the Zambian chongololo guilty of having a fake accent, but he or she is also guilty of going to the extreme in mimicking European dress and behavior. This takes on class dimensions, as one university student told me, "A chongololo is the child of an *apamwamba* [upper class person]." Another put it more extremely: "'Chongies' are victims of bourgeois capitalist ideology. They speak with American accents."[18] The negative behavior of the chongololo thus extends beyond a verbal style of "speak[ing] in tongues" to include the desire for a bourgeois lifestyle that is beyond the reach of most Zambians. Indeed, the actual content of the *Chongololo* program itself – observing birds in nature, appreciation of the world of insects, tourism within Zambia, and concern with wildlife preservation – emblematizes this essentially un-Zambian outlook.

What kinds of semiotic processes are at work in this recontextualization of a program title as a personal stereotype? First, there are certain formal linguistic conditions that support it. Analogous to the Kitwe example, this recontextualization is based on both metonymy and the existence of a shared lexical category (proper name). The program name *Chongololo* is also the club name, and club members – or people like them – are metonymically designated as *chongololos* or *chongies*. In addition, the recycling imports several features of the original radio context into its negative connotations: the mode of speaking, upper-class leisure activities, and a Western-oriented outlook. Moreover, the very concept of the radio program *as a club* that can be joined furthers the implicit critique that the show and the chongololo represent an exclusive sector of Zambian society. The Chongololo Radio Club of the Air, as a club for chongololos, in essence constitutes a distinct speech community where members share a common norm of English language usage (i.e., RP). The point of contention, and what motivates the negative stereotype, is whether this speech community has the rightful claim to also represent the linguistic community of English within Zambia. While the program's speakers do adhere to a "culture of the standard" (Silverstein 1987) and view themselves as exemplifying proper English usage – particularly as they are guided by a male British program host – most Zambians reject this as a model for how Zambians should speak English.

Poaching from Personalities

In contrast to the *Chongololo* show, numerous other radio programs provide very attractive models of speech styles which are emulated and invoked in more positive ways. In many cases, these styles and linguistic innovations are actually the trademarks of a particular radio personality. The uniqueness of such radio personalities is to a great degree built upon this verbal creativity, a creativity that is at the same time relatively predictable since it is recognizable as a personal style. In many instances this very reputation and visibility is what subsequently propels the adoption of broadcasters' linguistic innovations within popular culture (see Gumperz 1971: 223). Some of these recycled innovations retain the indexical link to the individual broadcaster's speech style, and others have been absorbed more widely into popular usage. In the following we look at a few examples of this popular adoption of broadcasters' speech innovations and habits.

Dennis Liwewe, Zambia's most famous sports announcer, is renowned for his fast speech, innovative descriptions, and dramatic delivery. His broadcasts are almost always in English, and his mode of speaking has become a model and a reference point for certain phrasings, even beyond the area of sports. For example, one very common Liwewe phrase during football (soccer) games combines the word *situation* with one or two numbers:

(4) It's a one-zero situation.
(5) Bwalya comes into the Zaire zone. It's a one-two situation.

In utterance (4), *situation* refers to the score. A one-zero situation is thus a score of one to zero. In (5), *situation* refers to the *positions* on the playing field. That is, there is one offensive player – Bwalya on the Zambian team – moving in against two defensive players in the Zaire zone.

Zambians have picked up on this usage of *situation* and have applied it outside the realm of sports, to refer to contexts where some numerical quantity is involved. For example, I was at the University of Zambia snack bar, and a young man had been at the counter trying to get some matches to light a cigarette. He was unsuccessful and walked back to his friend, saying:

(6) *Ifya*matches, zero situation   "Things [boxes] of matches, zero situation."
                                     "About the matches, zero situation."

The "zero situation" in this case is the unavailability of matches. While one might interpret *situation* here as meaning "predicament," it also has a sense analogous to the sports-specific forms in (4) and (5), as "score" or "position." The young man came up empty-handed in the search for matches; he thus failed to score and found that nothing was in position.

The recycling of the Liwewe formula "[number(-number)] situation" outside of sports talk is highly marked as creative language use. While recontextualized, it still retains an important indexical link back to its original source. This is not just a link of attribution, that is, the identification of Liwewe as the originator of the expression, but one that carries the broader associations of a "Liweweism," a phrasing that is dramatic, lively, and somewhat hyperbolic in the manner of the famous Liwewe.[19] The usage of ChiBemba-English code-mixing in (6) lends an additional air of trendiness to the expression.

Other examples of linguistic innovations stemming from specific radio personalities include the words *get* and *dig* as idioms for "understand" that, as discussed earlier, have been incorporated into the code-mixed slang expressions "Naugeta?" (Do ya get me?) and "Namudiga?" (Do you dig it?). These words emanate from the most popular Radio Zambia DJs, who are themselves recyclers, as they extract popular American and British slang from song lyrics while exhorting their listeners, talking up the records, and making segues between selections. Many DJs also exemplify the pronunciations characteristic of informal American English usage (for example, strongly nasalized "gonna," "wanna," and "ya know"), and these expressions circulate quite widely among Zambian youths. The following excerpt from Radio 4 disc jockey Leonard Kantumoya, also known as "The Groove Maker" or "The GM," illustrates some of these media sources of urban slang:

Ah, when you hear the GM playing instrumentals and keeping a little quiet, you just know the hour is about to arrive and I'm about to *hit the road* for home, because I see my good friend Swidden Hangaala is already in.
He's *dug* in already and he's trying to *dig* in even further. [*Laughs.*]
He's *gonna* sweep me out of my DJ saddle.
[Radio 4, February 3, 1989, emphasis added]

With this kind of fast-paced, exciting style, Zambian DJs play a pivotal role in introducing an English-language vocabulary that speaks to the mood and tempo of the modern condition. Contemporary Zambian English is replete with such words and idioms, many of which are not restricted to subcultural usage and many of which have origins as far back as the 1940s. Some of the most popular of these are the words *jive, jazz, super, live, nonstop, beat*, and *rap*. In this sense, radio – in conjunction with popular music that is often the original site of such vocabulary – has played a key role not only in introducing new lexical items but in structuring an entire semantic field that denotes excitement and entertainment.

Broadcasters' Recyclings: The Case of Personal Titles

The preceding discussion has touched on several instances where media professionals themselves recontextualize and reanimate phrases that originate in other contexts, for example, program titles that stem from indigenous oral traditions and Western media sources, and disc-jockey speech registers that draw from popular song lyrics and the styles of DJs heard on foreign stations. In this sense, not only does radio serve as a model of normative language use and as a springboard for linguistic innovations within popular culture, it is also a dynamically intertextual site in which an existing repertoire of public words is continually being modified and elaborated upon. This section examines one final case of broadcasters' recyclings, one that illustrates the possibilities of political parody within broadcasting.

All radio disc jockeys have at least one nickname that they regularly use; most of these are boasts of some sort, and many are creative twists on political titles or other titles associated with high status. For example, the late Peter Mweemba went by the name "Brother PM," a combination of his personal initials and an American-derived term for solidary males.[20] In the Zambian context, this coinage is particularly striking, because PM also designates the third highest ranking politician in the country, the Prime Minister.[21] As he cultivated his own style of casual and trendy familiarity, Brother PM played off the fact that the real PM is surrounded by the exact opposite: an aura of extreme deference and seriousness. Exploiting the full force of this contrast, ZNBC management actually orchestrated the meeting of Brother PM and the real PM on national radio, by inviting the then-Prime Minister to preside over the inauguration of a new radio channel. Peter Mweemba was the DJ on duty:

Right, this is your DJ, Brother PM,
behind the microphone hoping you're ready for us,
as we bring it to you, the biggest and best on FM stereo.
Right, in just a few minutes' time from now,
the Right Honorable Prime Minister, Kebby Musokotwane
will be walking into Radio Mulungushi stereo studio,
to officially switch on Radio Mulungushi.
[Radio 4, February 1, 1989]

After the Prime Minister inaugurates the new radio channel, Peter Mweemba interviews him at length about the role of broadcasting. In the exchange, the two address each other as "Right Honorable Prime Minister" and "Peter." Later in the interview, Mweemba personalizes the discussion and focuses on the musical tastes of the Prime Minister. The PM is asked if he has any favorites to request, and by the end of the interview, he is integrated like any other avid radio listener into the popular radio format of the deejayed greeting/request program:

Well, before I spin your records, Right Honorable Prime Minister,
finally, any special greetings to your friends and family?
I realize you are a national leader;
so I suppose there are one or two people you'd like to say hello to.

Of course, the integration is not really complete. Mweemba does not refer to himself as "Brother PM" during this exchange, nor would we expect the real PM to use this phrase. Moreover, the list of people whom the Prime Minister wishes to greet and thank is rather unusual. He first greets his wife, then his "colleagues in Cabinet," the Zambian people, and finally the President.

In an interesting twist on both Peter Mweemba's innovation and another political abbreviation, the broadcaster Margaret Phiri uses the initials "MP" as her DJ trademark. In common parlance, MP designates a Member of Parliament. Phiri is a rather low-key broadcaster and does not really play up the political connotations of her nickname. Many listeners feel that she rather uncreatively copied Mweemba's model. Behind this, however, are some basic gender differences and expectations about speaking styles. Projecting a strong lively personality on national airwaves and, especially, the playfulness and boasting that is inherent in many DJ nicknames (e.g., "The Sweet Sensation" and "The Man with the Longest Queue in Town") is deemed more appropriate for Zambian men and less appropriate for Zambian women.

One popular radio DJ who is constantly promoting himself and coining new phrases is Leonard Kantumoya ("The Groove Maker" or "The GM"). Behind the microphone, Kantumoya talks quite a lot and often uses American slang (circa 1970), as illustrated above. The wordplay, or abbreviation play, in his nickname builds on the fact that, in Zambia, GM is one of the most pervasive labels for the highest-ranking office in business and industry: the general manager. Using another abbreviation, Kantumoya dubs his music "PPS" (People Pleasing Sounds). PPS with GM is somewhat of a mixed metaphor (or mixed bureaucracy), but it is amusing in any case as it invokes the well-known title "Provincial Political Secretary."[22]

In their recontextualizations of these abbreviations designating bureaucratic structures and high offices, Zambian broadcasters display a distinctive sense of humor. They never directly refer to the original source of their nicknames; they only allude to it. But like political leaders and top level bureaucrats, they are, in their own realm, at the controls. They are in charge of spinning the records and making the announcements. In terms of their pragmatic structure, such DJ nicknames are most apt as uniquely identifying radio trademarks or signatures, because they already have a built-in definiteness. The initials themselves presuppose the existence of a specific nonabbreviated form, and these nonabbreviated forms specifically designate the holder of a particular office or position.

As recyclings of tropes of the nation-state, these DJ nicknames illustrate a more general point about the public sphere in Zambia. The knowledge of acronyms and abbreviations is an important part of communicative competence in Zambia, and this is essentially part of the postcolonial legacy.[23] For example, in modern-day Zambia the most prominent positions, institutions, and interests – from government offices and state services to multinational corporations and foreign donor agencies – are designated by a proliferation of acronyms such as UNZA, TAZARA, ZESCO, INDECO, ZNBC, DANIDA, SIDO, FTJ, KK, PM, MP, GM, and DG.[24] What appears to be a virtual alphabet soup for the uninitiated is actually a very concrete mapping and populating of the public sphere. With their own initials, Brother PM, MP, and the GM thus index not only their conversancy and sense of humor about this public sphere but also their unique membership in it: to be initialed in this way is to have a uniquely identifying description and to be counted among the ranks of the nation's leading figures.

Conclusion

This article has attempted to open up a relatively unexplored area of research at the intersection of language and culture, by investigating the social circulation of media discourse and its implications for the mediation of communities. I have argued that broadcasting functions as a common reservoir and reference point for various kinds of linguistic innovations in Zambia, ranging from the subcultural to the mainstream, from the fleeting to the perduring, and from the parodic to the mundane. Radio is a source for lexical coinage (e.g., *chongies* and *kabuusha*), idiomatic expressions (e.g., "Waikata line?"), and distinctive modes of verbal interaction (e.g., "Over to you"). It is also a resource for innovative tropes and analogies: for example, *BaSix Koloko* (The Six o'Clockers) as a name for members of ethnic groups whose newscasts begin daily at 6 a.m., or "Hello, Kitwe" as an address form for someone who is hard of hearing.

In addition to documenting these processes, I have made some broader semiotic generalizations about the types of media discourse that circulate and the types of conditions that enable this circulation. For example, metapragmatic discourse and, in particular, various kinds of interpersonal routines and framing devices are readily seized upon in creative reworkings of media language. I have proposed that features such as transparency of form and function and prominence (via frequent repetition or association with dramatic moments) create a "prepared-for detachability" (Bauman and Briggs 1990:74) that enables such discourse to be circulated across communities. I have also suggested that the language of proper names and definite description (including place-names, nicknames, and abbreviations), as well as generic names for social types, figure importantly in socially circulating media discourse, because they function to locate and populate a shared world, much in a manner analogous to the processes described by Anderson (1983) in reference to the 18th-century novel. And finally, I have suggested that these processes of circulation operate within a much larger context of a very dynamic verbal culture which itself is playful, ironic, and highly intertextual.

Addressing the thorny question of the construction of communities is a much more difficult task than discovering the various semiotic and cultural conditions that propel the social circulation of media discourse. I have claimed that mass media provide common reference points for the production of shared linguistic knowledge and that the social circulation of media discourse is just one case of the subtle linguistic connections that exist across populations that stretch over regional and national boundaries. I have proposed that criteria such as frequency of media consumption and large-scale exposure to a common media source enter into this equation and that the speech community concept can be productively refined by including these features.

As the cases considered here have intimated, the communities mediated by radio broadcasting are several. Since media discourse is not uniformly accessible or even uniformly seized upon and interpreted in the same ways, all kinds of outcomes are possible. In some instances the social circulation of media discourse occurs at the subcultural level (e.g., "Waikata line?" among urban youths), and in some instances it is more general (e.g., "Imbila ya Bulanda" and "Ofata yu"). Still other instances may be highly idiosyncratic, as suggested by the case of "Hello, Kitwe." Further research into the sociolinguistic distribution of recycled media discourse across age, gender, class, locale, and language is really required to answer such questions about communities more concretely.

One enduring issue throughout the discussion has been how to characterize the status of these phrases that circulate across and through mass media and popular culture. Following other work in linguistic anthropology (Bauman and Briggs 1990; Briggs and Bauman 1992; Lucy 1993; Silverstein and Urban 1996), I have attempted in each case to specify the various formal conditions on, and functional effects of, such recontextualized speech. In comparison to the better-known speech genres (e.g., narrative, oratory, ritual speech, and reported speech) that feature in such studies, many of the media fragments considered here exhibit (1) a much greater mobility through various social contexts, and (2) a peculiar built-in detachability and reproducibility, as stated above. As they thread through different contexts of use, giving people their own voices and aesthetic pleasures, such public words hearken to speakers and contexts which are in some ways larger than life. Indeed, it is this transportability, or detachability, that allows public words to seem to have lives of their own yet also be fibers of connection across various social situations and contexts.

While some scholars might attribute this circulation of media discourse more generally to the inherent nature of mass media and/or to a postmodern condition, I would challenge this. It may be true that the postmodern condition is characterized by an unprecedented fascination with icons, images, slogans, jingles, and other mass-produced objects that mass media disseminate and produce (Baudrillard 1983; Harvey 1989; Hebdige 1988; Jameson 1984). But the various practices that characterize active audiences such as media poaching and intertextuality (Certeau 1984; Jenkins 1992) do not seem to be particularly new. The evidence here suggests that recycling media discourse and even the existence of such "detachables" are part of a much more general process of language use, or social life of language, which intersects (but precedes) the postmodern, pop-culture era, and the advent of mass media as widespread, public communication forms. In fact, it seems equally the case that the radio recyclings discussed here are not really exemplars of a postmodern condition per se, but rather they are evidence of the more general heteroglossic nature of language. To quote Bakhtin:

[T]here are no "neutral" words and forms – words and forms that can belong to "no one"; language has been completely taken over, shot through with intentions and accents. For any individual consciousness living in it, language is not an abstract system of normative forms but rather a concrete heterglot conception of the world. All words have a "taste" of a profession, a genre ... a particular person, a generation, an age group, the day and hour. Each word tastes of the contexts in which it has lived its socially charged life. (1981:293)

As a far-reaching, ongoing, public communication form – which is itself a constant reanimator – radio broadcasting has the potential to magnify, and even create, this "socially charged life" of certain linguistic forms. I have suggested here that the study of media discourse in popular culture is one such avenue for examining the dynamism and mobility of language, and that this mobility (and mobilizability) has far-reaching implications for both language change and the construction of public cultures and speech communities which are vibrant and creative.

NOTES

Acknowledgements. The primary research for this article was carried out in 1988–90, supported by Fulbright-Hays and NSF fellowships, and facilitated by the Institute for African Studies (now INESOR) at the University of Zambia. I would like to extend my sincere thanks to these institutions. I am also grateful to the Spencer Foundation and the University Research Committee at Emory University for supporting various stages of this work. I am deeply indebted, as well, to many colleagues who have offered their valuable input at various writing stages, including, but not limited to, Mark Auslander, Misty Bastian, James Collins, Jane Hill, Bruce Knauft, Ben Lee, John Lucy, Mwelwa Musambachime, Bradd Shore, Michael Silverstein, and the anonymous reviewers for the *Journal of Linguistic Anthropology*.

1 As an adjective, *public* is used here (following Urban) in a fairly neutral sense to connote wide distribution and a general openness and availability. This definition contrasts in important ways with definitions of the noun *public*, or *the public*, as an ideological construct concerning state–citizen relations or corporation–consumer relations (Calhoun 1992; Gal 1995:417 f.; Gal and Woolard 1995; Spitulnik 1994a). For discussions of how these two are linked, that is, how public availability of certain communication forms figures into the ideological construction of publics, see Gal and Woolard 1995 and Spitulnik 1994a, 1994b.
2 For electronic media, the semantics of the term *broadcast* (which originated from the realm of agriculture) encapsulates this important sense of widespread distribution.
3 See Irvine 1987 for a discussion of the history of the speech community concept and its various definitions, revisions, shortcomings, and merits. Probably the most strongly debated issues concern the importance of shared knowledge of a linguistic code, including shared knowledge of norms for usage and interpretation (Gumperz 1971) and the related emphasis on the homogeneity of the speech community. For example, several scholars have pointed out that linguistic and sociolinguistic knowledge is not evenly shared across communities (Irvine 1987; Parkin 1994), despite a dominant ideology of sharedness in many cases (Silverstein 1987). In contrast, the criteria of density and frequency of interaction have been omitted, more

than debated, perhaps because of their problematic nature for large-scale societies and their behaviorist connotations stemming from Bloomfield, the originator of the speech community concept.

4   ChiBemba is the name for the language of the Bemba people, BaBemba, who constitute roughly 19 percent of Zambia's national population (Kashoki 1978a). More than half of the nation's 9.1 million inhabitants speak ChiBemba (56 percent of the national population, according to Kashoki 1978a), and at least one-quarter speak English (26 percent according to Kashoki 1978a, and 45 percent according to Claypole and Daka 1993). Approximately 69 percent of all national radio broadcasting is in English, and 6 percent is in ChiBemba (Spitulnik 1992).

5   According to a national media survey conducted in 1991, 57 percent of all Zambians own a working radio, 74 percent listen at least once per week, and 63 percent listen daily or almost daily. By sharp contrast, only 17 percent own TVs and 30 percent view TV at least once a week (Claypole and Daka 1993:63–4).

6   For a discussion of this last phrase, see Hill 1993 [and this volume].

7   Metapragmatic discourse is speech that is about the communication context or about the functions of language in context: for example, "Here's what I want to tell you …," "I didn't hear what you just said," and "Stop lecturing me." As speech about speaking, metapragmatic discourse functions to both regiment and frame the interpretation of the ongoing speech event (Silverstein 1976, 1993).

8   Media discourse about mistakes and failures is a common target of comic recycling. For example, ZNBC radio and TV frequently broadcast public service announcements for the national electric company regarding temporary power outages. The phrase "Any inconvenience caused is deeply regretted" is a standard feature of such announcements and can be humorously recast in other speech contexts. For an example on the World Wide Web, see Ranjit Warrier's rendering of the Zambian English version as "Any inconvenience caused is diply regraitted" in reference to his homepage's possibly strange appearance through non-Netscape browsers (Warrier 1996b).

9   The complex humor of this exchange is even more elaborate for those who know the etymology of the place-name "Kitwe" in Lamba, the language indigenous to the Copperbelt region. Kitwe is an abbreviation of a Lamba expression for "big ear." The place was named after an historical event involving an elephant.

10 In the late 1980s, versions of *Over to You* aired on Thursdays in Luvale, on Saturdays in English and ChiLunda, and on Sundays in ChiBemba, ChiNyanja, and ChiTonga.

11 Further investigation is required to determine the precise morpheme boundaries in these assimilated phrases. My representation is based on a hypothesis that the first three syllables are one word and that *you* is analyzed as a demonstrative pronoun for third-person singular, in an analogy with *yu* (ChiNyanja) and *uyu* (ChiBemba) "this person," "her," "him."

12 In the examples, italicized words are ChiBemba (unless otherwise noted), and nonitalicized words are English.

13 Further examples of foreign-derived titles on Radio Zambia include *This Is My Song, My Old Favorites, Yours for the Asking*, and other titles based on fill-in-the-blank formulas such as *X's Corner (Children's Corner, Women's Corner*, and *Poet's Corner)* and *X's Magazine (Women's Magazine)*.

14 More specific sociolinguistic questions about the significance of each form remain open for further research, since their usage and distribution were not systematically studied.

15 In addition to these more innovative names, Zambian media are also a popular source for personal names, for example, names for newborns and names that teenagers adopt for themselves. During the late 1980s the names Jeff and Pam were very popular, as they derived from the American television series *Dynasty* and *Dallas* running on TV-Zambia.

16 At the time, the party vigilantes were members of the country's ruling (and sole) party, the United National Independence Party (UNIP).

17 The closing song substitutes the last two verses with: "Now it's time to say good-bye to our friends far and near. Before we go let's give our wildlife a great big cheer. Yeah!"

18 This quote points to the difficulty in precisely defining the chongololo accent. In the radio program the broadcasters' accents are RP, and the children's accents approximate this. But

outside of radio, many forms of non-Zambian English count as chongololo accents, including ones that sound like a blend of American and British varieties. As one reviewer of this article noted, the perception that chongies have American accents may be linked, via ideological pressures, to the identification of speakers as "capitalists."

19 Liwewe's most famous phrase is his characteristic wild yell, "It's a goooooooooaaal!!!" For an electronic poaching of this, see Warrier 1996a.

20 Peter Mweemba's use of *brother* has several possible connotations and may stem from idioms of Christian brotherhood and/or from African American usage.

21 Political positions and rankings have changed somewhat under the current Chiluba government. At the time of fieldwork, during the one-party system, the secretary-general of the ruling party ranked second after the Zambian president.

22 During the period of one-party rule, this was the title for the second-highest government position at the provincial level.

23 The creative poaching of such abbreviations, acronyms, and state slogans is pervasive in Zambia and throughout much of Africa (Mbembe 1992; Spitulnik 1994b). One example of this is illustrated by the renderings of the abbreviation "IFA," which is on the front of the large Zambian army trucks manufactured by the IFA company (of the former East Germany). Because these vehicles are involved in so many fatal road accidents, the name is interpreted as designating "International Funeral Association/Ambassadors," or *inifwa* "death."

24 Respectively, these stand for University of Zambia, Tanzania-Zambia Railway, Zambia Electric Supply Corporation, Industrial Development Corporation, Zambia National Broadcasting Corporation, Danish International Development Agency, Small Industries Development Organisation, Frederick T. J. Chiluba (the current president), Kenneth Kaunda (the former president), Prime Minister, Member of Parliament, General Manager, and Director General.

REFERENCES

Anderson, Benedict (1983). *Imagined Communities: Reflections on the Origin and Spread of Nationalism*. London: Verso.

Bakhtin, Mikhail M. (1981[1934–35]). Discourse in the Novel. In *The Dialogic Imagination: Four Essays*. Michael Holquist and Caryl Emerson, trans.; Michael Holquist, ed., pp. 259–422. Austin: University of Texas Press.

Bakhtin, Mikhail M. (1986[1952–53]). The Problem of Speech Genres. In *Speech Genres and Other Late Essays*. Vern W. McGee, trans.; Caryl Emerson and Michael Holquist, eds., pp. 60–102. Austin: University of Texas Press.

Basso, Keith H. (1990a[1984]). "Stalking with Stories": Names, Places, and Moral Narratives among the Western Apache. In *Western Apache Language and Culture*, pp. 99–137. Tucson: University of Arizona Press.

Basso, Keith H. (1990b[1988]). "Speaking with Names": Language and Landscape among the Western Apache. In *Western Apache Language and Culture*, pp. 138–73. Tucson: University of Arizona Press.

Baudrillard, Jean (1983[1978]). The Implosion of Meaning in the Media. In *In the Shadow of the Silent Majorities*. Paul Foss, Paul Patton, and John Johnston, trans, pp. 95–110. New York: Semiotext(e).

Bauman, Richard, and Charles L. Briggs (1990). Poetics and Performance as Critical Perspectives on Language and Social Life. *Annual Review of Anthropology* 19:59–88.

Bhabha, Homi (1994). *The Location of Culture*. New York: Routledge.

Bourdieu, Pierre (1991[1982]). *Language and Symbolic Power*. Gino Raymond and Matthew Adamson, trans.; John B. Thompson, ed. Cambridge, MA: Harvard University Press.

Briggs, Charles L., and Richard Bauman (1992). Genre, Intertextuality, and Social Power. *Journal of Linguistic Anthropology* 2:131–72.

Calhoun, Craig (ed.) (1992). *Habermas and the Public Sphere*. Cambridge, MA: MIT Press.

Claypole, Andrew, and Given Daka (1993). Zambia. In *Global Audiences: Research in Worldwide Broadcasting 1993*. Graham Mytton, ed., pp. 59–70. London: John Libbey.

Certeau, Michel de (1984). *The Practice of Everyday Life*. Steven Rendall, trans. Berkeley: University of California Press.

Fischer, Michael M. J., and Mehdi Abedi (1990). *Debating Muslims: Cultural Dialogues in Postmodernity and Tradition*. Madison: University of Wisconsin Press.

Foucault, Michel (1972[1971]). The Discourse on Language. In *The Archaeology of Knowledge and the Discourse on Language*, pp. 215–37. Rupert Swyer, trans. New York: Harper & Row.

Gal, Susan (1989). Language and Political Economy. *Annual Review of Anthropology* 18:345–67.

Gal, Susan (1995). Language and the "Arts of Resistance." *Cultural Anthropology* 10:407–24.

Gal, Susan, and Kathryn A. Woolard (eds.) (1995). Constructing Languages and Publics. Theme issue. *Pragmatics* 5(2).

Gumperz, John J. (1971[1968]). The Speech Community. In *Language and Social Context*. Pier P. Giglioli, ed., pp. 219–31. New York: Viking Penguin.

Gumperz, John J. (1982). *Discourse Strategies*. Cambridge: Cambridge University Press.

Habermas, Jürgen (1989). *The Structural Transformation of the Public Sphere*. Thomas Burger, trans. Cambridge, MA: MIT Press.

Hanks, William F. (1996). *Language and Communicative Practices*. Boulder, CO: Westview.

Harvey, David (1989). *The Condition of Postmodernity: An Enquiry into the Origins of Cultural Change*. Cambridge, MA: Basil Blackwell.

Hebdige, Dick (1988). *Hiding in the Light: On Images and Things*. London: Comedia.

Hill, Jane H. (1993). Hasta La Vista, Baby: Anglo Spanish in the American Southwest. *Critique of Anthropology* 13:145–76.

Irvine, Judith T. (1987). Domains of Description in the Ethnography of Speaking: A Retrospective on the "Speech Community." In *Performance, Speech Community, and Genre*, pp. 13–24. Working Papers and Proceedings of the Center for Psychosocial Studies, 11. Chicago: Center for Psychosocial Studies.

Irvine, Judith T. (1996). Shadow Conversations: The Indeterminacy of Participant Roles. In *Natural Histories of Discourse*. Michael Silverstein and Greg Urban, eds, pp. 131–59. Chicago: University of Chicago Press.

Jameson, Fredric (1984). Postmodernism, or the Cultural Logic of Late Capitalism. *New Left Review* 146:53–92.

Jenkins, Henry (1992). *Textual Poachers: Television Fans and Participatory Culture*. London: Routledge.

Kashoki, Mubanga E. (1978a). The Language Situation in Zambia. In *Language in Zambia*. Sirarpi Ohannessian and Mubanga E. Kashoki, eds., pp. 9–46. London: International African Institute.

Kashoki, Mubanga E. (1978b). Lexical Innovation in Four Zambian Languages. *African Languages/Languages Africaines* 4:80–95.

Kroskrity, Paul V. (1992). Arizona Tewa Kiva Speech as a Manifestation of Linguistic Ideology. *Pragmatics* 2:297–309.

Lucy, John A. (ed.) (1993). *Reflexive Language: Reported Speech and Metapragmatics*. New York: Cambridge University Press.

Mbembe, Achille (1992). The Banality of Power and the Aesthetics of Vulgarity. *Public Culture* 4(2):1–30.

Myers-Scotton, Carol (1993). *Social Motivations for Codeswitching*. Oxford: Clarendon Press.

Parkin, David (1994). Language, Government and the Play on Purity and Impurity: Arabic, Swahili and the Vernaculars in Kenya. In *African Languages, Development and the State*. Richard Fardon and Graham Furniss, eds., pp. 227–45. London: Routledge.

Silverstein, Michael (1976). Shifters, Linguistic Categories and Cultural Description. In *Meaning in Anthropology*. Keith H. Basso and Henry A. Selby, eds., pp. 11–55. Albuquerque: University of New Mexico Press.

Silverstein, Michael (1987). *Monoglot "Standard" in America*. Working Papers and Proceedings of the Center for Psychosocial Studies, 13. Chicago: Center for Psychosocial Studies.

Silverstein, Michael (1992). The Indeterminacy of Contextualization: When Is Enough Enough? In *The Contextualization of Language*. Peter Auer and Aldo di Luzio, eds., pp. 55–76. Amsterdam: John Benjamins.

Silverstein, Michael (1993). Metapragmatic Discourse and Metapragmatic Function. In *Reflexive Language: Reported Speech and Metapragmatics*. John A. Lucy, ed., pp. 33–58. New York: Cambridge University Press.

Silverstein, Michael, and Greg Urban (eds.) (1996). *Natural Histories of Discourse*. Chicago: University of Chicago Press.

Spitulnik, Debra (1992). Radio Time Sharing and the Negotiation of Linguistic Pluralism in Zambia. *Pragmatics* 2:335–54.

Spitulnik, Debra (1993). Anthropology and Mass Media. *Annual Review of Anthropology* 22:293–315.

Spitulnik, Debra (1994a). Radio Culture in Zambia: Audiences, Public Words, and the Nation-State. Ph.D. dissertation, University of Chicago.

Spitulnik, Debra (1994b). Radio Cycles and Recyclings in Zambia: Public Words, Popular Critiques, and National Communities. *Passages* 8:10, 12, 14–16.

Swigart, Lee (1994). Cultural Creolisation and Language Use in Post-Colonial Africa: The Case of Senegal. *Africa* 64(2):75–89.

Urban, Greg (1991). *A Discourse-Centered Approach to Culture*. Austin: University of Texas Press.
Warrier, Ranjit (1996a). Memories from Zambia. Electronic document. http://www. latech. edu/~ranjitw/memory.html

Warrier, Ranjit (1996b). Ranjit Warrier's Home Page. Electronic document. http://www. latech.edu:80/~ranjitw/index.html

5

Communication of Respect in Interethnic Service Encounters

Benjamin Bailey

Conflict in face-to-face interaction between immigrant Korean retail merchants and their African American customers has been widely documented since the early 1980s. Newspapers in New York, Washington, DC, Chicago, and Los Angeles have carried stories on this friction; and the 1989 movie *Do the Right Thing* depicted angry confrontations of this type. By the time that the events of April 1992 – referred to variously as the Los Angeles "riots," "uprising," "civil disturbance" or, by many immigrant Koreans, *sa-i-gu* "April 29" – cast a media spotlight on such relations, there had already been numerous African American boycotts of immigrant Korean businesses in New York and Los Angeles; politicians had publicly addressed the issue; and academics (e.g. Ella Stewart 1989 and Chang 1990) had begun to write about this type of friction.

There are multiple, intertwined reasons for these interethnic tensions in small businesses. An underlying source is the history of social, racial, and economic inequality in American society. In this broader context, visits to any store can become a charged event for African Americans. Thus, according to Austin (1995:32),

Any kind of ordinary face-to-face retail transaction can turn into a hassle for a black person. For example, there can hardly be a black in urban America who has not been either denied entry to a store, closely watched, snubbed, questioned about her or his ability to pay for an item, or stopped and detained for shoplifting.

Specific features of small convenience/liquor stores, such as the ones studied here, exacerbate the potential for conflict. Prices in such stores are high, many customers have low incomes, and the storekeepers are seen by many as the latest in a long line of economic exploiters from outside the African American community (Drake & Cayton 1945; Sturdevant 1969; Chang 1990, 1993). Shoplifting is not uncommon, and the late hours and cash basis of the stores make them appealing targets for robbery. Nearly all the retailers interviewed had been robbed at gunpoint; this had led some to do business from behind bulletproof glass, making verbal interaction with customers difficult.

In this socially, racially, and economically charged context, subtle differences in the ways that respect is communicated in face-to-face interaction are of considerable significance, affecting relationships between groups. This article documents how differences in the ways that immigrant Korean storekeepers and African American customers communicate respect in service encounters have contributed to mutual, distinctively intense feelings of disrespect between the two groups, and serve as an ongoing source of tension. These contrasting practices for the display of politeness and respect are empirically evident in the talk and behavior that occur in stores, and the negative perceptions that result are salient in interviews of retailers and customers alike.

Respect

The issue of "respect" in face-to-face encounters has been stressed both in the media and in academic accounts of relations between African Americans and immigrant Korean retailers. Ella Stewart (1991:20) concludes that "respect" is important for both groups in service encounters:

Both groups declared rudeness as a salient inappropriate behavior. The underlined themes for both groups appear to be respect and courtesy shown toward each other. Each group felt that more respect should be accorded when communicating with each other, and that courtesy should be shown through verbal and nonverbal interaction by being more congenial, polite, considerate, and tactful toward each other.

Such analysis suggests that good intentions are all that is required to ameliorate relationships: each group simply has to show more "respect and courtesy" to the other. However, the data presented in this article suggest that, even when such good intentions seem to be present, respect is not effectively communicated and understood. The problem is that, in a given situation, there are fundamentally different ways of showing respect in different cultures. Because of different conventions for the display of respect, groups may feel respect for each other, and may continuously work at displaying their esteem – yet each group can feel that they are being disrespected. This type of situation, in which participants communicate at cross-purposes, has been analyzed most notably by Gumperz 1982a, b, 1992 regarding intercultural communication, though not regarding respect specifically.

The communication of respect is a fundamental dimension of everyday, face-to-face interaction. As Goffman says (1967:46), "the person in our urban secular world is allotted a kind of sacredness that is displayed and confirmed by symbolic acts." These symbolic acts are achieved, often unconsciously, through the manipulation of a variety of communicative channels including prosody, choice of words and topic, proxemic distance, and timing of utterances. Gumperz 1982a, 1992 has shown how cultural differences in the use of such contextualization cues – at levels ranging from the perception and categorization of sounds to the global framing of activities – can lead to misunderstandings in intercultural communication. The focus of this article is the ways in which constellations of interactional features can communicate (dis)-respect in service encounters.

The intercultural (mis)communication of respect between African American customers and immigrant Korean retailers is particularly significant for interethnic relations because behavior that is perceived to be lacking in respect is typically interpreted as actively threatening. Thus, according to Brown & Levinson (1987:33), "non-communication of the polite attitude will be read not merely as the absence of that attitude, but as the inverse, the holding of an aggressive attitude." When conventions for paying respect in service encounters differ between cultures, as they do between immigrant Koreans and African Americans, individuals may read each other's behavior as not simply strange or lacking in social grace, but as aggressively antagonistic.

Brown & Levinson posit a classification system for politeness practices that is useful for conceptualizing the contrasting interactional practices of immigrant Korean retailers and African American customers. Following Durkheim 1915 and Goffman 1971, they suggest two basic dimensions of individuals' desire for respect: NEGATIVE FACE wants and POSITIVE FACE wants. Negative face want is "the want of every 'competent adult member' that his actions be unimpeded by others," while positive face want is "the want of every member that his wants be desirable to at least some others" (Brown & Levinson, 62). Stated more simply, people do not want to be imposed on (negative face want); but they do want expressions of approval, understanding, and solidarity (positive face want). Because the labels "positive" and "negative" have misleading connotations, I use the word INVOLVEMENT to refer to positive politeness phenomena, and RESTRAINT to refer to negative politeness phenomena. These terms denote the phenomena to which they refer more mnemonically than the terms POSITIVE and NEGATIVE.

Strategies for paying respect include acts of "involvement politeness" and acts of "restraint politeness." Involvement politeness includes those behaviors which express approval of the self or "personality" of the other. It includes acts which express solidarity between interactors – e.g. compliments, friendly jokes, agreement, demonstrations of personal interest, offers, and the use of in-group identity markers. Data from store interactions show that these acts are relatively more frequent in the service encounter talk of African Americans than of immigrant Koreans.

Restraint politeness includes actions which mark the interactor's unwillingness to impose on others, or which lessen potential imposition. These strategies can include hedging statements, making requests indirect, being apologetic, or simply NOT demanding the other's attention to begin with. Restraint face wants are basically concerned with the desire to be free of imposition from others, where even the distraction of one's attention can be seen as imposition. Behaviors that minimize the communicative demands on another – e.g. NOT asking questions, NOT telling jokes that would call for a response, and NOT introducing personal topics of conversation – can be expressions of restraint politeness or respect. Such acts of restraint are typical of the participation of immigrant Korean store-owners in service encounters.

Methods

Fieldwork for this study took place in Los Angeles between July 1994 and April 1995. Data collection methods included ethnographic observation and interviewing in immigrant Korean stores, interviews with African Americans outside of store contexts, and videotaping of service encounters in stores.

I made repeated visits to six stores in the Culver City area, five in South Central, and two in Koreatown. Visits to stores typically lasted from one-half hour to two hours; with repeated visits, I spent over 10 hours at each of three stores in Culver City and one in South Central, and over five hours in one Koreatown store.

Service encounters in two immigrant Korean stores, one in Culver City and one in Koreatown, were videotaped for a total of four hours in each store. Video cameras were set up in plain view, but drew virtually no attention, perhaps because there were already multiple surveillance cameras in each store. The tapes from the Koreatown store are used for the current study because the Culver City store had no Korean customers and a lower proportion of African American customers. During the four hours of taping in this Koreatown store, there were 12 African American customers and 13 immigrant Korean customers.

The encounters with African American customers were transcribed using the conventions of conversation analysis (Atkinson & Heritage 1984),[1] resulting in over 30 pages of transcripts. The encounters in Korean were transcribed by a Korean American bilingual assistant according to McCune–Reischauer conventions, and then translated into English. Transcription and translation of Korean encounters were accompanied by interpretation and explanation – some of which was audio-recorded – by the bilingual assistant while watching the videotapes. In addition, the storekeeper who appears throughout the four hours of videotape watched segments of the tapes and gave background information on some of the customers appearing in the tapes, e.g. how regularly they came to the store. Transcripts of encounters in Korean comprise over 25 pages.

Service Encounter Interaction

In the following sections, I first consider the general structure of service encounters as an activity, delineating two types: SOCIALLY MINIMAL VS. SOCIALLY EXPANDED service encounters. Second, I consider the characteristics of convenience store service encounters between immigrant Koreans, presenting examples from transcripts that show socially minimal service encounters to be the common form. Third, I consider the characteristics of service encounters between immigrant Korean storekeepers and African American customers, using transcripts of two such encounters to demonstrate the contrasting forms of participation in them.

Merritt (1976:321) defines a service encounter as:

an instance of face-to-face interaction between a server who is "officially posted" in some service area and a customer who is present in that service area, that interaction being oriented to the satisfaction of the customer's presumed desire for some service and the server's obligation to provide that service. A typical service encounter is one in which a customer buys something at a store...

Service encounters in stores fall under the broader category of institutional talk, the defining characteristic of which is its goal-orientation (Drew & Heritage 1992a). Levinson (1992:71) sees the organization, or structure, of such activities as flowing directly from their goals: "wherever possible I would like to view these structural elements as rationally and functionally adapted to the point or goal of the activity in question, that is the function or functions that members of the society see the activity as having."

The structural differences between Korean–Korean service encounters and those with African American customers that will be described below suggest that the two groups have different perceptions of the functions of such encounters. Even when goals are seen to overlap, participants in intercultural encounters frequently utilize contrasting means of achieving those goals (Gumperz 1992:246). Although African American customers and immigrant Korean shopkeepers might agree that they are involved in a service encounter, they have different notions of the types of activities that constitute a service encounter and the appropriate means for achieving those activities.

The service encounters involving immigrant Koreans and African Americans that are transcribed in this article took place in a Koreatown liquor store between 3 p.m. and 7 p.m. on a Thursday in April 1995. The store does not use bulletproof glass, and from the cash register one has an unobstructed line of sight throughout the store. The cashier is a 31-year-old male employee with an undergraduate degree from Korea; he attended graduate school briefly, in both Korea and the US, in microbiology. He has been in the US for four years and worked in this store for about three and a half years.

Service encounters in this corpus vary widely both in length and in the types of talk they contain. They range from encounters that involve only a few words, and last just seconds, to interactions that last as long as seven minutes and cover such wide-ranging topics as customers' visits to Chicago, knee operations, and race relations. More common than these two extremes, however, are encounters like the following, in which an immigrant Korean woman of about 40 buys cigarettes:

Cash: *Annyŏng haseyo.*
       "Hello/How are you?" ((Customer has just entered store.))
Cust: *Annyŏng haseyo.*
       "Hello/How are you?"
Cust: *Tambae!*
       "Cigarettes!"
Cash: *Tambae tŭryŏyo?*
       "You would like cigarettes?" ((Cashier reaches for cigarettes under counter.))
Cash: *Yŏgi issŭmnida.*
       "Here you are." ((Cashier takes customer's money and hands her cigarettes; customer turns to leave.))
Cash: *Annyŏnghi kaseyo.*
       "Good-bye."
Cust: *Nye.*
       "Okay."

The basic communicative activities of this encounter are: (a) greetings or openings, (b) negotiation of the business exchange, and (c) closing of the encounter.

Greetings, as "access rituals" (Goffman 1971:79), mark a transition to a period of heightened interpersonal access. In these stores, greetings typically occur as the customer passes through the doorway, unless the storekeeper is already busy serving another customer. Greetings in these circumstances include *Hi, Hello, How's it going, How are you?* – or, in Korean, *Annyŏng haseyo* "Hello/How are you?"

The second basic activity is the negotiation of the business transaction, which includes such elements as naming the price of the merchandise brought to the counter by the customer, or counting out change as it is handed back to the customer. While explicit verbal greetings and closings do not occur in every recorded encounter, each contains a verbal negotiation of the transaction. The negotiation of the business exchange can be long and full of adjacency pairs (Schegloff & Sacks 1973) – involving, e.g., requests for a product from behind the counter, questions about a price, repairs (Schegloff et al. 1977), and requests or offers of a bag. Merritt calls these adjacency pairs "couplets," and she gives a detailed structural flow chart (1976:345) that shows the length and potential complexity of this phase of a service encounter.

The third and final activity of these encounters, the closing, often includes formulaic exchanges: *See you later, Take care, Have a good day*, or *Annyŏnghi kaseyo* "Goodbye." Frequently, however, the words used to close the negotiation of the business exchange also serve to close the entire encounter:

Cash: One two three four five ten twenty ((Counting back change.))
Cash: (Thank you/okay)
Cust: Alright.

This type of encounter – limited to no more than greetings/openings, negotiation of the exchange, and closings – I call a SOCIALLY MINIMAL service encounter. The talk in it refers almost entirely to aspects of the business transaction, the exchange of goods for money; it does not include discussion of more sociable, interpersonal topics, e.g. experiences outside the store or the customer's unique personal relationship with the storekeeper.

However, many service encounters do NOT match this socially minimal pattern. SOCIALLY EXPANDED service encounters typically include the basic elements described above, but also include activities that highlight the interpersonal relationship between customers and storekeepers. These socially expanded encounters are characterized by practices that increase interpersonal involvement, i.e. involvement politeness strategies such as making jokes or small-talk, discussing personal experiences from outside the store, and explicitly referring to the personal relationship between customer and storekeeper.

The initiation of a social expansion of a service encounter is evident in the following excerpt. The African American customer has exchanged greetings with the Korean owner and cashier of the store; the cashier has retrieved the customer's habitual purchase, and begins to ring it up. The customer, however, then reframes the activity in which they are engaged, initiating (marked in boldface) a new activity – a personable discussion of his recent sojourn in Chicago – which lasts for several minutes.

Cash: That's it?
Cust: Tha:t's it ((Cashier rings up purchases.)) ((1.5))
Cust: **I haven't seen you for a while**
Cash: hehe Where you been
Cust: Chicago. ((Cashier bags purchase.))
Cash: Oh really?

The customer's comment *I haven't seen you for a while* instantiates and initiates a new type of activity and talk. The discussion of the customer's time in Chicago is a fundamentally different type of talk from that of socially minimal service encounters. Specifically, it is characterized by talk that is not directly tied to the execution of the business transaction at hand, but rather focuses on the ongoing relationship between the customer and storekeeper. Discussing the customer's trip to Chicago both indexes this personal relationship and, at the same time, contributes to its maintenance.

Such sharing of information helps constitute social categories and co-membership. To quote Sacks (1975:72),

Information varies as to whom it may be given to. Some matters may be told to a neighbor, others not; some to a best friend, others, while they may be told to a best friend, may only be told to a best friend after another has been told, e.g., a spouse.

In introducing talk of his trip to Chicago, the customer asserts solidarity with the cashier: they are co-members of a group who can not only exchange greetings and make business exchanges, but who can also talk about personal experiences far removed from the store.

This type of talk, which indexes and reinforces interpersonal relationships, distinguishes socially expanded service encounters from minimal ones. My data contain a wide range of such talk which enhances personal involvement. Specific practices include, among many others, talk about the weather and current events (*Some big hotel down in Hollywood, all the windows blew out*), jokes (*I need whiskey, no soda, I only buy whiskey*), references to commonly known third parties (*Mr. Choi going to have some ice?*), comments on interlocutors' demeanor (*What's the matter with you today?*), and direct assertions of desired intimacy (*I want you to know me.*)[2] Through their talk, customers and retailers create, maintain, or avoid intimacy and involvement with each other. These individual service encounters – an everyday form of contact between many African Americans and immigrant Koreans – are fundamental, discrete social activities that shape the nature and tenor of interethnic relations on a broader scale.

Service Encounters between Immigrant Koreans

Before examining immigrant Korean interaction with African Americans, I consider service encounters in which the customers as well as the storekeepers are immigrant Koreans. These Korean–Korean interactions provide a basis for comparison with African American encounters with Koreans. If, for example, the taciturnity and restraint of retailers in their interaction with African Americans were due solely to racism, one would expect to find retailers chatting and joking with their Korean customers and engaging in relatively long, intimate conversations.

In fact, the retailers in Korean–Korean encounters display the same taciturn, impersonal patterns of talk and behavior that they display with African American customers, even in the absence of linguistic and cultural barriers. The Korean–Korean interactions are even shorter and show less intimacy than the corresponding interactions with African American customers. Ten of the 13 service encounters with immigrant Korean customers were socially minimal, while only 3 of the 12 encounters with African Americans were socially minimal. Unlike their African American counterparts, immigrant Korean customers generally do not engage in practices through which they could display and develop a more personal relationship during the service encounter, e.g. making small talk or introducing personal topics. The example of a Korean woman buying cigarettes, transcribed above, is typical of encounters between Korean merchants and customers. Racism or disrespect are not necessarily reasons for what African Americans perceive as distant, laconic behavior in service encounters.[3]

I have no recorded data of service encounters involving African American store-owners with which to compare these encounters with immigrant Korean ones. I did, however, observe many interactions between African American customers and African American cashiers who were employed in stores owned by immigrant Koreans. Interactions between customers and such African American cashiers were consistently longer, and included more social expansions and affective involvement, than the corresponding encounters with immigrant Korean cashiers in the same stores.

Of the three socially expanded service encounters among immigrant Koreans, two involve personal friends of the cashier from contexts outside the store, and the third is with a child of about 10 years who is a regular customer at the store. According to Scollon & Scollon (1994:137), the communicative behavior that East Asians display toward those whom they know and with whom they have an ongoing personal relationship ("insiders") differs drastically from the behavior displayed toward those in relatively anonymous service encounters ("outsiders"):

One sees quite a different pattern [from "inside" encounters] in Asia when one observes "outside" or service relationships. These are the situations in which the participants are and remain strangers to each other, such as in taxis, train ticket sales, and banks. In "outside" (or nonrelational encounters) one sees a pattern which if anything is more directly informational than what one sees in the West. In fact, Westerners often are struck with the contrast they see between the highly polite and deferential Asians they meet in their business, educational, and governmental contacts and the rude, pushy, and aggressive Asians [by Western standards for subway-riding behavior] they meet on the subways of Asia's major cities.

In my data, service encounter communicative behavior among Korean adults could be predicted by the presence or absence of personal friendship from contexts outside the store. Socially expanded encounters with immigrant Korean adults occurred only when those adults were personal friends of the cashier, with whom he had contact outside the store. The cashier did not have a relationship with the child customer outside the store; but criteria for expanding encounters with children, and the nature of the expansions, may be different than for adults. In this case, the social expansion included a lecture to the child on the necessity of working long hours, and the child formally asked to be released from the interaction before turning to go.

Even in socially expanded service encounters among adult Korean friends, interlocutors may at times display a relatively high degree of restraint. For example, in the following segment, the cashier encounters a former roommate whom he has not seen in several years, who has by chance entered the store as a customer. The cashier and this customer had shared an apartment for two months in Los Angeles, more than three years prior to this encounter, and the customer had later moved away from Los Angeles.

When the customer enters the store, he displays no visible surprise or emotion at this chance encounter with his former roommate. He initially gives no reply to the cashier's repeated queries, "Where do you live?", and gazes away from the cashier as if nothing had been said. After being asked five times where he lives, he gives a relatively uninformative answer, "Where else but home?"

Cash: Ŏ:!
      "He:y!" ((Recognizing customer who has entered store. Cashier reaches out and takes customer's hand. Customer pulls away and opens cooler door.)) ((3.0))
Cash: Ŏdi sarŏ
      "Where are you living?"
Cash: Ŏ?
      "Huh?" ((7.0))
Cash: Ŏdi sarŏ.
      "Where are you living?" ((.5))
Cash: Ŏdi sarŏ.
      "Where are you living?" ((Cashier and customer stand at the counter across from each other.)) ((2.5))
Cash: Ŏ?
      "Huh?" ((Customer gazes at display away from cashier. Cashier gazes at customer.))
Cash: Ŏdi sarŏ::
      "C'mon, where are you living?" ((1.0))
Cust: ( )
Cash: Ŏ?
      "Huh?" ((Cashier maintains gaze toward customer; customer continues to gaze at display.)) ((7.0))
Cash: Ŏdi sanyanikka?
      "So, where are you living?" ((3.0))
Cust: Ŏdi salgin, chibe salji.
      "Where else, but home?" ((1.0))
Cash: Ŏ?
      "Huh?"
Cash: Chibi ŏdi nyago?
      "So where is your house?"

In this opening segment of transcript, the cashier has asked the customer six times where he lives – 10 times if the follow-up *Huh?'s* are included. The customer does not reveal to his former roommate where he lives, even as he stands three feet away from him, directly across the counter.

The customer's initial unresponsiveness in this encounter is striking by Western standards of conversational cooperation (Grice 1975). The cashier, however, does not seem to treat the customer's behavior as excessively uncooperative, e.g. by becoming angry or demanding an explanation for his interlocutor's lack of engagement.

A Korean American consultant suggested that the customer's restraint was a sign not of disrespect, but of embarrassment (perhaps regarding his lack of career progress), which could explain the cashier's relative patience with uninformative responses.

This apparent resistance to engagement, however, is precisely the type of behavior cited by African Americans as insulting, and as evidence of racism on the part of immigrant Korean storekeepers:

When I went in they wouldn't acknowledge me. Like if I'm at your counter and I'm looking at your merchandise, where someone would say "Hi, how are you today, is there anything I –" they completely ignored me. It was like they didn't care one way or the other.

They wouldn't look at you at all. They wouldn't acknowledge you in any way. Nothing. You were nobody... They'd look over you or around you. (46-year-old African American woman)

...to me, many, not all, many of them perceive Blacks as a non-entity. We are treated as if we do not exist. (50-year-old African American male gift shop owner)

The customer's reluctance to acknowledge the cashier verbally or to respond to his questions – and the cashier's lack of anger at this – indicate that, at least in some situations, relatively dispassionate and impassive behavior is not interpreted by Koreans as insulting or disrespectful.

The taciturnity of the customer in this interaction, and of immigrant Korean storekeepers and customers more generally, is consistent with descriptions of the importance of *nunch'i* among Koreans – roughly "perceptiveness", "studying one's face", or "sensitivity with eyes" (M. Park 1979; Yum 1987). It is a Korean interactional ideal to be able to understand an interlocutor with minimal talk, to be able to read the other's face and the situation without verbal reference. Speaking, and forcing the interlocutor to react, can be seen as an imposition: "to provide someone with something before being asked is regarded as true service since once having asked, the requester has put the other person in a predicament of answering 'yes' or 'no'" (Yum 1987:80).

This ideal, of communicating and understanding without talk, is present in the two most important religio-philosophical traditions of Korea – Confucianism and Buddhism. Confucian education stresses reading and writing, rather than speaking. Talk cannot be entirely trusted and is held in relatively low regard:

To read was the profession of scholars, to speak that of menials. People were warned that "A crooked gem can be straightened even by rubbing; but a single mistake in your speech cannot be corrected. There is no one who can chain your tongue. As one is liable to make a mistake in speech, fasten your tongue at all times. This is truly a profound and urgent lesson..." (Yum 1987:79)

In Buddhism, communication through words is generally devalued: "there is a general distrust of communication, written or spoken, since it is incomplete, limited, and ill-equipped to bring out true meaning" (Yum 1987:83). Enlightenment and understanding in Korean Buddhism is achieved internally, unmediated by explicit utterances: "The quest for wordless truth – this has been the spirit of Korean Buddhism, and it still remains its raison d'être" (Keel 1993:19).

The data from service encounters presented here suggest that this cultural ideal, of understanding without recourse to words, exists not only in religio-philosophical traditions, but may extend in certain situations to ideals of behavior in everyday face-to-face interaction.

Service Encounters between Immigrant Koreans and African Americans

As noted above, the service encounters with African American customers are characterized by more personal, sociable involvement and talk than the Korean–Korean encounters. While social expansions with Korean adult customers occurred only with personal friends of the cashier from contexts outside the store, only one of the nine African American customers in socially expanded encounters was friends with the cashier outside the store context.

Although the encounters with African Americans are longer and in many ways more intimate than the corresponding ones with Korean customers, close examination reveals consistently contrasting forms of participation in the service encounters. Overwhelmingly, it is the African American customers who make the conversational moves that make the encounters more than terse encounters focusing solely on the business transaction. Repeatedly, African American customers, unlike the immigrant Korean storekeepers and customers, treat the interaction not just as a business exchange, but as a sociable, interpersonal activity – by introducing topics for small-talk, making jokes, displaying affect in making assessments, and explicitly referring to the interpersonal relationship between cashier and customer.

Immigrant Korean retailers in these encounters are interactionally reactive, rather than proactive, in co-constructing conversation. Videotaped records reveal, for example, repeated instances where African American customers finish turns when discussing issues not related to the business transaction, and then re-initiate talk when no reply is forthcoming from the storekeepers. African American customers carry the burden of creating and maintaining the interpersonal involvement.

When immigrant Korean storekeepers do respond to talk, many responses display an understanding of referential content of utterances – but no alignment with the emotional stance, of the customer's talk, e.g. humor or indignation. Consider the reaction to ASSESSMENTS, i.e. evaluative statements that show one's personal alignment toward a phenomenon (Goodwin & Goodwin 1992). These are not met by storekeepers with second-assessments of agreement. When they do respond to assessments with affect, e.g. smiling at a customer's joke and subsequent laughter, their displayed levels of affect and interpersonal involvement are typically not commensurate with those of the customers.

The relative restraint of storekeepers in interaction with African American customers is not only a function of cultural preference for socially minimal service encounters and situated, interactional restraint; it also reflects limited English proficiency. It is more difficult to make small-talk, to joke, or to get to know the details of a customer's life if communication is difficult. Restraint politeness can be expressed by NOT using the verbal channel, i.e. silence; but involvement politeness requires more complex verbal activities – e.g. using in-group identity markers, showing interest in the other's interests, and joking.

The phonological, morphological, and syntactic differences between Korean, an Altaic language, and English, an Indo-European one, make it difficult to achieve fluency, and store-owners have limited opportunities for study. Even among those who have been in America for 20 years, many cannot understand English spoken at native speed, and many express embarrassment about speaking it because of limited proficiency.[4]

Videotaped records of interaction do NOT reveal constant hostility and confrontations between immigrant Korean retailers and African American customers; this finding is consistent with many hours of observation in stores. Some relationships, particularly those between retailers and regular customers, are overtly friendly: customers and storekeepers greet each other, engage in some small-talk, and part amicably. Observation and videotape do not reveal the stereotype of the inscrutably silent, non-greeting, gaze-avoiding, and non-smiling Korean storekeepers which were cited by African Americans in media accounts and in interviews with me. However, videotaped records do reveal subtle but consistent differences between African Americans and immigrant Koreans in the forms of talk and behavior in service encounters. These differences, when interpreted through culture-specific frameworks, can contribute to and reinforce pejorative stereotypes of store-owners as unfriendly and racist, and of customers as selfish and poorly bred.

In the following section I detail these differences in interactional patterns in transcripts of two socially expanded service encounters. The first interaction is with a middle-aged African American man who is a regular at the store. The cashier was able to identify him immediately on videotape in a follow-up interview; he said that the customer had been coming to the store two or three times a week for at least three and a half years. This encounter shows notably good and comfortable relations, typical of encounters with regular customers, but at the same time it displays the asymmetrical pattern of involvement described above. The second interaction is a much longer one that occurs with a 54-year-old customer who is new to the area and the store, and who may be under the influence of alcohol at the time. Contrasting forms of participation are particularly evident in this second interaction.

Encounter 1

In this interaction, a neatly dressed African American man in his 40s, carrying a cellular phone, comes into the store to buy a soda and some liquor. He is a regular at the store, but at the time of videotaping he had been away in Chicago for a month. The cashier is behind the counter, and the store-owner is standing amid displays in the middle of the store. The store-owner, about 40, has been in America for 20 years. He received his undergraduate degree from the University of California, Los Angeles; he studied math and computer science, he told me, because his English was not good enough for other subjects. He is more outgoing and talkative with customers than most of the storekeepers of his age, or older, who were observed.

Following greetings, the customer begins to treat the activity not just as a business transaction, but as an opportunity to be sociable, e.g. by introducing personal narratives about his long absence from Los Angeles and his experiences in Chicago:

((Customer enters store and goes to soda cooler.))
Cust: [Hi   ]
Own: [How ar]e you?
((Customer takes soda toward cash register and motions toward displays.)) ((7.5))
Cust: Wow you guys moved a lot of things around
Cash: Hello:, ((Cashier stands up from where he was hidden behind the counter.))
Cash: Heh heh
Cash: How are you? ((Cashier retrieves customer's liquor and moves toward register))
Cust: What's going on man? ((Cashier gets cup for customer's liquor.)) ((.8))
Cust: How've you been?
Cash: Sleeping
Cust: eh heh heh ((1.8))
Cash: That's it?
Cust: Tha:t's it ((Cashier rings up purchases.)) ((1.5))
Cust: I haven't seen you for a while
Cash: hehe Where you been
Cust: Chicago. ((Cashier bags purchase.))
Cash: Oh really?
Cust: [yeah]
Cash: [How] long?
Cust: For about a month ((1.2))
Cash: How's there.
Cust: Co:l'!
Cash: [Co:ld?]
Cust: [heh   ] heh heh heh
Own: Is Chicago cold?
Cust: u::h! ((lateral headshakes)) ((1.4)) man I got off the plane and walked out the airport
        I said "Oh shit."
Cust: heh heh heh
Own: I thought it's gonna be nice spring season over there
Cust: Well not now this is about a month– I been there– I was there for about a month but
        you know (.) damn ((lateral headshakes))
        ((Customer moves away from cash register toward owner.)) ((1.4))
Cust: Too co:l'
Cust: I mean this was really cold
Own: (They have snowy) season there
Cust: I've known it to snow on Easter Sunday ((.))
Cust: Alright this Sunday it'll be Easter ((.))
Cust: I've seen it snow Easter Sunday
((15-second discussion, not clearly audible, in which the owner asks if there are mountains in
Chicago, and the customer explains that there are not.))
Cust: See th– this– California weather almost never changes.
Cust: ((Spoken slowly and clearly as for non-native speaker.)) back there it's a seasonal
        change, you got fall, winter, spring
Own: mm hm
Cust: You know
Cust: But back there the weather sshhh ((lateral headshake))
Cust: It's cold up until June
Cust: I mean these guys like they– they wearing lon:g john:s from September until June
Own: (It's hot season, June)
Cust: He– here it's hot, but there it's ((lateral headshake))
Cust: (Really) ((Customer moves toward exit.))
Own: Kay   [see you later]

Cust: [see you later]
Cust: Nice talking to you

   Although this customer has come into the store to buy a soda and liquor, he also displays interest in chatting, particularly about his sojourn in Chicago and the climate there. After the initial greetings, he comments on how much the store displays have changed: *Wow you guys moved a lot of things around*. This comment is consistent with the fact that he's been away; it provides an opening for a reply such as *We moved those a long time ago*, or another such comment that would display acknowledgment that the customer hasn't been in the store for some time. But neither cashier nor owner responds to his comment. The customer's use of the present perfect tense (*How've you been?*) – as opposed to present tense (*How are you?* or *How ya doing?*) – draws attention to the fact that he hasn't had contact with these storekeepers for a period of time beginning in the past and ending as he speaks; again this invites discussion of the fact that he hasn't been to the store for an unusually long time. The cashier answers the question *How've you been?* with *Sleeping*, treating it as referring to the present. The English present perfect tense is expressed with a past tense form in Korean, and may have led the cashier to interpret the question as a form of present tense.
   The cashier places the customer's habitually preferred liquor on the counter without the customer's requesting the item. In doing so, the cashier, without talk, shows that he knows the customer, at least his business exchange habits. As the cashier rings up the purchase, the customer again uses the present perfect tense, indexing his relatively long absence from the store, commenting: *I haven't seen you for a while*. This comment not only indexes his long absence from the store, but draws the cashier into conversation. The comment is typically made by a person who has remained in one place while another has left and come back. In this case there is no indication that the cashier has been away. In fact, as an immigrant Korean working in a liquor store, he probably spends 80 or more hours a week in the store, up to 52 weeks each year.
   The customer's seeming reversal of roles – speaking as if the cashier, rather than he, had been away – has the function, however, of drawing the cashier into conversation. The customer does not simply introduce the topic he wants to discuss; he compels the cashier to ask him about the topic. If the customer had simply stated, *I've been in Chicago for a month and it was cold*, his audience could simply have nodded and acknowledged it. Instead the speaker chooses an interactional strategy that compels a question from his interlocutors, increasing interpersonal involvement.
   The customer's delivery displays a relatively high level of affective personal involvement: he uses profanity (*Oh shit*), falsetto voice, hyperbole (*they wearing long johns from September until June*), elements of African American English syntax (*they wearing*) and phonology (*col'*), and relatively high-volume laughter. The cashier and owner, however, do not display such a high level of affective personal involvement in the interaction, even through channels which are not dependent on linguistic proficiency. They do not laugh during the encounter, for example, and the owner is looking down unsmiling when the customer recounts his reaction (*Oh shit*) when getting off the plane in Chicago.

This disparity in levels of personal involvement is particularly apparent as the customer makes repeated assessments that display his alignment toward the weather in Chicago. According to Goodwin & Goodwin (1992:166),

this alignment can be of some moment in revealing such significant attributes of the actor as his or her taste and the way in which he or she evaluates the phenomena he or she perceives. It is therefore not surprising that displaying congruent understanding can be an issue of some importance to the participants.

Assessments provide a locus for interlocutors to show a common understanding and orientation through verbal and/or non-verbal markers of agreement with the assessment. Even when an individual has little knowledge of the referent of an assessment, positive response to the assessment will show emotional understanding and alignment with the assessor.

Explicit practices for displaying this alignment are highly developed among African Americans in the interactional pattern of "call-and-response," in which one actor's words or actions receive an immediate, often overlapping, response and confirmation from others (Smitherman 1977). Call-and-response marks involvement and congruent understanding with explicit vocal and non-verbal acts. Responses that overlap the caller's action are not seen as disrespectful interruptions, but rather as a means of displaying approval and of bringing caller and responder closer together.

While most often studied in formal performances – e.g. concerts, speeches, or sermons – relatively animated back-channel responses also characterize everyday talk of (and particularly among) many African Americans. Smitherman (1977:118) points out that differing expectations and practices of back-channel responses can lead to the breakdown of interethnic communication:

"call-response" can be disconcerting to both parties in black–white communication... When the black person is speaking, the white person... does not obviously engage in the response process, remaining relatively passive, perhaps voicing an occasional subdued "Mmmmmmhhm." Judging from the white individual's seeming lack of involvement, the black communicator gets the feeling that the white isn't listening... the white person gets the feeling that the black person isn't listening, because he "keeps interrupting and turning his back on me."

In the encounter under consideration, the storekeepers display little reaction to the customer's assessments – much less animated, overlapping responses. The customer makes repeated assessments of the extreme cold of Chicago, e.g. *Co:l'!*; *Oh shit*; *damn*; *Too col'*; *this was really cold*; *back there the weather sshhh*; *it's cold up until June*; *they wearing lon:g john:s from September until June*; and *there it's* [lateral headshake]. The cashier smiles at the customer's *Oh shit* and immediately succeeding laughter, but other assessments get no such show of appreciation. The owner's responses to these dramatic assessments tend toward checks of facts: *Is Chicago cold?*; *I thought it's gonna be nice spring season over there*; and *It's hot season, June*. The Korean storekeepers show little appreciation for the cold of Chicago, thereby failing to align themselves and display solidarity with the customer making these assessments.

Following two of these assessments (*co:l'* and *I got off the plane and walked out the airport I said "Oh shit"*), the customer laughs. According to Jefferson (1979:93),

Laughter can be managed as a sequence in which speaker of an utterance invites recipient to laugh and recipient accepts that invitation. One technique for inviting laughter is the placement, by speaker, of a laugh just at completion of an utterance, and one technique for accepting that invitation is the placement, by recipient, of a laugh just after onset of speaker's laughter.

The customer's laughter following his utterances matches this pattern precisely, but cashier and owner do not accept the invitation to laugh. Not only do they fail to accept the invitation to laugh, but the owner actively declines the invitation to laugh. He does this not through silence, which would allow the speaker to pursue recipient laughter further, but by responding to the customer's laughter with serious talk of facts, i.e. the temperature in Chicago: *Is Chicago cold?* and *I thought it's gonna be nice spring season over there.* As Jefferson says,

In order to terminate the relevance of laughter, recipient must actively decline to laugh. One technique for declining a postcompletion invitation to laugh is the placement of speech, by recipient, just after onset of speaker's laughter, that speech providing serious pursuit of topic as a counter to the pursuit of laughter.

The owner's response to the customer's invitation to laugh serves as an effective counter to the invitation.

Finally, the customer's comment upon leaving (*Nice talking to you*) suggests his attitude toward this service encounter: it wasn't just an encounter about doing a business transaction, it was a time to enjoy talking personally and make connections to people. Such an attitude is consistent with observations and videotaped records, which show African American customers consistently engaging in a relatively high degree of sociable, interpersonal interaction in service encounters.

The customer's parting comment, *Nice talking to you*, has no equivalent in Korean. The closest expression might be *sugo haseo*, which has a literal meaning close to "Keep up the good work," but is used to mean "Thank you and goodbye." Reference to work may serve as a more appropriate social currency ("Keep up the good work") than reference to talk ("Nice talking to you"), consistent with cultural ideals of relative taciturnity in service encounters.

This asymmetrical pattern of interaction occurs despite apparent attempts by both parties to accommodate to the perceived style or linguistic proficiency of the other. Both cashier and owner, for example, make repeated inquiries about the customer's trip to Chicago (*How long?*; *How's there*) and the weather there (*Is Chicago cold?*; *They have snowy season there*). Showing interest in one's interlocutor's interests is a basic form of involvement politeness (Brown & Levinson 1987:103), and one that is absent in the encounters between immigrant Koreans that do not involve intimate friends or children. The cashier and owner are adopting a relatively involved style. The customer also appears to adapt his speech behavior to his interlocutors, in this case for non-native speakers. He explains and repeats his assessments after they draw no second-assessment of agreement (*I've known it to snow on Easter Sunday... Alright this Sunday it'll be Easter... I've seen it snow Easter Sunday*); and he shifts to a slow and enunciated register to explain the seasonal weather of Chicago (*back there it's a* *seasonal* *change, you got fall, winter, spring*). Thus both parties accommodate to the other, narrowing differences in communication patterns; but the accommodation is not necessarily of the type or degree that can be appreciated by the other, to result in a more synchronous, symmetrical interaction.

Encounter 2

This second encounter of a Korean immigrant shop-owner and cashier with an African American customer is much longer, lasting about 7 minutes, with distinct episodes – including two instances when the customer moves to the exit as if to leave, and then returns to re-initiate conversation. Five excerpts from the encounter are presented and discussed.

The customer's talk and communicative behavior are in sharp contrast to that of immigrant Korean customers. He not only engages in interactional practices that increase interpersonal involvement, e.g. talk of personal topics; he also explicitly states that he wants the storekeepers to know him, and he pledges extreme solidarity with them – e.g. he tells them to call him to their aid if their store is threatened in future "riots." His interaction with the storekeepers suggests that he has different ideas about the relationship between customers and storekeepers than do immigrant Koreans, and different ideas about the corresponding service encounter style.

This customer's explicit expressions of solidarity and intimacy with the store-keepers are matched with an interactional style that includes many of the character-istics – e.g. relatively high volume, volubility, and use of profanity – that immigrant Korean retailers have characterized as disrespectful (Ella Stewart 1989, 1991; Bailey 1996). While this customer's interactional style is "emotionally intense, dynamic, and demonstrative" (Kochman 1981:106), relative to most of the African American customers at this Koreatown store, it shares many features with the style regularly observed in stores in low-income South Central Los Angeles.

The customer, a male in his 50s, has visited the store just once before, the previous night. He is accompanied by his nephew, who does not speak during the encounter. The customer is wearing a warm-up suit and has sunglasses resting on top of his head. His extreme expressions of co-membership with the storekeepers as he talks to them, along with the jerkiness of some of his arm motions, suggest that he may have been drinking. It is not uncommon for customers at mom-and-pop liquor stores to display signs of alcohol use when they are at the store. This customer's speech is not slurred, however, and he does not appear to be unsteady on his feet.

This new customer arrives at the store speaking to his nephew at relatively high volume. The encounter proceeds as a socially minimal service encounter until the African American customer, following the pattern described above, reframes the activity by introducing a personal topic from outside the store context (his recent move to the area) and referring to his personal relationship with the cashier:

((Customer arrives talking to his companion, who is later identified as his nephew.))
Cust: ( ) thirty-seven years old (in this) ass
Cust: Motherfucker ((1.0))
Cash: Hi ((Customer approaches counter.)) ((.2))

Cust: How's it going partner? euh ((Cashier nods.)) ((1.0))
Cust: You got them little bottles?
Cash: (eh) ((Customer's gaze falls on the little bottles.)) ((3.5))
Cust: One seventy-fi:ve! ((Customer gazes at display of bottles.)) ((2.0))
Cust: You ain't got no bourbon? ((1.2))
Cash: No: we don't have bourbon ((1.0))
Cust: I'll get a beer then.
Cust: ((turns to nephew)) What would you like to drink? what do you want? ((Customer
        selects beverages and brings them to the cash register.)) ((7.5))
Cash: Two fifty ((Cashier rings up purchase and bags beer.)) ((4.5))
Cust: I just moved in the area. I talked to you the other day. You [remember me]?
Cash: [Oh yesterday] last night
Cust: Yeah
Cash: [(O:h yeah   )] ((Cashier smiles and nods.))
Cust: [Goddamn, shit] [then you don't–]
Own: [new neighbor, huh?] ((Customer turns halfway to the side toward
                        the owner.))
Cust: Then you don't know me
Cash: [(I know you)] ((Cashier gets change at register.))
Cust: [I want you to know] me so when I walk in here you'll know me. I smoke Winstons.
        Your son knows me
Cash: [Ye::ah]
Cust: [The yo]ung guy
Cash: There you go ((Cashier proffers change.))
Cust: [Okay then]
Cash: [Three four] five ten ((Cashier steps back from counter.))

The interaction with the storekeepers proceeds as a socially minimal service encounter until the customer volunteers personal information about himself (*I just moved in the area*) and raises the history of his relationship with the cashier (*I talked to you the other day. You remember me?*) Although the cashier shows that he remembers the customer (*Oh yesterday, last night*), the customer continues as if the cashier didn't know or remember him. The customer's *goddamn, shit . . . then you don't know me* is spoken at high volume, but with a smile, suggesting humor rather than anger.

Though the cashier acknowledges having seen the customer before, his turns are oriented toward completing the transaction. Except for the words *last night*, his acknowledgements of this customer's history with the store (*Oh yeah, I know you, Yeah*) are spoken in overlap with the customer's words, and only in response to the customer's assertions.

The customer does not acknowledge it when the cashier shows that he remembers him. Perhaps the recognition does not count when it requires prompting (*Then you don't know me*), but rather must be done immediately and spontaneously. The customer then explicitly states that he wants the cashier and the owner to know him (he moves his gaze back and forth between them): *I want you to know me so when I walk in here you'll know me. I smoke Winstons. Your son knows me.* This customer is concerned with the storekeepers "knowing" him: he wants them to know him now and on future store visits, and he finds it worth noting that one of the other employees (*your son*), already knows him.

Knowing a customer's habitual purchases and brand preferences (e.g. Winstons) is one way of "knowing" the customer, and storekeepers frequently ready a customer's cigarettes or liquor without being asked; minimally, this customer wants to be known in this way. Subsequent talk, however, suggests that "knowing" him will involve a more personal, intimate relationship, and one that involves specific types of talk and behavior.

The data presented here suggest that immigrant Korean retailers and African American customers have differing notions of what it means to "know" someone in a convenience store context, and differing ideas about the kinds of speech activities entailed by "knowing" someone in this context. Different ideas about what it means to know someone may apply not just to service encounters, as described above, but to any encounter between relative strangers. Thus M. Park (1979:82) suggests that, by Western standards, Koreans are restrained and impersonal with those who are not intimate friends or part of a known group:

The age-old cliché, "Koreans are the most courteous people in the East" is rather rightly applied only to inter-personal interaction among ingroups or hierarchical groups. Koreans tend to be [by Western standards] impolite or even rude when they interact with outgroups like outsiders or strangers. Everyone outside the ingroup is likely to be treated with curiosity or caution or even a bit of suspicion...

It may be difficult for these storekeepers to extend what for them is an intimate communicative style to a relative stranger.

In America, many communicative activities – e.g. greetings, smiles, and small-talk – occur in interactions both with friends and with relative strangers. The communicative style extended to both strangers and friends relatively emphasizes the expression of casual solidarity and explicit recognition of personal details.

Personal treatment in American life includes use of the first name, recognition of biographical details and acknowledgements of specific acts, appearances, preferences and choices of the individual. Cultural models are given by salesmen and airline hostesses. Their pleasant smiles, feigned and innocuous invasions of privacy, "kidding" and swapping of personal experiences constitute stereotypes of personal behavior... Signs of friendship, the glad handshake, the ready smile, the slap on the back...have become part of the normal way of behavior. (Edward Stewart 1972:55, 58)

Everyday speech behavior among strangers in America includes practices that would be reserved for talk among relative intimates in Korea.

Such differing assumptions about appropriate communicative style in service encounters, and about the relationship between customer and server, may underlie the contrasting forms of participation in the encounter under consideration. When the customer states that he wants the storekeepers to know him, the cashier's *Yeah* and subsequent *There you go*, as he hands back change, fail to engage the topic of knowing the customer. The cashier is reframing the activity as a business transaction, specifically the closing of the business negotiation component, and perhaps the entire encounter. The return and counting of change (*There you go; Three four five ten*) is used in many service encounters as a way of closing not only the business negotiation, but also the entire interaction.

The customer, however, does not treat this as the end of the encounter. Instead, he treats this as a time to discuss details of his life outside the store:

Cust: And then I– I've got three months to be out here.
Cash: How's [here   ] ((Cashier steps back from counter and gazes down.))
Cust: [I'm going] to school
Cash: How's here
Cust: I'm going to– (.2) locksmith school
Cash: Oh really
Cust: Yeah. so after that– because I had a (.) knee operation ((Customer rolls up pant leg to
        show scars.)) ((4.2))
Cust: I had a total knee so my company is retiring my– old black ass at fifty-four
        ((Customer smiles and gazes at owner.)) ((.6))
Own: (mmh) ((Owner shakes his head laterally and gazes away from the customer.))
Cust: And they give me some money
Cash: Huh ((Cashier bares his teeth briefly in a smile.))
Cust: So I'm spending my money at your store on liquor heh heh heh heh hah hah hah hah
        hah ((Customer laughs animatedly, turning toward the owner who does not smile,
        but who continues lateral headshakes as he takes a few steps to the side.))
Own: You still can work?

The business exchange has been completed, and the customer initiates discussion of a series of personal topics. He volunteers how long he will be in Los Angeles, what he is doing there, details of his medical history, and his current employment status. He goes so far as to roll up his pant-leg to show the scars from his knee replacement operation. He has said that he wants these storekeepers to "know" him, and he's giving them some of the information they need to know him. In doing so he is treating them as co-members of an intimate group, i.e. the circle of people who can see his knee scars, even though by some standards they are virtual strangers. The customer is treating the social distance between himself and the storekeepers as small; his interactional style increases involvement between him and the store-keepers.

The cashier's talk displays some interest in the interaction, e.g. his initial query *How's here* displays understanding of the customer's statement (*I've got three months to be out here*) and invites further comment. The customer, however, does not answer the question. The non-standard form *How's here* (for "How do you like it here?") may not have been understood by the customer, and comprehension may have been further hindered by the cashier's non-verbal actions. During the first *How's here*, the cashier's arm is in front of his face, and his gaze is not on the customer; during the second, he's shifting his weight to lean on a counter to the side. The even intonation contour of *How's here* may also prevent the customer from realizing that a question is being asked. Even when a storekeeper expresses involve-ment in an interaction, his or her limited English proficiency may prevent the customer from understanding the expression of interest.

The customer concludes this introduction with a joke that stresses the humorous nature of his relationship with the liquor store owners: he is sharing the proceeds from his disability payments with them. His smile and laughter at this situation are an invitation to his audience to share in his laughter (Jefferson 1979). The store-owner and cashier fail to join in this laughter; the cashier displays a fleeting, stiff smile, and the owner none at all. Not only do cashier and owner fail to accept the invitation to laughter, but as in the previous encounter, the owner, through his subsequent question, ACTIVELY DECLINES the invitation to laughter. His question *You still can work?* is a serious pursuit of a topic that effectively counters the customer's pursuit of laughter. The question proves his comprehension of the customer's prior talk, but displays no affective alignment or solidarity with the customer's humor. Even though the store-owner can understand the referential content of the words, he does not participate in the interactional activity of laughing – the preferred response to the customer's laughter.

It is also, of course, possible that the owner is displaying a dispreferred response because he does NOT want to display alignment: perhaps he thinks that people take advantage of social programs when they could support themselves through their own work – a sentiment voiced in interviews with immigrant Korean retailers in a variety of forms. This active declination to laugh, however, also occurs in my data during talk about morally less sensitive topics, e.g. the weather, with both African American and Korean customers; this suggests a pattern of declining invitations to laughter that is unrelated to personal opinions about the topic at hand.

In the next two minutes of talk and interaction (not transcribed here), the customer gets change for a five-dollar bill, and then explains to the owner that his former employer doesn't want him to work for fear that they would have to redo his knee operation if he resumed work. The customer takes his bag of purchases from the counter, and moves to the door as if to leave (the owner says *See ya*); but he stops in the doorway, then re-enters the store to resume talking. He discusses the exact amount of money he receives per month for his disability, compares it to the amount of money he made previously, and reiterates that if he goes to work now, his disability benefits will be cut off.

In the next segment, transcribed below, the customer explains that he is being re-trained for a new job. He begins to depart, and then once again returns from the threshold of the exit door to re-initiate talk:

Cust: So I gotta get another trade. Just like if you get hurt in the liquor store business, you gotta go get another trade. So I gotta go get another trade. For them to pay me the money. So I'm gonna get another trade. But then like– after I get another trade they pay me (a sum) a lump sum of money? And I'm gonna do what I wanna do. ((.8))
Cust: They only gonna give me about sixty or seventy thousand. ((1.4))
Cust: Plus– my schooling– ((1.0))
Cust: So:– I got to take it easy for a little bit. ((Customer moves toward exit.))
Cust: That's why I'm gonna buy enough of your liquor (so I can take it)
Own: Alright, take care
Cust: Okay ((Customer pauses in doorway.))

This segment is characterized by dramatically asymmetrical contributions to the interaction. Not only does the customer do most of the talking, but there is a noticeable absence of response to his statements. He gives up his turn at talk five times in this short segment, but receives a verbal response only once. The customer only gets verbal collaboration, in this segment, in leaving the store – which suggests that these storekeepers may be more proficient at closing interactions with customers than they are at sociable, personal discussion with them.

The lack of verbal response to the customer's talk is particularly noteworthy because he is making statements that invite easy responses. The fact that he's going to get a lump sum of money and *do what I wanna do* makes relevant such questions as: *How much are you going to get?* or *What are you going to do when you get the money?* The amount of money he's going to get (*sixty or seventy thousand*) similarly invites comment, e.g. *That's great*, or *That's a lot of money*, or again, *What are you going to do with it?* The customer's *Plus my schooling* invites questions about the details of the schooling, beyond the fact (stated earlier) that it's locksmith school. The customer's reference to buying *enough of your liquor* also provides an opening for storekeeper recognition of his patronage, e.g. *We appreciate your business*. The silence of the storekeepers displays restraint, but not interest or involvement.

The immigrant Korean storekeepers' lack of overt response to the customer's talk forms a stark contrast with the African American pattern of call-and-response described above. Smitherman (1977:108) emphasizes the importance of responding to a speaker, regardless of the form of the response: "all responses are 'correct'; the only 'incorrect' thing you can do is not respond at all." By this standard, the store-keepers' lack of response is inappropriate.

In the next segment, although the customer has once again moved to the door, and the owner has said goodbye, the customer re-enters the store and more talk follows. After learning the storekeepers' names, the customer invokes the events of April 1992. He tells the store-owners that he will come to their aid if they have problems in the future, and goes on to discuss his philosophy of race relations:

Cust: What's your name? ((Customer re-enters store and approaches the owner.))
Own: Han Choi ((.6))
Cust: Han? ((Customer shakes hands with the owner.)) ((1.2))
Cust: What's your name? ((Customer shakes cashier's hand.))
Cash: Shin
Cust: Chin?
Cash: No, [Shin]
Cust: [Okay] (.) Shin?
Cash: Yeah
Own: What's yours (then)?
Cust: Larry
Own: Larry
Cust: I'm a gangsta from Chicago, Larry Smith. Anybody fuck with you, this black– I seen them riots and things and they was fucking up with the Korean stores and the– and the what's his name stores? And I was in Vietnam and everything like that
Own: [(Our) neighbors friendly (here)]
Cust: [Well-(.) well let me] tell you something– nobody fuck with your store, if I catch 'em making fuck with your store (.) you just ca:ll me: dow:n
Own: Alright
Cust: I:'ll fuck 'em up ((Customer reaches out and shakes the owner's hand; the owner's arm is limp and he is pulled off balance by the handshake.)) ((.8))
Cust: Because I believe in people not Koreans, not Blacks, not Whites, not this, I believe in people. ((.4))
Cust: Right there. ((Customer taps the owner on the chest twice, in rhythm with the two words *right there*))

The customer, who has created and emphasized solidarity with the storekeepers throughout their interaction, continues to reinforce his solidarity and co-membership with them. After learning their names and shaking their hands – an act of physical intimacy – he makes two explicit assertions of solidarity.

His initial assertion of solidarity is dramatic: he promises with high volume and affect that he will respond to their call for help, and "fuck up" anyone who is harming them or their store. He has seen the havoc of Los Angeles in April 1992 on TV; but he is a Vietnam veteran, so he has the capacity to deal with such events. The storekeepers' enemies are his enemies; he and the storekeepers are co-members of an intimate group, a group whose members will risk harm to protect each other.

He reiterates this sentiment of solidarity by explaining his readiness to act on their behalf based on his personal philosophy: *Because I believe in people not Koreans, not Blacks, not Whites.* Social distance between him and these storekeepers is low; race is not a barrier. He emphasizes his intimacy with the store-owner by tapping him on the chest, once more making physical contact, and citing this specific store-owner as an example of the people in whom he has faith.

Following the segment transcribed above, there are two minutes of talk (not transcribed here) during which the customer discusses his beliefs about the basic sameness of people, regardless of race, and his criticisms of those who make society racist. The customer utters more than 10 words for each of the store-owner's words during this period. The service encounter comes to an end with the following turns:

((The customer speaks with high volume and animation, and sounds almost angry during these penultimate two turns. He is gesticulating so strongly that his sunglasses become dislodged from atop his head and he has to reposition them as he talks.))

Cust: Okay what I'm saying is (.) if you throw five kids (in the middle of the floor) and don't tell them what they are nothing like that they just grow up to be people ((.))
Cust: They don't even know (.) that they Black. they don't even know they Korean they don't know that they White they don't know this and that. It have to be an old person like you or me, George Washington and all these motherfuckers. Martin Luther King and all these motherfuckers.
((The customer has begun moving toward the exit. His vocal register shifts suddenly to one of low volume and affect for his final turn. He gazes first at the owner and then the cashier as he waves goodbye.))
Cust: Anyway– have a good day.
Own: Later ((Customer turns and exits.))

As this interaction progresses, the storekeepers become more and more reticent while the customer becomes more and more outspoken. Although the customer has dominated the talk throughout the interaction, his volume and affect level get higher as it progresses, and he holds the floor an ever higher proportion of the time. In the final two minutes of talk, the customer is literally following the owner from place to place in the store, leaning over the shorter man, and repeatedly touching him on the chest as he makes his points.

This asymmetry in participation occurs despite apparent efforts at accommodation by both customer and storekeepers. Thus the storekeepers ask more questions that display interest in the customer – *How's here*; *You still can work?* – than they ask of non-intimate adult Korean customers. The customer adapts his speech for non-natives, e.g. by using an example to explain his job retraining (*Just like if you get hurt in the liquor store business, you gotta go get another trade*); and he introduces a topic that might be of particular interest to them, e.g. Los Angeles civil unrest that could threaten their store. As in the first encounter, however, the mutual accommodation may not be of the degree or type that can be fully appreciated by the other party, or can result in more symmetrical participation in the encounter.

Mismatch in politeness orientations can have a self-reinforcing, spiraling effect that exaggerates differences in politeness style as interaction continues; this can exacerbate misunderstandings and mutual negative evaluations. The more this African American customer cheerfully talks and stresses his camaraderie with the store-owner, the more the retailer withdraws and declines involvement. This may be a more general phenomenon in interethnic communication. Borrowing a term from Bateson 1972, Tannen (1981:138) concludes that speakers from backgrounds with contrasting linguistic practices frequently respond to each other in "complementary schismogenetic fashion"; i.e., "the verbal devices used by one group cause speakers of the other group to react by intensifying the opposing behavior, and vice versa."

Since, for many African-Americans the nature of good and respectful service encounter relations involves relatively great personal involvement, this customer may be redoubling his efforts to create solidarity as he encounters the retailers' increasing reticence. For the store-owner, the appropriate response to a customer's increasing intimacy may be the silence or avoidance that demonstrates restraint. In this instance, the pattern does not escalate out of control. The owner maintains a degree of engagement, although he appears uncomfortable at times; and the customer does not react as if he is being ignored, although his increasing affect as the interaction proceeds may well be related to the low level of response he gets from the storekeepers.

However, this self-escalating cycle may contribute to confrontations that have occurred elsewhere. Media and informant accounts of confrontations between retailers and African Americans often stress the seeming suddenness with which storekeepers, perceived to be inscrutably impassive, suddenly explode in anger at customers. As customers persist in behaviors that the retailer perceives as invasive, the storekeeper will remain silent; the customer will not know that he or she is doing something that the storekeeper finds inappropriate, and will increase the intensity of the involvement behaviors in reaction to the restraint of storekeepers. When the weight of the trespass against sensibilities becomes too grave, the store-owner will feel justified in lashing out (Kochman 1981:118, 1984:206). Conversely, the increasingly restrained behavior of store-owners, as customers express ever-greater friendliness, can lead to customer outbursts and accusations of storekeeper racism. Storekeepers report repeated instances in which customers have suddenly (and to the storekeepers, inexplicably) accused them of being racists.

Conclusion

Divergent practices for displaying respect in service encounter interaction are an ongoing cause of tension between immigrant Korean retailers and their African American customers. The two groups have different concepts of the relationship between customer and storekeeper, and different ideas about the speech activities that are appropriate in service encounters. The talk of immigrant Koreans focuses almost exclusively on the business transaction at hand, while the talk of African American customers includes efforts toward more personal, sociable interaction.

The interactional patterns that are apparent in videotaped records are consistent with data that come from dozens of hours of observation in various stores, and from interviews with store-owners, customers, and consultants. The seeming avoidance of involvement on the part of immigrant Koreans is frequently seen by African Americans as the disdain and arrogance of racism. The relative stress on interpersonal involvement among African Americans in service encounters is typically perceived by immigrant Korean retailers as a sign of selfishness, interpersonal imposition, or poor breeding (Bailey 1996).

The focus of this article on miscommunication should not be taken to mean that immigrant Korean merchants and African American customers can never communicate effectively, or never have friendly relationships. The overwhelming majority of African American customers and immigrant Korean retailers that I observed get along, and relationships between retailers and regular customers (40–80% of the clientele at stores I visited) are often very positive. Retailers often know regular customers' family members and other details of their lives; and many retailers engage in friendly small-talk with such customers, even when limited English proficiency make it difficult. This type of relationship, which often results only after longer contact, can change mutual perceptions, as described by an African American woman in her 50s:

I find that they shy away from you until you get to know them. Like this lady, the Korean store, I've been in the neighborhood for years and years, and she's friendly with everybody cause she knows everybody but when they don't know you, they're shy, and you think they're prejudice. They might be, but you just have to get to know them. They're nice people once you get to know them.

This article has focused on one source of interethnic tensions: miscommunication due to cultural and linguistic differences. Socio-historical conditions – e.g. social, economic, and racial inequality – are also clearly sources of tensions between African Americans and immigrant Korean storekeepers. Within a social and historical context, however, there are specific linguistic and cultural practices that can ameliorate or exacerbate tensions between groups. The goal of this essay has been to shed light on communicative processes that can lead to tensions between groups in face-to-face interaction, in the hope that understanding linguistic and cultural bases of differences in communication patterns can make these differences less inflammatory.

NOTES

Initial fieldwork for this research was funded by a Research Institute for Man/Landes Training Grant. Many thanks to Alessandro Duranti for extensive comments on repeated drafts of the UCLA M.A. thesis on which this article is based. Thanks also to Jae Kim, who transcribed and translated the Korean service encounters, and who shared much with me about the language, lives, and perceptions of Korean immigrants in Los Angeles.

1   Transcription conventions are as follows: Speakers are identified with an abbreviation in the far left column, e.g. "Cust" for "Customer," "Cash" for "Cashier," and "Own" for "Owner." A question mark in this column indicates that the speaker's identity is not clear to the transcriber. Descriptions of non-verbal activities are in double parentheses, e.g. ((Customer enters store.)) Note also the following:

((4.3))   Numbers in parentheses indicate the length of time in seconds during which there is no talk. Single parentheses are used for intra-turn silences, double parentheses for silences between turns.

(.)   A period in parentheses or double parentheses indicates a stretch of time, lasting no more than two-tenths of a second, during which there is no talk.

:   A colon indicates that the preceding sound was elongated in a marked pronunciation.

?   A question mark indicates a marked rising pitch.

.   A period indicates a marked falling pitch.

( )   Parentheses that are empty indicate that something was said at that point, but it is not clear enough to transcribe. Parentheses around words indicate doubt about the accuracy of the transcribed material. A slash between words in parentheses indicates alternate possibilities.

hhh   *h*'s connected to a word indicate breathiness, usually associated with laughter.

[ ]   Brackets enclose those portions of utterances that are spoken in overlap with other talk. The overlapping portions of talk are placed immediately above or below each other on the page.

!   An exclamation point indicates an exclamatory tone.

,   A comma indicates a marked continuing intonation in the sound(s) preceding the comma.

–   Text that is underlined was pronounced with emphasis, i.e. some combination of higher volume, pitch, and greater vowel length.

'   A single apostrophe replaces a letter that was not pronounced, e.g. *col'* for *cold*, when the *d* is not pronounced.

–   A hyphen or dash indicates that speech was suddenly cut-off during or after the preceding word.

Transcriptions of Korean data follow Martin et al. (1967:xv).

2   This category includes practices that might seem to vary significantly in degree of intimacy; however, immigrant Koreans do not treat such distinctions as relevant in most encounters with immigrant Korean customers. As described in the section on encounters between immigrant Koreans, small-talk about the weather (for example) does not occur independently of, or more frequently than, talk of more personal matters.

3   This is not meant to deny the role of racism in tensions between African Americans and immigrant Korean retailers. Racism permeates American society; and it provides a cogent explanation for a wide variety of historical, social, and economic phenomena, including behavior in face-to-face interaction. Quotes from store-owners interviewed in other studies (e.g. Ella Stewart 1989; K. Park 1995), attest the blatant racism of some storekeepers. The point here is not that immigrant Korean merchants are or are not racist, but rather that many immigrant Korean interactional practices upon which African American customers base assumptions of racism are not valid indices of racism, because retailers use identical practices with immigrant Korean customers.

4   The difficulty of mastering English for adult speakers of Korean is suggested by the grammatical interference evident in the following utterance by a storekeeper who had been in Los Angeles over 20 years. When asked where her husband was, she replied: *Husband some merchandise buy* (i.e. "My husband is buying some merchandise.") The subject–object–verb word order of Korean is used, rather than the subject–verb–object word order of English. The present tense form of *buy* is used, rather than present progressive; this parallels Korean usage, in which the present tense form of action verbs can indicate present progressive meaning. The possessive pronoun *my* is elided, since it would be understood from context in Korean (Lee 1989:90).

REFERENCES

Atkinson, J. Maxwell, & Heritage, John (1984) (eds.) *Structures of Social Action: Studies in Conversation Analysis*. Cambridge & New York: Cambridge University Press.

Austin, Regina (1995). Moving beyond deviance: Expanding Black people's rights and reasons to shop and to sell. *Penn Law Journal* 30:30–4.

Bailey, Benjamin (1996). Communication of Respect in Service Encounters between Immigrant Korean Retailers and African-American Customers. M.A. thesis, University of California, Los Angeles.

Bateson, Gregory (1972). *Steps to an Ecology of Mind*. New York: Ballantine.

Brown, Penelope, & Levinson, Stephen (1987). *Politeness: Some Universals in Language Usage*. Cambridge & New York: Cambridge University Press.

Chang, Edward (1990). New Urban Crisis: Korean–Black Conflicts in Los Angeles. Dissertation, University of California, Berkeley.

Chang, Edward (1993). Jewish and Korean merchants in African American neighborhoods: A comparative perspective. *Amerasia Journal* 19:5–21.

Drake, St. Clair, & Cayton, Horace (1945). *Black Metropolis: A Study of Negro Life in a Northern City*. New York: Harper & Row.

Drew, Paul, & Heritage, John (1992a). Analyzing talk at work: An introduction. In Drew & Heritage (eds.), 3–65.

Drew, Paul, and Heritage, John (1992b) (eds.) *Talk at Work: Interaction in Institutional Settings*. Cambridge & New York: Cambridge University Press.

Duranti, Alessandro, & Goodwin, Charles (1992), (eds.) *Rethinking Context: Language as an Interactive Phenomenon*. Cambridge & New York: Cambridge University Press.

Durkheim, Emile (1915). *The Elementary Forms of the Religious Life*. London: Allen & Unwin.

Goffman, Erving (1967). The nature of deference and demeanor. In his *Interaction Ritual: Essays on Face-to-Face Behavior*, 47–95. New York: Pantheon.

Goffman, Erving (1971). *Relations in Public: Microstudies of the Public Order*. New York: Basic Books.

Goodwin, Charles & Goodwin, Marjorie H. (1992). Assessments and the construction of context. In Duranti & Goodwin (eds.), 147–90.

Grice, Paul (1975). Logic and conversation. In Peter Cole & Jerry Morgan (eds.), *Syntax and Semantics*, 3:41–58. New York: Academic Press.

Gumperz, John (1982a). *Discourse Strategies*. Cambridge & New York: Cambridge University Press.

Gumperz, John (1982b) (ed.). *Language and Social Identity*. Cambridge & New York: Cambridge University Press.

Gumperz, John (1992). Contextualization and understanding. In Duranti & Goodwin (eds.), 229–52.

Jefferson, Gail (1979). A technique for inviting laughter and its subsequent acceptance/declination. In George Psathas (ed.), *Everyday Language: Studies in Ethnomethodology*, 79–96. New York: Irvington.

Keel, Hee-Sung (1993). Word and wordlessness: The spirit of Korean Buddhism. *Korea Journal* 33:11–19.

Kochman, Thomas (1981). *Black and White Styles in Conflict*. Chicago: University of Chicago Press.

Kochman, Thomas (1984). The politics of politeness: Social warrants in mainstream American public etiquette. *Georgetown University Roundtable on Languages and Linguistics* 1984:200–9.

Lee, Hyon-Bok (1989). *Korean Grammar*. Oxford & New York: Oxford University Press.

Levinson, Stephen (1992). Activity types in language. In Drew & Heritage (eds.), 66–100.

Martin, Samuel, et al. (1967). *A Korean–English dictionary*. New Haven, CT: Yale University Press.

Merritt, Marilyn (1976). On questions following questions (in service encounters). *Language in Society* 5:315–57.

Park, Kyeyoung (1995). The re-invention of affirmative action: Korean immigrants' changing conceptions of African Americans and Latin Americans. *Urban Anthropology* 24:59–92.

Park, Myung-Seok (1979). *Communication Styles in Two Different Cultures: Korean and American*. Seoul: Han Shin.

Sacks, Harvey (1975). Everyone has to lie. In Mary Sanches & Ben Blount (eds.), *Sociocultural Dimensions of Language Use*, 57–79. New York: Academic Press.

Schegloff, Emanuel, Jefferson, Gail, & Sacks, Harvey (1977). The preference for self-correction in the organization of repair in conversation. *Language* 53:361–82.

Schegloff, Emanuel, & Sacks, Harvey (1973). Opening up closings. *Semiotica* 7:289–327.

Scollon, Ron, & Scollon, Suzanne Wong (1994). Face parameters in East–West discourse. In Stella Ting-Toomey (ed.), *The Challenge of Facework*, 133–58. Albany: State University of New York Press.

Smitherman, Geneva (1977). *Talkin' and Testifyin': The Language of Black America*. Boston: Houghton Mifflin.

Stewart, Edward (1972). *American Cultural Patterns*. Chicago: Intercultural Press.

Stewart, Ella (1989). Ethnic Cultural Diversity: An Interpretive Study of Cultural Differences and Communication Styles between Korean Merchants/Employees and Black Patrons in South Los Angeles. M.A. thesis, California State University, Los Angeles.

Stewart, Ella (1991). Ethnic Cultural Diversity: Perceptions of Intercultural Communication Rules for Interaction between Korean Merchants/Employees and Black Patrons in South Los Angeles. Paper presented to the 19th Annual Conference of the National Association for Ethnic Studies at California State Polytechnic University, Pomona, CA.

Sturdevant, Frederick (1969) (ed.), *The Ghetto Marketplace*. New York: Free Press.

Tannen, Deborah (1981). New York Jewish conversational style. *International Journal of the Sociology of Language* 30:133–49.

Yum, June-Ock (1987). Korean philosophy and communication. In D. Lawrence Kincaid (ed.), *Communication Theory: Eastern and Western Perspectives*, 71–86. San Diego: Academic Press.

Part II

The Performance of Language: Acts, Events, and Activities

Introduction

There is a long tradition in Western philosophy to think of utterances as statements that can be valued in terms of their truth. A more recent tradition, initiated by the Oxford philosopher J. L. Austin, looks at utterances as acts, with the force to do things in the world (e.g. inform, request, scold, approve, fire, promote, apologize, offend). For linguistic anthropologists to think about the work done by language means to start from where language happens, that is, from the events, activities, and acts within which language is used. This methodological choice has important theoretical implications, one of the most important of which is that speakers are not seen as information-processing machines but as social actors whose utterances matter for both their content and their form. The articles in Part II show that the style in which a message is delivered is crucial to its meaning and that ambiguity and other creative devices that are usually associated with poetry are also found in everyday conversation (Mitchell-Kernan). Hence the view of language as performance is an analytical attitude, that is, a perspective through which to examine what people say to whom, when, and how (Bauman). An important consequence of this attitude is that speaking is shown to be culturally organized, whether in highly structured events (Irvine) or in looser everyday encounters where the exchange of greetings is the only observable use of language (Duranti). In the production of linguistic messages, people simultaneously employ language, body, and material culture to activate or reproduce shared views about hierarchy, gender, intimacy (Goodwin and Goodwin).

Questions about the Performance of Language

1   What is "signifying" and how is it manifested? Is there anything similar to signifying in the speech communities you are familiar with?

2   What properties of language does "signifying" illustrate?
3   What defines a stretch of talk as artful? Can you think of examples of everyday talk that would qualify as artful according to Bauman's definition?
4   What are the four properties of formality discussed by Irvine? Can you apply them to events you are familiar with to assess their "formality"?
5   What are the universal properties of greetings proposed by Duranti? Using those properties, how many kinds of greetings can you identify?
6   How can you assess whether what people say during greetings is meant to be taken literally?
7   Most of the time speakers do not explicitly say whether they like or dislike something or whether they approve or not what has been done, and yet we are able to infer such evaluations. Use Goodwin and Goodwin's article to list some of the criteria on the basis of which we make such inferences.
8   How can the claim that emotions are located in human interaction affect our view of how to handle conflict and misunderstanding?
9   Can you identify thematic, methodological, and theoretical connections between the chapters in Part I and those in Part II?

Suggestions for Further Reading

For a philosophical perspective on language as action: Austin, J. L. (1975). *How to Do Things with Words* (2nd edn.), J. O. Urmson and Marina Sbisà, editors. Cambridge, MA: Harvard University Press; Wittgenstein, L. (1958). *Philosophical Investigations*, edited by G. E. M. Anscombe and R. Rhees, translated by G. E. M. Anscombe (2nd edn.). Oxford: Blackwell; Grice, H. P. (1989). *Study in the Way of Words*. Cambridge, MA: Harvard University Press; Searle, J. R. (1969). *Speech Acts: An Essay in the Philosophy of Language*. Cambridge: Cambridge University Press.

A good introduction to pragmatics, covering speech acts, conversational maxims, and conversation analysis is: Levinson, S. C. (1983). *Pragmatics*. Cambridge: Cambridge University Press.

An important anthropological contribution on language as action is found in the second volume of: Malinowski, B. (1935). *Coral Gardens and Their Magic*. London: Allen & Unwin.

The acquisition of the pragmatic force of language is discussed in the contributions to: Ochs, E., and Schieffelin, B. B. (1979). *Developmental Pragmatics*. New York: Academic Press.

A good collection of short essays on verbal art is: Bauman, R. (ed.) (1992). *Folklore, Cultural Performances, and Popular Entertainments*. New York: Oxford University Press.

Ethnographic studies of verbal art include: Sherzer, J. (1983). *Kuna Ways of Speaking: An Ethnographic Perspective*. Austin: University of Texas Press; Tedlock, D. (1983). *The Spoken Word and the Work of Interpretation*. Philadelphia: University of Pennsylvania Press; Briggs, C. L. (1988). *Competence in Performance: The Creativity of Tradition in Mexicano Verbal Art*. Philadelphia: University of Pennsylvania Press; Kuipers, J. C. (1990). *Power in Performance: The Creation of Textual Authority in Weyewa Ritual Speech*. Philadelphia: University of Pennsylvania Press; Graham, L. R. (1995). *Performing Dreams: Discourses of Immortality among the Xavante of Central Brazil*. Austin: University of Texas Press.

The interaction between language and context is reanalyzed in: Duranti, A., and Goodwin, C. (eds.) (1992). *Rethinking Context: Language as an Interactive Phenomenon*. Cambridge: Cambridge University Press.

6

Signifying and Marking: Two Afro-American Speech Acts

Claudia Mitchell-Kernan

In a linguistic community which is bilingual or bidialectal, the code in which messages are conveyed is likely to be highly salient both to members of the community and to the ethnographer. The languages spoken tend to be named, and individual speakers, who speak one or the other dialect in particular settings, identified as belonging to one or more groups. The fact that more than one language is spoken, that various social categories of people use specific languages in certain settings when discussing particular topics with members of other social categories, is a significant point of departure.

Aside from language or grammar *per se*, there are, however, other aspects of the communicative competence of such a group which require analysis. The appropriate beginning point for an investigation may be the analysis of the components which are emphasized by elaboration in a variety of speech forms. Well-elaborated components comprise a basis for selection among alternates. The pattern of such selection reveals crucial social information.

Hymes (1967) notes that precedence of components may differ from case to case, and such differences may be a basis for the classification of sociolinguistic systems. Such hierarchies of precedence may depend not simply on apparent causal direction in the interrelationships between components but also on the cultural focus (salience-emphasis) upon one or more of the components.

The artistic component is significant in black English. The salience of consideration of the artistic characteristics of speech acts in black English is evidenced by both the proliferation of terms which deal with aspects of verbal style and the common occurrence of speech routines which may be labeled by these terms. The artistic characteristics of a speech act are the characteristics that have to do with the *style* of the speech act, i.e., with the way in which something is said rather than with such components as the topic or the interlocutors. Moreover, the very term art carries connotations of value or judgment of appreciation (or non-appreciation).

The speech acts which will be described here are among the many which are given labels in black English. The terms themselves are sometimes descriptive of the style of the speech act. A partial list of such terms is: *signifying, rapping, sounding, playing the dozens, woofing, marking, loud-talking, shucking*, and *jiving*. Some of these terms are variants used in particular geographic areas. Undoubtedly, other variants exist.

I shall deal in detail with two of these speech acts, treat their stylistic aspects, and attempt to relate the artistic characteristics to the other components which together comprise the speech act. I will describe how these speech acts are used and demonstrate that concern with style and value of artistic merit on the part of speakers of black English influences the other components. Specifically, I will show that this concern has a direct effect upon the choice of the linguistic code in certain conversational settings and frequently explains the use of black dialect forms.

Value regarding verbal art in black English is evident not only from the high frequency of occurrences of nameable artistic variants but also from the comments on such variants in ongoing conversations, including stated values regarding speech use and judgments of the ability of particular speakers that are based upon considerations of artistic merit and style. Concern with verbal art is a dominant theme in black culture, and while these speech acts do not have style as their sole component, style is nevertheless the criterion which determines their effective use.

Signifying

A number of individuals interested in black verbal behavior have devoted attention to the "way of talking" which is known in many black communities as *signifying* (see Abrahams 1964; Kochman 1969). Signifying can be a tactic employed in game activity – verbal dueling – which is engaged in as an end in itself, and it is signifying in this context which has been the subject of most previous analyses. Signifying, however, also refers to a way of encoding messages or meanings in natural conversations which involves, in most cases, an element of indirection. This kind of signifying might be best viewed as an alternative message form, selected for its artistic merit, and may occur embedded in a variety of discourses. Such signifying is not focal to the linguistic interaction in the sense that it does not define the entire speech event. While the primacy of either of these uses of the term *signifying* is difficult to establish, the latter deserves attention due to its neglect in the literature.

The standard English concept of signifying seems etymologically related to the use of this term within the black community. An audience, e.g., may be advised to signify "yes" by standing or to signify its disapproval of permissive education by saying "aye." It is also possible to say that an individual signifies his poverty by wearing rags. In the first instance we explicitly state the relationship between the meaning and the act, informing the audience that in this context the action or word will be an adequate and acceptable means of expressing approval. In the second instance, the relationship between rags and poverty is *implicit* and stems from conventional associations. It is in this latter sense that standard English and black usage have the most in common.

In the context of news analyses and interpretation we hear the rhetorical question, "What does all of this signify?" Individuals posing this question proceed to tell us what some words or events mean by placing major emphasis on the implications of the thing which is the subject of interpretation and, more often than not, posing inferences which are felt to logically follow. Such interpretations rely on the establishment of context, which may include antecedent conditions and background knowledge as well as the context in which the event occurred.

The black concept of *signifying* incorporates essentially a folk notion that dictionary entries for words are not always sufficient for interpreting meanings or messages, or that meaning goes beyond such interpretations. Complimentary remarks may be delivered in a left-handed fashion. A particular utterance may be an insult in one context and not in another. What pretends to be informative may intend to be persuasive. Superficially, self-abasing remarks are frequently self-praise. The hearer is thus constrained to attend to all potential meaning carrying symbolic systems in speech events – the total universe of discourse. The context embeddedness of meaning is attested to by both our reliance on the given context and, most importantly, our inclination to construct additional context from our background knowledge of the world. Facial expression and tone of voice serve to orient us to one kind of interpretation rather than another. Situational context helps us to narrow meaning. Personal background knowledge about the speaker points us in different directions. Expectations based on role or status criteria enter into the sorting process. In fact, we seem to process all manner of information against a background of assumptions and expectations. Thus, no matter how sincere the tone of voice affected by the used car salesman, he is always suspect.

Labeling a particular utterance as signifying thus involves the recognition and attribution of some implicit content or function, which is potentially obscured by the surface content or function. The obscurity may lie in the relative difficulty it poses for interpreting (1) the meaning or message the speaker is adjudged as intending to convey; (2) the addressee – the person or persons to whom the message is directed; (3) the goal orientation or intent of the speaker. A precondition for the application of the term *signifying* to some speech act is the assumption that the meaning decoded was consciously and purposely formulated at the encoding stage. In reference to function the same condition must hold.

The following examples of signifying are taken from natural conversations recorded in Oakland, California. Each example will be followed by interpretations, intended to clarify the messages and meanings being conveyed in each case.

(1) The interlocutors here are Barbara, an informant; Mary, one of her friends; and the researcher. The conversation takes place in Barbara's home and the episode begins as I am about to leave.

Barbara: What are you going to do Saturday? Will you be over here?
R: I don't know.
Barbara: Well, if you're not going to be doing anything, come by. I'm going to cook some chit'lins. [Rather jokingly] Or are you one of those Negroes who don't eat chit'lins?
Mary: [Interjecting indignantly] That's all I hear lately – soul food, soul food. If you say you don't eat it you get accused of being saditty [affected, considering oneself superior].
  [Matter of factly] Well, I ate enough black-eyed peas and neck-bones during the depression that I can't get too excited over it. I eat prime rib and T-bone because I

like to, not because I'm trying to be white. [Sincerely] Negroes are constantly trying to find some way to discriminate against each other. If they could once get it in their heads that we are all in this together maybe we could get somewhere in this battle against the man.

[Mary leaves.]

Barbara: Well, I wasn't signifying at her, but like I always say, if the shoe fits, wear it.

While the manifest topic of Barbara's question was food, Mary's response indicates that this is not a conversation about the relative merits of having one thing or another for dinner. Briefly, Barbara was, in the metaphors of the culture, implying that Mary (and/or I) is an assimilationist.

Let us first deal with the message itself, which is somewhat analogous to an allegory in that the significance or meaning of the words must be derived from known symbolic values. An outsider or nonmember (perhaps not at this date) might find it difficult to grasp the significance of eating chit'lins or not eating chit'lins. Barbara's "one of those Negroes who" places the hearer in a category of persons which, in turn, suggests that the members of that category may share other features, in this case, negatively evaluated ones, and indicates that there is something here of greater significance than mere dietary preference.

Chit'lins are considered a delicacy by many black people, and eating chit'lins is often viewed as a traditional dietary habit of black people. Changes in such habits are viewed as gratuitous aping of whites and are considered to imply derogation of these customs. The same sort of sentiment often attaches to other behaviors such as changes in church affiliation of upwardly mobile blacks. Thus, not eating or liking chit'lins may be indicative of assimilationist attitudes, which in turn imply a rejection of one's black brothers and sisters. It is perhaps no longer necessary to mention that assimilation is far from a neutral term intraculturally. Blacks have traditionally shown ambivalence toward the abandonment of ethnic heritage. Many strong attitudes attached to certain kinds of cultural behavior seem to reflect a fear of cultural extermination.

It is not clear at the outset to whom the accusation of being an assimilationist was aimed. Ostensibly, Barbara addressed her remarks to me. Yet Mary's response seems to indicate that she felt herself to be the real addressee in this instance. The signifier may employ the tactic of obscuring his addressee as part of his strategy. In the following case the remark is, on the surface, directed toward no one in particular.

(2)   I saw a woman the other day in a pair of stretch pants, she must have weighed 300 pounds. If she knew how she looked she would burn those things.

Such a remark may have particular significance to the 235-pound member of the audience who is frequently seen about town in stretch pants. She is likely to interpret this remark as directed at her, with the intent of providing her with the information that she looks singularly unattractive so attired.

The technique is fairly straightforward. The speaker simply chooses a topic which is selectively relevant to his audience. A speaker who has a captive audience, such as a minister, may be accused of signifying by virtue of his text being too timely and selectively apropos to segments of his audience.

It might be proposed that Mary intervened in the hope of rescuing me from a dilemma by asserting the absence of any necessary relationships between dietary habits and assimilationist attitudes. However, Barbara's further remarks lend credence to the original hypothesis and suggest that Mary was correct in her interpretation, that she *was* the target of the insinuation.

Barbara: I guess she was saying all that for your benefit. At least, I hope she wasn't trying to fool me. If she weren't so worried about keeping up with her saditty friends, she would eat less T-bone steak and buy some shoes for her kids once in a while.

Although Mary never explicitly accuses Barbara of signifying, her response seems tantamount to such an accusation, as is evidenced by Barbara's denial. Mary's indignation registers quite accurately the spirit in which some signifying is taken.

This brings us to another feature of signifying: The message often carries some negative import for the addressee. Mary's response deserves note. Her retaliation also involves signifying. While talking about obstacles to brotherhood, she intimates that behavior such as that engaged in by Barbara is typical of artificially induced sources of schism which are in essence superficial in their focus, and which, in turn, might be viewed as a comment on the character of the individual who introduces divisiveness on such trivial grounds.

Barbara insulted Mary, her motive perhaps being to injure her feelings or lower her self-esteem. An informant asked to interpret this interchange went further in imputing motives by suggesting possible reasons for Barbara's behavior. He said that the answer was buried in the past. Perhaps Barbara was repaying Mary for some insult of the past, settling a score, as it were. He suggested that Barbara's goal was to raise her own self-esteem by asserting superiority of a sort over Mary. Moreover, he said that this kind of interchange was probably symptomatic of the relationship between the two women and that one could expect to find them jockeying for position on any number of issues. "Barbara was trying to *rank* Mary," to put her down by typing her. This individual seemed to be defining the function of signifying as the establishment of dominance in this case.

Messages like the preceding are indirect not because they are cryptic (i.e., difficult to decode) but because they somehow force the hearer to take additional steps. To understand the significance of not eating chit'lins, one must voyage to the black social world and discover the characteristics of social types referred to and the cultural values and attitudes toward them.

The indirect message may take any number of forms, however, as in the following example:

(3)   The relevant background information lacking in this interchange is that the husband is a member of the class of individuals who do not wear suits to work.
Wife: Where are you going?
Husband: I'm going to work.
Wife: (You're wearing) a suit, tie, and white shirt? You didn't tell me you got a promotion.

The wife, in this case, is examining the truth value of her husband's assertion (A) "I'm going to work" by stating the obvious truth that (B) he is wearing a suit.

Implicit is the inappropriateness of this dress as measured against shared background knowledge. In order to account for this discrepancy, she advances the hypothesis (C) that he has received a promotion and is now a member of the class of people who wear suits to work. B is obviously true, and if C is not true, then A must also be false. Having no reason to suspect that C is true, she is signifying that he is not going to work and moreover, that he is lying about his destination.

Now the wife could have chosen a more straightforward way of finding an acceptable reason for her husband's unusual attire. She might have asked, e.g., "Why are you wearing a suit?" And he could have pleaded some unusual circumstances. Her choice to entrap him suggests that she was not really seeking information but more than likely already had some answers in mind. While it seems reasonable to conclude that an accusation of lying is implicit in the interchange, and one would guess that the wife's intent is equally apparent to the husband, this accusation is never made explicit.

This brings us to some latent advantages of indirect messages, especially those with negative import for the receiver. Such messages, because of their form – they contain both explicit and implicit content – structure interpretation in such a way that the parties have the option of avoiding a real confrontation (Brown (1958:314) provides a similar discussion). Alternately, they provoke confrontations without at the same time exposing unequivocally the speaker's intent. The advantage in either case is for the speaker because it gives him control of the situation at the receiver's expense. The speaker, because of the purposeful ambiguity of his original remark, reserves the right to subsequently insist on the harmless interpretation rather than the provocative one. When the situation is such that there is no ambiguity in determining the addressee, the addressee faces the possibility that if he attempts to confront the speaker, the latter will deny the message or intent imputed, leaving him in the embarrassing predicament of appearing contentious.

Picture, if you will, the secretary who has become uneasy about the tendency of her knee to come into contact with the hand of her middle-aged boss. She finally decides to confront him and indignantly informs him that she is not that kind of a girl. He responds by feigning hurt innocence: "How could you accuse me of such a thing?" If his innocence is genuine, her misconstrual of the significance of these occasions of body contact possibly comments on her character more than his. She has no way of being certain, and she feels foolish. Now a secretary skilled in the art of signifying could have avoided the possibility of "having the tables turned" by saying "Oh, excuse me Mr. Smith, I didn't mean to get my knee in your way." He would have surely understood her message if he were guilty, and a confrontation would have been avoided. If he were innocent, the remark would have probably been of no consequence.

When there is some ambiguity with reference to the addressee, as in the first example, the hearer must expose himself as the target before the confrontation can take place. The speaker still has the option of retreating and the opportunity, while feigning innocence, to jibe, "Well, if the shoe fits, wear it." The individual who has a well-known reputation for this kind of signifying is felt to be sly and, sometimes, not man or woman enough to come out and say what he means.

Signifying does not, however, always have negative valuations attached to it; it is clearly thought of as a kind of art – a clever way of conveying messages. In fact, it does not lose its artistic merit even when it is malicious. It takes some skill to construct messages with multilevel meanings, and it sometimes takes equal expertise in unraveling the puzzle presented in all of its many implications. Just as in certain circles the clever punster derives satisfaction and is rewarded by his hearers for constructing a multisided pun, the signifier is also rewarded for his cleverness.

(4) The following interchange took place in a public park. Three young men in their early twenties sat down with the researcher, one of whom initiated a conversation in this way:

I: Mama, you sho is fine.
R: That ain' no way to talk to your mother.
[Laughter]
I: You married?
R: Um hm.
I: Is your husband married?
[Laughter]
R: Very.
[The conversation continues with the same young man doing most of the talking. He questions me about what I am doing and I tell him about my research project. After a couple of minutes of discussing "rapping," he returns to his original style.]
I: Baby, you a real scholar. I can tell you want to learn. Now if you'll just cooperate a li'l bit, I'll show you what a good teacher I am. But first we got to get into my area of expertise.
R: I may be wrong but seems to me we already in your area of expertise.
[Laughter]
I: You ain' so bad yourself, girl. I ain't heard you stutter yet. You a li'l fixated on your subject though. I want to help a sweet thang like you all I can. I figure all that book learning you got must mean you been neglecting other areas of your education.
II: Talk that talk! [Gloss: Olé]
R: Why don't you let me point out where I can best use your help.
I: Are you sure you in the best position to know?
[Laughter]
I: I'mo leave you alone, girl. Ask me what you want to know. Tempus fugit, baby.
[Laughter]

The folk label for the kind of talking engaged in by I is *rapping*, defined by Kochman as "a fluent and lively way of talking characterized by a high degree of personal style," which may be used when its function is referential or directive – to get something from someone or get someone to do something. The interchange is laced with innuendo – signifying because it alludes to and implies things which are never made explicit.

The utterance which initiated the conversation was intended from all indications as a compliment and was accepted as such. The manner in which it was framed is rather stylized and jocularly effusive, and as such makes the speaker's remarks less bold and presumptuous and is permissive of a response which can acknowledge the compliment in a similar and jokingly impersonal fashion. The most salient purpose of the compliment was to initiate a conversation with a strange woman. The response served to indicate to the speaker that he was free to continue; probably any response (or none at all) would not have terminated his attempt to engage the hearer, but the present one signaled to the speaker that it was appropriate to continue in his original style. The factor of the audience is crucial because it obliges the speaker to continue attempting to engage the addressee once he has begun. The speaker at all points has a surface addressee, but the linguistic and nonlinguistic responses of the other two young men indicate that they are very aware of being integral participants in this interchange. The question "Is your husband married?" is meant to suggest to the hearer, who seeks to turn down the speaker's advances by pleading marital ties, that such bonds should not be treated as inhibitory except when one's husband has by his behavior shown similar inhibition.

The speaker adjusts his rap to appeal to the scholarly leanings of his addressee, who responds by suggesting that he is presently engaging in his area of virtuosity. I responds to this left-handed compliment by pointing out that the researcher is engaging in the same kind of speech behavior and is apparently an experienced player of the game – "I ain't heard you stutter yet." – which is evidenced by her unfaltering responses. At the same time he notes the narrowness of the speaker's interests, and states the evidence leading him to the conclusion that there must be gaps in her knowledge. He benevolently offers his aid. His maneuvers are offensive and calculated to produce defensive responses. His repeated offers of aid are intended ironically. A member of the audience interjects, "Talk that talk!" This phrase is frequently used to signal approval of some speaker's virtuosity in using language skillfully and colorfully and, moreover, in using language which is appro-priate and effective to the social context.

The content of the message is highly directive. Those unfamiliar with black cultural forms might in fact interpret the message as threatening. But there are many linguistic cues that suggest that the surface meaning is not to be taken seriously. Note particularly the use of such expressions as "scholar," "cooperate," "area of expertise," "fixated on your subject," and "neglecting other areas of your education." All these relatively formal or literary expressions occur in sentences spoken with typically black phonology and black grammar (e.g., "I ain't heard..." and "Are you sure you in the best position to know?"). By his code selection and by paralinguistic cues such as a highly stylized leer, the speaker indicates that he is parodying a tête-à-tête and not attempting to engage the researcher in anything other than conversation. He is merely demonstrating his ability to use persuasive language, "playing a game," as it were. The researcher signals acknowledgment by her use of black forms such as "That ain' no way...", and "...we already in...". The speaker indicates that the game is over by saying, "I'mo leave you alone," and redirects the conversation. The juxtaposition of the lexical items "tempus fugit" and "baby," which typically are not paired, is meant to evoke more humor by accentu-ating the stylistic dissonance of the speech sequence.

Signifying as a Form of Verbal Art

All other conditions permitting, a style which has artistic merit is more likely to be selected than one which does not because of positive cultural values assigned to the skillful use of speech. Having discussed some of the characteristics of signifying, I would now like to examine briefly the artistic characteristics of signifying.

No attempt will be made here to formulate an all-encompassing definition of art. That individuals may differ in their conceptions of art is made patently clear, e.g., by

Abrahams's (1964:54) summarizing statement that signifying is "many facets of the smart-alecky attitude." That my appreciation differs has, more than likely, been communicated in these pages. For present purposes, what is art is simply what native speakers judge witty, skillful, and worthy of praise. This is a working definition at best. It nevertheless serves to limit our field of discourse and, more importantly, to base our judgments on the native speaker's own point of view.

It is true that poor attempts at signifying exist. That these attempts are poor art rather than non-art is clear from comments with which some of them are met. Needless and extreme circumlocution is considered poor art. In this connection, Labov has made similar comments about sounding (Labov et al. 1968). He cites peer group members as reacting to some sounds with such metalinguistic responses as "That's phony" and "That's lame." Signifying may be met with similar critical remarks. Such failures, incidentally, are as interesting as the successes, for they provide clues as to the rules by violating one or more of them while, at the same time, meeting other criteria.

One of the defining characteristics of signifying is its indirect intent or metaphorical reference. This indirection appears to be almost purely stylistic. It may sometimes have the function of being euphemistic or diplomatic, but its art characteristics remain in the forefront even in such cases. Without the element of indirection, a speech act could not be considered signifying. Indirection means here that the correct semantic (referential interpretation) or signification of the utterance cannot be arrived at by a consideration of the dictionary meaning of the lexical items involved and the syntactic rules for their combination alone. The apparent significance of the message differs from its real significance.

Meaning conveyed is not apparent meaning. Apparent meaning serves as a key which directs hearers to some shared knowledge, attitudes, and values or signals that reference must be processed metaphorically. The words spoken may actually refer to this shared knowledge by contradicting it or by giving what is known to be an impossible explanation of some obvious fact. The indirection, then, depends for its decoding upon shared knowledge of the participants, and this shared knowledge operates on two levels.

It must be employed, first of all, by the participants in a speech act in the recognition that signifying is occurring and that the dictionary-syntactical meaning of the utterance is to be ignored. Second, this shared knowledge must be employed in the reinterpretation of the utterance. It is the cleverness used in directing the attention of the hearer and audience to this shared knowledge upon which a speaker's artistic talent is judged.

Topic may have something to do with the artistic merit of an act of signifying. Although practically any topic may be signified about, some topics are more likely to make the overall act of signifying more appreciated. Sex is one such topic. For example, an individual offering an explanation for a friend's recent grade slump quipped, "He can't forget what happened to him underneath the apple tree," implying that the young man was preoccupied with sex at this point in his life and that the preoccupation stemmed from the relative novelty of the experience. A topic which is suggested by ongoing conversation is appreciated more than one which is peripheral. Finally, an act of *signifying* which tops a preceding one, in a verbal dueling sense, is especially appreciated.

Kochman cites such an example in the context of a discussion of *rapping:*

A man coming from the bathroom forgot to zip his pants. An unescorted party of women kept watching him and laughing among themselves. The man's friends hip (inform) him to what's going on. He approaches one woman – "Hey, baby, did you see that big Cadillac with the full tires, ready to roll in action just for you?" She answers, "No, mother-fucker, but I saw a little gray Volkswagen with two flat tires." (1969:27)

As mentioned earlier, signifying may be a tactic used in rapping, defined by Kochman as "a fluent and lively way of talking, always characterized by a high degree of personal style" (1969:27).

Verbal dueling is clearly occurring; the first act of signifying is an indirect and humorous way of referring to shared knowledge – the women have been laughing at the man's predicament. It is indirect in that it doesn't mention what is obviously being referred to. The speaker has cleverly capitalized on a potentially embarrassing situation by taking the offensive and at the same time, displaying his verbal skill. He emphasizes the sexual aspect of the situation with a metaphor that implies power and class. However, he is, as Kochman says, "capped." The woman wins the verbal duel by replying with an act of signifying which builds on the previous one. The reply is indirect, sexual, and appropriate to the situation. In addition, it employs the same kind of metaphor and is, therefore, very effective.

Motherfucker is a rather common term of address in such acts of verbal dueling. The term *nigger* also is common in such contexts, e.g., "Nigger, it was a monkey one time wasn't satisfied till his ass was grass" and "Nigger, I'm gon be like white on rice on you ass."

These two examples are illustrative of a number of points of good signifying. Both depend on a good deal of shared cultural knowledge for their correct semantic interpretation. It is the intricacy of the allusion to shared knowledge that makes for the success of these speech acts. The first refers to the toast "The Signifying Monkey." The monkey signified at the lion until he got himself in trouble. A knowledge of this toast is necessary for an interpretation of the message. "Until his ass was grass" – meaning "until he was beaten up" – can only be understood in the light of its common use in the speech of members of the culture and occurs in such forms as "His ass was grass and I was the lawnmower." What this example means is something like: You have been signifying at me and, like the monkey, you are treading on dangerously thin ice. If you don't stop, I am likely to become angry and beat you!

"Nigger, I'm gon be like white on rice on your ass" is doubly clever. A common way of threatening to beat someone is to say, "I'm gonna be all over your ass." And how is white on rice? – all over it. Metaphors such as these may lose their effectiveness over time due to overuse. They lose value as clever wit.

The use of the term *nigger* in these examples is of considerable linguistic interest. It is often coupled with code features which are far removed from standard English. That is, the code utilizes many linguistic markers which differentiate black speech from standard English or white speech. Frequently, more such markers than might ordinarily appear in the language of the speaker are used. Thus participants in these speech acts must show at least some degree of bidialectalism in black and standard English. They must be able to shift from one code to another for stylistic effect.

Note, e.g., that the use of the term *nigger* with other black English markers has the effect of "smiling when you say that." The use of standard English with *nigger*, in the words of an informant, represents "the wrong tone of voice" and may be taken as abusive.

Code selection and terminological choice thus have the same function. They highlight the fact that black English is being used and that what is being engaged in is a black speech act. More is conveyed here than simple emphasis on group solidarity. The hearer is told that this is an instance of black verbal art and should be interpreted in terms of the subcultural rules for interpreting such speech acts.

Code and content serve to define the style being used, to indicate its tone, and to describe the setting and participants as being appropriate to the use of such an artistic style. Further, such features indicate that it should be recognized that a verbal duel is occurring and that what is said is meant in a joking, perhaps also threatening, manner. A slight switch in code may carry implications for other components in the speech act. Because verbal dueling treads a fine line between play and real aggression, it is a kind of linguistic activity which requires strict adherence to sociolinguistic rules. To correctly decode the message, a hearer must be finely tuned to values which he observes in relation to all other components of the speech act. He must rely on his conscious or unconscious knowledge of the sociolinguistic rules governing this usage.

Marking

A common black narrative tactic in the folk tale genre and in accounts of actual events is the individuation of characters through the use of direct quotation. When in addition, in reproducing the words of individual actors, a narrator affects the voice and mannerisms of the speakers, he is using the style referred to as *marking* (clearly related to standard English "mocking"). Marking is essentially a mode of characterization. The marker attempts to report not only what was said but the way it was said, in order to offer implicit comment on the speaker's background, personality, or intent. Rather than introducing personality or character traits in some summary form, such information is conveyed by reproducing or sometimes inserting aspects of speech ranging from phonological features to particular content which carry expressive value. The meaning in the message of the marker is signaled and revealed by his reproduction of such things as phonological or grammatical peculiarities, his preservation of mispronounced words or provincial idioms, dialectal pronunciation, and, most particularly, paralinguistic mimicry.

The marker's choice to reproduce such features may reflect only his desire to characterize the speaker. It frequently signifies, however, that the characterization itself is relevant for further processing the meaning of the speaker's words. If, e.g., some expressive feature has been taken as a symbol of the speaker's membership in a particular group, his credibility may come into question on these grounds alone.

The marker attempts to replay a scene for his hearers. He may seek to give the implications of the speaker's remarks, to indicate whether the emotions and affect displayed by the speaker were genuine or feigned, in short to give his audience the full benefit of all the information he was able to process by virtue of expressive or context cues imparted by the speaker. His performance may be more in the nature of parody and caricature than true imitation. But the features selected to overplay are those which are associated with membership in some class. His ability to get his message across, in fact, relies on folk notions of the covariance of linguistic and nonlinguistic categories, combined, of course, with whatever special skill he possesses for creating imagery.

The kind of context most likely to elicit marking is one in which the marker assumes his hearers are sufficiently like himself to be able to interpret this metaphoric communication. Since there is, more likely than not, something unflattering about the characterization, and the element of ridicule is so salient, the relationship between a marker and his audience is likely to be one of familiarity and intimacy and mutual positive affect.

An informant quoted a neighbor to give me an appreciation of her dislike for the woman. She quoted the following comment from Pearl in a style carefully articulated to depict her as "putting on the dog," parodying gestures which gave the impression that Pearl is preposterously affected: "You know my family owns their own home and I'm just living here temporarily because it is more beneficial to collect the rent from my own home and rent a less expensive apartment." "That's the kind of person she is," my informant added, feeling no need for further explanation. This is, incidentally, a caricature of a social type which is frequently the object of scorn and derision. The quote was delivered at a pitch considerably higher than was usual for the informant, and the words were enunciated carefully so as to avoid loss of sounds and elision characteristic of fluid speech. What was implied was not that the phonological patterns mimicked are to be associated with affectation in a one–one relationship but that they symbolize affectation here. The marker was essentially giving implicit recognition to the fact that major disturbances in fluency are indexes of "monitored" speech. The presence of the features are grounds for the inference that the speaker is engaged in impression management which is contextually inappropriate. Individuals who are characterized as "trying to talk proper" are frequently marked in a tone of voice which is rather falsetto.

A marker wishing to convey a particular impression of a speaker may choose to deliver a quotation in a style which is felt to best suit what he feels lies underneath impression management or what is obscured by the speaker's effective manipulation of language. In the following example, the marker departs radically from the style of the speaker for purposes of disambiguation. The individuals here, with the exception of S_1, had recently attended the convention of a large corporation and had been part of a group which had been meeting prior to the convention to develop some strategy for putting pressure on the corporation to hire more blacks in executive positions. They had planned to bring the matter up at a general meeting of delegates, but before they had an opportunity to do so, a black company man spoke before the entire body. S_2 said, "After he spoke our whole strategy was undermined, there was no way to get around his impact on the whites."

S_1: What did he say?

S_2: [Drawling] He said, "Ah'm so-o-o happy to be here today. First of all, ah want to thank all you good white folks for creatin so many opportunities for us niggers and ya'll can be sho that as soon as we can git ourselves qualified we gon be filin our applications. Ya'll done done what we been waiting for a long time. Ya'll done give a colored man a good job with the company."

S$_1$: Did he really say that?

S$_3$: Um hm, yes he said it. Girl, where have you been. [Put down by intimating S$_1$ was being literal]

S$_1$: Yeah, I understand, but what did he really say?

S$_4$: He said, "This is a moment of great personal pride for me. My very presence here is a tribute to the civil rights movement. We now have ample evidence of the good faith of the company and we must now begin to prepare ourselves to handle more responsible positions. This is a major step forward on the part of the company. The next step is up to us." In other words, he said just what [S$_2$] said he said. He sold us out by accepting that kind of tokenism.

S$_2$ attempted to characterize the speaker as an Uncle Tom by using exaggerated stereotyped southern speech coupled with content that was compromising and denigrating. It would certainly be an overstatement to conclude that southern regional speech is taken by anyone as a sign of being an "Uncle Tom," but there is an historical association with the model of this stereotype being southern.

The characterization of individuals according to the way they speak is, of course, not peculiar to black people, although the implicit association of particular ways of speaking with specific social types may be more elaborated than elsewhere.

The parodying of southern regional black speech may sometimes serve as a device for characterizing a speaker as uneducated or unintelligent, and sometimes it is used to underscore the guilelessness of the speaker. The marker encodes his subjective reactions to the speaker and is concerned with the expressive function of speech more than its referential function.

Because marking relies on linguistic expression for the communication of messages, it is revealing of attitudes and values relating to language. It frequently conveys many subtleties and can be a significant source of information about conscious and unconscious attitudes toward language. An individual, on occasion, may mark a nonblack using exaggerated black English, with the emphasis clearly being on communicating that the subject was uneducated and used nonstandard usages. Perhaps more than anything, marking exhibits a finely tuned linguistic awareness in some areas and a good deal of verbal virtuosity in being able to reproduce aspects of speech which are useful in this kind of metaphorical communication.

Conclusion

Signifying and marking exemplify the close relationship of message form to content and function which characterizes black verbal behavior. Meaning, often assumed by linguists to be signaled entirely through code features, is actually dependent upon a consideration of other components of a speech act (cf. Gumperz 1964). A remark taken in the spirit of verbal dueling may, e.g., be interpreted as an insult by virtue of what on the surface seems to be merely a minor change in personnel, or a minor change in code or topic. Crucially, paralinguistic features must be made to conform to the rules. Change in posture, speech rate, tone of voice, facial expression, etc., may signal a change in meaning. The audience must also be sensitive to these cues. A change in meaning may signal that members of the audience must shift their responses, and that metalinguistic comments may no longer be appropriate.

It is this focus in black culture – the necessity of applying sociolinguistic rules, in addition to the frequent appeal to shared background knowledge for correct semantic interpretation – that accounts for some of the unique character and flavor of black speech. Pure syntactic and lexical elaboration is supplemented by an elaboration of the ability to carefully and skillfully manipulate other components of the speech act in order to create new meanings.

REFERENCES

Abrahams, Roger (1964). *Deep Down in the Jungle. Negro Narrative Folklore from the Streets of Philadelphia*. Hatboro, PA: Folklore Associates.

Brown, Roger W. (1958). *Words and Things*. New York: Free Press.

Gumperz, John J. (1964). Linguistic and Social Interaction in Two Communities. In John J. Gumperz and Dell Hymes (eds.), The Ethnography of Communication. *American Anthropologist* 66, 6, pt. II:137–54.

Hymes, Dell (1967). Models of the Interaction of Language and Social Setting. *Journal of Social Issues* 23 (2):8–28.

Kochman, Thomas (1969). "Rapping" in the Black Ghetto. *Trans-Action*, February 1969:26–34.

Labov, William, Paul Cohen, Clarence Robins, and John Lewis (1968). *A Study of Non-standard English of Negro and Puerto Rican Speakers in New York City*, Vol. II, pp. 76–152. Department of Linguistics, Columbia University, New York.

7

Verbal Art as Performance[1]

Richard Bauman

We will be concerned in this paper to develop a conception of verbal art as performance, based upon an understanding of performance as a mode of speaking. In constructing this framework for a performance-centered approach to verbal art, we have started from the position of the folklorist, but have drawn concepts and ideas from a wide range of disciplines, chiefly anthropology, linguistics, and literary criticism. Each of these disciplines has its own distinctive perspective on verbal art, and a long tradition of independent scholarship in its study. From at least the time of Herder, however, there has been an integrative tradition as well in the study of verbal art, manifested in the work of such figures as Edward Sapir, Roman Jakobson, and Dell Hymes, scholars who have operated at an intellectual level beyond the boundaries which separate academic disciplines, sharing an interest in the esthetic dimension of social and cultural life in human communities as manifested through the use of language. The present paper is offered in the spirit of that integrative tradition.

In a recent collection of conceptual and theoretical essays in folklore, assembled to indicate a range of new perspectives in the field, it was emphasized in the Introduction that the contributors shared a common concern with performance as an organizing principle (Bauman 1972a). The term performance was employed there, as it was by several of the contributors to the collection, because it conveyed a dual sense of artistic *action* – the doing of folklore – and artistic *event* – the performance situation, involving performer, art form, audience, and setting – both of which are central to the developing performance approach to folklore. This usage accorded well with the conventional meaning of the term "performance," and served to point up the fundamental reorientation from folklore as materials to folklore as communication which characterized the thinking of the contributors. Conventional meanings can carry scholarship just so far, however, before the lack of conceptual rigor begins to constrain analytical insight rather than advancing it. In view of the centrality of performance to the orientation of increasing numbers of folklorists and anthropologists interested in verbal art,[2] the time seems opportune for efforts aimed at expanding the conceptual content of folkloric performance as a communicative phenomenon, beyond the general usage that has carried us up to this point. That is the purpose of this essay.

One orientational and terminological point before proceeding: consistent with the chiefly sociolinguistic and anthropological roots of the performance approach, the terms "verbal art" and "oral literature" provide a better frame of reference, at least as a point of departure for the ideas to be advanced here, than the more diffuse and problematic term "folklore." "Spoken art" might be even better, insofar as this paper is concerned solely with a way of speaking and its attendant phenomena, but the term has never achieved currency in any of the disciplines where it might have served a useful purpose – folklore, anthropology, or linguistics.[3] Many things have been studied under the name of folklore, but verbal art has always been at or near the center of the larger domain, and has constituted the chief common ground between anthropological folklorists and those of other persuasions. Accordingly, the shift from the "folklore" of the preceding paragraph to the "verbal art" of those to follow is neither unprecedented nor arbitrary, but will serve, hopefully, to make somewhat clearer the universe of discourse within which the ideas which follow have been formulated.

Let us make explicit as well that a great deal more is intended here than a convenient relabeling of what is already known. The conception of performance to be developed in these pages is not simply an alternative perspective on the familiar genres of oral literature long studied by folklorists and anthropologists. It is that, but it is more than that as well. Performance, as we conceive of it and as our examples have been selected to illustrate, is a unifying thread typing together the marked, segregated esthetic genres and other spheres of verbal behavior into a general unified conception of verbal art as a way of speaking. Verbal art may comprehend both myth narration and the speech expected of certain members of society whenever they open their mouths, and it is performance that brings them together in culture-specific and variable ways, ways that are to be discovered ethnographically within each culture and community.

The Nature of Performance

Modern theories of the nature of verbal art, whether in anthropology, linguistics, or literature, tend overwhelmingly to be constructed in terms of special usages or patterning of formal features within texts. General formulations identify a primary "focus on the message for its own sake" (Jakobson 1960:356; Stankiewicz 1960:14–15) or a "concern with the form of expression, over and above the needs of communication" (Bascom 1955:247) as the essence of verbal art. Others are more specific about the nature or consequences of such a focus or concern, suggesting, for example, that the touchstone of verbal art lies in a maximized "use of the devices of the language in such a way that this use itself attracts attention and is perceived as uncommon" (Havránek 1964:10). Among certain linguists, the idea has some currency that verbal art "in some way deviates from norms which we, as members of society, have learnt to expect in the medium used" (Leech 1969:56; cf. Stankiewicz 1960:12; Durbin 1971), while others of their colleagues make a point of the "multiplicity of *additional formal laws* restricting the poet's free choice of expressions" (Fónagy 1965:72; italics in original).

Whatever their differences, of focus or emphasis, all of these approaches make for a conception of verbal art that is text-centered. For all, the artful, esthetic quality of an utterance resides in the way in which language is used in the construction of the textual item. To be sure, it may be considered necessary, at least implicitly, to assess the text against the background of general linguistic norms, but it is the text itself that remains the unit of analysis and point of departure for proponents of these approaches. This in turn places severe constraints on the development of a meaningful framework for the understanding of verbal art as performance, as a species of situated human communication, a way of speaking.

It is, of course, possible to move from artistic texts, identified in formal or other terms, to performance, by simply looking at how such texts are rendered, in action terms. But this is to proceed backwards, by approaching phenomena whose primary social reality lies in their nature as oral communication in terms of the abstracted textual products of the communicative process. As we shall see, oral literary texts, though they may fulfill the formal measures of verbal art, be accurately recorded, and bear strong associations with performance in their conventional contexts, may nevertheless not be the products of performance, but of rendition in another communicative mode. How many of the texts in our collections represent recordings of informants' abstracts, resumés, or reports of performances and performance forms rather than true performances (cf. Tedlock 1972)? By identifying the nature of performance and distinguishing it from other ways of speaking, we will have, among other things, a measure of the authenticity of collected oral literary texts.

A performance-centered conception of verbal art calls for an approach through performance itself. In such an approach, the formal manipulation of linguistic features is secondary to the nature of performance, per se, conceived of and defined as a mode of communication.

There is a very old conception of verbal art as communication which goes back at least to Plato's insistence that literature is lies. The notion, also manifest in Sir Philip Sidney's oft-quoted dictum, "the poet nothing affirmth" (Ohmann 1971:5) holds that whatever the propositional content of an item of verbal art, its meaning is somehow cancelled out or rendered inoperative by the nature of the utterance as verbal art. A more recent expression of this conception is to be found in the writings of the British Ordinary Language philosopher, J. L. Austin. Austin maintains, "of any and every utterance," that it will be *"in a peculiar way* hollow or void if said by an actor on the stage ... or spoken in soliloquy." He continues, "language in such circumstances is in special ways – intelligibly – used not seriously, but in ways *parasitic* upon its normal use – ways which fall under the doctrine of *etiolations* of language" (Austin 1962:21–2; italics in original).[4]

Leaving aside the unfortunate suggestion that the uses Austin mentions exert a weakening influence on language, a product of his particular bias, we may abstract from the cited passage the suggestion that performance represents a transformation of the basic referential ("serious," "normal" in Austin's terms) uses of language. In other words, in artistic performance of this kind, there is something going on in the communicative interchange which says to the auditor, "interpret what I say in some special sense; do not take it to mean what the words alone, taken literally, would convey." This may lead to the further suggestion that performance sets up, or represents, an interpretative frame within which the messages being communicated are to be understood, and that this frame contrasts with at least one other frame, the literal.

In employing the term "frame" here, I am drawing not upon Austin, but on the powerful insights of Gregory Bateson, and the more recent and equally provocative work of Erving Goffman (1974). Bateson first developed systematically on the notion of frame as a defined interpretive context providing guidelines for discriminating between orders of message (1972 [1956]:222), in his seminal article, "A Theory of Play and Fantasy" (1972 [1955]:177–93). We shall return to aspects of this theory, and of Goffman's, in more detail below.[5]

Although the notion of performance as a frame was introduced above, in connection with Austin's thinking, as contrasting with literal communication, it should be made clear from the beginning that many other such frames besides these two may be identified. For example:

– *insinuation*, in which the words spoken are to be interpreted as having a covert and indirect relation to the meaning of the utterance (cf. Austin 1962:121);
– *joking*, in which the words spoken are to be interpreted as not seriously meaning what they might otherwise mean (cf. Austin 1962:121);
– *imitation*, in which the manner of speaking is to be interpreted as being modeled after that of another person or persona;
– *translation*, in which the words spoken are to be interpreted as the equivalent of words originally spoken in another language or code;
– *quotation*, in which the words spoken are to be interpreted as the words of someone other than the speaker (cf. Weinreich 1966:162).

This is a partial and unelaborated list, which does not even adequately sample, much less exhaust, the range of possible interpretive frames within which communication may be couched. It should be noted, moreover, that frames listed may be used in combination, as well as singly. It should also be stressed that although theorists like Austin suggest that the literal frame somehow has priority over all the others – is more "normal" – this is not necessary to the theory, and in fact biases it in unproductive ways (Fish 1973). The notorious difficulty of defining literalness aside, there is growing evidence that literal utterances are no more frequent or "normal" in situated human communication than any of the other frames, and indeed that in spoken communication no such thing as naked literalness may actually exist (Burns 1972; Goffman 1974). For our purposes, all that is necessary is the recognition of performance as a distinctive frame, available as a communicative resource along with the others to speakers in particular communities.[6]

The first major task, then, is to suggest what kind of interpretive frame performance establishes or represents. How is communication that constitutes performance to be interpreted? The following represents a very preliminary attempt to specify the interpretive guidelines set up by the performance frame.

Fundamentally, performance as a mode of spoken verbal communication consists in the assumption of responsibility to an audience for a display of communicative competence. This competence rests on the knowledge and ability to speak in socially appropriate ways. Performance involves on the part of the performer an assumption of accountability to an audience for the way in which communication is carried out, above and beyond its referential content. From the point of view of the audience, the act of expression on the part of the performer is thus marked as subject to evaluation for the way it is done, for the relative skill and effectiveness of the performer's display of competence.[7] Additionally, it is marked as available for the enhancement of experience, through the present enjoyment of the intrinsic qualities of the act of expression itself. Performance thus calls forth special attention to and heightened awareness of the act of expression, and gives license to the audience to regard the act of expression and the performer with special intensity.[8]

Thus conceived, performance is a mode of language use, a way of speaking. The implication of such a concept for a theory of verbal art is this: it is no longer necessary to begin with artful texts, identified on independent formal grounds and then reinjected into situations of use, in order to conceptualize verbal art in communicative terms. Rather, in terms of the approach being developed here, performance becomes *constitutive* of the domain of verbal art as spoken communication.

Some examples may be useful at this point, to demonstrate in empirical terms the application of the notion of performance we have proposed. In several of her writings on the people of the plateau area of the Malagasy Republic (Keenan 1973, 1974), Elinor Keenan delineates the two major ways of speaking identified by this group. The first, called in native terminology *resaka*, may be loosely defined as informal conversation, described by native elders as "everyday talk," or "simple talk." The other way of speaking, *kabary*, is the one of principal interest to us here. *Kabary* is glossed by Keenan as "ceremonial speech, what we might call oratory." The following are excerpts from Keenan's description:

Kabary as a focal point of tradition and as a focal point of artistic expression is ... regarded with great interest. It is not uncommon to see groups of elders evaluating the skills and approaches of speechmakers following a *kabary* performance. A speechmaker who pleases his audience is rewarded with praise such as: "He is a very sharp speechmaker." "He is prepared." "He is a true speechmaker, a child of his father." His words are said to be "well-arranged" and "balanced." His performance is described as "satisfying". ... Evaluations are based on both skill in handling winding speech and on one's ability to follow certain rules governing the sequence and content of particular oratory. (1973:226–7)

And further, "*kabary* performances ... are platforms for exhibiting knowledge of traditional oratory" (1973:229). Wedding *kabary*, in particular, "is the most developed art form in the culture and a source of great delight and interest to all participants" (1973:242).

It is clear from this description that *kabary* represents for the plateau Malagasy a domain of performance. To engage in *kabary* is to assume responsibility to one's audience for a display of competence in the traditional *kabary* forms, to render one's speech subject to evaluation for the quality of one's speaking. One is judged as a speechmaker, for the way one's words are arranged. *Kabary* performances are keenly attended to and actively evaluated, with good performances indeed serving as a source of enjoyment and satisfaction to the auditors, for the way they are done. The ethnography of verbal art among the plateau Malagasy thus becomes centrally the ethnography of *kabary*.

Among the Ilongot of the Philippines, by contrast with the above, there are three major speech styles, described by Michelle Rosaldo: the stylistically unmarked "straight speech" (*qube:nata qupu*), invocatory speech (*nawnaw*), and a third style, *qambaqan*, described as "crooked" or witty talk (Rosaldo 1973). It is not wholly clear from Rosaldo's account whether *nawnaw* involves performance, but *qambaqan* very clearly does. *Qambaqan* is "artful, witty, charming," "a language of display, performance, pose" (Rosaldo 1973:197–8). What is especially noteworthy about speaking among the Ilongot, within our present context, is that the telling of tales, always included in *a priori* text-centered definitions of verbal art, is classified as a kind of "straight speech." That is, storytelling for the Ilongot is not a form of performance, thus in culture-specific communicative terms, not a form of verbal art. The domain of speaking among the Ilongot is to this extent, among many others, organized differently from that of the many cultures in which storytelling does involve performance.

Japanese professional storytellers, for example, as described by Hrdličková, are certainly performers in our sense of the term. For their audiences, "it is not seldom more important *how* a story is told than *what* the story relates. . . . Storytellers regard the mastery of [storytelling] elements as a necessary preliminary stage prior to any successful practicing of their art in public, since the audience not only expects of them an established manner of interpretation, but also rates them according to the degree of artistry the artists command" (Hrdličková 1969:193; italics in original). That is, storytelling involves a display of competence in the manner of telling the story, which is subject to evaluation for the way it is done. The audience derives enjoyment from the performance in proportion to the skill of the narrator (1969:193).

The point to be emphasized here is that just as speaking itself as a cultural system (or as part of cultural systems defined in other terms) will vary from speech community to speech community, so too will the nature and extent of the realm of performance and verbal art (Bauman 1972b). One of the principal questions one must ask in the ethnography of performance is what range of speech activity is regarded as susceptible to performance and what range is conventionally performed, that is, conventionally expected by members of the community to be rendered in a performance mode.[9] For the St. Vincentians, for example, performance may be invoked across a very wide spectrum of speech activity, from oratory, to storytelling, to gossip – even to speaking with a speech impediment – while the seventeenth century Quakers, because of basic attitudes toward speaking in general, restricted performance to an extremely narrow range of activity (Abrahams 1970; Abrahams and Bauman 1971; Bauman 1974, 1975). In performance terms, it is not possible to assert *a priori* that verbal art consists of "folktales, myths, legends, proverbs, riddles, and other 'literary forms'" defined solely in formal terms (Bascom 1955:245). We will return to the culture-specific nature of verbal art as performance below.

The Keying of Performance

Before embarking upon a discussion of the further implications of the notion of performance put forward above, there is one major element integral to the conception of performance as a frame which must be delineated, i.e., the way in which framing is accomplished, or, to use Goffman's term for the process by which frames are invoked and shifted, how performance is *keyed* (Goffman 1974). Here again, we may draw on Bateson's powerful insight, that it is characteristic of communicative interaction that it include a range of explicit or implicit messages which carry instructions on how to interpret the other message(s) being communicated. This communication about communication Bateson termed metacommunication (Ruesch and Bateson 1968:209). In Bateson's terms, "a frame is metacommunicative. Any message which either explicitly or implicitly defines a frame, *ipso facto* gives the receiver instructions or aids in his attempt to understand the messages included within the frame" (Bateson 1972 [1955]:188). All framing, then, including performance, is accomplished through the employment of culturally conventionalized metacommunication. In empirical terms, this means that each speech community will make use of a structured set of distinctive communicative means from among its resources in culturally conventionalized and culture-specific ways to key the performance frame, such that all communication that takes place within that frame is to be understood as performance within that community.

An etic list of communicative means that have been widely documented in various cultures as serving to key performance is not difficult to compile. Such a list would include at least the following:

(1) special codes, e.g., archaic or esoteric language, reserved for and diagnostic of performance (e.g., Toelken 1969; Sherzer 1974);
(2) special formulae that signal performance, such as conventional openings and closings, or explicit statements announcing or asserting performance (e.g., Crowley 1966; Reaver 1972; Uspensky 1972:19; Babcock-Abrahams 1974);
(3) figurative language, such as metaphor, metonymy, etc. (e.g., Keenan 1973, 1974; Fox 1974; Rosaldo 1973; Sherzer 1974);
(4) formal stylistic devices, such as rhyme, vowel harmony, other forms of parallelism (Jakobson 1966, 1968; Stankiewicz 1960:15; Austerlitz 1960; Gossen 1972, 1974; Fox 1974; Sherzer and Sherzer 1972);
(5) special prosodic patterns of tempo, stress, pitch (e.g., Lord 1960; Tedlock 1972);
(6) special paralinguistic patterns of voice quality and vocalization (e.g., Tedlock 1972; McDowell 1974);
(7) appeal to tradition (e.g., Innes 1974:145);
(8) disclaimer of performance (e.g., Darnell 1974; Keenan 1974).

The formal and conventional nature of the devices listed above bears an important relation to the very nature of performance itself. Burke has alerted us to the power of formal patterns to elicit the participation of an audience through the arousal of "an attitude of collaborative expectancy.... Once you grasp the trend of the form, it invites participation." This "yielding to the formal development, surrendering to its symmetry as such" (Burke 1969[1950]:58) fixes the attention of the audience more strongly on the performer, binds the audience to the performer in a relationship of dependence that keeps them caught up in his display. A not insignificant part of the capacity of performance to transform social structure, to be discussed at the end of this paper, resides in the power that the performer derives from the control over his audience afforded him by the formal appeal of his performance.

A list of the kind given above, however, is ultimately of only limited utility, for the essential task in the ethnography of performance is to determine the culture-specific constellations of communicative means that serve to key performance in particular communities. Features such as those listed above may figure in a variety of ways in the speech economy of a community. Rhyme, for example, may be used to key performance, or it may simply be a formal feature of the language, as when it figures in certain forms of reduplication, or it may appear in speech play (which may or may not involve performance). It may even be inadvertent. Interestingly, when this happens in English, there is a traditional formula which may be invoked to disclaim performance retroactively: "I'm a poet and I don't know it; my feet show it, they're longfellows." This is an indication that rhyme often does in fact key performance in English.

The basic point here is that one must determine empirically what are the specific conventionalized means that key performance in a particular community, and that these will vary from one community to another (though one may discover areal and typological patterns, and universal tendencies may exist). Let us consider some examples.

The telling of traditional folktales, or "old stories," in the Bahamas, as described by Daniel J. Crowley, characteristically involves performance. Narrators assume responsibility for the way they render their stories, and their performances are attended to for the enjoyment to be derived from the telling, and evaluated as displays of competence (for evidence of this see Crowley 1966:37, 137–9). Old story performances are keyed by a complex system of communicative means.

One of the most distinctive of these is the word "Bunday," which serves as a "trademark" for old stories, "since its mere mention is the sign for an old story to begin. . . . To the Bahamians, 'Bunday ain't nothing, it just mean is old story.'" Crowley identifies five conventional functions served by "Bunday" as a marker of old story performance: (1) as a means of announcing one's intention to tell a story and testing the audience's willingness to hear it; (2) as a means of recapturing audience attention (the better the storyteller, the less often he must have recourse to this device, but all storytellers must use it occasionally); (3) for emphasis and punctuation; (4) as a filler to cover pauses and other gaps in the narration; (5) as a signal that the story is ended.

In addition to "Bunday," storytelling performance is further signaled by opening and closing formulae. Some of these, such as "Once upon a time, a very good time, monkey chew tobacco, and he spit white lime," are stylistically developed in their own right, while others, like "Once upon a time," are more simple. Closing formulae are more individualized, with the closing "Bunday" coming before, between, or after the formula. To take one characteristic example, which brings the narrative back to the occasion of its telling: "I was passing by, and I say 'Mister Jack, how come you so smart?' And he make at me, and I run, causing me to come here tonight to tell you this wonderful story" (Crowley 1966:35–6).

The keying devices for old story performance further include special words and phrases (e.g., "one more day than all . . . " to begin a new motif), special pronunciations, elaborate onomatopoeia, and a range of metanarrational devices, such as the following of an impossible statement by "If I was going to tell you a story," and then another even more impossible statement (Crowley 1966:26–7). Finally, old story performance is keyed by distinctive paralinguistic and prosodic shifts for the purpose of characterization (e.g., Crowley 1966:67). In sum, this one segment of the Bahamian performance domain is keyed by a complex system of mutually reinforcing means, serving together to signal that an old story is being performed.

As we have noted, the foregoing inventory of keys to old story performance pertains to but a single genre. A full and ideal ethnography of performance would encompass the entire domain, viewing speaking and performance as a cultural system and indicating how the whole range of performance is keyed. Gary Gossen's elegant analyses of Chamula genres of verbal behavior come closest to any work in the literature known to the author to achieving such a description (Gossen 1972, 1974). Within the overall domain of "people's speech" (*sk'op kirsano*), Chamula identify three macro-categories of speech: "ordinary speech" (*loʔil k'op*), "speech for people whose hearts are heated" (*k'op sventa sk'isnah yoʔnlon yuʔun li kirsanoe*), and "pure speech" (*puru k'op*). Ordinary speech is conceived of by the people as unmarked, not special in any way. It is not associated with performance. Speech for people whose hearts are heated and pure speech, on the other hand, are strongly relevant to our discussion.?

As an overall category, what distinguishes speech for people whose hearts are heated from ordinary speech is that it is stylistically marked by a degree of verbatim repetition of words, phrases and metaphors, and in certain sub-categories, or genres, by parallelism in syntax and metaphorical couplets. Pure speech is distinguished in turn from speech for people whose hearts are heated by its relative fixity of form and the greater density of parallelism, either through proliferation of syntactically parallel lines or the "stacking" of metaphorical couplets.

From Gossen's description, it is evident that repetition and parallelism constitute keys to performance for the Chamula. Both speech for people whose hearts are heated and pure speech involve the display of competence, contribute to the enhancement of experience, and are subject to evaluation for the way they are done. There is a crucial point to be made here, however. Speech for people whose hearts are heated is idiosyncratic, unfixed, and markedly less saturated with those features that signal performance. The user of speech for people whose hearts are heated is less fully accountable for a display of competence, his expression is less intensely regarded by the audience, his performance has less to contribute to the enhancement of the audience's experience than the one who uses the forms of pure speech. The performance frame may thus be seen to operate with variable intensity in Chamula speaking.

It is worth underscoring this last point. Art is commonly conceived as an all-or-nothing phenomenon – something either is or is not art – but conceived as performance, in terms of an interpretive frame, verbal art may be culturally defined as varying in intensity as well as range. We are not speaking here of the relative quality of a performance – good performance versus bad performance – but the degree of intensity with which the performance frame operates in a particular range of culturally defined ways of speaking. When we move beyond the first level discrimination of culturally-defined ways of speaking that do not conventionally involve performance (e.g., Chamula ordinary speech, Malagasy *resaka*) versus ways of speaking that do characteristically involve performance (e.g., Chamula speech for people whose hearts are heated and pure speech, Malagasy *kabary*), we need to attend to the relative saturation of the performance frame attendant upon the more specific categories of ways of speaking within the community.

The variable range of performance in Chamula is confirmed by the metalanguage employed by the Chamula in their evaluation of performance. Because of the importance of the evaluative dimension of performance as communication, such metalanguages and the esthetic standards they express constitute an essential consideration in the ethnography of performance; the range of application of such esthetic systems may be the best indicator of the extent of the performance domain within a community (Dundes 1966; Babcock-Abrahams 1974). Increased fixity of form, repetition, and parallelism, which serve as measures of increasing intensity of performance, also signal for the Chamula increasing "heat." Heat is a basic metaphor for the Chamula, symbolizing the orderly, the good, and the beautiful, by derivation from the power of the sun deity. The transition from ordinary speech to speech for people whose hearts are heated to pure speech thus involves a progressive increase in heat and therefore of esthetic and ethical value in speaking.[10]

The Patterning of Performance

Our discussion of Chamula performance has centered upon the way in which performance is keyed, the communicative means that signal that a particular act of expression is being performed. We may advance our considerations still further by recognizing that it is only as these means are embodied in particular genres that they figure in the performance system of the Chamula themselves. That is, the Chamula organize the domain of speaking in terms of genres, i.e., conventionalized message forms, formal structures that incorporate the features that key performance. The association of performance with particular genres is a significant aspect of the patterning of performance within communities. This association is more problematic than text-centered, etic approaches to verbal art would indicate (Ben-Amos 1969).

In the ethnography of performance as a cultural system, the investigator's attention will frequently be attracted first by those genres that are conventionally performed. These are the genres, like the Chamula genres of pure speech or Bahamian old stories, for which there is little or no expectation on the part of members of the community that they will be rendered in any other way. He should be attentive as well, however, for those genres for which the expectation or probability of performance is lower, for which performance is felt to be more optional, but which occasion no surprise if they are performed. A familiar example from contemporary American society might be the personal narrative, which is frequently rendered in a simply repertorial mode, but which may well be highlighted as performance. There will, of course, in any society, be a range of verbal genres that are not rendered as performances. These will be viewed as not involving the kind of competence that is susceptible to display, not lending themselves for the enhancement of experience. Not to be forgotten are those genres that are considered by members of the community to be performance forms, but that are nevertheless not performed, as when there is no one left who is competent to perform them, or conditions for appropriate performance no longer exist. A related phenomenon is what Hymes calls performance in a perfunctory key (personal communication), in which the responsibility for a display of communicative competence is undertaken out of a sense of cultural duty, traditional obligation, but offering, because of changed circumstances, relatively little pleasure or enhancement of experience. One thinks, for example, of some masses in Latin. Such performances may, however, be a means of preserving performance forms for later reinvigoration and restoration to the level of full performance.

It should be noted, with reference to the native organization of the domain of speaking and cultural expectations for performance, that the members of a community may conceptualize speech activity in terms of acts rather than genres. The St. Vincentians are a case in point (Abrahams and Bauman 1971). Speech acts and genres are, of course, analytically distinct, the former having to do with speech behavior, the latter with the verbal products of that behavior. For an oral culture, however, the distinction between the act of speaking and the form of the utterance tends characteristically not to be significant, if it is recognized at all. Thus a particular performance system may well be organized by members of the community in terms of speech acts that conventionally involve performance, others that may or may not, and still others for which performance is not a relevant consideration.

We view the act of performance as situated behavior, situated within and rendered meaningful with reference to relevant contexts. Such contexts may be identified at a variety of levels – in terms of settings, for example, the culturally-defined places where performance occurs. Institutions too – religion, education, politics – may be viewed from the perspective of the way in which they do or do not represent contexts for performance within communities. Most important as an organizing principle in the ethnography of performance is the event, or scene, within which performance occurs (see, e.g., Kirshenblatt-Gimblett 1974).

There are, first of all, events for which performance is required, for which it is a criterial attribute, such that performance is a necessary component for a particular event to count as a valid instance of the class. These will be what Singer calls "cultural performances" (Singer 1972:71). They may be organized and conducted primarily for entertainment, such as Bahamian old story sessions or Vincentian tea meetings, or they may have some other stated primary purpose, like Malagasy bride-price meetings, but performance will be as integral a component for the latter as for the former.

As with genres and acts, there are other events for which performance is an optional feature, not necessary or invariably expected, but not unexpected or surprising, as when someone tells jokes at a party. Again, there will be a further range of events in which performance is extraneous, not a relevant variable insofar as people categorize and participate in the events of their culture.

The structure of performance events is a product of the interplay of many factors, including setting, act sequence, and ground rules of performance. These last will consist of the set of cultural themes and social-interactional organizing principles that govern the conduct of performance (Bauman and Sherzer 1974, Sect. III). As a kind of speaking, performance will be subject to a range of community ground rules that regulate speaking in general, but there will also be a set of ground rules specific to performance itself. Basic, too, to the structure of performance events are the participants, performer(s), and audience. Performance roles constitute a major dimension of the patterning of performance within communities.

As with events, certain roles will incorporate performance as a definitive attribute. Performance is necessary to establish oneself in the role, such that one cannot be considered an incumbent of the role without being a performer of verbal art, like the *sgealai*, the traditional Irish storyteller (Delargy 1945). Other roles may be more loosely associated with performance, such that members of the community have a certain expectation of performance from a person in a particular role, but it is neither required of everyone in the role, nor surprising when it does not occur. Salesmen may serve as an example here, in that there is a loose expectation in contemporary American culture that salesmen are often good performers of jokes, but no one requires or expects this skill on the part of all salesmen. And, as above, other roles will have nothing to do with performance, either as definitive criterion or optional attribute.

Eligibility for and recruitment to performance roles vary cross-culturally in interesting ways. One dimension along which this variation occurs has to do with conceptions of the nature of the competence required of a performer and the way such competence is acquired. Does it, for example, require special aptitude, talent, or training? Among the Limba, storytelling is a form of performance, but it is not considered to require the special talent called for in drumming and dancing. Anyone is a potential storyteller, and it calls for no special training to become one (Finnegan 1967:69–70). By contrast, the Japanese storytellers who perform *rakugo* or *kodan* must undergo a long and arduous period of training and apprenticeship before they are considered ready to practice their art (Hrdličková 1969).

Also to be taken into account in the analysis of performance roles is the relationship, both social and behavioral, between such roles and other roles played by the same individual. We have in mind here the way and extent to which the role of performer and the behavior associated with it may dominate or be subordinate to the other roles he may play. To illustrate one extreme possibility, we may cite Keil's assertion that in Afro-American society the role of bluesman assimilates or overshadows all other roles an adult male may normally be expected to fulfill (Keil 1966:143, 153–5). Sammy Davis, Jr., tellingly reveals the encompassing power of his role as entertainer in his statement that, "as soon as I go out the front door of my house in the morning, I'm on, Daddy, I'm on" (quoted in Messinger 1962:98–9).

The foregoing list of patterning factors for performance has been presented schematically, for analytical and presentational convenience, but it should not be taken as a mere checklist. It should be self-evident that performance genres, acts, events, and roles cannot occur in isolation, but are mutually interactive and interdependent. Any of the above factors may be used as a point of departure or point of entry into the description and analysis of the performance system of a community, but the ultimate ethnographic statement one makes about performance as part of social life must incorporate them all in some degree. It will be useful to consider one extended example here, drawn from Joel Sherzer's description of three major ceremonial traditions of the San Blas Cuna, to give some indication how the organizing features of a performance system fit together in empirical terms (Sherzer 1974).

Abstracting from Sherzer's rich description of the three traditions, we may note that each is associated with a type of event, within which specific functionaries perform particular genres in a characteristic performance mode. Thus, in the type of congress known as *omekan pela* (the women and everybody), the chiefs (*sakla*) chant (*namakke*) long chants called *pap ikar*. The chants, in turn, are interpreted to the assembled participants in the congress house by special spokesmen (*arkar*), whose speaking (*sunmakke*) also involves performance, though different from that of the chiefs. In curing rituals, a special *ikar*-knower (*ikar wisit*) speaks (*sunmakke*) the particular curing chant (each a type of *ikar*) for which he is a specialist and which is called for by the ailment from which the patient is suffering. In the third type of event, the girls' puberty ceremony, the specialist (*kantule*) in girls' puberty chants (*kantur ikar*) shouts (*kormakke*) the chants for the participants. The three perform-ance traditions may be summarized in tabular form thus:

Event	*Act*	*Role*	*Genre*
congress	chant	chief	chief's chant
(*omekan pela*)	(*namakke*)	(*sakla*)	(*pap ikar*)
	speak	spokesman	interpretation
	(*sunmakke*)	(*arkar*)	
curing ritual	speak	special *ikar*-knower	medicine chant
	(*sunmakke*)	(*ikar wisit*)	(*kapur ikar, kurkin ikar*, etc.)
girls' puberty	shout	specialist in	girls' puberty chant
ceremony	(*kormakke*)	girls' puberty chant	(*kantur ikar*)
		(*kantule*)	

For each ceremony or ritual to count as a valid instance of its class, the appropriate form must be rendered in the appropriate way by the appropriate functionary. That *namakke*, the *sunmakke* of the *arkar*'s interpretation and the *sunmakke* of the medicine chants, and *kormakke* all represent ways of performing for the Cuna is clear from Sherzer's description. All four roles, *sakla, arkar, ikar wisit*, and *kantule*, are defined in essential part in terms of competence in these specific ways of perform-ing their respective genres. There is thus, in these ceremonial traditions, a close and integral relationship between performance and specific events, acts, roles, and genres, and the configuration created by the interrelationships among these factors must be close to the center of an ethnography of performance among the Cuna.

Constellations such as Sherzer describes, involving events, acts, genres, and roles in highly structured and predictable combinations, constitute the nucleus of an ethnography of performance among the Cuna, and are aptly made the focus of Sherzer's paper. However, it is crucial to establish that not all performance related to the system Sherzer describes is captured within the framework of conventional interrelationships outlined above. We have noted, for example, that the performance of curing *ikar* by the *ikar-wisit* has its conventional locus in the curing ritual; such performance is obligatory for the *ikar wisit* to fulfill the demands of his role and for the curing ritual to be conducted at all. Against this background, then, it is note-worthy that the *ikar-wisit* may also be asked to perform his *ikar* during a chicha festival associated with the girls' puberty rites, purely for entertainment. That is, the performance that has its primary place in a particular context, in which it is obligatory, may be an optional feature of another kind of event, extended to the latter because of the esthetic enjoyment to be derived from it. The association between performer and genre is maintained, but the context, and of course the function, are different.

Though optional, the performance of curing *ikar* at puberty rite festivities is no less institutionalized than the obligatory performance of these chants in curing rituals. There is no surprise or novelty in the performance of curing *ikar* at the chicha festivals. Beyond the institutionalized system, however, lies one of the most important outlets for creative vitality within the performance domain. Consider the following circumstance, involving a group of small girls whom Sherzer was using as linguistic informants. On one occasion, knowing that he was interested in the performance forms of the community, the little girls launched spontaneously into a rendition of an *arkar*'s performance as they were being recorded (Sherzer, personal communication). The remarkableness of this is apparent when one considers that the role of *arkar* is restricted to adult men, and performances of the kind the girls imitated belonged, in conventional terms, to the congress and the congress house. Though the little girls' rendition was framed as imitation, a reframing of the *arkar*'s performance, it constituted performance in its own right as well, in which the girls assumed responsibility to an audience for a display of competence.

Consider one further observation made by Sherzer in his study of the Cuna. The congresses (*omekan pela*) discussed above, in which the chiefs chant their *pap ikar* and the *arkars* interpret them to the audience, are held in the congress house during the evening. During the daytime, however, when congresses are not in session, individuals who find themselves in the congress house may occasionally sit in a chief's hammock and launch into an attempt at a chief's chant, just for the fun of it (Sherzer, personal communication). Here we have what is a conventional perform-ance doubly reframed as imitation and more importantly as play, in which there is no assumption of responsibility for a display of communicative competence, nor any assumption of responsibility for or susceptibility to evaluation for the way in which the act of expression is done.

What are the implications of these two circumstances? The little girls' perform-ance of an *arkar*'s interpretation represents a striking instance of the use of an element from the conventional, structured performance system of the community in a novel, creative, and unexpected way to fashion a new kind of performance. The playful imitation of the chief's chant involves the reframing of what is convention-ally a performance genre into another mode of communication – in this case the performance genre is not performed but is rendered in another frame.[11] In both cases, the participants are using the structured, conventional performance system itself as a resource for creative manipulation, as a base on which a range of com-municative transformations can be wrought (cf. Sacks 1974). The structured system stands available to them as a set of conventional expectations and associations, but these expectations and associations are further manipulated in innovative ways, by fashioning novel performances outside the conventional system, or working various transformational adaptations which turn performance into something else. This is a very poorly documented aspect of performance systems, but one richly deserving of study, as a key to the creative vitality and flexibility of performance in a community.

The Emergent Quality of Performance

By stressing the creative aspect of optative performance, and the normative, structured aspect of conventional performance, we do not mean to imply that the latter is fixed and frozen while creativity is confined to the former. Rather, the argument developed up to this point to highlight creativity in the use of the performance frame itself as a resource for communication provides the entree for the final theme to be developed in this paper, the emergent quality of all performance.[12] The concept of emergence is necessary to the study of performances as a means toward comprehending the uniqueness of particular performances within the context of performance as a generalized cultural system in a community (cf. Georges 1969:319). The ethnographic construction of the structured, conventionalized performance system standardizes and homogenizes description, but all performances are not the same, and one wants to be able to appreciate the individuality of each, as well as the community-wide patterning of the overall domain.

The emergent quality of performance resides in the interplay between communicative resources, individual competence, and the goals of the participants, within the context of particular situations. We consider as resources all those aspects of the communication system available to the members of a community for the conduct of performance. Relevant here are the keys to performance, genres, acts, events, and ground rules for the conduct of performance that make up the structured system of conventionalized performance for the community. The goals of the participants include those that are intrinsic to performance – the display of competence, the focusing of attention on oneself as performer, the enhancement of experience – as well as the other desired ends toward which performance is brought to bear; these latter will be highly culture- and situation-specific. Relative competence, finally, has to do with relative degrees of proficiency in the conduct of performance.

One of the first works to conceptualize oral literature in terms of emergent structures was Albert Lord's influential book, *The Singer of Tales* (1960), a study of Serbo-Croatian oral epic poetry for the light it sheds on the classic Homeric epic. Consider the following passage:

Whether the performance takes place at home, in the coffee house, in the courtyard, or in the halls of a noble, the essential element of the occasion of singing that influences the form of the poetry is the variability and instability of the audience.

The instability of the audience requires a marked degree of concentration on the part of the singer in order that he may sing at all; it also tests to the utmost his dramatic ability and his narrative skill in keeping the audience as attentive as possible. But it is the length of a song which is most affected by the audience's restlessness. The singer begins to tell his tale. If he is fortunate, he may find it possible to sing until he is tired without interruption from the audience. After a rest he will continue, if his audience still wishes. This may last until he finishes the song, and if his listeners are propitious and his mood heightened by their interest, he may lengthen his tale, savoring each descriptive passage. It is more likely that, instead of having this ideal occasion the singer will realize shortly after beginning that his audience is not receptive, and hence he will shorten his song so that it may be finished within the limit of time for which he feels the audience may be counted on. Or, if he misjudges, he may simply never finish the song. Leaving out of consideration for the moment the question of the talent of the singer, one can say that the length of the song depends upon the audience. (Lord 1960: 16–17)

The characteristic context for the performance of the oral epics that Lord describes is one in which the singer competes for the attention of his audience with other factors that may engage them, and in which the time available for performance is of variable duration. The epic form is remarkably well-suited to the singer's combined need for fluency and flexibility. The songs are made up of ten-syllable, end-stopped lines with a medial caesura after the fourth syllable. In attaining competence, the singer must master a personal stock of line and half-line formulas for expressing character, action, and place, develop the capacity to generate formulaic expressions on the model of his fixed formulas, and learn to string together his lines in the development of the narrative themes out of which his epic songs are built. The ready-madeness of the formulas makes possible the fluency required under performance conditions, while the flexibility of the form allows the singer to adapt his performance to the situation and the audience, making it longer and more elaborate, or shorter and less adorned, as audience response, his own mood, and time constraints may dictate. And of course, the poetic skill of the singer is a factor in how strongly he can attract and hold the attention of the audience, how sensitively he can adapt to their mood, and how elaborate he can make his song if conditions allow. Lord recorded sung versions of the same narratives from the same singer and from different singers that varied in length by as much as several thousand lines.

Ultimately, one of Lord's chief contributions is to demonstrate the unique and emergent quality of the oral text, composed in performance. His analysis of the dynamics of the tradition sets forth what amounts to a generative model of epic performance. Although it has been argued that perhaps all verbal art is generated anew in the act of performance (Maranda 1972), there is also ample evidence to show that rote memorization and insistence on word-for-word fidelity to a fixed text do play a part in the performance system of certain communities (see, e.g., Friedman 1961). The point is that completely novel and completely fixed texts represent the poles of an ideal continuum, and that between the poles lies the range of emergent text structures to be found in empirical performance. The study of the factors contributing to the emergent quality of the oral literary text promises to bring about a major reconceptualization of the nature of the text, freeing it from the apparent fixity it assumes when abstracted from performance and placed on the written page, and placing it within an analytical context which focuses on the very source of the empirical relationship between art and society (cf. Georges 1969:324).

Other aspects of emergent structure are highlighted in Elinor Keenan's ethnography of the Malagasy marriage *kabary*,[13] an artful oratorical negotiation surrounding a marriage request (Keenan 1973). The *kabary* is conducted by two speechmakers, one representing the boy's family and one the girl's. The boy's speaker initiates each step of the *kabary*, which is then evaluated by the speaker for the girl. The latter may indicate that he agrees with and approves of that step, urging his opposite number on to the next, or he may state that the other's words are not according to tradition, that he has made an error in the *kabary*. The boy's speaker must then be able to justify what he has said, to show that no error has been made, or, if he admits error, he must correct it by repeating the step the right way and paying a small fine to the girl's family.

Keenan discovered, however, that there is no one unified concept of what constitutes a correct *kabary* shared by all members of the community. Rather, there are regional, familial, generational, individual, and other differences of conception and style. This being so, how is it decided what constitutes an error? There is, first of all, a preliminary meeting between the families, often with their respective speech-makers present, to establish the ground rules for the *kabary*. These are never fully conclusive, however, and it is a prominent feature of the *kabary* that arguments concerning the ground rules occur throughout the event, with appeals to the preliminary negotiations becoming simply one set of the range of possible appeals to establish authoritative performance.

Much of the impetus toward argument derives from conflicting pressures on the boy's speechmaker, who is obliged to admit to a certain range of errors, out of courtesy to the girl's family, but who is at the same time actuated by the motives of good performance, i.e., to establish his virtuosity as a performer. The girl's speech-maker, desirous of representing the family to best advantage, is likewise concerned to display his own skill as speechmaker.

The arguments, as noted, concern the ground rules for the *kabary* with each party insisting on the obligatoriness of particular rules and features by appeal to various standards drawn from pre-*kabary* negotiation, generational, regional, and other stylistic differences. Of particular interest is the fact that the strength of the participants' insistence on the rightness of their own way, their structural rigidity, is a function of the mood of the encounter, increasing as the tension mounts, decreasing as a settlement is approached. Ultimately, however, the practical goal of establishing an alliance between the two families involved takes precedence over all the speech-makers' insistence upon the conventions of *kabary* performance and their desire to display their performance skills; if the *kabary* threatens the making of the alliance, many are willing to reject the rules entirely to accomplish the larger goal.

The most striking feature of the marriage request *kabary* as described by Keenan is the emergent structure of the performance event itself. The ground rules for performance, as negotiated and asserted by the participants, shift and fluctuate in terms of what they bring to the event and the way it proceeds once under way. This is an extreme case, in which the competitive dimension and conflicting pressures make for an especially variable and shifting event structure, but here again the question is one of degree rather than kind, for all but the most ideally stereotyped of performance events will have discernibly variable features of act sequence and/or ground rules for performance. The emergent structure of performance events is of special interest under conditions of change, as participants adapt established patterns of performance to new circumstances (Darnell 1974).

In addition to text and event structure, we may uncover a third kind of structure emergent in performance, namely, social structure. To be sure, the emergent quality of social structure is not specific to situations involving performance. Indeed, there is an important line of inquiry in contemporary sociology which concerns itself with the creation of social structures in the course of and through all social interaction.

The principle addressed here is related to Raymond Firth's articulation, some years ago, of the distinction between social structure and social organization, in which the former is an abstract conception of ideal patterns of group relations, of conventional expectations and arrangements, and the latter has to do with "the systematic ordering of social relations by acts of choice and decision" in concrete activity. In Firth's terms, social organization is the domain of "variation from what has happened in apparently similar circumstances in the past.... Structural forms set a precedent and provide a limitation to the range of alternatives possible ... but it is the possibility of alternatives that makes for variability. A person chooses, consciously or unconsciously, which course he will follow" (Firth 1961:40).

What is missing from Firth's formulation is the centrality of situated social interaction as the context in which social organization, as an emergent, takes form. The current focus on the emergence of social structures in social interaction is principally the contribution of ethno-methodology, the work of Garfinkel, Cicourel, Sacks, and others. For these sociologists, "the field of sociological analysis is anywhere the sociologist can obtain access and can examine the way the 'social structure' is a meaningful ongoing accomplishment of members" (Phillipson 1972:162). To these scholars too is owed, in large part, the recognition that language is a basic means through which social realities are intersubjectively constituted and communicated (Phillipson 1972:140). From this perspective, insofar as performance is conceived of as communicative interaction, one would expect aspects of the social structure of the interaction to be emergent from the interaction itself, as in any other such situation. Rosaldo's explication of the strategic role-taking and role-making she observed in the course of a meeting to settle a dispute over brideprice among the Ilongot illuminates quite clearly the emergent aspect of social structure in that event (Rosaldo 1973). The conventions of such meetings and the oratorical performances of the interactants endow the interaction with a special degree of formalization and intensity, but the fact that artistic verbal performance is involved is not functionally related to the negotiation of social structure on the level Rosaldo is concerned with. Rather she focuses on such matters as the rhetorical strategies and consequences of taking the role of father in a particular event, thus placing your interlocutor in the role of son, with its attendant obligations.

There is, however, a distinctive potential in performance which has implications for the creation of social structure in performance. It is part of the essence of performance that it offers to the participants a special enhancement of experience, bringing with it a heightened intensity of communicative interaction which binds the audience to the performer in a way that is specific to performance as a mode of communication. Through his performance, the performer elicits the participative attention and energy of his audience, and to the extent that they value his performance, they will allow themselves to be caught up in it. When this happens, the performer gains a measure of prestige and control over the audience – prestige because of the demonstrated competence he had displayed, control because the determination of the flow of the interaction is in his hands. When the performer gains control in this way, the potential for transformation of the social structure may become available to him as well (Burke 1969[1950]:58–9). The process is manifest in the following passage from Dick Gregory's autobiography:

I got picked on a lot around the neighborhood...I guess that's when I first began to learn about humor, the power of a joke...
   At first...I'd just get mad and run home and cry when the kids started. And then, I don't know just when, I started to figure it out. They were going to laugh anyway, but if I made the jokes they'd laugh *with* me instead of *at* me. I'd get the kids off my back, on my side. So I'd come off that porch talking about myself....
   Before they could get going, I'd knock it out first, fast, knock out those jokes so they wouldn't have time to set and climb all over me....And they started to come over and listen to me, they'd see me coming and crowd around me on the corner....
   Everything began to change then....The kids began to expect to hear funny things from me, and after a while I could say anything I wanted. I got a reputation as a funny man. And then I started to turn the jokes on them. (Gregory 1964:54–5; italics in original)

Through performance, Gregory is able to take control of the situation, creating a social structure with himself at the center. At first he gains control by the artful use of the deprecatory humor that the other boys had formerly directed at him. The joking is still at his own expense, but he has transformed the situation, through performance, into one in which he gains admiration for his performance skills. Then, building on the control he gains through performance, he is able, by strategic use of his performance skills, to transform the situation still further, turning the humor aggressively against those who had earlier victimized him. In a very real sense, Gregory emerges from the performance encounters in a different social position *vis-à-vis* the other boys from the one he occupied before he began to perform, and the change is a consequence of his performance in those encounters.

The consideration of the power inherent in performance to transform social structures opens the way to a range of additional considerations concerning the role of the performer in society. Perhaps there is a key here to the persistently documented tendency for performers to be both admired and feared – admired for their artistic skill and power and for the enhancement of experience they provide, feared because of the potential they represent for subverting and transforming the status quo. Here too may lie a reason for the equally persistent association between performers and marginality or deviance, for in the special emergent quality of performance the capacity for change may be highlighted and made manifest to the community (see, e.g., Abrahams and Bauman 1971, n.d.; Azadovskii 1926:23–5; Glassie 1971:42–52; Szwed 1971:157–65). If change is conceived of in opposition to the conventionality of the community at large, then it is only appropriate that the agents of that change be placed away from the center of that conventionality, on the margins of society.

Conclusion

The discipline of folklore (and to an extent, anthropology as well) has tended throughout its history to define itself in terms of a principal focus on the traditional remnants of earlier periods, still to be found in those sectors of society that have been outdistanced by the dominant culture. To this extent, folklore has been largely the study of what Raymond Williams has recently termed "residual culture," those "experiences, meanings and values which cannot be verified or cannot be expressed in terms of the dominant culture, [but] are nevertheless lived and practised on the basis of the residue – cultural as well as social – of some previous social formation" (Williams 1973:10–11). If the subject matter of the discipline is restricted to the residue of a specific cultural or historical period, then folklore anticipates its own demise, for when the traditions are fully gone, the discipline loses its *raison d'être* (cf. Hymes 1962:678; Ben-Amos 1972:14). This need not be the case, however, for as Williams defines the concept, cultural elements may become part of residual culture as part of a continual social process, and parts of residual culture may be incorporated into the dominant culture in a complementary process. At best, though, folklore as the discipline of residual culture looks backward to the past for its frame of reference, disqualifying itself from the study of the creations of contemporary culture until they too may become residual.

Contrasted with residual culture in Williams' provocative formulation is "emergent culture," in which "new meanings and values, new practices, new significances and experiences are continually being created" (Williams 1973:11). This is a further extension of the concept of emergence, as employed in the preceding pages of this article, but interestingly compatible with it, for the emergent quality of experience is a vital factor in the generation of emergent culture. Emergent culture, though a basic element in human social life, has always lain outside the charter of folklore, perhaps in part for lack of a unified point of departure or frame of reference able to comprehend residual forms and items, contemporary practice, and emergent structures. Performance, we would offer, constitutes just such a point of departure, the nexus of tradition, practice, and emergence in verbal art. Performance may thus be the cornerstone of a new folkloristics, liberated from its backward-facing perspective, and able to comprehend much more of the totality of human experience.

NOTES

1 In the development of the ideas presented in this essay I have profited greatly from discussions with many colleagues and students over the past several years, among whom Barbara Babcock-Abrahams, Dan Ben-Amos, Marcia Herndon, Barbara Kirshenblatt-Gimblett, John McDowell, Norma McLeod, Américo Paredes, Dina Sherzer, and Beverly Stoeltje deserve special mention and thanks. My greatest debt, however, is to the three individuals who have stimulated and influenced my thinking most profoundly: Dell Hymes, for imparting to me the ethnographic perspective on verbal art and for his ideas on the nature of performance; Roger D. Abrahams, for focusing my attention on performance as an organizing principle for the study of folklore; and Joel Sherzer for sharing in the intellectual process all along the way.

2 Particularly important for folklorists is the seminal essay by Jansen (1957), and Lomax (1968), and Abrahams (1968, 1972). Two collections which reflect the performance orientation are Paredes and Bauman (1972) and Ben-Amos and Goldstein (1975). Bauman and Sherzer (1974) reflects a wider performance orientation, of which performance in verbal art is one aspect. Singer (1958a, 1958b, 1972) represents the perspective of an anthropologist on "cultural performances." Colby and Peacock (1973) contains a section on Performance Analysis which, however, ignores the work of folklorists in this field, an omission which is perhaps to be expected in an article on narrative which announces its deliberate neglect of folklore journals.

3 The term "spoken art" was suggested by Thomas Sebeok in discussion of Bascom's ideas on verbal art (Bascom 1955:246, n. 9; see also Dorson 1972:9).

4   Richard Ohmann, in two recent articles, employs the same passage from Austin as a point of
    departure for the formulation of a theory of literature based on Austin's theory of speech acts
    (Ohmann 1971, 1972). Ohmann's argument is interesting in places, but its productiveness is
    severely limited by his failure – like Austin's – to recognize that the notion of strictly referential,
    "literal" meaning has little, if any, relevance to the use of spoken language in social life. For a
    strong critique of the concept of "ordinary language," and the impoverishing effect it has on
    definitions of literature, see Fish (1973).
5   The notion of frame, though not necessarily the term, is used in a similar manner by other writers
    (see, e.g., Huizinga 1955; Milner 1955:86; Smith 1968; Uspensky 1972; Fish 1973:52–3).
6   Concerning the ecological model of communication underlying this formulation, are Sherzer
    and Bauman (1972) and Bauman and Sherzer (1974).
7   Note that it is *susceptibility* to evaluation that is indicated here; in this formulation the status
    of an utterance as performance is independent of *how* it is evaluated, whether it is judged good
    or bad, beautiful or ugly, etc. A bad performance is nonetheless a performance. On this point,
    see Hymes (1973:189–90).
8   I have been influenced in this formulation by Hymes (1974, 1975), d'Azevedo (1958:706),
    Mukařovský (1964:19, 1970:21), and Goffman (1974). A similar conception of performance
    is developed in an unfinished paper by my former colleague Joseph Doherty (Doherty n.d.),
    whose recent tragic and untimely death occurred before he was able to complete his work, and
    prevented me from benefiting from discussions we planned but never had. Elli Köngäs
    Maranda seems to be operating in terms of a conception of verbal art which is similar in
    certain central respects to the one developed here (Maranda 1974:6). Compare also Fish's
    conception of literature (Fish 1973).
       A special word should be said of the use of "competence" and "performance" in the above
    formulation. Use of these terms, especially in such close juxtaposition, demands at least some
    acknowledgement of Noam Chomsky's contribution of both to the technical vocabulary of
    linguistics (Chomsky 1965:3–4). It should be apparent, however, that both terms are employed
    in a very different way in the present work – competence in the sense advanced by Hymes
    (1971 [and this volume]), and performance as formulated above.
9   The aspect of conventionality will be discussed below.
10 Ethics and esthetics are not always as coterminous as Gossen suggests, in summing up his
    analysis of the Chamula. In St. Vincent, for example, the domain "talking nonsense" is
    negatively valued in terms of ethics, but encompasses a range of speech activities with a strong
    performance element about them that is highly valued and much enjoyed in esthetic terms
    (Abrahams and Bauman 1971). Real, as against ideal, moral systems often accommodate more
    disreputability than anthropologists give them credit for, and the association between perform-
    ance and disreputability has often been remarked (see Abrahams and Bauman n.d.). Another
    case that underscores the complexity of the relationship between ethics and esthetics is that of
    the seventeenth century Quakers, for whom fundamental moral principles against putting
    oneself forward, speaking things that were in a strict sense "not the truth," and gratifying the
    earthly man, severely limited the potential and actual domain of artistic verbal performance,
    leaving but a few very special kinds of outlets for performance at all (Bauman 1970, 1974,
    1975). The whole matter of the relationship between ethics and esthetics is one that badly
    needs investigation from an anthropological point of view.
11 Hymes (1975) applies the term "metaphrasis" to this phenomenon.
12 The concept of emergence is developed in McHugh (1968). The emergent quality of perform-
    ance is emphasized in Hymes (1975).
13 *Kabary* designates both a way of speaking and the forms in which it is manifested.

REFERENCES

Abrahams, Roger D. (1968). Introductory Remarks to a Rhetorical Theory of Folklore. *Journal of American Folklore* 81:143–8.
Abrahams, Roger D. (1970). A Performance-Centered Approach to Gossip. *Man* 5:290–301.

Abrahams, Roger D. (1972). Folklore and Literature as Performance. *Journal of the Folklore Institute* 8:75–94.

Abrahams, Roger D., and Richard Bauman (1971). Sense and Nonsense in St. Vincent. *American Anthropologist* 73:762–72.

Abrahams, Roger D., and Richard Bauman (n.d.). Ranges of Festival Behavior. In *The Reversible World: Essays on Symbolic Inversion*. Barbara Babcock-Abrahams, ed.

Austerlitz, Robert (1960). Parallelismus. In *Poetics, Poetyka*, поетика. The Hague: Mouton.

Austin, J. L. (1962). *How to Do Things with Words*. New York: Oxford University Press.

Azadovskii, Mark (1926). *Eine Sibirische Märchenerzählerin*. Helsinki: Folklore Fellows Communication No. 68. English translation by James R. Dow. Austin, TX: Center for Intercultural Studies in Folklore and Oral History (in press).

Babcock-Abrahams, Barbara (1974). The Story in the Story: *Metanarration* in Folk Narrative. Paper delivered at the VI Folk Narrative Congress, Helsinki, June 17.

Bascom, William (1955). Verbal Art. *Journal of American Folklore* 68:245–52.

Bateson, Gregory (1972). *Steps to an Ecology of Mind*. New York: Ballantine.

Bauman, Richard (1970). Aspects of Seventeenth Century Quaker Rhetoric. *Quarterly Journal of Speech* 56:67–74.

Bauman, Richard (1972a). Introduction. In *Toward New Perspectives in Folklore*. Américo Paredes and Richard Bauman, eds. Austin: University of Texas Press.

Bauman, Richard (1972b). The La Have Island General Store: Sociability and Verbal Art in a Nova Scotia Community. *Journal of American Folklore* 85: 330–43.

Bauman, Richard (1974). Speaking in the Light: The Role of the Quaker Minister. In *Explorations in the Ethnography of Speaking*. Richard Bauman and Joel Sherzer, eds. New York: Cambridge University Press.

Bauman, Richard (1975). Quaker Folk Linguistics and Folklore. In *Folklore: Communication and Performance*. Dan Ben-Amos and Kenneth Goldstein, eds. The Hague: Mouton.

Bauman, Richard, and Joel Sherzer (eds.) (1974). *Explorations in the Ethnography of Speaking*. New York: Cambridge University Press.

Ben-Amos, Dan (1969). Analytical Categories and Ethnic Genres. *Genre* 2:275–301.

Ben-Amos, Dan (1972). Toward a Definition of Folklore in Context. In *Toward New Perspectives in Folklore*. Américo Paredes and Richard Bauman, eds. Austin: University of Texas Press.

Ben-Amos, Dan, and Kenneth Goldstein (eds.) (1975). *Folklore: Communication and Performance*. The Hague: Mouton.

Burke, Kenneth (1969). *A Rhetoric of Motives*. Berkeley & Los Angeles: University of California Press.

Burns, Elizabeth (1972). *Theatricality*. New York: Harper.

Chomsky, Noam (1965). *Aspects of the Theory of Syntax*. Cambridge, MA: MIT Press.

Colby, Benjamin, and James Peacock (1973). Narrative. In *Handbook of Social and Cultural Anthropology*. John J. Honigmann, ed. Chicago: Rand McNally.

Crowley, Daniel J. (1966). *I Could Talk Old Story Good*. Berkeley & Los Angeles: University of California Press.

Darnell, Regna (1974). Correlates of Cree Narrative Performance. In *Explorations in the Ethnography of Speaking*. Richard Bauman and Joel Sherzer, eds. New York: Cambridge University Press.

d'Azevedo, Warren (1958). A Structural Approach to Esthetics: Toward a Definition of Art in Anthropology. *American Anthropologist* 60:702–14.

Delargy, James H. (1945). The Gaelic Story-Teller. London: *Proceedings of the British Academy* 31:177–221.

Doherty, Joseph (n.d.). Towards a Poetics of Performance. Manuscript.

Dorson, Richard M. (1972). *African Folklore*. New York: Doubleday Anchor.

Dundes, Alan (1966). Metafolklore and Oral Literary Criticism. *The Monist* 50:505–16.

Durbin, Mridula (1971). Transformational Models Applied to Musical Analysis: Theoretical Possibilities. *Ethnomusicology* 15:353–62.

Finnegan, Ruth (1967). *Limba Stories and Storytelling*, Oxford: Oxford University Press.

Firth, Raymond (1961). *Elements of Social Organization* (3rd edn.). Boston: Beacon Press (paperback 1963).

Fish, Stanley E. (1973). How Ordinary Is Ordinary Language? *New Literary History* 5:40–54.

Fónagy, Ivan (1965). Form and Function of Poetic Language. *Diogenes* 51:72–110.

Fox, James (1974). Our Ancestors Spoke in Pairs. In *Explorations in the Ethnography of Speaking*. Richard Bauman and Joel Sherzer, eds. New York: Cambridge University Press.

Friedman, Albert (1961). The Formulaic Improvisation Theory of Ballad Tradition – A Counterstatement. *Journal of American Folklore* 74:113–15.

Georges, Robert (1969). Toward an Understanding of Storytelling Events. *Journal of American Folklore* 82:313–28.

Glassie, Henry (1971). Take that Night Train to Selma: An Excursion to the Outskirts of Scholarship. In *Folksongs and Their Makers*, by Henry Glassie, Edward D. Ives, and John F. Szwed. Bowling Green, OH: Bowling Green University Popular Press.

Goffman, Erving (1974). *Frame Analysis*. New York: Harper Colophon.

Gossen, Gary (1972). Chamula Genres of Verbal Behavior. In *Toward New Perspectives in Folklore*. Américo Paredes and Richard Bauman, eds. Austin: University of Texas Press.

Gossen, Gary (1974). To Speak with a Heated Heart: Chamula Canons of Style and Good Performance. In *Explorations in the Ethnography of Speaking*. Richard Bauman and Joel Sherzer, eds. New York: Cambridge University Press.

Gregory, Dick (1964). *Nigger: An Autobiography*. New York: Dutton.

Havránek, Bohuslav (1964). The Functional Differentiation of the Standard Language. In *A Prague School Reader on Esthetics, Literary Structure, and Style*. Paul L. Garvin, ed. Washington, DC: Georgetown University.

Hrdličková, V. (1969). Japanese Professional Storytellers. *Genre* 2:179–210.

Huizinga, Johan (1955). *Homo Ludens*. Boston: Beacon.

Hymes, Dell (1962). Review of *Indian Tales of North America*, by T. P. Coffin. *American Anthropologist* 64:676–9.

Hymes, Dell (1971). Competence and Performance in Linguistic Theory. In *Language Acquisition: Models and Methods*. Renira Huxley and Elisabeth Ingram, eds. London and New York: Academic Press.

Hymes, Dell (1973). An Ethnographic Perspective. *New Literary History* 5:187–201.

Hymes, Dell (1974). Ways of Speaking. In *Explorations in the Ethnography of Speaking*. Richard Bauman and Joel Sherzer, eds. New York: Cambridge University Press.

Hymes, Dell (1975). Breakthrough into Performance. In *Folklore: Communication and Performance*. Dan Ben-Amos and Kenneth Goldstein, eds. The Hague: Mouton.

Innes, Gordon (1974). *Sunjata: Three Mandinka Versions*. London: School of Oriental and African Studies, University of London.

Jakobson, Roman (1960). Linguistics and Poetics. In *Style in Language*. Thomas A. Sebeok, ed. Cambridge, MA: MIT Press.

Jakobson, Roman (1966). Grammatical Parallelism and Its Russian Facet. *Language* 42:399–429.

Jakobson, Roman (1968). Poetry of Grammar and Grammar of Poetry. *Lingua* 21:597–609.

Jansen, William Hugh (1957). Classifying Performance in the Study of Verbal Folklore. In *Studies in Folklore*. W. Edson Richmond, ed. Bloomington, In: Indiana University Press.

Keenan, Elinor (1973). A Sliding Sense of Obligatoriness: The Poly-Structure of Malagasy Oratory. *Language in Society* 2:225–43.

Keenan, Elinor (1974). Norm Makers, Norm Breakers: Uses of Speech by Men and Women in a Malagasy Community. In *Explorations in the Ethnography of Speaking*. Richard Bauman and Joel Sherzer, eds. New York: Cambridge University Press.

Keil, Charles (1966). *Urban Blues*. Chicago: University of Chicago Press.

Kirshenblatt-Gimblett, Barbara (1974). The Concept and Varieties of Narrative Performance in East European Jewish Culture. In *Explorations in the Ethnography of Speaking*. Richard Bauman and Joel Sherzer, eds. New York: Cambridge University Press.

Leech, Geoffrey (1969). *A Linguistic Guide to English Poetry*. London: Longmans.

Lomax, Alan (1968). *Folksong Style and Culture*. Washington, DC: American Association for the Advancement of Science.

Lord, Albert B. (1960). *The Singer of Tales*. Cambridge, MA: Harvard University Press.

Maranda, Elli Köngäs (1972). Theory and Practice of Riddle Analysis. In *Toward New Perspectives in Folklore*. Américo Paredes and Richard Bauman, eds. Austin: University of Texas Press.

Maranda, Elli Köngäs (1974). Individual and Tradition. Paper delivered at the VI Folk Narrative Congress, Helsinki, June 20.

McDowell, John (1974). *Some Aspects of Verbal Art in Bolivian Quechua*. Folklore Annual of the University Folklore Association (University of Texas, Austin), No. 6.

McHugh, Peter (1968). *Defining the Situation*. Indianapolis, IN: Bobbs-Merrill.

Messinger, Sheldon L. (1962). Life as Theater: Some Notes on the Dramaturgic Approach to Social Reality. *Sociometry* 25:98–110.

Milner, Marion (1955). Role of Illusion in Symbol Formation. In *New Directions in Psycho-analysis*. Melanie Klein, ed. New York: Basic Books.

Mukařovský, Jan (1964). Standard Language and Poetic Language. In *A Prague School Reader on Esthetics Literary Structure, and Style*. Paul L. Garvin, ed. Washington, DC: Georgetown University.

Mukařovský, Jan (1970). *Aesthetic Function, Norm and Value as Social Facts*. Ann Arbor: Department of Slavic Languages and Literature, University of Michigan.

Ohmann, Richard (1971). Speech Acts and the Definition of Literature. *Philosophy and Rhetoric* 4:1–19.

Ohmann, Richard (1972). Speech, Literature, and the Space Between. *New Literary History* 4:47–63.

Paredes, Américo, and Richard Bauman (eds.) (1972). *Toward New Perspectives in Folklore*. Austin: University of Texas Press.

Phillipson, Michael (1972). Phenomenological Philosophy and Sociology. In *New Directions in Sociological Theory*, by Paul Filmer, Michael Phillipson, David Silverman, and David Walsh. Cambridge, MA: MIT Press.

Reaver, J. Russell (1972). From Reality to Fantasy: Opening-Closing Formulas in the Structures of American Tall Tales. *Southern Folklore Quarterly* 36:369–82.

Rosaldo, Michelle Z. (1973). I Have Nothing to Hide: The Language of Ilongot Oratory. *Language in Society* 2:193–223.

Ruesch, Jurgen, and Gregory Bateson (1968). *Communication*. New York: Norton.

Sacks, Harvey (1974). An Analysis of the Course of a Joke's Telling in Conversation. In *Explorations in the Ethnography of Speaking*. Richard Bauman and Joel Sherzer, eds. New York: Cambridge University Press.

Sherzer, Dina, and Joel Sherzer (1972). Literature in San Blas: Discovering the Cuna *Ikala*. *Semiotica* 6:182–99.

Sherzer, Joel (1974). *Namakke, Sunmakke, Kormakke*: Three Types of Cuna Speech Events. In *Explorations in the Ethnography of Speaking*. Richard Bauman and Joel Sherzer, eds. New York: Cambridge University Press.

Sherzer, Joel, and Richard Bauman (1972). Areal Studies and Culture History: Language as a Key to the Historical Study of Culture Contact. *Southwestern Journal of Anthropology* 28:131–52.

Singer, Milton (1958a). From the Guest Editor. *Journal of American Folklore* 71:191–204.

Singer, Milton (1958b). The Great Tradition in a Metropolitan Center: Madras. *Journal of American Folklore* 71:347–88.

Singer, Milton (1972). *When a Great Tradition Modernizes*. New York: Praeger.

Smith, Barbara H. (1968). *Poetic Closure*. Chicago: University of Chicago.

Stankiewicz, Edward (1960). Poetic Language and Non-Poetic Language in their Interrelation. In *Poetics, Poetyka, поетика*. The Hague: Mouton.

Szwed, John F. (1971). Paul E. Hall: A Newfoundland Song-Maker and Community of Song. In *Folksongs and Their Makers*, by Henry Glassie, Edward D. Ives, and John F. Szwed. Bowling Green, OH: Bowling Green University Popular Press.

Tedlock, Dennis (1972). On the Translation of Style in Oral Narrative. In *Toward New Perspectives in Folklore*. Américo Paredes and Richard Bauman, eds. Austin: University of Texas Press.

Toelken, J. Barre (1969). The "Pretty Language" of Yellowman: Genre, Mode, and Texture in Navaho Coyote Narratives. *Genre* 2:211–35.

Uspensky, B. A. (1972). Structural Isomorphism of Verbal and Visual Art. *Poetics* 5:5–39.

Weinreich, Uriel (1966). On the Semantic Structure of a Language. In *Universals of Language*. Joseph Greenberg, ed. Cambridge, MA: MIT Press.

Williams, Raymond (1973). Base and Superstructure in Marxist Cultural Theory. *New Left Review* 82:3–16.

8

Formality and Informality in Communicative Events

Judith T. Irvine

Formality and its opposite, informality, are concepts frequently used in the ethnography of communication, in sociolinguistics, and in social anthropology to describe social occasions and the behavior associated with them. This paper examines the usefulness of those concepts in description and comparison. What might one mean by *formality*, in terms of observable characteristics of human social interaction? How might formality correspond to the cultural categories with which other peoples describe their own social occasions? Are the relevant distinctions best formulated as dichotomy (as the contrast formality/informality might suggest), or as a continuum ranging between two poles, or as something more complex? Do whatever distinctions we decide are involved in formality/informality apply to every society? Will the same kinds of behavioral differences, or the same kinds of cultural categories, emerge everywhere?

I pose these questions in an attempt to further the development of a more precise analytical vocabulary, particularly for the ethnography of communication, which has perhaps invoked those concepts most often (although their relevance is not limited to that field). We now have a small number of case-history descriptions of ways of speaking in particular speech communities. But the terms in which those descriptions are made are often vague, lacking in explicit analytical content, too close to our own folk categories – inadequate for cross-cultural comparison, or even for description itself. Many anthropologists (and I include myself) have used terms such as formality without defining them or thinking about their definitions, simply assuming that the meanings are clear, when in fact the usages are vague and quite variable.

My object, then, is to give our usages more substance and to explore how they might then better serve cross-cultural comparison. I shall first consider what has been meant by formality and informality in the recent literature – that is, what various authors seem to have intended those terms to describe. The literature I draw upon comes mainly from sociolinguistics and the ethnography of speaking although some works in other fields will be cited as well. I shall then restate these various senses of formality in what I hope is a more explicit fashion and argue for the usefulness of the more detailed formulation for comparison, both within and between speech communities. A third section of the paper attempts a more extended comparison; it examines the formality of certain social occasions in two African societies, the Wolof and the Mursi, and compares them with a third society, the Ilongots of the northern Philippines. The fourth, and final, section, asks whether the cover term formality remains useful at all.

The last section also considers some broader issues in social theory to which these terms and concepts relate. Actually, this is the larger object of the essay. Refining an analytical vocabulary is not simply a matter of improving the quality of empirical data; the terminology also reflects and incorporates more general assumptions about the nature of the social order. To discuss the descriptive and analytical vocabulary, therefore, is also to address those assumptions.

What Has Been Meant by Formality in the Literature

A look at some recent literature in sociolinguistics, the ethnography of speaking, and related fields (e.g., Gumperz and Hymes 1972; Bauman and Sherzer 1974; Sanches and Blount 1975; Fishman 1968; Bloch 1975; Kirshenblatt-Gimblett 1976; papers in *Language in Society; Working Papers in Sociolinguistics*) suggests three principal senses of formality, which are potentially confused with each other. These different senses have to do with whether the formality concerns properties of a communicative code, properties of the social setting in which a code is used, or properties of the analyst's description.

For instance, many authors use formality in the sense of an increased structuring and predictability of discourse. Here, formality is an aspect of code, such that the discourse is subject to extra rules or some greater elaboration of rules. In this vein, for example, Bricker (1974:388) and Gossen (1974:412), both writing on the Maya, and Fox (1974:73) who writes on the Rotinese, all describe "formal speech" as marked by special structuring – notably redundancy, and syntactic or semantic parallelism. Others have emphasized the predictability of structured discourse; they have argued that a "formal style" reduces the variability and spontaneity of speech (see Joos 1959 and Wolfson 1976). For example, Rubin's (1968) paper on bilingualism in Paraguay discusses formality in terms of limitations on the kinds of behaviors that are acceptable and on the amount of allowable variation (conceived as deviation from a norm).

Other authors use formality/informality as a way of describing the characteristics of a social situation, not necessarily the kind of code used in that situation. The relevant characteristics of the situation may have something to do with a prevailing affective tone, so that a formal situation requires a display of seriousness, politeness, and respect. For instance, Fischer (1972), describing ways of speaking among Trukese and Ponapeans, discusses the use of "respect vocabulary" and "formal etiquette" as displays of politeness marking a formal situation. In Fishman's (1972:51) discussion of "lecturelike or formal situations," formality seems to be understood as the opposite of levity and intimacy. Ervin-Tripp (1972:235), too, relates formality to politeness and "the seriousness of such situations." Not all authors agree on just what formality means about a situation, however. Rubin (1968) lists formality as a situational variable separate from "degree of intimacy" and "degree of seriousness." For Labov (1972: 113), formality of situational context is what makes a speaker pay increased attention to his or her speech.

Finally, many authors use formal to refer to a technical mode of description, in which the analyst's statement of the rules governing discourse is maximally explicit. Although most linguists apply this sense of formality (as "explicitness") only to the statements made by an outside observer,[1] some anthropologists also apply it to a people's own analysis of their social order. When Murphy (1971:159), for instance, speaks of "the formal, conscious models of society held by its members," he refers to those conceptions of society and behavior that informants can present in explicit verbal statements. For other anthropologists the explicit statements need not be verbal; see Leach's (1965:15–16) discussion of nonverbal ritual as a way in which social structure, or a people's ideas about social structure, are made explicit and "formally recognized."

These three senses of formality have often been merged or interrelated. For example, when formality is conceived as an aspect of social situations, it is common to extend the term to the linguistic varieties used in such situations, regardless of what those varieties happen to be like otherwise. Formal and informal pronouns are a case in point. Their formality lies in what they connote about a social setting in which they are appropriately used; they do not necessarily differ in the number or elaboration of syntactic (or other) rules governing their use.

Some authors go further, blending all three senses of formality and arguing that formal descriptions are most suitable (or only suitable) for the more structured discourse that occurs in ceremoniallike formal situations. Here, one wonders whether it is not just the use of the single term formal for a kind of description, a kind of discourse, and a kind of situation that makes the three appear necessarily related. Discourse that is spontaneous is still rule-governed, as linguists working with syntax have been at pains to point out; indeed, a major effort of linguists in the past 20 years has been to show how and why rules of grammar permit the utterance and comprehension of sentences that have never occurred before. Explicit formulation of those rules cannot, therefore, be limited to specially rigidified or redundant discourse. So, with Halliday (1964), I would seek to avoid confusing the technical sense of formality (explicitness of the observer's description) with senses that concern the behavior and conceptual systems of the people described.

Still, some ways of interrelating different senses of formality are potentially fruitful. Maurice Bloch (1975) has recently argued, for instance, that code structuring and situational formality are causally related, so that increased structuring of discourse necessarily brings about increased politeness and a greater display of respect for a traditional, normative social order (and perhaps a coercive political establishment). That argument has various antecedents in social anthropology, although they are less clearly articulated and do not give particular attention to speech. One such forerunner is Durkheim's conception of ritual, as expressing and confirming the solidarity of the group and constraining the individual to conformity. A related matter, too, is the widespread view in structural-functional anthropology that connects structure with norm and tradition, and with order, coherence, and stability – a view of structure as essentially static.

Bloch's argument is an important one and I shall return to it later. Now, however, the point is that these basic questions about structure and action in discourse can be addressed only if the relevant variables are first disentangled. Arguments that do so (such as Bloch's) are much more useful than those that merely slide from one sense of formality to another, leaving implicit the connection between formal situations and frozen, rigidified speech (or other behavior).

Four Aspects of Formality that Apply Cross-Culturally

Leaving aside questions of causal relationships for now, I will restate, in a more detailed way, what considerations one may have in mind when describing social occasions as formal or informal. A search of some available ethnographic evidence, inadequate as it is for the purpose – and filtered as it is through ethnographers' descriptive vocabularies – suggests that the discourse aspect and the situational aspect of formality should be broken down into finer distinctions. Four different aspects of formality emerge that seem to apply to a wide variety of speech communities, perhaps to all. The four kinds of formality often co-occur in the same social occasion though not always (hence their presentation as separate variables).

Increased code structuring

This aspect of formality concerns the addition of extra rules or conventions to the codes that organize behavior in a social setting. Although I focus on the linguistic, any code (such as dress, gesture, or spatial organization) can, of course, be subject to degrees of structuring. It is important to recognize, however, that a social occasion involves many codes that operate at once, and the degrees of structuring that they variously display may differ. Even within the linguistic code one should distinguish among the various levels of linguistic organization that may be subject to the additional or elaborated structuring, such as intonation (including pitch contour, meter, loudness, and speed of talk), phonology, syntax, the use of particular sets of lexical items, fixed-text sequences, and turn taking. Increased structuring need not affect all these aspects of linguistic organization equally or at the same time.[2] Some speech events formalize different parts of the linguistic system and so cannot be lined up on a simple continuum from informality to formality.

For instance, among the Wolof[3] there are two distinct speech events, *woy* ("praise-singing") and *xaxaar* ("insult sessions"), which differ from ordinary conversations in their structuring of intonational patterns (among other things). But different aspects of intonation are affected. In praise-singing, the pitch contour of utterances is more structured than in ordinary talk but meter remains relatively loose; in insult sessions, meter is strictly regulated (with drum accompaniment), while pitch remains loose. It would be impossible to say that one form of discourse is more formalized than the other, although one could say that both are more formalized than ordinary conversation (and less formalized than some types of religious singing, which structure both pitch and rhythm).

Similarly, among the Yoruba, two speech events, both associated with the Iwi Egungun cult celebrations, formalize different aspects of the discourse (Davis 1976). In one event, speakers use highly structured utterances, often fixed texts, on conventional topics, whereas turn taking among speakers is unpredictable, with much of the interest for the audience residing in the speakers' competition for the floor. In the other type of speech event, turn taking is quite strictly regulated (as though in a play), but the topics can be creative and novel. The formalization of discourse here cannot be thought of as just a progressive rigidifying and restriction on creative potential. Instead, what is involved is a focusing of creativity onto a certain aspect of talk, which is highlighted because other aspects are redundant and predictable.

Code consistency

A second kind of formalization involves co-occurrence rules. At many different levels of linguistic organization and in other avenues of communicative expression as well, speakers select from among alternatives that have contrasting social significance. Co-occurrence rules provide for the extent to which these choices must be consistent. In the kinds of discourse that ethnographers have labeled more formal, consistency of choices (in terms of their social significance) seems to be greater than in ordinary conversation, where speakers may be able to recombine variants to achieve special effects.

For example, among the Wolof, differences of pitch, loudness, and speed of talk (as well as other discourse features) may connote something about the speaker's social rank: high pitch, high volume, and high speed all suggest low social rank, while low pitch, low volume, and a laconic slowness suggest high social rank. Sometimes a speaker can mix choices (e.g., high pitch + low volume + low speed seems to indicate baby talk, used by adults to address infants; for some other mixes and their uses, see Irvine 1974); but in some kinds of discourse – which one might call the more formal – choices for each discourse feature are consistent in their social connotations.

Another example comes from Friedrich's (1972) paper on Russian pronouns. Friedrich notes that usage of the second-person pronouns *ty* and *vy* (for singular addressee) can be consistent or inconsistent with facial expressions. More formal situations are characterized by greater consistency – as opposed to "ironic" uses that combine the pronoun *vy* (usually called the formal pronoun) with a contemptuous expression ("paralinguistic *ty*"). Similarly, Jackson (1974:63) indicates that among the Vaupés Indians, "language-mixing" – for example, the use of Tuyuka words in a conversation that is syntactically Bará (and Bará in the rest of the lexicon) – is likely to occur only in informal discourse. In settings that she calls "more formal," co-occurrence rules are stricter so that the social connotations of lexicon and syntax are consistent (connotations of longhouse and descent-unit identity).

Because many authors describe co-occurrence violations with terms such as *irony, levity, humor,* or *local color,* it appears that some of what is meant by the "seriousness" of formal situations is actually a matter of behavioral consistency and adherence to a set of co-occurrence rules that apply to these situations and not to others. As Ervin-Tripp remarks (1972:235), co-occurrence rules are especially strict in formal styles of discourse "because of the seriousness of such situations."

But why should co-occurrence rules and "seriousness" be linked? Perhaps the clue lies in the fact that code-switching and code inconsistencies are so often used as distancing devices – ways of setting off a quotation, making a parenthetic aside, mimicking someone, or enabling a speaker to comment on his or her own behavior (see Goffman 1961; Irvine 1974; and the code-switching literature summarized in Timm 1975). By code inconsistency the speaker can detach himself from the social persona implied by one type of usage and suggest that that persona is not to be taken quite "for real"; the speaker has another social persona as well. Code inconsistency, then, may be a process of framing or undercutting one message with another that qualifies it and indicates that in some sense, or from some point of view, it doesn't really count (cf. Bateson 1972; Goffman 1961, 1974). In contrast, the code-consistent message has to count; it has to be taken "seriously" because no alternative message or social persona is provided. Each aspect of the speaker's behavior shows the same kind and degree of involvement in the situation.[4]

Invoking positional identities

A third aspect of formality has to do with the social identities of participants in a social gathering. More a property of the situation than of code *per se*, it concerns which social identity (of the many that an individual might have) is invoked on a particular kind of occasion. Formal occasions invoke positional and public, rather than personal, identities (to use a term proposed by Mead [1937] and applied to speech events by Hymes [1972]).[5] Public, positional identities are part of a structured set likely to be labeled and widely recognized in a society (that is, it is widely recognized that the set of identities exists and that persons X, Y, and Z have them). Personal identities, on the other hand, are individualized and depend more on the particular history of an individual's interactions. They are perhaps less likely to be explicitly recognized or labeled and less likely to be common knowledge in the community at large.

This aspect of formality is involved in what many authors have interpreted as the formal event's emphasis on social distance (as opposed to intimacy) and respect (for an established order of social positions and identities). For example, Albert (1972), writing on the Burundi, distinguishes two speech events that she calls formal and informal visiting. Formal visiting requires an open acknowledgement of differences in social rank, and it usually occurs between persons whose positions are clearly ranked in a publicly known, apparently indisputable sense (such as feudal lord and vassal). Formal visiting is characterized by other aspects of formality as well: special structuring and planning of the discourse; use of formulas; special stance; and "seriousness" (which I take to imply some constraints on topic, intonation, facial expressions, and gestures, and consistency of these with social rank).

Because positional identities and formal (structured) discourse go together in the example just cited, one might suppose that this type of social identity is necessarily invoked by the structuring of discourse and need not be considered an independent variable. But another part of Albert's description suggests otherwise. Here, Albert discusses a speech event she calls "semiformalized quarreling," a "symbolic fight" between persons who represent the bride's and groom's families at a wedding. It seems that the major factor contrasting "semiformalized quarreling" with other (unformalized) quarreling is that the identities of the participants are positional rather than personal. True, enough information is not really given to know whether there are also differences in the organization of discourse in these two kinds of quarrels. But Albert's statement that there is always a great danger that the symbolic fight might become a real fight suggests that the major difference between them lies less in the organization of the discourse than in whether it applies to personal identities.

Of course, societies can be compared as to what social identities are structured in this positional (or formal) sense; and, within a society, communicative events can be compared as to which positional sets are invoked and the scope of the social relations organized in them. For instance, among the Wolof, kinship positions, although publicly known, organize relations among a smaller group of persons than do society-wide identities, such as caste. An individual Wolof man is patrilateral cross-cousin to only a certain group of people, and that identity is relevant only to his interaction with them, whereas his caste identity is relevant to his interaction with everyone. Whether the identities invoked in a Wolof communicative event are society-wide or not has consequences for many aspects of the participants' behavior. It is convenient to say that the wider, or more public, the scope of the social identities invoked on a particular occasion, the more formal the occasion is, in this third sense of the term.

Emergence of a central situational focus

A fourth aspect of formality concerns the ways in which a main focus of attention – a dominant mutual engagement that encompasses all persons present (see Goffman 1963:164) – is differentiated from side involvements. Probably all conversations display this differentiation to some extent. Jefferson (1972) shows that even ordinary conversations between two persons clearly mark off certain sets of utterances as side sequences and distinguish them from the main, or focal, sequence. When a social gathering has a larger number of participants, however, it may or may not be organized around a central focus of attention that engages, or might engage, the whole group. An American cocktail party, for example, is usually decentralized, with many small groups whose conversations are not meant to concern the gathering as a whole; but a lecture is centralized even if members of the audience mutter asides to each other during the lecturer's performance.

The emergence of a central focus of attention for a social gathering parallels the process of focusing mentioned above for aspects of code. Participation in the central, focal activity is regulated and structured in special ways. For instance, it may be that only certain persons have the right to speak or act in the main sequence, with others restricted to the side sequences. In the main sequence, speech is governed by constraints on topic, continuity, and relevance that do not apply (or not to the same extent) in the side sequences (cf. Ervin-Tripp 1972:243).

This focusing process can be seen at work in the organization of events at a Wolof naming-day ceremony. Much of the ceremony involves decentralized participation: the guests sit in small groups, chatting and eating. At various points, however, a *griot* (praise-singer) may start shouting bits of praise-poems in an effort to capture the attention of the crowd and establish a focus of attention for his performance. If he succeeds, the situation changes character, altering the patterns of movement and talk for all participants, and bringing caste identities (rather than more personal relations) into the foreground.

Similarly, David Turton (1975), in his writing on the Mursi of southern Ethiopia, distinguishes among three kinds of political speech events according to criteria that seem to resemble this focusing process. Turton calls the difference between "chatting," "discussion," and "debate" in Mursi society a difference in "degree of formality": what the more formal events entail is a process of setting off a single central (onstage) speaker from his audience, by spatial arrangements and verbal cues. Only men of certain age-grades may speak in the main (focal) sequence; other persons are relegated to the audience or to side sequences.[6] In this way, central activities and central actors are differentiated from peripheral activities and actors.

For any society, that only certain kinds of activities and actors will be able to command center stage can be expected. At the least, the activities must be ones that all participants recognize as relevant to them. Because these distinctions are made by the participants themselves in the ways they direct their attention and in the ways they do or do not perform, the organization of a formal occasion must reflect ideas that the participants hold about their own social life. In this sense a people's own analysis of its social order is intrinsic to the emergence of a central situational focus, the fourth aspect of formality, just as it was intrinsic to the explicit labels for, and public knowledge of, positional identities.

A Cross-Cultural Comparison: Wolof, Mursi, and Ilongot Political Meetings

I have suggested that these four aspects of formality may apply universally – that all speech communities may have social occasions that show different degrees of formality according to each of these criteria or combinations of them. These four aspects of formality are useful for comparing communicative events within a given sociocultural system, as the previous examples are meant to illustrate. But how might communities differ with respect to formality and informality in social occasions? For cross-cultural comparison both the similarities and the differences among societies need to be seen in some systematic fashion. Using the definitions of formality here proposed, one can say that speech communities may differ: (a) in the specific details of each variable or aspect of formality (e.g., what social identities are available, or precisely which linguistic phenomena are subject to additional structuring?); (b) in the ways the four aspects of formality combine or are interdependent; (c) in additional factors that correlate with formality in a given community (that is, when formality in one or all aspects is greatest, what other characteristics will the social occasion display in that community?).

To show how such differences might work and what kinds of factors might explain them, I shall compare in more detail two societies, the Wolof and the Mursi (from Turton 1975), with respect to the organization of political discourse and action. Each of these African societies has special speech events concerned with politics, including some events that are more formal than others. In other respects the two societies are quite different. The Wolof have a large-scale, complex organization of castes and centralized political authority, with a strong emphasis on social rank and inequality. The Mursi are a small-scale society, with an acephalous political system, and recognize no fundamental differences in rank other than those based on sex and age.

The comparison between Wolof and Mursi will be supplemented with a comparison with a third society, the Ilongots of the northern Philippines (from Rosaldo 1973), that shows certain resemblances to each of the other two. This part of the discussion will allow me to return to some earlier questions about relations between formality and political coercion.

Wolof and Mursi political speech events

Both the Wolof and the Mursi distinguish more formal political "discussions" or "meetings" (*methe* in Mursi, *ndaje* in Wolof)[7] from casual "chat" about political topics. The more formal events contrast with the chats in all four of the ways that are being discussed.

First, the more formal events show a greater degree of structuring, both in spatial arrangements and in the discourse. Spatially, the Wolof participants are arranged according to rank; within this arrangement the speaker in the focal sequence stands (near the center) while others sit (or stand around the sidelines). The Mursi participants are spatially arranged by age-grades, with the focal speaker standing separately and pacing back and forth. In the discourse, in both societies each speaker opens with conventional phrases. Among the Wolof there are also conventional interjections by griots in the audience, and sometimes special repetitions by griots acting as spokesmen for high-caste speakers.

The more formal events also show greater consistency in the selection among alternative forms in all communicative modes. Among the Wolof, a speaker's movements, gestures, intonation, amount of repetition, and degree of syntactic elaboration are all consistent with his social rank, particularly his caste (and so will differ according to whether he is a griot or a noble, for instance), whereas in informal chatting he might vary one or more of these modes for special purposes. Among the Mursi, although Turton gives few details, it appears that the successful speaker is one who performs in a manner fully consistent with the social image of a wise elder. The speaker's movements should be forceful but he should not show "excitement," repetitiousness, or "unintelligible" enunciation – from which I infer that there are co-occurring constraints on gesture and facial expression, intonation, rapidity of speech, choice of phonological variants, and the organization of his discourse.

In the more formal events in both societies there is a single main focal sequence, in which participation is specially regulated: only certain persons really have the right to speak "on stage," and that right has to do with their publicly recognized social identities. Among the Mursi, these positional identities involve sex and membership in particular age-grades; among the Wolof, they involve generation, caste, and tenure of labeled political offices.

There are, however, some clear differences between formal meetings of the Wolof and of the Mursi, differences that concern the organization and nature of participation among those persons who have the right to speak onstage. One difference lies in the regulation of turn taking. In Wolof meetings turn taking is relatively highly structured; the order of speakers may be announced at the beginning, or there may be a person who acts as a master of ceremonies. That is, there is usually one person who has the right to control the order of speakers in the focal sequence. In Mursi meetings, however, speakers compete for turns, and interruptions are frequent. A speaker may not be able to finish what he wants to say before the audience or another speaker interrupts him.

Another contrast concerns the nature of the speaking roles themselves. Among the Wolof, the more formal a speech event is (according to any of the four criteria, and depending on whether or not the occasion is explicitly concerned with politics), the more likely it is that the speaking roles will divide into complementary sets, associated with high and low social rank. That is, even among those who participate in the main sequence of discourse, participation is differentiated into two asymmetric roles. All levels of linguistic organization show this differentiation. There will always be some participants who speak louder, at higher pitch, with more repetitive and more emphatic constructions (usages that connote low social rank), while other participants speak more softly, at lower pitch, with fewer emphatic constructions, and so on (usages that connote high social rank). This asymmetry of speaking roles is always a concomitant of formality in Wolof speech events. But I call it a concomitant because one would not want to say it is part of a *definition* of formality that might apply cross-culturally, since the Mursi speaking roles, for instance, seem to be more symmetrical. Among the Mursi there are no structured differences among speaking roles at political meetings. Even the behavioral differences between speaker and audience are fewer than among the Wolof because the Mursi audience interrupts and interjects loud comments in a way that the Wolof audience would not.

What aspects of social or political organization, which (as has been noted) are quite different for the two peoples, might be reflected in the differing organization of their formal speech events? One possible explanation for the Wolof asymmetry of speaking roles is that Wolof society shows a greater degree of role differentiation altogether. But that is not a sufficient explanation for a contrast in speech-event organization that is qualitative, not quantitative (asymmetry vs. symmetry, not really as a matter of degree). Rather, I think the explanation lies in the Wolof preoccupation with rank and hierarchy, as opposed to the Mursi outlook, which is more egalitarian – the only structured inequalities being sex and age. The rural Wolof view society as composed of complementary unequal ranks where the upper has a natural right to command the lower.[8] Political decisions are culturally seen as initiated and decreed from above, by a recognized leader; the role of followers is only to advise and consent.

As a result, Wolof village political meetings are convened not for the purpose of decision making but for announcing decisions made from above and answering questions about them. The complementarity of ranks is the source of the asymmetrical speaking roles; the centralization and autocracy of political authority is the source of the master of ceremonies's right to determine the order of speakers. There is no competition among speakers for the opportunity to express opinions, since the expression of opinions and counterarguments is not the purpose of the meeting. Among the Wolof the expression of opinion and the exercise of debate go on in private, as does the leader's decision-making process.

Mursi political meetings, in contrast, are convened for the express purpose of decision making, by consensus, about future collective action. Each man of sufficient age has an equal right to participate in the consensus and to try to influence what consensus will be reached.

From the differences between Wolof and Mursi formal political meetings, however, it is not logical to conclude that political decision making is *actually* despotic among the Wolof and democratic among the Mursi. Wolof leaders need consensus support for their decisions, or their followers may fail to cooperate or may abandon them for other leaders. Conversely, for the Mursi, Turton notes that the decisions arrived at in formal meetings are sometimes such foregone conclusions that they were not reached during the course of the meeting at all. Private lobbying is as much a factor in some Mursi decisions as it is in the Wolof decision-making process.[9]

The differences between Wolof and Mursi formal political meetings do not reflect differences in the actual decision-making process so much as they reflect contrasts between what can be shown onstage and what happens offstage. The formality of the meetings has to do with what can be focused upon publicly; and it is in this sense that formality can often connote a social order, or forms of social action, that is publicly recognized and considered legitimate (regardless of whether political power actually operates through that public, formal social order or not). The organization of these meetings reflects political ideology, therefore, but it does not necessarily reflect political actuality.

Ilongot political meetings

We have seen that the Wolof and Mursi political meetings are both more formal, in all respects, than ordinary conversation about political matters. But is one *kind* of meeting more formal than the other? If so, does the more formal kind place greater restrictions on its participants' political freedom, as Bloch (1975) suggests? These questions are addressed more easily by turning from the Wolof and Mursi to a third society, the Ilongots of the northern Philippines (as described by Rosaldo 1973), among whom both kinds of meetings are found. One Ilongot subgroup holds political meetings that, in certain ways, resemble the Mursi *methe*; another subgroup holds meetings that resemble the Wolof *ndaje*. Many aspects of language and cultural context remain the same for both Ilongot subgroups, however. For this reason, whatever difference the form of the meeting might make should emerge more clearly than it did in the initial comparison of Wolof and Mursi.

According to Rosaldo, the Ilongots are an acephalous, egalitarian society in the process of being incorporated into a larger Philippine national polity that is both more hierarchical and more authoritarian. This process has not affected all Ilongot communities equally, however; it has gone much further among coastal communities than it has inland. Ilongots are divided, therefore, into two subgroups, the "modern" and the "traditional," which contrast in a number of ways (and see themselves as distinct). Among other things, the two subgroups differ in their conceptions of how a political meeting should be organized. Like the Mursi, traditional Ilongots hold meetings in which there is no master of ceremonies. Speakers compete for the floor and interrupt each other frequently. Like the Mursi, too, speaking roles are relatively undifferentiated. Although some men "speak for" others, no one is bound by what another says, and the relevant parties may also speak for themselves. Modern Ilongots, on the other hand, disapprove of interruptions. In their meetings a master of ceremonies calls on speakers one by one; and the people he calls on are "captains," who speak on behalf of their "soldiers" (men from their respective localities). The soldiers, who remain silent, are considered bound to uphold what their captain says. In the regulation of turn taking and differentiation of complementary behavioral roles, therefore, modern Ilongot meetings have come to resemble the Wolof meetings described above.

As among the Wolof, this centralized type of meeting coincides, for the modern Ilongots, with a new ideological emphasis on rank and authority. The connection is surely not accidental. In fact, one of the interesting things about the Ilongot example is its implication that the kinds of political meetings seen among the Wolof and Mursi actually correspond to two very basic kinds of political ideology that are widely found in societies around the world.[10]

But which kind of meeting is more formal? The modern Ilongot meeting has a more centralized focus of attention: only one person speaks at a time, and the differentiation of central from peripheral participants is apparently maintained throughout, unlike the traditional meeting (Rosaldo 1973:204–5). In one sense, therefore, the modern meeting seems to be the more formal (that is, in terms of the fourth aspect of formality listed in this article). Yet, the opposite is suggested by linguistic aspects of the discourse. Oratory in traditional meetings displays much more linguistic elaboration and redundancy, such as repetitions of utterances and parts of utterances, reduplicative constructions, formulaic expressions, and so on. Modern Ilongot oratory lacks those elaborations although it does have a few stylistic conventions of its own. So, in terms of linguistic structuring (the first aspect of formality), the traditional meeting is the more formal. The Ilongots themselves perhaps recognize that linguistic elaboration when they call modern oratory "straight speech" and traditional oratory "crooked speech." From an analytical perspective, therefore, one could not say that one type of meeting is altogether "more formal" than the other. The two are just formalized in different ways. For the Ilongots, at least, the two ways seem to be complementary (and hence, mutually exclusive). Rosaldo suggests (1973:220) that much of the linguistic elaboration and redundancy in traditional oratory is a matter of maintaining continuity and relevance in the central sequence of utterances, and keeping that sequence distinct from peripheral discourse. Linguistic elaboration, in other words, is a way of organizing speakers' access to the floor, in the absence of a master of ceremonies; it is his functional equivalent in this respect, and one would not expect to find both extreme linguistic elaboration and extreme centralization in the same communicative event.

Because the various aspects of formality are not maximized on the same social occasions, formality/informality is not a single continuum, at least not for the Ilongots. Therefore, if one type of meeting somehow restricts the political freedom of its participants more than the other, it is not formality in general that brings restrictions, but only one aspect of formality (either centralization of attention or increased structuring of code). That the more elaborated, redundant oratorical style is found, among the Ilongots, in the less authoritarian political system suggests that increased code structuring (the first aspect of formality) is not necessarily an instrument of coercion manipulated by a political leadership. As Rosaldo comments (1973:222), "Linguistic elaboration, and a reflective interest in rhetoric, belongs to societies in which no one can command another's interest or attention, let alone enforce his compliance." In contrast, the centralization of attention in modern

Ilongot meetings, with a master of ceremonies who not only prevents interruptions but determines which persons may be central speakers and which only peripheral, is the more restrictive of political expression, at least for some participants. Defined as peripheral, the Ilongot "soldiers" are not allowed to speak at the meeting at all. Their opportunities for creative statement are virtually nil.

Yet what the Ilongot "soldier" can or cannot do onstage in the meeting tells little about what he might do offstage. That the captain speaks for his men does not show whether he is a tyrant or a mere figurehead. As among the Wolof and Mursi, the formal organization of political meetings among the Ilongots is more directly related to political ideology – conscious models of the way society ought to work, as held by its members – than to the way political decisions are actually made. It is not clear, therefore, that either kind of meeting has a coercive effect on its participants in the long run, although the modern Ilongot meeting does seem to restrict some participants' opportunities for creative expression during the meeting itself.

In sum, the argument that formalizing a social occasion reduces its participants' political freedom can hold true only in limited ways. (a) Only certain aspects of formality (particularly the fourth, centralization of attention) are relevant to it; structuring of the linguistic aspects of the discourse (the first aspect of formality) is less relevant. (b) Not all participants are necessarily affected. (c) Possibly, formalization is coercive only if a society's political ideology, which the formal meeting's organization expresses, is authoritarian. (d) Finally, any restrictions on participation in formal meetings do not necessarily apply to other contexts, which may be the ones where political decision making actually occurs and where political freedom is, therefore, more at issue.

"Formality" as a Concept in Social Theory

Formality and social stasis

The foregoing discussion has concerned relations between formality (of social occasions) and political coercion. But there remains a broader kind of constraint: the force of tradition. Does formalizing a social occasion inevitably tend to reinforce a normative, traditional social order (regardless of whether that tradition prescribes an authoritarian political leadership)? Does formality always imply rigidity, stability, or conservatism?

To address those questions, the various aspects of formality must be distinguished from each other, since formality represents not just one, but several dimensions along which social occasions can vary. Not all aspects of formalization necessarily concern the public social order at all. The structured discourse of poetry, for instance, does not automatically have a special relationship to the social establishment. It need not have a public audience or a public subject matter. Nor do the ways in which the discourse in poetry is structured necessarily have to be traditional ways. If formality in speech events reflects, and in that sense supports, a traditional social system, it is the other aspects of formality that do so, not the structuring of discourse in itself. With the other three aspects of formality, the relation to an established public social system is more evident, since the social occasions that could be called formal in these respects would be those that invoke social identities and modes of participation that are publicly recognized and considered appropriate.

Certainly, these occasions concern the publicly known social system; they may even call attention to it. What is not quite so clear is whether they therefore *reinforce* it. By mentioning a thesis, for instance, one does in a certain sense support it, more than if it were allowed to fall into oblivion; but mentioning it does not mean that one agrees with it. Calling attention to something can also be a way of altering it – as when a rite of passage calls attention to an individual's social identity in order to transform it into another. Some anthropologists have argued that it is the very formality of such ritual occasions, which minimize personal histories and focus on the relevant social relationships, that makes the creative transformation possible (see, for example, Douglas 1966:77–9).[11]

Now it might be objected that the transformation of social identities that goes on in a rite of passage, although a kind of creativity, is a superficial kind in that it operates only *within* a traditional system. It is not the same thing as change in that system, to which formalization might still be inimical. But formalization can be thought inimical to change only if one has a certain view of the social system to which formal occasions call attention – a view that the social system is monolithic, that the structure of a society prevents its members from conceiving of alternatives, and that all members of society have exactly identical conceptions of the social order. If members' political ideologies, for instance, differ, there can scarcely be a situation in which such differences become more apparent than in formal meetings whose organization, as we saw for the Wolof, Mursi, and Ilongot, is ideologically based. This ideological clash is just what happens among the Ilongots, when people from coastal ("modern") communities and people from inland ("traditional") communities have to hold joint meetings. When, on such an occasion, the Ilongots found they did not agree on how a meeting should be run, assumptions about how and why meetings are organized could not be left unquestioned. They had to be discussed (and, one gathers, some accommodation reached; see Rosaldo 1973:219). That is, the process of formalization forces the recognition of conflicting ideas and in so doing may impel their change. (There is also, of course, the inverse situation, in which a group with internal conflicts tries to avoid holding the formal meetings that might oblige those conflicts to be faced. Stability and communal harmony are thus achieved by *not* formalizing. See, e.g., the Israeli *moshav* described by Abarbanel 1975:152.)

The Ilongot example represents an acculturative situation, where the ideational conflict comes about because new ideas are introduced from outside. I do not want to suggest, however, that outside influence is necessary before formalization can induce change. To the extent that ideas about the social order vary according to the social position of those who hold them, any social system will generate differences of opinion, and that is quite apart from the possibility that the ideas themselves might be ambiguous, contradictory, or indeterminate. The point is that formalization does not automatically support stability and conservatism unless the social relations it articulates are fully agreed on by everyone and admit no alternatives. Whether that is the case depends on the particular social relations and on the cultural system in question; it is not implicit in the analytical concept of formality itself.[12]

Is "formality" useful as a cover term?

The various aspects of formality distinguished in this paper concern quite different kinds of social phenomena. Some concern properties of code while others concern properties of a social situation; some focus on observable behavior while others invoke the conceptual categories of social actors. For purposes of description and analysis, all such matters can and should be considered separately. But their separation in a research strategy does not mean that they are all fully independent variables. In fact, they must be interdependent, to the extent that cultural definitions of social situations and social identities must have a behavioral content.

This interdependence is something that social actors can exploit by altering their behavior to bring about a redefinition of the situation and of the identities that are relevant to it. The Wolof griot (praise-singer) who tries to capture the guests' attention at a naming-day ceremony illustrates this process (see the section on the emergence of a central situational focus). If he succeeds in attracting the attention of all the guests, a situation that began as a multifocused gathering coalesces into a single all-encompassing engagement; and, in consequence, positional identities whose scopes are wide enough to include all persons present will be invoked. Normally, caste identities are the relevant ones, especially since the griot is acting in accordance with his own caste specialization. Because high-caste persons in general owe largesse to griots, invoking caste identities places high-caste guests under obligation to reward the praise-singer even if the words of his performance do not mention them. (Some high-caste Wolof report that in the hope that they will not have to pay, they pretend not to notice the griot unless he already has a large audience.)

In this example, the Wolof naming-day ceremony, the third aspect of formality (positional identities) is entailed by the fourth (emergence of a centralized situational focus). In fact, it is reasonable to suppose that centralization is always likely to entail positional identities if a large number of persons are present, because positional identities are the ones that are widely recognized and that organize people on a systematic and broad scale. Similarly, the third aspect of formality is also entailed by the second (code consistency), because the sociolinguistic variants among which the speaker selects usually express categorical, not individual, identities. Complete code consistency would mean, for instance, that a Wolof man who uses an intonational pattern associated with griots (extreme speed, loudness, high pitch) will consistently express griot identity in all other aspects of his behavior as well (syntax, posture, movements, and so on). Little scope would be left for individuality.

Yet, if there are certain ways in which the various aspects of formality are interdependent, there are other ways in which they are not. In the first place, the entailments just mentioned do not seem to be reversible. Thus no. 4 entails no. 3, but no. 3 does not have to entail no. 4. The griot can invoke caste identities even when privately addressing a single high-caste individual, and he can do so simply by declaring, "I am a griot." Although some of his intonational and gestural usages must be consistent with this statement if it is not to sound like a joke, not all of them need be. For instance, his speed of talk might be slow, unlike the rapid tempo normally associated with griots. By such means he can distance himself enough from the griot role to make some personal comment on it, even if he still intends caste identities to define the situation and to suggest his interlocutor's course of action.

Finally, there is no intrinsic reason why code consistency, positional identities, or centralization (no. 2, 3, or 4) should entail a change in the degree of structuring to which a code is subjected (criterion no. 1) or vice versa. Linguistic aspects of discourse in poetry are structured, for instance, but a poem's subject matter can be entirely private. Moreover, code switches and code inconsistencies in poetry are frequent and can contribute significantly to the poem's special effect. The first aspect of formality seems, therefore, to be independent of the other three; and this was also suggested by the Ilongot example, in which the same event cannot maximize both linguistic structuring (formality no. 1) and centralization (formality no. 4).

Is there, after all this, any sense in which all four aspects of formality are related – a sense in which *formality* remains useful as a cover term? I think there is, but it is so general that it is not very useful as an analytical tool. The only thing all four criteria have in common is that all of them concern the degree to which a social occasion is systematically organized. This sense of formality as "degree of organization" has some resemblance to Goffman's (1963:199) definition of formality/informality as "tightness"/"looseness." The thrust of my argument, however, is that being organized in one way does not necessarily mean being organized in other ways to the same degree or at the same time. In fact, the various ways in which a communicative event is organizable may be complementary or even antithetical, rather than additive.

I suspect, therefore, that it is appropriate in few instances to speak of "formality" generally without specifying more precisely what one has in mind. Otherwise, there is too great a risk of mistaking one kind of formality for another or assuming that kinds of formality are really the same. That an ordinary English word has multiple meanings – as we have seen in its multiple uses in the sociolinguistic literature – does not make those meanings essentially homogeneous, nor should we unwittingly elevate this word's polysemy to a social theory. As Leach has remarked (1961:27), "We anthropologists...must reexamine basic premises and realize that English language patterns of thought are not a necessary model for the whole of human society."

NOTES

Acknowledgment. I am indebted to Ben Blount, Dell Hymes, Joel Sherzer, Maurice Bloch, and David Turton for their helpful comments on an earlier version of this paper.

1   The application is made except insofar as the linguist acts as his or her own informant and so combines the roles of observer and subject.
2   Actually, to equate the relevant aspects of code structuring with addition of or elaboration of existing rules presents some problems. The notion seems to apply well enough to examples such as the Wolof insult sessions described in the section *Increased Code Structuring*, because speech rhythms in those sessions must not only conform to the usual metric principles of stress and length in ordinary speech but be further organized to fit a precise and repetitive drum rhythm. But it is not clear that redundancies of meter, rhyme, or syntactic parallelism in poetry should always be interpreted in terms of addition of rules. For instance, Sherzer's (1974)

description of Cuna congress chants proposes that syntactic parallelism and redundancy are achieved by retaining underlying representations, i.e., by *not* following the usual transformational rules that would zero out redundant noun phrases and verb phrases. This suggests that the special aesthetic structure of chants is achieved by using fewer rules, rather than more. Yet, how do the rules of chanting provide for the fact that the usual reductions are not to occur? Is there any assurance that this provision is not best analyzed via extra rules that reinsert the redundant forms, since that analysis might better conform to general principles of markedness (if the chants are to be considered as marked discourse forms)? A similar problem arises for types of Western poetry in which, it is sometimes said, structuring of meter and rhyme is accompanied by syntactic and semantic "poetic licence." This argument suggests that extra structuring in one aspect of the discourse might be accompanied by loosening of structure in another. It is not clear, however, that "licence" is really the appropriate conception of poetic syntax and semantics. The issues here are complex and they reach far beyond the scope of this paper.

3   Since my fieldwork was conducted in rural areas of the Préfecture de Tivaouane, when I speak of "the Wolof" I can, of course, mean only the villages I have myself observed and the extent to which they may be representative of Wolof villages more generally. This caveat is necessary because "Wolof" as an ethnic category now includes a numerous and diverse population, urban as well as rural, elite as well as peasant. I believe my comments here apply to the *Communautés Rurales* (Senegalese rural administrative units) in the core regions of Wolof occupation; they do not necessarily apply to urban Wolof.

4   See Goffman's discussion (1963:198–215) relating formality/informality to degree of involvement in a situation.

5   Other authors describe a similar distinction in somewhat different terms. Geertz (1966), for example, speaks of the "anonymization of individuals" in ceremonialized interaction.

6   For another example, see Tyler's (1972) paper on the Koya of central India. A number of behavioral differences, including lexical choices, differentiate central from peripheral actors in Koya formal events.

7   The occasions I refer to are public meetings conducted in rural villages or *Communautés Rurales*. Increasingly, Wolof call these meetings by the French term *réunion*, which (in Senegalese usage) distinguishes them more definitively from casual encounters than does the Wolof term *ndaje*.

8   I leave aside the relation of the priesthood (*Imans* and *marabouts*), which ranks highest in a religious sense, to political decision making.

9   On this point, Turton comments (personal communication) that "although the Mursi do indeed see their debates as decision-making procedures, I am less and less convinced that, from the point of view of the outside observer, they should be thus characterized."

10 I do not mean to suggest that these two societal types, if types they are, exhaust all possibilities of political ideology and organized political discussion; our own society probably fits neither. Nor, on the basis of materials presented in this paper, do I propose to match such types to points on an evolutionary scale. That two forms of political discourse have a certain historical relationship among the Ilongots does not mean they will have the same relationship everywhere.

11 See also Firth (1975) on "the *experimental* aspect of [formal] oratory" in Tikopia (emphasis in original). Firth argues that public meetings and formal oratory emerge in Tikopia under conditions of crisis and social change, not during periods of stability. The Tikopia *fono* (formal assembly of titled elders) cannot be dismissed as merely a reactionary reaffirmation of a threatened tradition. It is also a means of publicly exploring important issues, and a way for Tikopia leaders to find out whether a new proposal is likely to be acceptable (1975:42–3).

12 Sally Falk Moore (1975:231) makes a similar point: "It is important to recognize that processes of regularization, processes having to do with rules and regularities, may be used to block change or to produce change. The fixing of rules and regularities are as much tools of revolutionaries as they are of reactionaries. It is disastrous to confuse the analysis of processes of regularization with the construction of static social models."

REFERENCES

Abarbanel, Jay (1975). The Dilemma of Economic Competition in an Israeli Moshav. In *Symbol and Politics in Communal Ideology*. Sally Falk Moore and Barbara Myerhoff, eds., pp. 144–65. Ithaca: Cornell University Press.

Albert, Ethel (1972). Cultural Patterning of Speech Behavior in Burundi. In *Directions in Sociolinguistics*. John Gumperz and Dell Hymes, eds., pp. 72–105. New York: Holt, Rinehart, and Winston.

Bateson, Gregory (1972). *Steps to an Ecology of Mind*. San Francisco: Chandler.

Bauman, Richard, and Joel Sherzer (eds.) (1974). *Explorations in the Ethnography of Speaking*. London: Cambridge University Press.

Bloch, Maurice (ed.) (1975). *Political Language and Oratory in Traditional Society*. New York: Academic Press.

Bricker, Victoria (1974). The Ethnographic Context of Some Traditional Mayan Speech Genres. In *Explorations in the Ethnography of Speaking*. Richard Bauman and Joel Sherzer, eds., pp. 368–88. London: Cambridge University Press.

Davis, Ermina (1976). In Honor of the Ancestors: The Social Context of Iwi Egungun Chanting in a Yoruba Community. Ph. D. dissertation, Brandeis University.

Douglas, Mary (1966). *Purity and Danger*. Baltimore: Penguin.

Ervin-Tripp, Susan (1972). On Sociolinguistic Rules: Alternation and Co-occurrence. In *Directions in Sociolinguistics*. John Gumperz and Dell Hymes, eds., pp. 213–50. New York: Holt, Rinehart, and Winston.

Firth, Raymond (1975). Speech-making and Authority in Tikopia. In *Political Language and Oratory in Traditional Society*. Maurice Bloch, ed., pp. 29–44. New York: Academic Press.

Fischer, John (1972). The Stylistic Significance of Consonantal Sandhi in Trukese and Ponapean. In *Directions in Sociolinguistics*. John Gumperz and Dell Hymes, eds., pp. 498–511. New York: Holt, Rinehart, and Winston.

Fishman, Joshua (ed.) (1968). *Readings in the Sociology of Language*. The Hague: Mouton.

Fishman, Joshua (1972). *Sociolinguistics: A Brief Introduction*. Rowley, Mass.: Newbury House.

Fox, James (1974). "Our Ancestors Spoke in Pairs": Rotinese Views of Language, Dialect, and Code. In *Explorations in the Ethnography of Speaking*. Richard Bauman and Joel Sherzer, eds., pp. 65–85. London: Cambridge University Press.

Friedrich, Paul (1972). Social Context and Semantic Feature: The Russian Pronominal Usage. In *Directions in Sociolinguistics*. John Gumperz and Dell Hymes, eds, pp. 270–300. New York: Holt, Rinehart, and Winston.

Geertz, Clifford (1966). *Person, Time and Conduct in Bali: An Essay in Cultural Analysis*. Yale Southeast Asia Program, Cultural Report Series, No. 14. New Haven.

Goffman, Erving (1961). *Encounters: Two Studies in the Sociology of Interaction*. Indianapolis, IN: Bobbs-Merrill.

Goffman, Erving (1963). *Behavior in Public Places*. New York: Free Press.

Goffman, Erving (1974). *Frame Analysis*. New York: Harper and Row.

Gossen, Gary (1974). To Speak with a Heated Heart: Chamula Canons of Style and Good Performance. In *Explorations in the Ethnography of Speaking*. Richard Bauman and Joel Sherzer, eds., pp. 389–413. London: Cambridge University Press.

Gumperz, John, and Dell Hymes (eds.) (1972). *Directions in Sociolinguistics*. New York: Holt, Rinehart, and Winston.

Halliday, Michael (1964). The Users and Uses of Language. In *The Linguistic Sciences and Language Teaching*. Halliday, McIntosh, and Strevens, eds. London: Longmans. (Reprinted in Fishman 1968, pp. 139–69.)

Hymes, Dell (1972). Models of the Interaction of Language and Social Life. In *Directions in Sociolinguistics*. John Gumperz and Dell Hymes, eds., pp. 35–71. New York: Holt, Rinehart, and Winston.

Irvine, Judith (1974). Strategies of Status Manipulation in the Wolof Greeting. In *Explorations in the Ethnography of Speaking*. Richard Bauman and Joel Sherzer, eds., pp. 167–91. London: Cambridge University Press.

Jackson, Jean (1974). Language Indentity of the Colombian Vaupés Indians. In *Explorations in the Ethnography of Speaking*. Richard Bauman and Joel Sherver, eds., pp. 50–64. London: Cambridge University Press.

Jefferson, Gail (1972). Side Sequences. In *Studies in Social Interaction*. David Sudnow, ed., pp. 294–338. New York: Free Press.

Joos, Martin (1959). *The Isolation of Styles*. Monograph Series on Languages and Linguistics 12:107–13. Washington, D.C.: Georgetown University. (Reprinted in Fishman 1968, pp. 185–91.)

Kirshenblatt-Gimblett, Barbara (ed.) (1976). *Speech Play*. Philadelphia: University of Pennsylvania Press.

Labov, William (1972). Some Principles of Linguistic Methodology. *Language in Society* 1:97–120.

Leach, Edmund (1961). *Rethinking Anthropology*. London: Athlone.

Leach, Edmund (1965). *Political Systems of Highland Burma*. Boston: Beacon Press.

Mead, Margaret (1937). Public Opinion Mechanisms Among Primitive Peoples. *Public Opinion Quarterly* 1:5–16.

Moore, Sally Falk (1975). Epilogue: Uncertainties in Situations, Indeterminacies in Culture. In *Symbol and Politics in Communal Ideology*. Sally Falk Moore and Barbara Myerhoff, eds., pp. 210–39. Ithaca: Cornell University Press.

Murphy, Robert (1971). *The Dialectics of Social Life*. New York: Basic Books.

Rosaldo, Michelle Z. (1973). I Have Nothing to Hide: The Language of Ilongot Oratory. *Language in Society* 2:193–224.

Rubin, Joan (1968). Bilingual Usage in Paraguay. In *Readings in the Sociology of Language*. Joshua Fishman, ed., pp. 512–30. The Hague: Mouton.

Sanches, Mary, and Ben Blount (eds.) (1975). *Sociocultural Dimensions of Language Use*. New York: Academic Press.

Sherzer, Joel (1974). Namakke, Sunmakke, Kormakke: Three Types of Cuna Speech Event. In *Explorations in the Ethnography of Speaking*. Richard Bauman and Joel Sherzer, eds., pp. 263–82. London: Cambridge University Press.

Timm, L. A. (1975). Spanish-English Code-Switching: El Porqué y How-Not-To. *Romance Philology* 28:473–82.

Turton, David (1975). The Relationships Between Oratory and the Exercise of Influence Among the Mursi. In *Political Language and Oratory in Traditional Society*. Maurice Bloch, ed., pp. 163–84. New York: Academic Press.

Tyler, Stephen (1972). Context and Alternation in Koya Kinship Terminology. In *Directions in Sociolinguistics*. John Gumperz and Dell Hymes, eds., pp. 251–69. New York: Holt, Rinehart, and Winston.

Wolfson, Nessa (1976). Speech Events and Natural Speech: Some Implications for Sociolinguistic Methodology. *Language in Society* 5:189–210.

9

Universal and Culture-Specific Properties of Greetings

Alessandro Duranti

There is widespread evidence that greetings are an important part of the communicative competence necessary for being a member of any speech community.[1] They are often one of the first verbal routines learned by children and certainly one of the first topics introduced in foreign language classes. They are also of great interest to analysts of social interaction, who see them as establishing the conditions for social encounters. It is not surprising, then, to find out that there is a considerable number of ethological, linguistic, sociological, and ethnographic studies of greetings. But despite the attention greetings have received in the social sciences, there is to date no generalizable definition of greetings and therefore no systematic way for deciding what qualifies as "greetings" in a particular speech community. Nonetheless, researchers have felt at ease identifying "greetings" in different languages and providing hypotheses about what greetings "do" for or to people. In this article, I suggest that this has been possible due to the widespread belief that greetings are verbal formulas with virtually no propositional content (Searle 1969) or zero referential value (Youssouf et al. 1976). Students of greetings have argued that people are either not believed to "mean" whatever they say during greetings or they are seen as "lying" (see Sacks 1975). In fact, I will argue, these claims are not always tenable. As I will show, not all greetings are completely predictable and devoid of propositional content. Before making such a claim, however, I must establish some independent criteria by which to determine whether a given expression or exchange should qualify as a "greeting." Short of such criteria, critics might always argue that the apparent counterexamples are not greetings at all.

In what follows I first briefly review the existing literature on greetings in a variety of fields and identify some of the factors that contributed to the common belief that greetings are formulas with no propositional content. Then I introduce six criteria for identifying greetings across languages and speech communities. Using these criteria, I go on to identify four types of verbal greetings in one community where I worked, in [formerly] Western Samoa. In discussing the fourth Samoan greeting, the "Where are you going?" type, I will argue that it blatantly violates the common expectation of greetings as phatic, predictable exchanges, and I show that it functions as an information-seeking and action-control strategy. Finally, I examine a Samoan expression that has been translated as a greeting in English but seems problematic on the basis of ethnographic information, and I show that, as we would expect, it does not qualify for some of the criteria proposed in this article.

Previous Studies

The literature on greetings can be divided along several methodological and theoretical lines. In what follows, I will briefly review the contribution of human ethologists, ethnographers, conversation analysts, and speech act theorists.

In the ethological tradition, exemplified by Irenäus Eibl-Eibesfeldt's work, greetings are studied as a means to uncovering some of the evolutionary bases of human behavior. By comparing humans with other species and adult–adult interaction with mother–child interaction (Eibl-Eibesfeldt 1977), greetings are defined as rituals of appeasing and bonding that counteract potentially aggressive behavior during face-to-face encounters. The presupposition here is that humans and animals alike live in a permanent, phylogenetically encoded condition of potential aggression (or fear of aggression) and, were it not for such adaptive rituals as greetings, individuals would be tearing each other apart. Fear of aggression is also used by Kendon and Ferber (1973) to explain eye-gaze aversion during certain phases of human encounters – people look away just as primates and other animals do to avoid the threat of physical confrontation – and by Firth (1972) and others to interpret the common gesture of handshake across societies as a symbol of trust in the other. This line of research is characterized by three features: (i) a focus on nonverbal communication (for example, Eibl-Eibesfeldt's 1972 study of the eyebrow flash), which is often analyzed independently of the talk that accompanies it; (ii) the assumption of shared goals between humans and other species; and (iii) the assumption that the same type of greeting behavior will have the same origin, motivation, or explanation across situations. The focus on nonverbal communication has been important in counterbalancing the logocentric tendency of other studies of greetings (see below) and has revealed commonalities across cultures that would have been missed were researchers concentrating exclusively on verbal behavior. The second feature, namely, the assumption that humans and animals share similar goals, presents certain problems. It might be easy to accept that all species share a concern for survival and safety, but it is less easy to believe that the meaning of such a concern could be the same across species. For instance, Firth (1972), Goffman (1971), and others suggested that greetings in all societies are about continuity of relationships, but the representation, conceptualization, and perception of continuity by humans are likely to be much more complex than those found in other species, partly due to the use of human language (Leach 1972). Furthermore, without minimizing the aggressive potential of human psyche and human action, we must remember that there are other things in life besides fighting or avoiding fights. Hence, even if we accept that greeting behavior might have phylogenetically originated from avoidance behavior, we still must demonstrate that such an origin is relevant to the specific context in which a particular greeting is used.

A second set of studies of greetings is ethnographically oriented. These studies tend to be descriptive in nature, focusing on culture-specific aspects of greeting behaviors, but they also share an interest in a few potentially universal dimensions such as the sequential properties of greeting exchanges and the importance of status definition and manipulation. This is particularly true of two classic studies of African greetings: Esther Goody's (1972) comparison of greeting and begging among the Gonja and the Lodagaa – a stratified and an acephalous society respectively – and Judith Irvine's (1974) study of Wolof greetings.

Ethnographically oriented studies tend to highlight the importance of identity definition in greetings. Some of them also reveal the subtle ways in which greetings are connected to or part of the definition of the ongoing (or ensuing) activity. This is especially the case in Caton's (1986) and Milton's (1982) studies, which provide clear examples not only of the religious dimensions of greetings in some societies but also of how what is said during greetings both presupposes and entails a particular type of social encounter (see also Duranti 1992a).

The emphasis on the sequential nature of greeting exchanges is the most important contribution of the work of conversation analysts. Schegloff and Sacks's work on conversational openings and closings, for instance, shows that greetings should not be analyzed as isolated acts but as a series of pairs, adjacency pairs, whereby the uttering of the first part by one party calls for and at the same time defines the range of a possible "next turn" by a second party, the recipient (Sacks 1992; Schegloff 1968, 1986; Schegloff and Sacks 1973). Sacks's (1975) study of "How are you?" as a "greeting substitute" in English provides a stimulating description of the interactional implications of choosing to greet and choosing to answer in a particular way; we learn why answering "fine" has different consequences from answering "lousy," and hence we are provided with a sociological justification for lying. As I will show later, the extension of these insights into another language and a different speech community shows that it is not always as easy to determine what is a greeting "substitute." Nor is it always the case that routinized questions can be easily answered by lying.

Finally, greetings have been analyzed by speech act theorists, who focused on their function as acknowledgment of another person's presence. Searle (1969) and Searle and Vanderveken (1985) proposed to analyze English greetings as an example of the "expressive" type of speech act,[2] aimed at the "courteous indication of recognition" of the other party (Searle and Vanderveken 1985:216), and Bach and Harnish (1979) classified greetings as "acknowledgments," their reformulation of Austin's "behabitives"[3] and Searle's "expressives." In line with authors in other research traditions, Searle (1969) and Searle and Vanderveken (1985) also assume that greetings have no propositional content, while Bach and Harnish (1979:51–2) interpret the act of greeting as an expression of "pleasure at seeing (or meeting)" someone. The claim that greetings have no propositional content – or almost zero referential value (Youssouf et al. 1976) – is at least as old as Malinowski's (1923:315–16) introduction of the notion of "phatic communion," a concept that was originally meant to recast speech as a mode of action, a form of social behavior that establishes or confirms social relations and does not necessarily communicate "new ideas." The problem with the characterization of greetings as "phatic," and hence merely aimed at establishing or maintaining "contact" (Jakobson 1960), is that it makes it difficult to account for differences across and within communities in what people say during greetings. Finally, the view of greeting as an act that displays pleasure might make sense in some contexts and especially in those situations where verbal greetings are accompanied by smiles and other nonverbal as well as verbal displays of positive affect (for example, the English "Nice to see you"), but it might not be generalizable beyond such cases.

The interest in the biological basis of greetings, their social functions, their sequential organization, and their illocutionary force have revealed a number of recurrent properties of greetings and have presented interesting hypotheses about the form and function of greetings. At the same time, the emphasis on the "social functions" of greetings has contributed to the trivialization of what people actually talk about during greetings. If the only or main goal of greeting is to acknowledge another person's presence, what is actually said during a greeting may be seen as socially insignificant. In this article I argue that this lack of consideration of the propositional content of greetings presents considerable empirical problems, and I suggest that we need ethnographically grounded analyses of greeting expressions to solve such problems.

One of the problems in ignoring the content of verbal greetings is that it establishes loose connections between social functions and the talk used to achieve them. As a consequence, differences in what people say can be ignored and we end up supporting the view that "once you've seen a greeting, you've seen them all," a corollary of the more general principle "once you've seen a ritual, you've seen them all." (Hence, why bother with the study of different societies, given that all you need can be found in your own backyard?)

The context for understanding what people say during greetings is nothing more or nothing less than the culture that supports and is supported by the encounters in which greetings occur or that are constituted by them. The method by which such encounters need to be studied must then minimally include (1) ethnography,[4] (2) the recording of what is actually said, and (3) at least a working definition of the phenomenon that is being investigated. Too many of the existing studies of greetings are based either on observation, interviews, or field notes, without the support of film or electronic recording or on recordings without proper ethnographic work (see Duranti 1997a: ch. 5).

The Universality of Greetings

The starting assumption in this study is that we must be open to all kinds of conventional openings in social encounters as potential cases of greetings. Although some speech communities have activity-specific items that are used only for greetings (the American English "hi!" and the Italian "ciao," for example[5]), the existing literature shows that many communities do not have such expressions, and what people say during greetings might be identical to what is being said during other kinds of speech activities, the English "how're you doing?" being an example of such a type. For this reason, to concentrate only on lexical items and phrases exclusively reserved for greetings (or, more generally, salutations) would be tantamount to admitting that many languages do not have greetings or have a much restricted set of types. The criteria provided below are offered as a solution to this problem.

Criteria for Identifying Greetings across Languages

Building on the studies mentioned above and a few others, it is possible to extract a set of six recurring features to be used as criteria for the identification of greetings in a speech community:

1   near-boundary occurrence;
2   establishment of a shared perceptual field;
3   adjacency pair format;
4   relative predictability of form and content;
5   implicit establishment of a spatiotemporal unit of interaction; and
6   identification of the interlocutor as a distinct being worth recognizing.

As it will become apparent in the following discussion, some of these features could be grouped into larger categories. For example, features 3, 4, and 6 cover what is actually said in greetings, whereas features 2, 5, and 6 are reformulations of what other authors have identified as potential functions of greetings. In addition, features 1 and 5 (and in some ways, 2) define the spatial and temporal organization of the exchange. Although future studies may prove the need to regroup or even eliminate some of the distinctions that I am proposing, for the purpose of this article I have chosen to keep the six criteria distinct to ensure a broader spectrum of potentially relevant cases. Finally, I should mention that although both verbal and nonverbal aspects of greeting behavior were taken into consideration in the choice of defining features, later on in the article, I will favor verbal over nonverbal aspects of greetings. This is simply due to my efforts in this case to draw attention to the importance of the specific verbal expressions used in greetings and is not meant to undermine the importance of gestures and motion in the analysis of social encounters, which I have addressed elsewhere (Duranti 1992a) and intend to return to in the future.

Criterion 1: Near-boundary occurrence

Greetings are routinely expected to occur at the beginning of a social encounter, although they may not always be the very first words that are exchanged between parties. This first feature of greetings is related to their potential function as attention-getting devices and their ability to establish a shared field of interaction (see criteria 2 and 5). As defined here, greetings must then be distinguished from closing salutations or leave takings, despite the fact that in some cases the same expression might function as both opening and closing salutation.[6]

Criterion 2: Establishment of a shared perceptual field

Greetings either immediately follow or are constitutive of the interactants' public recognition of each other's presence in the same perceptual field,[7] as shown by the fact that they are usually initiated after the parties involved have sighted each other (Duranti 1992a; Kendon and Ferber 1973). In some cases, making recognition visually available to the other party may constitute the greeting itself (viz., with a toss of the head, a nod, or an eyebrow flash); in other cases, visual recognition is followed by verbal recognition. There are differences, however, in the timing of the verbal exchange vis-à-vis other forms of mutual recognition or verbal interaction. In some cases, talk may be exchanged before the actual greeting takes place. This is the case, for instance, in the Samoan ceremonial greetings (see below), where participants may exchange jokes, questions, or a few brief remarks before starting to engage in what is seen as the official greeting. A possible hypothesis here is that the more formal – or the more institutionally oriented – the encounter, the more delayed the greeting, and that the more delayed the greeting, the more elaborate the language used. Thus we would expect brief and casual opening salutations to occur simultaneously with or at least very close to mutual sighting and long and elaborate greetings to occur after the parties have had a chance to previously recognize each other's presence in some way. One of the most extreme examples of this delayed greeting is the one described by Sherzer (1983) among the Kuna, where a visiting "chief" who has come to the "gathering house" is greeted after he and his entourage ("typically consisting of his wife, his 'spokesman,' and one of his 'policemen,'") have been taken to someone's house to bathe.

Then they return to the "gathering house," where the visiting "chief" and one of the host village "chiefs," sitting beside one another in hammocks, perform *arkan kae* (literally handshake), the ritual greeting. (Sherzer 1983:91)

Such chanted greetings are quite extended, including a long sequence of verses that are regularly responded to by the other chief, who chants *teki* "indeed".

Observationally, this property of greetings is a good index of the function of the greeting and the type of context and participants involved. Immediate and short greetings tend to index an ordinary encounter, whereas delayed and long greetings tend to index something special in the occasion, the social status of the participants, their relationships, or any combination of these various aspects.

This idea of greetings as reciprocal recognitions could be an argument in favor of Bach and Harnish's (1979) classification of greetings as "acknowledgments." Greeting would be a response to finding oneself within someone's visual and/ or auditory range – if such a person is a candidate for recognition. As we shall see, the view of greetings as acknowledgments does not imply the acceptance of Bach and Harnish's view of greeting as a universal expression of attitudes or feelings.

Criterion 3: Adjacency pair format

Although it is possible to speak of a "greeting" by one person, greetings are typically part of one or more sets of adjacency pairs (see Schegloff and Sacks 1973), that is, two-part sequences in which the first pair part by one party (A) invites, constrains, and creates the expectation for a particular type of reply by another party (B); see examples 1, 4, and 6 below. The adjacency pair structure makes sense if greetings are exchanges in which participants test each other's relationship (e.g., Are we still on talking terms? Are we still friends? Do I still recognize your authority? Do I still acknowledge my responsibility toward you?). The sequential format of the adjacency pair allows participants to engage in a joint activity that exhibits some evidence of mutual recognition and mutual understanding. The number, utterance type, and participant structure of these pairs vary both within and across communities (see Duranti 1992a:660–2).[8] For example, some African greetings are organized in several adjacency pairs (Irvine 1974).

If we take the adjacency pair format to be a defining feature of greetings, a one-pair-part greeting – not as uncommon as one might think – would be "defective" or in need of an explanation.

Criterion 4: Relative predictability of form and content

Since what is said during a greeting or part of a greeting exchange is highly predictable compared to other kinds of interactions, researchers have often assumed that greetings have no propositional content and their denotational value (to be assessed in terms of truth) can be largely ignored. Whether people say "hi," "good morning," or "how are you?" has been seen as an index of properties of the context (for example, the relationship between the parties, the nature of the social encounter) rather than as a concern participants manifest toward gaining access to new information about their interlocutors. This aspect of greetings needs to be further qualified in at least three ways. First, it should be made clear that information is exchanged in human encounters regardless of whether there is talk. Even when there is no speech, there are usually plenty of semiotic resources in an encounter for participants to give out information about themselves and make inferences about others. Such semiotic resources are based on or include participants' mere physical presence, their gestures, posture, and movements, their clothes, the objects they carry or the tools they are using. Second, there is information exchanged beyond the propositional content of what is said. For example, prosodic and paralinguistic features are a rich source of cues for contextualization (Gumperz 1992). Finally, even common formulaic expressions can be informative. In fact, if we start from the assumption that what is said and done in any human encounter lives along a formulaic–creative continuum, greetings might simply be interactions that tend to fall toward the formulaic side. We cannot, however, in principle assume that, because greetings are formulaic, (i) they are always completely predictable, (ii) they have no information value, and (iii) participants have nothing invested in the propositional value of what is said. First, the fact of considering an exchange highly routinized does not make its content completely predictable or uninteresting for social analysis, a point well illustrated by Bourdieu's (1977) analysis of gift exchange and Schegloff's (1986) discussion of telephone openings. It is still important to ascertain how participants manage to achieve the expected or preferred outcome. Second, the occurrence of certain routine and highly predictable questions and answers during greetings does not imply that the parties involved do not exchange some new information. Third, whether or not the participants are interested in the information that is being exchanged should be an empirical question and not an unquestioned assumption.

Criterion 5: Implicit establishment of a spatiotemporal unit of interaction

The occurrence of greetings defines a unit of interaction. Sacks (1975) alluded to this feature of greetings by saying that they occur only once in an interaction and that they can constitute a "minimal proper conversation." More generally, greetings clearly enter into the definition of larger units of analysis such as a day at work, different parts of the day with family members, or even extended interactions over several months – for example, when done through electronic mail (Duranti 1986). That the "unit" is something more complex than a continuous stretch of time (e.g., a day) is shown by the fact that two people meeting in two different places during the same day may in fact exchange greetings again. An empirical investigation of when greetings are exchanged throughout a day by a given group of people who repeatedly come into each other's interactional space might provide important clues on how they conceptualize the different space-time zones in which they operate. It might also give us a sense of the relation between natural units (such as a day–night cycle) versus cultural units (such as a meeting).

Criterion 6: Identification of the interlocutor as a distinct being worth recognizing

The occurrence of greetings and the ways in which they are carried out typically identify a particular class of people. Syntagmatically, a greeting item (e.g., English "hello," "hi," "hey, how're you doing," "what's up") might be accompanied by address terms or other context-dependent and context-creating signs that identify participants as belonging to social groups of various sorts. Paradigmatically, the very use of greetings (as opposed to their absence) identifies a group of people as members of the class of individuals with whom we communicate in public or private arenas. That this is more than a tautology may be shown in various ways, including Sacks's (1975) arguments that in English the people we greet with the (substitute) greeting "how are you?" constitute a class he called "proper conversationalists." Even in those societies in which apparently *any* two people entering the same perceptual field would be expected to exchange greetings, distinctions are in fact made. Thus, for instance, among the Tuareg, according to Youssouf et al. (1976:801), once two people are seen progressing toward one another, the parties *must* meet, and once they have met, they must greet each other. Such moral imperatives, however, must be understood against the background of a social world in which avoiding greeting would be interpreted as a potentially threatening situation:

The desert people have a history of intertribal warfare and intratribal feuds. If the Targi meets another, or others, in [the desert], the identification of the other – as early as possible – is critically important. For, once another person is sighted on a intersecting trajectory, there is no turning aside ... for that can be interpreted as a sign of either fear or potential treachery and ambush, which invites countermeasures. (Youssouf et al. 1976:801)

This means that, implicitly, the use of greetings can distinguish between Us and Them, insiders and outsiders, friends and foes, valuable and nonvaluable interactants.

For example, in many societies children and servants are not greeted. The absence of greetings then marks these individuals not only as nonproper conversationalists or strangers but also as not worth the attention implied by the use of greetings.

An Empirical Case Study

Any proposal for universal criteria needs empirical investigations to support it. In the rest of this article, I will offer a brief discussion of Samoan greetings as a way of assessing and refining some of the claims made so far. In particular, I will be concerned with two main issues: (i) the relationship between universal features and culture-specific instantiations of such features, and (ii) the distinction between verbal expressions that are greetings and those that, although they might look like potential candidates, are not greetings.

It should be understood that what follows is not an exhaustive study of Samoan greetings. Such a study would require a project expressively designed with the goal of collecting all types of greetings used in Samoan communities;[9] in fact, as far as I know, such a comprehensive project has never been attempted for any speech community. Although the data discussed here are drawn from a range of interactions originally recorded for other purposes, they do contain a considerable number of exchanges that qualify as greetings according to the above mentioned criteria. Furthermore, in using Samoan data, I have the advantage of relying on previous studies of language in context carried out by myself or other researchers.

Four Types of Samoan Greetings

On the basis of the criteria mentioned above, I examined audio- and videotaped data collected in a Samoan community during three periods for a total of a year and a half of fieldwork.[10] I identified four types of exchanges that can qualify as "greetings": (1) *tālofa* greetings; (2) ceremonial greetings; (3) *mālō* greetings; and (4) "where are you going?" greetings.[11] The analysis presented here is also based on my own observation of and participation in hundreds if not thousands of Samoan greeting exchanges.

Before discussing these four types of greetings, I need to mention a few basic facts about the community where I worked; more detailed information on this community may be found in Duranti 1981 and 1994 and in Ochs 1988. (For a more comprehensive ethnography of Samoan social life, see Shore 1982.)

Despite modernization and a considerable amount of syncretism in religious and political practices, members of the Samoan community where I carried out research still hang on to traditional Polynesian values of family relations and mutual dependence. Their society is still divided between titled individuals (*matai*) and untitled ones (*taulele'a*), and the matai are distinguished according to status (chiefs, orators) and rank (high chief, lower-ranking chiefs). Having a title usually comes with rights over land and its products and the duty to participate in decision-making processes such as the political meetings called *fono* (see Duranti 1994). Status and rank distinctions are pervasive in everyday and ceremonial life in a Samoan village. The language marks such distinctions in a number of ways, the most obvious of which is a special lexicon called *'upu fa'aaloalo* "respectful words" used in addressing people of high status and in talking about them in certain contexts (see Duranti 1992b; Milner 1961; Shore 1982). Such words are part of some of the greeting exchanges that I will discuss below.

None of the greetings I discuss qualifies as the most "basic" or unmarked greeting item or exchange in Samoan society. As I will show below, the greeting that is the highest on the "formulaic" end of the formulaic-creative continuum, and hence with the least propositional content, "tālofa," is the rarest in everyday life and hence is an unlikely candidate for the role of the most basic type or the one the other greetings are substituting for.

The tālofa greeting

This greeting can be used in a number of settings, including open and closed areas (for example, either outside or inside a house), whenever two people become visibly and acoustically accessible to each other. Unlike the other Samoan greetings I will discuss below, the tālofa greeting is at times accompanied by handshaking, a gesture likely borrowed from past Western visitors and colonial authorities. In fact, this is a greeting that is today most commonly used with foreigners. Contrary to what was described by Margaret Mead (1928:14), people from the same village today rarely greet each other with "tālofa" (see Holmes 1987:112),[12] which is reserved for people who have not seen each other for a while or have never met before (hence its common use with foreigners and guests from abroad). In an hour-long audiotape of an "inspection committee" (asiasiga) going around the village and meeting dozens of people, I found three examples of "tālofa." All three examples involve only one member of the inspection committee (Chief S, the highest ranking chief of the group) who initiates the greeting. In one case, "tālofa" was exchanged with a group of chiefs from another village waiting for the bus. Although I have no information on the people who were greeted with "tālofa" in the other two cases, the interaction is not incompatible with the hypothesis that the parties involved had not seen each other for a while or are not very familiar with one another.[13]

Like the expressions used in the other Samoan greetings, tālofa may occur by itself or may be accompanied by an address term, either a name or a title, for example, "tālofa ali'i!," or "greetings sir(s)!" Here is an example that shows the adjacency pair format of the greeting and its rather simple AB structure:

(1) [*Inspection, December 1978: While standing outside, the committee members have been interacting with a woman who is inside the house, when Chief S directly addresses another woman from the same family, Kelesia.*]

Chief S: tālofa Kelesia!
           Hello Kelesia!
           (0.2)
Kelesia: tālofa!
           Hello!
Chief S: ((*chuckles*)) hehe.

Tālofa is homophonous with and probably derived from the expression *tālofa* or *tālofae* – usually pronounced /kaalofa/ and /kaalofae/, respectively[14] (see the appendix) – used to display empathy for someone who is judged to be suffering or under any form of distress (see also Ochs 1988:173). This other use of the expression *tālofa* is found in the following excerpt from the same transcript, where a member of the inspection committee invites the others to feel sorry for the old woman Litia, who got up at dawn in order to clean her lawn in time for the committee's inspection. As shown by the following comment by Chief S, Tūla'i's sympathy is not shared by everyone else. In the next turn, Chief S proposes, albeit with some hesitation, to fine Litia.

(2) [*Inspection: The orator Tūla'i sees the old woman Litia, here pronounced /Likia/, cutting the grass.*][15]

1	Tūla'i:	kālofa sē ia Likia- 'ua uso pō e-
		empathy Voc Emp Litia Perf rise rise night Comp
		Hey, feel sorry for Litia. (She) got up at dawn to –
2	Chief S:	'ae- 'ae- 'ae- 'ae kakau ga // sala
		but but but but ought to fine
		But, but, but, but she should be fined.
3	Litia:	e sēsē mātou i le faimea taeao.
		Pres wrong we:excl-pl in Art do-thing morning
		We shouldn't be doing things in the morning.

This example shows that it is not the occurrence of a particular expression that defines an utterance as a greeting. Whereas in (1) Chief S uses *tālofa* as the first pair part of a greeting exchange with Kelesia, in (2) the orator Tūla'i uses *tālofa* as an attempt to draw sympathy for the old woman Litia (pronounced /Likia/ in line 1) but not to greet her. In fact, the ensuing interaction with Litia does not contain a greeting. In an apparent response to the men's comments, Litia's first turn in line 3 is a negative assessment of her being up and running early in the morning, which could be interpreted as veiled apology.

In his Samoan–English dictionary, G.B. Milner (1966) suggests that *tālofa* is a compound made out of the words *tā* "strike" and *alofa* "love, have compassion." *Ta* could also be the first-person singular, positive-affect pronoun. In this case the long /aa/ (spelled *ā*) would be accounted for by the combination of two consecutive /a/ : *ta + alofa* → / taalofa /, originally meaning "(poor) me feels sorry." Although *tālofa* as a greeting does not have the same meaning of *tālofa* as an expression of empathy and therefore looks like a good candidate for a word with very little or no propositional content, specialized for greetings, its rarity in everyday life makes it an unlikely candidate as the unmarked greeting in a Samoan speech community.

The mālō greeting

In my data, this greeting is most commonly used when one party (A) arrives at a site where the other party (B) already is. It has the structure given in (3).

(3)   *Mālō-greeting*:

A: mālō (+ intensifier) (+ address + title or name)
B: mālō (+ intensifier) (+ address + title or name)

The word *mālō* has several meanings in Samoan. Its use as an opening salutation is closely related to its use as a compliment or encouragement to people who are working or have just finished doing something (see below).[16] An example of the *mālō* greeting is provided in (4), from an audiorecording of the "Inspection" tape mentioned above:

(4) [*Inspection: The committee members, including Afoa, a chief, and Tūla'i, an orator, arrive at the orator Taipī's family compound and see Taipī's wife Si'ilima.*]

1	Afoa:	mālō Si'ilima!
		Congratulations/hello Si'ilima!
2		(0.5)
3	Si'ilima:	mālō!
		Congratulations/hello!
4		(0.5)
5	Afoa:	'ua lelei mea 'uma!
		Everything is fine!

6   Tūla'i: [
                                                  māgaia – (0.3) māgaia le- (0.5) le fagua: –
                                                 Nice – the land looks nice –[17]

7		Si'ilima
		Si'ilima
8		(2.5)
9	Tūla'i:	fea le koeaiga?
		Where (is) the old man? [...]

Here, line 1 contains the first pair part, and line 3 contains the second pair part. In this case, the structure of the exchange is:

(5)

A: mālō + Name (first pair part)
B: mālō (second pair part)

In other cases, we might find more complex turns not only with names but also with titles and intensifiers (e.g., *lava* "much, indeed").

(6) [*Inspection*]

Tūla'i:	mālō ali'i Faikaumakau!	(mālō + address + title)
	Congratulations, Mr. Faitaumatau!	
Faitaumatau:	mālō lava.	(mālō + intensifier)
	Much congratulations.	

In most cases, the exchange is initiated by the arriving party. This makes sense if we interpret this use of *mālō* as a greeting as an extension of the use of *mālō* as an expression of congratulation to someone who is engaged in a task or has just successfully completed one. In the latter case, called the "*mālō* exchange" in Duranti and Ochs (1986), the first *mālō* recognizes one party's work or activity and the second *mālō* recognizes the role played by the supporter(s) (*tāpua'i*). The second *mālō* in this case is usually followed by the adverb (intensifier) *fo'i* "quite, also," which further underscores the reciprocity of the exchange. Differently from the greeting *mālō*, the complimenting *mālō* typically occurs in the middle of an interaction; hence it does not conform to the first two criteria described above (near-boundary occurrence and establishment of a shared perceptual field). But when the complimenting *mālō* does occur at the beginning of an encounter, it can function as both a compliment and a greeting. An example of this use of *mālō* is provided in excerpt (7), where the woman Amelia surprises the inspecting committee (see the "repair" particle *'oi* in Tūla'i's response) by initiating the interaction with a congratulating "mālō." This *mālō* is followed by the display of the reason for her congratulations, namely, their "inspecting" or "visiting." (*le asiasi* is the nominalization of the predicate *asiasi* "visit, inspect."[18])

(7)   [*Inspection*]

Amelia: mālō ā le asiasi!
               congratulations Emp Art visit
               Congratulations indeed (for) the inspecting!
Tūla'i: 'oi / / mālō!
               oh! // congratulations!
Chief Afoa: mālō fo'i.
               Congratulations also (to you).
Tūla'i: 'ua 'ou iloa::-
               I realize that –
Amelia: pulegu'u ma oukou kōfā i le komiki!
               mayor and you-all honorable (orators) in the committee
               (To the) mayor and you honorable (orators) in the committee!
Tūla'i: mālō / / lava iā ke 'oe le kigā!
               congratulations Emp to you the mother
               Congratulations indeed to you, the mother (of the family)!
               [...]

In this case, the exchange is enacted as a series of reciprocal compliments, as shown by the syntax of the last utterance by Tūla'i: "*mālō* indeed to you, the mother (of the family)!," but it also works as a greeting. This is predictable given that it conforms to the six criteria introduced earlier and no other greeting with Amelia follows.

In 1978, I was told by a Samoan instructor who had taught Peace Corps volunteers not to use *mālō* as a greeting. He, like other adult Samoans with whom I spoke, considered the use of *mālō* as a greeting a relatively recent and degenerate extension of the use of *mālō* as a compliment. (This view is supported by the fact that *mālō* is not mentioned as a greeting in any of the earlier ethnographic accounts.)

How can we explain the extension of the *mālō* from one context to the other? In the mālō greeting, the party who is about to enter another's living space calls out to the other by starting an exchange of mutual support and recognition. Since the other is likely to be busy doing something or to have just finished doing something, *mālō* is an extension of the one used in those contexts in which one party is more explicitly seen as "doing something" and the other as "supporting the other party's efforts." When the mālō exchange is started by the person who is stationary (e.g., inside a house), it could be seen as an extension of a congratulatory act to the newcomer for having made it to the present location, overcoming whatever obstacles he encountered or could have encountered.

In its ambiguous state between a congratulating act and a greeting act, this Samoan greeting shares certain similarities with the English "How are you?" discussed by Sacks (1975) and others. In both cases, we have a greeting item that is not exclusively used for greeting and in fact is imported, as it were, into the greeting exchange from other uses and contexts. In both cases, we have a relative or incomplete ritualization of the term so that it can be still taken "literally." There still is, in other words, some of the force of the mālō compliment in the mālō greeting. At the same time, differently from the English "How are you?," we cannot define the mālō greeting as a "greeting substitute" because there is no other obvious candidate for the same types of situations.

Ceremonial greetings

Ceremonial greetings are typically exchanged when a high status person (e.g., a titled individual [or *matai*], a government official, a minister of the church, a deacon, a head nurse) arrives at what is either foreseen or framed as an official visit or formal event. As discussed in Duranti (1992a), ceremonial greetings (CGs) only take place after the newly arrived party goes to sit down in the "front region" of the house. CGs are the most complex among the four types of Samoan greetings discussed here. They are made of two main parts, a first pair part, the "welcoming," and a second pair part, the "response."

(8)
A: [WELCOMING]
B: [RESPONSE]

Each of these two parts may, in turn, be divided in two major subcomponents, a predicate and an address.

(9)
WELCOMING   RESPONSE
a. Welcoming predicate   a. Responding predicate
b. Address   b. Address

The welcoming predicates recognize the arrival of the new party and welcome him or her into the house. They are the same predicates that in different contexts function as verbs of motion meaning "arrive, come." A list of some such verbs is given in table 9.1, with information relative to the specific social status indexed by each term. Whereas *maliu* and *sosopo* are said to (and imply that the addressee is) an orator (*tulāfale*), the verb *afio* is used with (and implies that the addressee is) a chief (*ali'i*). The deictic particle *mai*, which accompanies all of them, expresses an action toward the speaker or, more precisely, toward the deictic center (see Platt 1982), which in all the cases discussed here is the totality of the shared space already occupied by the welcoming party and defined according to the physical shape of the house (see Duranti 1992a).

The responding predicate exhibits less variation and is often omitted. The address is the most complex part and the one that allows for more variation. It can also be repeated when the speaker differentiates among the addressees:

(10) Address:

a. Address form
b. Generic title
c. Name (specific) title
d. Ceremonial attributes (taken from *fa'alupega*[19])

The address may have up to these four parts. The address form (see table 9.2) shows distinctions similar to the ones found in the welcoming predicates. Some of the forms are in fact nominalizations of those predicates. The distinction between what I call a generic title and a name title is found only in some cases. In the village of Falefā, where I conducted my research, there were two orator title names (Iuli and Moe'ono) that also had a generic title, Matua, which I have elsewhere translated as "senior orator" (Duranti 1981, 1994).

Table 9.1 Welcoming predicates used during ceremonial greetings (CGs)

Samoan term	English translation	Social index
maliu mai	"welcome"	<orator>
sosopo mai	"welcome"	<orator>
afio mai	"welcome"	<chief>
susū mai	"welcome"	<chief or orator>[a]

[a] This particular verb is used with the holders of titles descending from the high chief Malietoa and can be used with either a chief or an orator. It is also the most commonly used term for high status individuals who are not matai, e.g. pastors, school teachers, doctors, government officials. It is thus often used as an "unmarked" term when one is not sure of the social identity of the addressee or when one knows that the addressee does not have a title but wishes to treat him or her with deference. In my living experience in a Samoan village I moved from being addressed with *susū mai* in the earlier stages to more specific terms such as *afio mai* later on in my stay.

Table 9.2 Address forms according to status

Samoan term	English translation	Social index
lau tōfā	"your honor/highness"	<orator>
lau afioga	"your honor/highness"	<chief>
lau susuga	"your honor/highness"	<chief or orator>

Any of the following combinations were commonly used during CGs and other formal exchanges in addressing the people holding the Iuli or Moe'ono title:

• an address form (*lau tōfā* "your honor")
• address form + generic title
  (*lau tōfā* + *le Matua* "your honor + the senior orator")[20]
• address form + generic title + name title
  (*lau tōfā* + *le Matua* + *Iuli* "your honor + the senior orator + Iuli" or *lau tōfā* + *le Matua* + *Moe'ono* "your honor + the senior orator + Moe'ono").

If a person has a *matai* title, the name given at birth (called *igoa taule'ale'a* "untitled name") will not be used in the CG. Only those who do not have a *matai* title – such as pastors, some government officials, and foreigners – might be greeted with the address form followed by the birth name. For example, a pastor whose untitled name is Mareko would be addressed as "lau susuga Mareko" (your honorable Mareko). In this case, the proper name replaces the "name title." If a person does not have a *matai* title and does not hold a religious or administrative office and his name is not known to the welcoming party, a title must be found for the CG to be complete. The title may be borrowed from someone else in the family. (E.g., he might be greeted as if he were a titled person to whom he is related; this is a convention used with untitled people when they perform ceremonial roles on behalf of their family, village, or religious congregation.) Other times, an ad hoc "title" is created on the spot based on whatever information about the newcomer is contextually available. For example, people who did not know me personally often referred to me as "the guest from abroad" (*le mālō mai i fafo*). If they saw me filming, I became "the cameraman": *le ali'i pu'e ata*, lit. "the (gentle)man (who) takes pictures."

The adjacency pair structure of the CGs is hard to perceive at first, and these greetings are particularly hard to transcribe because they are typically performed by several people at once and never in unison. This means that the speech of the different participants typically overlaps and interlocks, producing a nonchanted fugue (Duranti 1997b). Here is an example from a meeting of the village council (*fono*). One of the two senior orators in the village, Moe'ono, has just arrived and gone to sit in the front part of the house. The orator Falefā, who is the village "mayor" (*pulenu'u*) and whose house is being used for the meeting, initiates the greeting and is followed by a few other members of the council. (I have here slightly simplified the transcript for expository reasons.)

(11) [*Monday Fono, August 1988; ceremonial greeting of senior orator Moe'ono*]

Falefā:	ia'. māliu mai lau kōfā i le Makua
	Well. Welcome your highness, the senior orator.
Malaga:	lau kōfā i le Makua
	Your highness, the senior orator
	(2.0)
?:	lau kōfā i le Makua
	Your highness, the senior orator
	(2.0)
Moe'ono:	ia'. ('e'e ka'ia) le kākou gu'u
	Well. ((I) submit to) our village
	[
??:	(lau kōfā le Ma:kua)
	(*Your highness, the senior orator*)
	(7.0)
Moe'ono:	mamalu i le- (1.0) susuga a le ali'i pulegu'u gei
	dignity of the – (1.0) highness of Mr. Mayor here
	(7.0)

This exchange seems to qualify easily as a greeting, according to the six criteria established above. Like other exchanges I have either witnessed or recorded, this one occurs a little after the newcomer, Moe'ono, has arrived to the house (criterion 1) (but see more on this later). It also defines a shared perceptual field, as defined by the welcoming predicate with its deictic particle *mai* (criterion 2). The greeting is sequentially organized as an adjacency pair (criterion 3). The expressions used in greeting are predictable but not completely so (criterion 4). The exchange establishes the ensuing interaction as a formal one in which public identities will be evoked, in this case, a formal meeting of the village council (criterion 5 [see Irvine, this volume]). Moe'ono is recognized as a distinct interlocutor (criterion 6). Sometimes, however, other greetings or greetinglike items precede or follow the CG. For example, before the CG shown in (11) above, one of the people in the house uses a *mālō* with Moe'ono – although no audible response can be heard – and a few minutes later, Moe'ono himself exchanges *mālō* with an orator who has just come in and has already been greeted with a CG. My hypothesis is that these other greetings or greetinglike exchanges are between different social personae and that they are performing a different kind of work. The CG recognizes the party's positional identity that is judged relevant to the forthcoming activity, typically a formal type of exchange (e.g., a political or business meeting, a ceremonial exchange), and is done between an individual as a representative of a group and a collectivity (the people already in the house).[21] The *mālō* greeting, on the other hand, although it may be addressed to collectivities,[22] usually is a preliminary to short and relatively informal exchanges. Its use projects a sense of immediacy and is a prelude to some business that can be easily dealt with, without even entering the house. Example (12) below reproduces some of the verbal interaction preceding the CG illustrated in (11). Senior orator Moe'ono and the orator Talaitau have arrived at the same time, but only Moe'ono goes to sit in the front region of the house; this transcript starts a few seconds before the one in (11) above and shows that the notion of "acknowledgment" or "recognition" proposed by speech act theorists as the illocutionary force of greetings must be qualified. We need to specify what is being acknowleged. Physical presence? Status? Social role in the ensuing interaction? For example, when we enlarge the context of the CG in (11), we find out that both Moe'ono's physical presence and his status have already been recognized before the CG is produced. After Moe'ono's remark about the presence of the videocamera in lines 5 and 6, the orator Manu' a provides a justification for the presence of the videocamera (lines 13–15), which starts with a formulaic apology (starting with the expression "vaku...") indexing Moe'ono's higher rank. Manu'a might be apologizing for a number of things, including his speaking at all to such a high-status person before proper greetings have been exchanged, his speaking about such nondignified matters as videotaping, or his (and the other matai's) failure to ask for Moe'ono's approval before allowing the camera to be used.[23]

(12)   [*Monday Meeting, August 1988*]

1	Moe'ono:	(he) sole!
		(Hey) brother!
2	?:	((to a woman outside)) (ai) suga!
		(?) Sister!
3	?:	(??)
4	Manu'a:	'e- mālō lava!
		Tns- congratulation Emph
		Is – hello, hello!
5	Moe'ono:	māgaia ali'i le- lea ke va'ai aku ali'i
		Nice sir, the – that I see sir(s),

		e fai le pu'ega aka ali'i (o le –)
		there are pictures taken sirs (of the –)
		[
7	Talaitau:	(?sē)
		(?Hey)
8		oi. oi sole!
		Uh-oh, brother!
		[
9	Moe'ono:	o le kākou fogo ali'i
		of our meeting sirs
10	Talaitau:	ai 'o le ā le mea lea ga ili ai le pū a le pulenu'u.
		Maybe that's why the horn of the mayor was blown.
		[
11	Manu'a:	(leai fa'afekai)
		(No thanks.)
12		(0.7)
13		'e vaku lau kōfā le Makua,
		With due respect, your highness the senior orator,
14		(2.0)
15		'o si koe – 'o si koe'iga e sau e pu'e – se aka o (le –)
		The dear old ma – the dear old man comes to film (the –)
16		(1.0)
17	?Moe'ono:	((Sigh)) haaaa!
		Haaaa!
18	Manu'a:	o:: –
19	?:	(??lea)
20		(3.0)
21	??:	(??fagu?)
22	?:	(leai!)
		(No!)
23	??:	(???)
		[
24	Moe'ono:	e lelei kele le ali'i 'o Falefā
		Mr. Falefā is very good
25	Falefā:	ia'. māliu mai lau kōfā i le Makua
		Well. Welcome your highness, the senior orator.

If acknowledgments of physical presence, status, and rank have already been done, the CG, which is started by the orator and mayor Falefā in line 25, must do something more. I suggest that the CG allows the people present to *collectively* recognize Moe'ono's presence *as* the senior orator, someone who has specific rights and duties within the forthcoming event, the meeting of the fono. Conversely, the CG gives Moe'ono the opportunity to recognize the presence and hence future role played by the rest of the assembly. *It is as social actors engaged or about to be engaged in a particular (and to some extent predictable) type of interaction that participants' presence is recognized by means of a CG.*

It is, of course, possible to argue that CGs are not *real* greetings and a distinction should be made between "greetings" and "welcomings," with the CGs being an example of the latter. The translation of the predicates used in the first pair part would support this hypothesis. My experience in this community, however, makes me reluctant to accept this hypothesis. Rather, I would favor seeing CGs as the type of greeting exchange that is appropriate for high-ranking individuals who meet in a closed area, which is likely to be the site for further activities also involving or indexing their positional roles. This position is supported by a number of observations.

In Samoa, I heard high-ranking persons who met on the road, for example, while inside a car, apologize for the improper way in which they find themselves in each other's presence. The expression used is "leaga tātou te feiloa'i i le auala" ([too] bad [that] we meet on the road). This expression was explained to me by a person who had just used it to imply that meeting on the road is not the proper way for high-ranking people to come together. In other words, the implication is "we should have met elsewhere." Where? For instance, at someone's house. If such a meeting had taken place, ceremonial greetings would have been exchanged (as well as food and perhaps gifts). This, to me, indicates that for high-ranking Samoans ceremonial greetings are part of what makes an encounter proper or canonical.

The formality or ritualistic nature of the CGs is not a reason for not considering them greetings. For one thing, such formality is quite common in everyday encounters. As documented by Bradd Shore, Margaret Mead, and other ethnographers, Samoans are used to rapidly shifting, within the same setting, from an apparently casual exchange to a much more formal one, in which fancy epithets and metaphors are used and individuals get addressed with longer names, inside of longer turns at talk. In other words, CGs are much more routine than we might think and, in fact, statistically much more common than the tālofa greeting. In Western Samoa, whenever I went to visit persons of high status, if I entered their house and sat on the floor in the "front region" (see Duranti 1992a, 1994), I would be greeted with a CG. No matter how hard I tried at times to avoid the CG by acting informally and engaging my hosts in conversation, I was rarely able to avoid it. After a few seconds of my arrival, someone would clear his or her voice and start a CG with the usual shifting activity marker *ia'* "well, so." Only kids or young, untitled folks may enter and leave a house without being the target of CGs. Part of this sharp social asymmetry is still at work in the Samoan community in Los Angeles, where young and untitled members of the families I visited are never introduced to me and do not expect to participate in the greeting rituals that in American society often include the youngest children in the family.

The "where are you going?" greeting

When two parties, at least one of whom is ostensibly going somewhere, cross one another's visual field of perception and are close enough for their voices to be heard by one another (the volume of the parties' voices being adjusted proportionally to the physical distance between them), they may engage in what I will call the "where are you going?" greeting:[24]

(13)   Scheme of "where are you going?" greeting

1 A: Where are you going?
2 B: I'm going to [goal].

This goal may be either a place or a task.

First, we must recognize that the adjacency pair in the scheme in (13) conforms to the criteria introduced earlier for greetings. It is typically used when party B is seen moving along the road or a nearby path by party A, who is stationary (e.g., inside a house, in front of a store), but it can also be found in cases in which A and B pass each other on the road. Under these circumstances, the initiator usually stops to address the other (moving party), who may or not also stop to respond. (This is different from the Mehinaku greeting discussed in Gregor 1977.)

The greeting may continue with a leave-taking exchange of the following kind:

(14)   Leave-taking after "where are you going?" greeting

3 A: Then go.
4 B: I/we go.

The existence of "where are you going?" greetings in Samoan and other languages (see Firth 1972; Gregor 1977; Hanks 1990) suggests that we cannot easily extend to other speech communities Searle's analysis of English greetings as an expressive type of speech act (see above). As may be gathered by an examination of its content, the "where are you going?" greeting is more than an expression of a psychological state. It is an attempt to sanction the reciprocal recognition of one another's presence with some specific requests of information that may or may not receive satisfactory response. Although they are highly predictable and conventional, "where are you going?" greetings force participants to deal with a wide range of issues including an individual's or group's right to have access to information about a person's where-abouts, culture-specific expectations about the ethics of venturing into public space, the force of questioning as a form of social control and hence the possibility of withholding information as a form of resistance to public scrutiny and moral judgment (Keenan 1976). As in the neighboring language of Tokelau (Hoëm 1993:143, 1995:29), Samoan speakers who greet with the "where are you going?" question feel that they have the right to an answer, and the question itself is a form of social control. With the last part of the exchange, shown in (14), the questioner formally grants the other party permission to go. The speech act analysis proposed for English greetings, then, cannot be easily extended to these greetings, given that to initiate a "where are you going?" greeting is definitely more than (or different from) a "courteous indication of recognition" (Searle and Vanderveken 1985:216) or a conventional expression of pleasure at the sight of someone (Bach and Harnish 1979:51–2). To ask "where are you going?" is a request for an account, which may include the reasons for being away from one's home, on someone else's terri-tory, or on a potentially dangerous path. To answer such a greeting may imply that one commits oneself not only to the truthfulness of one's assertion but also to the appropriateness of one's actions. It is not by accident, then, that in some cases speakers might try to be as evasive as possible. Samoans, for instance, often reply to the "where are you going?" greeting question with the vague "to do an errand" (*fai le fe'au*). Even when they give what appear to be more specific statements such as "I'm going to buy something," "I'm going to wait for the bus," and "I'm going to Apia," speakers are still holding on to their right to release only a minimum amount of information – with bragging being an obvious exception ("I'm going down to the store to buy a five pound can of corn beef for Alesana!"). Just as in the Malagasy situation discussed by Elinor Ochs Keenan (1976), the tendency in these encounters is to violate Grice's (1975) cooperative principle and not to be too informative.

The violation of this principle, however, does not have the same implications discussed by Sacks (1975) regarding the American passing-by greeting "How are you?". In the American case, the common assumption is that the party who asks the question as a greeting is not really interested in an accurate or truthful answer. It is this lack of interest that justifies what Sacks sees as a social justification for "lying." People are expected to provide a positive assessment (*fine, good, okay*) regardless of how they are actually doing or feeling at the moment. In the Samoan case, instead, questioners would like to know as much as possible about the other's whereabouts, and the vagueness in the answer is an attempt by the responding party to resist the information-seeking force of the greeting. Furthermore, the consequences of one's answer are also different. Whereas in the American English greeting substitute "How are you?," as argued by Sacks, a lie is a preferred answer regardless of its truth value, in the case of the Samoan "Where are you going?" greeting, vagueness is conventionally accepted, but violation of truth is potentially problematic if later detected.

That the Samoan "Where are you going?" greeting is, at least in part, about rights and duties, expectations, and possible violations is shown by the fact that, when questioned by someone with higher authority, Samoan speakers might be expected to give more specific answers. Likewise, they might display their uneasiness about a situation in which they have been placed, uneasiness about the very fact of being visible and hence vulnerable to public questioning by someone with authority. This is indeed the case in (15) below. In this example, the inspection committee encounters a group of young men on the road. One of the members of the committee, the orator Tūla'i, recognizes a young man from his extended family and addresses him:

(15)   *[Inspection]*

A   1   Tūla'i: fea (a)li('i) a alu iai le kou – kegi 'i ukā?
                         Where (sir) are you going inland with your pals?
B   2   Young man: sē vage afioga ali'i ma kulāfale mākou ke ō aku 'i ukā
                         With your permission, honorable chiefs and orators, we are going inland
    3   e – (0.8) e kapega mai le – (0.2) suāvai – (0.2) – o le Aso Sā.
                         to – (0.8) prepare the – (0.2) food (0.2) – for Sunday.
A   4   Tūla'i: ia' ō loa ('ā)
                         Okay, go then,
B   5   Other man: (mākou) ō.
                         (We) go.

The way in which this exchange is played out illustrates a number of important points about the social organization presupposed by the encounter, as well as the social organization achieved by it. First, the content displays a noticeable status asymmetry between A and B (which is represented by more than one speaker). Despite the relatively polite questioning by orator Tūla'i (the address form "ali'i" he uses does not have the gender and age selectional restrictions as the English "sir" or the Spanish "señor" but does convey some consideration for the person addressed),[25] there is no question that in lines 2 and 3 the young speaker does his best to show appreciation of the specific statuses represented by the members of the inspection committee, since the respectful term /afioga ali'i/ refers to the chiefs in the committee and the term /kulaafale/ refers to the orators. These terms are in contrast with the casual, almost "slang" word /kegi/, a borrowing from the English *gang*, used by the orator Tūla'i in referring to the young man's group. Furthermore, the young man also indicates through his opening remark /vage/, an apologetic expression for an unbecoming (past or future) act (corresponding to the /vaku/ we saw earlier in (12), line 13) that anything he might do or say to such a distinguished audience is likely going to be inappropriate. In fact, even his group's presence in front of the committee may be seen as an inappropriate interference in the chiefs' and orators' actions, or at least in their interactional space. There are some remnants here of possible avoidance relations with people of high *mana* that have been characterized as typical of ancient Polynesia (Valeri 1985).

Despite the conventionality of the exchange, what is said and how it is said is extremely important. The illocutionary point or goal of the greeting is not just "a courteous indication of recognition, with the presupposition that the speaker has just encountered the hearer" (Searle and Vanderveken 1985:215). Although recognition is certainly involved, the exchange plays out a set of social relations and cultural expectations about where parties should be at a particular time of the day and what they should be doing then, all expressed through an actual exchange of information about the parties' whereabouts. It is the higher status party, that is, the orator Tūla'i in this case, who asks the question. The only thing the young men can do is answer as quickly and as politely as possible and hope for a quick and uneventful exchange. In this interpretive frame, the final granting of permission to go ("ia' ō loa") is also ambiguous between a formulaic closure (corresponding to the English "See you" or "Good-bye") and a meaningful sanction of the young men's goals and destination by a man of higher authority.

Expressions That Are Not Greetings

Given my claim that the six criteria introduced above should allow researchers to identify greetings across languages and communities, it is important to establish whether the same criteria can allow us to exclude words and exchanges that are *not* greetings. A good candidate for such a test is the Samoan term *tulouna* or *tulouga*.[26] In Augustine Krämer's (1902–03) extensive ethnography of Samoan history and social life, *tulouga* was translated to the German *gegrüsst*, the past participle of the verb *grüssen* "greet." The English version of the German text done by Theodore Verhaaren (Krämer 1994) mirrors the same translation with the English *greeted*. Here is an example from Krämer's book; (16) shows the original, and (17), the English translation. The passage is taken from the beginning part of the *fa'alupega* (ceremonial address of the village of Falefā, which is the site of the exchanges analyzed in this article).

(16)

Tulouga a 'oe le faleatua	Gegrüsst du das Haus von Atua
tulouga a 'oe le 'a'ai o Fonotī	gegrüsst die Stadt des Fonotī

(Krämer 1902:277)

(17)

| Tulouga a 'oe le faleatua | Greeted you, the house of Atua |
| tulouga a 'oe le 'a'ai o Fonotī | greeted Fonotī's city |

(Krämer 1994:360)

The translation of *tulouga* with "greeted" at the beginning of each phrase achieves the goal of mirroring the word order of Samoan (verb first). But the translation is problematic first of all on empirical grounds, given that *tulouga* is not used in any of the ceremonial greetings I described above. For example, *tulouga* is never mentioned in the ceremonial greetings despite the fact that they are quite formal and, as we saw above, include sections of the ceremonial address (*fa'alupega*) of the village, the context in which *tulouna* appears in Krämer's text. Instead, I found *tulouga* (pronounced /kulouga/; see the appendix) in the first speech given during the meetings of the fono. In this context, as I suggested in Duranti 1981, it makes sense to translate it to "acknowledgement" or "recognition":[27]

(18)   *[April 1, 1979: first speech of the meeting, by orator Loa]*

Loa: ia'.
         Well,
         (2.0)
         kulouga ia (1.0) a le aofia ma le fogo,
         recognition indeed...of the assembly and the council,
         (3.0)
         kulouga le viligia ma – kulouga le saukia,
         recognition (of) the suffering and – recognition (of) the early arrival,
         (2.0)
         kulouga Moamoa 'o kua o Lalogafu'afu'a
         recognition (of) Moamoa,[28] the back of Lalogafu'afu'a[29]
         [...]

The translation of *tulouna* (or *tulouga*) with *recognition* (one might even consider the term *apology*, given its obvious relation to the expression "tulou!" [excuse (me)][30]) is consistent with the description provided in Milner's dictionary:

Expression used before mentioning important names or titles (esp. when making a speech). It implies that the speaker makes a formal acknowledgement of their importance, expresses his deference and respect for the established order, and apologizes for any offence he might inadvertently give when speaking before the distinguished assembly. (N.B. This expression is used repeatedly in uttering the ceremonial style and address of a social group or village [*fa'alupega*]). (1966:286–7)

When we match *tulouga* against the six criteria provided above, we find that it matches only two or perhaps three of the criteria for identifying greetings:

(i)   It is part of a relatively predictable part of a speech (criterion 4).
(ii)   It contributes in part to the establishment of a spatiotemporal unit of interaction (to the extent to which it contributes to clarifying the type of encounter in which it occurs) (criterion 5).
(iii)   It identifies the interlocutors as distinct and yet related beings (criterion 6).

But *tulouga* does not qualify according to the three remaining criteria:

(a) It does not occur close to an interactional boundary (criterion 1). Instead, it is used in the middle of a speech.
(b) It does not establish a shared perceptual field (criterion 2). Such a field has already been established by a number of other expressions and rituals.
(c) It is not in the form of an adjacency pair (criterion 3). There is no immediate or obvious response to the particular section of the speech in which the speaker uses *tulouga*.

Conclusions

The analysis of greetings presented here shows that semantic analysis must be integrated with ethnographic information if we want to provide an adequate pragmatic analysis of speech activities within and across speech communities. Whatever greetings accomplish, they do it by virtue of the participants' ability to match routine expressions with particular sociohistorical circumstances. To say that greetings are constituted by formulaic expressions only tells half of the story. The other half is how such formulaic expressions may be adapted to, and at the same time help establish, new contexts.

I have argued that we cannot compare greetings across speech communities unless we come up with a universal definition of what constitutes a greeting exchange. After proposing such a universal definition consisting of six criteria, I have shown that the tendency to see greetings as devoid of propositional content or expressing "phatic communion" is too limiting and, in fact, inaccurate. Greetings are, indeed, toward the formulaic end of the formulaic–creative continuum that runs across the full range of communicative acts through which humans manage their everyday life, but they can also communicate new information to participants through the types of questions they ask and the kinds of answers they produce. My analysis of four different types of Samoan greetings offers an empirical corroboration of the six criteria and proposes some new hypotheses about the work that is done during greetings in human encounters. In particular, I have shown the following:

1. The notion of "greeting substitute" used for English greetings such as "How are you?" may not be extendable to other speech communities. I showed that in Samoan, since no particular greeting can be identified as the most basic or unmarked one, there is no sense in claiming that any of the expressions used in greetings are "greeting substitutes."

2. In certain types of greetings, most noticeably ceremonial ones, recognition has already taken place before greetings are exchanged. This means that "acknowledgment" of another's presence per se cannot be the function of greeting, unless we redefine the notion of "acknowledgment" to make it more culture- and context-specific. For example, physical recognition might have taken place (i.e., participants might be signaling that they have sighted one another), but context-specific social recognition might still be needed; that is, participants need to be acknowledged for what they represent or embody in a particular situation or course of action. The act of greeting, in other words, does not necessarily imply that the speaker has *just* encountered the hearer, as proposed by Searle and Vanderveken (1985:216), but that

the encounter is taking place *under particular sociohistorical conditions* and the parties are relating to one another *as particular types of social personae*. This is the case across a number of greetings. It undermines the possibility of cross-culturally extending speech act theorists' analysis of English greetings as an "expressive" type of speech act aimed at the "courteous indication of recognition" of the other party (Searle and Vanderveken 1985:216).

3. Contrary to what is assumed by most existing studies of greetings, greetings are not necessarily devoid of propositional content; they can be used to gather information about a person's identity or whereabouts. The Samoan "Where are you going?" greeting, for example, is seeking information about the addressee and, unlike what is argued by Sacks (1975) about the English "How are you?," in answering the Samoan greeting, a lie is not the "preferred" answer, or at least not preferred by the one who asks the question. The questioner would rather find out as much as possible about the other party's whereabouts. For this reason, the "Where are you going?" greeting can also work as a form of social control and therefore be quite the opposite of Bach and Harnish's (1979:51–2) view of the act of greeting (in English only?) as an expression of "pleasure at seeing (or meeting)" someone.

NOTES

1   Although the absence of greetings or their relatively rare occurrence in certain societies has been mentioned at times – the classic example being American Indian groups such as the Western Apache studied by Basso (1972), who are said to prefer "silence" during phases of encounters that other groups would find ripe for greetings (see also Farnell 1995) – there is overwhelming evidence at this point that most speech communities do have verbal expressions that conform to the criteria I define in this article, although their use and frequency may vary both across and within communities. (See Hymes's comments about North American Indians in Youssouf et al. 1976:817 fn. 6.)

2   Although Searle and Vanderveken claim to be discussing the English verb *greet*, as shown by the following quote, they in fact treat *greet* and *hello* as part of the same class:

> "Greet" is only marginally an illocutionary act since it has no propositional content. When one greets someone [but usually one does not greet by using the verb *greet!* A.D.], for example, by saying "Hello," one indicates recognition in a courteous fashion. So we might define greeting as a courteous indication of recognition, with the presupposition that the speaker has just encountered the hearer. (1985:215–16)

3   Austin defined behabitives as "reactions to other people's behaviour and fortunes and . . . attitudes and expressions of attitudes to someone else's past conduct or imminent conduct" (1962:159).

4   By *ethnography* I mean here the study of human action within a particular community through participant-observation of spontaneous encounters for the purpose of gaining an understanding of the participants' perspective on what is going on in such encounters. For a review of ethnographic methods applied to the study of verbal interaction, see Duranti (1997a: ch. 4).

5   Italians use *ciao* for both opening and closing salutations.

6   This statement is ambiguous. It should be understood as meaning either one of the following scenarios: (i) in a given speech community, the same verbal expression may be used in both greeting (viz. opening salutation) and leave-taking; or (ii) a greeting item can exhaust the encounter and in that sense function as both an opening and closing expression. An example of the first situation is the word *ciao* as used in Italy. An example of the second situation is the English question "How're you doing?" when it is not followed by an answer.

7 The use of the notion of *perceptual field* allows for the inclusion of visual and auditory access. The issue of technologies that allow for nonreal time communication (writing in general) is left out of the present discussion. (But see Duranti 1986 for a brief discussion of greetings in electronic mail.)

8 Philips (1972:377) used the notion *participant structure* in referring to structural arrangements of interaction. For the related notion of "participation framework," see Goffman 1981:226 and M. H. Goodwin 1990.

9 I am avoiding here the term *Samoan society*, given the existence of many communities around the world where Samoan is regularly spoken, including two independent countries, (formerly Western) Samoa and American Samoa, each of which with different kinds of language policies and language practices, including different levels of bilingualism.

10 July 1978–July 1979, March–May 1981, August 1988.

11 As I said earlier, these four types of greetings do not exhaust the typology of Samoan greetings. There is at least one more possible candidate, the informal "'ua 'e sau?" (Have you come?), said to someone who has just come into the house. (For a similar greeting in Tikopia, see Firth 1972.) The lack of personal experience with this greeting and the absence of examples of this greeting in my data have prevented me from including it in the discussion. One of the reviewers also suggested the expression *uā* as an abbreviation of the same greeting.

12 It is possible of course that the use of this greeting has changed over the years and that Mead witnessed an earlier usage of the term.

13 The laughter that follows excerpt (1) could be interpreted as an index of the awkwardness of the exchange under the present circumstances.

14 Although I have no quantitative data at this moment to support such a statement, I must mention that the greeting *tālofa* is one of the few Samoan terms that can be pronounced with the initial /t/ even in the "bad speech" pronunciation (see the appendix); in other words, it does not necessarily change to /kālofa/ even in those contexts in which all other /t/ sounds disappear. This feature of *tālofa* might be related to its common use with foreigners.

15 For abbreviations used in interlinear glosses, see the appendix.

16 This meaning makes the Samoan *mālō* related to the homophonous Tongan term *mālō*, meaning "(to be) laudable, worthy of thanks or praise" as well as "thank you" (Churchward 1959:325), and to the Hawaiian *mahalo* "thanks, gratitude, to thank" (Pukui and Elbert 1986:218).

17 Given the different word order of English and Samoan, it is impossible to adequately reproduce here the pauses in the English translation. Samoans say "is nice the land" rather than "the land is nice." This explains why many examples of repairs are in the predicate phrase.

18 Samoan distinguishes in this case between *le asiasi* "the inspecting/visiting" and *asiasiga* "the visit/inspection" or the "visiting/inspecting party".

19 What I call "ceremonial attributes" here are parts of the *fa'alupega* "ceremonial style of address" for people of high status or their entire community. (There is a *fa'alupega* of the entire country.) They include metaphorical expressions that identify particular titles and their connections to ancestors, places, and important events in Samoan history. See Duranti 1981, 1994; Mead 1930; and Shore 1982. Krämer 1902–03 (and 1994) contains all the *fa'alupega* as known at the time of his study.

20 Syntactically, the name of the title may be simply juxtaposed next to the addressed term, as in "lau kōfā le Makua," or be linked to it with an oblique preposition (e.g. 'i/i or 'iā/iā), as in "lau kōfā i le Makua" (literally, "your honor from the senior orator"). The word *kōfā* also means "opinion (of a chief)." Orators are expected to present the position of their chief.

21 It is also possible to have CGs exchanged between two groups, for example, when two or more individuals arrive simultaneously. In these cases, however, the individuals, especially when their number is low, are each addressed within the same extended CG (Duranti 1997b).

22 Here is an example of a response by an individual to all the members of the inspection committee:

Tūla'i: mālō (Timi)! // (?)

Timi: mālō (1.0) afioga i ali'i – ma failāuga!

    (3.0)   *Congratulations (1.0) honorable chiefs – and orators!*

Tūla'i: 'ua lē faia lou lima iga 'ua 'ē ka'oko!
           You haven't done your hand [i.e., played cards] since you've been operated on
           [i.e., you've gotten a tattoo]!

23 This third hypothesis makes this exchange similar to another one that took place a decade earlier, when another matai spoke on my behalf to explain to the Moe'ono of those days – the father of the person holding the Moe'ono title in this interaction – what I was writing on my notebook (see Duranti 1992b:91–2).

24 Given its context of use, this type of exchange is the most difficult to catch on tape unless the researcher carefully plans the use of the audiorecorder or videocamera having in mind this type of greeting. Given that the decision to systematically study greetings was made after returning from the field, although I witnessed and participated in hundreds if not thousands of these exchanges, I have very few clear and reliable "where are you going" greetings in my corpus. Despite this limitation, however, I think that some hypotheses may be made about their organization and in particular about the importance of their propositional content.

25 The term *ali'i*, which historically comes from the Polynesian term for "chief" (Proto-Polynesian *aliki*), maintains in Samoan this meaning for the higher-ranking *matai*. In (15), instead, it is used as a separate address form. It may also be used like a title in English and other Indo-European languages: for example, before a first name (*ali'i Alesana* "Mr. Alesana") and as a descriptor (*le ali'i lea* "this gentleman/fellow"). In contemporary Samoa, the term does not have restrictions in terms of age, gender, or animacy. Thus *ali'i* may be used with a young child, a woman (e.g. *ali'i Elenoa* "Ms. Elinor"), or even an object (*le ali'i lea* can mean "that person" or "that thing"). Such a variety of uses makes it difficult to provide a translation of its use in the first line of (15), but it is clear that it should be understood as showing some form of respect, however minimum, of the addressee's social persona. It contrasts, for instance, with the informal address terms *sole* (for male recipients) and *suga* (for female recipients), which may be translated with English terms such as *lad*, *brother*, or *man* and *lassie*, *sister*, or *girl*, respectively (see example (12), line 2).

26 The alternative spelling and pronunciation is probably due to hypercorrection resulting from the sociolinguistic variation between *n* ([n]) and *ng* ([ŋ]) (see Duranti 1990; Duranti and Ochs 1986; Hovdhaugen 1986; Shore 1982).

27 The English *acknowledgment* parallels the way in which *tulouga* is sometimes used by Samoan speakers, who seem to treat it as a nominalization as well. For example, in example (18), the first *tulouga* is followed by a genitive phrase "a le aofia ma le fogo" (of the assembly and the council).

28 Moamoa is the name of the *malae* "ceremonial green" of the village of Falefā.

29 Lalogafu'afu'a is the name of the malae of the village of Lufilufi, the capital of the subdistrict of Anoama'a East where Falefā is located. The spatial metaphor "the back of" is meant to convey the idea that the people of Falefā are expected to support and protect the people of Lufilufi.

30 "Tulou!" (Excuse me!) is commonly used to excuse oneself for inappropriately entering the interactional space occupied by others (Duranti 1981).

REFERENCES

Austin, J. L. (1962). *How to Do Things with Words*. Oxford: Oxford University Press.

Bach, Kent, and Robert M. Harnish (1979). *Linguistic Communication and Speech Acts*. Cambridge, MA: MIT Press.

Basso, Keith (1972). "To Give Up on Words": Silence in Western Apache Culture. In *Language and Social Context*. P. P. Giglioli, ed., pp. 67–86. Harmondsworth, England: Penguin Books.

Bourdieu, Pierre (1977). *Outline of a Theory of Practice*. Richard Nice, trans. Cambridge: Cambridge University Press.

Caton, Steven C. (1986). Salam Tahiyah: Greetings from the Highlands of Yemen. *American Ethnologist* 13:290–308.

Churchward, C. Maxwell (1959). *Tongan Dictionary*. Tonga: Government Printing Press.

Duranti, Alessandro (1981). *The Samoan Fono: A Sociolinguistic Study*. Pacific Linguistics Monographs, Series B, 80. Canberra: Australian National University, Department of Linguistics, Research School of Pacific Studies.

Duranti, Alessandro (1986). Framing Discourse in a New Medium: Openings in Electronic Mail. *Quarterly Newsletter of the Laboratory of Comparative Human Cognition* 8(2): 64–71.

Duranti, Alessandro (1990). Code Switching and Conflict Management in Samoan Multiparty Interaction. *Pacific Studies* 141:1–30.

Duranti, Alessandro (1992a). Language and Bodies in Social Space: Samoan Ceremonial Greetings. *American Anthropologist* 94:657–91.

Duranti, Alessandro (1992b). Language in Context and Language as Context: The Samoan Respect Vocabulary. In *Rethinking Context: Language as an Interactive Phenomenon*. A. Duranti and C. Goodwin, eds., p. 77–99. Cambridge: Cambridge University Press.

Duranti, Alessandro (1994). *From Grammar to Politics: Linguistic Anthropology in a Western Samoan Village*. Berkeley and Los Angeles: University of California Press.

Duranti, Alessandro (1997a). *Linguistic Anthropology*. Cambridge: Cambridge University Press.

Duranti, Alessandro (1997b). Polyphonic Discourse: Overlapping in Samoan Ceremonial Greetings. *Text* 17(3):349–81.

Duranti, Alessandro, and Elinor Ochs (1986). Literacy Instruction in a Samoan Village. In *Acquisition of Literacy: Ethnographic Perspectives*. B. B. Schieffelin and P. Gilmore, eds., pp. 213–32. Norwood, NJ: Ablex.

Eibl-Eibesfeldt, Irenäus (1972). Similarities and Differences between Cultures in Expressive Movements. In *Non-Verbal Communication*. R. A. Hinde, ed., pp. 297–312. Cambridge: Cambridge University Press.

Eibl-Eibesfeldt, Irenäus (1977). Patterns of Greetings in New Guinea. In *New Guinea Area Languages and Language Study*, vol. 3. S. A. Wurm, ed., pp. 209–47. Canberra: Australian National University, Department of Linguistics, Research School of Pacific Studies.

Farnell, Brenda (1995). *Do You See What I Mean?: Plains Indian Sign Talk and the Embodiment of Action*. Austin: University of Texas Press.

Firth, Raymond (1972). Verbal and Bodily Rituals of Greeting and Parting. In *The Interpretation of Ritual: Essays in Honour of A. I. Richards*. J. S. La Fontaine, ed., pp. 1–38. London: Tavistock.

Goffman, Erving (1971). *Relations in Public: Microstudies of the Public Order*. New York: Harper and Row.

Goffman, Erving (1981). *Forms of Talk*. Philadelphia: University of Pennsylvania Press.

Goodwin, Marjorie Harness (1990). *He-Said-She-Said: Talk as Social Organization among Black Children*. Bloomington: Indiana University Press.

Goody, Esther (1972). "Greeting", "Begging", and the Presentation of Respect. In *The Interpretation of Ritual*. J. S. La Fontaine, ed., pp. 39–71. London: Tavistock.

Gregor, Thomas (1977). *The Mehinaku: The Drama of Everyday Life in a Brazilian Indian Village*. Chicago: University of Chicago Press.

Grice, H. P. (1975). Logic and Conversation. In *Syntax and Semantics*, vol. 3, *Speech Acts*. P. Cole and N. L. Morgan, eds., pp. 41–58. New York: Academic Press.

Gumperz, John J. (1992). Contextualization and Understanding. In *Rethinking Context*. A. Duranti and C. Goodwin, eds., pp. 229–52. Cambridge: Cambridge University Press.

Hanks, William F. (1990). *Referential Practice: Language and Lived Space among the Maya*. Chicago: University of Chicago Press.

Hoëm, Ingjerd (1993). Space and Morality in Tokelau. *Pragmatics* 3:137–53.

Hoëm, Ingjerd (1995). A Sense of Place: The Politics of Identity and Representation. Doctoral thesis, University of Oslo.

Holmes, Lowell D. (1987). *Quest for the Real Samoa: The Mead/Freeman Controversy and Beyond*. South Hadley, MA: Bergin and Garvey.

Hovdhaugen, Even (1986). The Chronology of Three Samoan Sound Changes. In *Papers from the Fourth International Conference on Austronesian Linguistics*. P. Geraghty, L. Carrington, and S. A. Wurm, eds., pp. 313–33. Pacific Linguistics, Series C, 93–4. Canberra: Research School of Pacific Studies, Australian National University.

Irvine, Judith (1974). Strategies of Status Manipulation in Wolof Greeting. In *Explorations in the Ethnography of Speaking*. R. Bauman and J. Sherzer, eds., pp. 167–91. Cambridge: Cambridge University Press.

Jakobson, Roman (1960). Closing Statement: Linguistics and Poetics. In *Style in Language*. T. A. Sebeok, ed., pp. 398–429. Cambridge, MA: MIT Press.

Keenan, Elinor Ochs [Also see Ochs, Elinor] (1976). The Universality of Conversational Postulates. *Language in Society* 5:67–80.

Kendon, Adam, and Andrew Ferber (1973). A Description of Some Human Greetings. In *Comparative Ecology and Behaviour of Primates*. R. P. Michael and J. H. Crook, eds., pp. 591–668. London: Academic Press.

Krämer, Augustine (1902–03). *Die Samoa-Inseln*. Stuttgart, Germany: Schwertzerbartsche.

Krämer, Augustine (1994). *The Samoa Islands. An Outline of a Monograph with Particular Consideration of German Samoa*, vol. 1. Theodore Verhaaren, trans. Honolulu: University of Hawaii Press.

Leach, Edmund (1972). The Influence of Cultural Context on Non-Verbal Communication in Man. In *Non-Verbal Communication*. R. Hinde, ed., pp. 315–47. Cambridge: Cambridge University Press.

Malinowski, Bronislaw (1923). The Problem of Meaning in Primitive Languages. In *The Meaning of Meaning*. C. K. Ogden and I. A. Richards, eds., pp. 296–336. New York: Harcourt, Brace and World.

Mead, Margaret (1928). *Coming of Age in Samoa*. New York: William Morrow.

Mead, Margaret (1930). *Social Organization of Manu'a*. Honolulu, HI: Bishop Museum Press.

Milner, G. B. (1961). The Samoan Vocabulary of Respect. *Journal of the Royal Anthropological Institute* 91:296–317.

Milner, G. B. (1966). *Samoan Dictionary: Samoan–English English–Samoan*. London: Oxford University Press.

Milton, Kay (1982). Meaning and Context: The Interpretation of Greetings in Kasigau. In *Semantic Anthropology*. D. Parkin, ed., pp. 261–77. London: Academic Press.

Ochs, Elinor [Also see Keenan, Elinor Ochs] (1985). Variation and Error: A Sociolinguistic Study of Language Acquisition in Samoa. In *The Crosslinguistic Study of Language Acquisition*. D. I. Slobin, ed., pp. 783–838. Hillsdale, NJ: Erlbaum.

Ochs, Elinor (1988). *Culture and Language Development: Language Acquisition and Language Socialization in a Samoan Village*. Cambridge: Cambridge University Press.

Philips, Susan U. (1972). Participant Structures and Communicative Competence: Warm Springs Children in Community and Classroom. In *Functions of Language in the Classroom*. C. B. Cazden, V. P. John, and D. Hymes, eds., pp. 370–94. New York: Columbia Teachers Press.

Platt, Martha (1982). Social and Semantic Dimensions of Deictic Verbs and Particles in Samoan Child Language. Ph.D. dissertation, University of Southern California.

Pukui, Mary Kawena, and Samuel H. Elbert (1986). *Hawaiian Dictionary. Hawaiian–English English–Hawaiian*. Revised and enlarged edn. Honolulu: University of Hawaii Press.

Sacks, Harvey (1975). Everyone Has to Lie. In *Sociocultural Dimensions of Language Use*. M. Sanches and B. G. Blount, eds., pp. 57–80. New York: Academic Press.

Sacks, Harvey (1992). *Lectures on Conversation*, vol. 1. Cambridge, MA: Blackwell.

Sacks, Harvey, Emanuel A. Schegloff, and Gail Jefferson (1974). A Simpler Systematics for the Organization of Turn-Taking for Conversation. *Language* 50:696–735.

Schegloff, Emanuel (1968). Sequencing in Conversational Openings. *American Anthropologist* 70:1075–95.

Schegloff, Emanuel (1986). The Routine as Achievement. *Human Studies* 9:111–51.

Schegloff, Emanuel A., and Harvey Sacks (1973). Opening Up Closings. *Semiotica* 8:289–327.

Searle, John R. (1969). *Speech Acts: An Essay in the Philosophy of Language*. Cambridge: Cambridge University Press.

Searle, John R., and Daniel Vanderveken (1985). *Foundations of Illocutionary Logic*. Cambridge: Cambridge University Press.

Sherzer, Joel (1983). *Kuna Ways of Speaking: An Ethnographic Perspective*. Austin: University of Texas Press.

Shore, Bradd (1982). *Sala'ilua: A Samoan Mystery*. New York: Columbia University Press.

Valeri, Valerio (1985). *Kingship and Sacrifice*. Chicago: University of Chicago Press.

Youssouf, Ibrahim Ag, Allen D. Grimshaw, and Charles S. Bird (1976). Greetings in the Desert. *American Ethnologist* 3:797–824.

Appendix

Transcription conventions

All Samoan examples are taken from transcripts of spontaneous interactions recorded by the author in Western Samoa at different times between 1978 and 1988. In the transcripts presented in the article, I adopt the conventions introduced by Gail Jefferson for conversation analysis (see Sacks et al. 1974), with a few modifications.

[*Inspection*]	A name in brackets before the text of an example refers to the name of the transcript.
Tūla'i:	Speakers' names (or general descriptors) are separated from their utterances by colons.
?:	A question mark instead of a name indicates that no good guess could be made as to the identity of the speaker.
??:	Repeated question marks indicate additional unidentified speakers.
?Tūla'i:	A question mark before the name of the speaker stands for a probable, but not safe, guess.
(2.5)	Numbers between parentheses indicate length of pauses in seconds and tenths of seconds.
[	A square bracket between turns indicates the point at which overlap by another speaker starts.
//	Parallel slashes are an alternative symbol indicating point of overlap.
=	The equal signs indicate that two utterances are latched immediately to one another with no pause.
=[	The equal signs before a square bracket between turns signals that the utterance above and the one below are both latched to the prior one.
(I can't do)	Talk between parentheses represents the best guess of a stretch of talk which was difficult to hear.
(??)	Parentheses with question marks indicate uncertain or unclear talk of approximately the length of the blank spaces between parentheses.
(( ))	Material between double parentheses provides extralinguistic information.
[...]	An ellipsis between square brackets indicates that parts of the original transcript or example have been omitted or that the transcript starts or ends in the middle of further talk.
o::	Colons, single or double, indicate lengthening of the sound they follow.

Abbreviations in interlinear glosses

Art = article; Comp = complementizer; Emp = emphatic particle; excl = exclusive; incl = inclusive; Perf = perfective aspect marker; pl = plural (as opposed to singular or dual); Pres = present tense; Voc = vocative particle.

"Good speech" and "bad speech"

Samoan has two phonological registers, called by Samoans *tautala lelei* "good speech" and *tautala leaga* "bad speech." "Good speech" is strongly associated with Christianity, written language (e.g., the Bible), and Western education (Duranti and Ochs 1986; Ochs 1988; Shore 1982). It is thus required of children and adults most of the time in the schools and during church services and most church-related activities. "Bad speech" is used in everyday encounters in the homes, at the store, or on the road and is also characteristic of most formal contexts in which traditional speechmaking is used, including the ceremonial greetings discussed in this article. There is also a considerable amount of shifting between these two registers (Duranti 1990; Ochs 1985, 1988). All the examples reproduced here are given with the pronunciation originally used by the speakers, which is usually "bad speech." When discussing words or phrases in the text of the article, I have usually used "good speech," unless I am referring to words actually used by people, in which case I put them between obliques to frame them as different from traditional orthography, e.g. /lau kōfā/ and /fogo/ instead of *lau tōfā* and *fono*, respectively. This means that the same word may be found in two different versions: for example, the expression *tulouga* is /kulouga/ in the transcript of a speech in a fono in which it was used. I followed standard Samoan orthography: the letter *g* stands for a velar nasal ([ŋ]). The apostrophe (') stands for a glottal stop ([ʔ]).

10

Emotion within Situated Activity

Marjorie H. Goodwin and Charles Goodwin

In this chapter, we will look at emotion as situated practices lodged within specific sequential positions in interaction. We argue that the relevant unit for the analysis of emotion is not the individual or the semantic system of a language, but instead the sequential organization of action. In contrast to a considerable body of research on emotion and language focusing on **emotion vocabulary** (Wierzbicka, 1992, 1995), the way people identify, classify, and recognize emotions (called "emotionology" by Stearns and Stearns (1988) and Harré and Gillett (1994)), this chapter focuses on a range of embodied practices deployed by participants to visibly take up stances toward phenomena being evaluated within the midst of situated interaction.

As linguistic anthropologists, we are interested in analyzing the **practices** through which people build the actions and scenes that constitute their lifeworlds. While in the 1960s cognitive anthropologists were concerned with mental models of culture as procedural and propositional **knowledge** (cognitive structures lodged within the individual mind), we view language as a social **tool** for organizing groups, for shaping alignment, and social identities of participants. Such a perspective is consistent with Malinowski's (1959) early formulations of language as "a mode of social action rather than a mere reflection of thought." For example, utterance structure can invoke participation frameworks for the organization of action, encompassing both occasion-relevant identities for participants and forms of talk. In analyzing the structure of opening accusation statements of he-said-she-said disputes among urban African American children, M. H. Goodwin (1990) has shown how a single utterance such as "Kerry said you said I wasn't gonna go around Poplar no more" can be used to invoke a confrontation in important political processes among girls – ways of sanctioning inappropriate behavior that lead to ostracism from the neighborhood peer group. Such analysis of situated social action can be informed by long-term fieldwork, and more generally, data obtained within contexts of naturally occurring discourse.

The approach we adopt for understanding the orderliness of human interaction is conversation analysis, a field established by the late Harvey Sacks in collaboration with Emanuel Schegloff and Gail Jefferson (Sacks, Schegloff, & Jefferson, 1974; Schegloff, Jefferson, & Sacks, 1977; for a history of the field, see Clayman & Maynard, 1994; Heritage, 1984, 1995; Levinson, 1983). Conversation analysis investigates the procedures participants employ to construct and make intelligible their talk, and the events that occur within it (Sacks, 1984). Displaying the orderliness of talk is not primarily an analytic problem for the researcher but rather one of the central tasks that participants themselves face in producing conversational moves (Schegloff & Sacks, 1973). As argued by Sacks, Schegloff, and Jefferson (1974):

But while understandings of other turns' talk are displayed to coparticipants, they are available as well to professional analysts, who are thereby provided a proof criterion (and a search procedure) for the analysis of what a turn's talk is occupied with. Since it is the parties' understandings of prior turns' talk that is relevant to their construction of next turns, it is their understandings that are warranted for analysis. (pp. 728–9)

Because participants in conversation display their analysis of prior talk, the sequential organization of conversation provides rigorous, empirical ways of understanding how participants themselves make sense of the talk they are engaged in.

Our methods combine extensive ethnographic research with video recording. The video camera makes it possible to record mundane talk, visible behavior and some relevant features of the settings where members of a society actually constitute their lives.

The approach of conversation analysis provides a thoroughly social rather than individual perspective on language. In our view, rather than being lodged exclusively within the psychology of the individual, we find that the cognitive resources participants deploy to construct consequential action are situated within both language practices and the cultural (Duranti, 1994, 1997; Ochs, 1988) and material features (Hutchins, 1995; Latour, 1996) of the settings where action occurs. In a study of communication in the operations room of a mid-sized airport (Goodwin & Goodwin, 1996), we found that in formulating answers to pilots, Flight Trackers make use of multiple modalities, including the Flight Information Display screen in front of them, a radio log on their desk, and a bank of monitors in the room relaying images of activity at the gates of the terminal. Likewise, scientists probing the sea at the mouth of the Amazon rely on the instruments, computer displays, and activity across several teams of science, including physical oceanographers as well as geochemists, in order to conduct scientific investigation (Goodwin, 1995b). As Duranti (1997) has argued, culture includes both material objects and ideational objects such as belief systems and linguistic codes, for both "are instruments through which humans mediate their relationship with the world" (p. 41). This chapter will investigate how girls playing hopscotch build actions that require the integrated use of both particular language formats and the semiotic field provided by the hopscotch grid, which shapes and defines actions being contested.

Fieldwork within particular settings is important if we want to investigate the full linguistic repertoire of a speech community. For example, most studies in the psychological and sociological literature have found that girls are less able than boys to incorporate argumentative talk or forceful imperative forms within their interaction (thus positing a view of girls as powerless actors). In contrast, during her fieldwork over a year and a half in urban Philadelphia, M. H. Goodwin (1998) found that girls can select from a range of different types of actions to construct widely different forms of social organization, depending on the particular situation of the moment. Fieldwork also allows us to investigate how speech forms are consequential for extensive social projects extending beyond the immediate encounter; something not possible when single encounters of talk are recorded or talk is elicited.

Emotion as Embodied Performance

Budwig (2000) has argued that if we are to view children as agents in constructing their social worlds then we need to look at how language is used by children to position themselves in actual interactive situations. The following provides a first example of how emotion is situated within children's language activity. Three bilingual Spanish- and English-speaking girls (primarily second-generation Central Americans) in grades 2–5 in an elementary school located in the Pico Union/Korea-town district, near downtown Los Angeles, are playing hopscotch. Data are transcribed using the conventions of Sacks, Schegloff, and Jefferson (1974) described in the Appendix.

Illustrated in figure 10.1, Carla says that she will take the next turn. This is immediately answered by a very strong display of opposition from Gloria, who claims that Carla is usurping her turn.

The oppositional turn contains no emotional words whatsoever. Nonetheless it vividly displays a strong emotional stance on the part of its speaker, for example, what we might gloss as outraged indignation at the despicable behavior of the first

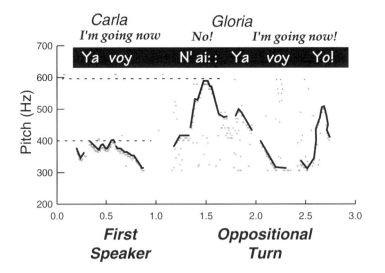

Figure 10.1

speaker. How is this stance made visible? The oppositional turn begins with a **preface**, "N'ai," announcing at the earliest possible opportunity in the turn that the prior move is being objected to. Moreover this preface is spoken with a dramatic pitch excursion. Such forms of "emphatic speech style" resemble what Selting (1994) has described as "peaks of involvement" within the domain of storytelling, places in a story where the speaker suddenly shifts to a marked emphatic style. Within the single syllable of the preface the second speaker's voice leaps from 400 to 600 Hz. The display of outrage, with its associated emotional components, is made visible as an embodied performance – that is, through the way in which the second speaker controls her voice and intonation.

However, pitch height does not function as an isolated, decontextualized display. Instead it becomes visible as a specific, meaningful event, by virtue of the way in which it is embedded within a particular sequence of action. Not only the turn preface, but also the squeal of outrage, are indexically tied to the immediately prior action that constitutes the point of departure for the display of opposition. The second speaker builds her moves within a field of meaning that has been brought into existence by the conditional relevance (Schegloff, 1968) of the prior action. On the level of sound structure itself, the pitch height becomes visible as a salient action through the way in which it vividly contrasts with the talk preceding it. In essence, a single participant's display of emotion must be analyzed by embedding it within a larger sequence of action.

Sequential slots for the production of relevant responses provide participants with a place where they can use a range of different kinds of embodied activity to build appropriate action. In figure 10.2, Carla uses not only pitch, but also posture and gesture, to accuse another girl, Sandra (at the left of the frame grid), of having landed on a line while making a jump in hopscotch.

Carla: OUT! OUT!

Figure 10.2

Once again no emotion words are found in the semantic structure of the talk that occurs here. Nonetheless Carla vividly displays heightened affect as she accuses her opponent of being *out*. Some of the organizational frameworks that make such emotion visible and relevant will be briefly described. First, Carla's action occurs in a particular sequential position: immediately after Sandra's jump, the precise place where an assessment of the success or failure of that jump is due. By virtue of such positioning, Carla's talk is heard as an evaluation of Sandra's performance. Second, Carla's evaluation is produced immediately, without any delay after the jump. Through such quick uptake, and the lack of doubt or mitigation in the call, there is an unambiguous assertion that a clear violation did in fact occur. Third, the two *Out!* calls are spoken with markedly raised pitch, as illustrated in figure 10.3.

The normal pitch of the girls is between 250 and 350 Hz; here, however, Carla's voice leaps dramatically to 663 and 673 Hz over the two *Outs*. Fourth, while saying *Out!* Carla points a condemning finger at Sandra. The accusation can be found not only in her talk, but also visibly in the gesture she uses. In short, affect is lodged within embodied sequences of action. Moreover, the phenomena that provide organization for both affect and action are distributed through multiple media within a larger field of action.

To further explore the scope of the field providing organization for the actions found here, consider the constitution of an *Out* in hopscotch. Speech action, and cognition more generally, are frequently assumed to lie within the domain of *mental* representations. However, an *Out* is defined by the placement of the jumper's body on an external representation: an actual grid drawn in the asphalt of the playground. The task of seeing an *Out* seamlessly integrates nonmaterial rules with actual embodied performance and cognitive artifacts (the game grid) that have a material existence at a specific place in the local environment. Consistent with the arguments of Hutchins (1995; see also Latour, 1996; Užgiris, 1996), cognition is not lodged exclusively within the head of an isolated actor, but instead within a distributed system, one that includes both other participants and meaningful artifacts, such as the hopscotch grid, which defines a public, visible arena for the constitution of specific types of action. Such objects, artifacts, and tools are not incidental but critical in the framing of human experience (Latour, 1996).

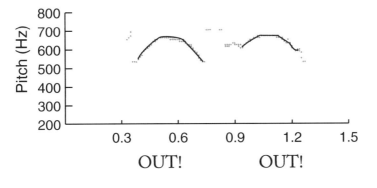

Figure 10.3

Crucial components of the cognitive activities in progress are located in the setting and in the performed actions of participants' bodies. Indeed, a moment later, Carla justifies her *Out* by walking to the grid and using her own body to "replay" the activity just seen. In much the way that a speaker can report another's speech, the feet of the judge, Carla, both replay and comment upon the errors made by Sandra's feet.

Sandra:	((*jumps and lands on some lines*))	**Problematic Move**
Carla:	OUT! OUT!	**Out!** ((*finger point*))
	PISASTE LA DE AQUÍ	**Explanation**
	You stepped on this one	((*demonstration*))
	Y LA DE ACÁ.	
	and this one.	

Judges not only state verbally their objections to a player's moves in the game. In addition, in conjunction with their talk, they may provide nonvocal accounts that consist of replaying past moves to add further grounding for their positions. In challenging the player Sandra's move, Carla animatedly provides a rendition of Sandra's past mistake. As she states that Sandra had stepped on "this one" (*la de aquí*) and "this one" (*la de acá*), Carla reenacts Sandra's movement through space, challenging the player's prior move. The demonstration – involving a fully embodied gestural performance in an inscribed space – could not have been done without the grid, as it provides the relevant background – the necessary tool – for locating violations. From a slightly different perspective, recent work on deixis (Agha, 1996) has argued that an indexical term such as "this one" requires a relevant spatial superimposition in order to become meaningful. Here the indexical term in the stream of the speech, the gesture and the grid, as a semiotic field in its own right, mutually elaborate each other (see also Goodwin, 1995b, 1996a).

Turns of judges such as these display a clear orientation towards forms of "aggravated correction" (Goodwin, 1983), and thus contrast strongly with what has been described in the literature about the preference for agreement in both male and female *adult* conversation. Yaeger-Dror (1986) notes that intonation over disagreement is frequently nonsalient. Sacks (1973/1987) and Pomerantz (1984) find that in adult polite conversation disagreement is a dispreferred activity that is minimized through various features of turn design including (1) delays before the production of a disagreement and (2) prefaces that mitigate the disagreement. Sometimes these prefaces take the form of agreements that were followed by the disagreement.

A: She doesn't uh usually come in on Friday, does she?
B: Well, yes she does, sometimes.

Here, disagreement is mitigated by both the hesitant "Well" that precedes it and the qualifier "sometimes" that follows it.

By way of contrast, in the game of hopscotch, when calling an *Out* or a *Foul*, opposition occurs immediately, positioning the affective stance at the earliest possible place with respect to the prior turn. This is frequently followed by an

Figure 10.4   Carla: PISASTE LA DE AQUÍ

Figure 10.5   Carla: Y LA DE ACÁ

emotionally charged, pejorative description of the party who committed the offense, for example, *Chiriona* ("cheater").

Gloria:	((*jumps from square two to one changing feet*))	**Problematic Move**
Carla:	NO CHIRIONA!	**Polarity Expression +**
		Negative Person Descriptor
	No Cheater!	
	YA NO SE VALE ASÍ.	**Explanation**
	That way is no longer valid!	
Gloria:	((*takes a turn out of turn*))	**Problematic Move**
Carla:	AY: TÚ CHIRIONA!	**Response Cry + Negative**
		Person Descriptor
	Hey You Cheater!	
	EH NO PISES AQUÍ	**Explanation**
	Hey don't step here.	
	PORQUE AQUÍ YO VOY!	
	Because I'm going here.	
Gloria:	((*jumps from square 3 to 2 changing feet*))	**Problematic Move**
Carla:	!EY::! !CHIRIONA! !MIRA!	**Response Cry + Negative**
		Person Descriptor
	Hey! Cheater! Look!	
	TE VENISTES DE AQUÍ ASÍ!	**Explanation**
	You came from here like this.	
	((*demonstrating how Gloria jumped changing feet*))	

With these examples we see that the display of a form of affect is made relevant by the structure of *practices for performing* the out call – that is, within a specific sequential position in the midst of an activity: reacting to a violation. Rather than viewing emotion as lodged within specific semantic categories, we see how it is conveyed through affective intensity (Bradac, Mulac, & Thompson, 1995) or highlighting (Goodwin, 1994) as indicated through pitch leaps, vowel lengthening, and raised volume. Unlike delayed disagreement observable in adult conversation (Pomerantz, 1984; Sacks, 1973/1987), the girls, through their intonation and gestures (such as extended hand points) display in a forceful, integrated manner that opposition is occurring, thus countering many of the stereotypical views of female language use (see also Goodwin, 1998).

The way in which an *Out* is defined by embodied action occurring at a particular location in space provides organization for the body of the judge prior to the call. In order to assess the success or failure of the player's move she must position herself so that she can clearly see the player's feet landing on the grid. A moment before the jump Carla has moved to just such a position. Indeed, the reason she is pointing with her accusing finger from a crouch is that she has bent down to look carefully at the place where the jumper will land. It is only by virtue of such perceptual access to the events being evaluated that the judge's call can be heard as a valid action (for example, if she hadn't seen the landing, her call would not be heard as a legitimate claim about what had happened). Her affect presupposes an actor positioned to assess the events being challenged. We shall see in a moment that establishing such access is a crucial feature of many other assessments as well.

Emotion Without a Vocabulary

Analysis will now focus on interaction in the family of a man, Rob, with severe nonfluent aphasia. A stroke to the left hemisphere of his brain has left Rob with the ability to speak only four words *Yes, No, And*, and *Oh*. By varying his intonation and attending to sequential organization Rob is actually able to construct a range of quite diverse action with what might appear to be a very restricted vocabulary. Indeed, when embodiment and context are taken into account, it can be plausibly argued that variants of *Yes*, such as *Yeah*, with a range of different intonation contours in fact provide him with a substantially larger set of meaningful terms for communication with his interlocutors (Goodwin, 1995a). Thus, despite the extraordinary scarceness of his vocabulary Rob is a most active participant in conversation. Moreover, one of his main communicative resources is the ability to display appropriate, changing emotional alignment to the talk of others. How is this possible? His vocabulary contains no emotion words at all.

The hopscotch data revealed that powerful emotional statements could be built through use of the following: (1) sequential position, (2) resources provided by the setting where action occurs, and (3) artful orchestration of a range of embodied actions (intonation, gesture, timing, etc.). To explore such phenomena further we will investigate the activity of assessment (see Goodwin & Goodwin, 1987), that is, affectively evaluating some relevant current event, available either in the local scene or through a report in the talk of the moment. The following provide two examples of a basic action structure used to do assessment.

In figure 10.6, Jere is holding up a calendar with photographs of birds that Pat has received as a present. Between the first and second line Jere changes the calendar so that a new bird picture appears.

Immediately upon seeing the first bird, Pat produces an audible in-breath (transcribed as "*hhh"). Our transcription is not able to capture the precise way in which the voice quality of this in-breath, a deep inhale, displays vivid, spontaneous appreciation of what she has just seen. The in-breath is immediately followed by "*Wow!*" Pat's audible reaction to the picture constitutes what Goffman (1981) has called a *response cry*, an embodied display that the party producing it has been so moved by a triggering event that they temporarily "flood out" with a brief emotional expression. This is followed a moment later by a fully formed syntactic phrase which accounts for and explicates the speaker's reaction by describing something that is remarkable in the event being responded to (see Goodwin, 1996b). When a new picture appears, this same pattern occurs a second time. Of particular relevance to the present analysis is the way in which the Reactive Particle, occurring in a specific sequential position (for example, right after the event it is heard as responding to), provides one systematic practice for making a precisely placed and appropriate display of emotion with minimal lexical resources.

We will now look at the actions of Rob, the man with aphasia, in this sequence (figure 10.7). In response to the first bird picture, Rob produces a series of nonlexical syllables, "Dih-dih-dih-dih." Our transcription is not able to adequately capture the

Pat:	*hhh **Wow**!	Those are **great** pictures.
	Triggering Event **Reactive Particle**	**Elaborating Sentence**
Pat: Jere:	Oh my °god.	Look ⌐at that color. ⌐Look at those colors.

Figure 10.6

voice quality through which enthusiastic appreciation is displayed in the way these syllables are spoken. When Jere flips to the second picture, Rob immediately changes his response to a rich, appreciative "*YEAH:*."

As Pat's response cries here demonstrate [figure 10.7], the slot right after a triggering event provides a place where speakers can produce a relevant display of emotion with minimal lexical resources. Rob uses this structure to coparticipate in the activity of assessing the pictures with an appropriate emotional response to them.

However, Rob's initial response "*Dih-dih-dih-dih*" does not occur until well after Pat's reaction. When the videotape is examined, we see that during Pat's "*Wow*," Rob is looking down at his food. On hearing the "*Wow*" (which could be considered an "emphatic unit" calling for a relevant response, in Selting's (1994) terms), he immediately starts to raise his gaze. However, he does not move it toward the speaker who produced the "*Wow*," but instead to the calendar Pat is reacting to. Such gaze movement demonstrates that Rob is not simply responding to a salient bid for attention (in which case movement toward the sound and its producer would be appropriate). Instead, he analyzes the "*Wow*" as a component of a specific, recognizable

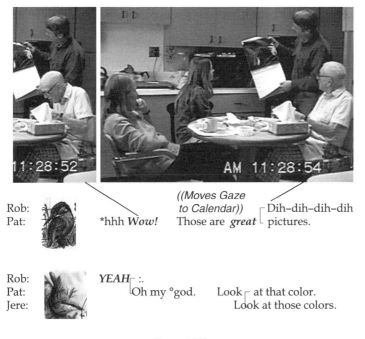

Figure 10.7

activity – reacting to an assessible object in the local scene – and moves his gaze to the object being commented upon. This movement takes time. Only when it has been completed and Rob has had the opportunity to see the picture himself does he begin his appreciative emotional response to it.

Goffman's (1967) elegant, but perhaps infelicitous term *response cry* might lead one to see a party's emotional reaction to a triggering event as a matter of "natural" contingency. The event is so powerful that an actor spontaneously "floods out" on encountering it and emits an involuntary, emotionally charged response cry. The present data allow us to see that the relationship between triggering event and response cry is a matter of visible organization rather than haphazard contingency. Triggering event and response cry are fitted to each other as subcomponents of a larger activity system; each implies the other. On hearing the cry, Rob looks for what might have triggered it. It would be quite possible physically for Rob to immediately follow Pat's "*Wow*" with a congruent reaction of his own, for example, rapidly produce an assessment without waiting to actually see the object being commented on. Indeed, because of her severe Parkinson's disease, Rob's wife does precisely this. She frequently produces sequentially appropriate assessments of events she hasn't actually witnessed. However, Rob doesn't do this. Instead he works to put himself in a position where he can independently assess the picture and only then reacts to it. The very simple lexical and syntactic structure of response cries masks a more elaborate grammar of practice.

Central to the organization of response cries is a particular kind of experience that requires appropriate access to the event being responded to. The nature of that access can vary. On some occasions, the assessable event might be visible, on others it might be tasted, on still others it might be made available through the report of another speaker, and so on. However, despite variation in mode of access, the party producing the response cry is making an embodied assessment of something they know in a relevant way. In these data we can observe an actor actively working to put himself in a position where he has appropriate access before producing a response that agrees with an assessment just made by his coparticipant.

Stressing the importance of looking at communication as a multimodal activity that involves more than spoken language, Užgiris (1996) has argued that "affectivity, action contours, and the patterning of exchanges during interaction are a means for communication without explicit symbols" (p. 23). In the data being examined here, despite the complete absence of emotion vocabulary Rob is able to participate in an intricate emotional conversation by making use of the larger sequential structures and embodied practices through which emotion is organized as an interactive process. His family considers him a fully alert, active coparticipant. The present data reveal some of the resources that make this possible. To briefly summarize some of the practices used by Rob in this sequence: (1) he uses the slot after a triggering event to make an emotionally colored response to that event through intonation and other embodied displays; (2) like his speaking partners, he changes his response the moment a new assessable appears (moving from "*Dih-dih-dih-dih*" to "*YEAH*" as soon as the page is flipped to a new picture), and thus demonstrates through action that he is closely attending to the changing particulars of the events being assessed; (3) he recognizes that Pat's "*Wow!*" indexes a specific kind of activity that calls for particular actions on his part if he is to coparticipate in it; (4) he attends to the grammar of response cries as embedded within a language game, a situated activity system (Goffman, 1967) that requires specific kinds of experience and forms of access to the entities being assessed. Thus, he delays production of his response until he has moved to a position where he has appropriate acces to the calendar. Though he is not able to describe emotions with semantic labels, Rob participates in the social organization of locally relevant emotionally charged assessments through intricate, temporally unfolding sequences of embodied action.

Rob's ability to control his intonation provides him with a central resource for building meaningful action. Given the importance of assessments, he has developed patterned ways of displaying appreciation through a recognizable contour. His ability to produce different kinds of syllables is quite limited; the same syllables are thus used to perform many different kinds of actions (assessments, commenting on stories, requesting attention, announcing a new topic, and so on). However, he uses a quite distinctive intonation pattern to do assessment and appreciation. A comparatively large number of syllables, typically five, is produced as a single breath group. The primary function of the syllables seems to be carrying a distinctive pitch contour. This contour varies to show Rob's engagement and enjoyment or appreciation of the entity being assessed. Characteristically, appreciations are done with relatively high pitch. Frequently, the last syllable is elongated, or in other ways marked as different from the syllables that preceded it. This seems in part a practice for displaying that the unit is coming to a point of possible completion. Here are several examples (while the contour systematically represents some aspects of what he is doing, we would like to emphasize that much of the appreciative character of

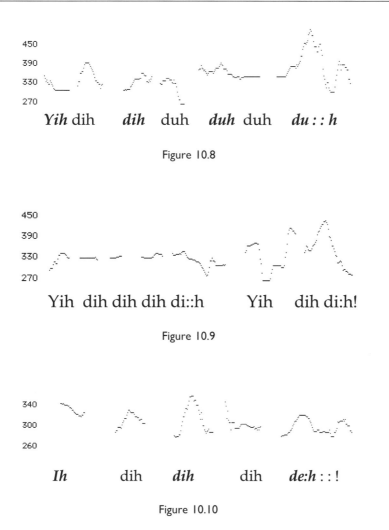

Figure 10.8

Figure 10.9

Figure 10.10

his voice is not captured by the pitch tracks). In figure 10.8, Rob, eating with his wife, has just taken the first bite of a cheese Danish.

In figure 10.9, Rob is looking at a plate of fresh Danish pastries.

Rob is looking at a hummingbird photograph in Pat's calendar. Note the continual pitch variation throughout the assessment in figure 10.10.

Further evidence for Rob's pragmatic competence and his ability to track and coparticipate in what others are doing through talk is visible in the differentiated responses he provides to structurally different kinds of talk. Not only does he display enthusiasm and excitement for events being assessed; contrastively, he can affirm his disapproval and displeasure for persons and events being evaluated. In the following, we find Rob participating in an assessment sequence in which speakers are critiquing rather than appreciating the assessable object. His granddaughter Susan tells family members that the next day she will be visiting her boyfriend and his mother.

```
 1  Chad:    So Sue. When are you going to go see your be-
 2           boyfriend.
 3  Susan:   Tomorrow morning. heh! ((exhales/sighing and smiling))
 4  Rob:     Ah dah dah! ((falsetto, eyebrows go up))
 5  Chad:    Well this is a big thing to meet his parents.=
 6           [isn't it?
 7  Rob:     [Myeah! ((slight nod of head))=
 8  Susan:   Ye::s. Well – I mean I've met his father?
 9           but his big thing's to meet his mother?
10           Because he wouldn't tell his mother about us
11           at fi(hh)rst. eh heh!
```

In this sequence, we find a range of different affective stances being taken up by Rob as he tracks the unfolding events in a story in fine detail. Susan answers Chad's question about when she is going to her boyfriend's with "Tomorrow morning" followed by a sigh. Rob quickly enters the conversation with an appreciative uptake "Ah dah *dah!*" (line 4). Chad's next question provides a sentential equivalent to this action, a request for elaboration of the story: "Well this is a *big thing* to meet his parents" (line 5). The request is addressed to Susan.

One way that Rob routinely displays his tracking of unfolding events is to provide a parasitic comment in the slot designated for another speaker affectively commenting on the import of the action. At line 7, Rob provides such a comment in the slot where Susan is to reply to Chad's question, an emotionally charged "Myeah!" This matches the affective tone of the "Ye::s." that begins Susan's turn in line 8. With respect to issues of Rob's pragmatic competence note the precision timing of this move (Jefferson, 1973), the way in which it begins exactly at the first possible completion of Chad's turn and thus overlaps the appended tag question. As the sequence develops further, Rob markedly changes his coparticipation to track the unfolding structure of Susan's story:

```
 8  Susan:   Ye::s. Well – I mean I've met his father?
 9           but his big thing's to meet his mother?
10           Because he wouldn't tell his mother about us
11           at fi(hh)rst. eh heh!
12  Rob:     °ah [nah.
13  Chad:        [Ah:.
14  Susan:   [Because he didn't want to deal with her.=
15  Chad:    [Why not.
16  Susan:   I don't know. It sounds like she's not qui(hh)te,
17           th(hh)e be(hh)st person. I don't know. ((shoulder shrug))
18  Rob:     ((shrugs his head, looks away, mirroring Susan's gesturing body))
19  Susan:   *hh She sounds a little – ((throat clear))
20           a little protective and –
21  Rob:     No. No. No. ((shaking his head)) ((taps Susan's elbow))
22  Rob:     N[o no no no no. ((shaking head, waving hand))
23  Susan:    [Doesn't want her son – going out with-]
    Rob:     ((shaking head, waving, tapping))
24  Rob:     [No(h) no no no    [no(hh)o.
25  Susan:   [anyone in college. [eh heh!
26  Chad:                        [°yeah hmph-heh-heh-heh-heh!
27  Susan:   ((looks over towards Rob))
```

28 Jessica: Col [lege?
29 Susan: [A little scary.

When Susan inserts laughter at the conclusion of line 11, "Because he wouldn't tell his mother about us at fi(hh)rst. eh heh!," both Rob and Chad (lines 12 and 13) join in a small assessment with Susan at this story segment juncture.

When Susan further elaborates why her boyfriend wouldn't tell his mother, "She's not qui(hh)te, th(hh)e be(hh)st person. I don't know." (lines 16–17) she nonvocally comments with a small shoulder shrug. This is mirrored by Rob's head shrug and look-away. When Susan further amplifies her complaints against the mother, stating that she is a "little protective" (lines 19–20) Rob escalates his assessment. He produces a series of "no's" while shaking his head and tapping Susan's hand (line 21). As Rob initiates a new series of "no's" (line 22) this time accompanied by not only shaking his head but also waving his hand, Susan adds a new segment to her talk (line 23) and the two collaboratively assess the event as something they both find deplorable (see also Goodwin, 1980). In the final segment of co-appreciation (line 24), Rob inserts laugh particles [markedy by "(h)"] (Jefferson, 1979), which generate laughter from Susan upon the completion of her turn.

Though his repertoire of words seems to consist largely of binary opposites – *yes* and *no* – through selection from this set and reduplication of words, he can make visible a range of differentiated stances (Goodwin, 1995a). By combining these words with gestures, head shakes, and hand waves he can make evident through multiple semiotic resources specific commentary on the events in progress. His "no's" in line 24 are timed to overlap Susan's talk, ending when it does (see Goodwin, 1986); he is thus able to show that both of them are assessing the event being described in a similar way, as something of which they disapprove.

The precision with which Rob coparticipates in this sequence, coming in and ending at breath group boundaries and tracking through differentiated participation displays the unfolding drama of this narrative, challenges many descriptions of slowness in aphasic speech because of problems with processing.

Conclusion

In this chapter, we have examined how emotion is a *social* phenomenon. It is organized and made visible as a consequential event through systematic practices that are lodged within the processes of situated interaction, used by participants to build in concert with each other the events that make up their lifeworld. Two different kinds of settings were investigated: first, preadolescent girls playing hopscotch and second, interaction in the family of a man with severe aphasia.

However, despite the differences in these settings, a small, general activity system for the organization of assessments was found in both. In each a triggering event made relevant a subsequent assessment.

[Triggering Event] + [Assessment]

The public nature of the assessment makes possible an interactive organization of *co-experience*. Participants treat the assessment slot as a place for heightened mutual orientation and action.

In hopscotch, subsequent assessments provide a place for displaying a range of differentiated stances. These stances, whether outraged indignation, glee, and so on, involve fully embodied practices, integrating syntactic choice, intonation, timing, and the tenor of a girl's body into a powerful display of emotionally charged action. Such strong position-taking challenges the traditional portrayal of girls and their play in the psychological literature. According to Leaper (1991), while boys seek "independence, competition, and dominance" in their interactions with others, girls strive for "closeness, cooperation, and interpersonal harmony" (p. 798; see also Maccoby, 1990). Rather than structuring their game playing on principles of co-operative interaction or a morality based on relatedness, equity, or responsibility, we instead find girls vividly producing their out calls to construct opposition.

Analysis of the actual talk of participants, rather than reports of talk (see, for example, Lever, 1978), permits us to view how displays of emotion emerge within interaction and have strong social consequences; thus, through powerful displays of righteous indignation girls show a strong orientation to the possibilities that games provide for testing, negotiating, and challenging rules and their situated applications. Piaget (1965) argued that the legal sense is little developed among young girls. By way of contrast, here we find young girls pursuing powerful legal debate about the scope of rules and their application. This is quite consistent with earlier findings (Goodwin, 1990) about how the he-said-she-said of African American girls constitutes a vernacular legal process, one that was far more powerful and extended than anything found in the interaction of the boys they played with.

In the aphasia data, the assessment organized different forms of appreciation, approval and disapproval. Across all cases, what is called for is an *embodied performance* of affect through intonation, gesture, body posture and timing. An explicit emotion vocabulary is not necessary for powerful displays of emotion with language in its full pragmatic environment. This is particularly crucial for Rob, who because of his aphasia, has no lexical terms for emotion. Though his possibilities for speech are limited, by varying what tokens he does have at relevant moments within the stream of interaction, Rob is able to demonstrate through his visible coparticipation finely placed ongoing analysis of changes in the events he is engaged in.

Within a Bakhtinian, textually biased theory of language practice that focuses exclusive attention on phenomena within the stream of speech, Rob appears as a severely limited actor, someone who quite literally talks in nonsense syllables. Similarly, if participation is conceptualized simply as a structural position within a speech event, a point within a typology, then the intricate analysis Rob is performing of the organization of ongoing activities, his cognitive life as a participant in a relevant course of action, remains inaccessible to study. However, when utterances are analyzed as participation frameworks which invoke a domain of temporally unfolding embodied action through which multiple practices build in concert with each other the events that constitute their lifeworld, then Rob emerges as a competent actor capable of finely coordinated participation in the activities that make up a state of talk.

Through assessments like these, participants are able to display that their minds are together – that they evaluate the events being assessed in a similar way. Within such a framework, language resides within a community of interacting participants rather than in the syntactic abilities of an isolated speaker. Though unable to speak himself, Rob uses structure visible in the language of others to participate in a state of talk by co-constructing relevant action.

From a slightly different perspective, focus on participation lodges embodiment within socially organized practices. Recently, Tyler (1995) observed critically that despite contemporary interest in the notion of embodiment much of it remains

little more than expressions of faith, and evidence of the continuing hold of Cartesianism on our minds, for the idea of embodiment is little more than an unthinking ego, constructing itself out of its own body in lonely isolation from all other bodies. (p. 569)

By way of contrast, all the data examined here demonstrate how the body becomes a site for visible meaningful action by being embedded with the participation frameworks used to build relevant action within endogenous settings.

Appendix: Transcription Conventions

Data are transcribed according to a modified version of the system developed by Jefferson and described in Sacks, Schegloff, and Jefferson (1974).

Cut offs: A dash (–) marks a sudden cut-off of the current sound.
Bold: Boldface indicates some form of emphasis.
Overlap Bracket: A left bracket ([) marks the point at which the current talk is overlapped by other talk.
Lengthening: Colons (::) indicate that the sound immediately preceding has been noticeably lengthened.
Intonation: Punctuation symbols are used to mark intonation changes rather than as grammatical symbols: A period indicates a falling contour, a question mark indicates a rising contour, and a comma indicates a falling–rising contour.
In-breath: An *h* preceded by an asterisk (*h) marks an in-breath.
Comments: Double parentheses (( )) enclose material that is not part of the talk being transcribed, frequently indicating gesture or body position.
Silence: Numbers in parentheses (0.6) mark silences in seconds and tenths of seconds.
Increased volume: Capitals (CAPS) indicate increased volume.
Breathiness, laughter: An *h* in parentheses (hhh) indicates plosive aspiration, which could result from breathiness or laughter.
Problematic hearing: Material in single parentheses indicates a hearing the transcriber was uncertain about.
Italics: Italics are used in two situations: (1) to distinguish comments in parentheses about nonvocal aspects of the interaction and (2) for English translations.

REFERENCES

Agha, A. (1996). Scheme and superposition in spatial deixis. *Anthropological Linguistics* 38(4), 643–82.

Bradac, J. J., Mulac, A., & Thompson, S. A. (1995). Men's and women's use of intensifiers and hedges in problem-solving interaction: Molar and molecular analyses. *Research on Language in Social Interaction* 28(2), 93–116.

Budwig, N. (2000). Language and the construction of self. In N. Budwig, I. C. Uzgiris, & J. V. Wertsch (eds.), *Communication: An Arena of Development* (pp. 195–214). Stamford, CT: Ablex.

Clayman, S. E., & Maynard, D. W. (1994). Ethnomethodology and conversation analysis. In P. ten Have & G. Psathas (eds.), *Situated Order: Studies in the Social Organization of Talk and Embodied Activities* (pp. 1–30). Washington, DC: University Press of America.

Duranti, A. (1994). *From Grammar to Politics: Linguistic Anthropology in a Western Samoan Village*. Los Angeles: University of California Press.

Duranti, A. (1997). *Linguistic Anthropology*. Cambridge: Cambridge University Press.

Goffman, E. (1967). *Interaction Ritual: Essays in Face to Face Behavior*. Garden City, NY: Doubleday.

Goffman, E. (1981). *Forms of Talk*. Philadelphia: University of Pennsylvania Press.

Goodwin, C. (1986). Between and within: Alternative treatments of continuers and assessments. *Human Studies* 9, 205–17.

Goodwin, C. (1994). Professional vision. *American Anthropologist* 96(3), 606–33.

Goodwin, C. (1995a). Co-constructing meaning in conversations with an aphasic man. *Research on Language and Social Interaction* 28(3), 233–60.

Goodwin, C. (1995b). Seeing in depth. *Social Studies of Science* 25, 237–74.

Goodwin, C. (1996a). Practices of color classification. *Ninchi Kagaku (Cognitive Studies: Bulletin of the Japanese Cognitive Science Society* 3(2), 62–82.

Goodwin, C. (1996b). Transparent vision. In E. Ochs, E. A. Schegloff, & S. Thompson (eds.), *Interaction and Grammar* (pp. 370–404). Cambridge: Cambridge University Press.

Goodwin, C., & Goodwin, M. H. (1987). Concurrent operations on talk: Notes on the interactive organization of assessments. *IPrA Papers in Pragmatics* 1(1), 1–52.

Goodwin, C., & Goodwin, M. H. (1996). Seeing as a situated activity: Formulating planes. In Y. Engeström & D. Middleton (eds.), *Cognition and Communication at Work* (pp. 61–95). Cambridge: Cambridge University Press.

Goodwin, M. H. (1980). Processes of mutual monitoring implicated in the production of description sequences. *Sociological Inquiry* 50, 303–17.

Goodwin, M. H. (1983). Aggravated correction and disagreement in children's conversations. *Journal of Pragmatics* 7, 657–77.

Goodwin, M. H. (1990). *He-Said-She-Said: Talk as Social Organization among Black Children*. Bloomington, IN: Indiana University Press.

Goodwin, M. H. (1998). Games of stance: Conflict and footing in hopscotch. In S. Hoyle & C. T. Adger (eds.), *Kid's Talk: Strategic Language Use in Later Childhood* (pp. 23–46). New York: Oxford University Press.

Harré, R., & Gillett, G. (1994). *The Discursive Mind*. Thousand Oaks, CA: Sage.

Heritage, J. (1984). *Garfinkel and Ethnomethodology*. Cambridge: Polity Press.

Heritage, J. (1995). Conversation analysis: Methodological aspects. In U. M. Quasthoff (ed.), *Aspects of Oral Communication* (pp. 391–418). Berlin: Walter de Gruyter.

Hutchins, E. (1995). *Cognition in the Wild*. Cambridge, MA: MIT Press.

Jefferson, G. (1973). A case of precision timing in ordinary conversation: Overlapped tag-positioned address terms in closing sequences. *Semiotica* 9, 47–96.

Jefferson, G. (1979). A technique for inviting laughter and its subsequent acceptance/declination. In G. Psathas (ed.), *Everyday Language: Studies in Ethnomethodology* (pp. 79–96). New York: Irvington.

Latour, B. (1996). Perusing the discussion of interobjectivity with a few friends. *Mind, Culture and Activity* 3(4), 266–9.

Leaper, C. (1991). Influence and involvement in children's discourse: Age, gender and partner effects. *Child Development* 62, 797–811.

Lever, J. R. (1978). Sex differences in the complexity of children's play and games. *American Sociological Review* 43, 471–83.

Levinson, S. C. (1983). *Pragmatics*. Cambridge: Cambridge University Press.

Maccoby, E. E. (1990). Gender and relationships: A developmental account. *American Psychologist* 45(4), 513–20.

Malinowski, B. (1959). The problem of meaning in primitive languages. In C. K. Ogden & I. A. Richards (eds.), *The Meaning of Meaning* (pp. 296–336). New York: Harcourt, Brace and World. (Original work published 1923.)

Ochs, E. (1988). *Culture and Language Development: Language Acquisition and Language Socialization in a Samoan Village*. Cambridge: Cambridge University Press.

Piaget, J. (1965). *The Moral Judgment of the Child*. New York: Free Press.

Pomerantz, A. (1984). Agreeing and disagreeing with assessments: Some features of preferred/dispreferred turn shapes. In J. M. Atkinson & J. Heritage (eds.), *Structures of Social Action: Studies in Conversation Analysis* (pp. 57–101). Cambridge: Cambridge University Press.

Sacks, H. (1984). Notes on methodology. In J. M. Atkinson & J. Heritage (eds.), *Structures of Social Action* (pp. 21–7). Cambridge: Cambridge University Press.

Sacks, H. (1987). On the preferences for agreement and contiguity in sequences in conversation. In G. Button & J. R. E. Lee (eds.), *Talk and Social Organisation* (pp. 54–69). Clevedon, England: Multilingual Matters. (Original work published 1973.)

Sacks, H., Schegloff, E. A., & Jefferson, G. (1974). A simplest systematics for the organization of turn-taking for conversation. *Language 50*, 696–735.

Schegloff, E. A. (1968). Sequencing in conversational openings. *American Anthropologist 70*, 1075–95.

Schegloff, E. A., Jefferson, G., & Sacks, H. (1977). The preference for self-correction in the organization of repair in conversation. *Language 53*, 361–82.

Schegloff, E. A., & Sacks, H. (1973). Opening up closings. *Semiotica 8*, 289–327.

Selting, M. (1994). Emphatic speech style with special focus on the prosodic signaling of heightened emotive involvement in conversation. *Journal of Pragmatics 22*, 375–408.

Stearns, C. Z., & Stearns, P. W. (1988). *Emotion and Social Change*. New York: Holmes and Meier.

Tyler, S. (1995). The semantics of time and space. *American Anthropologist 97*(3), 567–9.

Užgiris, I. Č. (1996). Together and apart: The enactment of values in infancy. In E. S. Reed, E. Turiel, & T. Brown (eds.), *Values and Knowledge* (pp. 17–39). Mahwah, NJ: Lawrence Erlbaum.

Wierzbicka, A. (1992). Defining emotion concepts. *Cognitive Science 16*, 539–81.

Wierzbicka, A. (1995). Emotion and facial expression: A semantic perspective. *Culture and Psychology 1*, 227–58.

Yaeger-Dror, M. (1986). Intonational prominence on negatives in English. *Language and Speech 28*, 197–230.

Part III

Language Socialization and Literacy Practices

Introduction

If language is such an important part of culture, the process through which children acquire language must be a fundamental part of the process whereby children become competent members of their society. And yet, despite the fact that language acquisition has been of great interest to linguists and psychologists, only recently have researchers started to pay attention to the cultural prerequisites and the cultural implications of language acquisition. The field of language socialization is meant to provide the theoretical and methodological foundations for the study of how children are socialized through language and to language (Ochs and Schieffelin). Language socialization does not stop after the child has learned to talk (primary language socialization). It continues throughout the life span as individuals participate in different activities and institutional settings that require them to use language in new ways (secondary socialization). An important and by now almost universal site for secondary language socialization is participation in literacy activities, that is, activities where individuals are introduced to and must learn to engage with written (e.g. print) material. Three of the chapters of Part III deal with this important experience in children's life. The authors of two of those chapters try to make sense of the differences in school performance among different ethnic groups by looking at the social organization of classroom interaction (Philips) and by comparing the type of relationship established with texts within families from different social classes and ethnic groups (Heath). The last chapter examines the use of the same story in the construction of ethnic identity in two religious classes, one in Spanish and the other in English (Baquedano-López).

Questions about Language Socialization and Literacy Practices

1   What are the three "developmental stories" told by Ochs and Schieffelin and how do they help build a model of different styles of socialization?
2   How is "baby talk" related to other kinds of verbal and non-verbal behavior some adults engage in?
3   What is the process of Warm Springs Children's acquisition of competence as described by Philips? How does it differ from the modes of interaction experienced in the classroom?
4   What differences did Philips observe in the role of speaking among North American Indians and non-Indians?
5   How does the concept of "literacy event" help us understand the differences Heath found in literacy skills across three communities?
6   What kind of bookreading is "mainstream school-oriented" and why?
7   How many kinds of literacy events do you engage in throughout the day?
8   How different are the narratives about Nuestra Señora de Guadalupe in the two classes observed by Baquedano-López? How are those differences involved in the construction of the children's social identity?

Suggestions for Further Reading

A good collection of essays on language socialization in different speech communities is: Schieffelin, B. B., and Ochs, E. (1986). *Language Socialization across Cultures*. Cambridge: Cambridge University Press.

A broad review of the literature on children's acquisition of grammar and communicative competence is: Romaine, S. (1984). *The Language of Children and Adolescents: The Acquisition of Communicative Competence*. New York: Basil Blackwell.

A wide range of perspectives on child language is found in: Fletcher, P., and MacWhinney, B. (eds.) (1995). *The Handbook of Child Language*. Oxford: Blackwell.

Model case studies of language socialization are: Miller, P. (1982). *Amy, Wendy, and Beth: Learning Language in South Baltimore*. Austin: University of Texas Press; Ochs, E. (1988). *Culture and Language Development: Language Acquisition and Language Socialization in a Samoan Village*. Cambridge: Cambridge University Press; Schieffelin, B. B. (1990). *The Give and Take of Everyday Life: Language Socialization of Kaluli Children*. Cambridge: Cambridge University Press; Kulick, D. (1992). *Language Shift and Cultural Reproduction: Socialization, Self, and Syncretism in a Papua New Guinean Village*. Cambridge: Cambridge University Press; Zentella, A. C. (1997). *Growing Up Bilingual: Puerto Rican Children in New York*. Oxford: Blackwell.

The broader cultural context of early childhood is investigated in: LeVine, R. A., Dixon, S., LeVine, S., Richman, A., Leiderman, P. H., Keefer, C. H., and Brazelton, T. B. (1996). *Childcare and Culture: Lessons from Africa*. Cambridge: Cambridge University Press; Stephens, S. (ed.) (1995). *Children and the Politics of Culture*. Princeton, NJ: Princeton University Press; Woodhead, M., Faulkner, D., and

Littleton, K. (eds.) (1998). *Cultural Worlds of Early Childhood*. London: Routledge & The Open University.

The literature on literacy is vast. Earlier influential essays are found in: Goody, J. (ed.) (1968). *Literacy in Traditional Societies*. Cambridge: Cambridge University Press; see also Goody, J. (1977). *The Domestication of the Savage Mind*. Cambridge: Cambridge University Press; and Goody, J. (1986). *The Logic of Writing and the Organization of Society*. Cambridge: Cambridge University Press. For an alternative view to Goody's model: Street, B. V. (1984). *Literacy in Theory and Practice*. Cambridge: Cambridge University Press.

Ethnographically oriented studies of literacy are: Scollon, R., and Scollon, S. B. K. (1981). *Narrative, Literacy, and Face in Interethnic Communication*. Norwood, NJ: Ablex; Besnier, N. (1995). *Literacy, Emotion, and Authority: Reading and Writing on a Polynesian Atoll*. Cambridge: Cambridge University Press; the essays in Cook-Gumperz, J. (ed.) (1986). *The Social Construction of Literacy*. Cambridge: Cambridge University Press; Schieffelin, B. B., and Gilmore, P. (1986). *The Acquisition of Literacy: Ethnographic Perspectives*. Norwood, NJ: Ablex; and Langer, J. A. (ed.) (1987). *Language, Literacy, and Culture: Issues of Society and Schooling*. Norwood, NJ: Ablex.

A study that successfully used both psychological and anthropological methods is: Scribner, S., and Cole, M. (1981). *Psychology of Literacy*. Cambridge, MA: Harvard University Press.

An ethnographic perspective on the use of language in the classroom is analyzed in: Cazden, C., John, V., and Hymes, D. (eds.) (1972). *Functions of Language in the Classroom*. New York: Teachers College Press; Philips, S. (1983). *The Invisible Culture: Communication in Classroom and Community on the Warm Springs Indian Reservation*. New York: Longman.

11

Language Acquisition and Socialization: Three Developmental Stories and Their Implications

Elinor Ochs and Bambi B. Schieffelin

This chapter addresses the relationship between communication and culture from the perspective of the *acquisition of* language and socialization *through language*. Heretofore the processes of language acquisition and socialization have been considered as two separate domains. Processes of language acquisition are usually seen as relatively unaffected by cultural factors such as social organization and local belief systems. These factors have been largely treated as "context," something that is *separable* from language and its acquisition. A similar attitude has prevailed in anthropological studies of socialization. The language used both *by* children and *to* children in social interactions has rarely been a source of information on socialization. As a consequence, we know little about the role that language plays in the acquisition and transmission of sociocultural knowledge. Neither the forms, the functions, nor the message content of language have been documented and examined for the ways in which they *organize* and *are organized by* culture.

Our own backgrounds in cultural anthropology and language development have led us to a more integrated perspective. Having carried out research on language in several societies (Malagasy, Bolivian, white middle-class American, Kaluli [Papua New Guinea], and Western Samoan), focusing on the language of children and their caregivers in three of them (white middle-class American, Kaluli, Western Samoan), we have seen that the primary concern of caregivers is to ensure that their children are able to display and understand behaviors appropriate to social situations. A major means by which this is accomplished is through language. Therefore, we must examine the language of caregivers primarily for its socializing functions, rather than for only its strict grammatical input function. Further, we must examine the prelinguistic and linguistic behaviors of children to determine the ways they are continually and selectively affected by values and beliefs held by those members of society who interact with them. What a child says, and how he or she says it, will be influenced by local cultural processes in addition to biological and social processes that have universal scope. The perspective we adopt is expressed in the following two claims:

1   The process of acquiring language is deeply affected by the process of becoming a competent member of a society.
2   The process of becoming a competent member of society is realized to a large extent through language, by acquiring knowledge of its functions, social distribution, and interpretations in and across socially defined situations, i.e., through exchanges of language in particular social situations.

In this chapter, we will support these claims through a comparison of social development as it relates to the communicative development of children in three societies: Anglo-American white middle class, Kaluli, and Samoan. We will present specific theoretical arguments and methodological procedures for an ethnographic approach to the development of language. Our focus at this point cannot be comprehensive, and therefore we will address developmental research that has its interests and roots in language development rather than anthropological studies of socialization.[1]

Approaches to Communicative Development

Whereas interest in language structure and use has been a timeless concern, the child as a language user is a relatively recent focus of scholarly interest. This interest has been located primarily in the fields of linguistics and psychology, with the wedding of the two in the establishment of developmental psycholinguistics as a legitimate academic specialization. The concern here has been the relation of language to thought, both in terms of conceptual categories and in terms of cognitive processes (such as perception, memory, recall). The child has become one source for establishing just what that relation is. More specifically, the language of the child has been examined in terms of the following issues:

1   The relation between the relative complexity of conceptual categories and the linguistic structures produced and understood by young language-learning children at different developmental stages.[2]
2   Processes and strategies underlying the child's construction of grammar.[3]
3   The extent to which these processes and strategies are language universal or particular.[4]
4   The extent to which these processes and strategies support the existence of a language faculty.[5]
5   The nature of the prerequisites for language development.[6]
6   Perceptual and conceptual factors that inhibit or facilitate language development.[7]

Underlying all these issues is the question of the *source* of language, in terms of not only what capacities reside within the child but the relative contributions of biology (nature) and the *social* world (nurture) to the development of language. The relation between nature and nurture has been a central theme around which theoretical positions have been oriented. B. F. Skinner's (1957) contention that the child brings relatively little to the task of learning language and that it is through responses to specific adult stimuli that language competence is attained provided a formulation that was subsequently challenged and countered by Chomsky's (1959) alternative position. This position, which has been termed nativist, innatist, rationalist (see Piattelli-Palmarini 1980), postulates that the adult verbal environment is an inadequate source for the child to inductively learn language. Rather, the rules and principles for constructing grammar have as their major source a genetically determined language faculty:

Linguistics, then, may be regarded as that part of human psychology that is concerned with the nature, function, and origin of a particular "mental organ." We may take UG (Universal Grammar) to be a theory of the language faculty, a common human attribute, genetically determined, one component of the human mind. Through interaction with the environment, this faculty of mind becomes articulated and refined, emerging in the mature person as a system of knowledge of language. (Chomsky 1977:164)

It needs to be emphasized that an innatist approach does not eliminate the adult world as a source of linguistic knowledge; rather, it assigns a different role (vis-à-vis the behaviorist approach) to that world in the child's attainment of linguistic competence: The adult language presents the relevant information that allows the child to select from the Universal Grammar those grammatical principles specific to the particular language that the child will acquire.

One of the principal objections that could be raised is that although "the linguist's grammar is a theory of this [the child's] attained competence" (Chomsky 1977:163), there is no account of *how* this linguistic competence is attained. The theory does not relate the linguist's grammar(s) to processes of acquiring grammatical knowledge. Several psycholinguists, who have examined children's developing grammars in terms of their underlying organizing principles, have argued for similarities between these principles and those exhibited by other cognitive achievements (Bates et al. 1979; Bever 1970).

A second objection to the innatist approach has concerned its characterization of adult speech as "degenerate," fragmented, and often ill formed (McNeill 1966; Miller & Chomsky 1963). This characterization, for which there was no empirical basis, provoked a series of observational studies (including tape-recorded documentation) of the ways in which caregivers speak to their young language-acquiring children (Drach 1969; Phillips 1973; Sachs, Brown, & Salerno 1976; Snow 1972). Briefly, these studies indicated not only that adults use well-formed speech with high frequency but that they modify their speech to children in systematic ways as well. These systematic modifications, categorized as a particular speech register called baby-talk register (Ferguson 1977), include the increased (relative to other registers) use of high pitch, exaggerated and slowed intonation, a baby-talk lexicon (Garnica 1977; Sachs 1977; Snow 1972, 1977b), diminutives, reduplicated words, simple sentences (Newport 1976), shorter sentences, interrogatives (Corsaro 1979), vocatives, talk about the "here-and-now," play and politeness routines – peek-a-boo, hi–good-bye, say "thank you" (Andersen 1977; Gleason & Weintraub 1978), cooperative expression of propositions, repetition, and expansion of one's own and the child's utterances. Many of these features are associated with the expression of positive affect, such as high pitch and diminutives. However, the greatest emphasis in the literature has been placed on these features as evidence that caregivers *simplify* their speech in addressing young children (e.g., slowing down, exaggerating intonation, simplifying sentence structure and length of utterance). The scope of the effects on grammatical development has been debated in a number of studies. Several studies have supported Chomsky's position by demonstrating that caregiver speech facilitates the acquisition of only language-specific features but not those features widely (universally) shared across languages (Feldman, Goldin-Meadow, & Gleitman 1978; Newport, Gleitman, & Gleitman 1977). Other studies, which do not restrict the role of caregiver speech to facilitating only language-specific grammatical features (Snow 1977b, 1979), report that caregivers appear to adjust their speech to a child's cognitive and linguistic capacity (Cross 1977). And as children become more competent, caregivers use fewer features of the baby-talk register. Whereas certain researchers have emphasized the direct facilitating role of caregiver speech in the acquisition of language (van der Geest 1977), others have linked the speech behavior of caregivers to the caregiver's desire to communicate with the child (Brown 1977; Snow 1977a, 1977b, 1979). In this perspective, caregivers simplify their own speech in order to make themselves understood when speaking to young children. Similarly, caregivers employ several verbal and nonverbal strategies to understand what the child is trying to communicate. For example, the caregiver attends to what the child is doing, where the child is looking, and the child's behavior to determine the child's communicative intentions (Foster 1981; Golinkoff 1983; Keenan, Ochs, & Schieffelin 1976). Further, caregivers often request clarification by repeating or paraphrasing the child's utterance with a questioning intonation, as in Example 1 (Bloom 1973:170):

Example 1[*]
Mother   *Allison* (16 mos 3 wks)
(*A* picks up a jar, trying to open it)   more wídə/ə wídə/
                                                      ə wídə/ ə wídə/
(*A* holding jar out to *M*)   up/ Mama/ Mama/
                                                      Mama ma ə wídə/
                                                      Mama Mama ə wídə/
What, darling?
                                                      Mama wídə/ Mama/
                                                      Mama wídə/ Mama/
                                                      Mama wídə/
What do you want Mommy to do?
                                                      — /ə wídə/ ə wídə/
(*A* gives jar to *M*)   — /here/
(*A* tries to turn top on jar in *M*'s hand)
                                                      Mama/ Mama/ ə wídə/
Open it up?
                                                      up/
Open it? OK.
(*M* opens it)

[*] Examples 1–5 follow transcription conventions in Bloom and Lahey 1978.

In other cases, the caregiver facilitates communication by jointly expressing with the child a proposition. Typically, a caregiver asks a question to which the child supplies the missing information (often already known to the caregiver), as in Example 2 (Bloom 1973:153):

Example 2
Mother   *Allison*
What's Mommy have (*M* holding cookies)
(*A* reaching for cookie)   cookie/
Cookie! OK. Here's a cookie for you
(*A* takes cookie; reaching with other hand
toward others in bag)   more/
There's more in here. We'll have it in a little while.
(*A* picking up bag of cookies)   bag/

These studies indicate that caregivers make extensive accommodations to the child, assuming the perspective of the child in the course of engaging him or her in conversational dialogue. Concurrent research on interaction between caregivers and prelinguistic infants supports this conclusion (Bruner 1977; Bullowa 1979; Lock 1978; Newson 1977, 1978; Schaffer 1977; Shotter 1978). Detailed observation of white middle-class mother–infant dyads (English, Scottish, American, Australian, Dutch) indicates that these mothers attempt to engage their very young infants (starting at birth) in "conversational exchanges." These so-called protoconversations (Bullowa 1979) are constructed in several ways. A protoconversation may take place when one party responds to some facial expression, action, and/or vocalization of the other. This response may be nonverbal, as when a gesture of the infant is "echoed" by his or her mother.

As a rule, prespeech with gesture is watched and replied to by exclamations of pleasure or surprise like "Oh, my my!", "Good heavens!", "Oh, what a big smile!", "Ha! That's a big one!" (meaning a story), questioning replies like, "Are you telling me a story?", "Oh really?", or even agreement by nodding "Yes" or saying "I'm sure you're right" . . . . A mother evidently perceives her baby to be a person like herself. Mothers interpret baby behavior as not only intended to be communicative, but as verbal and meaningful. (Trevarthen 1979a:339)

On the other hand, mother and infant may respond to one another through verbal means, as, for example, when a mother expresses agreement, disagreement, or surprise following an infant behavior. Social interactions may be sustained over several exchanges by the mother assuming both speaker roles. She may construct an exchange by responding on behalf of the infant to her own utterance, or she may verbally interpret the infant's interpretation. A combination of several strategies is illustrated in Example 3 (Snow 1977a:12).

Example 3
Mother   *Ann* (3 mos)
                                                 (smiles)
Oh what a nice little smile!
Yes, isn't that nice?
There.
There's a nice little smile.   (burps)
What a nice wind as well!
Yes, that's better, isn't it?
Yes.
Yes.   (vocalizes)
Yes!
There's a nice noise.

These descriptions capture the behavior of white middle-class caregivers and, in turn, can be read for what caregivers believe to be the capabilities and predispositions of the infant. Caregivers evidently see their infants as sociable and as capable of intentionality, particularly with respect to the intentional expression of emotional and physical states. Some researchers have concluded that the mother, in interpreting an infant's behaviors, provides meanings for those behaviors that the infant will ultimately adopt (Lock 1981; Ryan 1974; Shotter 1978) and thus emphasize the active role of the mother in socializing the infant to her set of interpretations. Other approaches emphasize the effect of the infant on the caregiver (Lewis & Rosenblum 1974), particularly with respect to the innate mechanisms for organized, purposeful action that the infant brings to interaction (Trevarthen 1979b).

These studies of caregivers' speech to young children have all attended to what the child is learning from these interactions with the mother (or caregiver). There has been a general movement away from the search for *direct* causal links between the ways in which caregivers speak to their children and the emergence of grammar. Instead, caregivers' speech has been examined for its more general communicative functions, that is, how meanings are negotiated, how activities are organized and accomplished, and how routines and games become established. Placed within this broader communicative perspective, language development is viewed as one of several achievements accomplished through verbal exchanges between the caregiver and the child.

The Ethnographic Approach

Ethnographic orientation

To most middle-class Western readers, the descriptions of verbal and nonverbal behaviors of middle-class caregivers with their children seem very familiar, desirable, and even natural. These descriptions capture in rich detail what goes on, to a greater or lesser extent, in many middle-class households. The characteristics of caregiver speech (baby-talk register) and comportment that have been specified are highly valued by members of white middle-class society, including researchers, readers, and subjects of study. They are associated with good mothering and can be spontaneously produced with little effort or reflections. As demonstrated by Shatz and Gelman (1973), Sachs and Devin (1976), and Andersen and Johnson (1973), children as young as 4 years of age often speak and act in these ways when addressing small children.

From our research experience in other societies as well as our acquaintance with some of the cross-cultural studies of language socialization[8] the general patterns of white middle-class caregiving that have been described in the psychological literature are characteristic neither of all societies nor of all social groups (e.g., all social classes within one society). We would like the reader, therefore, to reconsider the descriptions of caregiving in the psychological literature as ethnographic descriptions.

By ethnographic, we mean descriptions that take into account the perspective of members of a social group, including beliefs and values that underlie and organize their activities and utterances. Ethnographers rely heavily on observations and on formal and informal elicitation of members' reflections and interpretations as a basis for analysis (Geertz 1973). Typically, the ethnographer is not a member of the group under study. Further, in presenting an ethnographic account, the researcher faces the problem of communicating world views or sets of values that may be unfamiliar and strange to the reader. Ideally, such statements provide for the reader a set of organizing principles that give coherence and an analytic focus to the behaviors described.

Psychologists who have carried out research on the verbal and nonverbal behavior of caregivers and their children draw on both methods. However, unlike most ethnographers, the psychological researcher *is* a member of the social group under observation. (In some cases, the researcher's own children are the subjects of study.) Further, unlike the ethnographer, the psychologist addresses a readership familiar with the social scenes portrayed.

That the researcher, reader, and subjects of study tend to have in common a white middle-class literate background has had several consequences. For example, by and large, the psychologist has not been faced with the problem of cultural translation, as has the anthropologist. There has been a tacit assumption that readers can provide the larger cultural framework for making sense out of the behaviors documented, and, consequently, the cultural nature of the behaviors and principles presented have not been explicit. From our perspective, language and culture as bodies of knowledge, structures of understanding, conceptions of the world, and collective representations are extrinsic to any individual and contain more information than any individual could know or learn. Culture encompasses variations in knowledge between individuals, but such variation, although crucial to what an individual may know and to the social dynamic between individuals, does not have its locus within the individual. Our position is that culture is not something that can be considered separately from the accounts of caregiver–child interaction; rather, it is what organizes and gives meaning to that interaction. This is an important point, as it affects the definition and interpretation of the behaviors of caregivers and children. How caregivers and children speak and act toward one another is linked to cultural patterns that extend and have consequences beyond the specific interactions observed. For example, how caregivers speak to their children may be linked to other institutional adaptations to young children. These adaptations, in turn, may be linked to how members of a given society view children more generally (their "nature," their social status and expected comportment) and to how members think children develop.

We are suggesting here that the sharing of assumptions between researcher, reader, and subjects of study is a mixed blessing. In fact, this sharing represents a paradox of familiarity. We are able to apply without effort the cultural framework for interpreting the behavior of caregivers and young children in our own social group; indeed, as members of a white middle-class society, we are socialized to do this very work, that is, interpret behaviors, attribute motives, and so on. Paradoxically, however, in spite of this ease of effort, we can not easily isolate and make explicit these cultural principles. As Goffman's work on American society has illustrated, the articulation of norms, beliefs, and values is often possible only when faced with violations, that is, with gaffes, breaches, misfirings, and the like (Goffman 1963, 1967; Much & Shweder 1978).

Another way to see the cultural principles at work in our own society is to examine the ways in which *other* societies are organized in terms of social interaction and of the society at large. In carrying out such research, the ethnographer offers a point of contrast and comparison with our own everyday activities. Such comparative material can lead us to reinterpret behaviors as cultural that we have assumed to be natural. From the anthropological perspective, every society will have its own cultural constructs of what is natural and what is not. For example, every society has its own theory of procreation. Certain Australian Aboriginal societies believe that a number of different factors contribute to conception. Von Sturmer (1980) writes that among the Kugu-Nganychara (West Cape York Peninsula, Australia) the spirit of the child may first enter the man through an animal that he has killed and consumed. The spirit passes from the man to the woman through sexual intercourse, but several sexual acts are necessary to build the child (see also Hamilton 1981; Montagu 1937). Even within a single society there may be different beliefs concerning when life begins and ends, as the recent debates in the United States and Europe concerning abortion and mercy killing indicate. The issue of what is nature and what is nurtured (cultural) extends to patterns of caregiving and child development. Every society has (implicitly or explicitly) given notions concerning the capacities and temperament of children at different points in their development (see, e.g., Dentan 1978; Ninio 1979; Snow, de Blauw, & van Roosmalen 1979), and the expectations and responses of caregivers are directly related to these notions.

Three developmental stories

At this point, using an ethnographic perspective, we will recast selected behaviors of white middle-class caregivers and young children as pieces of one "developmental story." The white middle-class developmental story that we are constructing is based on various descriptions available and focuses on those patterns of interaction (both verbal and nonverbal) that have been emphasized in the literature. This story will be compared with two other developmental stories from societies that are strikingly different: Kaluli (Papua New Guinea) and Western Samoan.

A major goal in presenting and comparing these developmental stories is to demonstrate that communicative interactions between caregivers and young children are culturally constructed. In our comparisons, we will focus on three facets of communicative interaction: (1) the social organization of the verbal environment of very young children, (2) the extent to which children are expected to adapt to situations or that situations are adapted to the child, (3) the negotiation of meaning by caregiver and child. We first present a general sketch of each social group and then discuss in more detail the consequences of the differences and similarities in communicative patterns in these social groups.

These developmental stories are not timeless but rather are linked in complex ways to particular historical contexts. Both the ways in which caregivers behave toward young children and the popular and scientific accounts of these ways may differ at different moments in time. The stories that we present represent ideas currently held in the three social groups.

The three stories show that there is more than one way of becoming social and using language in early childhood. All normal children will become members of their own social group, but the process of becoming social, including becoming a language user, is culturally constructed. In relation to this process of construction, every society has its own developmental stories that are rooted in social organization, beliefs, and values. These stories may be explicitly codified and/or tacitly assumed by members.

An Anglo-American white middle-class developmental story. The middle class in Britain and the United States includes a broad range of lower middle-, middle middle-, and upper middle-class white-collar and professional workers and their families.[9] The literature on communicative development has been largely based on middle middle- and upper middle-class households. These households tend to consist of a single nuclear family with one, two, or three children. The primary caregiver almost without exception is the child's natural or adopted mother. Researchers have focused on communicative situations in which one child interacts with his or her mother. The generalizations proposed by these researchers concerning mother–child communication could be an artifact of this methodological focus. However, it could be argued that the attention to two-party encounters between a mother and her child reflects the most frequent type of communicative interaction to which most young middle-class children are exposed. Participation in two-party as opposed to multiparty interactions is a product of many considerations, including the physical setting of households, where interior and exterior walls bound and limit access to social interaction.

Soon after an infant is born, many mothers hold their infants in such a way that they are face-to-face and gaze at them. Mothers have been observed to address their infants, vocalize to them, ask questions, and greet them. In other words, from birth on, the infant is treated as a *social being* and as an *addressee* in social interaction. The infant's vocalizations and physical movements and states are often interpreted as meaningful and are responded to verbally by the mother or other caregiver. In this way, protoconversations are established and sustained along a dyadic, turn-taking model. Throughout this period and the subsequent language-acquiring years, caregivers treat very young children as communicative partners. One very important procedure in facilitating these social exchanges is the mother's (or other caregiver's) taking the perspective of the child. This perspective is evidenced in her own speech through the many simplifying and affective features of the baby-talk register that have been described and through the various strategies employed to identify what the young child may be expressing.

Such perspective taking is part of a much wider set of accommodations by adults to young children. These accommodations are manifested in several domains. For example, there are widespread material accommodations to infancy and childhood in the form of cultural artifacts designed for this stage of life, for example, baby clothes, baby food, miniaturization of furniture, and toys. Special behavioral accommodations are coordinated with the infant's perceived needs and capacities, for example, putting the baby in a quiet place to facilitate and ensure proper sleep; "baby-proofing" a house as a child becomes increasingly mobile, yet not aware of, or able to control, the consequences of his or her own behavior. In general, the pattern appears to be one of prevention and intervention, in which situations are adapted or modified to the child rather than the reverse. Further, the child is a focus of attention, in that the child's actions and verbalizations are often the starting point of social interaction with more mature persons.

Although such developmental achievements as crawling, walking, and first words are awaited by caregivers, the accommodations have the effect of keeping the child dependent on, and separate from, the adult community for a considerable period of time. The child, protected from those experiences considered harmful (e.g., playing with knives, climbing stairs), is thus denied knowledge, and his or her competence in such contexts is delayed.

The accommodations of white middle-class caregivers to young children can be examined for other values and tendencies. Particularly among the American middle class, these accommodations reflect a discomfort with the competence differential between adult and child. The competence gap is reduced by two strategies. One is for the adult to simplify her/his speech to match more closely what the adult considers to be the verbal competence of the young child. Let us call this strategy the self-lowering strategy, following Irvine's (1974) analysis of inter-caste demeanor. A second strategy is for the caregiver to richly interpret (Brown 1973) what the young child is expressing. Here the adult acts *as if* the child were more competent than his behavior more strictly would indicate. Let us call this strategy the child-raising (no pun intended!) strategy. Other behaviors conform to this strategy, such as when an adult cooperates in a task with a child but treats that task as an accomplishment of the child.

For example, in eliciting a story from a child, a caregiver often cooperates with the child in the telling of the story. This cooperation typically takes the form of posing questions to the child, such as "Where did you go?" "What did you see?" and so on, to which the adult knows the answer. The child is seen as telling the story even though she or he is simply supplying the information the adult has preselected and organized (Greenfield & Smith 1976; Ochs, Schieffelin & Platt 1979; Schieffelin & Eisenberg 1984). Bruner's (1978) description of scaffolding, in which a caregiver constructs a tower or other play object, allowing the young child to place the last block, is also a good example of this tendency. Here the tower may be seen by the caregiver and others as the child's own work. Similarly, in later life, caregivers playing games with their children let them win, acting as if the child can match or more than match the competence of the adult.

The masking of incompetence applies not only in white middle-class relations with young children but also in relations with mentally, and to some extent to physically, handicapped persons as well. As the work of Edgerton (1967) and the film *Best Boy* indicate, mentally retarded persons are often restricted to protected environments (family households, sheltered workshops or special homes) in which trained staff or family members make vast accommodations to their special needs and capacities.

A final aspect of this white middle-class developmental story concerns the willingness of many caregivers to interpret unintelligible or partially intelligible utterances of young children (cf. Ochs 1982c), for example, the caregiver offers a paraphrase (or "expansion"; Brown & Bellugi 1964; Cazden 1965), using a question intonation. This behavior of caregivers has continuity with their earlier attributions of intentionality to the ambiguous utterances of the infant. For both the prelinguistic and language-using child, the caregiver provides an explicitly verbal interpretation.

This interpretation or paraphrase is potentially available to the young child to affirm, disconfirm, or modify.

Through exposure to, and participation in, these clarification exchanges, the young child is socialized into several cultural patterns. The first of these recognizes and defines an utterance or vocalization that may not be immediately understood. Second, the child is presented with the procedures for dealing with ambiguity. Through the successive offerings of possible interpretations, the child learns that more than one understanding of a given utterance or vocalization may be possible. The child is also learning who can make these interpretations and the extent to which they may be open to modification. Finally, the child is learning how to settle upon a possible interpretation and how to show disagreement or agreement. This entire process socializes the child into culturally specific modes of organizing knowledge, thought, and language.[10]

A Kaluli developmental story. A small (population approximately 1,200), non-literate egalitarian society (E. Schieffelin 1976), the Kaluli people live in the tropical rain forest on the Great Papuan Plateau in the southern highlands of Papua New Guinea.[11] Most Kaluli are monolingual, speaking a non-Austronesian verb final ergative language. They maintain large gardens and hunt and fish. Traditionally, the sixty to ninety individuals that comprise a village lived in one large longhouse without internal walls. Currently, although the longhouse is maintained, many families live in smaller dwellings that provide accommodations for two or more extended families. It is not unusual for at least a dozen individuals of different ages to be living together in one house consisting essentially of one semipartitioned room.

Men and women use extensive networks of obligation and reciprocity in the organization of work and sociable interaction. Everyday life is overtly focused around verbal interaction. Kaluli think of, and use, talk as a means of control, manipulation, expression, assertion, and appeal. Talk gets you what you want, need, or feel you are owed. Talk is a primary indicator of social competence and a primary means of socializing. Learning how to talk and become independent is a major goal of socialization.

For the purpose of comparison and for understanding something of the cultural basis for the ways in which Kaluli act and speak to their children, it is important first to describe selected aspects of a Kaluli developmental story constructed from various ethnographic data. Kaluli describe their babies as helpless, "soft" (*taiyo*), and "having no understanding" (*asugo andoma*). They take care of them, they say, because they "feel sorry for them." Mothers, the primary caregivers, are attentive to their infants and physically responsive to them. Whenever an infant cries, it is offered the breast. However, while nursing her infant, a mother may also be involved in other activities, such as food preparation, or she may be engaged in conversation with individuals in the household. Mothers never leave their infants alone and only rarely with other caregivers. When not holding their infants, mothers carry them in netted bags suspended from their heads. When the mother is gardening, gathering wood, or just sitting with others, the baby sleeps in the netted bag next to the mother's body.

Kaluli mothers, given their belief that infants "have no understanding," never treat their infants as partners (speaker/addressee) in dyadic communicative interactions.

Although they greet their infants by name and use expressive vocalizations, they rarely address other utterances to them. Furthermore, a mother and infant do not gaze into each other's eyes, an interactional pattern that is consistent with adult patterns of not gazing when vocalizing in interaction with one another. Rather than facing their babies and speaking to them, Kaluli mothers tend to face their babies outward so that they can see, and be seen by, other members of the social group. Older children greet and address the infant, and the mother responds in a high-pitched nasalized voice "for" the baby while moving the baby up and down. Triadic exchanges such as that in Example 4 are typical (Golinkoff 1983).

Example 4

Mother is holding her infant son Bage (3 mo). Abi (35 mo) is holding a stick on his shoulder in a manner similar to that in which one would carry a heavy patrol box (the box would be hung on a pole placed across the shoulders of the two men).

Mother	Abi
	(to baby)
	Bage/ do you see my box here?/
	Bage/ ni bokisi we badaya?/
	Do you see it?/
	olibadaya?/
(high nasal voice talking as if she is the baby, moving the baby who is facing Abi):	
My brother, I'll take half, my brother.	
nao, hɛbɔ ni diɛni, nao.	
	(holding stick out)
	mother give him half/
	nɔ hɛbɔ emɔ dimina/ *mother,*
	my brother here/here take half/
	nao we/we hɛbɔ dima/
(in a high nasal voice as baby):	
My brother, what half do I take?	
nao, hɛbɔ diɛni hɛh?	
What about it? my brother, put it on the shoulder!	
Wangaya? nao, kɛlɛnɔ wɛla diɛfoma!	
(to Abi in her usual vo*ice):*	
Put it on the shoulder.	
kɛlɛnɔ wɛla diɛfɔndo.	
	(rests stick on baby's shoulder)
There, carefully put it on.	
ko dinafa diɛfoma. (stick accidentally pokes baby)	
Feel sorry, stop.	
Heyɔ, kadɛfoma.	

When a mother takes the speaking role of an infant she uses language that is well formed and appropriate for an older child. Only the nasalization and high-pitch mark it as "the infant's." When speaking as the infant to older children, mothers speak assertively, that is, they never whine or beg on behalf of the infant. Thus, in taking this role the mother does for the infant what the infant cannot do for itself, that is, appear to act in a controlled and competent manner, using language. These kinds of interactions continue until a baby is between 4 and 6 months of age.

Several points are important here. First, these triadic exchanges are carried out primarily for the benefit of the older child and help create a relationship between the two children. Second, the mother's utterances in these exchanges are not based on, nor do they originate with, anything that the infant has initiated – either vocally or gesturally. Recall the Kaluli claim that infants have no understanding. How could someone with "no understanding" initiate appropriate interactional sequences?

However, there is an even more important and enduring cultural construct that helps make sense out of the mother's behaviors in this situation and in many others as well. Kaluli say that "one cannot know what another thinks or feels." Although Kaluli obviously interpret and assess one another's available behaviors and internal states, these interpretations are not culturally acceptable as topics of talk. Individuals often talk about their own feelings (I'm afraid, I'm happy, etc.). However, there is a cultural dispreference for talking about or making claims about what another might think, what another might feel, or what another is about to do, especially if there is no external evidence. As we shall see, these culturally constructed behaviors have several important consequences for the ways in which Kaluli caregivers verbally interact with their children and are related to other pervasive patterns of language use, which will be discussed later.

As infants become older (6–12 months), they are usually held in the arms or carried on the shoulders of the mother or an older sibling. They are present in all ongoing household activities, as well as subsistence activities that take place outside the village in the bush. During this time period, babies are addressed by adults to a limited extent. They are greeted by a variety of names (proper names, kin terms, affective and relationship terms) and receive a limited set of both negative and positive imperatives. In addition, when they do something they are told not to do, such as reach for something that is not theirs to take, they will often receive such rhetorical questions such as "who are you?!" (meaning "not someone to do that") or "is it yours?!" (meaning "it is not yours") to control their actions by shaming them (*sasidiab*). It should be stressed that the language addressed to the preverbal child consists largely of "one-liners" that call for no verbal response but for either an action or termination of an action. Other than these utterances, very little talk is directed to the young child by the adult caregiver.

This pattern of adults treating infants as noncommunicative partners continues even when babies begin babbling. Although Kaluli recognize babbling (*dabedan*), they call it noncommunicative and do not relate it to the speech that eventually emerges. Adults and older children occasionally repeat vocalizations back to the young child (age 12–16 months), reshaping them into the names of persons in the household or into kin terms, but they do not say that the baby is saying the name nor do they wait for, or expect, the child to repeat those vocalizations in an altered form. In addition, vocalizations are not generally treated as communicative and given verbal expression except in the following situation. When a toddler shrieks in protest of the assaults of an older child, mothers say "I'm unwilling" (using a quotative particle), referring to the toddler's shriek. These are the only circumstances in which mothers treat vocalizations as communicative and provide verbal expression for them. In no other circumstances did the adults in the four families in the study provide a verbally expressed interpretation of a vocalization of a preverbal child. Thus, throughout the preverbal period very little language is directed to the child, except for imperatives, rhetorical questions, and greetings. A child who by Kaluli terms has not yet begun to speak is not expected to respond either verbally or vocally. As a result, during the first 18 months or so very little sustained dyadic verbal exchange takes place between adult and infant. The infant is only minimally treated as an addressee and is not treated as a communicative partner in dyadic exchanges. Thus, the conversational model that has been described for many white middle-class caregivers and their preverbal children has no application in this case. Furthermore, if one defines language input as language directed to the child then it is reasonable to say that for Kaluli children who have not yet begun to speak there is very little. However, this does not mean that Kaluli children grow up in an impoverished verbal environment and do not learn how to speak. Quite the opposite is true. The verbal environment of the infant is rich and varied, and from the very beginning the infant is surrounded by adults and older children who spend a great deal of time talking to one another. Furthermore, as the infant develops and begins to crawl and engage in play activities and other independent actions, these actions are frequently referred to, described, and commented upon by members of the household, especially older children, to each other. Thus the ongoing activities of the preverbal child are an important topic of talk among members of the household, and this talk about the here-and-now of the infant is available to the infant, though it is not talk addressed to the infant. For example, in referring to the infant's actions, siblings and adults use the infant's name or kin term. They say, "Look at Seligiwo! He's walking." Thus the child may learn from these contexts to attend the verbal environment in which he or she lives.

Every society has its own ideology about language, including when it begins and how children acquire it. The Kaluli are no exception. Kaluli claim that language begins at the time when the child uses two critical words, "mother" (nɔ) and "breast" (bo). The child may be using other single words, but until these two words are used, the beginning of language is not recognized. Once a child has used these words, a whole set of interrelated behaviors is set into motion. Once a child has begun to use language, he or she then must be "shown how to speak" (Schieffelin 1979). Kaluli show their children language in the form of a teaching strategy, which involves providing a model for what the child is to say followed by the word ɛlɛma, an imperative meaning "say like that." Mothers use this method of direct instruction to teach the social uses of assertive language (tcasing, shaming, requesting, challenging, reporting). However, object labeling is never part of an ɛlɛma sequence, nor does the mother ever use ɛlɛma to instruct the child to beg or appeal for food or objects. Begging, the Kaluli say, is natural for children. They know how to do it. In contrast, a child must be taught to be assertive through the use of particular linguistic expressions and verbal sequences.

A typical sequence using ɛlɛma is triadic, involving the mother, child (20–36 months), and other participants, as in Example 5 (Schieffelin 1979).

Example 5

Mother(M), daughter Binalia(B) (5 yrs), cousin Mama ($3\frac{1}{2}$ yrs), and son Wanu(W) (27 mos) are at home, dividing up some cooked vegetables. Binalia has been begging for some, but her mother thinks that she has had her share.
M → W —> B:[*]

Whose is it?! say like that.
Abɛnowo?! ɛlɛma.

whose is it?!/
abɛnowo?!/

Is it yours?! say like that.
Gɛnowo?! ɛlɛma.

Is it yours?!/
gɛnowo?!/

Who are you?! say like that.
ge oba?! ɛlɛma.

who are you?!/
ge oba?!/

Mama → W →> B:
Did you pick?! say like that.
gi suwo?! ɛlɛma.

did you pick?!/
gi suwo?!/

M → W →> B:
My grandmother picked! say like that.
ni nuwɛ suke! ɛlɛma.

My grandmother picked!/
ni nuwɛ suke!/

Mama → W →> B:
This my g'mother picked! say like that
we ni nuwɛ suke! ɛlɛma.

This my g'mother picked!/
we ni nuwɛ suke!/

*→ = speaker to addressee
→> = addressee to intended addressee

In this situation, as in many others, the mother does not modify her language to fit the linguistic ability of the young child. Instead, her language is shaped so as to be appropriate (in terms of form and content) for the child's intended addressee. Consistent with the way she interacts with her infant, what a mother instructs her young child to say usually does not have its origins in any verbal or nonverbal behaviors of the child but in what the mother thinks should be said. The mother pushes the child into ongoing interactions that the child may or may not be interested in and will at times spend a good deal of energy in trying to get the child verbally involved. This is part of the Kaluli pattern of fitting (or pushing) the child into the situation rather than changing the situation to meet the interests or abilities of the child. Thus mothers take a directive role with their young children, teaching them what to say so that they may become participants in the social group.

In addition to instructing their children by telling them what to say in often extensive interactional sequences, Kaluli mothers pay attention to the form of their children's utterances. Kaluli correct the phonological, morphological, or lexical form of an utterance or its pragmatic or semantic meaning. Because the goals of language acquisition include the development of a competent and independent child who uses mature language, Kaluli use no baby-talk lexicon, for they said (when I asked about it) that to do so would result in a child sounding babyish, which was clearly undesirable and counterproductive. The entire process of a child's development, in which language acquisition plays a very important role, is thought of as a hardening process and culminates in the child's use of "hard words" (Feld & Schieffelin 1982).

The cultural dispreference for saying what another might be thinking or feeling has important consequences for the organization of dyadic exchanges between caregiver and child. For one, it affects the ways in which meaning is negotiated during an exchange. For the Kaluli, the responsibility for clear expression is with the speaker, and child speakers are not exempt from this. Rather than offering possible interpretations or guessing at the meaning of what a child is saying, caregivers make extensive use of clarification requests such as "huh?" and "what?" in an attempt to elicit clearer expression from the child. Children are held to what they say and mothers will remind them that they in fact have asked for food or an object if they don't act appropriately on receiving it. Because the responsibility of expression lies with the speaker, children are also instructed with ɛlɛma to request clarification (using similar forms) from others when they do not understand what someone is saying to them.

Another important consequence of not saying what another thinks is the absence of adult expansions of child utterances. Kaluli caregivers put words into the mouths of their children, but these words originate from the caregiver. However, caregivers do not elaborate or expand utterances initiated by the child. Nor do they jointly build propositions across utterances and speakers except in the context of sequences with ɛlɛma in which they are constructing the talk for the child.

All these patterns of early language use, such as the lack of expansions and the verbal attribution of an internal state to an individual are consistent with important cultural conventions of adult language usage. The Kaluli avoid gossip and often indicate the source of information they report. They make extensive use of direct quoted speech in a language that does not allow indirect quotation. They use a range of evidential markers in their speech to indicate the source of speakers' information, for example, whether something was said, seen, heard or gathered from other kinds of evidence. These patterns are also found in a child's early speech and, as such, affect the organization and acquisition of conversational exchanges in this face-to-face egalitarian society.

A Samoan developmental story. In American and Western Samoa, an archipelago in the southwest Pacific, Samoan, a verb-initial Polynesian language, is spoken.[12] The following developmental story draws primarily on direct observations of life in a large, traditional village on the island of Upolu in Western Samoa; however, it incorporates as well analyses by Mead (1927), Kernan (1969), and Shore (1982) of social life, language use, and childhood on other islands (the Manu'a islands and Savai'i).

As has been described by numerous scholars, Samoan society is highly stratified. Individuals are ranked in terms of whether or not they have a title, and if so, whether it is an orator or a chiefly title – bestowed on persons by an extended family unit (*'āthiga potopoto*) – and within each status, particular titles are reckoned with respect to one another.

Social stratification characterizes relationships between untitled persons as well, with the assessment of relative rank in terms of generation and age. Most relevant to the Samoan developmental story to be told here is that caregiving is also socially stratified. The young child is cared for by a range of untitled persons, typically the child's older siblings, the mother, and unmarried siblings of the child's mother. Where more than one of these are present, the older is considered to be the higher ranking caregiver and the younger the lower ranking caregiver (Ochs 1982c). As will be discussed in the course of this story, ranking affects how caregiving tasks are carried out and how verbal interactions are organized.

From birth until the age of 5 or 6 months, an infant is referred to as *pepemeamea* (baby thing thing). During this time, the infant stays close to his or her mother, who is assisted by other women and children in child-care tasks. During this period, the infant spends the periods of rest and sleep near, but somewhat separated from, others, on a large pillow enclosed by a mosquito net suspended from a beam or rope. Waking moments are spent in the arms of the mother, occasionally the father, but most often on the hips or laps of other children, who deliver the infant to his or her mother for feeding and in general are responsible for satisfying and comforting the child.

In these early months, the infant is talked *about* by others, particularly in regard to his or her physiological states and needs. Language addressed *to* the young infant tends to be in the form of songs or rhythmic vocalizations in a soft, high pitch. Infants at this stage are not treated as conversational partners. Their gestures and vocalizations are interpreted for what they indicate about the physiological state of the child. If verbally expressed, however, these interpretations are directed in general not to the infant but to some other more mature member of the household (older child), typically in the form of a directive.

As an infant becomes more mature and mobile, he or she is referred to as simply *pepe* (baby). When the infant begins to crawl, his or her immediate social and verbal environment changes. Although the infant continues to be carried by an older sibling, he or she is also expected to come to the mother or other mature family members on his or her own. Spontaneous language is directed to the infant to a much greater extent. The child, for example, is told to "come" to the caregiver.

To understand the verbal environment of the infant at this stage, it is necessary to consider Samoan concepts of childhood and children. Once a child is able to locomote himself or herself and even somewhat before, he or she is frequently described as cheeky, mischievous, and willful. Very frequently, the infant is negatively sanctioned for his actions. An infant who sucks eagerly, vigorously, or frequently at the breast may be teasingly shamed by other family members. Approaching a guest or touching objects of value provokes negative directives first and mock threats second. The tone of voice shifts dramatically from that used with younger infants. The pitch drops to the level used in causal interactions with adult addressees and voice quality becomes loud and sharp. It is to be noted here that caregiver speech is largely talk directed *at* the infant and typically caregivers do not engage in "conversations" *with* infants over several exchanges. Further, the language used by caregivers is not lexically or syntactically simplified.

The image of the small child as highly assertive continues for several years and is reflected in what is reported to be the first word of Samoan children: *tae* (shit), a curse word used to reject, retaliate, or show displeasure at the action of another. The child's earliest use of language, then, is seen as explicitly defiant and angry. Although caregivers admonish the verbal and nonverbal expression of these qualities, the qualities are in fact deeply valued and considered necessary and desirable in particular social circumstances.

As noted earlier, Samoan children are exposed to, and participate in, a highly stratified society. Children usually grow up in a family compound composed of several households and headed by one or more titled persons. Titled persons conduct themselves in a particular manner in public, namely, moving slowly or being stationary, and they tend to disassociate themselves from the activities of lower status persons in their immediate environment. In a less dramatic fashion, this demeanor characterizes high ranking caregivers in a household as well, who tend to leave the more active tasks, such as bathing, changing, and carrying an infant to younger persons (Ochs 1982c).

The social stratification of caregiving has its reflexes in the verbal environment of the young child. Throughout the day, higher ranking caregivers (e.g., the mother) direct lower ranking persons to carry, put to sleep, soothe, feed, bathe, and clothe a child. Typically, a lower ranking caregiver waits for such a directive rather than initiate such activities spontaneously. When a small child begins to speak, he or she learns to make his or her needs known to the higher ranking caregiver. The child learns not to necessarily expect a direct response. Rather, the child's appeal usually generates a conversational sequence such as the following:

Child appeals to high ranking caregiver	(A → B)
High ranking caregiver directs lower ranking caregiver	(B → C)
Lower ranking caregiver responds to child	(C → A)

These verbal interactions differ from the ABAB dyadic interactions described for white middle-class caregivers and children. Whereas a white middle-class child is often alone with a caregiver, a Samoan child is not. Traditional Samoan houses have no internal or external walls, and typically conversations involve several persons inside and outside the house. For the Samoan child, then, multiparty conversations are the norm, and participation is organized along hierarchical lines.

The importance of status and rank is expressed in other uses of language as well. Very small children are encouraged to produce certain speech acts that they will be expected to produce later as younger (i.e., low ranking) members of the household. One of these speech acts is reporting of news to older family members. The reporting of news by lower status persons complements the detachment associated with relatively high status. High status persons ideally (or officially) receive information through reports rather than through their own direct involvement in the affairs of others. Of course, this ideal is not always realized. Nonetheless, children from the one-word stage on will be explicitly instructed to notice others and to provide information to others as Example 6 illustrates.

Example 6

Pesio, her peer group including Maselino 3 yrs 4 mos, and Maselino's mother, Iuliana, are in the house. They see Alesana (member of research project) in front of the trade store across the street. Iuliana directs the children to notice Alesana.

Pesio (2 yrs 3 mos)	*Others*
	Iuliana: Va'ai Alesana.
	Look (at) Alesana!
ā?/	
Huh?	
	Iuliana: Alesana
	Maselino: Alesaga/
ai Alesaga/	
Look (at) Alesana	
	Iuliana: Vala'au Alesana
	Call (to) Alesana.
((very high, loud))	
SAGA?/	((high, soft))
Alesana!	Iuliana: Mālō.
	(*Congratulations/hello*)
((loud))	
ALŌ!	
(*Congratulations/hello*)	
	Iuliana: (Fai) o Elegoa lea.
	(Say) prt. Elenoa here.
	(*say*) *"Elenoa [is] here."*
Sego lea/	
Elenoa here	
Elenoa [is] here.	

The character of these instructions is similar to that of the triadic exchanges described in the Kaluli developmental story. A young child is to repeat an utterance offered by a caregiver to a third party. As in the Kaluli triadic exchanges, the utterance is designed primarily for the third party. For example, the high, soft voice quality used by Iuliana expresses deference in greeting Alesana, the third party. Caregivers use such exchanges to teach children a wide range of skills and knowedge. In fact, the task of repeating what the caregiver has said is *itself* an object of knowledge, preparing the child for his or her eventual role as messenger. Children at the age of 3 are expected to deliver *verbatim* messages on behalf of more mature members of the family.

The cumulative orientation is one in which even very young children are oriented toward others. In contrast to the white middle-class tendencies to accommodate situations to the child, the Samoans encourage the child to meet the needs of the situation, that is, to notice others, listen to them, and adapt one's own speech to their particular status and needs.

The pervasiveness of social stratification is felt in another, quite fundamental aspect of language, that of ascertaining the meaning of an utterance. Procedures for clarification are sensitive to the relative rank of conversational participants in the following manner. If a high status person produces a partially or wholly unintelligible utterance, the burden of clarification tends to rest with the hearer. It is not inappropriate for high status persons to produce such utterances from time to time. In the case of orators in particular, there is an expectation that certain terms and expressions will be obscure to certain members of their audiences. On the other hand, if a low status person's speech is unclear, the burden of clarification tends to be placed more on the speaker.

The latter situation applies to most situations in which young children produce ambiguous or unclear utterances. Both adult and child caregivers tend not to try to determine the message content of such utterances by, for example, repeating or expanding such an utterance with a query intonation. In fact, unintelligible utterances of young children will sometimes be considered as not Samoan but another language, usually Chinese, or not language at all but the sounds of an animal. A caregiver may choose to initiate clarification by asking "What?" or "Huh?" but it is up to the child to make his or her speech intelligible to the addressee.

Whereas the Samoans place the burden of clarification on the child, white middle-class caregivers assist the child in clarifying and expressing ideas. As noted in the white middle-class developmental story, such assistance is associated with good mothering. The good mother is one who responds to her child's incompetence by making greater efforts than normal to clarify his or her intentions. To this end, a mother tries to put herself in the child's place (take the perspective of the child). In Samoa good mothering or good caregiving is almost the reverse: A young child is encouraged to develop an ability to take the perspective of higher ranking persons in order to assist them and facilitate their well-being. The ability to do so is part of showing *fa'aaloalo* (respect), a most necessary demeanor in social life.

We can not leave our Samoan story without touching on another dimension of intelligibility and understanding in caregiver–child interactions. In particular, we need to turn our attention to Samoan attitudes toward motivation and intentionality (cf. Ochs 1982c). In philosophy, social science, and literary criticism, a great deal of ink has been spilled over the relation between act and intention behind an act. The pursuit and ascertaining of intentions is highly valued in many societies, where acts are objects of interpretation and motives are treated as explanations. In traditional Samoan society, with exceptions such as teasing and bluffing, actions are not treated as open to interpretation. They are treated for the most part as having one assignable meaning. An individual may not always know what that meaning is, as in the case of an oratorical passage; in these cases, one accepts that there is one meaning that he may or may not eventually come to know. For the most part as well, there is not a concern with levels of intentions and motives underlying the performance of some particular act.

Responses of Samoan caregivers to unintelligible utterances and acts of young children need to be understood in this light. Caregivers tend not to guess, hypothesize, or otherwise interpret such utterances and acts, in part because these procedures are not generally engaged in, at least explicitly, in daily social interactions within a village. As in encounters with others, a caregiver generally treats a small child's utterances as either clear or not clear, and in the latter case prefers to wait until the meaning becomes known to the caregiver rather than initiate an interpretation.

When young Samoan children participate in such interactions, they come to know how "meaning" is treated in their society. They learn what to consider as meaningful (e.g., clear utterances and actions), procedures for assigning meaning to utterances and actions, and procedures for handling unintelligible and partially intelligible utterances and actions. In this way, through language use, Samoan children are socialized into culturally preferred ways of processing information. Such contexts of experience reveal the interface of language, culture, and thought.

Implications of developmental stories: three proposals

Interactional design reexamined.   We propose that infants and caregivers do not interact with one another according to one particular "biologically designed choreography" (Stern 1977). There are many choreographies within and across societies, and cultural as well as biological systems contribute to their design, frequency, and significance. The biological predispositions constraining and shaping the social behavior of infants and caregivers must be broader than thus far conceived in that the use of eye gaze, vocalization, and body alignment are orchestrated differently in the social groups we have observed. As noted earlier, for example, Kaluli mothers do not engage in sustained gazing at, or elicit and maintain direct eye contact with, their infants as such behavior is dispreferred and associated with witchcraft.

Another argument in support of a broader notion of a biological predisposition to be social concerns the variation observed in the participant structure of social interactions. The literature on white middle-class child development has been oriented, quite legitimately, toward the two-party relationship between infant and caregiver, typically infant and mother. The legitimacy of this focus rests on the fact that this relationship is primary for infants within this social group. Further, most communicative interactions are dyadic in the adult community. Although the mother is an important figure in both Kaluli and Samoan developmental stories, the interactions in which infants are participants are typically triadic or multiparty. As noted, Kaluli mothers organize triadic interactions in which infants and young children are oriented away from their mothers and toward a third party. For Samoans, the absence of internal and external walls, coupled with the expectation that others will attend to, and eventually participate in, conversation, makes multiparty interaction far more common. Infants are socialized to participate in such interactions in ways appropriate to the status and rank of the participants.

This is not to say that Kaluli and Samoan caregivers and children do not engage in dyadic exchanges. Rather, the point is that such exchanges are not accorded the same significance as in white middle-class society. In white middle-class households that have been studied, the process of becoming social takes place predominantly through dyadic interactions, and social competence itself is measured in terms of the young child's capacity to participate in such interactions. In Kaluli and Samoan households, the process of becoming social takes place through participation in dyadic, triadic, and multiparty social interactions, with the latter two more common than the dyad.

From an early age, Samoan and Kaluli children must learn how to participate in interactions involving a number of individuals. To do this minimally requires attending to more than one individual's words and actions and knowing the norms for when and how to enter interactions, taking into account the social identities of at least three participants. Further, the sequencing of turns in triadic and multiparty interactions has a far wider range of possibilities vis-à-vis dyadic exchanges and thus requires considerable knowledge and skill. Whereas dyadic exchanges can only be ABABA..., triadic or multiparty exchanges can be sequenced in a variety of ways, subject to such social constraints as speech content and the status of speaker (as discussed in the Samoan developmental story). For both the Kaluli and the Samoan child, triadic and multiparty interactions constitute their earliest social experiences and reflect the ways in which members of these societies routinely communicate with one another.

Caregiver register reexamined.   A second major proposal based on these three developmental stories is that the simplifying features of white middle-class speech are not necessary input for the acquisition of language by young children. The word "input" itself implies a directionality toward the child as information processor. The data base for the child's construction of language is assumed to be language directed *to* the child. It is tied to a model of communication that is dyadic, with participation limited to the roles of speaker and addressee. If we were to apply this strict notion of input (language addressed to the child) to the Kaluli and Samoan experiences, we would be left with a highly restricted corpus from which the child is expected to construct language. As we have emphasized in these developmental stories, the very young child is less often spoken to than spoken about. Nonetheless, both Kaluli and Samoan children become fluent speakers within the range of normal developmental variation.

Given that the features of caregivers' speech cannot be accounted for primarily in terms of their language-facilitating function, that is, as input, we might ask what can account for the special ways in which caregivers speak to their children. We suggest that the particular features of the caregiver register are best understood as an expression of a basic sociological phenomenon. Every social relationship is associated with a set of behaviors, verbal and nonverbal, that set off that relationship from other relationships. Additionally, these behaviors indicate to others that a particular social relationship is being actualized. From this point of view, the "special" features of caregiver speech are not special at all, in the sense that verbal modifications do occur wherever social relationships are called into play. This phenomenon has been overlooked in part because in describing the language of caregivers to children it is usually contrasted with a generalized notion of the ways in which adults talk to everyone else. The most extreme example of this is found in interviews with adults in which they are asked to describe special ways of talking to babies (Ferguson 1977). A less extreme example is found in the procedure of comparing caregiver speech to children with caregiver speech to the researcher/ outsider (Newport, Gleitman, & Gleitman 1977). In the latter case, only one adult–adult relationship is used as a basis of comparison, and this relationship is typically formal and socially distant.

The social nature of caregiver speech has been discussed with respect to its status as a type of speech register. Nonetheless, the language-simplifying features have been emphasized more than any other aspect of the register. The dimension of simplification is significant with respect to the white middle-class caregiver registers documented; however, the notion of simplification has been taken as synonymous with the caregiver register itself. More to the point of this discussion is the apparent tendency to see simplification as a universal, if not natural, process. Ferguson's insightful parallel between caregiver speech and foreigner talk (1977) has been taken to mean that more competent speakers everywhere spontaneously accommodate their speech to less competent interactional partners, directly influencing language change in contact situations (pidgins in particular) as well as in acquisition of a foreign language. Ferguson's own discussion of "simplified registers" does not carry with it this conclusion, however. Further, the stories told here of Kaluli and Samoan caregiver speech and comportment indicate that simplification is culturally organized in terms of when, how, and extent. In both stories, caregivers do not speak in a dramatically more simplified manner to very young children. They do not do so for different cultural reasons: The Kaluli do not simplify because such speech is felt to inhibit the development of competent speech, the Samoans because such accommodations are dispreferred when the addressee is of lower rank than the speaker.

The cultural nature of simplification is evidenced very clearly when we compare Samoan speech to young children with Samoan speech to foreigners (*pālangi*). As discussed by Duranti (1981), "foreigner talk" *is* simplified in many ways, in contrast to "baby talk." To understand this, we need only return to the social principle of relative rank. Foreigners typically (and historically) are persons to whom respect is appropriate – strangers or guests of relatively high status. The appropriate comportment toward such persons is one of accommodation to their needs, communicative needs being basic. The Samoan example is an important one, because we can use it to understand social groups for whom speaking to foreigners is like speaking to children. That is, we can at least know where to *start* the process of understanding this speech phenomenon; to see the phenomenon as expressive of cultural beliefs and values. Just as there are cultural explanations for why and how Samoans speak differently to young children and foreigners, so there are cultural explanations for why and how white middle-class adults modify their speech in similar ways to these two types of addressees. These explanations go far beyond the attitudes discussed in the white middle-class story. Our task here is not to provide an adequate cultural account but rather to encourage more detailed research along these lines. An understanding of caregiver or baby-talk register in a particular society will never be achieved without a more serious consideration of the sociological nature of register.

What caregivers do with words. In this section we build on the prior two proposals and suggest that:

1   A functional account of the speech of both caregiver and child must incorporate information concerning cultural knowledge and expectations;
2   Generalizations concerning the relations between the behavior and the goals of caregivers and young children should not presuppose the presence or equivalent significance of particular goals across social groups.

In each of these developmental stories we saw that caregivers and children interacted with one another in culturally patterned ways. Our overriding theme has been that caregiver speech behavior must be seen as part of caregiving and socialization more generally. What caregivers say and how they interact with young children are motivated in part by concerns and beliefs held by many members of the local community. As noted earlier, these concerns and beliefs may not be conscious in all cases. Certain beliefs, such as the Kaluli notions of the child as "soft" and socialization as "hardening" the child, are explicit. Others, such as the white middle-class notions of the infant and small child as social and capable of acting intentionally (expressing intentions), are not explicitly formulated.

To understand what any particular verbal behavior is accomplishing, we need to adopt ethnographic procedures, namely, to relate particular behaviors to those performed in other situations. What a caregiver is doing in speaking to a child is obviously related to what she or he does and/or others do in other recurrent situations. We have suggested, for example, that the accommodations that middle-class (particularly American) caregivers make in speaking to young children are linked to patterned ways of responding to incompetence in general (e.g., handicapped persons, retardates). Members of this social group appear to adapt situations to meet the special demands of less competent persons to a far greater extent than in other societies, for example, Samoan society. We have also suggested that the heavy use of expansions by middle-class caregivers to query or confirm what a child is expressing is linked to culturally preferred procedures for achieving understanding, for example, the recognition of ambiguity, the formulation and verification of hypotheses (interpretations, guesses). In participating in interactions in which expansions are used in this way, the child learns the concepts of ambiguity, interpretation, and verification, and the procedures associated with them.

A common method in child language research has been to infer function or goal from behavior. The pitfalls of this procedure are numerous, and social scientists are acutely aware of how difficult it is to establish structure–function relations. One aspect of this dilemma is that one cannot infer function on the basis of a structure in isolation. Structures get their functional meaning through their relation to contexts in which they appear. The "same" structure may have different functions in different circumstances. This is true within a society, but our reason for mentioning it here is that it is true also across societies and languages. Although caregivers in two different societies may expand their children's utterances, it would not necessarily follow that the caregivers shared the same beliefs and values. It is possible that their behavior is motivated by quite different cultural processes. Similarly, the absence of a particular behavior, such as the absence of expansions among caregivers, may be motivated quite differently across societies. Both the Kaluli and the Samoan caregivers do not appear to rely on expansions, but the reasons expansions are dispreferred differ. The Samoans do not do so in part because of their dispreference for guessing and in part because of their expectation that the burden of intelligibility rests with the child (as lower status party) rather than with more mature members of the society. Kaluli do not use expansions to resay or guess what a child may be expressing because they say that "one cannot know what someone else thinks," regardless of age or social status.

Our final point concerning the structure–function relation is that the syntax of our claims about language acquisition must be altered to recognize variation across societies. The bulk of research on communicative development has presupposed or asserted the universality of one or another function, for example, the input function, the communicative function, and the illustrated verbal and nonverbal behaviors that follow from, or reflect, that function. Our three stories suggest that generalizations must be context-restricted. Thus, for example, rather than assuming or asserting that caregivers desire to communicate with an infant, the generalization should be expressed: "Where caregivers desire communication with an infant, then..." or "If it is the case that caregivers desire communication with an infant then..."

A Typology of Socialization and Caregiver Speech Patterns

At this point, with the discussion nearing its conclusion, we have decided to stick our necks out a bit further and suggest that the two orientations to children discussed in the developmental stories – adapting situations to the child and adapting the child to situations – distinguish more than the three societies discussed in this chapter. We believe that these two orientations of mature members toward children can be used to create a typology of socialization patterns. For example, societies in which children are expected to adapt to situations may include not only Kaluli and Samoan but also white and black working-class Americans (Heath 1983; Miller 1982; Ward 1971).

The typology of course requires a more refined application of these orienting features. We would expect these orientations to shift as children develop; for example, a society may adapt situations to meet the needs of a very small infant, but as the infant matures, the expectation may shift to one in which the child should adapt to situations. Indeed, we could predict such a pattern for most, if not all, societies. The distinction between societies would be in terms of *when* this shift takes place and in terms of the *intensity* of the orientation at any point in developmental time.

Having stuck our necks out this far, we will go a little further and propose that these two orientations will have systematic reflexes in the organization of communication between caregivers and young children across societies: We predict, for example, that a society that adapts or fits situations to the needs (perceived needs) of young children will use a register to the children that includes a number of simplifying features, for example, shorter utterances, with a restricted lexicon, that refer to here-and-now. Such an orientation is also compatible with a tendency for caregivers to assist the child's expression of intentions through expansions, clarification requests, cooperative proposition building and the like. These often involve the caregiver's taking the perspective of a small child and correlate highly with allowing a small child to initiate new topics (evidencing child-centered orientation).

On the other hand, societies in which children are expected to meet the needs of the situation at hand will communicate differently with infants and small children. In these societies, children usually participate in multiparty situations. Caregivers will socialize children through language to notice others and perform appropriate (not necessarily polite) speech acts toward others. This socialization will often take

Table 11.1   Two orientations toward children and their corresponding caregiver speech patterns

Adapt situation to child	Adapt child to situation
Simplified register features baby-talk lexicon	Modeling of (unsimplified) utterances for child to repeat to third party (wide range of speech act, not simplified)
Negotiation of meaning via expansion and paraphrase	
Cooperative proposition building between caregiver and child	Child directed to notice others
Utterances that respond to child-initiated verbal or nonverbal act	Topics arise from range of situational circumstances to which caregiver wishes child to respond
Typical communicative situation: two-party	Typical communicative situation: multiparty

the form of modeling, where the caregiver says what the child should say and directs the child to repeat. Typically, the child is directed to say something to someone other than the caregiver who has modeled the original utterance. From the Kaluli and Samoan cases, we would predict that the utterances to be repeated would cover a wide range of speech acts (teasing, insulting, greeting, information requesting, begging, reporting of news, shaming, accusations, and the like). In these interactions, as in other communicative contexts with children, the caregivers do not simplify their speech but rather shape their speech to meet situational contingencies (table 11.1).

A Model of Language Acquisition through Socialization (the Ethnographic Approach)

Cultural organization of intentionality

Like many scholars of child language, we believe that the acquisition of language is keyed to accomplishing particular goals (Bates et al. 1979; Greenfield & Smith 1976; Halliday 1975; Lock 1978; Shotter 1978; Vygotsky 1962). As Bates and her colleagues (1979) as well as Carter (1978) and Lock (1981) have pointed out, small children perform communicative acts such as drawing attention to an object and requesting and offering before conventional morphemes are produced. They have acquired knowledge of particular social acts before they have acquired language in even the most rudimentary form. When language emerges, it is put to use in these and other social contexts. As Bates and her colleagues suggest, the use of language here is analogous to other behaviors of the child at this point of development; the child is using a new means to achieve old goals.

Although not taking a stand as to whether or not language is like other behaviors, we support the notion that language is acquired in a social world and that many aspects of the social world have been absorbed by the child by the time language emerges. This is not to say that functional considerations determine grammatical structure but rather that ends motivate means and provide an orienting principle for producing and understanding language over developmental time. Norman (1975), as well as Hood, McDermott, and Cole (1978), suggests that purpose/function is a mnemonic device for learning generally.

Much of the literature on early development has carefully documented the child's capacity to react and act intentionally (Harding & Golinkoff 1979). The nature and organization of communicative interaction is seen as integrally bound to this capacity. Our contribution to this literature is to spell out the social and cultural systems in which intentions participate. The capacity to express intentions is human but which intentions can be expressed by whom, when, and how is subject to local expectations concerning the social behavior of members. With respect to the acquisition of competence in language use, this means that societies may very well differ in their expectations of what children can and should communicate (Hymes 1967). They may also differ in their expectations concerning the capacity of young children to understand intentions (or particular intentions). With respect to the particular relationship between a child and his or her caregivers, these generalizations can be represented as follows:

Social expectations and language acquisition

| Expectations | *Influence* | Participation in social situations | How & which intentions are expressed by child *Influences* How & which intentions are expressed by caregiver | Structure of child language *Influence* Structure of caregiver language |

Let us consider examples that illustrate these statements. As noted in the Samoan development story, Samoans have a commonly shared expectation that a child's first word will be *tae* (shit) and that its communicative intention will be to curse and confront (corresponding to the adult for *'ai tae* (eat shit)). Whereas a range of early consonant-vowel combinations of the child are treated as expressing *tae* and communicative, other phonetic strings are not treated as language. The Kaluli consider that the child has begun to use language when he or she says "mother" and "breast." Like the Samoans, the Kaluli do not treat other words produced before these two words appear as part of "language," that is, as having a purpose.

Another example of how social expectations influence language acquisition comes from the recent work by Platt (1980) on Samoan children's acquisition of the deictic verbs "come," "go," "give," "take." The use of these verbs over developmental time is constrained by social norms concerning the movement of persons and objects. As noted in the Samoan story, higher ranking persons are expected to be relatively inactive in the company of lower ranking (e.g., younger) persons. As a consequence, younger children who are directed to "come" and who evidence comprehension of this act, tend not to perform the same act themselves. Children are socially constrained not to direct the more mature persons around them to move in their direction. On the other hand, small children are encouraged to demand and give out goods (particularly food). At the same developmental point at which the children are *not* using "come," they *are* using "give" quite frequently. This case is interesting because it indicates that a semantically more complex form ("give" – movement of object and person toward deictic center) may appear in the speech of a child earlier than a less complex form ("come" – movement of person toward deictic center) because of the social norms surrounding its use (Platt 1980).

Although these examples have focused on children's speech, we also consider caregiver speech to be constrained by local expectations and the values and beliefs that underlie them. The reader is invited to draw on the body of this chapter for examples of these relationships, for example, the relation between caregivers who adapt to young children and use of a simplified register. Indeed, the major focus of our developmental stories has been to indicate precisely the role of sociocultural processes in constructing communication between caregiver and child.

Sociocultural knowledge and code knowledge

In this section we will build on our argument that children's language is constructed in socially appropriate and culturally meaningful ways. Our point will be that the process of acquiring language must be understood as the process of integrating code knowledge with sociocultural knowledge.

Sociocultural knowledge is generative in much the same way that knowledge about grammar is generative. Just as children are able to produce and understand utterances that they have never heard before, so they are able to participate in social situations that don't exactly match their previous experiences. In the case of social situations in which language is used, children are able to apply both grammatical and sociocultural principles in producing and comprehending novel behavior. Both sets of principles can be acquired out of conscious awareness.

$$\begin{array}{c}
\textit{Developmental time} \uparrow \\
\end{array}
\qquad
\begin{array}{l}
\text{Sociocultural} \rightarrow \text{code} \\
\text{knowledge} \quad \leftarrow \text{knowledge}
\end{array}$$

In the case of infants and young children acquiring their first language(s), sociocultural knowledge is acquired hand-in-hand with the knowledge of code properties of a language. Acquisition of a foreign or second language by older children and adults may not necessarily follow this model. In classroom foreign-language learning, for example, a knowledge of code properties typically precedes knowledge of the cultural norms of code use. Even where the second language is acquired in the context of living in a foreign culture, the cultural knowledge necessary for appropriate social interaction may lag behind or never develop, as illustrated by Gumperz (1977) for Indian speakers in Great Britain.

Another point to be mentioned at this time is that the sociocultural principles being acquired are not necessarily shared by all native speakers of a language. As noted in the introduction, there are variations in knowledge between individuals and between groups of individuals. In certain cases, for example, children who are members of a nondominant group, growing up may necessitate acquiring different cultural frameworks for participating in situations. American Indian and Australian Aboriginal children find themselves participating in interactions in which the language is familiar but the interactional procedures and participant structures differ from earlier experiences (Philips 1983). These cases of growing up monolingually but biculturally are similar to the circumstances of second-language learners who enter a cultural milieu that differs from that of first socialization experiences.

On the unevenness of language development

The picture we have built up suggests that there is quite a complex system of norms and expectations that the young language acquirer must attend to, and does attend to, in the process of growing up to be a competent speaker-hearer. We have talked about this system as affecting structure and content of children's utterances at different points in developmental time. One product of all this is that children come to use and hear particular structures in certain contexts but not in others. In other words, children acquire forms in a subset of contexts that has been given "priority" by members.

Priority contexts are those in which children are encouraged to participate. For example, Kaluli and Samoan children use affect pronouns, for example, "poor-me," initially in begging, an activity they are encouraged to engage in. The use of affect pronouns in other speech acts is a later development. Similarly, many white middle-class children use their first nominal forms in the act of labeling, an activity much encouraged by caregivers in this social group. Labeling is not an activity which Kaluli and Samoan caregivers and children engage in. Each social group will have its preferences, and these, in turn, will guide the child's acquisition of language.

On lack of match between child and caregiver speech

Those who pursue the argument concerning how children acquire language often turn to correlational comparisons between children's and caregivers' speech strategies. Lack of match is taken as support for some input-independent strategy of the child and as evidence that some natural process is at work. We suggest that this line of reasoning has flaws.

If the reader has accepted the argument that societies have ideas about how children can and should participate in social situations and that these ideas differ in many respects from those concerning how more mature persons can and should behave, then the reader might further accept the conclusion that children may speak and act differently from others because they have learned to do so. Why should we equate input exclusively with imitation, that is, with a match in behavior? Of course there are commonalities between child and adult behavior, but that does not imply that difference is not learned. In examining the speech of young children, we should not necessarily expect their speech and the functions to which it is put to match exactly those of caregivers. Children are neither expected nor encouraged to do many of the things that older persons do, and, conversely, older persons are neither expected nor encouraged to do many of the things that small children do. Indeed, unless they are framed as "play," attempts to cross these social boundaries meet with laughter, ridicule, or other forms of negative sanctioning.

A note on the role of biology

Lest the reader think we advocate a model in which language and cognition are the exclusive product of culture, we note here that sociocultural systems are to be considered as *one* force influencing language acquisition. Biological predispositions, of course, have a hand in this process as well. The model we have presented should be considered as a subset of a more general acquisition model that includes both influences.

Social expectations		Language over
	Influence	developmental time
Biological predispositions		

Conclusions

This is a chapter with a number of points but one message: That the process of acquiring language and the process of acquiring sociocultural knowledge are intimately tied. In pursuing this generalization, we have formulated the following proposals:

1   The specific features of caregiver speech behavior that have been described as simplified register are neither universal nor necessary for language to be acquired. White middle-class children, Kaluli children, and Samoan children all become speakers of their languages within the normal range of development and yet their caregivers use language quite differently in their presence.
2   Caregivers' speech behavior expresses and reflects values and beliefs held by members of a social group. In this sense, caregivers' speech is part of a larger set of behaviors that are culturally organized.
3   The use of simplified registers by caregivers in certain societies may be part of a more general orientation in which situations are adapted to young children's perceived needs. In other societies, the orientation may be the reverse, that is, children at a very early age are expected to adapt to requirements of situations. In such societies, caregivers direct children to notice and respond to other's actions. They tend not to simplify their speech and frequently model appropriate utterances for the child to repeat to a third party in a situation.
4   Not only caregivers' but children's language as well is influenced by social expectations. Children's strategies for encoding and decoding information, for negotiating meaning, and for handling errors are socially organized in terms of who does the work, when, and how. Further, every society orchestrates the ways in which children participate in particular situations, and this, in turn, affects the form, the function, and the content of children's utterances. Certain features of the grammar may be acquired quite early, in part because their use is encouraged and given high priority. In this sense, the process of language acquisition is part of the larger process of socialization, that is, acquiring social competence.

Although biological factors play a role in language acquisition, sociocultural factors have a hand in this process as well. It is not a trivial fact that small children develop in the context of organized societies. Cultural conditions for communication organize even the earliest interactions between infants and others. Through participation as audience, addressee, and/or "speaker," the infant develops a range of skills, intuitions, and knowledge enabling him or her to communicate in culturally preferred ways. The development of these faculties is an integral part of becoming a competent speaker.

Coda

This chapter should be in no way interpreted as proposing a view in which socialization determines a fixed pattern of behavior. We advocate a view that considers human beings to be flexible and able to adapt to change, both social and linguistic, for example, through contact and social mobility. The ways in which individuals change is a product of complex interactions between established cultural procedures and intuitions and those the individual is currently acquiring. From our perspective, socialization is a continuous and open-ended process that spans the entire life of an individual.

NOTES

This chapter was written while the authors were research fellows at the Research School of Pacific Studies, the Australian National University. We would like to thank Roger Keesing and the Working Group in Language and Its Cultural Context. Ochs's research was supported by the National Science Foundation and the Australian National University. Schieffelin's research was supported by the National Science Foundation and the Wenner-Gren Foundation for Anthropological Research. We thank these institutions for their support.

1   For current socialization literature, the reader is recommended to see Briggs 1970; Gallimore, Boggs, & Jordon 1974; Geertz 1959; Hamilton 1981; Harkness & Super 1980; Korbin 1978; Leiderman, Tulkin, & Rosenfeld 1977; LeVine 1980; Levy 1973; Mead & MacGregor 1951; Mead & Wolfenstein 1955; Montagu 1978; Munroe & Munroe 1975; Richards 1974; Wagner & Stevenson 1982; Weisner & Gallimore 1977; Whiting 1963; Whiting & Whiting 1975; Williams 1969; and Wills 1977.

2   Bloom 1970, 1973; Bowerman 1977, 1981; Brown 1973; Clark 1974; Clark & Clark 1977; Greenfield & Smith 1976; Karmiloff-Smith 1979; MacNamara 1972; Nelson 1974; Schlesinger 1974; Sinclair 1971; Slobin 1979.

3   Bates 1976; Berko 1958; Bloom, Hood, & Lightbown 1974; Bloom, Lightbown, & Hood 1975; Bowerman 1977; Brown & Bellugi 1964; Brown, Cazden, & Bellugi 1969; Dore 1975; Ervin-Tripp 1964; Lieven 1980; MacWhinney 1975; Miller 1982; Scollon 1976; Shatz 1978; Slobin 1973.

4   Berman 1985; Bowerman 1973; Brown 1973; Clancy 1985; Clark 1985; Johnston & Slobin 1979; MacWhinney & Bates 1978; Ochs 1982b, 1985; Slobin 1981, 1985; Aksu-Koç & Slobin 1985.

5   Chomsky 1959, 1968, 1977; Fodor, Bever, & Garrett 1974; Goldin-Meadow 1977; McNeill 1970; Newport 1981; Newport, Gleitman, & Gleitman 1977; Piattelli-Palmarini 1980; Shatz 1981; Wanner & Gleitman 1982.

6   Bates et al. in press; Bloom 1973; Bruner 1975, 1977; Bullowa 1979; Carter 1978; de Lemos 1981; Gleason & Weintraub 1978; Golinkoff 1983; Greenfield & Smith 1976; Harding & Golinkoff 1979; Lock 1978, 1981; Sachs 1977; Shatz 1983; Slobin 1983; Snow 1979; Snow & Ferguson 1977; Vygotsky 1962; Werner & Kaplan 1963.

7   Andersen, Dunlea, & Kekelis 1982; Bever 1970; Greenfield & Smith 1976; Huttenlocher 1974; Menyuk & Menn 1979; Piaget 1955/1926; Slobin 1981; Sugarman 1984; Wanner & Gleitman 1982.

8   Blount 1972; Bowerman 1981; Clancy 1985; Eisenberg 1982; Fischer 1970; Hamilton 1981; Harkness 1975; Harkness & Super 1977; Heath 1983; Miller 1982; Philips 1983; Schieffelin & Eisenberg 1984; Scollon & Scollon 1981; Stross 1972; Ward 1971; Watson-Gegeo & Gegeo 1982; Wills 1977.

9   This story is based on the numerous accounts of caregiver–child communication and interaction that have appeared in both popular and scientific journals. Our generalizations regarding language use are based on detailed reports in the developmental psycholinguistic literature, which are cited throughout. In addition, we have drawn on our own experiences and intuitions as mothers and members of this social group. We invite those with differing perceptions to comment on our interpretations.

10   We would like to thank Courtney Cazden for bringing the following quotation to our attention: "It seems to us that a mother in expanding speech may be teaching more than grammar; she may be teaching something like a world-view" (Brown & Bellugi 1964).

11 This analysis is based on the data collected in the course of ethnographic and linguistic fieldwork among the Kaluli in the Southern Highlands Province between 1975 and 1977. During this time, E. L. Schieffelin, a cultural anthropologist, and S. Feld, an ethnomusicologist, were also conducting ethnographic research. This study of the development of communicative competence among the Kaluli focused on four children who were approximately 24 months old at the start of the study. However, an additional twelve children were included in the study (siblings and cousins in residence), ranging in age from birth to 10 years. The spontaneous conversations of these children and their families were tape-recorded for one year at monthly intervals with each monthly sample lasting from 3 to 4 hours. Detailed contextual notes accompanied the taping, and these annotated transcripts, along with interviews and observations, form the data base. A total of 83 hours of audio-tape were collected and transcribed in the village. Analyses of Kaluli child acquisition data are reported in Schieffelin 1981, 1985, and 1990.

12 The data on which this analysis is based were collected from July 1978 to July 1979 in a traditional village in Western Samoa (now Samoa). The village, Falefa, is located on the island of Upolu, approximately 18 miles from the capital, Apia. The fieldwork was conducted by Alessandro Duranti, Martha Platt, and Elinor Ochs. Our data collection consisted of two major projects. The language development project, carried out by Ochs and Platt, was a longitudinal documentation, through audio- and videotape, of young children's acquisition of Samoan. This was accomplished by focusing on six children from six different households, from 19 to 35 months of age at the onset of the study. These children were observed and taped every five weeks, approximately three hours each period. Samoan children live in compounds composed of several households. Typically, numerous siblings and peers are present and interact with a young child. We were able to record the speech of seventeen other children under the age of 6, who were part of the children's early social environment. A total of 128 hours of audio and 20 hours of video recording were collected. The audio material is supplemented by handwritten notes detailing contextual features of the interactions recorded. All the audio material has been transcribed in the village by a family member or family acquaintance and checked by a researcher. Approximately 18,000 pages of transcript form the child language data base. Analyses of Samoan child language are reported in Ochs 1982a, 1982b, and 1985.

REFERENCES

Aksu-Koç, A., & Slobin, D. I. (1985). Acquisition of Turkish. In D. I. Slobin (ed.), *The Crosslinguistic Study of Language Acquisition*. Hillsdale, N.J.: Erlbaum.

Andersen, E. (1977). Learning to Speak with Style. Unpublished doctoral dissertation, Stanford University.

Andersen, E. S., Dunlea, A., & Kekelis, L. (1982). Blind Children's Language: Resolving Some Differences. Paper presented at the Stanford Child Language Research Forum, Stanford, Calif.

Andersen, E. S., & Johnson, C. E. (1973). Modifications in the speech of an eight-year-old to younger children. *Stanford Occasional Papers in Linguistics*, No. 3:149–60.

Bates, E. (1976). *Language and Context: The Acquisition of Pragmatics*. New York: Academic Press.

Bates, E., Beeghly-Smith, M., Bretherton, I., & McNew, S. (In press). Social bases of language development: A reassessment. In H. W. Reese & L. P. Lipsitt (eds.), *Advances in Child Development and Behavior*, vol. 16. New York: Academic Press.

Bates, E., Benigni, L., Bretherton, I., Camaioni, L., & Volterra, V. (1979). *The Emergence of Symbols*. New York: Academic Press.

Berko, J. (1958). The child's learning of English morphology. *Word* 14:150–77.

Berman, R. (1985) Acquisition of Hebrew. In D. I. Slobin (ed.), *The Crosslinguistic Study of Language Acquisition*. Hillsdale, N.J.: Erlbaum.

Bever, T. (1970). The cognitive basis for linguistic structure. In J. R. Hayes (ed.), *Cognition and the Development of Language*. New York: Wiley.

Bloom, L. (1970). *Language Development: Form and Function in Emerging Grammars*. Cambridge, Mass.: MIT Press.

Bloom, L. (1973). *One Word at a Time*. The Hague: Mouton.

Bloom, L., Hood, L., & Lightbown, P. (1974). Imitation in language development: If, when, and why? *Cognitive Psychology* 6:380–420.

Bloom, L., & Lahey, M. (1978). *Language Development and Language Disorders*. New York: Wiley.

Bloom, L., Lightbown, P., & Hood, L. (1975). Structure and variation in child language. *Monographs of the Society for Research in Child Development* 40(2, serial no. 160).

Blount, B. (1972). Aspects of socialization among the Luo of Kenya. *Language in Society* 1:235–48.

Bowerman, M. (1973). *Early Syntactic Development: A Cross-linguistic Study with Special Reference to Finnish*. Cambridge: Cambridge University Press.

Bowerman, M. (1977). Semantic and syntactic development: A review of what, when and how in language acquisition. In R. Schiefelbusch (ed.), *Bases of Language Intervention*. Baltimore: University Park Press.

Bowerman, M. (1981). Language development. In H. Triandis & A. Heron (eds.), *Handbook of Cross-cultural Psychology*, vol. 4. Boston: Allyn & Bacon.

Briggs, J. L. (1970). *Never in Anger: Portrait of an Eskimo Family*. Cambridge, Mass.: Harvard University Press.

Brown, R. (1973). *A First Language: The Early Stages*. Cambridge, Mass.: Harvard University Press.

Brown, R. (1977). Introduction. In C. Snow & C. Ferguson (eds.), *Talking to Children: Language Input and Acquisition*. Cambridge: Cambridge University Press.

Brown, R., & Bellugi, U. (1964). Three processes in the child's acquisition of syntax. *Harvard Educational Review* 34:133–51.

Brown, R., Cazden, C., & Bellugi, U. (1969). The child's grammar from I to III. In J. P. Hill (ed.), *Minnesota Symposium on Child Psychology*, vol. 2. Minneapolis: University of Minnesota Press.

Bruner, J. S. (1975). The ontogenesis of speech acts. *Journal of Child Language* 2:1–19.

Bruner, J. S. (1977). Early social interaction and language acquisition. In H. R. Schaffer (ed.), *Studies in Mother–Infant Interaction*. London: Academic Press.

Bruner, J. S. (1978). The role of dialogue in language acquisition. In A. Sinclair, R. J. Jarvella, & W. J. M. Levelt (eds.), *The Child's Conception of Language*. New York: Springer-Verlag.

Bullowa, M. (1979). Introduction: Prelinguistic communication: A field for scientific research. In M. Bullowa (ed.), *Before Speech: The Beginnings of Interpersonal Communication*. Cambridge: Cambridge University Press.

Carter, A. L. (1978). From sensori-motor vocalizations to words. In A. Lock (ed.), *Action, Gesture and Symbol: The Emergence of Language*. London: Academic Press.

Cazden, C. (1965). Environmental Assistance to the Child's Acquisition of Grammar. Unpublished doctoral dissertation, Harvard University.

Chomsky, N. (1959). Review of *Verbal Behavior* by B. F. Skinner. *Language* 35:26–58.

Chomsky, N. (1965). *Aspects of the Theory of Syntax*. Cambridge, Mass.: MIT Press.

Chomsky, N. (1968). *Language and Mind*. New York: Harcourt Brace Jovanovich.

Chomsky, N. (1975). *Reflections on Language*. Glasgow: Fontana/Collins.

Chomsky, N. (1977). *Essays on Form and Interpretation*. New York: North Holland.

Clancy, P. (1985). Acquisition of Japanese. In D. I. Slobin (ed.), *The Cross-linguistic Study of Language Acquisition*. Hillsdale, N.J.: Erlbaum.

Clark, E. V. (1974). Some aspects of the conceptual basis for first language acquisition. In R. L. Schiefelbusch & L. Lloyd (eds.), *Language Perspectives: Acquisition, Retardation and Intervention*. Baltimore: University Park Press.

Clark, E. V. (1985). Acquisition of Romance, with special reference to French. In D. I. Slobin (ed.), *The Crosslinguistic Study of Language Acquisition*. Hillsdale, N.J.: Erlbaum.

Clark, H. H., & Clark, E. V. (1977). *Psychology and Language*. New York: Harcourt Brace Jovanovich.

Corsaro, W. (1979). Sociolinguistic patterns in adult–child inter-action. In E. Ochs & B. B. Schieffelin (eds.), *Developmental Pragmatics*. New York: Academic Press.

Cross, T. (1977). Mothers' speech adjustments: The contributions of selected child listener variables. In C. Snow & C. Ferguson (eds.), *Talking to Children: Language Input and Acquisition*. Cambridge: Cambridge University Press.

de Lemos, C. (1981). Interactional processes in the child's construction of language. In W. Deutsch (ed.), *The Child's Construction of Language*. London: Academic Press.

Dentan, R. K. (1978). Notes on childhood in a nonviolent context: The Semai case. In A. Montagu (ed.), *Learning Non-aggression: The Experience of Nonliterate Societies*. Oxford: Oxford University Press.

Dore, J. (1975). Holophrases, speech acts and language universals. *Journal of Child Language* 2:21–40.

Drach, K. (1969). *The Language of the Parent*. Working paper 14, Language Behavior Research Laboratory, University of California, Berkeley.

Duranti, A. (1981). *The Samoan Fono: A Sociolinguistic Study*. Pacific Linguistic Series B, vol. 80. Canberra: Australian National University.

Edgerton, R. (1967). *The Cloak of Competence: Stigma in the Lives of the Mentally Retarded*. Berkeley: University of California Press.

Eisenberg, A. (1982). Language Acquisition in Cultural Perspective: Talk in Three Mexicano Homes. Unpublished doctoral dissertation, University of California, Berkeley.

Ervin-Tripp, S. (1964). Imitation and structural change in children's language. In E. Lenneberg (ed.), *New Directions in the Study of Language*. Cambridge, Mass.: MIT Press.

Feld, S., & Schieffelin, B. B. (1982). Hard words: A functional basis for Kaluli discourse. In D. Tannen (ed.), *Analyzing Discourse: Talk and Text*. Washington, D.C.: Georgetown University Press.

Feldman, H., Goldin-Meadow, S., & Gleitman, L. (1978). Beyond Herodotus: The creation of language by linguistically deprived deaf children. In A. Lock (ed.), *Action, Gesture and Symbol*. London: Academic Press.

Ferguson, C. (1977). Baby talk as a simplified register. In C. Snow & C. Ferguson (eds.), *Talking to Children: Language Input and Acquisition*. Cambridge: Cambridge University Press.

Fischer, J. (1970). Linguistic socialization: Japan and the United States. In R. Hill & R. Konig (eds.), *Families in East and West*. The Hague: Mouton.

Fodor, J., Bever, T., & Garrett, M. (1974). *The Psychology of Language*. New York: McGraw-Hill.

Foster, S. (1981). The emergence of topic type in children under 2,6: A chicken and egg problem. *Papers and Reports in Child Language Development*, No. 20. Stanford, Calif.: Stanford University Press.

Gallimore, R., Boggs, J., & Jordan, C. (1974). *Culture, Behavior and Education: A Study of Hawaiian Americans*. Beverly Hills, Calif.: Sage.

Garnica, O. (1977). Some prosodic and para-linguistic features of speech to young children. In C. Snow & C. Ferguson (eds.), *Talking to Children: Language Input and Acquisition*. Cambridge: Cambridge University Press.

Geertz, C. (1973). *The Interpretation of Cultures*. New York: Basic Books.

Geertz, H. (1959). The vocabulary of emotion: A study of Javanese socialization processes. *Psychiatry* 22:225–37.

Gleason, J. B., & Weintraub, S. (1978). Input language and the acquisition of communicative competence. In K. Nelson (ed.), *Children's Language*, vol. 1. New York: Gardner Press.

Goffman, E. (1963). *Behavior in Public Places*. New York: Free Press.

Goffman, E. (1967). *Interaction Ritual: Essays on Face to Face Behavior*. Garden City, N.Y.: Doubleday (Anchor Books).

Goldin-Meadow, S. (1977). Structure in a manual language system developed without a language model: Language without a helping hand. In H. Whitaker & H. A. Whitaker (eds.), *Studies in Neurolinguistics*, vol. 4. New York: Academic Press.

Golinkoff, R. (ed.) (1983). *The Transition from Prelinguistic to Linguistic Communication*. Hillsdale, N.J.: Erlbaum.

Goody, E. (1978). Towards a theory of questions. In E. Goody (ed.), *Questions and Politeness*. Cambridge: Cambridge University Press.

Greenfield, P. (1979). Informativeness, presupposition and semantic choice in single-word utterances. In E. Ochs & B. B. Schieffelin (eds.), *Developmental Pragmatics*. New York: Academic Press.

Greenfield, P. M., & Smith, J. H. (1976). *The Structure of Communication in Early Language Development*. New York: Academic Press.

Gumperz, J. (1977). The conversational analysis of interethnic communication. In E. L. Ross (ed.), *Interethnic Communication. Proceedings of the Southern Anthropological Society.* Athens: University of Georgia Press.

Halliday, M. A. K. (1975). *Learning How to Mean: Explorations in the Development of Language.* London: Arnold.

Hamilton, A. (1981). *Nature and Nurture: Aboriginal Childrearing in North-Central Arnhem Land.* Canberra, Australia: Institute of Aboriginal Studies.

Harding, C., & Golinkoff, R. M. (1979). The origins of intentional vocalizations in prelinguistic infants. *Child Development* 50:33–40.

Harkness, S. (1975). Cultural variation in mother's language. In W. von Raffler-Engel (ed.), *Child Language – 1975, Word* 27:495–8.

Harkness, S., & Super, C. (1977). Why African children are so hard to test. In L. L. Adler (ed.), *Issues in Cross Cultural Research: Annals of the New York Academy of Scences* 285:326–31.

Harkness, S., & Super, C. (eds.) (1980). *Anthropological Perspectives on Child Development.* New Directions for Child Development, no. 8. San Francisco: Jossey-Bass.

Heath, S. B. (1983). *Ways with Words: Language, Life and Work in Communities and Classroom.* Cambridge: Cambridge University Press.

Hood, L., McDermott, R., & Cole, M. (1978). Ecological Niche-picking (Working Paper 14). Unpublished manuscript, Rockefeller University, Laboratory of Comparative Human Cognition, New York.

Huttenlocher, J. (1974). The origins of language comprehension. In R. L. Solso (ed.), *Theories of Cognitive Psychology.* Hillsdale, N.J.: Erlbaum.

Hymes, D. (1967). Models of the interaction of language and social setting. *Journal of Social Issues* 23(2):8–28.

Hymes, D. (1974). *Foundations in Sociolinguistics: An Ethnographic Approach.* Philadelphia: University of Pennsylvania Press.

Irvine, J. (1974). Strategies of status manipulation in the Wolof greeting. In R. Bauman & J. Sherzer (eds.), *Explorations in the Ethnography of Speaking.* Cambridge: Cambridge University Press.

Johnston, J. R., & Slobin, D. I. (1979). The development of locative expressions in English, Italian, Serbo-Croatian and Turkish. *Journal of Child Language* 6:529–45.

Karmiloff-Smith, A. (1979). *A Functional Approach to Child Language.* Cambridge: Cambridge University Press.

Keenan, E., Ochs, E., & Schieffelin, B. B. (1976). Topic as a discourse notion: A study of topic in the conversations of children and adults. In C. Li (ed.), *Subject and Topic.* New York: Academic Press.

Kernan, K. T. (1969). The Acquisition of Language by Samoan Children. Unpublished doctoral dissertation, University of California, Berkeley.

Korbin, J. 1978. Caretaking Patterns in a Rural Hawaiian Community. Unpublished doctoral dissertation, University of California, Los Angeles.

Leiderman, P. H., Tulkin, S. R., & Rosenfeld, A. (eds.) (1977). *Culture and Infancy.* New York: Academic Press.

LeVine, R. (1980). Anthropology and child development. *Anthropological Perspectives on Child Development.* New Directions for Child Development, no. 8. San Francisco: Jossey-Bass.

Levy, R. (1973). *The Tahitians.* Chicago: University of Chicago Press.

Lewis, M., & Rosenblum, L. A. (eds.) (1974). *The Effect of the Infant on its Caregiver.* New York: Wiley.

Lieven, E. (1980). Different routes to multiple-word combinations? *Papers and Reports in Child Language Development,* no. 19, Standford University, Stanford, Calif.

Lock, A. (ed.) (1978). *Action, Gesture and Symbol.* London: Academic Press.

Lock, A. (1981). *The Guided Reinvention of Language.* London: Academic Press.

MacNamara, J. (1972). The cognitive basis of language learning in infants. *Psychological Review* 79:1–13.

McNeill, D. (1966). The creation of language by children. In J. Lyons & R. J. Wales (eds.), *Psycholinguistic Papers.* Edinburgh: Edinburgh University Press.

McNeill, D. (1970). *The Acquisition of Language.* Harper & Row.

MacWhinney, B. (1975). Rules, rote and analogy in morphological formation by Hungarian children. *Journal of Child Language* 2:65–77.

MacWhinney, B., & Bates, E. (1978). Sentential devices for conveying givenness and newness: A cross-cultural developmental study. *Journal of Verbal Learning and Verbal Behavior* 17:539–58.

Mead, M. (1927). *Coming of Age in Samoa*. New York: Blue Ribbon Books.

Mead, M. (1975). *Growing Up in New Guinea*. New York: Morrow. (Originally published 1935.)

Mead, M., & MacGregor, F. (1951). *Growth and Culture*. New York: Putnam.

Mead, M., & Wolfenstein, M. (1955). *Childhood in Contemporary Cultures*. Chicago: University of Chicago Press.

Menyuk, P. & Menn, L. (1979). Early strategies for the perception and production of words and sounds. In P. Fletcher & M. Garman (eds.), *Language Acquisition*. Cambridge: Cambridge University Press.

Miller, G., & Chomsky, N. (1963). Finitary models of language users. In R. Bush, E. Galanter, & R. Luce (eds.), *Handbook of Mathematical Psychology*, vol. 2. New York: Wiley.

Miller, P. (1982). *Amy, Wendy and Beth: Learning Language in South Baltimore*. Austin: University of Texas Press.

Montagu, A. (1937). *Coming into Being Among the Australian Aborigines: A Study of the Procreation Beliefs of the Native Tribes of Australia*. London: Routledge.

Montagu, A. (ed.) (1978). *Learning Non-aggression: The Experience of Nonliterate Societies*. Oxford: Oxford University Press.

Much, N., & Shweder, R. (1978). Speaking of rules: The analysis of culture in breach. In W. Damon (ed.), *Moral Development*. New Directions for Child Development, no. 2. San Francisco: Jossey-Bass.

Munroe, R. L., & Munroe, R. N. (1975). *Cross Cultural Human Development*. Monterey, Calif.: Brooks/Cole.

Nelson, K. (1974). Concept, word and sentence: Interrelations in acquisition and development. *Psychological Review* 81:267–85.

Newport, E. L. (1976). Motherese: The speech of mothers to young children. In N. J. Castellan, D. B. Pisoni, & G. R. Potts (eds.), *Cognitive Theory*, vol. 2. Hillsdale, N.J.: Erlbaum.

Newport, E. L. (1981). Constraints on structure: Evidence from American sign language and language learning. In W. A. Collins (ed.), *Minnesota Symposium on Child Psychology*, vol. 14. Hillsdale, N.J.: Erlbaum.

Newport, E. L., Gleitman, H., & Gleitman, L. R. (1977). Mother, I'd rather do it myself: Some effects and non-effects of maternal speech style. In C. Snow & C. Ferguson (eds.), *Talking to Children: Language Input and Acquisition*. Cambridge: Cambridge University Press.

Newson, J. (1977). An intersubjective approach to the systematic description of mother–infant interaction. In H. R. Schaffer (ed.), *Studies in Mother–Infant Interaction*. London: Academic Press.

Newson, J. (1978). Dialogue and development. In A. Lock (ed.), *Action, Gesture and Symbol*. London: Academic Press.

Ninio, A. (1979). The naive theory of the infant and other maternal attitudes in two subgroups in Israel. *Child Development* 50:976–80.

Norman, D. A. (1975). Cognitive organization and learning. In P. M. A. Rabbitt & S. Dornic (eds.), *Attention and Performance V*. New York: Academic Press.

Ochs, E. (1982a). Affect in Samoan Child Language. Paper presented to the Stanford Child Language Research Forum, Stanford, Calif.

Ochs, E. (1982b). Ergativity and word order in Samoan child language: A sociolinguistic study. *Language* 58:646–71.

Ochs, E. (1982c). Talking to children in Western Samoa. *Language in Society* 11:77–104.

Ochs, E. (1985). Variation and error: A sociolinguistic study of language acquisition in Samoa. In D. I. Slobin (ed.), *The Crosslinguistic Study of Language Acquisition*. Hillsdale, N.J.: Erlbaum.

Ochs, E., Schieffelin, B. B., & Platt, M. (1979). Propositions across utterances and speaker. In E. Ochs & B. B. Schieffelin (eds.), *Developmental Pragmatics*. New York: Academic Press.

Philips, S. (1983). *The Invisible Culture*. New York: Longman.

Phillips, J. (1973). Syntax and vocabulary of mothers' speech to young children: Age and sex comparisons. *Child Development* 44:182–5.

Piaget, J. (1955). *The Language and Thought of the Child*. London: Routledge & Kegan Paul. (Originally published 1926.)

Piattelli-Palmarini, M. (ed.) (1980). *Language and Learning: The Debate Between Jean Piaget and Noam Chomsky*, Cambridge, Mass.: Harvard University Press.

Platt, M. (1980). The acquisition of "come," "give," and "bring" by Samoan children. *Papers and Reports in Child Language Development*, no. 19. Stanford, Calif.: Stanford University.

Richards, M. P. M. (ed.) (1974). *The Integration of a Child into a Social World*. Cambridge: Cambridge University Press.

Ryan, J. (1974). Early language development: Towards a communicational analysis. In M. P. M. Richards (ed.), *The Integration of a Child into a Social World*. Cambridge: Cambridge University Press.

Sachs, J. (1977). Adaptive significance of input to infants. In C. Snow & C. Ferguson (eds.), *Talking to Children: Language Input and Acquisition*. Cambridge: Cambridge University Press.

Sachs, J., Brown, R., & Salerno, R. (1976). Adults' speech to children. In W. von Raffler-Engel & Y. Lebrun (eds.), *Baby Talk and Infant Speech*. Lisse: Riddler Press.

Sachs, J., & Devin, J. (1976). Young children's use of age-appropriate speech styles. *Journal of Child Language* 3:81–98.

Schaffer, H. R. (ed.) (1977). *Studies in Mother–Infant Interaction*. London: Academic Press.

Schieffelin, B. B. (1979). Getting it together: An ethnographic approach to the study of the development of communicative competence. In E. Ochs & B. B. Schieffelin (eds.), *Developmental Pragmatics*. New York: Academic Press.

Schieffelin, B. B. (1981). A developmental study of pragmatic appropriateness of word order and case marking in Kaluli. In W. Deutsch (ed.), *The Child's Construction of Language*. London: Academic Press.

Schieffelin, B. B. (1985). Acquisition of Kaluli. In D. I. Slobin (ed.), *The Crosslinguistic Study of Language Acquisition*. Hillsdale, N.J.: Erlbaum.

Schieffelin, B. B. (1990). *The Give and Take of Everyday Life: Language Socialization of Kaluli Children*. Cambridge: Cambridge University Press.

Schieffelin, B. B., & Eisenberg, A. (1984). Cultural variation in children's conversations. In R. L. Schiefelbusch & J. Pickar (eds.), *Communicative Competence: Acquisition and Intervention*. Baltimore: University Park Press.

Schieffelin, E. L. (1976). *The Sorrow of the Lonely and the Burning of the Dancers*. New York: St. Martin's Press.

Schlesinger, I. M. (1974). Relational concepts underlying language. In R. Schiefelbusch & L. Lloyd (eds.), *Language Perspectives – Acquisition, Retardation and Intervention*. Baltimore: University Park Press.

Scollon, R. (1976). *Conversations with a One Year Old*. Honolulu: University Press of Hawaii.

Scollon, R. & Scollon, S. (1981). The literate two-year old: The fictionalization of self. Abstracting themes: a Chipewyan two-year-old. *Narrative, Literacy and Face in Interethnic Communication*. Vol. 7 of R. O. Freedle (ed.), *Advances in Discourse Processes*. Norwood, N.J.: Ablex.

Shatz, M. (1978). The relationship between cognitive processes and the development of communication skills. In C. B. Keasey (ed.), *Nebraska Symposium on Motivation*, vol. 25. Lincoln: University of Nebraska Press.

Shatz, M. (1981). Learning the rules of the game: Four views of the relation between social interaction and syntax acquisition. In W. Deutsch (ed.), *The Child's Construction of Language*. London: Academic Press.

Shatz, M. (1983). Communication. In P. Mussen, J. H. Flavell, & E. M. Markman (eds.), *Handbook of Child Psychology* (4th edn.), Volume III: *Cognitive Development*. New York: John Wiley & Sons.

Shatz, M., & Gelman, R. (1973). The development of communication skills: Modifications in the speech of young children as a function of listener. *Monographs of the Society for Research in Child Development*, 152 (38, serial no. 5).

Shore, B. (1982). *Sala' ilua: A Samoan Mystery*. New York: Columbia University Press.

Shotter, J. (1978). The cultural context of communication studies: Theoretical and methodological issues. In A. Lock (ed.), *Action, Gesture and Symbol*. London: Academic Press.

Sinclair, H. (1971). Sensorimotor action patterns as a condition for the acquisition of syntax. In R. Huxley & E. Ingram (eds.), *Language Acquisition: Models and Methods*. New York: Academic Press.

Skinner, B. F. (1957). *Verbal Behavior*. New York: Appleton-Century-Crofts.

Slobin, D. I. (1973). Cognitive prerequisites for grammar. In C. Ferguson & D. I. Slobin (eds.), *Studies in Child Language Development*. New York: Holt, Rinehart, and Winston.

Slobin, D. I. (1979). *Psycholinguistics*, 2nd edn. Glenview, Ill.: Scott Foresman.

Slobin, D. I. (1981). The origin of grammatical encoding of events. In W. Deutsch (ed.), *The Child's Construction of Language*. London: Academic Press.

Slobin, D. I. (1982). Universal and particular in the acquisition of language. In E. Wanner & L. R. Gleitman (eds.), *Language Acquisition: The State of the Art*. Cambridge: Cambridge University Press.

Slobin, D. I. (ed.) (1967). *A Field Manual for Cross-cultural Study of the Acquisition of Communicative Competence*. Language Behavior Research Laboratory, University of California, Berkeley.

Slobin, D. I. (ed.) (1985). *The Crosslinguistic Study of Language Acquisition*. Hillsdale, N.J.: Erlbaum.

Snow, C. (1972). Mothers' speech to children learning language. *Child Development* 43:549–65.

Snow, C. (1977a). The development of conversation between mothers and babies. *Journal of Child Language* 4:1–22.

Snow, C. (1977b). Mothers' speech research: From input to inter-action. In C. Snow & C. Ferguson (eds.), *Talking to Children: Language Input and Acquisition*. Cambridge: Cambridge University Press.

Snow, C. (1979). Conversations with children. In P. Fletcher & M. Garman (eds.), *Language Acquisition*. Cambridge: Cambridge University Press.

Snow, C., de Blauw, A., & van Roosmalen, G. (1979). Talking and playing with babies: The role of ideologies of child-rearing. In M. Bullowa (ed.), *Before Speech: The Beginnings of Interpersonal Communication*. Cambridge: Cambridge University Press.

Snow, C., & Ferguson, C. (eds.) (1977). *Talking to Children: Language Input and Acquisition*. Cambridge: Cambridge University Press.

Stern, D. (1977). *The First Relationship: Infant and Mother*. Cambridge, Mass.: Harvard University Press.

Stross, B. (1972). Verbal processes in Tzeltal speech socialization. *Anthropological Linguistics* 14:1.

Sugarman, S. (1984). The development of preverbal communication: Its contribution and limits in promoting the development of language. In R. L. Schiefelbusch & J. Pickar (eds.), *Communicative Competence: Acquisition and Intervention*. Baltimore: University Park Press.

Trevarthen, C. (1979a). Communication and cooperation in early infancy: A description of primary intersubjectivity. In M. Bullowa (ed.), *Before Speech: The Beginnings of Interpersonal Communication*. Cambridge: Cambridge University Press.

Trevarthen, C. (1979b). Instincts for human understanding and for cultural cooperation: Their development in infancy. In M. von Cranach, K. Foppa, W. Lepenies, & D. Ploog (eds.), *Human Ethology: Claims and Limits of a New Discipline*. Cambridge: Cambridge University Press.

van der Geest, T. (1977). Some interactional aspects of language acquisition. In C. Snow & C. Ferguson (eds.), *Talking to Children: Language Input and Acquisition*. Cambridge: Cambridge University Press.

von Sturmer, D. E. (1980). Rights in Nurturing. Unpublished master's thesis, Australian National University, Canberra.

Vygotsky, L. S. (1962). *Thought and Language*. Cambridge, Mass.: MIT Press.

Wagner, D., & Stevenson, H. W. (eds.) (1982). *Cultural Perspectives on Child Development*. San Francisco: Freeman.

Wanner E., & Gleitman, L. R. (eds.) (1982) *Language Acquisition: The State of the Art*. Cambridge: Cambridge University Press.

Ward, M. (1971). *Them Children: A Study in Language Learning*. New York: Holt, Rinehart, and Winston.

Watson-Gegeo, K., & Gegeo, D. (1982). Calling Out and Repeating: Two Key Routines in Kwara'ae Children's Language Acquisition. Paper presented at the American Anthropological Association meetings, Washington, D.C.

Weisner, T. S., & Gallimore, R. (1977). My brother's keeper: Child and sibling caretaking. *Current Anthropology* 18(2):169–90.

Werner, H., & Kaplan, B. (1963). *Symbol Formation*. New York: Wiley.

Whiting, B. (ed.) (1963). *Six Cultures: Studies of Child Rearing*. New York: Wiley.

Whiting, B., & Whiting, J. (1975). *Children of Six Cultures*. Cambridge, Mass.: Harvard University Press.

Williams, T. R. (1969). *A Borneo Childhood: Enculturation in Dusun Society*. New York: Holt, Rinehart, and Winston.

Wills, D. (1977). Culture's Cradle: Social Structural and Interactional Aspects of Senegalese Socialization. Unpublished doctoral dissertation, University of Texas, Austin.

12

Participant Structures and Communicative Competence: Warm Springs Children in Community and Classroom

Susan U. Philips

Introduction

Recent studies of North American Indian education problems have indicated that in many ways Indian children are not culturally oriented to the ways in which classroom learning is conducted. The Wax–Dumont study (Wax et al., 1964) of the Pine Ridge Sioux discusses the lack of interest children show in what goes on in school and Wolcott's (1967) description of a Kwakiutl school tells of the Indian children's organized resistance to his ways of structuring classroom learning. Cazden and John (1968) suggest that the "styles of learning" through which Indian children are enculturated at home differ markedly from those to which they are introduced in the classroom. And Hymes (1967) has pointed out that this may lead to sociolinguistic interference when teacher and student do not recognize these differences in their efforts to communicate with one another.

On the Warm Springs Indian Reservation in central Oregon, where I have been carrying out research in patterns of speech usage, teachers have pointed to similar phenomena, particularly in their repeated statements that Indian children show a great deal of reluctance to talk in class, and that they participate less and less in verbal interaction as they go through school. To help account for the reluctance of the Indian children of Warm Springs (and elsewhere as well) to participate in classroom verbal interactions, I am going to demonstrate how some of the social conditions governing or determining when it is appropriate for a student to speak in the classroom differ from those that govern verbal participation and other types of communicative performances in the Warm Springs Indian community's social interactions.

The data on which discussion of these differences will be based are drawn, first of all, from comparative observations in all-Indian classes in the reservation grammar school and non-Indian or white classes in another grammar school at the first- and sixth-grade levels. The purpose here is to define the communicative contexts in which Indian and non-Indian behavior and participation differ, and to describe the ways in which they differ.

After defining the situations or social contexts in which Indian students' verbal participation is minimal, discussion will shift to consideration of the social conditions in Indian cultural contexts that define when speaking is appropriate, attending to children's learning experiences both at home and in the community-wide social activities in which they participate.

The end goal of this discussion will be to demonstrate that the social conditions that define when a person uses speech in Indian social situations are present in classroom situations in which Indian students use speech a great deal, and absent in the more prevalent classroom situations in which they fail to participate verbally.

There are several aspects of verbal participation in classroom contexts that should be kept in mind during the discussion of why Indians are reluctant to talk. First of all, a student's use of speech in the classroom during structured lesson sessions is a communicative performance in more than one sense of "performance." It involves demonstration of sociolinguistic competency, itself a complex combination of linguistic competency and social competency involving knowledge of when and in what style one must present one's utterances, among other things. This type of competency, however, is involved in every speech act. But in the classroom there is a second sense in which speaking is a performance that is more special although not unique to classroom interactions. In class, speaking is the first and primary mode for communicating competency in all of the areas of skill and knowledge that schools purport to teach. Children communicate what they have learned to the teacher and their fellow students through speaking; only rarely do they demonstrate what they know through physical activity or creation of material objects. While writing eventually becomes a second important channel or mode for communicating knowledge or demonstrating skills, writing, as a skill, is to a great extent developed through verbal interaction between student and teacher, as is reading.

Consequently, if talk fails to occur, then the channel through which learning sessions are conducted is cut off, and the structure of classroom interaction that depends on dialogue between teacher and student breaks down and no longer functions as it is supposed to. Thus, while the question "Why don't Indian kids talk more in class?" is in a sense a very simple one, it is also a very basic one, and the lack of talk a problem that needs to be dealt with if Indian children are to learn what is taught in American schools.

Cultural and Educational Background of the Warm Springs Indians

Before embarking on the main task of the discussion outlined above, some background information on the setting of the research, the Warm Springs Indian Reservation, is necessary to provide some sense of the extent to which the cultural, linguistic, and educational situation there may be similar to or different from that of North American Indians in other parts of the country.

Today the reservation of 564,209 acres is populated by some 1,500 descendants of the "bands" of Warm Springs Sahaptin, Wasco Chinook, and Paiute Indians who gradually settled there after the reservation was established in 1855. The Warm Springs Indians have always been the largest group numerically, followed by the Wasco, with the Paiutes so small in number that their influence in the culture of the reservation has been of relatively small significance. Although they spoke different languages, the Warm Springs and Wasco groups were geographically quite close to one another before the reservation was established and were culturally similar in many respects. Thus, after over a hundred years together on the reservation, they presently share approximately the same cultural background.

The "tribe," as the Indians of Warm Springs now refer to themselves collectively, today comprises a single closely integrated community with strong tribal leadership, which receives the full backing of the people. Until after World War II the Indians here experienced considerable poverty and hardship. Since that time, however, tribal income from the sale of reservation timber has considerably improved the economic situation, as has tribal purchase of a sawmill and a small resort, which provide jobs for tribal members.

With the income from these enterprises, and drawing as well on various forms of federal aid available to them, the tribe has developed social programs to help members of the tribe in a number of ways. Chief among their concerns is the improvement of the education of their children, whom they recognize to be less successful in school than their fellow non-Indian students. Tribal leaders have taken numerous important steps to increase the educational opportunities of their young people, including the establishment of a scholarship program for college students and a tribal education office with half a dozen full-time employees supervising the tribally sponsored kindergarten, study halls, and community center courses as well as the federally sponsored programs such as VISTA, Head Start, and Neighborhood Youth Corps. The education office employees also act as liaisons between parents of children with problems in school and the administrators and teachers of the public schools the children attend. In sum, the tribe is doing a great deal to provide the Warm Springs children with the best education possible.

Despite their efforts, and those of the public school officials, who are under considerable pressure from tribal leaders to bring about changes in the schools that will result in the improvement of the academic performance of Indian students, the Indians continue to do poorly in school when compared to the non-Indian students in the same school system.

One of the most important things to know about the schools the Indian children attend is the "ethnic" composition of their classes. For the first six grades, Warm Springs children attend a public school that is located on the reservation. Here their classmates are almost all Indians and their teachers are all non-Indians or whites. After the first six grades, they are bused into the town of Madras, a distance of fifteen to thirty miles, depending on where they live on the reservation. Here, encountering their fellow white students for the first time, the Indian students are outnumbered by a ratio of five to one. From the point of view of tribal leaders, it is only when they reach the high school, or ninth grade, that the Indian students' "problems" really become serious, for it is at this point that hostility between Indian and non-Indian is expressed openly, and the Indian students' failure to participate in classroom discussions and school activities is recognized by everyone.

There is, however, abundant evidence that Indian students' learning difficulties begin long before they reach the high school. The statistics that are available on their educational achievements and problems are very similar to those which have been reported for Indians in other parts of the country (Berry, 1969). On national achievement tests the Warm Springs Indian children consistently score lower than the national average in skills tested. Their lowest scores are in areas involving verbal competencies, and the gap between their level of performance on such tests and the national averages widens as they continue into the higher grade levels (Zentner, 1960).

Although many people on the reservation still speak an Indian language, today all of the Warm Springs children in school are monolingual speakers of English. The dialect of English they speak, however, is not the Standard English of their teachers, but one that is distinctive to the local Indian community, and that in some aspects of grammar and phonology shows influence from the Indian languages spoken on the reservation.

In addition, there is some evidence that many children are exposed to talk in the Indian languages that may affect their acquisition of English. Because older people on the reservation are very concerned about the Indian languages' dying out, many of them make a concerted effort to teach young children an Indian language, particularly the Warm Springs Sahaptin. Thus some infants and young children are spoken to consistently in both Warm Springs and English. Every Indian child still knows some Indian words, and many informants report that while their children refuse to speak the Warm Springs Sahaptin – particularly after they start school – they understand much of what is said to them in it.

The effects of the acquisition of a very local dialect of English and the exposure to the Warm Springs language on classroom learning are difficult for local educators to assess because children say so little in the presence of the teachers. Observations of Indian children's verbal interactions outside the classroom indicate a control and productive use of linguistic rules that is manifested infrequently in classroom utterances, indicating that the appropriate social conditions for speech use, from the Indians' point of view, are lacking. It is this problem with appropriate social contexts for speaking that will now be considered in greater detail.

Conditions for Speech Use in School Classrooms

When the children first enter school, the most immediate concern of the teachers is to teach them the basic rules for classroom behavior upon which the maintenance of continuous and ordered activity depends. One of the most important of these is the distinction between the roles of teacher and student. In this there is the explicit and implicit assumption that the teacher controls all of the activity taking place in the classroom and the students accept and are obedient to her authority. She determines the sociospatial arrangements of all interactions; she decrees when and where movement takes place within the classroom. And most important for our present concern with communication, she determines who will talk and when they will talk.

While some class activities are designed to create the sense of a class of students as an organized group with class officers, or student monitors carrying out various responsibilities contributing to the group, actual spontaneous organization within the student group that has not been officially designated by the teacher is not encouraged. It interferes with the scheduling of activities as the teacher has organized them. The classroom situation is one in which the teacher relates to the students as an undifferentiated mass, much as a performer in front of an audience. Or she relates to each student on a one-to-one basis, often with the rest of the class as the still undifferentiated audience for the performance of the individual child.

In comparing the Indian and non-Indian learning of these basic classroom distinctions which define the conditions in which communication will take place, differences are immediately apparent. Indian first-graders are consistently slower to begin acting in accordance with these basic arrangements. They do not remember to raise their hands and wait to be called on before speaking, they wander to parts of the room other than the one in which the teacher is conducting a session, and they talk to other students while the teacher is talking, much further into the school year than do students in non-Indian classes. And the Indian children continue to fail to conform to classroom procedure much more frequently *through* the school year.

In contrast to the non-Indian students, the Indian students consistently show a great deal more interest in what their fellow students are doing than in what the teacher is doing. While non-Indian students constantly make bids for the attention of their teachers, through initiating dialogue with them as well as through other acts, Indian students do very little of this. Instead they make bids for the attention of their fellow students through talk. At the first-grade level, and more noticeably (with new teachers only) at the sixth-grade level, Indian students often act in deliberate organized opposition to the teacher's directions. Thus, at the first-grade level, if one student is told not to put his feet on his chair, another will immediately put his feet on his chair, and he will be imitated by other students who see him do this. In non-Indian classrooms, such behavior was observed only at the sixth-grade level in interaction with a substitute teacher.

In other words, there is, on the part of Indian students, relatively less interest, desire, and/or ability to internalize and act in accordance with some of the basic rules underlying classroom maintenance of orderly interaction. Most notably, Indian students are less willing than non-Indian students to accept the teacher as director and controller of all classroom activities. They are less interested in developing the one-to-one communicative relationship between teacher and student, and more interested in maintaining and developing relationships with their peers, regardless of what is going on in the classroom.

Within the basic framework of teacher-controlled interaction, there are several possible variations in structural arrangements of interaction, which will be referred to from here on as "participant structures." Teachers use different participant structures, or ways of arranging verbal interaction with students, for communicating different types of educational material, and for providing variation in the presentation of the same material to hold children's interest. Often the notion that different kinds of materials are taught better and more efficiently through one sort of participant structuring rather than another is also involved.

In the first type of participant structure the teacher interacts with all of the students. She may address all of them, or a single student in the presence of the rest of the students. The students may respond as a group or chorus in unison, or individually in the presence of their peers. And finally, student verbal participation may be either voluntary, as when the teacher asks who knows the answer to her question, or compulsory, as when the teacher asks a particular student to answer, whether his hand is raised or not. And always it is the teacher who determines whether she talks to one or to all, receives responses individually or in chorus, and voluntarily or without choice.

In a second type of participant structure, the teacher interacts with only some of the students in the class at once, as in reading groups. In such contexts participation is usually mandatory rather than voluntary, individual rather than chorus, and each student is expected to participate or perform verbally, for the main purpose of such smaller groups is to provide the teacher with the opportunity to assess the knowledge acquired by each individual student. During such sessions, the remaining students who are not interacting with the teacher are usually working alone or independently at their desks on reading or writing assignments.

A third participant structure consists of all students working independently at their desks, but with the teacher explicitly available for student-initiated verbal interaction, in which the child indicates he wants to communicate with the teacher by raising his hand, or by approaching the teacher at her desk. In either case, the interaction between student and teacher is not witnessed by the other students in that they do not hear what is said.

A fourth participant structure, and one that occurs infrequently in the upper primary grades, and rarely, if ever, in the lower grades, consists of the students' being divided into small groups that they run themselves, though always with the more distant supervision of the teacher, and usually for the purpose of so-called "group projects." As a rule such groups have official "chairmen," who assume what is in other contexts the teacher's authority in regulating who will talk when.

In observing and comparing Indian and non-Indian participation or communicative performances in these four different structural variations of contexts in which communication takes place, differences between the two groups again emerge very clearly.

In the first two participant structures where students must speak out individually in front of the other students, Indian children show considerable reluctance to participate, particularly when compared to non-Indian students. When the teacher is in front of the whole class, they volunteer to speak relatively rarely, and teachers at the Warm Springs grammar school generally hold that this reluctance to volunteer to speak out in front of other students increases as the children get older.

When the teacher is with a small group, and each individual must give some kind of communicative verbal performance in turn, Indian children much more frequently refuse, or fail to utter a word when called upon, and much less frequently, if ever, urge the teacher to call on them than the non-Indians do. When the Indian children do speak, they speak very softly, often in tones inaudible to a person more than a few feet away, and in utterances typically shorter or briefer than those of their non-Indian counterparts.

In situations where the teacher makes herself available for student-initiated communication during sessions in which students are working independently on assignments that do not involve verbal communication, students at the first-grade level in the Indian classes at first rarely initiate contact with the teachers. After a few weeks in a classroom they do so as frequently as the non-Indian students. And at the sixth-grade level Indian students initiate such relatively private encounters with teachers much more frequently than non-Indian students do.

When students control and direct the interaction in small group projects, as described for the fourth type of participant structure, there is again a marked contrast between the behavior of Indian and non-Indian students. It is in such contexts that Indian students become most fully involved in what they are doing, concentrating completely on their work until it is completed, talking a great deal to one another within the group, and competing, with explicit remarks to that effect, with the other groups. Non-Indian students take more time in "getting organized," disagree and argue more regarding how to go about a task, rely more heavily on appointed chairmen for arbitration and decision-making, and show less interest, at least explicitly, in competing with other groups from their class.

Observations of the behavior of both Indian and non-Indian children outside the classroom during recess periods and teacher-organized physical education periods provide further evidence that the differences in readiness to participate in interaction are related to the way in which the interaction is organized and controlled.

When such outside-class activity is organized by the teachers, it is for the purpose of teaching children games through which they develop certain physical and social skills. If the games involve a role distinction between leader and followers in which the leader must tell the others what to do – as in Simon Says, Follow the Leader, Green Light Red Light, and even Farmer in the Dell – Indian children show a great deal of reluctance to assume the leadership role. This is particularly true when the child is appointed leader by the teacher and must be repeatedly urged to act in telling the others what to do before doing so. Non-Indian children, in contrast, vie eagerly for such positions, calling upon the teacher and/or other students to select them.

If such playground activity is unsupervised, and the children are left to their own devices, Indian children become involved in games of team competition much more frequently than non-Indian children. And they sustain such game activities for longer periods of time and at younger ages than non-Indian children. While non-Indian children tend more to play in groups of two and three, and in the upper primary grades to form "friendships" with one or two persons from their own class in school, Indian children interact with a greater number of children consistently, and maintain friendships and teams with children from classes in school other than their own.

In reviewing the comparison of Indian and non-Indian students' verbal participation under different social conditions, two features of the Warm Springs children's behavior stand out. First of all, they show relatively less willingness to perform or participate verbally when they must speak alone in front of other students. Second, they are relatively less eager to speak when the point at which speech occurs is dictated by the teacher, as it is during sessions when the teacher is working with the whole class or a small group. They also show considerable reluctance to be placed in the "leadership" play roles that require them to assume the same type of dictation of the acts of their peers.

Parallel to these negative responses are the positive ones of a relatively greater willingness to participate in group activities that do not create a distinction between individual performer and audience, and a relatively greater use of opportunities in which the point at which the student speaks or acts is determined by himself, rather than by the teacher or a "leader."

It is apparent that there are situations arising in the classroom that do allow for the Indian students to verbalize or communicate under or within the participant structures their behavior indicates they prefer; otherwise it would not have been possible to make the distinctions between their behavior and that of non-Indians in the areas just discussed. However, the frequency of occurrence of such situations in the classroom is very low when compared to the frequency of occurrence of the type of participant structuring in which Indian students fail to participate verbally, particularly in the lower grades.

In other words, most verbal communication that is considered part of students' learning experience does take the structure of individual students' speaking in front of other students. About half of this speaking is voluntary insofar as students are invited to volunteer to answer, and half is compulsory in that a specific student is called on and expected to answer. In either case, it is the teacher who establishes when talk will occur and within what kind of participant structure.

There are many reasons why most of the verbal communication takes place under such conditions. Within our particular education system, a teacher needs to know how much her students have learned or absorbed from the material she has presented. Students' verbal responses provide one means – and the primary means, particularly before students learn to write – of measuring their progress, and are thus the teacher's feedback. And, again within our particular educational system, it is not group but individual progress with which our teachers are expected to be concerned.

In addition, it is assumed that students will learn from each others' performances both what is false or wrong, and what is true or correct. Another aspect of this type of public performance that may increase educators' belief in its efficacy is the students' awareness that these communicative acts *are* performances, in the sense of being demonstrations of competency. The concomitant awareness that success or failure in such acts is a measure of their worth in the eyes of those present increases their motivation to do well. Thus they will remember when they made a mistake and try harder to do well to avoid public failure, in a way they would not were their performances in front of a smaller number of people. As I will try to demonstrate further on, however, the educators' assumption of the validity or success of this type of enculturation process, which can briefly be referred to as "learning through public mistakes," is not one the Indians share, and this has important implications for our understanding of Indian behavior in the classroom.

The consequences of the Indians' reluctance to participate in these speech situations are several. First of all, the teacher loses the primary means she has of receiving feedback on the children's acquisition of knowledge, and is thus less able to establish at what point she must begin again to instruct them, particularly in skills requiring a developmental sequencing, as in reading.

A second consequence of this reluctance to participate in speech situations requiring mandatory individual performances is that the teachers in the Warm Springs grammar school modify their teaching approach whenever possible to accommodate, in a somewhat ad hoc fashion, what they refer to as the Indian students' "shyness." In the first grade it is not easy to make very many modifications because of what teachers perceive as a close relationship between the material being taught and the methods used to teach it. There is some feeling, also, that the teaching methods that can be effective with children at age six are somewhat limited in range. However, as students go up through the grades, there is an increasing tendency for teachers to work with the notion, not always a correct one, that given the same body of material there are a number of different ways of "presenting" it, or in the terms being used here, a range of different participant structures and modes of communication (e.g., talking versus reading and writing) that can be used.

Even so, at the first-grade level there are already some changes made to accommodate the Indian children that are notable. When comparing the Indian first-grade classes with the non-Indian first-grade classes, one finds very few word games being used that involve students' giving directions to one another. And even more conspicuous in Indian classes is the absence of the ubiquitous "show and tell" or "sharing," through which students learn to get up in front of the class, standing where the teacher stands, and presenting, as the teacher might, a monologue relating an experience or describing a treasured object that is supposed to be of interest to the rest of the class. When asked whether this activity was used in the classroom, one teacher explained that she had previously used it, but so few children ever volunteered to "share" that she finally discontinued it.

By the time the students reach the sixth grade, the range of modes and settings for communication has increased a great deal, and the opportunity for elimination of some participant structures in preference to others is used by the teachers. As one sixth-grade teacher put it, "I spend as little time in front of the class as possible." In comparison with non-Indian classes, Indian classes have a relatively greater number of group "projects." Thus, while non-Indian students are learning about South American history through reading texts and answering the teacher's questions, Indian students are doing group-planned and -executed murals depicting a particular stage in Latin American history; while non-Indian students are reading science texts and answering questions about how electricity is generated, Indian students are doing group-run experiments with batteries and motors.

Similarly, in the Indian classes "reports" given by individual students are almost nonexistent, but are a typical means in non-Indian classes for demonstrating knowledge through verbal performance. And finally, while in non-Indian classes students are given opportunities to ask the teacher questions in front of the class, and do so, Indian students are given fewer opportunities for this because when they do have the opportunity, they don't use it. Rather, the teacher of Indians allows more periods in which she is available for individual students to approach her alone and ask their questions where no one else can hear them.

The teachers who make these adjustments, and not all do, are sensitive to the inclinations of their students and want to teach them through means to which they most readily adapt. However, by doing so they are avoiding teaching the Indian children how to communicate in precisely the contexts in which they are least able but most need to learn if they are to "do well in school." The teachers handicap themselves by setting up performance situations for the students in which they are least able to arrive at the evaluations of individual competence upon which they rely for feedback to establish at what level they must begin to teach. And it is not at all clear that students do acquire the same information through one form of communication as they do through another. Thus these manipulations of communication settings and participant structures, which are intended to transmit knowledge to the students creatively through the means to which they are most adjusted, may actually be causing the students to miss completely types of information their later high school teachers will assume they picked up in grammar school.

The consequences of this partial adaptation to Indian modes of communication become apparent when the Indian students join the non-Indian students at the junior and senior high school levels. Here, where the Indian students are outnumbered five to one, there is no manipulation and selection of communication settings to suit the inclinations of the Indians. Here the teachers complain that the Indian students never talk in class, and never ask questions, and everyone wonders why.

It does not necessarily follow from this that these most creative teachers at the grade school level should stop what they are doing. Perhaps it should be the teachers at the junior and senior high school levels who make similar adaptations. Which of these occurs (or possibly there are *other* alternatives) depends on the goals the Indian community has for its youngsters, an issue that will be briefly considered in the conclusion of the paper.

Conditions for Speech Use in the Warm Springs Indian Community

To understand why the Warm Springs Indian children speak out readily under some social conditions but fail to do so under others, it is necessary to examine the sociolinguistic assumptions determining the conditions for communicative performances, particularly those involving explicit demonstrations of knowledge or skill, in the Indian community. It will be possible here to deal with only some of the many aspects of communication involved. Attention will focus first on the social structuring of learning situations or contexts in which knowledge and skills are communicated to children in Indian homes. Then some consideration will be given to the underlying rules or conditions for participation in the community-wide social events that preschool children, as well as older children, learn through attending such events with their families.

The Indian child's preschool and outside-school enculturation at home differs from that of many non-Indian or white middle-class children's in that a good deal of the responsibility for the care and training of children is assumed by persons other than the parents of the children. In many homes the oldest children, particularly if they are girls, assume these responsibilities when the parents are at home, as well as when they are not. Frequently, also, grandparents, uncles, and aunts assume the full-time responsibility for care and instruction of children. Children thus become accustomed to interacting with and following the instructions and orders of a greater number of people than is the case with non-Indian children. Equally important is the fact that all of the people with whom Indian children form such reciprocal nurturing and learning relationships are kinsmen. Indian children are rarely, if ever, taken care of by "baby-sitters" from outside the family. Most of their playmates before beginning school are their siblings and cousins, and these peer relationships typically continue to be the strongest bonds of friendship through school and adult life, later providing a basis for reciprocal aid in times of need, and companionship in many social activities.

Indian children are deliberately taught skills around the home (for girls) and in the outdoors (for boys) at an earlier age than many middle-class non-Indian children. Girls, for example, learn to cook some foods before they are eight, and by this age may be fully competent in cleaning a house without any aid or supervision from adults.

There are other areas of competence in which Indian children are expected to be proficient at earlier ages than non-Indian children, for which the means of enculturation or socialization are less visible and clear-cut. While still in grammar school, at the age of ten or eleven, some children are considered capable of spending afternoons and evenings in the company of only other children, without the necessity of accounting for their whereabouts or asking permission to do whatever specific activity is involved. At this same age many are also considered capable of deciding where they want to live, and for what reasons one residence is preferable to another. They may spend weeks or months at a time living with one relative or another, until it is no longer possible to say that they live in any particular household.

In general, then, Warm Springs Indian children become accustomed to self-determination of action, accompanied by very little disciplinary control from older relatives, at much younger ages than middle-class white children do.

In the context of the household, learning takes place through several sorts of somewhat different processes. First of all, children are present at many adult interactions as silent but attentive observers. While it is not yet clear how adult activities in which children are not full participants are distinguished from those in which children may participate fully, and from those for which they are not allowed to be present at all, there are clearly marked differences. What is most remarkable, however, is that there are many adult conversations to which children pay a great deal of silent, patient attention. This contrasts sharply with the behavior of non-Indian children, who show little patience in similar circumstances, desiring either to become a full participant through verbal interaction, or to become completely involved in some other activity.

There is some evidence that this silent listening and watching was, in the Warm Springs culture, traditionally the first step in learning skills of a fairly complex nature. For example, older women reminisce about being required to watch their elder relatives tan hides when they were very young, rather than being allowed to play. And certainly the winter evening events of myth-telling, which provided Indian children with their first explicitly taught moral lessons, involved them as listening participants rather than as speakers.

A second type of learning involves the segmentation of a task by an older relative, and the partial carrying out of the task or one of its segments by the child. In household tasks, for example, a child is given a very simple portion of a job (e.g., in cleaning a room the child may begin by helping move the furniture) and works in cooperation with and under the supervision of an older relative. Such activities involve a small amount of verbal instruction or direction from the older relative, and allow for questions on the part of the child. Gradually the child comes to learn all of the skills involved in a particular process, consistently under the supervision of an older relative who works along with him.

This mode of instruction is not unique to the Warm Springs Indians, of course; many non-Indian parents use similar methods. However, there are aspects of this type of instruction that differ from its use among non-Indians. First of all, when it occurs among the Indians it is likely to be preceded by the long periods of observation just described. The absence of such observation among non-Indian children is perhaps replaced by elaborate verbal instructions outlining the full scope of a task before the child attempts any part of it.

A second way in which this type of instruction among the Warm Springs Indians differs from that of non-Indians is the absence of "testing" of the child's skill by the instructing kinsman before the child exercises the skill unsupervised. Although it is not yet clear how this works in a diversity of situations, it appears that in many areas of skill, the child takes it upon himself to test the skill unsupervised and alone, without other people around. In this way, if he is unsuccessful his failure is not seen by others. If he is successful, he can show the results of his success to those by whom he has been taught, whether it be in the form of a deer that has been shot, a hide tanned, a piece of beadwork completed, or a dinner on the table when the adults come home from work.

Again there is some evidence that this type of private individual's testing of competency, followed by public demonstration only when competency is fully developed and certain, has been traditional in the Warm Springs Indian culture. The most dramatic examples of this come from the processes of acquisition of religious and ritual knowledge. In the vision quests through which adolescents, or children of even younger ages, acquired spirit power, individuals spent long periods in isolated mountain areas from which they were expected to emerge with skills they had not previously demonstrated. While some of these abilities were not fully revealed until later in life, the child was expected to be able to relate some experience of a supernatural nature that would prove that he had, in fact, been visited by a spirit. Along the same lines, individuals until very recently received and learned, through dreams and visions, ritual songs that they would sing for the first time in full and completed form in the presence of others.

The contexts described here in which learning takes place can be perceived as an idealized sequence of three steps: (1) observation, which of course includes listening; (2) supervised participation; and (3) private, self-initiated self-testing. It is not the case that all acquisition of skills proceed through such phases, however, but rather only some of these skills that Indian adults consciously and deliberately teach their children, and which the children consciously try to learn. Those which are learned through less deliberate means must to some extent invoke similar structuring, but it is difficult to determine to what extent.

The use of speech in the process is notably minimal. Verbal directions or instructions are few, being confined to corrections and question-answering. Nor does the final demonstration of skill particularly involve verbal performance, since the validation of skill so often involves display of some material evidence or non-verbal physical expression.

This process of Indian acquisition of competence may help to explain, in part, Indian children's reluctance to speak in front of their classmates. In the classroom, the processes of *acquisition* of knowledge and *demonstration* of knowledge are collapsed into the single act of answering questions or reciting when called upon to do so by the teacher, particularly in the lower grades. Here the assumption is that one will learn, and learn more effectively, through making mistakes in front of others. The Indian children have no opportunity to observe others performing successfully before they attempt it, except for their fellow classmates who precede them and are themselves uninitiated. They have no opportunity to "practice," and to decide for themselves when they know enough to demonstrate their knowledge; rather, their performances are determined by the teacher. And finally, their only channel for communicating competency is verbal, rather than non-verbal.

Turning now from learning processes in the home to learning experiences outside the home, in social and ritual activities involving community members other than kinsmen, there is again considerable evidence that Indian children's understanding of when and how one participates and performs individually, and thus demonstrates or communicates competence, differs considerably from what is expected of them in the classroom.

Children of all ages are brought to every sort of community-wide social event sponsored by Indians (as distinct from those sponsored by non-Indians). There is rarely, if ever, such a thing as an Indian community event that is attended by adults only. At many events children participate in only certain roles, but this is true of everyone. Sociospatially and behaviorally, children must always participate minimally, as do all others, in sitting quietly and attentively alongside their elders.

One of the social features that characterizes social events that are not explicitly kin group affairs, including activities like political general councils, social dinners, and worship dances, is that they are open to participation by all members of the Warm Springs Indian community. While different types of activities are more heavily attended by certain Indians rather than others, and fairly consistently sponsored and arranged by certain individuals, it is always clear that everyone is invited, both by community knowledge of this fact and by explicit announcements on posters placed in areas where most people pass through at one time or another in their day-to-day activities.

A second feature of such activities is that there is usually no one person directing the activity verbally, or signaling changes from one phase to another. Instead the structure is determined either by a set procedure or ritual, or there is a group of people who in various complementary ways provide such cuing and direction. Nor are there any participant roles that can be filled or are filled by only one person. In dancing, singing, and drumming there are no soloists, and where there are performers who begin a sequence, and are then joined by others, more than one performer takes a turn at such initiations. The speaking roles are handled similarly. In contexts where speeches are appropriate, it is made clear that anyone who wants to may "say a few words." The same holds true for political meetings, where the answerer to a question is not necessarily one who is on a panel or council, but rather the person who feels he is qualified, by his knowledge of a subject, to answer. In all situations thus allowing for anyone who wants to to speak, no time limit is set, so that the talking continues until everyone who wants to has had the opportunity to do so.

This does not mean that there are never any "leaders" in Indian social activities, but rather that leadership takes quite a different form from that in many non-Indian cultural contexts. Among the people of Warm Springs, a person is not a leader by virtue of holding a particular position, even in the case of members of the tribal council and administration. Rather, he is a leader because he has demonstrated ability in some sphere and activity, and many individuals choose to follow his suggestions because they have independently each decided they are good ones. If, for example, an individual plans and announces an activity, but few people offer to help him carry it out or attend it, then that is an indication that the organizer is not a respected leader in the community at the present time. And the likelihood that he will repeat his efforts in the near future is reduced considerably.

This type of "leadership," present today among the people of Warm Springs, is reminiscent of that which was described by Hoebel for the Comanche chiefs:

In matters of daily routine, such as camp moving, he merely made the decisions himself, announcing them through a camp crier. Anyone who did not like his decision simply ignored it. If in time a good many people ignored his announcements and preferred to stay behind with some other man of influence, or perhaps to move in another direction with that man, the chief had then lost his following. He was no longer chief, and another had quietly superseded him. (Hoebel, 1954, p. 132)

A final feature of Indian social activities, which should be recognized from what has already been said, is that all who do attend an activity may participate in at least some of the various forms participation takes for the given activity, rather than there being a distinction made between participants or performers and audience. At many Indian gatherings, particularly those attended by older people, this aspect of the situation is reflected in its sociospatial arrangement: People are seated in such a way that all present are facing one another, usually in an approximation of a square, and the focus of activity is either along one side of the square, or in its center, or a combination of the two.

And each individual chooses the degree of his participation. No one, other than, perhaps, those who set up the event, is committed to being present beforehand, and all participating roles beyond those of sitting and observing are determined by the individual at the point at which he decides to participate, rather than being pre-scheduled.

In summary, the Indian social activities to which children are early exposed outside the home generally have the following properties: (1) they are community-wide, in the sense that they are open to all Warm Springs Indians; (2) there is no single individual directing and controlling all activity, and, to the extent that there are "leaders," their leadership is based on the choice to follow made by each person; (3) participation in some form is accessible to everyone who attends. No one need be exclusively an observer or audience, and there is consequently no sharp distinction between audience and performer. And each individual chooses for himself the degree of his participation during the activity.

If one now compares the social conditions for verbal participation in the classroom with the conditions underlying many Indian events in which children participate, a number of differences emerge.

First of all, classroom activities are not community-wide, and, more importantly, the participants in the activity are not drawn just from the Indian community. The teacher, as a non-Indian, is an outsider and a stranger to these events. In addition, by virtue of her role as teacher, she structurally separates herself from the rest of the participants, her students. She places herself outside the interaction and activity of the students. This encourages their cultural perceptions of themselves as the relevant community, in opposition to the teacher, perhaps much as they see themselves in opposition to other communities, and on a smaller scale, as one team is in opposition to another. In other words, on the basis of the Indians' social experiences, one is either a part of a group or outside it. The notion of a single individual being structurally set apart from all others, in anything other than an observer role, and yet still a part of the group organization, is one that children probably encounter for the first time in school, and continue to experience only in non-Indian-derived activities (e.g., in bureaucratic, hierarchically structured occupations). This helps to explain why Indian students show so little interest in initiating interaction with the teacher in activities involving other students.

Second, in contrast to Indian activities where many people are involved in determining the development and structure of an event, there is only one single authority directing everything in the classroom, namely the teacher. And the teacher is not the controller or leader by virtue of the individual students' choices to follow her, as in the case in Indian social activities, but rather by virtue of her occupation of the role of teacher. This difference helps to account for the Indian children's frequent indifference to the directions, orders, and requests for compliance with classroom social rules that the teacher issues.

Third, it is not the case in the classroom that all students may participate in any given activity, as in Indian community activities. Nor are they given the opportunity to choose the degree of their participation, which, on the basis of evidence discussed earlier, would in Indian contexts be based on the individual's having already ascertained in private that he was capable of successful verbal communication of competence. Again these choices belong to the teacher.

Conclusion

In summary, Indian children fail to participate verbally in classroom interaction because the social conditions for participation to which they have become accustomed in the Indian community are lacking. The absence of these appropriate social conditions for communicative performances affects the most common and everyday speech acts that occur in the classroom. If the Indian child fails to follow an order or answer a question, it may not be because he doesn't understand the linguistic structure of the imperative and the interrogative, but rather because he does not share the non-Indian's assumption in such contexts that use of these syntactic forms by definition implies an automatic and immediate response from the person to whom they were addressed. For these assumptions are sociolinguistic assumptions that are not shared by the Indians.

Educators cannot assume that because Indian children (or any children from cultural backgrounds other than those that are implicit in American classrooms) speak English, or are taught it in the schools, that they have also assimilated all of the sociolinguistic rules underlying interaction in classrooms and other non-Indian social situations where English is spoken. To the extent that existing cultural variation in sociolinguistic patterning that is not recognized by the schools results in learning difficulties and feelings of inferiority for some children, changes in the structuring of classroom learning situations are needed. Ultimately the nature of the changes to be made should be determined by the educational goals of the particular communities where this type of problem exists.

If, as may be the case on the Warm Springs Indian Reservation, the people's main concern is to enable Indian children to compete successfully with non-Indians, and to have the *choice* of access to the modes of interaction and life styles of non-Indians, then there should be a conscious effort made in the schools to teach the children the modes for appropriate verbal participation that prevail in non-Indian classrooms. Thus, rather than shifting away from situations in which children perform individually in front of their peers only with great reluctance, conscious emphasis on and encouragement of participation in such situations should be carried out in the early grades.

If, on the other hand, as also may be the case in Warm Springs (there are strong differences of opinion here on this issue that complicate the teachers' actions), there is strong feeling in the community that is culturally distinctive modes of communication should be maintained and encouraged to flourish rather than be eliminated through our educational system's apparent pursuit of cultural uniformity throughout the country, then quite a different shift in the orientation of classroom modes of instruction would be called for. Here an effort to adapt the community's conditions for appropriate speech usage to the classroom should be made, not in an ad hoc and partial fashion as at Warm Springs, but consistently and systematically. And where the classroom situation is one in which children of more than one cultural background come together, efforts should be made to allow for a complementary diversity in the modes of communication through which learning and measurement of "success" take place.

BIBLIOGRAPHY

Berry, Brewton (1969). *The Education of American Indians: A Survey of the Literature*. Prepared for the Special Subcommittee on Indian Education of the Committee on Labor and Public Welfare, United States Senate. Washington, D.C.: Government Printing Office.

Cazden, Courtney B., and John, Vera P. (1968). Learning in American Indian Children. In *Styles of Learning among American Indians: An Outline for Research*. Washington, D.C.: Center for Applied Linguistics.

Hoebel, E. Adamson (1954). *The Law of Primitive Man*. Cambridge, Mass.: Harvard University Press.

Hymes, Dell [this volume]. On Communicative Competence. In Renira Huxley and Elizabeth Ingram (eds.), *Mechanisms of Language Development*. London: Centre for Advanced Study in the Developmental Science and CIBA Foundation. (Article first appeared 1967.)

Wax, Murray, Wax, Rosalie, and Dumont, Robert V., Jr. (1964). *Formal Education in an American Indian Community*. Social Problems Monograph No. 1. Kalamazoo, Mich.: Society for the Study of Social Problems.

Wolcott, Harry (1967). *A Kwakiutl Village and School*. New York: Holt, Rinehart, and Winston.

Zentner, Henry (1960). *Oregon State College Warm Springs Research Project*. Vol. II: *Education*. Corvallis: Oregon State College.

13

What No Bedtime Story Means: Narrative Skills at Home and School

Shirley Brice Heath

In the preface to *Introduction to S/Z*, Roland Barthes's work on ways in which readers read, Richard Howard writes: "We require an education in literature . . . in order to discover that *what we have assumed* – with the complicity of our teachers – *was nature is in fact culture, that what was given is no more than a way of taking*" (emphasis not in the original; Howard 1974:ix).[1] This statement reminds us that the *culture* children learn as they grow up is, in fact, "ways of taking" meaning from the environment around them. The means of making sense from books and relating their contents to knowledge about the real world is but one "way of taking" that is often interpreted as "natural" rather than learned. The quote also reminds us that teachers (and researchers alike) have not recognized that ways of taking from books are as much a part of learned behavior as are ways of eating, sitting, playing games, and building houses.

As school-oriented parents and their children interact in the preschool years, adults give their children, through modeling and specific instruction, ways of taking from books that seem natural in school and in numerous institutional settings such as banks, post offices, businesses, and government offices. These *mainstream* ways exist in societies around the world that rely on formal educational systems to prepare children for participation in settings involving literacy. In some communities these ways of schools and institutions are very similar to the ways learned at home; in other communities the ways of school are merely an overlay on the home-taught ways and may be in conflict with them.[2]

Yet little is actually known about what goes on in storyreading and other literacy-related interactions between adults and preschoolers in communities around the world. Specifically, though there are numerous diary accounts and experimental studies of the preschool reading experiences of mainstream middle-class children, we know little about the specific literacy features of the environment upon which the school expects to draw. Just how does what is frequently termed "the literate tradition" envelop the child in knowledge about interrelationships between oral and written language, between knowing something and knowing ways of labeling and displaying it? We have even less information about the variety of ways children from *nonmainstream* homes learn about reading, writing, and using oral language to display knowledge in their preschool environment. The general view has been that whatever it is that mainstream school-oriented homes have, these other homes do not have it; thus these children are not from the literate tradition and are not likely to succeed in school.

A key concept for the empirical study of ways of taking meaning from written sources across communities is that of *literacy events*: occasions in which written language is integral to the nature of participants' interactions and their interpretive processes and strategies. Familiar literacy events for mainstream preschoolers are bedtime stories; reading cereal boxes, stop signs, and television ads; and interpreting instructions for commercial games and toys. In such literacy events, participants follow socially established rules for verbalizing what they know from and about the written material. Each community has rules for socially interacting and sharing knowledge in literacy events.

This paper briefly summarizes the ways of taking from printed stories families teach their preschoolers in a cluster of mainstream school-oriented neighborhoods of a city in the southeastern region of the United States. I then describe two quite different ways of taking used in the homes of two English-speaking communities in the same region that do not follow the school-expected patterns of bookreading and reinforcement of these patterns in oral storytelling. Two assumptions underlie this paper and are treated in detail in the ethnography of these communities (Heath 1983): (1) Each community's ways of taking from the printed word and using this knowledge are interdependent with the ways children learn to talk in their social interactions with caregivers; (2) there is little or no validity to the time-honored dichotomy of "the literate tradition" and "the oral tradition." This paper suggests a frame of reference for both the community patterns and the paths of development children in different communities follow in their literacy orientations.

Mainstream School-oriented Bookreading

Children growing up in mainstream communities are expected to develop habits and values that attest to their membership in a "literate society." Children learn certain customs, beliefs, and skills in early enculturation experiences with written materials: The bedtime story is a major literacy event that helps set patterns of behavior that reoccur repeatedly through the life of mainstream children and adults.

In both popular and scholarly literature, the bedtime story is widely accepted as a given – a natural way for parents to interact with their child at bedtime. Commercial publishing houses, television advertising, and children's magazines make much of this familiar ritual, and many of their sales pitches are based on the assumption that in spite of the intrusion of television into many patterns of interaction between parents and children, this ritual remains. Few parents are fully conscious of what bedtime storyreading means as preparation for the kinds of learning and displays of knowledge expected in school. Ninio & Bruner (1978), in their longitudinal study of one mainstream middle-class mother–infant dyad in joint picturebook reading, strongly suggest a universal role of bookreading in the achievement of labeling by children.

In a series of "reading cycles," mother and child alternate turns in a dialogue: The mother directs the child's attention to the book and/or asks what-questions and/or labels items on the page. The items to which the what-questions are directed and labels given are two-dimenstional representations of three-dimensional objects, so that the child has to resolve the conflict between perceiving these as two-dimensional objects and as representations of a three-dimensional visual setting. The child does so "by assigning a privileged, autonomous status to pictures as visual objects" (1978:5). The arbitrariness of the picture, its decontextualization, and its existence as something that cannot be grasped and manipulated like its "real" counterparts are learned through the routines of structured interactional dialogue in which mother and child take turns playing a labeling game. In a "scaffolding" dialogue (cf. Cazden 1979), the mother points and asks "What is x?" and the child vocalizes and/or gives a nonverbal signal of attention. The mother then provides verbal feedback and a label. Before the age of 2, the child is socialized into the initiation–reply–evaluation sequences repeatedly described as the central structural feature of classroom lessons (e.g., Sinclair & Coulthard 1975; Griffin & Humphry 1978; Mehan 1979). Teachers ask their students questions to which the answers are prespecified in the mind of the teacher. Students respond, and teachers provide feedback, usually in the form of an evaluation. Training in ways of responding to this pattern begins very early in the labeling activities of mainstream parents and children.

Maintown ways

This patterning of "incipient literacy" (Scollon & Scollon 1979) is similar in many ways to that of the families of fifteen primary-level schoolteachers in Maintown, a cluster of middle-class neighborhoods in a city of the Piedmont Carolinas. These families (all of whom identify themselves as "typical," "middle-class," or "mainstream") had preschool children, and the mother in each family was either teaching in local public schools at the time of the study (early 1970s) or had taught in the academic year preceding participation in the study. Through a research dyad approach, using teacher-mothers as researchers with the ethnographer, the teacher-mothers audiorecorded their children's interactions in their primary network – mothers, fathers, grandparents, maids, siblings, and frequent visitors to the home. Children were expected to learn the following rules in literacy events in these nuclear households:

1   As early as 6 months of age, children *give attention to books and information derived from books*. Their rooms contain bookcases and are decorated with murals, bedspreads, mobiles, and stuffed animals that represent characters found in books. Even when these characters have their origin in television programs, adults also provide books that either repeat or extend the characters' activities on television.

2   Children, from the age of 6 months, *acknowledge questions about books*. Adults expand nonverbal responses and vocalizations from infants into fully formed grammatical sentences. When children begin to verbalize about the contents of

books, adults extend their questions from simple requests for labels ("What's that?" "Who's that?") to ask about the attributes of these items ("What does the doggie say?" "What color is the ball?")

3   From the time they start to talk, children *respond to conversational allusions to the content of books; they act as question-answerers who have a knowledge of books*. For example, a fuzzy black dog on the street is likened by an adult to Blackie in a child's book: "Look, there's a Blackie. Do you think *he's* looking for a boy?" Adults strive to maintain with children a running commentary on any event or object that can be book-related, thus modeling for them the extension of familiar items and events from books to new situational contexts.

4   Beyond 2 years of age, children *use their knowledge of what books do to legitimate their departures from "truth."* Adults encourage and reward "book talk," even when it is not directly relevant to an ongoing conversation. Children are allowed to suspend reality, to tell stories that are not true, to ascribe fiction-like features to everyday objects.

5   Preschool children *accept book and book-related activities as entertainment*. When preschoolers are "captive audiences" (e.g., waiting in a doctor's office, putting a toy together, or preparing for bed), adults reach for books. If there are no books present, they talk about other objects as though they were pictures in books. For example, adults point to items and ask children to name, describe, and compare them to familiar objects in their environment. Adults often ask children to state their likes or dislikes, their view of events, etc. at the end of the captive-audience period. These affective questions often take place while the next activity is already under way (e.g., moving toward the doctor's office, putting the new toy away, or being tucked into bed), and adults do not insist on answers.

6   Preschoolers *announce their own factual and fictive narratives* unless they are given in response to direct adult elicitation. Adults judge as most acceptable those narratives that open by orienting the listener to setting and main character. Narratives that are fictional are usually marked by formulaic openings, a particular prosody, or the borrowing of episodes in storybooks.

7   When children are about 3 years old, adults discourage the highly interactive participative role in bookreading children have hitherto played and children *listen and wait as an audience*. No longer does either adult or child repeatedly break into the story with questions and comments. Instead, children must listen, store what they hear, and, on cue from the adult, answer a question. Thus children begin to formulate "practice" questions as they wait for the break and the expected formulaic questions from the adult. It is at this stage that children often choose to "read" to adults rather than be read to.

A pervasive pattern of all these features is the authority that books and book-related activities have in the lives of both the preschoolers and members of their primary network. Any initiation of a literacy event by a preschooler makes an interruption, an untruth, a diverting of attention from the matter at hand (whether it be an uneaten plate of food, a messy room, or an avoidance of going to bed) acceptable. Adults jump at openings their children give them for pursuing talk about books and reading.

In this study, writing was found to be somewhat less acceptable as an "anytime activity," since adults have rigid rules about times, places, and materials for writing. The only restrictions on bookreading concern taking good care of books: They should not be wet, torn, drawn on, or lost. In their talk to children about books and in their explanations of why they buy children's books, adults link school success to "learning to love books," "learning what books can do for you," and "learning to entertain yourself and to work independently." Many of the adults also openly expressed a fascination with children's books "nowadays." They generally judged them as more diverse, wide-ranging, challenging, and exciting than books they had as children.

The mainstream pattern

A close look at the way bedtime-story routines in Maintown taught children how to take meaning from books raises a heavy sense of the familiar in all of us who have acquired mainstream habits and values. Throughout a lifetime, any school-success-ful individual moves through the same processes described above thousands of times. Reading for comprehension involves an internal replaying of the same types of questions adults ask children about bedtime stories. We seek *what-explanations*, asking what the topic is, establishing it as predictable and recognizing it in new situational contexts by classifying and categorizing it in our minds with other phenomena. The what-explanation is replayed in learning to pick out topic sentences, write outlines, and answer standardized tests that ask for the correct titles to stories, and so on. In learning to read in school, children move through a sequence of skills designed to teach what-explanations. There is a tight linear order of instruction that recapitulates the bedtime-story pattern of breaking down the story into small bits of information and teaching children to handle sets of related skills in isolated sequential hierarchies.

In each individual reading episode in the primary years of schooling, children must move through what-explanations before they can provide *reason-explanations* or *affective commentaries*. Questions about why a particular event occurred or why a specific action was right or wrong come at the end of primary-level reading lessons, just as they come at the end of bedtime stories. Throughout the primary-grade levels, what-explanations predominate, reason-explanations come with increasing frequency in the upper grades, and affective comments most often come in the extra-credit portions of the reading workbook or at the end of the list of suggested activities in textbooks across grade levels. This sequence characterizes the total school career. Highschool freshmen who are judged poor in compositional and reading skills spend most of their time on what-explanations and practice in advanced versions of bedtime-story questions and answers. They are given little or no chance to use reason-giving explanations or assessments of the actions of stories. Reason-explanations result in configurational rather than hierarchical skills, are not predictable, and thus do not present content with a high degree of redundancy. Reason-giving explanations tend to rely on detailed knowledge of a specific domain. This detail is often unpredictable to teachers, and is not as highly valued as is knowledge that covers a particular area of knowledge with less detail but offers opportunity for extending the knowledge to larger and related concerns. For example, a primary-level student whose father owns a turkey farm may respond with reason-explanations to a story about a turkey. His knowledge is intensive and covers details perhaps not known to the teacher and not judged as relevant to the story. The knowledge is unpredictable and questions about it do not continue to repeat the common core of content knowledge of the story. Thus such configured knowledge is encouraged only for the "extras" of reading – an extra-credit oral report or a creative picture and story about turkeys. This kind of knowledge is allowed to be used once the hierarchical what-explanations have been mastered and displayed in a particular situation and, in the course of one's academic career, only when one has shown full mastery of the hierarchical skills and subsets of related skills that underlie what-explanations. Thus reliable and successful participation in the ways of taking from books that teachers view as natural must, in the usual school way of doing things, precede other ways of taking from books.

These various ways of taking are sometimes referred to as "cognitive styles" or "learning styles." It is generally accepted in the research literature that they are influenced by early socialization experiences and correlated with such features of the society in which the child is reared as social organization, reliance on authority, male–female roles, and so on. These styles are often seen as two contrasting types, most frequently termed "field independent–field dependent" (Witkin et al. 1966) or "analytic–relational" (Kagan, Sigel & Moss 1963; Cohen 1968, 1969, 1971). The analytic/field-independent style is generally presented as that which correlates positively with high achievement and general academic and social success in school. Several studies discuss ways in which this style is played out in school – in preferred ways of responding to pictures and written text and selecting from among a choice of answers to test items.

Yet we know little about how behaviors associated with either of the dichotomized cognitive styles (field-dependent/relational and field-independent/analytic) were learned in early patterns of socialization. To be sure, there are vast individual differences that may cause an individual to behave so as to be categorized as having one or the other of these learning styles. But much of the literature on learning styles suggests that a preference for one or the other is learned in the social group in which the child is reared and in connection with other ways of behaving found in that culture. But how is a child socialized into an analytic/field-independent style? What kinds of interactions does he enter into with his parents and the stimuli of his environment that contribute to the development of such a style of learning? How do these interactions mold selective attention practices such as "sensitivity to parts of objects," "awareness of obscure, abstract, nonobvious features," and identification of "abstractions based on the features of items" (Cohen 1969:844–5)? Since the predominant stimuli used in school to judge the presence and extent of these selective attention practices are written materials, it is clear that the literacy orientation of preschool children is central to these questions.

The foregoing descriptions of how Maintown parents socialize their children into a literacy orientation fit closely those provided by Scollon & Scollon for their own child, Rachel. Through similar practices, Rachel was "literate before she learned to read" (1979:6). She knew, before the age of 2, how to focus on a book and not on herself. Even when she told a story about herself, she moved herself out of the text and saw herself as author, as someone different from the central character of her story. She learned to pay close attention to the parts of objects, to name them, and to provide a running commentary on features of her environment. She learned to manipulate the contexts of items, her own activities, and language to achieve book-like, decontextualized, repeatable effects (such as puns). Many references in her talk were from written sources; others were modeled on stories and questions about these stories. The substance of her knowledge, as well as her ways of framing knowledge orally, derived from her familiarity with books and bookreading. No doubt this development began by labeling in the dialogue cycles of reading (Ninio & Bruner 1978), and it will continue for Rachel in her preschool years along many of the same patterns described by Cochran Smith (1984) for a mainstream nursery school. There teacher and students negotiated storyreading through the scaffolding of teachers' questions and running commentaries that replayed the structure and sequence of storyreading learned in their mainstream homes.

Close analyses of how mainstream school-oriented children come to learn to take from books at home suggest that such children learn not only how to take meaning from books, but also how to talk about it. In doing the latter, they repeatedly practice routines that parallel those of classroom interaction. By the time they enter school, they have had continuous experience as information givers; they have learned how to perform in those interactions that surround literate sources through-out school. They have had years of practice in interaction situations that are the heart of reading – both learning to read and reading to learn in school. They have developed habits of performing that enable them to run through the hierarchy of preferred knowledge about a literate source and the appropriate sequence of skills to be displayed in showing knowledge of a subject. They have developed ways of decontextualizing and surrounding with explanatory prose the knowledge gained from selective attention to objects.

They have learned to listen, waiting for the appropriate cue that signals it is their turn to show off this knowledge. They have learned the rules for getting certain services from parents (or teachers) in the reading interaction (Merritt 1979). In nursery school, they continue to practice these interaction patterns in a group rather than in a dyadic situation. There they learn additional signals and behaviors necessary for getting a turn in a group and for responding to a central reader and to a set of centrally defined reading tasks. In short, most of their waking hours during the preschool years have enculturated them into: (1) all those habits associated with what-explanations, (2) selective attention to items of the written text, *and* (3) appro-priate interactional styles for orally displaying all the know-how of their literate orientation to the environment. This learning has been finely tuned and its habits are highly interdependent. Patterns of behaviors learned in one setting or at one stage reappear again and again as these children learn to use oral and written language in literacy events and to bring their knowledge to bear in school-acceptable ways.

Alternative Patterns of Literacy Events

But what corresponds to the mainstream pattern of learning in communities that do not have this finely tuned, consistent, repetitive, and continuous pattern of training? Are there ways of behaving that achieve other social and cognitive aims in other sociocultural groups?

The data below are summarized from an ethnography of two communities – Roadville and Trackton – located only a few miles from Maintown's neighborhoods in the Piedmont Carolinas. Roadville is a white working-class community of families steeped for four generations in the life of the textile mill. Trackton is a working-class black community whose older generations have been brought up on the land, either farming their own land or working for other landowners. However, in the past decade, they have found work in the textile mills. Children of both communities are unsuccessful in school; yet both communities place a high value on success in school, believing earnestly in the personal and vocational rewards school can bring and urging their children "to get ahead" by doing well in school. Both Roadville and Trackton are literate communities in the sense that the residents of each are able to read printed and written materials in their daily lives, and on occasion they produce written messages as part of the total pattern of communication in the community. In both communities, children go to school with certain expectancies of print and, in Trackton especially, children have a keen sense that reading is something one does to learn something one needs to know (Heath 1980). In both groups, residents turn from spoken to written uses of language and vice versa as the occasion demands, and the two modes of expression seem to supplement and reinforce each other. Nonetheless there are radical differences between the two communities in the ways in which children and adults interact in the preschool years; each of the two communities also differs from Maintown. Roadville and Trackton view children's learning of language from two radically different perspectives: In Trackton, children "learn to talk"; in Roadville, adults "teach them how to talk."

Roadville

In Roadville, babies are brought home from the hospital to rooms decorated with colorful, mechanical, musical, and literacy-based stimuli. The walls are decorated with pictures based on nursery rhymes, and from an early age children are held and prompted to "see" the wall decorations. Adults recite nursery rhymes as they twirl the mobile made of nursery-rhyme characters. The items of the child's environment promote exploration of colors, shapes, and textures: A stuffed ball with sections of fabrics of different colors and textures is in the crib; stuffed animals vary in texture, size, and shape. Neighbors, friends from church, and relatives come to visit and talk to the baby and about him to those who will listen. The baby is fictionalized in the talk to him: "But this baby wants to go to sleep, doesn't he? Yes, see those little eyes gettin' heavy." As the child grows older, adults pounce on wordlike sounds and turn them into "words," repeating the "words," and expanding them into well-formed sentences. Before they can talk, children are introduced to visitors and prompted to provide all the expected politeness formulas, such as "Bye, bye," "Thank you," and so forth. As soon as they can talk, children are reminded about these formulas, and book or television characters known to be "polite" are involved as reinforcement.

In each Roadville home, preschoolers first have cloth books, featuring a single object on each page. They later acquire books that provide sounds, smells, and different textures or opportunities for practicing small motor skills (closing zippers, buttoning buttons, etc.). A typical collection for a 2-year-old consisted of a dozen or so books – eight featured either the alphabet or numbers; others were books of nursery rhymes, simplified Bible stories, or "real-life" stories about boys and girls (usually taking care of their pets or exploring a particular feature of their environment). Books based on Sesame Street characters were favorite gifts for 3- and 4-year-olds.

Reading and reading-related activities occur most frequently before naps or at bedtime in the evening. Occasionally an adult or older child will read to a fussy child while the mother prepares dinner or changes a bed. On weekends, fathers sometimes read with their children for brief periods of time, but they generally prefer to play games or play with the children's toys in their interactions. The following episode illustrates the language and social interactional aspects of these bedtime events; the episode takes place between Wendy (2;3 at the time of this episode) and Aunt Sue, who is putting her to bed.

[Aunt Sue (AS) picks up book, while Wendy crawls about the floor, ostensibly looking for something]

W: Uh uh

AS: Wendy, we're gonna read, uh, read this story, come on, hop up here on this bed. [Wendy climbs up on the bed, sits on top of the pillow, and picks up her teddy bear. Aunt Sue opens book, points to puppy]

AS: Do you remember what this book is about? See the puppy? What does the puppy do? [Wendy plays with the bear, glancing occasionally at pages of the book, as Aunt Sue turns. Wendy seems to be waiting for something in the book]

AS: See the puppy?
       [Aunt Sue points to the puppy in the book and looks at Wendy to see if she is watching]

W: Uh huh, yea, yes ma'am

AS: Puppy sees the ant, he's a li'l [Wendy drops the bear and turns to book] fellow. Can you see that ant? Puppy has a little ball.

W: Ant bite puppy [Wendy points to ant, pushing hard on the book]

AS: No, the ant won't bite the puppy, the [turns page] puppy wants to play with the ant, see? [Wendy tries to turn the page back; AS won't let her, and Wendy starts to squirm and fuss]

AS: Look here, here's someone else, the puppy [Wendy climbs down off the bed and gets another book]

W: Read this one

AS: Okay, you get back up here now. [Wendy gets back on bed]

AS: This book is your ABC book. See the A, look, here, on your spread, there's an A. You find the A. [The second book is a cloth book, old and tattered, and long a favorite of Wendy's. It features an apple on the cover, and its front page has an ABC block and ball. Through the book, there is a single item on each page, with a large representation of the first letter of the word commonly used to name the item. As AS turns the page, Wendy begins to crawl about on her quilt, which shows ABC blocks interspersed with balls and apples. Wendy points to each of the A's on the blanket and begins talking to herself. As reads the book, looks up, and sees Wendy pointing to the A's in her quilt]

AS: That's an A, can you find the A on your blanket?

W: There it is, this one, there's the hole too. [Pokes her finger through a place where the threads have broken in the quilting]

AS: [Points to ball in book] Stop that, find the ball, see, here's another ball.

This episode characterizes the early orientation of Roadville children to the written word. Bookreading time focuses on letters of the alphabet, numbers, names of basic items pictured in books, and simplified retellings of stories in the words of the adult.

If the content or story plot seems too complicated for the child, the adult tells the story in short, simple sentences, frequently laced with requests that the child give what-explanations.

Wendy's favorite books are those with which she can participate; that is, those to which she can answer, provide labels, point to items, give animal sounds, and "read" the material back to anyone who will listen to her. She memorizes the passages and often knows when to turn the pages to show that she is "reading." She holds the book in her lap, starts at the beginning, and often reads the title – "Puppy."

Adults and children use either the title of the book (or phrases such as "the book about a puppy") to refer to reading material. When Wendy acquires a new book, adults introduce the book with phrases such as "This is a book about a duck, a little yellow duck. See the duck. Duck goes quack quack." On introducing a book, adults sometimes ask the child to recall when they have seen a real specimen of the one treated in the book: "Remember the duck on the College lake?" The child often shows no sign of linking the yellow fluffy duck in the book with the large brown and gray mallards on the lake, and the adult makes no effort to explain that two such disparate-looking objects go by the same name.

As Wendy grows older, she wants to "talk" during the stories and Bible stories, and carry out the participation she so enjoyed with the alphabet books. However, by the time she reaches $3\frac{1}{2}$, Wendy is restrained from such wide-ranging participation. When she interrupts, she is told: "Wendy, stop that, you be quiet when someone is reading to you" or "You listen; now sit still and be quiet." Often Wendy will immediately get down and run away into the next room, saying "No, no." When this happens, her father goes to get her, pats her bottom, and puts her down hard on the sofa beside him. "Now you're gonna learn to listen." During the third and fourth years, this pattern occurs more and more frequently; only when Wendy can capture an aunt who does not visit often does she bring out the old books and participate with them. Otherwise, parents, Aunt Sue, and other adults insist that she be read a story and that she "listen" quietly.

When Wendy and her parents watch television, eat cereal, visit the grocery store, or go to church, adults point out and talk about many types of written material. On the way to the grocery, Wendy (3;8) sits in the back seat, and when her mother stops at a corner, Wendy says, "Stop." Her mother says, "Yes, that's a stop sign." Wendy has, however, misread a yield sign as a stop. Her mother offers no explanation of what the actual message on the sign is, yet when she comes to the sign she stops to yield to an oncoming car. Her mother, when asked why she had not given Wendy the word "yield," said it was too hard, Wendy would not understand, and "It's not a word we use like *stop.*"

Wendy recognized animal-cracker boxes as early as 10 months, and later, as her mother began buying other varieties, Wendy would see the box in the grocery store and yell, "Cook cook." Her mother would say, "Yes, those are cookies. Does Wendy want a cookie?" One day Wendy saw a new type of cracker box, and screeched, "Cook cook." Her father opened the box and gave Wendy a cracker and waited for her reaction. She started the "cookie," then took it to her mother, saying, "You eat." The mother joined in the game and said, "Don't you want your *cookie*?" Wendy said, "No cookie. You eat." "But Wendy, it's a cookie box, see?" and her mother pointed to the C of "crackers" on the box. Wendy paid no attention and ran off into another room.

In Roadville's literacy events, the rules for cooperative discourse around print are repeatedly practiced, coached, and rewarded in the preschool years. Adults in Roadville believe that instilling in children the proper use of words and understanding of the meaning of the written word are important for both their educational and religious success. Adults repeat aspects of the learning of literacy events they have known as children. In the words of one Roadville parent, "It was then that I began to learn...when my daddy kept insisting I *read* it, *say* it right. It was then that I *did* right, in his view."

The path of development for such performance can be described in three overlapping stages. In the first, children are introduced to discrete bits and pieces of books – separate items, letters of the alphabet, shapes, colors, and commonly represented items in books for children (apple, baby, ball, etc.). The latter are usually decontextualized, and they are represented in two-dimensional, falt line drawings. During this stage, children must participate as predictable information givers and respond to questions that ask for specific and discrete bits of information about the written matter. In these literacy events, specific features of the two-dimensional items in books that are different from their real counterparts are not pointed out. A ball in a book is flat; a duck in a book is yellow and fluffy; trucks, cars, dogs, and trees talk in books. No mention is made of the fact that such features do not fit these objects in reality. Children are not encouraged to move their understanding of books into other situational contexts or to apply it in their general knowledge of the world about them.

In the second stage, adults demand an acceptance of the power of print to entertain, inform, and instruct. When Wendy could no longer participate by contributing her knowledge at any point in the literacy event, she learned to recognize bookreading as a performance. The adult exhibited the book to Wendy: She was to be entertained, to learn from the information conveyed in the material, and to remember the book's content for the sequential follow-up questioning, as opposed to ongoing cooperative, participatory questions.

In the third stage, Wendy was introduced to preschool workbooks that provided story information and was asked questions or provided exercises and games based on the content of the stories or pictures. Follow-the-number coloring books and preschool push-out-and-paste workbooks on shapes, colors, and letters of the alphabet reinforced repeatedly that the written word could be taken apart into small pieces and one item linked to another by following rules. She had practice in the linear, sequential nature of books: Begin at the beginning, stay in the lines for coloring, draw straight lines to link one item to another, write your answers on lines, keep your letters straight, match the cutout letter to diagrams of letter shapes.

The differences between Roadville and Maintown are substantial. Roadville adults do not extend either the content or the habits of literacy events beyond bookreading. They do not, upon seeing an item or event in the real world, remind children of a similar event in a book and launch a running commentary on similarities and differences. When a game is played or a chore done, adults do not use literate sources. Mothers cook without written recipes most of the time; if they use a recipe from a written source, they do so usually only after confirmation and alteration by friends who have tried the recipe. Directions to games are read, but not carefully followed, and they are not talked about in a series of questions and answers that try to establish their meaning. Instead, in the putting together of toys or the playing of games, the abilities or preferences of one party prevail. For example, if an adult knows how to put a toy together, he does so; he does not talk about the process, refer to the written material and "translate" for the child, or try to sequence steps so the child can do it.[3] Adults do not talk about the steps and procedures of how to do things; if a father wants his preschooler to learn to hold a miniature bat or throw a ball, he says, "Do it this way." He does not break up "this way" into such steps as "Put your fingers around here," "Keep your thumb in this position," "Never hold it above this line." Over and over again, adults do a task and children observe and try it, being reinforced only by commands such as "Do it like this" and "Watch that thumb."

Adults at tasks do not provide a running verbal commentary on what they are doing. They do not draw the attention of the child to specific features of the sequences of skills or the attributes of items. They do not ask questions of the child, except questions which are directive or scolding in nature ("Did you bring the ball?" "Didn't you hear what I said?"). Many of their commands contain idioms that are not explained: "Put it up" or "Put that away now" (meaning "Put it in the place where it usually belongs") or "Loosen up," said to a 4-year-old boy trying to learn to bat a ball. Explanations that move beyond the listing of names of items and their features are rarely offered by adults. Children do not ask questions of the type "But I don't understand? What is that?" They appear willing to keep trying, and if there is ambiguity in a set of commands, they ask a question such as "You want me to do this?" (demonstrating their current efforts), or they try to find a way of diverting attention from the task at hand.

Both boys and girls during their preschool years are included in many adult activities, ranging from going to church to fishing and camping. They spend a lot of time observing and asking for turns to try specific tasks, such as putting a worm on the hook or cutting cookies. Sometimes adults say, "No, you're not old enough." But if they agree to the child's attempt at the task, they watch and give directives and evaluations: "That's right, don't twist the cutter." "Turn like this." "Don't try to scrape it up now, let me do that." Talk about the task does not segment its skills and identify them, nor does it link the particular task or item at hand to other tasks. Reason-explanations such as "If you twist the cutter, the cookies will be rough on the edge" are rarely given – or asked for.

Neither Roadville adults nor children shift the context of items in their talk. They do not tell stories that fictionalize themselves or familiar events. They reject Sunday school materials that attempt to translate Biblical events into a modern-day setting. In Roadville, a story must be invited or announced by someone other than the storyteller, and only certain community members are designated good storytellers. A story is recognized by the group as a story about one and all. It is a true story, an actual event that happened to either the storyteller or someone else present. The marked behavior of the storyteller and audience alike is seen as exemplifying the weaknesses of all and the need for persistence in overcoming such weaknesses. The sources of stories are personal experience. They are tales of transgressions that make the point of reiterating the expected norms of behavior of man, woman, fisherman, worker, and Christian. They are true to the facts of the event.

Roadville parents provide their children with books; they read to them and ask questions about the books' contents. They choose books that emphasize nursery rhymes, alphabet learning, animals, and simplified Bible stories, and they require their children to repeat from these books and to answer formulaic questions about their contents. Roadville adults also ask questions about oral stories that have a point relevant to some marked behavior of a child. They use proverbs and summary statements to remind their children of stories and to call on them for simple comparisons of the stories' contents to their own situations. Roadville parents coach children in their telling of a story, forcing them to tell about an incident as it has been precomposed or pre-scripted in the head of the adult. Thus in Roadville children come to know a story as either an accounting from a book or a factual account of a real event in which some type of marked behavior occurred and there is a lesson to be learned. Any fictionalized account of a real event is viewed as a *lie*; reality is better than fiction. Roadville's church and community life admit no story other than that which meets the definition internal to the group. Thus children cannot decontextualize their knowledge or fictionalize events known to them and shift them about into other frames.

When these children go to school they perform well in the initial stages of each of the three early grades. They often know portions of the alphabet, some colors and numbers, and can recognize their names and tell someone their address and their parents' names. They will sit still and listen to a story, and they know how to answer questions asking for what-explanations. They do well in reading workbook exercises that ask for identification of specific portions of words, items from the story, or the linking of two items, letters, or parts of words on the same page. When the teacher reaches the end of storyreading or the reading circle and asks questions such as "What did you like about the story?" relatively few Roadville children answer. If asked questions such as "What would you have done if you had been Billy [a story's main character]?" Roadville children most frequently say, "I don't know" or shrug their shoulders.

Near the end of each year, and increasingly as they move through the early primary grades, Roadville children can handle successfully the initial stages of lessons. But when they move ahead to extra-credit items or to activities considered more advanced and requiring more independence, they are stumped. They turn frequently to teachers, asking, "Do you want me to do this? What do I do here?" If asked to write a creative story or tell it into a tape recorder, they retell stories from books; they do not create their own. They rarely provide emotional or personal commentary on their accounting of real events or book stories. They are rarely able to take knowledge learned in one context and shift it to another; they do not compare two items or events and point out similarities and differences. They find it difficult either to hold one feature of an event constant and shift all others or to hold all features constant but one. For example, they are puzzled by questions such as "What would have happened if Billy had not told the policemen what happened?" They do not know how to move events or items out of a given frame. To a question such as "What habits of the Hopi Indians might they be able to take with them when they move to a city?" they provide lists of features of life of the Hopi on the reservation. They do not take these items, consider their appropriateness in an urban setting, and evaluate the hypothesized outcome. In general, they find this type of question impossible to answer, and they do not know how to ask teachers to help them take apart the questions to figure out the answers. Thus their initial successes in reading, being good students, following orders, and adhering to school norms of participating in lessons begin to fall away rapidly about the time they enter the fourth grade. As the importance and frequency of questions and reading habits with which they are familiar decline in the higher grades, they have no way of keeping up or of seeking help in learning what it is they do not even know they don't know.

Trackton

Babies in Trackton come home from the hospital to an environment that is almost entirely human. There are no cribs, car beds, or carseats, and only an occasional highchair or infant seat. Infants are held during their waking hours, occasionally while they sleep, and they usually sleep in the bed with parents until they are about 2 years of age. They are held, their faces fondled, their cheeks pinched, and they eat and sleep in the midst of human talk and noise from the television, stereo, and radio. Encapsulated in an almost totally human world, they are in the midst of constant human communication, verbal and nonverbal. They literally feel the body signals of shifts in emotion of those who hold them almost continuously; they are talked about and kept in the midst of talk about topics that range over any subject. As children make cooing or babbling sounds, adults refer to this as "noise," and no attempt is made to interpret these sounds as words or communicative attempts on the part of the baby. Adults believe they should not have to depend on their babies to tell them what they need or when they are uncomfortable; adults know, children only "come to know."

When a child can crawl and move about on his or her own, he or she plays with the household objects deemed safe for him or her – pot lids, spoons, plastic food containers. Only at Christmastime are there special toys for very young children; these are usually trucks, balls, doll babies, or plastic cars, but rarely blocks, puzzles, or books. As children become completely mobile, they demand ride toys or electronic and mechanical toys they see on television. They never request nor do they receive manipulative toys, such as puzzles, blocks, take-apart toys or literacy-based items, such as books or letter games.

Adults read newspapers, mail, calendars, circulars (political and civic-events-related), school materials sent home to parents, brochures advertising new cars, television sets, or other products, and the Bible and other church-related materials. There are no reading materials especially for children (with the exception of children's Sunday school materials), and adults do not sit and read to children. Since children are usually left to sleep whenever and wherever they fall asleep, there is no bedtime or naptime as such. At night, they are put to bed when adults go to bed or whenever the person holding them gets tired. Thus going to bed is not framed in any special routine. Sometimes in a play activity during the day an older sibling will read to a younger child, but the latter soon loses interest and squirms away to play. Older children often try to "play school" with younger children, reading to them from books and trying to ask questions about what they have read. Adults look on these efforts with amusement and do not try to persuade the small child to sit still and listen.

Signs from very young children of attention to the nonverbal behaviors of others are rewarded by extra fondling, laughter, and cuddling from adults. For example, when an infant shows signs of recognizing a family member's voice on the phone by bouncing up and down in the arms of the adult who is talking on the phone, adults comment on this to others present and kiss and nudge the child. Yet when children utter sounds or combinations of sounds that could be interpreted as words, adults pay no attention. Often by the time they are 12 months old, children approximate words or phrases of adults' speech; adults respond by laughing or giving special attention to the child and crediting him with "sounding like" the person being imitated. When children learn to walk and imitate the walk of members of the community, they are rewarded by comments on their activities: "He walks just like Toby when he's tuckered out."

Children between the ages of 12 and 24 months often imitate the tune or "general Gestalt" (Peters 1977) of complete utterances they hear around them. They pick up and repeat chunks (usually the ends) or phrasal and clausal utterances of speakers around them. They seem to remember fragments of speech and repeat these without active production. In this first stage of language learning, the *repetition* stage, they imitate the intonation contours and general shaping of the utterances they repeat. Lem (1;2) in the following example illustrates this pattern.

Mother [talking to neighbor on porch while Lem plays with a truck on the porch nearby]: But they won't call back, won't happen=
Lem: =call back
Neighbor: Sam's going over there Saturday, he'll pick up a form=
Lem: =pick up on, pick up on [Lem here appears to have heard "form" as "on"]

The adults pay no attention to Lem's "talk," and their talk, in fact, often overlaps his repetitions.

In the second stage, *repetition with variation*, Trackton children manipulate pieces of conversation they pick up. They incorporate chunks of language from others into their own ongoing dialogue, applying productive rules, inserting new nouns and verbs for those used in the adults' chunks. They also play with rhyming patterns and varying intonation contours.

Mother: She went to the doctor again.
Lem (2;2):   Went to de doctor, doctor, tractor, dis my tractor, [in a singsong fashion] doctor on a tractor, went to de doctor.

Lem creates a monologue, incorporating the conversation about him into his own talk as he plays. Adults pay no attention to his chatter unless it gets so noisy as to interfere with their talk.

In the third stage, *participation*, children begin to enter the ongoing conversations about them. They do so by attracting the adult's attention with a tug on the arm or pant leg, and they help make themselves understood by providing nonverbal reinforcements to help recreate a scene they want the listener to remember. For example, if adults are talking, and a child interrupts with seemingly unintelligible utterances, the child will make gestures or extra sounds, or act out some outstanding features of the scene he is trying to get the adult to remember. Children try to create a context, a scene, for the understanding of their utterance.

This third stage illustrates a pattern in the children's response to their environment and their ways of letting others know their knowledge of the environment. Once they are in the third stage, their communicative efforts are accepted by community members, and adults respond directly to the child instead of talking to others about the child's activities as they have done in the past. Children continue to practice for conversational participation by playing, when alone, both parts of dialogues, imitating gestures as well as intonation patterns of adults. By 2;6 all children in the community can imitate the walk and talk of others in the community or of frequent visitors such as the man who comes around to read the gas meters. They can feign anger, sadness, fussing, remorse, silliness, or any of a wide range of expressive behaviors. They often use the same chunks of language for varying effects, depending on nonverbal support to give the language different meanings or cast it in a different key (Hymes 1972). Girls between 3 and 4 years of age take part in extraordinarily complex stepping and clapping patterns and simple repetitions of handclap games played by older girls. From the time they are old enough to stand alone, they are encouraged in their participation by siblings and older children in the community. These games require anticipation and recognition of cues for upcoming behaviors, and the young girls learn to watch for these cues and to come in with the appropriate words and movements at the right time.

Preschool children are not asked for what-explanations of their environment. Instead, they are asked a preponderance of analogical questions that call for non-specific comparisons of one item, event, or person with another: "What's that like?" Other types of questions ask for specific information known to the child but not the adults: "Where'd you get that from?" "What do you want?" "How come you did that?" (Heath 1982b). Adults explain their use of these types of questions by expressing their sense of children: They are "comers," coming into their learning by experiencing what knowing about things means. As one parent of a 2-year-old boy put it: "Ain't no use me tellin' 'im, 'Learn this, learn that, what's this, what's that?' He just gotta learn, gotta know; he see one thing one place one time, he know how it go, see sump'n like it again, maybe it be the same, maybe it won't." Children are expected to learn how to know when the form belies the meaning, and to know contexts of items and to use their understanding of these contexts to draw parallels between items and events. Parents do not believe they have a tutoring role in this learning; they provide the experiences on which the child draws and reward signs of their successfully coming to know.

Trackton children's early stories illustrate how they respond to adult views of them as "comers." The children learn to tell stories by drawing heavily on their abilities to render a context, to set a stage, and to call on the audience's power to join in the imaginative creation of story. Between the ages of 2 and 4 years, the children, in a monologue-like fashion, tell stories about things in their lives, events they see and hear, and situations in which they have been involved. They produce these spontaneously during play with other children or in the presence of adults. Sometimes they make an effort to attract the attention of listeners before they begin the story, but often they do not. Lem, playing off the edge of the porch, when he was about $2\frac{1}{2}$ years of age, heard a bell in the distance.

He stopped, looked at Nellie and Benjy, his older siblings, who were nearby, and said:

Way
Far
Now
It a churchbell
Ringin'
Dey singin'
Ringin'
You hear it?
I hear it
Far
Now.

Lem had been taken to church the previous Sunday and had been much impressed by the churchbell. He had sat on his mother's lap and joined in the singing, rocking to and fro on her lap, and clapping his hands. His story, which is like a poem in its imagery and linelike prosody, is in response to the current stimulus of a distant bell. As he tells the story, he sways back and forth.

This story, somewhat longer than those usually reported from other social groups for children as young as Lem,[4] has some features that have come to characterize fully developed narratives or stories. It recapitulates in its verbal outline the sequence of events being recalled by the storyteller. At church, the bell rang while the people sang. In the line "It a churchbell," Lem provides his story's topic and a brief summary of what is to come. This line serves a function similar to the formulas often used by older children to open a story: "This is a story about (a church bell)." Lem gives only the slightest hint of story setting or orientation to the listener; where and when the story took place are capsuled in "Way / Far." Preschoolers in Trackton almost never hear "Once upon a time there was a ——" stories, and they rarely provide definitive orientations for their stories. They seem to assume listeners "know" the situation in which the narrative takes place. Similarly, preschoolers in Trackton do not close off their stories with formulaic endings. Lem poetically balances his opening and closing in an *inclusio*, beginning "Way / Far / Now" and ending "Far / Now." The effect is one of closure, but there is no clearcut announce-ment of closure. Throughout the presentation of action and result of action in their stories, Trackton preschoolers invite the audience to respond or evaluate the story's actions. Lem asks, "You hear it?" which may refer either to the current stimulus or to yesterday's bell, since Lem does not productively use past tense endings for any verbs at this stage in his language development.

Preschool storytellers have several ways of inviting audience evaluation and inter-est. They may themselves express an emotional response to the story's actions; they may have another character or narrator in the story do so, often using alliterative language play; or they may detail actions and results through direct discourse or sound effects and gestures. All these methods of calling attention to the story and its telling distinguish the speech event as a story, an occasion for audience and story teller to interact pleasantly and not simply to hear an ordinary recounting of events or actions.

Trackton children must be aggressive in inserting their stories into an ongoing stream of discourse. Storytelling is highly competitive. Everyone in a conversation may want to tell a story, so only the most aggressive wins out. The content ranges widely, and there is "truth" only in the universals of human experience. Fact is often hard to find, though it is usually the seed of the story. Trackton stories often have no point – no obvious beginning or ending; they go on as long as the audience enjoys and tolerates the storyteller's entertainment.

Trackton adults do not separate out the elements of the environment around their children to tune their attentions selectively. They do not simplify their language, focus on single-word utterances by young children, label items or features of objects in either books or the environment at large. Instead, children are continuously contextualized, presented with almost continuous communication. From this ongoing, multiple-channeled stream of stimuli, they must themselves select, practice, and determine rules of production and structuring. For language, they do so by first repeating, catching chunks of sounds and intonation contours, and practicing these without specific reinforcement or evaluation. But practice material and models are continuously available. Next, the children seem to begin to sort out the productive rules for the speech and practice what they hear about them with variation. Finally, they work their way into conversations, hooking their meanings for listeners into a familiar context by recreating scenes through gestures, special sound effects, and so on. These characteristics continue in their story-poems and their participation in jump-rope rhymes. Because adults do not select out, name, and describe features of the environment for the young, children must perceive situations, determine how units of the situations are related to each other, recognize these relations in other situations, and reason through what it will take to show their correlation of one situation with another. The children can answer questions such as "What's that like?" ("It's like Doug's car"), but they can rarely name the specific feature or features that make two items or events alike. For example, in saying a car seen on the street is "like Doug's car," a child may be basing the analogy on the fact that this car has a flat tire and Doug's also had one last week. But the child does not name (and is not asked to name) what is alike between the two cars.

Children seem to develop connections between situations or items not by specification of labels and features in the situations but by configuration links. Recognition of similar general shapes or patterns of links seen in one situation and connected to another seems to be the means by which children set scenes in their nonverbal representations of individuals, and later of their verbal chunking, and then their segmentation and production of rules for putting together isolated units. They do not decontextualize; instead they heavily contextualize nonverbal and verbal language. They fictionalize their "true stories," but they do so by asking the audience to identify with the story through making parallels from their own experiences. When adults read, they often do so in a group. One person, reading aloud, for example, from a brochure on a new car decodes the text and displays illustrations and photographs, and listeners relate the text's meaning to their experiences, asking questions and expressing opinions. Finally, the group as a whole synthesizes the written text and the negotiated oral discourse to construct a meaning for the brochure (Heath 1982a).

When Trackton children go to school, they face unfamiliar types of questions that ask for what-explanations. They are asked as individuals to identify items by name and to label features such as shape, color, size, number. The stimuli to which they are to give these responses are two-dimensional flat representations that are often highly stylized and bear little resemblance to the real items. Trackton children generally score in the lowest percentile range on the Metropolitan Reading Readiness tests. They do not sit at their desks and complete reading workbook pages; neither do they tolerate questions about reading materials that are structured in the usual lesson format. Their contributions are in the form of "I had a duck at my house one time"; "Why'd he do that?" or they imitate the sound effects teachers may produce in stories they read to the children. By the end of the first three primary grades, their general language-arts scores have been consistently low, except for those few who have begun to adapt to and adopt some of the behaviors they have had to learn in school. But the majority not only fail to learn the content of lessons, but also do not adopt the social-interactional rules for school literacy events. Print in isolation bears little authority in their world. The kinds of questions asked about reading books are unfamiliar. The children's abilities to link metaphorically two events or situations and to recreate scenes are not tapped in the school; in fact, *these abilities often cause difficulties*, because they enable children to see parallels teachers did not intend and, indeed, may not recognize until the children point them out (Heath 1978).

By the end of the lessons or by the time in their total school career when reason-explanations and affective statements call for the creative comparison of two or more situations, it is too late for many Trackton children. They have not picked up along the way the composition and comprehension skills they need to translate their analogical skills into a channel teachers can accept. They seem not to know how to take meaning from reading; they do not observe the rules of linearity in writing, and their expression of themselves on paper is very limited. Taped oral stories are often much better, but these rarely count as much as written compositions. Thus Trackton children continue to collect very low or failing grades, and many decide by the end of the sixth grade to stop trying and turn their attention to the heavy peer socialization that usually begins in these years.

From Community to Classroom

A recent review of trends in research on learning pointed out that "learning to read through using and learning from language has been less systematically studied than the decoding process" (Glaser 1979:7). Put another way, how children learn to use language to read to learn has been less systematically studied than decoding skills. Learning how to take meaning from writing before one learns to read involves repeated practice in using and learning from language through appropriate participation in literacy events such as exhibitor/questioner and spectator/respondent dyads (Scollon & Scollon 1979) or group negotiation of the meaning of a written text. Children have to learn to select, hold, and retrieve content from books and other written or printed texts in accordance with their community's rules or "ways of taking," and the children's learning follows community paths of language socialization. In each society, certain kinds of childhood participation in literacy events may precede others, as the developmental sequence builds toward the whole complex of home and community behaviors characteristic of the society. The ways of taking employed in the school may in turn build directly on the preschool development, may require substantial adaptation on the part of the children, or may even run directly counter to aspects of the community's pattern.

At home

In *Maintown* homes, the construction of knowledge in the earliest preschool years depends in large part on labeling procedures and what-explanations. Maintown families, like other mainstream families, continue this kind of classification and knowledge construction throughout the child's environment and into the school years, calling it into play in response to new items in the environment and in running commentaries on old items as they compare to new ones. This pattern of linking old and new knowledge is reinforced in narrative tales that fictionalize the teller's events or recapitulate a story from a book. Thus for these children the bedtime story is simply an early link in a long chain of interrelated patterns of taking meaning from the environment. Moreover, along this chain the focus is on the individual as respondent and cooperative negotiator of meaning from books. In particular, children learn that written language may represent not only descriptions of real events, but decontextualized logical propositions, and the occurrence of this kind of information in print or in writing legitimates a response in which one brings to the interpretation of written text selected knowledge from the real world. Moreover, readers must recognize how certain types of questions assert the priority of meanings in the written word over reality. The "real" comes into play only after prescribed decontextualized meanings; affective responses and reason-explanations follow conventional presuppositions that stand behind what-explanations.

Roadville also provides labels, features, and what-explanations, and prescribes listening and performing behaviors for preschoolers. However, Roadville adults do not carry on or sustain in continually overlapping and interdependent fashion the linking of ways of taking meaning from books to ways of relating that knowledge to other aspects of the environment. They do not encourage decontextualization; in fact, they proscribe it in their own stories about themselves and their requirements of stories from children. They do not themselves make analytic statements or assert universal truths, except those related to their religious faith. They lace their stories with synthetic (non-analytic) statements that express, describe, and synthesize real-life materials. Things do not have to follow logically so long as they fit the past experience of individuals in the community. Thus children learn to look for a specific moral in stories and to expect that story to fit their facts of reality explicitly. When they themselves recount an event, they do the same, constructing the story of a real event according to coaching by adults who want to construct the story as they saw it.

Trackton is like neither Maintown nor Roadville. There are no bedtime stories; in fact, there are few occasions for reading to or with children specifically. Instead, during the time these activities would take place in mainstream and Roadville homes, Trackton children are enveloped in different kinds of social interactions. They are held, fed, talked about, and rewarded for nonverbal, and later verbal, renderings of events they witness. Trackton adults value and respond favorably when children show they have come to know how to use language to show correspondence in function, style, configuration, and positioning between two different things or situations. Analogical questions are asked of Trackton children, although the implicit questions of structure and function these embody are never made explicit. Children do not have labels or names of attributes of items and events pointed out for them, and they are asked for reason-explanations, not what-explanations. Individuals express their personal responses and recreate corresponding situations with often only a minimal adherence to the germ of truth of a story. Children come to recognize similarities of patterning, though they do not name lines, points, or items that are similar between two items or situations. They are familiar with group literacy events in which several community members orally negotiate the meaning of a written text.

At school

In the early reading stages, and in later requirements for reading to learn at more advanced stages, children from the three communities respond differently, because they have learned different methods and degrees of taking from books. In contrast to Maintown children, Roadville children's habits learned in bookreading and toy-related episodes have not continued for them through other activities and types of reinforcement in their environment. They have had less exposure to both the content of books and ways of learning from books than have mainstream children. Thus their need in schools is not necessarily for an intensification of presentation of labels, a slowing down of the sequence of introducing what-explanations in connection with bookreading. Instead they need *extension of these habits to other domains* and to opportunities for practicing habits such as producing running commentaries, creating exhibitor/questioner and spectator/respondent roles, etc. Perhaps, most important, Roadville children need to have articulated for them *distinctions in discourse strategies and structures*. Narratives of real events have certain strategies and structures; imaginary tales, flights of fancy, and affective expressions have others. Their community's view of narrative discourse style is very narrow and demands a passive role in both creation of and response to the account of events. Moreover, these children have *to be reintroduced to a participant frame of reference to a book*. Though initially they were participants in bookreading, they have been trained into passive roles since the age of 3 years, and they must learn once again to be active information givers, taking from books and linking that knowledge to other aspects of their environment.

Trackton students present an additional set of alternatives for procedures in the early primary grades. Since they usually have few of the expected "natural" skills of taking meaning from books, they must not only learn these but also *retain their analogical reasoning practices* for use in some of the later stages of learning to read. They must *learn to adapt the creativity in language, metaphor, fictionalization, recreation of scenes, and exploration of functions and settings of items they bring to school*. These children already use narrative skills highly rewarded in the upper primary grades. They distinguish a fictionalized story from a real-life narrative. They know that telling a story can be in many ways related to play; it suspends reality and frames an old event in a new context; it calls on audience participation to recognize the setting and participants. They must now *learn as individuals to recount factual events in a straightforward way* and *recognize appropriate occasions for reason-explanations and affective expressions.* Trackton children seem to have skipped learning to label, list features, and give what-explanations. Thus they need to *have the mainstream or school habits presented in familiar activities with explanations related to their own habits of taking meaning* from the environment. Such "simple," "natural" things as distinctions between two-dimensional and three-dimensional objects may need to be explained to help Trackton children learn the stylization and decontextualization that characterize books.

To lay out in more specific detail how Roadville's and Trackton's ways of knowing can be used along with those of mainstreamers goes beyond the scope of this paper. However, it must be admitted that a range of alternatives to ways of learning and displaying knowledge characterizes all highly school-successful adults in the advanced stages of their careers. Knowing more about how these alternatives are learned at early ages in different sociocultural conditions can help the schools to provide opportunities for all students to avail themselves of these alternatives early in their school careers. For example, mainstream children can benefit from early exposure to Trackton's creative, highly analogical styles of telling stories and giving explanations, and they can add the Roadville true story with strict chronicity and explicit moral to their repertoire of narrative types.

In conclusion, if we want to understand the place of literacy in human societies and ways children acquire the literacy orientations of their communities, we must recognize two postulates of literacy and language development:

1   Strict dichotomization between oral and literate traditions is a construct of researchers, not an accurate portrayal of reality across cultures.
2   A unilinear model of development in the acquisition of language structures and uses cannot adequately account for culturally diverse ways of acquiring knowledge or developing cognitive styles.

Roadville and Trackton tell us that the mainstream type of literacy orientation is not the only type even among Western societies. They also tell us that the mainstream ways of acquiring communicative competence do not offer a universally applicable model of development. They offer proof of Hymes's assertion a decade ago that "it is impossible to generalize validly about 'oral' vs. 'literate' cultures as uniform types" (1974:54).

Yet in spite of such warnings and analyses of the uses and functions of writing in the specific proposals for comparative development and organization of cultural systems (cf. Basso 1974:432), the majority of research on literacy has focused on differences in class, amount of education, and level of civilization among groups having different literacy characteristics.

"We need, in short, a great deal of ethnography" (Hymes 1973) to provide descriptions of the ways different social groups "take" knowledge from the environment. For written sources, these ways of taking may be analyzed in terms of *types of literacy events*, such as group negotiation of meaning from written texts, individual "looking things up" in reference books, writing family records in Bibles, and the dozens of other types of occasions when books or other written materials are integral to interpretation in an interaction. These must in turn be analyzed in terms of the specific *features of literacy events*, such as labeling, what-explanation, affective comments, reason-explanations, and many other possibilities. Literacy events must also be interpreted in relation to the *larger sociocultural patterns* that they may exemplify or reflect. For example, ethnography must describe literacy events in their sociocultural contexts, so we may come to understand how such patterns as time and space usage, caregiving roles, and age and sex segregation are interdependent with the types and features of literacy events a community develops. It is only on the basis of such thoroughgoing ethnography that further progress is possible toward understanding cross-cultural patterns of oral and written language uses and paths of development of communicative competence.

NOTES

1   First presented at the Terman Conference on Teaching at Stanford University, 1980, this paper has benefited from cooperation with M. Cochran Smith of the University of Pennsylvania. She shares an appreciation of the relevance of Roland Barthes's work for studies of the socialization of young children into literacy; her research (1984) on the storyreading practices of a mainstream school-oriented nursery school provides a much-needed detailed account of early school orientation to literacy.

2   Terms such as *mainstream* and *middle-class* are frequently used in both popular and scholarly writings without careful definition. Moreover, numerous studies of behavioral phenomena (for example, mother–child interactions in language learning) either do not specify that the subjects being described are drawn from mainstream groups or do not recognize the importance of this limitation. As a result, findings from this group are often regarded as universal. For a discussion of this problem, see Chanan & Gilchrist 1974; Payne & Bennett 1977. In general, the literature characterizes this group as school-oriented, aspiring toward upward mobility through formal institutions, and providing enculturation that positively values routines of promptness, linearity (in habits ranging from furniture arrangement to entrance into a movie theatre), and evaluative and judgmental responses to behaviors that deviate from their norms. In the United States, mainstream families tend to locate in neighborhoods and suburbs around cities. Their social interactions center not in their immediate neighborhoods but in voluntary associations across the city. Thus a cluster of mainstream families (and not a community – which usually implies a specific geographic territory as the locus of a majority of social interactions) is the unit of comparison used here with the Trackton and Roadville communities.

3   Behind this discussion are findings from cross-cultural psychologists who have studied the links between verbalization of task and demonstration of skills in a hierarchical sequence, e.g., Childs & Greenfield 1980. See Goody 1979 on the use of questions in learning tasks unrelated to a familiarity with books.

4   Cf. Umiker-Sebeok's (1979) descriptions of stories of mainstream middle-class children, ages 3–5, and Sutton-Smith 1981.

REFERENCES

Basso, K. (1974). The ethnography of writing. In R. Bauman & J. Sherzer (eds.), *Explorations in the Ethnography of Speaking.* Cambridge: Cambridge University Press, pp. 425–32.

Cazden, C. B. (1979). Peekaboo as an instructional model: Discourse development at home and at school. *Stanford Papers and Reports in Child Language Development* 17:1–29.

Chanan, G. & Gilchrist, L. (1974). *What School Is For.* New York: Praeger.

Childs, C. P. & Greenfield, P. M. (1980). Informal modes of learning and teaching. In N. Warren (ed.), *Advances in Cross-Cultural Psychology,* vol. 2. London: Academic Press, pp. 269–316.

Cochran Smith, M. (1984). *The Making of a Reader.* Norwood, N.J.: Ablex.

Cohen, R. (1968). The relation between socio-conceptual styles and orientation to school requirements. *Sociology of Education* 41:201–20.

Cohen, R. (1969). Conceptual styles, culture conflict, and nonverbal tests of intelligence. *American Anthropologist* 71, 5:828–56.

Cohen, R. (1971). The influence of conceptual rule-sets on measures of learning ability. In C. L. Brace, G. Gamble, & J. Bond (eds.), *Race and Intelligence.* Anthropological Studies, no. 8. Washington, D.C.: American Anthropological Association, pp. 41–57.

Glaser, R. (1979). Trends and research questions in psychological research on learning and schooling. *Educational Researcher* 8, 10:6–13.

Goody, E. (1979). Towards a theory of questions. In E. N. Goody (ed.), *Questions and Politeness: Strategies in Social Interaction.* Cambridge: Cambridge University Press, pp. 17–43.

Griffin, P. & Humphry, F. (1978). Task and talk. In *The Study of Children's Functional Language and Education in the Early Years.* Final report to the Carnegie Corporation of New York. Arlington, Va.: Center for Applied Linguistics.

Heath, S. (1978). *Teacher Talk: Language in the Classroom.* Language in Education 9. Arlington, Va.: Center for Applied Linguistics.

Heath, S. (1980). The functions and uses of literacy. *Journal of Communication* 30, 1:123–33.

Heath, S. (1982a). Protean shapes: Ever-shifting oral and literate traditions. In Deborah Tannen (ed.), *Spoken and Written Language: Exploring Orality and Literacy.* Norwood, N.J.: Ablex, pp. 91–118.

Heath, S. (1982b). Questioning at home and at school: A comparative study. In George Spindler (ed.), *Doing Ethnography: Educational Anthropology in Action.* New York: Holt, Rinehart, & Winston, pp. 102–31.

Heath, S. (1983). *Ways with Words: Language, Life and Work in Communities and Classrooms.* Cambridge: Cambridge University Press.

Howard, R. (1974). A note on S/Z. In R. Barthes, *Introduction to S/Z,* trans. Richard Miller. New York: Hill & Wang, pp. ix–xi.

Hymes, D. H. (1972). Models of the interaction of language and social life. In J. J. Gumperz & D. Hymes (eds.), *Directions in Sociolinguistics.* New York: Holt, Rinehart, & Winston, pp. 35–71.

Hymes, D. H. (1973). Speech and language: On the origins and foundations of inequality among speakers. *Daedalus* 102:59–85.

Hymes, D. H. (1974). Speech and language: On the origins and foundations of inequality among speakers. In E. Haugen & M. Bloomfield (eds.), *Language as a Human Problem.* New York: Norton, pp. 45–71.

Kagan, J., Sigel, I., & Moss, H. (1963). Psychological significance of styles of conceptualization. In J. Wright & J. Kagan (eds.), *Basic Cognitive Processes in Children.* Monographs of the Society for Research in Child Development 28, 2:73–112.

Mehan, H. (1979). *Learning Lessons.* Cambridge, Mass.: Harvard University Press.

Merritt, M. (1979). Service-like Events during Individual Work Time and Their Contribution to the Nature of the Rules for Communication. NIE Report EP 78-0436.

Ninio, A. & Bruner, J. (1978). The achievement and antecedents of labelling. *Journal of Child Language* 5:1–15.

Payne, C. & Bennett, C. (1977). "Middle class aura" in public schools. *Teacher Educator* 13, 1:16–26.

Peters, A. (1977). Language learning strategies. *Language* 53:560–73.

Scollon, R. & Scollon, S. (1979). *The Literate Two-Year-Old: The Fictionalization of Self*. Working Papers in Sociolinguistics. Austin: Southwest Regional Laboratory.

Sinclair, J. M. & Coulthard, R. M. (1975). *Toward an Analysis of Discourse*. New York: Oxford University Press.

Sutton-Smith, B. (1981). *The Folkstories of Children*. Philadelphia: University of Pennsylvania Press.

Umiker-Sebeok, J. D. (1979). Preschool children's intraconversational narratives. *Journal of Child Language* 6, 1:91–110.

Witkin, H., Faterson, F., Goodenough, R., & Birnbaum, J. (1966). Cognitive patterning in mildly retarded boys. *Child Development* 37, 2:301–16.

14

Creating Social Identities through *Doctrina* Narratives

Patricia Baquedano-López

This study describes how teachers and students in *doctrina* class (a religious education class in Spanish) composed of Mexican immigrants at a Catholic parish in Los Angeles construct social identities in the course of telling the narrative of the apparition of *Nuestra Señora de Guadalupe* (Our Lady of Guadalupe). During the telling of this narrative, *doctrina* teachers at the parish of St. Paul[1] employ several discursive and interactional resources to represent a multiplicity of identities within a coherent collective narrative, establishing in this way links to traditional Mexican world views. Like narratives of personal experience, this traditional narrative organizes collective experience in a temporal continuum, extending past experience into the present (Heidegger, 1962; Ricoeur, 1985/1988; Polkinghorne, 1988; Bruner, 1990; Brockelman, 1992; Ochs, 1994; Ochs & Capps, 1996).

Narrating the Collectivity

Through narrative we relate not only events, but also stances and dispositions towards those events (Labov & Waletzky, 1968). While they emerge from experience, narratives also shape experience (Ochs & Capps, 1996); thus, we tell our stories for their potency to explain, rationalize, and delineate past, present, and possible experience. As collaborative undertakings, narratives are co-told and designed with the audience's input, addressing an audience's present and even future concerns (Duranti & Brenneis, 1986; Ochs, 1994). Stories of personal experience are told from present perspectives, from the here and now, evoking present emotions and creating present experiences for both narrator and audience (Capps & Ochs, 1995; Ochs and Capps, 1996; Heidegger, 1962; Ricoeur, 1985/1988). Collective narratives, which tell the experiences of a group, organize diversity in the collectivity. And while they tend to normalize the existing status quo, Chatterjee (1993) reminds us that they can also be expressions of resistances in the face of master story lines. Morgan (1995) has noted that certain narratives of African-American experience, in particular those alluding to the times of slavery, contest and resist both past and present experience. Through indirection and linguistic "camouflage," story-tellers describe and explain a collective history of African Americans as an economically exploited and socially marginalized minority group. Like these stories of African American collective experience, *doctrina* narratives of *Nuestra Señora de Guadalupe* also create explanations for the social worlds of *doctrina* teachers and students as a community with past experiences of oppression. This is achieved in part by *doctrina* classroom narrative activity in which narrated events are brought to bear upon ongoing class discussion, illustrating how past experience might continue to influence and shape the present. Indeed, at *doctrina*, a traditional religious narrative becomes not only a story to live by, it affirms and contests the community's past, present, and possible stories.

The narrative

In Los Angeles, a city with a large Mexican population, one does not need to journey far before noticing the ubiquity of popular written and pictorial versions of the narrative of *Nuestra Señora de Guadalupe* on bookmarks, greeting cards, candle vases in supermarket stores, and on city street wall murals. This narrative tells the story of a Mexican peasant, Juan Diego, who had a vision of the Virgin Mary at Mount Tepeyac, near Mexico City in the year 1531. The following excerpt, taken from the legend of a greeting card, represents one of many popular versions:

Ten years after the bloody Spanish conquest of Mexico, the Mother of God appeared to an Aztec craftsman named Juan Diego. She appeared as an Aztec herself and addressed him in Nahuatl, the Aztec tongue, in a manner one would address a prince. She appeared several miles outside of Mexico City, which had become the center of Spanish power; she insisted, however, that a shrine in her honor be built on that spot among the conquered people. She sent Juan Diego back to the Spanish clergy to "evangelize" them – [the] ones who felt they already had all the truth. In each of these ways she restored dignity and hope to native people who had been dehumanized by foreign oppression. A shrine was built where Mary appeared, and Juan Diego spent the remaining 17 years of his life there, repeating her message of hope and liberation to all who would come. About eight million Native Americans became Christians in response to this message. (Lentz, 1987)

While the master story line remains constant across versions, there is, inevitably, elaboration of details. Indeed, in *doctrina* classes, teachers craft particular renditions of the narrative emphasizing certain events. The message, however, is perennial; a Mexican Indian (and therefore, Mexico, the place of the apparition) was chosen as the recipient of an important message. Versions of the narrative are based on two relatively unknown written sources, one in Nahuatl and the other in Spanish, which date back to the 16th century (Rodriguez, 1994 and sources therein). Poole (1995) has most vigorously challenged the historical origins of the narrative concluding that manipulations of the narrative have served at various points in time to politically define and redefine Mexican identity. Indeed, *doctrina* narrative practices support his conclusion. Neither the Nahuatl nor the Spanish written text versions are mentioned during *doctrina* instruction; instead, a particular local version emerges from collaborative narrative activity.

Language Socialization in Religious Institutions

In its broadest sense, socialization is the process of becoming a competent member of society, of internalizing the norms, role expectations, and values of the community; in sum, of becoming culturally competent (Bernstein, 1970; Schieffelin & Ochs, 1986). Within this paradigm, language socialization constitutes socialization through language and socialization to use language (Schieffelin & Ochs, 1986). In this paper I concentrate on the discourse and interaction of teachers and students during religious instruction, and on the process of socialization in *doctrina* classes.

As some anthropologists have noted, a child's first exposure to literacy and other formal uses of his or her language can take place in churches. Heath (1983) described church literacy practices in the Piedmont Carolinas where interactions at church mirrored those of the home, reinforcing socialization practices learned in the home. Ethnographic research in Western Samoa has shown how Bible lessons socialize children not only to formal registers of Samoan, but also to the English language and American cultural norms (Duranti, 1994; Ochs, 1986; Duranti & Ochs, 1986). In turn, immigrant Samoan groups in the United States find the institution of the church to be an important link to their culture. Indeed, the teaching of the Samoan alphabet and numbers in a Samoan-American Sunday school in Southern California constitutes a nexus of cultural networks beyond the home and the church (Duranti, Ochs, & Ta'ase, 1995). The church in these immigrant situations is a powerful agent in the maintenance of the community's world views and language. As in the Samoan case, *doctrina* is a culturally significant space where both language and religious instruction take place. Through narrative activity enacted around the telling of the narrative of *Nuestra Señora de Guadalupe*, teachers link their students' present experiences to the experiences evoked in the narrative.

Language socialization at doctrina

Early records of *doctrina* instruction date back to the Spanish conquest. In colonial Mexico, *doctrina* classes were offered daily and were conducted in the native languages. Indeed, students were so numerous that the term "*doctrina*" was also used to describe entire towns of newly converted indigenous groups.[2] An ethnography of the town of Mexquitic in Central Mexico notes that in the year 1680, the number of converts was so large that a visiting bishop felt the need to declare Castillian Spanish the language of *doctrina* instruction to enforce the use of the colonizers' language. This decision, however, extended the use of Spanish to other aspects of public life in the town, concatenating linguistic and religious conversion (Frye, 1996). This move towards religious and linguistic uniformity was soon politically reinforced, and by the year 1770, a Spanish royal decree instituted the teaching of Castillian in Mexico, with the eventual goal of eliminating the native languages (Suárez, 1983). As this bit of historical background suggests, religious instruction is part of an institution which has socialized children not only to religious tenets but to dominant languages as well.

Religious instruction at St. Paul's

In Southern California, Catholic parishes with a large Spanish-speaking Latino membership often hold *doctrina* and religious services in Spanish. At St. Paul's Catholic church, *doctrina* classes were first offered in 1979 as a parallel to religious instruction classes offered in English, called catechism. The use of Spanish by the Latino membership of the St. Paul's parish is best explained in the words of a bilingual Latina parishioner, who, upon being asked her choice of language for religious practice categorically stated: "I talk to God in the language of the heart." For her and others in this parish, that language is Spanish. And while these Latinos reside in a state where English is the official language of the public sphere[3] children in *doctrina* are being socialized to use Spanish for what is close to the heart: for them, religious practice. Ironically, this situation illustrates the achieved goal of colonial Spanish friars, as today in this Los Angeles parish, in what constitutes a former Spanish colony, Spanish is the local indigenous language that now needs to be eradicated.

In April 1996, amid much local debate, the parish council at St. Paul's voted to eliminate *doctrina*. The major concern expressed by the leaders of this predominantly English-speaking parish was that *doctrina* and other Spanish-speaking activities fostered an image of separate parishes within what should be perceived as a single religious unit. Yet, when interviewed regarding this proposed change, both English- and Spanish-speaking parishioners often cited poor race relations as the main reason behind the decision to eliminate *doctrina*. During these interviews, parishioners expressed varying degrees of intolerance towards the religious practices of the Spanish-speaking group. A catechism teacher, whose class will be discussed in a later section of this paper, stated that Latinos were "too superstitious." Given the current race relations and conflicting perceptions of religious practice at St. Paul's, which reflect a generalized movement against multilingualism in the state of California, it comes as no surprise that English is being instituted as the language of instruction. The 1680 *doctrina* mandate of the Mexquitic town, which replaced Nahuatl with Spanish, is echoed 316 years later in the parish of St. Paul's decision to eliminate Spanish as the language of instruction in *doctrina* in favor of English.

Religious instruction classes at St. Paul's take place on Saturday mornings during the academic year in the classrooms of the St. Paul's Elementary School, the parish's private school located across the street from the main church building. Approximately 150 children participate in these religious education classes. Perhaps the most salient difference between *doctrina* and catechism can be summarized in the following terms: Whereas *doctrina* instructional policies seem to be more locally managed and community-oriented, often blending religious and cultural practice, the catechism curriculum follows a uniform format adhered to by parishes throughout the United States which concentrates on the teaching of Catholic precepts.

Doctrina

Student ages at *doctrina* range from 6–15. Most students come from working class families and attend public schools, as few can afford the costly monthly fees of the

St. Paul's Elementary School.[4] *Doctrina* children are bilingual speakers of Spanish and English, and only a few seem to be more competent in English. Most are recent immigrants from Mexico, with only a few of them being U.S.-born Latinos. The *doctrina* teachers, all of Mexican descent, tend to be monolingual Spanish speakers and long-time residents of Los Angeles. At *doctrina*, all interaction is carried out in Spanish, including the religious services associated with religious instructional activities.[5]

Catechism

English catechism classes meet an hour before *doctrina* classes begin, so that by the time *doctrina* students arrive, the catechism children have left, making the interaction between these two groups of children very limited. The children enrolled in catechism represent a variety of different ethnic backgrounds, including Latino, Asian-American, and European American. While it might seem surprising to find Latinos in the English catechism classes, these children are often second- and third-generation immigrants from Mexico and South America who are more proficient in English than Spanish.

The children's ages in catechism range from 6–9 constituting a considerably younger student population than that of *doctrina*. Because Catholic children who are enrolled in parochial schools must also receive religious instruction at their local parishes, many children who attend other parish schools attend St. Paul's Saturday instruction. In general, children in catechism come from a slightly higher socioeconomic level. The two catechism teachers at the time of the study were European American and conducted their classes entirely in English.

Data Base

Data for this paper are drawn from a corpus of video and audio recordings of *doctrina* and catechism classes, interviews, field notes, and on-going conversations with teachers, parents, and children collected over the span of twenty months of participant-observation, from September 1994 to May 1996. The *doctrina* class described here is composed of 42 students. Teresa, the teacher of the class, is a monolingual, Spanish-speaking woman who immigrated in her early twenties to the United States, and has lived in Los Angeles for over thirty years. The study also draws on one catechism class composed of 15 students. The catechism teacher, Nancy, is a monolingual, English-speaking woman in her late forties. She is a native of Los Angeles. The *doctrina* segments discussed in the next few paragraphs include transcribed[6] excerpts from the telling of the narrative of *Nuestra Señora de Guadalupe* in Teresa's *doctrina* class and illustrate how her class collaboratively constructs the identities of dark-skinned Mexicans with a history of oppression. In contrast, the catechism excerpt presented here is part of a lesson on the multiple apparitions of the Virgin Mary and illustrates a different ideology about Our Lady of Guadalupe[7] and ethnicity in general.

Constructing Social Identities through *Doctrina* Narratives

As previously noted, narratives are collaboratively told and socially organized. As such, in the course of telling a narrative version, participants take socially relevant roles as teller and listener. At *doctrina*, this activity is also highly affiliative. But the most significant characteristic of the telling of the narrative of *Nuestra Señora de Guadalupe* is that it serves as a locus of identity construction. Classroom interaction draws children into crafting narrative renditions of the apparition of *Nuestra Señora de Guadalupe* which encourage identification with the place of the apparition and the Virgin Mary. These classroom narratives describe the sociohistorical setting of colonial Mexico as a setting of past oppressive experience, which might reflect *doctrina* children's lives as ethnic minorities in the United States. The narration of events often spawns a great deal of questions about the students' lives. Similar to "whole language" approaches to literacy which are used in other formal classrooms, Teresa's teaching style contextualizes the narrative being presented, breaking it down into more manageable parts. She stops frequently in the course of telling the narrative to directly relate the experiences being described to those of the students in the class. This link is created both at the interactional level (through pauses, questions, and repetitions) and at the grammatical level (through predication and the temporal dynamics of tense and aspect).

The narrative construction of Mexican identity

Example (1) below illustrates how Teresa and her *doctrina* class collaboratively construct a Mexican identity. As Teresa begins to recount the events of the story, she first situates these events as taking place in colonial Mexico. She does this by stopping the narration, and through questions, determining how many of her students are from Mexico, the setting of the ongoing narrative. In this way, she includes her students from Mexico as part of the narrative in progress, making the telling relevant to the students' present lives. This also constitutes a highly affiliative activity, and as we will see, students who were not born in Mexico can claim participation in this collective identity through their parents' heritage:

Example (1)

Teresa:　↑ **Hace (.) muchos años que se   apareció**
　　　　　has been many   years that REFX appear-PAST-3Sg
　　　　　Many years ago appeared
　　　　　(0.8)
　　　　　la Santísima Virgen de Guadalupe
　　　　　the Blessed Virgin of Guadalupe
　　　　　en el   cerro (0.2) del Tepeyac,
　　　　　in the mount   of Tepeyac
　　　　　at mount Tepeyac
　　　　　(0.2)
　　　　　en la capital de México.
　　　　　in the capital of Mexico
　　　　　(0.8)

	>Quiénes	**son**		**de México.**	
	how many	be-PRES-Pl		from Mexico	
	who is from Mexico				
Class:	((raises hands))				
Teresa:	**Los demás**	**son**		**de**	**a ↑ quí**
	the rest	be-PRES-Pl		from	here
	the rest are from here				
	(1.0)				
Class:	**Sí:[:**				
	yes				
Teresa:	**[Quiénes**	**somos**	**de**	**México**	
	how many	be-1Pl	from	Mexico	
	how many of us are from Mexico				
Carlos:	**Mis pa- mi**	**madres**	**son**	**de**	**México,**
	my pa- my	mothers	be-3Pl	from	Mexico
	my fa- my mothers are from Mexico				
Teresa:	**A-Oh ↑ sí**				
	oh yes				
	(0.8)				
	Bueno. bajen		**la**	**manita**	
	good low-CMD		the	hand-DIM	
	good lower your little hand				

As Teresa begins to tell the events of the narrative, she establishes a link from the place where the Virgin Mary appeared, *la capital de México* ("the capital of Mexico"), to present times by relating the setting to the students' place of birth. In her question *Quiénes son de México* ("who is from Mexico") she asks her Mexican students to publicly identify as Mexicans couching this affiliative interaction in present tense, in the here and now. The first time a collectivity is invoked in this class, it describes two contrasting groups: those *de México* ("from Mexico") and those who are not – those *de aquí* ("from here") understood as from the United States.

Teresa's second invocation of a collective identity as Mexican is found in the utterance *Quiénes somos de México*, which now includes her, aligning with those students who first identified as *de México* ("from Mexico"). In her question *Quiénes somos de México* ("how many of us are from Mexico") Teresa uses a form of the verb to be, *somos* ("we are" the first person plural form), which in its inclusive form indexes a collective identity as Mexican. Such is the affiliative force of Teresa's question that Carlos, a student presumably *de aquí* ("from here"), states that his parents *son de México* ("are from Mexico"). Students like Carlos, whose parents come from Mexico (though we assume that he himself does not) are included in the evolving "we" as illustrated by Teresa's affirmative response *A-Oh ↑sí* ("Oh yes").

Narrative activity at *doctrina*, thus socializes children to identify as Mexican. Through questions about the students' place of birth, a group of Mexicans and a group *de aquí* ("from here") are identified. Though Teresa begins a classroom rendition by narrating the past, the *then* of the story, locating the place where the Virgin Mary appeared in Mexico, she then switches to the moment of the telling to collaboratively redefine the setting of the story in relation to the present participants. Thus the narrative is not only about the apparition of the Virgin Mary in the Mexico of many years ago, it is also a narrative about the Mexican students in this *doctrina* class as they have been made an integral part of the story.

The narrative construction of oppression

As Teresa continues to orchestrate a particular classroom narrative rendition, a history of oppression in colonial times is discursively constructed. Having identified as Mexicans, this class now collectively recounts its own colonial history. In Example (2), through temporal dynamics available in Spanish, in particular, through the use of the imperfective (IMPF) aspect, Teresa guides her class through an historical revisitation of the social landscape of colonial Mexico as she describes in more detail the setting at the time of the apparition of the Virgin Mary.

As a language that encodes tense and aspect morphologically, the imperfect in Spanish is realized in suffixation in the forms *-ía-*, *-aba*. The imperfective portrays actions as viewed from within and in progress, and stands in contrast to the perfective usually encoded in past tense, which denotes actions as completed, viewing a situation from the outside (Comrie, 1976). The choice of imperfective is thus a particularly effective resource which allows for a more vivid[8] and highly affiliative use of language to describe the setting of the story, a setting depicting a series of oppressive acts carried out by Spanish conquistadores which warranted intervention (as is often the case in postcolonial histories; see Chatterjee, 1993). The following example illustrates the imperfective as the vehicle through which the class travels the oppressive landscape of Sixteenth Century Mexico; a journey that stops abruptly with a contrasting switch to past tense to explain that the entire situation, the panorama of oppression which the class has now "witnessed," was untenable:

Example (2)

Teresa: Entonces este[9] (1.2)
          then
          fíjense   bien lo que les   voy   a   decir
          Attend-CMD   well it   that to you go-FUT   to   say-INF
          pay attention to what I'm going to say to you
          (1.2)
          cuando (0.5) en México había   mucha opresión, (.)
          when   in Mexico be-IMPF-Sg   much   oppression
          when in Mexico there was a lot of oppression
          por los   españoles
          by   the   Spaniards
          by the Spaniards
          (1.5)
          que a-oprimían   mucho al   indígena.
          who oppress-IMPF-Pl much   to+the   indian
          who oppressed the Indians a lot
          (1.5)
          Y entonces   e:ran (.)   muy   católicos
          and then   be-IMPF-Pl   very   catholic
          and they were very catholic

> porque	bueno	porque	nos	dejaban	muchas	iglesias <
because	well	because	to us	leave-IMPF-Pl	many	churches

because well because they left us many churches

en todo el país de México
in all the country of Mexico
(0.5)
es que también este (0.5)
is that too
it's that too

querían.	tener.	sometidos,	(.8) a (.)	a la gente	más	pobre
want-IMPF-Pl	have-INF	subjugated		to the people	more	poor

they [Spaniards] wanted to have subjugated the poorest people

o l-la	trabajaban	mu:cho	verdad,
or	work-IMPF-Pl	much	right

or they worked them hard, right

> pues	ellos	que	querían	más[10]
well	they	that	want-IMPF-Pl	more

well they wanted more

que (.)	los	indígenas
than	the	indians

than the Indians
(0.8)

ésto <u>no</u> (.)	le pareció	a	la	Virgen
that no	seem-PAST-Sg	to	the	virgin

that didn't seem [right] to the Virgin

First note that the orientation to the story, the detailed description of the setting is conveyed exclusively using the imperfective:

• en México **había** opresión	• in Mexico there was(IMPF) oppression
• los españoles **oprimían**	• the Spaniards oppressed(IMPF)
• **eran** católicos	• (they) were(IMPF) Catholic
• nos **dejaban** muchas iglesias	• they left(IMPF) us many churches
• **querían** tener sometidos	• They wanted(IMPF) to have subjugated
• la **trabajaban** mucho	• (they) worked(IMPF) (the people) hard
• ellos **querían** más	• they wanted(IMPF) more

Precisely at the end of this description, a switch to past tense, in *ésto no le pareció a la Virgen* ("this didn't seem [right] to the Virgin") summarizes the previous description (indicated in *ésto* "this") indicating a switch in action, the Virgin Mary's intervention. The grammatical resources in this narrative telling, including the use of the imperfective to access knowledge about the past, makes the description of Mexico's colonial setting not only more vivid but more affiliative. The unfolding of the oppressive events which describe the indigenous Mexicans as oppressed, subjugated, and overworked, immediately after this class has publicly identified as Mexican, is a powerful means for affiliating with that past.

The oppressive acts embedded in the setting of the story are so consequential in the making of this story of redemption that the teacher quizzes her students at the end of the class period precisely on those acts which motivated the Virgin Mary's appearance in Mexico. In Example (3) below, the socio-economic inequality of

colonial Mexico is emphasized again, this time co-narrated by the teacher and a
student named Enrique:

Example (3)

Teresa: Y   por qué se   quiso   aparecer   la Virgen   en México
          and   why REFX   want-PAST-3Sg   appear-INF   the virgin   in Mexico
          and why did the Virgin want to appear in Mexico
Enrique: Para   cuidar   a México ↑
          To   take care-INF   of Mexico
          to take care of Mexico
          (0.5)
Teresa: Claro.   para   rescatar a:::-a   los (0.5)   indígenas
          of course to   rescue-INF DO   the   indians
          Of course, to rescue the Indians
          de   la   opresión   de   los   españoles.
          from   the   oppression of   the   Spaniards
          from Spanish oppression.

In response to Teresa's question about the reason for the Virgin Mary's apparition in
Mexico, Enrique answers that she appeared in Mexico to take care of the country; a
response which Teresa accepts with *claro* ("of course") reformulating it from *para
cuidar a México* ("to take care of Mexico") into *para rescatar a los indígenas* ("to
take care of the Indians"). She further elaborates on Enrique's response, indicating
that the Indians needed to be rescued from Spanish oppression. Recall that Teresa's
class's journey to Mexico's past is a journey to a past that is now shared by the
Mexicans in her class; one which has described two groups of people, the Spaniards
and the Indians as actors from an unequal past. This interaction between Teresa and
Enrique emphasizes one distinguishing aspect of this class's narrative: that the Virgin
Mary chose to appear in Mexico not only to take care of Mexico, but also because
the Indians needed to be liberated from Spanish oppression. But what is also
interesting to note, is that these *doctrina* members have thus far identified as
Mexican in the present (recall that Teresa asks students to publicly identify as
Mexican) and as Indian in terms of a collaboratively constructed reference to an
oppressive past. This blurred distinction between a Mexican present and an Indian
past is emphasized again in the course of the narrative, as the class creates an identity
as dark-skinned people.

The narrative construction of skin color

As Teresa continues to narrate the story of *Nuestra Señora de Guadalupe*, she
describes the color of the Virgin Mary's skin establishing two skin colors representative of two groups of people. Example (4) below illustrates how a switch from the
narrated past to the moment of the telling creates yet another collective identity for
this class, this time making reference to skin color. Since current discussion in the
social sciences has been problematizing the boundaries between ethnic and racial
identity (Hollinger, 1995; Omi & Winant, 1993; Waters, 1990), it is particularly
revealing to see how at *doctrina*, ethnic identity is based on skin color. In the

example below, Teresa explains to her class the physical features of *Nuestra Señora de Guadalupe* as similar to their own:

Example (4)

Teresa:
la Santísima Virgen quiso ser (.)   se
the blessed   virgin want-PAST-3Sg be-INF REFX
The Blessed Virgin wanted to be
parecerse   morenita   como   nosotros.
look-INF-REFX   dark-DIM   like   Pro-1Pl
to look a little dark like us
(1.0)
porque la   Virgen, (.) de   Guadalupe
because the Virgin   of   Guadalupe
because the Virgin of Guadalupe
no es blanca   como (.) la   Virgen del   Carmen
no is white   like   the Virgin of   Carmen
is not white like the Virgin of Carmen
que se   apareció (.)
who REFX   appear-PAST-3Sg
who appeared
y   es la   patrona   de España,
and is the patroness of Spain
and is the patroness of Spain
la Virgen del Carmen es   blanca.
the Virgin of   Carmen is   white
the Virgin of Carmen is white
(0.5)
y   la   Virgen de   Guadalupe
and the Virgin of   Guadalupe
and the Virgin of Guadalupe
es morenita   como   nosotros
is dark-DIM like   Pro-1Pl
is a little dark like us

In this example, a particular shade of skin color, *morenita* ("a little dark"), is identified as the defining feature of the Virgin of Guadalupe, and the predicate construction *como nosotros* ("like us") embraces the *doctrina* class in a collectivity of dark-skinned peoples. By switching to the moment of the telling, the narration of past events and the description of the narrative's characters includes the dark-skinned *doctrina* people of the present. As the example illustrates, the Virgin of Guadalupe was/is (yesterday/today) dark like the people at *doctrina*.

It is also interesting to note that in this display of ethnic awareness with skin color as the most salient element of contrast, the Virgin of Guadalupe and the Virgin of Carmen co-exist in the present, that is, at the moment of the telling. Notice too that Teresa emphasizes that the Virgin of Guadalupe is not white like the Virgin of Carmen, implying that the Mexican children who look like the Virgin of Guadalupe are not white either. The description and emphasis through repetition, that the Virgin of Guadalupe is *morenita como nosotros* ("a little dark like us"), is indexical of the class of dark Mexicans, and, by extension, the oppressed dark Indians of the past. By disaffiliating her class from the white Virgin of Carmen, Teresa disaffiliates her class from the oppressor Spaniards of colonial Mexico who share the white Virgin's skin color, while at the same time, recognizing and claiming a dark skin color for her class.

This particular *doctrina* narrative telling is an example of how variation in narrative details respond to the recipient organization and the goals of the narrative activity. Clearly, Teresa keeps the main story line, compared, for example, to the plot depicted in the greeting card example I presented before, yet she elaborates on the setting and the skin color of the Virgin Mary. As Poole (1995) has noted, the narrative has served as a means for creating a Mexican identity. Through the continuous unfolding of the narrative, Teresa and her students represent their multiple identities in temporal blends: In the past, they were dark-skinned oppressed Indians in Mexico; they are now dark-skinned Mexicans; and they can also be people *de aquí* ("from here"). This tracing of identities along a temporal and spatial continuum illustrates the diasporic potential of narrative as it creates and explains life in the "borderlands" (Anzaldúa, 1987). *Doctrina* members are linked to Mexico through place, as the birth-place of the majority of the students; they are also linked to Mexico in time, as Indians of the past; and they are also people from here (be it the United States, Los Angeles, or the parish) *both* in time and place. The narrative renditions of the apparition of *Nuestra Señora de Guadalupe* are thus sites where *doctrina* children are socialized to Mexican identity.

Multi-ethnic Mary

As the parish of St. Paul's moves towards its own "English Only" policy, Latino children will probably join children in other religious instruction classes in which English is the medium of instruction. The effect this multiracial environment will have on *doctrina* students' experiences and on the collaborative telling of particular versions of the narrative of *Nuestra Señora de Guadalupe* remains to be assessed. As I have indicated before, English catechism classes at St. Paul's are racially diverse. On the day the classroom interaction described here was recorded, there were Latino, Asian, and Caucasian students present. A segment of classroom interaction depicted in Example (5) below, illustrates two distinct phenomena. First, the dynamics of tense and aspect are used differently, especially distinct from the *doctrina* class examples presented above. Second, Mexican ethnicity is positioned as one of many ethnicities representative of a generic model of American society. In Example (5), Nancy, the teacher, explains to her catechism class the many apparitions of the Virgin Mary:

Example (5)

Nancy: Now. (0.2) remember that Mary has appeared (0.2)
           in many many countries (.) to many many people,
           (0.5)
           d̲ifferently.
           (0.2)
           Our Lady of Guadalup̲e she appeared to the I̲ndian.
           she looked like an I̲ndian.
           °hh when she appeared over [he:re
                                       [(((walking towards cast statue on desk))
           (1.5)

uh (0.5) Our Lady of Grace
(0.8) [this is Our Lady of Grace
        [((touching statue))
(0.5)
she's crushing the snake, (0.5) with her ↑ feet
(0.5)
cause the snake represents the ↑ Devil
(0.5)
and she's standing on top of the world,
this is (.) Our Lady of Grace.
(0.5)
We have (0.5) uh (0.2) Our Lady of Mount Carmel.
We saw[11] the Pilgrim Virgin, (0.2) Our Lady of Fatima:,
(0.5)
She has appeared (.) to many many many many places.
(0.2)
She's appeared in Lourdes.
(.)
and when she was in ↑ Lourdes,
she wore the costume of the
French ladies, (.) she looked like a French lady.
(0.2)
when she appears in Japa:n, (.) she appears (0.2) Japa ↑ nese
(0.5)
When she appears in Hawaii: (0.2)
if she does. she'd appears Hawaiian,
(0.5)
So Our Lady can (.) can change her (0.5) features,
(.) to look like (.) the country that she is appearing in.

Let's consider first the temporal organization of this list. Present perfect is initially used to state that the Virgin Mary has appeared to several people in the past, in Nancy's words: *Mary has appeared in many many countries to many many people.* Nancy's first example of the Virgin Mary's apparition is Our Lady of Guadalupe who appear*ed* (past tense) to the Indian. In all cases in which the place (and manner) of apparition is mentioned, the past tense is used (*looked like an Indian; she wore the costume; she looked like a French lady*). Present tense variants are used to describe the different apparitions of the Virgin Mary, portraying what seem to be generic manifestations. This stands in contrast to the particularization observed in the *doctrina* narrative rendition, where the telling of the apparition of Our Lady of Guadalupe is embedded in a unique historical moment. Moreover, the emphasis in this catechism class seems to be on describing a generic, multi-ethnic Mary, which contrasts with the emphasis of the *doctrina* narrative discussed before to create a Mexican identity and describe Spanish oppression in colonial Mexico. While Nancy notes Mary's apparitions without making reference to specific historical contexts, in fact, this generic portrayal leaves the possibility open for a future apparition in Hawaii, she does make sure that the list recognizes many ethnicities, including Mexican, French, and Japanese. This teacher's teaching style[12] is certainly inclusive, yet it denies a particular historicity and the opportunity to organize and explain past and present experience of particular ethnic groups in the class. Moreover, Nancy's recitational style does not encourage participation from the students in her class.

Even though the two classes described in this paper cannot be compared in terms of the actual telling of the narrative, there is one important difference in the way in which both teachers make reference and assign meaning to Our Lady of Guadalupe. Whereas the narrative of *Nuestra Señora de Guadalupe* promotes affiliative activities and creates a unique Latino identity, a collective self and history, in Nancy's catechism class, Our Lady of Guadalupe is mentioned ahistorically as part of a list that becomes a representative sample of the multi-ethnic composition of the class and of society at large. Given the changes in language policy at St. Paul's, the *doctrina* children of the parish will be joining catechism classes, like Nancy's, where the opportunities to create a collective identity as Mexican are limited and where homogenizing and generic discourses pervade.

Implications

Doctrina teachers design collaborative narrative activities that socialize children to acquire and display knowledge of a collective class version of the narrative of *Nuestra Señora de Guadalupe*. That is, creating a collective version of the narrative not only promotes recall of information, it legitimizes the experiences of the *then* and *now* – both the experiences narrated in the story and those which include the teacher's and students' present lives. The study of the language socialization practices of this church community sheds explanatory light on the ways in which language is a potent way to either constitute or minimize identities. We have seen how a *doctrina* teacher orchestrates an oral collaborative rendition of the narrative of the apparition of *Nuestra Señora de Guadalupe* to socialize children to a range of social identities. We have also seen how a catechism teacher positions ethnic identities as part of a representative list.

The analysis of the practices of the *doctrina* community described in this article has implications for understanding the complexity of the social worlds in which the children of this community live, especially as school-aged minority children. Meaning-making in this Latino learning context is carried out differently. At *doctrina* children acquire and learn to verbally display socio-historical knowledge that is affiliative and which they share with their classmates and teachers. The language socialization practices of *doctrina* linguistically and interactionally reaffirm membership in a particular Latino community, linking children to the world views of their community. Yet these practices will become difficult to enact given the parish's mandate to use English as the medium of instruction. The practices at *doctrina* are examples of the ways in which a community not only retells its past, it affirms and claims social identities while gradually being relegated to the linguistic and cultural margins of a local parish in Los Angeles.

ACKNOWLEDGMENTS

I am indebted to Elinor Ochs for her insight and guidance. Many thanks to Betsy Rymes, Adrienne Lo, and the members of the UCLA Discourse, Identity, and Representation Collective (D.I.R.E) for their helpful commentary and suggestions.

Special thanks to Marcyliena Morgan. The research presented here was made possible by a grant from the UCLA Institute of American Cultures and the Chicano Studies Research Center. Any errors remaining are my own.

NOTES

1   All names have been changed.
2   *VOX Diccionario Manual Ilustrado de la Lengua Española*, 8th edition. Calabria, Barcelona: Biblograf. See also Frye, 1996 for a brief description of early colonial religious practices and life in Mexico.
3   Certain states, including California, have legally adopted "English Only" policies that restrict the use of languages other than English in public places such as the workplace and government offices.
4   For the academic year of 1995–96, tuition was $200.00 per month, not including books and other school supplies.
5   Most notably, First Communion preparation culminates with a celebratory religious service at the main church building.
6   Transcription symbols used in this paper: ↑ Indicates sharp rising intonation; a period at the end of words marks falling intonation; > indicates speech faster than normal cadence; underlining represents sounds pronounced with emphasis; colons indicate elongated sounds; ".hh" indicates inhalations; numbers in parentheses indicate time elapsed in tenths of seconds, with periods indicating micropauses or noticeable pauses that are less than two tenths of a second; brackets indicate overlapping speech; information contained in ((double parentheses)) indicates nonverbal behavior; CMD is command verbal form; DIM is diminutive suffix, often encoding affect; REFX is a reflexive pronoun; Sg denotes singular; Pl denotes plural; INF is the infinitive tense; IMPF is the imperfective (in Spanish both tense and aspect); DO is direct object.
7   I will be using the English name of Our Lady of Guadalupe when describing the catechism class.
8   Silva-Corvalán (1983) has noted that certain Spanish tenses, in particular the historical present (HP), provide "vividness" and act as an evaluative device. This same argument has been made for the HP in English by Schiffrin (1981). Here I extend Silva-Corvalán's claim to include the Spanish imperfective as functioning both as an evaluative and affiliative device.
9   Similar to American English "uhm."
10 From context it is understood that the Spaniards wanted more material goods than did the Indians.
11 On an earlier trip to the temple that morning, the class met a woman carrying the statue of the Pilgrim Virgin.
12 It remains unknown whether Nancy's choice of examples and descriptive attributes of the different Virgin Marys reflect more than instructional ideology; that is, whether the examples reflect personal and community attitudes towards different cultural groups.

REFERENCES

Anzaldúa, G. (1987). *Borderlands/La Frontera: The New Mestiza*. San Francisco: Aunt Lute Books.
Bernstein, B. (1970/1972). Social class, language, and socialization. In P. Gigioli (ed.), *Language and Social Context*. London: Penguin.
Brockelman, P. (1992). *The Inside Story: A Narrative Approach to Religious Understanding and Truth*. Albany: State University of New York Press.
Bruner, J. (1990). *Acts of Meaning*. Cambridge, MA: Harvard University Press.
Capps, L., & Ochs, E. (1995). *Constructing Panic: The Discourse of Agoraphobia*. Cambridge, MA: Harvard University Press.

Chatterjee, P. (1993). *The Nation and its Fragments: Colonial and Postcolonial Histories*. Princeton, NJ: Princeton University Press.

Comrie, B. (1976). *Aspect: An Introduction to the Study of Verbal Aspect and Related Problems*. Cambridge: Cambridge University Press.

Duranti, A. (1994). *From Grammar to Politics: Linguistic Anthropology in a Western Samoan Village*. Berkeley: University of California Press.

Duranti, A., & Brenneis, D. (eds.) (1986). The audience as co-author. Special Issue of *Text* (6.3). New York: Mouton de Gruyter.

Duranti, A., & Ochs, E. (1986). Literacy instruction in a Samoan village. In B. Schieffelin & P. Gilmore (eds.), *The Acquisition of Literacy: Ethnographic Perspectives* (pp. 213–32). Norwood, NJ: Ablex.

Duranti, A., Ochs, E., & Ta'ase, E. (1995). Change and Tradition in Literacy Instruction in a Samoan American Community. Paper presented at the Annual Meeting of the American Educational Research Association (AERA), San Francisco, California, April 18.

Frye, D. (1996). *Indians into Mexicans: History and Identity in a Mexican Town*. Austin: University of Texas Press.

Heath, S.B. (1983). *Ways with Words: Language, Life, and Work in Communities and Classrooms*. Cambridge: Cambridge University Press.

Heidegger, M. (1962). *Being and Time*. Trans. J. Macquarrie. & E. Robinson. New York: Harper & Row.

Hollinger, D. (1995). *Postethnic America: Beyond Multiculturalism*. New York: Basic Books.

Labov, W., & Waletzky, J. (1968). Narrative analysis. In W. Labov (ed.), *A Study of the Nonstandard English of Negro and Puerto Rican Speakers in New York City* (pp. 286–338). New York: Columbia University.

Lentz, R. (1987). *Nuestra Señora de Guadalupe/Our Lady of Guadalupe*. Burlington, VT: Bridge Building Images.

Morgan, M. (1995). Just to Have Something: Camouflaged Narratives of African American Life. Unpublished manuscript. University of California, Los Angeles.

Ochs, E. (1986). *Culture and Language Development: Language Acquisition and Language Socialization in a Samoan Village*. Cambridge: Cambridge University Press.

Ochs, E. (1994). Stories that step into the future. In D. Biber & E. Finegan (eds.), *Perspectives on Register: Situating Register Variation within Sociolinguistics* (pp. 106–35). Oxford: Oxford University Press.

Ochs, E., & Capps, L. (1996). Narrating the self. *Annual Review of Anthropology* 25: 19–43. Palo Alto, CA: Annual Reviews.

Omi, M., & Winant, H. (1993). On the theoretical concept of race. In C. McCarthy & W. Crichlow (eds.), *Race, Identity, and Representation in Education* (pp. 3–10). New York: Routledge.

Polkinghorne, D. (1988). *Narrative Knowing in the Human Sciences*. Albany: State University of New York Press.

Poole, S. (1995). *Our Lady of Guadalupe: The Origins and Sources of a Mexican National Symbol, 1531–1797*. Tucson: University of Arizona Press.

Ricoeur, P. (1985/1988). *Time and Narrative*. Chicago: University of Chicago Press.

Rodriguez, J. (1994). *Our Lady of Guadalupe: Faith and Empowerment among Mexican-American Women*. Austin: University of Texas Press.

Schiffrin, D. (1981). Tense variation in narrative, *Language* 57: 45–62.

Schieffelin, B., & Ochs, E. (eds.) (1986). *Language Socialization across Cultures*. Cambridge: Cambridge University Press.

Silva-Corvalán, C. (1983). Tense and aspect in oral Spanish narrative: Context and meaning. *Language* 59(4): 760–80.

Suárez, J. (1983). *The Mesoamerican Indian Languages*. New York: Cambridge University Press.

Waters, M. (1990). *Ethnic Options: Choosing Identities in America*. Berkeley: University of California Press.

Part IV

The Power of Language

Introduction

There are different ways of thinking about the power of language. One is in terms of the power that language itself (e.g. due to its conventions) has on its speakers. The other is in terms of the power that speakers can exert by means of linguistic conventions. The chapters in Part IV address both perspectives. Linguistic relativity, that is, the view that the language we speak has the power to affect our thinking and acting in the world is presented in chapter 15, which reproduces a classic paper by Whorf on the differences between the worldview implicit in a Native American language (Hopi) and the worldview implicit in a composite language which he calls "Standard Average European" (SAE). Whorf's work is extended and elaborated in chapter 16, where Silverstein identifies the features that should make it easier for speakers to have the ability to explicate the meaning implicit in the linguistic forms they routinely use, and in chapter 17, where Kroskrity discusses the strategies that speakers of Arizona Tewa use to stop innovation and shows the limits of what speakers can consciously control. Another way of thinking about the power of language is in terms of its role in the reproduction of social stereotypes and social inequality. The other three chapters in this Part address these aspects of language use. Gal warns us against reproducing certain stereotypes of gender differences in our own study and reminds us that we should think of gender as culturally constructed, with everyday talk playing a major part in such a construction. Ochs and Taylor look at the production of narratives at the dinner table and uncover how hierarchy is reproduced through the division of linguistic labor among participants, who assume a variety of roles (e.g. introducer, initial teller, primary recipient, problematizer, judge). Finally, by examining the cultural implications of the use of "Mock Spanish," Hill unveils the reproduction of racial stereotypes in everyday discourse.

Questions about the Power of Language

1 In what became a very famous and controversial paper, Whorf argued that European languages and Hopi have a radically different way of conceiving time. What was his hypothesis and what kind of evidence did he use to support it?
2 Try to extend Whorf's methodology to languages you are familiar with – e.g. compare how two languages express the same domain (e.g. time, space, causation, agency, natural events, emotions). Do you find similarities, differences, or both? Do you find yourself agreeing with Whorf's views?
3 What are the factors identified by Silverstein as relevant to native speakers' ability to reflect on the pragmatic force of their language (i.e. its ability to affect reality)?
4 On the basis of Kroskrity's discussion of the Arizona Tewa linguistic ideology, define (1) regulation by convention, (2) indigenous purism, and (3) strict compartmentalization by using examples from languages and speech communities you are familiar with.
5 How does the purism enforced in kiva ceremonies among the Tewa (and other Native American groups) relate to the discussion of features of formality done by Irvine in Part II?
6 How is the ideology of "Father knows best" illustrated by Ochs and Taylor reproduced through narrative activity?
7 Can you extend Ochs and Taylor's analysis of story-telling at the dinner table to other situations you are familiar with?
8 What are the attributes of "Mock Spanish" and why does Hill consider it an example of racist discourse?
9 What are other examples of ethnic stereotyping done through language that you are familiar with? Could you apply to them Hill's method of analysis?

Suggestions for Further Reading

Useful collections of articles by Edward Sapir and Benjamin Lee Whorf are: Mandelbaum, D. G. (ed.) (1949). *Selected Writings of Edward Sapir in Language, Culture, and Personality*. Berkeley and Los Angeles: University of California Press; and Carroll, J. B. (ed.) (1956). *Language, Thought, and Reality: Selected Writings of Benjamin Lee Whorf*. Cambridge, MA: MIT Press. For an intellectual biography of Sapir: Darnell, R. (1990). *Edward Sapir: Linguist, Anthropologist, Humanist*. Berkeley: University of California Press.

An in-depth review of a wide range of articles and books on linguistic relativity can be found in: Lucy, J. A. (1992). *Language Diversity and Cognitive Development: A Reformulation of the Linguistic Relativity Hypothesis*. Cambridge: Cambridge University Press; and Lee, P. (1996). *The Whorf Theory Complex: A Critical Reconstruction*. Amsterdam: John Benjamins.

A recent collection of contributions to linguistic relativity is: Gumperz, J. J., and Levinson, S. C. (eds.) (1996). *Rethinking Linguistic Relativity*. Cambridge: Cambridge University Press.

The work on metalinguistics and metapragmatics is found in a number of articles, some of which are collected in: Lucy, J. A. (ed.) (1993). *Reflexive Language: Reported Speech and Metapragmatics*. New York: Cambridge University Press; and Silverstein, M., and Urban, G. (eds.) (1996). *Natural Histories of Discourse*. Chicago: University of Chicago Press.

Some useful collections of essays on the language of politics and conflict across cultural contexts are: Bloch, M. (1975). *Political Language and Oratory in Traditional Society*. London: Academic Press; Brenneis, D. L., and Myers, F. (eds.) (1984). *Dangerous Words: Language and Politics in the Pacific*. New York: New York University Press; Watson-Gegeo, K., and White, G. (eds.) (1990). *Disentangling: Conflict Discourse in Pacific Societies*. Stanford, CA: Stanford University Press.

A powerful comparative study of the use of language for mediating differences in power is: Brown, P., and Levinson, S. C. (1987). *Politeness: Some Universals in Language Usage*. Cambridge: Cambridge University Press.

The literature on language and gender is quite vast. Here are some good collections of articles to start with: Philips, S., Steele, S., and Tanz, C. (eds.) (1987). *Language, Gender, and Sex in Comparative Perspective*. Cambridge: Cambridge University Press (a useful collection of essays on gender from a variety of perspectives); Tannen, D. (ed.) (1993). *Gender and Conversational Interaction*. New York: Oxford University Press (a set of good articles that critically review past literature and define new research agendas); Hall, K., and Bucholtz, M. (eds.) (1995). *Gender Articulated: Language and the Socially Constructed Self*. New York: Routledge; Bucholtz, M., Liang, A. C., and Sutton, L. A. (eds.) (1999). *Reinventing Identities: The Gendered Self in Discourse*. New York: Oxford University Press.

An in-depth study of differences between boys' and girls' discursive strategies in an African American speech community (which reverses several stereotyped views of gender differences) is: Goodwin, M. H. (1990). *He-Said-She-Said: Talk as Social Organization among Black Children*. Bloomington, IN: Indiana University Press.

15

The Relation of Habitual Thought and Behavior to Language

Benjamin Lee Whorf

Human beings do not live in the objective world alone, nor alone in the world of social activity as ordinarily understood, but are very much at the mercy of the particular language which has become the medium of expression for their society. It is quite an illusion to imagine that one adjusts to reality essentially without the use of language and that language is merely an incidental means of solving specific problems of communication or reflection. The fact of the matter is that the "real world" is to a large extent unconsciously built up on the language habits of the group. . . . We see and hear and otherwise experience very largely as we do because the language habits of our community predispose certain choices of interpretation.

Edward Sapir (1949:162)

There will probably be general assent to the proposition that an accepted pattern of using words is often prior to certain lines of thinking and forms of behavior, but he who assents often sees in such a statement nothing more than a platitudinous recognition of the hypnotic power of philosophical and learned terminology on the one hand or of catchwords, slogans, and rallying cries on the other. To see only thus far is to miss the point of one of the important interconnections which Sapir saw between language, culture, and psychology, and succinctly expressed in the introductory quotation. It is not so much in these special uses of language as in its constant ways of arranging data and its most ordinary everyday analysis of phenomena that we need to recognize the influence it has on other activities, cultural and personal.

The Name of the Situation as Affecting Behavior

I came in touch with an aspect of this problem before I had studied under Dr. Sapir, and in a field usually considered remote from linguistics. It was in the course of my professional work for a fire insurance company, in which I undertook the task of analyzing many hundreds of reports of circumstances surrounding the start of fires, and in some cases, of explosions. My analysis was directed toward purely physical conditions, such as defective wiring, presence or lack of air spaces between metal flues and woodwork, etc., and the results were presented in these terms. Indeed it was undertaken with no thought that any other significances would or could be revealed. But in due course it became evident that not only a physical situation *qua* physics, but the meaning of that situation to people, was sometimes a factor, through the behavior of the people, in the start of the fire. And this factor of meaning was clearest when it was a LINGUISTIC MEANING, residing in the name or the linguistic description commonly applied to the situation. Thus, around a storage of what are called "gasoline drums," behavior will tend to a certain type, that is, great care will be exercised; while around a storage of what are called "empty gasoline drums," it will tend to be different – careless, with little repression of smoking or of tossing cigarette stubs about. Yet the "empty" drums are perhaps the more dangerous, since they contain explosive vapor. Physically the situation is hazardous, but the linguistic analysis according to regular analogy must employ the word "empty," which inevitably suggests lack of hazard. The word "empty" is used in two linguistic patterns: (1) as a virtual synonym for "null and void, negative, inert," (2) applied in analysis of physical situations without regard to, e.g., vapor, liquid vestiges, or stray rubbish, in the container. The situation is named in one pattern (2) and the name is then "acted out" or "lived up to" in another (1), this being a general formula for the linguistic conditioning of behavior into hazardous forms.

In a wood distillation plant the metal stills were insulated with a composition prepared from limestone and called at the plant "spun limestone." No attempt was made to protect this covering from excessive heat or the contact of flame. After a period of use, the fire below one of the stills spread to the "limestone," which to everyone's great surprise burned vigorously. Exposure to acetic acid fumes from the stills had converted part of the limestone (calcium carbonate) to calcium acetate. This when heated in a fire decomposes, forming inflammable acetone. Behavior that tolerated fire close to the covering was induced by use of the name "limestone," which because it ends in "-stone" implies non-combustibility.

A huge iron kettle of boiling varnish was observed to be overheated, nearing the temperature at which it would ignite. The operator moved it off the fire and ran it on its wheels to a distance, but did not cover it. In a minute or so the varnish ignited. Here the linguistic influence is more complex; it is due to the metaphorical objectifying (of which more later) of "cause" as contact or the spatial juxtaposition of "things" – to analyzing the situation as "on" versus "off" the fire. In reality, the stage when the external fire was the main factor had passed; the overheating was now an internal process of convection in the varnish from the intensely heated kettle, and still continued when "off" the fire.

An electirc glow heater on the wall was little used, and for one workman had the meaning of a convenient coathanger. At night a watchman entered and snapped a switch, which action he verbalized as "turning on the light." No light appeared, and this result he verbalized as "light is burned out." He could not see the glow of the heater because of the old coat hung on it. Soon the heater ignited the coat, which set fire to the building.

A tannery discharged waste water containing animal matter into an outdoor settling basin partly roofed with wood and partly open. This situation is one that ordinarily would be verbalized as "pool of water." A workman had occasion to light a blowtorch near by, and threw his match into the water. But the decomposing waste matter was evolving gas under the wood cover, so that the setup was the reverse of "watery." An instant flare of flame ignited the woodwork, and the fire quickly spread into the adjoining building.

A drying room for hides was arranged with a blower at one end to make a current of air along the room and thence outdoors through a vent at the other end. Fire started at a hot bearing on the blower, which blew the flames directly into the hides and fanned them along the room, destroying the entire stock. This hazardous setup followed naturally from the term "blower" with its linguistic equivalence to "that which blows," implying that its function necessarily is to "blow." Also its function is verbalized as "blowing air for drying," overlooking that it can blow other things, e.g., flames and sparks. In reality, a blower simply makes a current of air and can exhaust as well as blow. It should have been installed at the vent end to DRAW the air over the hides, then through the hazard (its own casing and bearings), and thence outdoors.

Beside a coal-fired melting pot for lead reclaiming was dumped a pile of "scrap lead" – a misleading verbalization, for it consisted of the lead sheets of old radio condensers, which still had paraffin paper between them. Soon the paraffin blazed up and fired the roof, half of which was burned off.

Such examples, which could be greatly multiplied, will suffice to show how the cue to a certain line of behavior is often given by the analogies of the linguistic formula in which the situation is spoken of, and by which to some degree it is analyzed, classified, and allotted its place in that world which is "to a large extent unconsciously built up on the language habits of the group." And we always assume that the linguistic analysis made by our group reflects reality better than it does.

Grammatical Patterns as Interpretations of Experience

The linguistic material in the above examples is limited to single words, phrases, and patterns of limited range. One cannot study the behavioral compulsiveness of such material without suspecting a much more far-reaching compulsion from large-scale patterning of grammatical categories, such as plurality, gender and similar classifications (animate, inanimate, etc.), tenses, voices, and other verb forms, classifications of the type of "parts of speech," and the matter of whether a given experience is denoted by a unit morpheme, an inflected word, or a syntactical combination. A category such as number (singular vs. plural) is an attempted interpretation of a whole large order of experience, virtually of the world or of nature; it attempts to say how experience is to be segmented, what experience is to be called "one" and what "several." But the difficulty of appraising such a far-reaching influence is great because of its background character, because of the difficulty of standing aside from our own language, which is a habit and a cultural *non est disputandum*, and scrutinizing it objectively. And if we take a very dissimilar language, this language becomes a part of nature, and we even do to it what we have already done to nature. We tend to think in our own language in order to examine the exotic language. Or we find the task of unraveling the purely morphological intricacies so gigantic that it seems to absorb all else. Yet the problem, though difficult, is feasible; and the best approach is through an exotic language, for in its study we are at long last pushed willy-nilly out of our ruts. Then we find that the exotic language is a mirror held up to our own.

In my study of the Hopi language, what I now see as an opportunity to work on this problem was first thrust upon me before I was clearly aware of the problem. The seemingly endless task of describing the morphology did finally end. Yet it was evident, especially in the light of Sapir's lectures on Navaho, that the description of the LANGUAGE was far from complete. I knew for example the morphological formation of plurals, but not how to use plurals. It was evident that the category of plural in Hopi was not the same thing as in English, French, or German. Certain things that were plural in these languages were singular in Hopi. The phase of investigation which now began consumed nearly two more years.

The work began to assume the character of a comparison between Hopi and western European languages. It also became evident that even the grammar of Hopi bore a relation to Hopi culture, and the grammar of European tongues to our own "Western" or "European" culture. And it appeared that the interrelation brought in those large subsummations of experience by language, such as our own terms "time," "space," "substance," and "matter." Since, with respect to the traits compared, there is little difference between English, French, German, or other European languages with the POSSIBLE (but doubtful) exception of Balto-Slavic and non-Indo-European, I have lumped these languages into one group called SAE, or "Standard Average European."

That portion of the whole investigation here to be reported may be summed up in two questions: (1) Are our own concepts of "time," "space," and "matter" given in substantially the same form by experience to all men, or are they in part conditioned by the structure of particular languages? (2) Are there traceable affinities between (*a*) cultural and behavioral norms and (*b*) large-scale linguistic patterns? I should be the last to pretend that there is anything so definite as "a correlation" between culture and language, and especially between ethnological rubrics such as "agricultural, hunting," etc., and linguistic ones like "inflected," "synthetic," or "isolating."[1] When I began the study, the problem was by no means so clearly formulated, and I had little notion that the answers would turn out as they did.

Plurality and Numeration in SAE and Hopi

In our language, that is SAE, plurality and cardinal numbers are applied in two ways: to real plurals and imaginary plurals. Or more exactly if less tersely: perceptible spatial aggregates and metaphorical aggregates. We say "ten men" and also "ten days." Ten men either are or could be objectively perceived as ten, ten in one group perception[2] – ten men on a street corner, for instance. But "ten days" cannot be objectively experienced. We experience only one day, today; the other nine (or even all ten) are something conjured up from memory or imagination. If "ten days" be regarded as a group it must be as an "imaginary," mentally constructed group. Whence comes this mental pattern? Just as in the case of the fire-causing errors, from the fact that our language confuses the two different situations, has but one pattern for both. When we speak of "ten steps forward, ten strokes on a bell," or any similarly described cyclic sequence, "times" of any sort, we are doing the same thing as with "days." CYCLICITY brings the response of imaginary plurals. But a likeness of cyclicity to aggregates is not unmistakably given by experience prior to language, or it would be found in all languages, and it is not.

Our AWARENESS of time and cyclicity does contain something immediate and subjective – the basic sense of "becoming later and later." But, in the habitual thought of us SAE people, this is covered under something quite different, which though mental should not be called subjective. I call it OBJECTIFIED, or imaginary, because it is patterned on the OUTER world. It is this that reflects our linguistic usage. Our tongue makes no distinction between numbers counted on discrete entities and numbers that are simply "counting itself." Habitual thought then assumes that in the latter the numbers are just as much counted on "something" as in the former. This is objectification. Concepts of time lose contact with the subjective experience of "becoming later" and are objectified as counted QUANTITIES, especially as lengths, made up of units as a length can be visibly marked off into inches. A "length of time" is envisioned as a row of similar units, like a row of bottles.

In Hopi there is a different linguistic situation. Plurals and cardinals are used only for entities that form or can form an objective group. There are no imaginary plurals, but instead ordinals used with singulars. Such an expression as "ten days" is not used. The equivalent statement is an operational one that reaches one day by a suitable count. "They stayed ten days" becomes "they stayed until the eleventh day" or "they left after the tenth day." "Ten days is greater than nine days" becomes "the tenth day is later than the ninth." Our "length of time" is not regarded as a length but as a relation between two events in lateness. Instead of our linguistically promoted objectification of that datum of consciousness we call "time," the Hopi language has not laid down any pattern that would cloak the subjective "becoming later" that is the essence of time.

Nouns of Physical Quantity in SAE and Hopi

We have two kinds of nouns denoting physical things: individual nouns, and mass nouns, e.g., "water, milk, wood, granite, sand, flour, meat." Individual nouns denote bodies with definite outlines: "a tree, a stick, a man, a hill." Mass nouns denote homogeneous continua without implied boundaries. The distinction is marked by linguistic form; e.g., mass nouns lack plurals,[3] in English drop articles, and in French take the partitive article *du, de la, des*. The distinction is more widespread in language than in the observable appearance of things. Rather few natural occurrences present themselves as unbounded extents; "air" of course, and often "water, rain, snow, sand, rock, dirt, grass." We do not encounter "butter, meat, cloth, iron, glass," or most "materials" in such kind of manifestation, but in bodies small or large with definite outlines. The distinction is somewhat forced upon our description of events by an unavoidable pattern in language. It is so inconvenient in a great many cases that we need some way of individualizing the mass noun by further linguistic devices. This is partly done by names of body-types: "stick of wood, piece of cloth, pane of glass, cake of soap"; also, and even more, by introducing names of containers though their contents be the real issue: "glass of water, cup of coffee, dish of food, bag of flour, bottle of beer." These very common container formulas, in which "of" has an obvious, visually perceptible meaning ("contents"), influence our feeling about the less obvious type-body formulas: "stick of wood, lump of dough," etc. The formulas are very similar: individual noun plus a similar relator (English "of"). In the obvious case this relator denotes contents. In the inobvious one it "suggests" contents. Hence the "lumps, chunks, blocks, pieces," etc., seem to contain something, a "stuff," "substance," or "matter" that answers to the "water," "coffee," or "flour" in the container formulas. So with SAE people the philosophic "substance" and "matter" are also the naïve idea; they are instantly acceptable, "common sense." It is so through linguistic habit. Our language patterns often require us to name a physical thing by a binomial that splits the reference into a formless item plus a form.

Hopi is again different. It has a formally distinguished class of nouns. But this class contains no formal subclass of mass nouns. All nouns have an individual sense and both singular and plural forms. Nouns translating most nearly our mass nouns still refer to vague bodies or vaguely bounded extents. They imply indefiniteness, but not lack, of outline and size. In specific statements, "water" means one certain mass or quantity of water, not what we call "the substance water." Generality of statement is conveyed through the verb or predicator, not the noun. Since nouns are individual already, they are not individualized by either type-bodies or names of containers, if there is no special need to emphasize shape or container. The noun itself implies a suitable type-body or container. One says, not "a glass of water" but *kə·yi* "a water," not "a pool of water" but *pa·hə*,[4] not "a dish of cornflour" but *ŋəmni* "a (quantity of) cornflour," not "a piece of meat" but *sikʷi* "a meat." The language has neither need for nor analogies on which to build the concept of existence as a duality of formless item and form. It deals with formlessness through other symbols than nouns.

Phases of Cycles in SAE and Hopi

Such terms as "summer, winter, September, morning, noon, sunset" are with us nouns, and have little formal linguistic difference from other nouns. They can be subjects or objects, and we say "at sunset" or "in winter" just as we say "at a corner" or "in an orchard."[5] They are pluralized and numerated like nouns of physical objects, as we have seen. Our thought about the referents of such words hence becomes objectified. Without objectification, it would be a subjective experience of real time, i.e. of the consciousness of "becoming later and later" – simply a cyclic phase similar to an earlier phase in that ever-later-becoming duration. Only by imagination can such a cyclic phase be set beside another and another in the manner of a spatial (i.e. visually perceived) configuration. But such is the power of linguistic analogy that we do so objectify cyclic phasing. We do it even by saying "a phase" and "phases" instead of, e.g., "phasing." And the pattern of individual and mass nouns, with the resulting binomial formula of formless item plus form, is so general that it is implicit for all nouns, and hence our very generalized formless items like "substance, matter," by which we can fill out the binomial for an enormously wide range of nouns. But even these are not quite generalized enough to take in our phase nouns. So for the phase nouns we have made a formless item, "time." We have made it by using "a time," i.e. an occasion or a phase, in the pattern of a mass noun, just as from "a summer" we make "summer" in the pattern of a mass noun. Thus with our binomial formula we can say and think "a moment of time, a second of time, a year of time." Let me again point out that the pattern is simply that of "a bottle of milk" or "a piece of cheese." Thus we are assisted to imagine that "a summer" actually contains or consists of such-and-such a quantity of "time."

In Hopi however all phase terms, like "summer, morning," etc., are not nouns but a kind of adverb, to use the nearest SAE analogy. They are a formal part of speech by themselves, distinct from nouns, verbs, and even other Hopi "adverbs." Such a word is not a case form or a locative pattern, like "des Abends" or "in the morning." It contains no morpheme like one of "in the house" or "at the tree."[6] It means "when it is morning" or "while morning-phase is occurring." These "temporals" are not used as subjects or objects, or at all like nouns. One does not say "it's a hot summer" or "summer is hot"; summer is not hot, summer is only WHEN conditions are hot, WHEN heat occurs. One does not say "THIS summer," but "summer now" or "summer recently." There is no objectification, as a region, an extent, a quantity, of the subjective duration-feeling. Nothing is suggested about time except the perpetual "getting later" of it. And so there is no basis here for a formless item answering to our "time."

Temporal Forms of Verbs in SAE and Hopi

The three-tense system of SAE verbs colors all our thinking about time. This system is amalgamated with that larger scheme of objectification of the subjective experience of duration already noted in other patterns – in the binomial formula applicable to nouns in general, in temporal nouns, in plurality and numeration. This objectification enables us in imagination to "stand time units in a row." Imagination of time as like a row harmonizes with a system of THREE tenses; whereas a system of TWO, an earlier and a later, would seem to correspond better to the feeling of duration as it is experienced. For if we inspect consciousness we find no past, present, future, but a unity embracing complexity. EVERYTHING is in consciousness, and everything in consciousness IS, and is together. There is in it a sensuous and a nonsensuous. We may call the sensuous – what we are seeing, hearing, touching – the "present" while in the nounsensuous the vast image-world of memory is being labeled "the past" and another realm of belief, intuition, and uncertainty "the future"; yet sensation, memory, foresight, all are in consciousness together – one is not "yet to be" nor another "once but no more." Where real time comes in is that all this in consciousness is "getting later," changing certain relations in an irreversible manner. In this "latering" or "durating" there seems to me to be a paramount contrast between the newest, latest instant at the focus of attention and the rest – the earlier. Languages by the score get along well with two tenselike forms answering to this paramount relation of "later" to "earlier." We can of course CONTRAST AND CONTEMPLATE IN THOUGHT a system of past, present, future, in the objectified configuration of points on a line. This is what our general objectification tendency leads us to do and our tense system confirms.

In English the present tense seems the one least in harmony with the paramount temporal relation. It is as if pressed into various and not wholly congruous duties. One duty is to stand as objectified middle term between objectified past and objectified future, in narration, discussion, argument, logic, philosophy. Another is to denote inclusion in the sensuous field: "I SEE him." Another is for nomic, i.e. customarily or generally valid, statements: "We SEE with our eyes." These varied uses introduce confusions of thought, of which for the most part we are unaware.

Hopi, as we might expect, is different here too. Verbs have no "tenses" like ours, but have validity-forms ("assertions"), aspects, and clause-linkage forms (modes), that yield even greater precision of speech. The validity-forms denote that the speaker (not the subject) reports the situation (answering to our past and present) or that he expects it (answering to our future)[7] or that he makes a nomic statement (answering to our nomic present). The aspects denote different degrees of duration and different kinds of tendency "during duration." As yet we have noted nothing to indicate whether an event is sooner or later than another when both are REPORTED. But need for this does not arise until we have two verbs: i.e. two clauses. In that case the "modes" denote relations between the clauses, including relations of later to earlier and of simultaneity. Then there are many detached words that express similar relations, supplementing the modes and aspects. The duties of our three-tense system and its tripartite linear objectified "time" are distributed among various verb categories, all different from our tenses; and there is no more basis for an objectified time in Hopi verbs than in other Hopi patterns; although this does not in the least hinder the verb forms and other patterns from being closely adjusted to the pertinent realities of actual situations.

Duration, Intensity, and Tendency in SAE and Hopi

To fit discourse to manifold actual situations, all languages need to express durations, intensities, and tendencies. It is characteristic of SAE and perhaps of many other language types to express them metaphorically. The metaphors are those of spatial extension, i.e. of size, number (plurality), position, shape, and motion. We express duration by "long, short, great, much, quick, slow," etc.; intensity by "large, great, much, heavy, light, high, low, sharp, faint," etc.; tendency by "more, increase, grow, turn, get, approach, go, come, rise, fall, stop, smooth, even, rapid, slow"; and so on through an almost inexhaustible list of metaphors that we hardly recognize as such, since they are virtually the only linguistic media available. The nonmetaphorical terms in this field, like "early, late, soon, lasting, intense, very, tending," are a mere handful, quite inadequate to the needs.

It is clear how this condition "fits in." It is part of our whole scheme of OBJECTIFYING – imaginatively spatializing qualities and potentials that are quite nonspatial (so far as any spatially perceptive senses can tell us). Noun-meaning (with us) proceeds from physical bodies to referents of far other sort. Since physical bodies and their outlines in PERCEIVED SPACE are denoted by size and shape terms and reckoned by cardinal numbers and plurals, these patterns of denotation and reckoning extend to the symbols of nonspatial meanings, and so suggest an IMAGINARY SPACE. Physical shapes "move, stop, rise, sink, approach," etc., in perceived space; why not these other referents in their imaginary space? This has gone so far that we can hardly refer to the simplest nonspatial situation without constant resort to physical metaphors. I "grasp" the "thread" of another's arguments, but if its "level" is "over my head" my attention may "wander" and "lose touch" with the "drift" of it, so that when he "comes" to his "point" we differ "widely," our "views" being indeed so "far apart" that the "things" he says "appear" "much" too arbitrary, or even "a lot" of nonsense!

The absence of such metaphor from Hopi speech is striking. Use of space terms when there is no space involved is NOT THERE – as if on it had been laid the taboo teetotal! The reason is clear when we know that Hopi has abundant conjugational and lexical means of expressing duration, intensity, and tendency directly as such, and that major grammatical patterns do not, as with us, provide analogies for an imaginary space. The many verb "aspects" express duration and tendency of manifestations, while some of the "voices" express intensity, tendency, and duration of causes or forces producing manifestations. Then a special part of speech, the "tensors," a huge class of words, denotes only intensity, tendency, duration, and sequence. The function of the tensors is to express intensities, "strengths," and how they continue or vary, their rate of change; so that the broad concept of intensity, when considered as necessarily always varying and/or continuing, includes also tendency and duration. Tensors convey distinctions of degree, rate, constancy, repetition, increase and decrease of intensity, immediate sequence, interruption or sequence after an interval, etc., also QUALITIES of strengths, such as we should express metaphorically as smooth, even, hard, rough. A striking feature is their lack of resemblance to the terms of real space and movement that to us "mean the same." There is not even more than a trace of apparent derivation from space terms.[8] So, while Hopi in its nouns seems highly concrete, here in the tensors it becomes abstract almost beyond our power to follow.

Habitual Thought in SAE and Hopi

The comparison now to be made between the habitual thought worlds of SAE and Hopi speakers is of course incomplete. It is possible only to touch upon certain dominant contrasts that appear to stem from the linguistic differences already noted. By "habitual thought" and "thought world" I mean more than simply language, i.e. than the linguistic patterns themselves. I include all the analogical and suggestive value of the patterns (e.g., our "imaginary space" and its distant implications), and all the give-and-take between language and the culture as a whole, wherein is a vast amount that is not linguistic but yet shows the shaping influence of language. In brief, this "thought world" is the microcosm that each man carries about within himself, by which he measures and understands what he can of the macrocosm.

The SAE microcosm has analyzed reality largely in terms of what it calls "things" (bodies and quasibodies) plus modes of extensional but formless existence that it calls "substances" or "matter." It tends to see existence through a binomial formula that expresses any existent as a spatial form plus a spatial formless continuum related to the form, as contents is related to the outlines of its container. Nonspatial existents are imaginatively spatialized and charged with similar implications of form and continuum.

The Hopi microcosm seems to have analyzed reality largely in terms of EVENTS (or better "eventing"), referred to in two ways, objective and subjective. Objectively, and only if perceptible physical experience, events are expressed mainly as outlines, colors, movements, and other perceptive reports. Subjectively, for both the physical and nonphysical, events are considered the expression of invisible intensity factors, on which depend their stability and persistence, or their fugitiveness and proclivities. It implies that existents do not "become later and later" all in the same way; but some do so by growing like plants, some by diffusing and vanishing, some by a procession of metamorphoses, some by enduring in one shape till affected by violent forces. In the nature of each existent able to manifest as a definite whole is the power of its own mode of duration: its growth, decline, stability, cyclicity, or creativeness. Everything is thus already "prepared" for the way it now manifests by earlier phases, and what it will be later, partly has been, and partly is in act of being so "prepared." An emphasis and importance rests on this preparing or being prepared aspect of the world that may to the Hopi correspond to that "quality of reality" that "matter" or "stuff" has for us.

Habitual Behavior Features of Hopi Culture

Our behavior, and that of Hopi, can be seen to be coordinated in many ways to the linguistically conditioned microcosm. As in my fire casebook, people act about situations in ways which are like the ways they talk about them. A characteristic of Hopi behavior is the emphasis on preparation. This includes announcing and getting ready for events well beforehand, elaborate precautions to insure persistence of desired conditions, and stress on good will as the preparer of right results. Consider the analogies of the day-counting pattern alone. Time is mainly reckoned "by day" (taɭk, -tala) or "by night" (tok), which words are not nouns but tensors, the first formed on a root "light, day," the second on a root "sleep." The count is by ORDINALS. This is not the pattern of counting a number of different men or things, even though they appear successively, for, even then, they COULD gather into an assemblage. It is the pattern of counting successive reappearances of the SAME man or thing, incapable of forming an assemblage. The analogy is not to behave about day-cyclicity as to several men ("several days"), which is what WE tend to do, but to behave as to the successive visits of the SAME MAN. One does not alter several men by working upon just one, but one can prepare and so alter the later visits of the same man by working to affect the visit he is making now. This is the way the Hopi deal with the future – by working within a present situation which is expected to carry impresses, both obvious and occult, forward into the future event of interest. One might say that Hopi society understands our proverb "Well begun is half done," but not our "Tomorrow is another day." This may explain much in Hopi character.

This Hopi preparing behavior may be roughly divided into announcing, outer preparing, inner preparing, covert participation, and persistence. Announcing, or preparative publicity, is an important function in the hands of a special official, the Crier Chief. Outer preparing is preparation involving much visible activity, not all necessarily directly useful within our understanding. It includes ordinary practicing, rehearsing, getting ready, introductory formalities, preparing of special food, etc. (all of these to a degree that may seem overelaborate to us), intensive sustained muscular activity like running, racing, dancing, which is thought to increase the intensity of development of events (such as growth of crops), mimetic and other magic, preparations based on esoteric theory involving perhaps occult instruments like prayer sticks, prayer feathers, and prayer meal, and finally the great cyclic ceremonies and dances, which have the significance of preparing rain and crops. From one of the verbs meaning "prepare" is derived the noun for "harvest" or "crop": *na'twani* "the prepared" or the "in preparation."[9]

Inner preparing is use of prayer and meditation, and at lesser intensity good wishes and good will, to further desired results. Hopi attitudes stress the power of desire and thought. With their "microcosm" it is utterly natural that they should. Desire and thought are the earliest, and therefore the most important, most critical and crucial, stage of preparing. Moreover, to the Hopi, one's desires and thoughts influence not only his own actions, but all nature as well. This too is wholly natural. Consciousness itself is aware of work, of the feel of effort and energy, in desire and thinking. Experience more basic than language tells us that, if energy is expended, effects are produced. WE tend to believe that our bodies can stop up this energy, prevent it from affecting other things until we will our BODIES to overt action. But this may be so only because we have our own linguistic basis for a theory that formless items like "matter" are things in themselves, malleable only by similar things, by more matter, and hence insulated from the powers of life and thought. It is no more unnatural to think that thought contacts everything and pervades the universe than to think, as we all do, that light kindled outdoors does this. And it is not unnatural to suppose that thought, like any other force, leaves everywhere traces of effect. Now, when WE think of a certain actual rosebush, we do not suppose that our thought goes to that actual bush, and engages with it, like a searchlight turned upon it. What then do we suppose our consciousness is dealing with when we are thinking of that rosebush? Probably we think it is dealing with a "mental image" which is not the rosebush but a mental surrogate of it. But why should it be NATURAL to think that our thought deals with a surrogate and not with the real rosebush? Quite possibly because we are dimly aware that we carry about with us a whole imaginary space, full of mental surrogates. To us, mental surrogates are old familiar fare. Along with the images of imaginary space, which we perhaps secretly know to be only imaginary, we tuck the thought-of actually existing rosebush, which may be quite another story, perhaps just because we have that very convenient "place" for it. The Hopi thought-world has no imaginary space. The corollary to this is that it may not locate thought dealing with real space anywhere but in real space, nor insulate real space from the effects of thought. A Hopi would naturally suppose that his thought (or he himself) traffics with the actual rosebush – or more likely, corn plant – that he is thinking about. The thought then should leave some trace of itself with the plant in the field. If it is a good thought, one about health and growth, it is good for the plant; if a bad thought, the reverse.

The Hopi emphasize the intensity-factor of thought. Thought to be most effective should be vivid in consciousness, definite, steady, sustained, charged with strongly felt good intentions. They render the idea in English as "concentrating, holding it in your heart, putting your mind on it, earnestly hoping." Thought power is the force behind ceremonies, prayer sticks, ritual smoking, etc. The prayer pipe is regarded as an aid to "concentrating" (so said my informant). Its name, *na'twanpi*, means "instrument of preparing."

Covert participation is mental collaboration from people who do not take part in the actual affair, be it a job of work, hunt, race, or ceremony, but direct their thought and good will toward the affair's success. Announcements often seek to enlist the support of such mental helpers as well as of overt participants, and contain exhortations to the people to aid with their active good will.[10] A similarity to our concepts of a sympathetic audience or the cheering section at a football game should not obscure the fact that it is primarily the power of directed thought, and not merely sympathy or encouragement, that is expected of covert participants. In fact these latter get in their deadliest work before, not during, the game! A corollary to the power of thought is the power of wrong thought for evil; hence one purpose of covert participation is to obtain the mass force of many good wishers to offset the harmful thought of ill wishers. Such attitudes greatly favor cooperation and community spirit. Not that the Hopi community is not full of rivalries and colliding interests. Against the tendency to social disintegration in such a small, isolated group, the theory of "preparing" by the power of thought, logically leading to the great power of the combined, intensified, and harmonized thought of the whole community, must help vastly toward the rather remarkable degree of cooperation that, in spite of much private bickering, the Hopi village displays in all the important cultural activities.

Hopi "preparing" activities again show a result of their linguistic thought background in an emphasis on persistence and constant insistent repetition. A sense of the cumulative value of innumerable small momenta is dulled by an objectified, spatialized view of time like ours, enhanced by a way of thinking close to the subjective awareness of duration, of the ceaseless "latering" of events. To us, for whom time is a motion on a space, unvarying repetition seems to scatter its force along a row of units of that space, and be wasted. To the Hopi, for whom time is not a motion but a "getting later" of everything that has ever been done, unvarying repetition is not wasted but accumulated. It is storing up an invisible change that holds over into later events.[11] As we have seen, it is as if the return of the day were felt as the return of the same person, a little older but with all the impresses of yesterday, not as "another day," i.e. like an entirely different person. This principle joined with that of thought-power and with traits of general Pueblo culture is expressed in the theory of the Hopi ceremonial dance for furthering rain and crops, as well as in its short, piston-like tread, repeated thousands of times, hour after hour.

Some Impresses of Linguistic Habit in Western Civilization

It is harder to do justice in few words to the linguistically conditioned features of our own culture than in the case of the Hopi, because of both vast scope and difficulty of objectivity – because of our deeply ingrained familiarity with the attitudes to be analyzed. I wish merely to sketch certain characteristics adjusted to our linguistic binomialism of form plus formless item or "substance," to our metaphoricalness, our imaginary space, and our objectified time. These, as we have seen, are linguistic.

From the form-plus-substance dichotomy the philosophical views most traditionally characteristic of the "Western world" have derived huge support. Here belong materialism, psychophysical parallelism, physics – at least in its traditional Newtonian form – and dualistic views of the universe in general. Indeed here belongs almost everything that is "hard, practical common sense." Monistic, holistic, and relativistic views of reality appeal to philosophers and some scientists, but they are badly handicapped in appealing to the "common sense" of the Western average man – not because nature herself refutes them (if she did, philosophers could have discovered this much), but because they must be talked about in what amounts to a new language. "Common sense," as its name shows, and "practicality" as its name does not show, are largely matters of talking so that one is readily understood. It is sometimes stated that Newtonian space, time, and matter are sensed by everyone intuitively, whereupon relativity is cited as showing how mathematical analysis can prove intuition wrong. This, besides being unfair to intuition, is an attempt to answer offhand question (1) put at the outset of this paper, to answer which this research was undertaken. Presentation of the findings now nears its end, and I think the answer is clear. The offhand answer, laying the blame upon intuition for our slowness in discovering mysteries of the Cosmos, such as relativity, is the wrong one. The right answer is: Newtonian space, time, and matter are no intuitions. They are recepts from culture and language. That is where Newton got them.

Our objectified view of time is, however, favorable to historicity and to everything connected with the keeping of records, while the Hopi view is unfavorable thereto. The latter is too subtle, complex, and ever-developing, supplying no ready-made answer to the question of when "one" event ends and "another" begins. When it is implicit that everything that ever happened still is, but is in a necessarily different form from what memory or record reports, there is less incentive to study the past. As for the present, the incentive would be not to record it but to treat it as "preparing." But OUR objectified time puts before imagination something like a ribbon or scroll marked off into equal blank spaces, suggesting that each be filled with an entry. Writing has no doubt helped toward our linguistic treatment of time, even as the linguistic treatment has guided the uses of writing. Through this give-and-take between language and the whole culture we get, for instance:

1 Records, diaries, bookkeeping, accounting, mathematics stimulated by account-ing.
2 Interest in exact sequence, dating, calendars, chronology, clocks, time wages, time graphs, time as used in physics.
3 Annals, histories, the historical attitude, interest in the past, archaeology, atti-tudes of introjection toward past periods, e.g., classicism, romanticism.

Just as we conceive our objectified time as extending in the future in the same way that it extends in the past, so we set down our estimates of the future in the same shape as our records of the past, producing programs, schedules, budgets. The formal equality of the spacelike units by which we measure and conceive time leads us to consider the "formless item" or "substance" of time to be homogeneous and in ratio to the number of units. Hence our prorata allocation of value to time, lending itself to the building up of a commercial structure based on time-prorata values: time wages (time work constantly supersedes piece work), rent, credit, interest, depreciation charges, and insurance premiums. No doubt this vast system, once built, would continue to run under any sort of linguistic treatment of time; but that it should have been built at all, reaching the magnitude and particular form it has in the Western world, is a fact decidedly in consonance with the patterns of the SAE languages. Whether such a civilization as ours would be possible with widely different linguistic handling of time is a large question – in our civilization, our linguistic patterns and the fitting of our behavior to the temporal order are what they are, and they are in accord. We are of course stimulated to use calendars, clocks, and watches, and to try to measure time ever more precisely; this aids science, and science in turn, following these well-worn cultural grooves, gives back to culture an ever-growing store of applications, habits, and values, with which culture again directs science. But what lies outside this spiral? Science is beginning to find that there is something in the Cosmos that is not in accord with the concepts we have formed in mounting the spiral. It is trying to frame a NEW LANGUAGE by which to adjust itself to a wider universe.

It is clear how the emphasis on "saving time" which goes with all the above and is very obvious objectification of time, leads to a high valuation of "speed," which shows itself a great deal in our behavior.

Still another behavioral effect is that the character of monotony and regularity possessed by our image of time as an evenly scaled limitless tape measure persuades us to behave as if that monotony were more true of events than it really is. That is, it helps to routinize us. We tend to select and favor whatever bears out this view, to "play up to" the routine aspects of existence. One phase of this is behavior evincing a false sense of security or an assumption that all will always go smoothly, and a lack in foreseeing and protecting ourselves against hazards. Our technique of harnessing energy does well in routine performance, and it is along routine lines that we chiefly strive to improve it – we are, for example, relatively uninterested in stopping the energy from causing accidents, fires, and explosions, which it is doing constantly and on a wide scale. Such indifference to the unexpectedness of life would be disastrous to a society as small, isolated, and precariously poised as the Hopi society is, or rather once was.

Thus our linguistically determined thought world not only collaborates with our cultural idols and ideals, but engages even our unconscious personal reactions in its patterns and gives them certain typical characters. One such character, as we have seen, is CARELESSNESS, as in reckless driving or throwing cigarette stubs into waste paper. Another of different sort is GESTURING when we talk. Very many of the gestures made by English-speaking people at least, and probably by all SAE speakers, serve to illustrate, by a movement in space, not a real spatial reference but one of the nonspatial references that our language handles by metaphors of imaginary space. That is, we are more apt to make a grasping gesture when we speak of grasping an elusive idea than when we speak of grasping a doorknob. The gesture seeks to make a metaphorical and hence somewhat unclear reference more clear. But, if a language refers to nonspatials without implying a spatial analogy, the reference is not made any clearer by gesture. The Hopi gesture very little, perhaps not at all in the sense we understand as gesture.

It would seem as if kinesthesia, or the sensing of muscular movement, though arising before language, should be made more highly conscious by linguistic use of imaginary space and metaphorical images of motion. Kinesthesia is marked in two facets of European culture: art and sport. European sculpture, an art in which Europe excels, is strongly kinesthetic, conveying great sense of the body's motions; European painting likewise. The dance in our culture expresses delight in motion rather than symbolism or ceremonial, and our music is greatly influenced by our dance forms. Our sports are strongly imbued with this element of the "poetry of motion." Hopi races and games seem to emphasize rather the virtues of endurance and sustained intensity. Hopi dancing is highly symbolic and is performed with great intensity and earnestness, but has not much movement or swing.

Synesthesia, or suggestion by certain sense receptions of characters belonging to another sense, as of light and color by sounds and vice versa, should be made more conscious by a linguistic metaphorical system that refers to nonspatial experiences by terms for spatial ones, though undoubtedly it arises from a deeper source. Probably in the first instance metaphor arises from synesthesia and not the reverse; yet metaphor need not become firmly rooted in linguistic pattern, as Hopi shows. Nonspatial experience has one well-organized sense, HEARING – for smell and taste are but little organized. Nonspatial consciousness is a realm chiefly of thought, feeling, and SOUND. Spatial consciousness is a realm of light, color, sight, and touch, and presents shapes and dimensions. Our metaphorical system, by naming nonspatial experiences after spatial ones, imputes to sounds, smells, tastes, emotions, and thoughts qualities like the colors, luminosities, shapes, angles, textures, and motions of spatial experience. And to some extent the reverse transference occurs; for, after much talking about tones as high, low, sharp, dull, heavy, brilliant, slow, the talker finds it easy to think of some factors in spatial experience as like factors of tone. Thus we speak of "tones" of color, a gray "monotone," a "loud" necktie, a "taste" in dress: all spatial metaphor in reverse. Now European art is distinctive in the way it seeks deliberately to play with synesthesia. Music tries to suggest scenes, color, movement, geometric design; painting and sculpture are often consciously guided by the analogies of music's rhythm; colors are conjoined with feeling for the analogy to concords and discords. The European theater and opera seek a synthesis of many arts. It may be that in this way our metaphorical language that is in some sense a confusion of thought is producing, through art, a result of far-reaching value – a deeper esthetic sense leading toward a more direct apprehension of underlying unity behind the phenomena so variously reported by our sense channels.

Historical Implications

How does such a network of language, culture, and behavior come about historically? Which was first: the language patterns or the cultural norms? In main they have grown up together, constantly influencing each other. But in this partnership the nature of the language is the factor that limits free plasticity and rigidifies channels of development in the more autocratic way. This is so because a language is a system, not just an assemblage of norms. Large systematic outlines can change to something really new only very slowly, while many other cultural innovations are made with comparative quickness. Language thus represents the mass mind; it is affected by inventions and innovations, but affected little and slowly, whereas TO inventors and innovators it legislates with the decree immediate.

The growth of the SAE language–culture complex dates from ancient times. Much of its metaphorical reference to the nonspatial by the spatial was already fixed in the ancient tongues, and more especially in Latin. It is indeed a marked trait of Latin. If we compare, say Hebrew, we find that, while Hebrew has some allusion to not-space as space, Latin has more. Latin terms for nonspatials, like *educo, religio, principia, comprehendo*, are usually metaphorized physical references: lead out, tying back, etc. This is not true of all languages – it is quite untrue of Hopi. The fact that in Latin the direction of development happened to be from spatial to nonspatial (partly because of secondary stimulation to abstract thinking when the intellectually crude Romans encountered Greek culture) and that later tongues were strongly stimulated to mimic Latin, seems a likely reason for a belief, which still lingers on among linguists, that this is the natural direction of semantic change in all languages, and for the persistent notion in Western learned circles (in strong contrast to Eastern ones) that objective experience is prior to subjective. Philosophies make out a weighty case for the reverse, and certainly the direction of development is sometimes the reverse. Thus the Hopi word for "heart" can be shown to be a late formation within Hopi from a root meaning think or remember. Or consider what has happened to the word "radio" in such a sentence as "he bought a new radio," as compared to its prior meaning "science of wireless telephony."

In the Middle Ages the patterns already formed in Latin began to interweave with the increased mechanical invention, industry, trade, and scholastic and scientific thought. The need for measurement in industry and trade, the stores and bulks of "stuffs" in various containers, the type-bodies in which various goods were handled, standardizing of measure and weight units, invention of clocks and measurement of "time," keeping of records, accounts, chronicles, histories, growth of mathematics and the partnership of mathematics and science, all cooperated to bring our thought and language world into its present form.

In Hopi history, could we read it, we should find a different type of language and a different set of cultural and environmental influences working together. A peaceful agricultural society isolated by geographic features and nomad enemies in a land of scanty rainfall, arid agriculture that could be made successful only by the utmost perseverance (hence the value of persistence and repetition), necessity for collaboration (hence emphasis on the psychology of teamwork and on mental factors in general), corn and rain as primary criteria of value, need of extensive PREPARATIONS and precautions to assure crops in the poor soil and precarious climate, keen realization of dependence upon nature favoring prayer and a religious attitude toward the forces of nature, especially prayer and religion directed toward the ever-needed blessing, rain – these things interacted with Hopi linguistic patterns to mold them, to be molded again by them, and so little by little to shape the Hopi world-outlook.

To sum up the matter, our first question asked in the beginning is answered thus: Concepts of "time" and "matter" are not given in substantially the same form by experience to all men but depend upon the nature of the language or languages through the use of which they have been developed. They do not depend so much upon ANY ONE SYSTEM (e.g., tense, or nouns) within the grammar as upon the ways of analyzing and reporting experience which have become fixed in the language as integrated "fashions of speaking" and which cut across the typical grammatical classifications, so that such a "fashion" may include lexical, morphological, syntactic, and otherwise systemically diverse means coordinated in a certain frame of consistency. Our own "time" differs markedly from Hopi "duration." It is conceived as like a space of strictly limited dimensions, or sometimes as like a motion upon such a space, and employed as an intellectual tool accordingly. Hopi "duration" seems to be inconceivable in terms of space or motion, being the mode in which life differs from form, and consciousness *in toto* from the spatial elements of consciousness. Certain ideas born of our own time-concept, such as that of absolute simultaneity, would be either very difficult to express or impossible and devoid of meaning under the Hopi conception, and would be replaced by operational concepts. Our "matter" is the physical subtype of "substance" or "stuff," which is conceived as the formless extensional item that must be joined with form before there can be real existence. In Hopi there seems to be nothing corresponding to it; there are no formless extensional items; existence may or may not have form, but what it also has, with or without form, is intensity and duration, these being nonextensional and at bottom the same.

But what about our concept of "space," which was also included in our first question? There is no such striking difference between Hopi and SAE about space as about time, and probably the apprehension of space is given in substantially the same form by experience irrespective of language. The experiments of the Gestalt psychologists with visual perception appear to establish this as a fact. But the CONCEPT OF SPACE will vary somewhat with language, because, as an intellectual tool,[12] it is so closely linked with the concomitant employment of other intellectual tools, of the order of "time" and "matter," which are linguistically conditioned. We see things with our eyes in the same space forms as the Hopi, but our idea of space has also the property of acting as a surrogate of nonspatial relationships like time, intensity, tendency, and as a void to be filled with imagined formless items, one of which may even be called "space." Space as sensed by the Hopi would not be connected mentally with such surrogates, but would be comparatively "pure," unmixed with extraneous notions.

As for our second question: There are connections but not correlations or diagnostic correspondences between cultural norms and linguistic patterns. Although it would be impossible to infer the existence of Crier Chiefs from the lack of tenses in Hopi, or vice versa, there is a relation between a language and the rest of the culture of the society which uses it. There are cases where the "fashions of speaking" are closely integrated with the whole general culture, whether or not this be universally true, and there are connections within this integration, between the kind of linguistic analyses employed and various behavioral reactions and also the shapes taken by various cultural developments. Thus the importance of Crier Chiefs does have a connection, not with tenselessness itself, but with a system of thought in which categories different from our tenses are natural. These connections are to be found not so much by focusing attention on the typical rubrics of linguistic, ethnographic, or sociological description as by examining the culture and the language (always and only when the two have been together historically for a considerable time) as a whole in which concatenations that run across these departmental lines may be expected to exist, and, if they do exist, eventually to be discoverable by study.

NOTES

1 We have plenty of evidence that this is not the case. Consider only the Hopi and the Ute, with languages that on the overt morphological and lexical level are as similar as, say, English and German. The idea of "correlation" between language and culture, in the generally accepted sense of correlation, is certainly a mistaken one.

2 As we say, "ten at the SAME TIME," showing that in our language and thought we restate the fact of group perception in terms of a concept "time," the large linguistic component of which will appear in the course of this paper. *ə*

3 It is no exception to this rule of lacking a plural that a mass noun may sometimes coincide in lexeme with an individual noun that of course has a plural; e.g., "stone" (no pl.) with "a stone" (pl. "stones"). The plural form denoting varieties, e.g., "wines" is of course a different sort of thing from the true plural; it is a curious outgrowth from the SAE mass nouns, leading to still another sort of imaginary aggregates, which will have to be omitted from this paper.

4 Hopi has two words for water quantities; *kə·yi* and *pa·hə*. The difference is something like that between "stone" and "rock" in English, *pa·hə* implying greater size and "wildness"; flowing water, whether or not outdoors or in nature, is *pa·hə*; so is "moisture." But, unlike "stone" and "rock," the difference is essential, not pertaining to a connotative margin, and the two can hardly ever be interchanged.

5 To be sure, there are a few minor differences from other nouns, in English for instance in the use of the articles.

6 "Year" and certain combinations of "year" with name of season, rarely season names alone, can occur with a locative morpheme "at," but this is exceptional. It appears like historical detritus of an earlier different patterning, or the effect of English analogy, or both.

7 The expective and reportive assertions contrast according to the "paramount relation." The expective expresses anticipation existing EARLIER than objective fact, and coinciding with objective fact LATER than the status quo of the speaker, this status quo, including all the subsummation of the past therein, being expressed by the reportive. Our notion "future" seems to represent at once the earlier (anticipation) and the later (afterwards, what will be), as Hopi shows. This paradox may hint of how elusive the mystery of real time is, and how artificially it is expressed by a linear relation of past–present–future.

8 One such trace is that the tensor "long in duration," while quite different from the adjective "long" of space, seems to contain the same root as the adjective "large" of space. Another is that "somewhere" of space used with certain tensors means "at some indefinite time." Possibly however this is not the case and it is only the tensor that gives the time element, so that "somewhere" still refers to space and that under these conditions indefinite space means simply general applicability, regardless of either time or space. Another trace is that in the temporal (cycle word) "afternoon" the element meaning "after" is derived from the verb "to separate." There are other such traces, but they are few and exceptional, and obviously not like our own spatial metaphorizing.

9 The Hopi verbs of preparing naturally do not correspond neatly to our "prepare"; so that *na'twani* could also be rendered "the practiced-upon, the tried-for," and otherwise.

10 See, e.g., Ernest Beaglehole, *Notes on Hopi Economic Life* (Yale University Publications in Anthropology, no. 15, 1937), especially the reference to the announcement of a rabbit hunt, and on p. 30, description of the activities in connection with the cleaning of Toreva Spring – announcing, various preparing activities, and finally, preparing the continuity of the good results already obtained and the continued flow of the spring.

11 This notion of storing up power, which seems implied by much Hopi behavior, has an analog in physics: acceleration. It might be said that the linguistic background of Hopi thought equips it to recognize naturally that force manifests not as motion or velocity, but as cumulation or acceleration. Our linguistic background tends to hinder in us this same recognition, for having legitimately conceived force to be that which produces change, we then think of change by our linguistic metaphorical analog, motion, instead of by a pure motionless changingness concept, i.e. accumulation or acceleration. Hence it comes to our naïve feeling as a shock to find from physical experiments that it is not possible to define force by motion, that motion and speed, as also "being at rest," are wholly relative, and that force can be measured only by acceleration.

12 Here belong "Newtonian" and "Euclidean" space, etc.

REFERENCE

Sapir, E. (1949). The Status of Linguistics as a Science. In D. G. Mandelbaum (ed.), *Selected Writings of Edward Sapir in Language, Culture and Personality* (pp. 160–6). Berkeley and Los Angeles: University of California Press.

16

The Limits of Awareness

Michael Silverstein

In the course of field work, linguists, just like other anthropologists, spend a great deal of time listening to people talk about what they are doing. The resulting data form a corpus of speech about speech, a "meta-corpus" as it were, that consists of speech at the same time that it seems to talk about, or characterize, speech as a meaningful social action. In reply to our queries or spontaneously, people will utter descriptive statements about who has said or can say what to whom, when, why, and where, just like statements about who can give presents of certain kinds to whom, when, why, and where. But talking about "saying" is, for better or worse, also an example of "saying"; and such metalanguage, for the analyst of culture, is as much a part of the problem as part of the solution. As is readily apparent, all our efforts to differentiate "conscious native models" from "anthropologist's models," or "ethno-theories" and "ideologies" from "objective social reality," are attempts to come to grips with the metalanguage vs. language relationship, or its more general form, (meta-)language vs. action. So I hope that what I discuss here will be seen not as a crabbed and technical treatment whose relevance is bounded by linguistic and semiotic debate, but as a contribution to general anthropological theory and methodology, using the data of speech. And further, I hope that my title in terms of "limits" is not taken as purely negative, but rather as characterizing relative ease and relative difficulty. For the point I wish to make is that it is extremely difficult, if not impossible, to make a native speaker take account of those readily-discernible facts of speech as action that (s)he has no ability to describe for us in his or her own language. And I want to demonstrate by examples what dimensions of speech usage play a role in this relationship.

Let me now introduce the word "pragmatic" for how speech forms are used as effective action in specifiable cultural contexts. One dimension of the "meaning" of every speech form is pragmatic, exactly like any social action. From a semiotic point of view, all such meanings can be described as rules linking certain culturally-constituted features of the speech situation with certain forms of speech. To give those rules, or talk about them, is to engage in "meta-pragmatic" discourse, we should say. So the statement, "In our society, when a proper religious or judiciary functionary so empowered sincerely utters to a man and woman, 'I pronounce you husband and wife,' the latter are married," is a metapragmatic utterance describing the effective use of this formula. Whether or not it is a correct statement is, of course, not at issue; it is in any case intended as a description of some pragmatic meaning relation.

I can now formulate my hypothesis as follows. For the native speaker, the ease or difficulty of accurate metapragmatic characterization of the use of the forms of his or her own language seems to depend on certain general semiotic properties of the use in question. That is, the basic evidence we have for awareness of the pragmatic dimension of language use, susceptibility to conscious native testimony, is universally bounded by certain characteristics of the form and contextually-dependent function of the pragmatic markers in speech. I intend here to illustrate the dimensions I have so far isolated in field-based data, drawn from my own and from others' field work, and then to try to explain them. In each case, we will be interested in seeing why native speakers are able or unable to characterize the contextual appropriateness of speech, and to manipulate it for the investigator.

Let me start with a success story, reported in a number of publications about the Djirbal language of North Queensland, Australia, by R. M. W. Dixon.[1] Djirbal has two disjoint (non-overlapping) sets of vocabulary items, one that Dixon calls the "everyday" set of words, and the other, of contextually-specific usage, that he calls the "mother-in-law" set. As is widespread in Australia, when a person speaks within earshot of a classificatory "mother-in-law" – the details of the kin-reckoning need not concern us here – he must use all and only the vocabulary items of the special "mother-in-law" set, and none of those in the "everyday" set of items. Utterances in either style have exactly the same overt grammatical patterns, however. Now we should understand that a speaker is not necessarily talking about, or referring to, the mother-in-law, when using the special mother-in-law vocabulary; it is just that the use of this set of vocabulary items is obligatory in the context where speaker and audience are in a specified kin relationship, regardless of the topic of discourse. We would say that, in any given appropriate instance of speaking, the vocabulary items used have two independent kinds of meaning relations: (a) a context-independent word-"sense," in terms of how the Djirbalŋan refer to persons, things, events, and build statements using these words in grammatical arrangements; and (b) a context-dependent "indexical" value, that indicates whether or not a classificatory mother-in-law is present as an audience in the speech event. Note that every vocabulary item in Djirbal must be specified on both these dimensions.

Now, as it turns out, the number of vocabulary items in the everyday set is about four or five times that in the mother-in-law set, and so there seems to be a many-to-one relationship in terms of referring to any particular entity, as shown in (1). Where in everyday vocabulary, there are five separate words (of masculine gender class) for various lice and ticks, in the mother-in-law vocabulary there is only one term, that can refer to the same total range of things as the whole set of everyday items. Similarly, where the everyday vocabulary has six separate words (of the edible flora gender class) for loya vines of different species and stages of growth, the

(1) Vocabulary sets in "Everyday" style and in "Mother-in-law" style

"Everyday"		"Mother-in-law"
bayi maṛbu	"louse"	
bayi nuŋgan	"large louse"	
bayi mindilinj	"big tick"	↔ bayi dimaninj
bayi biya	"tick (sp.)"	
bayi daynjdjaṛ	"tick (sp.)"	
balam djuyu	"edible loya vine"	
balam gambay	"loya vine (sp.)"	
balam baygal	"loya vine (sp.)"	
balam djuŋgay	"green loya vine"	↔ balam ŋundjanum
balam guguṛ	"young shoots of *djuŋgay*"	
balam bugul	"thin loya vine"	

mother-in-law vocabulary has one cover term. As any structuralist knows, if there are a different number of elements that enter into referential opposition, dividing up an "ethno-classificatory" realm, then there must be different word-senses, a different structural contribution each item of everyday vs. mother-in-law vocabulary makes to sentences containing them. And yet, as shown in (2), from the point of view of Djirbal speakers, in actual situations of discourse there is equivalence of understood reference in the everyday and mother-in-law speech contexts, but there is difference in indexing or indicating mother-in-law as audience or not.

(2) Formulable use relations of the two styles

Pragmatic reference:	"Everyday" = "Mother-in-law"
Presence of affine:	"Everyday" ≠ "Mother-in-law" (no vs. yes)

Dixon brilliantly seized on this apparent contradiction in semantic structure vs. pragmatic implementation, in order to elucidate the meaning of Djirbal verbs. To do so, he had to rely on the native speakers' ability to engage in metapragmatic discourse about language use in these two situations, their ability, in other words, intentionally to talk about utterances that are equivalent in referential effect in these two contexts of use. He used a two-way elicitation procedure as follows. First, Dixon asked how to say the same thing as some given everyday utterance using the mother-in-law style, as shown in (3a): "'Bala baŋgul nudin' wiyaman djalŋuydja?" ("How does one say, 'Bala baŋgul nudin ["he cut it"]' in Djalŋuy [mother-in-law style]?") This stage of elicitation yields many-to-one relationships of various sets of everyday vocabulary items to one mother-in-law item, as shown for example in (3a) for verbs of "telling." Such sets were gathered together in orderly files from separately-elicited word equivalences. In the second stage of elicitation, Dixon asked speakers how to say the same thing as some given mother-in-law utterance, using the everyday style. This stage, remarkably, yielded one-to-one equivalences, as shown in (3b), the mother-in-law item *wuyuban* yielding everyday item *buwanju* and no others. Finally, Dixon's hypothesis that both of these styles must have distinct but compatible word-sense structures (deducible from the universal properties of grammar, and hence really just the assumption that Djirbal is a natural human language) led him to ask, for each item of vocabulary in the various everyday sets he generated in the first stage, how one would say that and only that in the mother-in-law style (there is a construction meaning "exactly" or "only" in Djirbal). In this third stage, he induced precisely the differences of referential value he suspected. The one item of everyday vocabulary that showed one-to-one translatability in stages one and two still had this characteristic, as shown in (3c), while the other items in each such set showed complex mother-in-law constructions with various grammatical structures of mother-in-law words used to indicate exact, context-independent referential distinctions. This last kind of data showed some variability, moreover, just as we would expect for attempts at folk-definition.

(3) Typical elicitation process for equivalence relations

  (a) " 'bala baŋgul nudin'   wiyaman   djalŋuydja?"
          it   he   cut   done-in-what-fashion in mother-in-law

"Everyday"		"Mother-in-law"
buwanju	"tell"	
djinganju	"tell a particular piece of news"	
		→ wuyuban
gindimban	"warn"	
ŋaran	"tell falsely that one lacks something"	

  (b) buwanju   ← wuyuban

  (c) buwanju   → wuyuban
       djinganju   → wuyuwuyuban [redup. "do to excess or iteratively (sc., to
                          many people)"]
       gindimban   → njungulmban wuyuban [njungul "one," -mbal "do (tr.)"]
       ŋaran   → wuyuban djilbuŋga [djilbu "nothing," -nga "locative"]

I must stress here that the native ability accurately and explicitly to formulate relations of use, the native ability to talk about utterances appropriate to specific contexts, is critical to Dixon's enterprise. Here, as shown, the speakers are aware of the pragmatic equivalence of referring with the specific terms of everyday style and the vague or general terms of mother-in-law style, and they are aware of the difference of context signalled by these vocabulary switches. Also, they are aware of the asymmetry of reference, as shown by the back-translation of stage two of the elicitation. And finally, they are aware of ways to make mother-in-law style referentially precise, which is not the custom in using this style, but can be, as in stage three, induced on the data. I want to claim that there are three crucial factors that play a necessary, though perhaps not sufficient, role in this awareness, this availability of everyday vs. mother-in-law styles of use for conscious metapragmatic discussion. The first I call their *unavoidable referentiality*; the second, their *continuous segmentability*; and the third, their *relative presuppositional* quality vis-à-vis the context of use. (See 4a, b, c.)

(4) Semiotic properties of these pragmatic forms

    (a) *Unavoidable referentiality*: in isolating the aspect of the signal that enters into the pragmatic opposition in question, we have thereby identified a constituent that enters into referential oppositions, e.g.,

        "formal" vs. "familiar" pronouns for hearer (French *vous* vs. *tu*, Russian *vy* vs. *ty*, German *Sie* vs. *du*)

      but not

        phonetic markers of socio-economic class affiliation of speaker (cf. W. Labov's *Sociolinguistic Patterns*, Philadelphia, 1972)

    (b) *Continuous segmentability*: the pragmatic signal can be identified as continuous stretches in actual speech, segmentable as overt meaningful units of the utterances in which they occur, e.g.,

        whole sentences: The man was walking down the street;

        continuous phrases: The man, Was walking down the street, Was walking, Down the street, The street;

        words: The, Man, Was, Walking, Down, The, Street;

        suffixes and prefixes: -Ing;

      but not

        Progressive Aspect, expressed by "Be -Ing" (Observe there is no "The man wasing walk down the street")

    (c) *Relative presupposition*: a specific effective instance of a pragmatic signal is linked to and requires, for its effect, some independently verifiable contextual factor or factors, e.g.,

        English demonstratives *this* and *that* (presupposing sight or sound of some entity, or co-occurring verbal description, or previous reference in temporally prior speech);

      but not

        phonological markers of class or regional affiliation of speaker (the "Hævəd Yæd" phenomenon),

        deference and politeness markers ("Roger" vs. "Prof. Brown").

Unavoidable referentiality is the property of those pragmatic (effective context-dependent) signals that are automatically identified by identifying the elements of speech that refer, or describe. Reference, or statement-value, is that aspect of the meaningfulness of speech which relates speaking to a logical calculus of propositions, ultimately related to the notions of truth and falsity. In general, our whole western view of grammar is based on this kind of meaningfulness, the detailed exposition of which I will not enter into here. But I will insist that the identification of so-called grammatical categories, sentence and construction types, and lexical items (or word stems) with various senses, all ultimately come from looking at language as a system of reference in this manner. Now, if, in identifying the utterance-fractions (or constituents) of speech that have some identifiable pragmatic function – that enter into pragmatic oppositions – we thereby also isolate utterance-fractions that form units of reference, these pragmatic utterance-fractions are unavoidably referential. Thus, one of the well-known pragmatic systems of many European languages signals (broadly) deference-to-hearer vs. solidarity-with-hearer by the alternation of two pronominal forms, say "second or third person plural" vs. "second person singular," e.g., French *vous* vs. *tu*, Russian *vy* vs. *ty*, German *Sie* vs. *du*. And these forms are at the same time the very units of referring to, or picking out, the hearer in a speech event. The deference vs. solidarity system is thus unavoidably referential. We can contrast on this dimension such pragmatic alternations as certain North American English phonetic markers of social stratification isolated by Labov in many famous studies, where the signals of socio-economic class affiliation of the speaker reside in subtle pronunciation effects within certain phonemic categories, which operate independent of any segmentation of speech by the criterion of reference. To be sure, we know from various psychological experiments of Wallace Lambert and others that these markers are readily understood by native speakers of English, inasmuch as the experimental subjects categorize the speakers of such alternate pronunciations quite readily. But, in isolating the relevant pragmatic signals, we do not thereby isolate units of language that play a role in the system of reference. In the Djirbal case under consideration, the alternation of everyday vs. mother-in-law forms in normal usage consists of a kind of word-by-word substitutability. The very lexical elements of reference to things and events are precisely isolated (up to but not including their grammatical inflections) in isolating the pragmatic speech-fractions at issue.

Continuous segmentability is the property of those pragmatic signals that can be identified as continuous stretches of actual speech, segmentable as overt meaningful units of the utterances in which they occur. Thus, any word-stem, prefix or suffix, word, continuous phrase, or even whole sentence is a continuously segmentable element. In any utterance, such units of language are realized as continuous stretches of overt signal behavior. Note that this criterion cross-cuts that of unavoidable referentiality. For example, take any statement of the sentence, *The man was walking down the street*, as a referential event, one that simply states this as a proposition. If we had recordings of such fluent executions, we would find that the whole utterance, "The man was walking down the street," would be, in our sense, continuously segmentable; it would be realized in a continuous temporal stretch of speech behavior. So also would be the phrases, "The man," "Was walking down the street," "Was walking," "Down the street," "The street." So also would be the words, "The," "Man," "Was," "Walking," "Down," "The," "Street." So also would be the suffix "-ing" on "walking." However, still under the hypothesis of referential (or propositional) meaning, the single referential unit expressing the Progressive aspect, the complex of forms "was -ing," is not continuously segmentable; it is a discontinuous combination of parts of the overt utterance that together signal the progressive aspect in English. That they form a referential unit is quite clear (Chomsky's 1957 *Syntactic Structures* is essentially a whole theoretical monograph built on this fact). But they can never be in continuous temporal order, as is easily seen from trying to say, "The man wasing walk down the street." Observe that the Djirbal case under discussion involves the alternation of word-stems as the effective pragmatic signal, and hence each of the alternants is continuously segmentable. Each word-stem occurs in a continuous time fraction of the utterance.

Relative presupposition is a relationship whereby a specific effective instance of a pragmatic signal is linked to and requires, for its effect, some independently verifiable contextual factor or factors. Relative creativity of a particular pragmatic signal, at the opposite pole of this continuum, essentially brings some contextual factor into existence, serving as the unique signal thereof. I hope that this dimension of contrast does not seem too terribly abstract; it is trying to capture the degree to which our knowledge of the contextual factors linked to specific pragmatic instances comes from other signals or depends on the occurrence of the very signal at issue. A pragmatic instance that depends on other signals for its effectiveness "presupposes" the establishment of some contextual factor by those other signals, whether they be signals in the same or some other sensory modality. Thus, for a valid pointing out of something with an instance of English "this" or "that," we presuppose one or more of the following: (a) non-speech verifiability of the presence of some entity, by sight or sound or whatever; (b) the presence of some entity that verifiably satisfies some verbal description that accompanies the "this" or "that"; or (c) prior reference (in the proper sequential position in speech itself) to some entity. Failing the satisfaction of one or more of these presuppositions, the instance of "this" or "that" fails to point. There is little creative potential in such linguistic units. Contrastively, elements of speech that signal class or regional affiliation of the speaker, or that enter into the so-called "politeness" system, are by and large the unique signals of these understood contextual dimensions to which they are linked; their creative potential is very great. In saying "Hævɨd Yǽd" (Harvard Yard in regional class accent) and similar forms, I communicate and establish my membership in a certain dialect group of American English. In addressing someone with a particular form of name, as Brown and Ford long ago showed, the speaker establishes the contextual dimensions of power relationships and familiarity between him/herself and the addressee. In the Djirbal case under discussion, one does not create a mother-in-law by the instantiation of the mother-in-law vocabulary. This relationship is known on other grounds for appropriate use in the first place. In other words, the mother-in-law style of vocabulary is relatively presupposing of the very aspect of the context to which it is pragmatically linked, the kin relationship between speaker and audience.

So, to sum up, this example of Djirbal mother-in-law vs. everyday vocabulary alternation is readily subject to accurate native metapragmatic testimony and manipulation. I want to claim that this is bound up with the three semiotic properties the alternation has as a pragmatic system, unavoidable referentiality, continuous segmentability, and relatively presuppositional usage. In contrast, I want to point out an elicitation failure, in my own Kiksht (Wasco-Wishram Chinookan) work, where direct appeal to native metapragmatic awareness leads nowhere, and where, interestingly enough, the situation differs on all three semiotic dimensions.[2]

In this Native American language of the Columbia River, as in many languages of the Western U.S., there is an alternation of forms that comes under the rubric of the gradation "augmentative"–"neutral"–"diminutive." Every form can be uttered in up to six different ways, as shown in (5), by changing certain features of the consonants, and, marginally, of the vowels, in entirely regular fashion, depending only on what are the shapes of the "neutral" forms

(5) Examples of gradation of forms ("augmentative" > "neutral" > "diminutive")

> i-mi-gáqšdaq > i-mi-q'áqštaq > i-mi-k'ak,stak > i-mi-k'ak'st'ak' "your head"
> id-mí-bž > id-mí-pš > it'-mi pls "your foot"
> i-[ia]-qbáiλ> i-[ia]-gáiλ > i-[ia]-gáic > i-[ia]-k'áic > i-[ia]-k'ʷáicɬ > i-[ia]-k'ʷɛitlθ   "enormous" … "tiny"
> a-ia-pkʲ'ʷ's "his immature penis" [dim., cf. a-ga-pkʷš "her nipple"]
> qalaqbáya! "damn!" [aug., cf. qanaga "just like, rather like"]

Notice that it is not a question of where consonants and vowels occur in words, nor what the words refer to, nor what grammatical units or classes are instantiated in the words. The augmentative–neutral–diminutive changes operate on the sounds of Wasco-Wishram wherever they happen to occur in forms, subject only to certain sequential constraints on consonant clusters that reduce the freedom of alternation in certain positions (see 6).

(6) Gradations in sound features (augmentative > neutral > diminutive)

      Consonants: voiced stops, affricates > voiceless > glottalized (b > p > pl)
                      nonstrident affricates > strident (λ > c)
                      hushing stridents > hissing stridents (š > s)
                      uvular > velar > labiovelar (q > k > k^w)
                      guttural + labial > labioguttural (qp > q^w)

      vowels: low > mid (a > ε)
                      mid > high (ε > i)

From textual evidence, from spontaneous recorded conversation, and from certain frozen (or "lexicalized") examples, the pragmatic meaning of this alternation is clear. Taking the neutral form as the point of departure, the augmentative form additionally expresses the speaker's feeling that the referent of some lexical item is large for what it is, or to excess, if an activity; that it is repulsive to the speaker – in short, a speaker evaluation of oversize, overmuch, and affectively negative. The diminutive form, on the other hand, expresses the speaker's feeling that the referent is small, or subtle; that it endears the speaker – in short, a speaker evaluation of undersize, restricted, and affectively positive. Baby-talk forms (including the child's kinterms) are in diminutive or super-diminutive shape; mocking and insulting speech is in augmentative.

    What can native speakers do when asked about these linguistic forms? Can they talk about the augmentative–neutral–diminutive gradations? Can they produce series of forms on demand, given one of the alternants? Can they accurately characterize the uses? Many attempts at direct systematic elicitation proved, ultimately, to be unsuccessful. Ever watchful for such forms, and for the opportunity to question consultants about them, I heard, in a piece of delicious gossip, the form "iǰamuqbál" "she with rotten old big belly" as an epithet for a loose woman, clearly the augmentative of the neutral form "ičamuq^{w}ál" "she with big belly" or "her paunch," as shown in (7).

(7) Attempted elicitation

    iǰamuqbál, aug. of i-ča-muq^{w}ál "her paunch," "she with big belly" occurs spontaneously;
    ičamuq^{w}ál, neut. form is "repeated" by informant, even to tape-recording;
    i-ia-gáiλ ičamuq^{w}ál "it-is-large her-paunch" given as translation equivalent.

Here was the opportunity to bring the consultant to conscious awareness of the changes! So I asked for a repetition, and, as you may guess by now, the consultant "repeated" "ičamuq^{w}ál," the neutral form. "But you just said '-muqbal' didn't you? That means 'great big one,' no?" I insist. "No, it's ičamuq^{w}ál." Playing the tape-recording back was of no avail. Eventually, I ask for the form: "Well, how do you say, 'her great big belly'?" "Oh, iagáiλ ičamuqʷál" – this last expression being a fully referential or descriptive phrase, "her belly is large" or "she has a big belly" (and note the neutral form of the word for "large" as well). What is subject to conscious manipulation is the referential or descriptive component of Wasco-Wishram, but the augmentative–neutral–diminutive gradations are beyond this kind of metapragmatic characterization. This particular consultant (whose name I can no longer give, since she has recently died) was one of the more sensitive in matters linguistic; on another occasion she could tell me, for example, that all the forms I produced with diminutive effects "sounded kinda cute," but she just could not grasp the metapragmatic task of producing them on demand, though her spontaneous speech was replete with examples.

This failure of metapragmatic elicitation is quite telling, in contrast to the Djirbal case of mother-in-law switches (or in contrast to my own ability to elicit mother-in-law vs. everyday forms among the Worora of northwestern Australia). For here we are dealing with pragmatic forms of speech that systematically contrast along all three dimensions we have so far seen. First, recall, the augmentative–neutral–diminutive alternations operate on certain sound properties (or "features") of consonants and of some vowels wherever and whenever they occur in free positions in speech. So, in isolating the signals of the alternations, we are isolating not segments of speech, but phonological features of some of the segments; we are not isolating thereby any units of language that themselves have referential value. So the gradations of form here are not unavoidably referential; they operate on utterance-fractions that are completely independent of the units of reference. Second, the proper formulation of the gradation is in terms of features of the sounds in speech that appear in the contrasts here-and-there in the course of speaking. In such forms as (augmentative) "-gáqšdaq" vs. (diminutive) "-kʼakʼstʼakʼ," the first, third, fourth, fifth, and final sound segments undergo feature change; the rest of the shape of the stem remains the same. So the gradations of form here are clearly not continuously segmentable. Third, the alternations of form here are essentially the unique signal of speaker attitude toward what is talked about; in using such an augmentative or diminutive (vs. neutral) form, the speaker communicates his attitude to the hearer, and this attitude becomes a contextual reality with effects on how the interaction then proceeds. (You don't tell a salacious story about someone who has just been referred to diminutively, at the risk of offending the prior speaker!) Such forms presuppose merely the constitution of a speech situation with speaker and hearer, something guaranteed just by the fact of speech occurring. Basically, then, the augmentative–neutral–diminutive shifts are highly creative elements of Kiksht.

I want to claim that these formal and functional differences in the two cases are, at least in part, characteristic of the causes of the difference in the way the pragmatics of languages are available for conscious metapragmatic discourse. But we are not finished. I want briefly to present two more dimensions of contrast of pragmatic forms, dimensions I have called *decontextualized deducibility* and *metapragmatic transparency*. The first three dimensions presented, in shorthand, referentiality, segmentability, and presupposition, deal with whether or not a native can give evidence of accurate metapragmatic awareness. These last two dimensions deal with how native speakers treat the forms in metapragmatic discourse.

The fourth dimension, decontextualized deducibility, can best be approached by asking the following question. Given the occurrence of some pragmatic form, what proposition expressible in language follows from the fact that the particular pragmatic form has occurred? In a logical sense, we would ask, what proposition formulable in language is entailed by the occurrence of this form, independent of anything in the context of speaking linked to (indexed by) the form? (Cf. 8.)

(8) A fourth dimension of metapragmatic contrast (cf. (4) above):

    (d) *Decontextualized deducibility*: what proposition, formulable in the language, is entailed (follows as true) by the effective occurrence of a pragmatic form? E.g.,
        In English, a truly referring noun phrase *My brother* ... entails *I have a brother*;
        In English, a truly referring noun phrase *The present King of France* ... entails
        There is now a King of France.

Suppose, for example, that the pragmatic form in question is an instance of the referring item, "My brother...," as contrasted pragmatically with the form, "I have a brother." If the form "my brother..." correctly refers to someone, then from this instance of correct reference we can deduce that I have a brother. Note that any occurrence of the statement, "I have a brother," entails no such consequences; it may be perfectly false, and the hearer of such a form can say, "Are you sure?" or "Wasn't that formerly your sister?" or some such. Philosophers talk always about Russell's classic example, "The present King of France is bald," and why it is odd. They speak in terms of the "presuppositions" of any utterance of this form, of what propositions must be true in order for the proposition coded in this utterance to have any truth value. The crux of the example is the noun phrase *the present King of France,* for, as we can now reformulate it, from any valid instance of referring with this phrase, picking out an actually existing entity, the proposition "There exists now a King of France" is deducible as true. And this, of course, was not true even in Russell's day. So there can be no valid instance of a truly referring form, "The present King of France"; for if there were, by the pragmatics of English the proposition about there now being a King of France would be entailed.

Such examples from English serve to introduce a rather nice parallel from Wasco-Wishram, attested in my field records. This involves what can be called the "evidential passive" form of the verb, a pragmatic alternant for saying that there is evidence in the situation of discourse, to the speaker's knowledge, that leads him or her to think that someone or something has been the object of someone's action. Let me outline its properties in terms of what we have seen so far in the other examples.

The evidential passive form is a particular configuration of the transitive verb with a special suffix *-ix.* It contrasts with several other possible verbal formations that have the same, or related referential effect. Note that for a typical transitive verb, such as "to boil," we can have a regular straightforward "active" form, as shown in (9), like English "he boiled them long ago," "ni-č-d-u-čxm"; a so-called "antipassive" form, like English "he was doing boiling long ago," "nig-i-k'i-čxm-al", that does not tell us what were the objects of his endeavors, just that he was engaged in some activity; an "indefinite agent" form, like English "somebody boiled them long ago," "ni-q-d-u-čxm"; a "collective agent" form, like English "they boiled them long ago," "ni-łk-d-u-čxm", used by contemporary Wasco-Wishram speakers in about the same way as the English nonanaphoric or generic "they"; and a "transitional passive" form, like English "they became boiled" or "they got boiled," "ni-d-u-čxm-xit".

(9) Conjugational forms in the Wasco-Wishram verbal paradigm:

Active:	ni	-$\check{c}_2$	-d_3- u-	√čxm	"he$_2$ boiled them$_3$ long ago"
Antipassive:	nig-	i_3-	kł i-	√čxm-al	"he$_3$ was doing boiling long ago"
Indefinite Agent:	ni	-q_2	-d_3- u-	√čxm	"somebody$_2$ boiled them$_3$ long ago"
Collective Agent:	ni	-łk$_2$	-d_3- u-	√čxm	"they$_2$ boiled them$_3$ long ago"
Transitional Passive:	ni -		d_3- u-	√čxm-xit	"they$_3$ became boiled long ago"
Evidential Passive:			d_3- u-	√čxm-ix	"they$_3$ must have been boiled"

Additionally, when the speaker sees some evidence in what he or she understands to be the results of some activity, (s)he can use the "evidential passive," "d-u-čxm-ix," which I translate as "they must have been boiled" (because, for example, (s)he sees that they are all mushy, or (s)he tastes that they are soft, or whatever).

Clearly, this form is isolable just by isolating the parts of utterances we are interested in from the point of view of reference; it consists of nothing but a transitive verb form inflected only with a prefix for the undergoer of the activity, plus a suffix *-ix* that occurs in a number of formations, with much the same referential value as the English deictic word "there." So we would say that the particular evidential passive construction is unavoidably referential. Next, since the particular form of an evidential passive, by contrast with all the other forms a verb might take, consists of a particular prefix configuration together with a suffix at the end of the verb, it is not continuous. The critical signals of the evidential passive are not uttered as a continuous unit in speech, and hence the evidential passive is not a continuously segmentable pragmatic form. If we had time, I could demonstrate how this gives consultants a great deal of difficulty in distinguishing the evidential forms from forms that mean "there is…". But by proper eliciting, where we know what we are looking for, we can get consultants to focus on this particular form. As to our third criterion of presupposition, we should note that any valid use of the evidential passive presupposes that in the context of use there will indeed be evidence of a nonlinguistic sort, available to both speaker and hearer. This presuppositional requirement seems to be fairly absolute, like the English examples of "this" and "that" introduced above.

We are in fairly good shape, then, insofar as guarantees of metapragmatic awareness are concerned. But when we ask consultants about the use of these forms, when we engage them in metapragmatic conversation, we find that they tell us about the presupposed contextual requirements, as we would expect, and then give the "meaning" of these forms as the deduced proposition which must be true if the evidential passive is validly used! Let us look at some field records, transcribed from continuous tape-recordings, with all but the actual forms under discussion translated into English (the work proceeded partly in English and partly in Kiksht).

In the first case, in (10a), I am trying to talk about the evidential passive of the form "cause someone to cry," which, as a morphological causative, is about as good a transitive verb as one can get. I start from a form gathered earlier in a text, "I made

(10) Elicitation of evidential passive forms

(a) Cns: Wonder how'd you say that now, nanugʷačaxəm – I made them cry. I'm real sure but it's kinda hard. ə˙m, you could say óne- for one- you can say nanu- naniug ʷičax̣-mida.

na-n-i-u-gʷičáx̣mid-a "I recently caused him to cry"

MS: naniu...

Cns: gʷičáx̣mida, I made him cry.

MS: naniugʷi...

Cns: čáx̣mida, I made him cry. Else nanu-nanugʷi – I guess you could say same way nanługič- čáx̣mida, see? I made them cry. nanługičáx̣mida. Now I got it. I made 'em cry nanługičáx̣mida. naniugičáx̣mida.   nanugičáx̣- mida.

na-n-ł-u-gʷičáx̣mid-a "I...them..."
na-n[a]-u-gʷičáx̣mid-a "I...her..."

MS: əhó. And how 'bout like if he made me cry. you say načnu...

Cns: naču-načnugʷičáx̣mida,   he made me cry.

na-č-n-u-gʷičáx̣mid-a "he...me..."

MS: I see. Interesting. əhó. Could you say like, ə˙, somebody made me cry; could I say, ə˙˙, nugʷičáx̣mi- dix?

? n-u-gʷičáx̣mid-ix "somebody made me cry"

Cns: nugʷičáx̣midix? O·h, person – the way you can tell a person, she looks like she was crying, igičáx̣mit –

MS: How?

Cns: ugʷičáx̣midix.

[a]-u-gʷičáx̣mid-ix "she must have been made to cry"

MS: əhó, –

Cns: Like if you see somebody, she been cryin', like it looks some- body she – she musta been cry- ing, see?

MS: – Yeah –

Cns: – ugičáx̣midix, her eyes shows it. ugičáx̣midix. iłgugičáx̣mid or somethin', they made her cry I guess.

i-łg-[a]-i-gʷičáx̣mit "they just made her cry"

them cry recently." The consultant volunteers "naniugʷičáx̣mida," a fully-inflected transitive verb form, meaning "I made him cry recently". Then she offers the form for a collective object, "nanługʷičáx̣mida" "I made the bunch cry recently". And, having gotten the hang of the form, we have several more examples, "I made her cry," "he made me cry," and so forth. Seeing that she controls the regular "active" inflection, I then ask for the first person evidential passive form by specifying it: "'somebody made me cry,' nugʷičáx̣midix." The form understood by the consultant is the feminine singular, "she must have been made to cry," "ugʷicáx̣midix," which is carefully explained in terms of the presupposed context for its occurrence – "she looks like she was crying... her eyes shows it" – and then in terms of the deduced proposition the truth of which is guaranteed by the proper usage of the evidential passive form – "iɬgugicáx̣mit... they made her cry, I guess."

A second case of this sort, shown in (10b), involves the verb for "pinching." Having established the regular "active" form, both iterative "I was pinching her" (insanxap'íyantk) and noniterative "I just pinched her" (insanxap'íyatk), the investigator asks for the evidential passive with a first person, "'I'm pinched'... snxap'íyatgix." Note that the consultant responds with the form, and gives the deduced proposition in the same breath – "snxap'íyatKix... iɬksnxap'íyatk 'they just pinched me'" – explaining that the meaning is "like" this. Now, pressing for the correctness or incorrectness of the evidential passive, I repeat the form, and the consultant says this could be used if the speaker shows the presupposed evidence – "if you show where you was pinched." Again, from the point of view of native speaker metapragmatic awareness, the evidential passive is characterized in terms of its presupposition of evidence in the context of speaking, and the deduced full propositional form which must be true if the form is to be used correctly.

(10b) Cns: – ənsanxap'íyantk, that means two   i-n-s-a-n-xap'íya-n-tk "I was just
             or three times I guess –   pinching her"
      MS: – Oh, I see –
      Cns: – But incáx̣-incanxap'íyatk that's   i-n-s-a-n-xap'íya-tk "I just pinched her"
             just ónce.
      MS: Can you also say like, ə˙ – ə˙ – could   ? s-n[-n]-xap'íya-tg-ix "I'm pinched"
             you say, I'm pinched? Could you
             say, snxap'íyatgix?
      Cns: Yeah –
      MS: – How? –
      Cns: I'm pinched. šnxaʔ-šnxap' –
      MS: -snx-
      Cns: -snxap'íyatKix. xsznxap'íyatk –   i-ɬk-s-n-[n]-xap'íya-tk "they just
             iɬksnxap'íyatk.   pinched me"
      MS: əhə́.
      Cns: Somebody pinched me like.
      MS: You could say snxap'íyatgix
             though?
      Cns: əhə́! If you show where you was
             pinched.
      MS: – on the behind.
      Cns: On the behind.

My final example of the evidential passive, as shown in (10c), is the verb "to bump into." Here, in the course of elicitation of some related item, the consultant volunteers "iníltʿəq" "I just bumped into it." Then, to check on whether the stem ends in a back qʷ or a front kʷ, I also ask for the future form, which turns out to show the former (anildagʷa). Now I ask after the evidential passive form, "ildáqux" "it must have been bumped into." Sure enough, the consultant characterizes it by the presupposed evidence – "like if he'll leave a mark or something" – plus the deduced proposition – "somebody run into it. That's what it means, somebody niłi·t'aq łga ['they probably came and bumped into it a while back']." And the consultant stresses once again the presupposed evidence, "it shóws where it's been bumped."

(10c) Cns: iníltəq too you can say you   i-n-i-l-√ta-q "I just bumped into it
              búmped into something, iní·lt'əq.   (masc.)"
       MS: əhə́. How 'bout I'm going to? –
              might –
       Cns: -dala?ax anildagᵂa.   dala?ax a-n-i-l-√da-gᵂ-a "perhaps I will
                                                                bump into it"
       MS: Is it -dagᵂa or -dagᵂa?
       Cns: -dagᵂa.
       MS: əhə́.
       Cns: dala?ax anildagᵂa.
       MS: əhə́. əhə́. Could you also say   ? i-l-√dá-qᵂ-x "it must have been bumped
              ildáqux? ildáqux.   into"
       Cns: ildáqux. O···h, like if he'll leave a
              mark or something somebody run
              into it. That's what it means,   ni-ł-i·-[t]-ta-q łga "they probably came
              somebody niłi·-λi·t'əq łga.   and bumped into it a
              – łiltə 'q-niłi·t 'əq'.   while back"
       MS: əhə́.
       Cns: ilt'əqux.
       MS: But could you say ildáqux?
       Cns: ildáqux, yeah! That's the same
              thing.
       MS: əhə́.
       Cns: ildə́qux it means that it shóws
              where it's been bumped.
       MS: əhə́.

So, as these examples show, the "meaning" of the evidential passive construction in Wasco-Wishram can be specified in terms of (a) the presupposed evidence that must be in the context of speaking, and (b) the communication of speaker estimate that the evidence is the result of some Agency, doing some specified action named by the verb stem used. The occurrence of an evidential passive allows the hearer (and the speaker) to deduce that "Somebody did such-and-such to the object that shows the evidence therefor." And, from the native speaker's point of view, this deducible entailed proposition *is* "the meaning" of the form. It is what is available to conscious metapragmatic discourse.

The final dimension of metapragmatic awareness I will discuss here is *metaprag-matic transparency*, as shown in (11). This is the degree of sameness between any metapragmatic utterances that could be used to talk about a pragmatic form, and the pragmatic form itself. Thus, a pragmatic form is metapragmatically transparent to the extent that, in metapragmatic discourse describing some use of speech, native speakers can duplicate the very forms under discussion. Consider the familiar speech event of a person giving a lecture and, noticing the audience becoming restless, saying the following: "Just a few more minutes." Now consider an identical situation, except that the speech event is signalled by "I promise to stop talking soon." The utterance "Just a few more minutes" may indeed function pragmatically in exactly the same way as the utterance "I promise to stop talking soon," in that they both communicate the speaker's commitment to cease and desist after a short interval starting at the moment of speaking. But the second utterance, "I promise to stop talking soon," is metapragmatically transparent, whereas the first utterance, "Just a few more minutes," is not. For, if asked to describe what went on in that speech event – what action, in other words, transpired that depended on speech – we could answer as native speakers, "He promised to stop talking soon," duplicating in the description the effective pragmatic forms of the second utterance at issue. Observe that this same metapragmatic description could be used for the first utterance, "Just a few more minutes," as well as several other possible descriptions, such as "He indicated that the lecture would not continue much longer," and so forth. But in each of these last instances of metapragmatic characterization, there is a radical difference between the form of the description and the form of the particular effective pragmatic signal. In short, when we seek the forms of possible metapragmatic descriptions to which it is susceptible, the utterance "Just a few more minutes" shows little metapragmatic transparency.

(11) A fifth dimension of metapragmatic contrast (cf. 4 and 8 above):

> (e) *Metapragmatic transparency*: a pragmatic form is so to the extent that in metapragmatic discourse describing its use, native speakers duplicate the form under discussion, e.g.,
> *I promise to stop talking soon*, uttered as a commitment of the speaker to stop talking soon after utterance;
> but not
> *Just a few more minutes*, uttered for precisely the same purpose.

Now obviously, given some occurrence of speech, some event instantiated as an effective speech signal in a certain context, there are many ways in which a native speaker can answer the question, "What happened?" or "What went on?" He or she can describe the event as a whole, if there is some means of referring to this totality; he or she can describe the presupposed context (as we have seen); he or she can describe the signal, in the most obvious case, that of so-called "direct quotation," just duplicating it, and in less obvious cases, so-called "indirect quotation," duplicating certain aspects of the signal. Or the native speaker can characterize the change(s) in the context effected by the speech signal in answer to the question, "What happened?" But for analytic purposes, the pragmatic meaning of any signal used in speech must be a statement of the presupposed and created contextual factors, that is, a description of what must independently be so about the context for the instance to be effective action, and what must be so about the context from the occurrence of the effective action. So any transparent pragmatic form is a signal that can be used both in effecting specific contextual changes and in describing them. And the description can focus on any of the components of the speech event: speaker, hearer, audience, referent, channel, signal, time, locus, or some relationship between these. And we would, in a fine-grained discussion of the matter, have to differentiate among these factors by their potential contributions to transparency, something we do not have space for in this discussion, but which emerges by example in the material now to be presented.

If we look at the last set of data, on English "directives" as analyzed by Susan Ervin-Tripp, we find that there are numerous directive forms, pragmatic signals for getting someone to do something.[3]

(12) Kinds of directive utterances in American English
    (a)   Need statements: "I'll need a routine culture and a specimen."
    (b)   Imperatives: "(You privates will) repeat the preparatory command and 'aye aye, Sir!'."
    (c)   Embedded imperatives: "Why don't you open the window?"
    (d)   Permission directives: "May I have change for a dollar?"
    (e)   Request questions: "Is Dean Lehrer in?"
    (f)   Hint: "Mrs. Terry, it's quite noisy in here."

As is shown in (12), these include (a) statements of what the speaker needs, some object of the addressee's action, such as "a routine culture and a specimen," or some action on the part of the addressee, "I'll need you to put your finger on the knot." They also include (b) our traditionally-analyzed "imperatives," which communicate just the action the addressee is to carry out; as well as (c) embedded imperatives, which are usually of the "Why don't you...?" question-form with embedded specification of the action the addressee is to do, but having distinct stress and intonation contours terminating in falling instead of level-or-rising pitch (and hence distinct from an interrogative form). Other forms collected include two interrogative types, (d) questions of permission for the speaker to accomplish something, and (e) questions of a seemingly informational content. Finally, there are (f) hints, which are statements about the context uttered with directive force. There is, to be sure, a finer subdivision possible on linguistic and other grounds, but this classification of Ervin-Tripp's will do for our purposes.

(13) Characteristics of directives

Type	Neutrali-zation	Discourse Comply	Constraints* Comply	No Comply	Obvious**	Social Features
(a) Need	no[1]	none		excuse	yes	subordinates
(b) Imperative	no	none		excuse	yes	subordinates, familiar equals
(c) Embedded Imperative	no	agree		excuse	yes	unfamiliar; or different rank; task extraordinary; compliance expected
(d) Permission	yes	agree		excuse	yes	superiors (?); unfamiliar
(e) Request	yes	answer/ inference		answer (=excuse)	no***	possible non-compliance
(f) Hint	yes	(reply + inference)		reply	no***	possible non-compliance; familiarity, or routine roles

*   Expected verbal response to adult; when complying or not complying.
**   Routinely understood as a directive under these social conditions.
***   Some are routinely understood as directives, depending on familiarity, etc.
Note 1: Ervin-Tripp codes "yes" here; but data do not show neutralization in first person.

What are the characteristics of use that Ervin-Tripp has discovered for these different kinds of directives in (Berkeley?) American English? We see in (13) that the formal and functional properties of these expressions can be scaled in a rather regular array. For each directive type, indicated in the rows of the chart, we give Ervin-Tripp's criteria in columnar fashion. Neutralization (indicated as "yes" or "no") means that the actual overt signal form potentially serves both as a directive and as some other pragmatic signal. Thus, imperative forms in row (b) never count as anything but directives, while "requestions" in row (e) are ambiguously either a directive or a request for a "yes" or "no" answer of an informational sort. (Remember the old joke, "Do you have Prince Albert in a can?" "Sure." "Well, let him out!") The discourse constraints on compliance or non-compliance with the directive indicate what the addressee of the directive must do in the way of verbal behavior, in either of these two situations. Thus, to an embedded imperative, such as the example (c) already given under (12), one either agrees with "Sure" or "All right" and opens the window, or one says why one cannot, e.g., "Sorry, my hands are full" (or "... full of —"). Note that to comply with a hint of type (f), one must infer what one must do that follows in some way from the situation described in the hint; not to comply, one must answer the statement with a contrary, such as, "It's not very noisy" or "... cold" or "Wait until the record stops," or "Wait until the noxious fumes clear from the air," or whatever. The social features of the speech situation describe what is presupposed about the relationship between speaker and addressee, or about the understood obligations of the addressee vis-à-vis the particular action demanded. Finally, in terms of these criteria, the obviousness of the utterance as a directive is indicated by "yes" or "no."

What interests us here is the metapragmatic transparency of these forms. If we look at the various types, and consider the way that a directive event would be specifically described, then the types of directives at the bottom of the chart are minimally transparent, and those at the top of the chart are maximally transparent. The hint of type (f) can be accurately described as "the speaker asking Mrs. Terry, the addressee, to be quiet" or "... to turn off the radio" or whatever (see 12f), using metapragmatic description that has no formal commonalty with the actual directive signal under consideration. On the other hand, the need statement of type (a) can be described as "the speaker asking the addressee to do whatever is routinely done to get a culture and a specimen," naming the goals that the mand requires of the addressee. This matches that part of the directive signal, "a routine culture and a specimen." Again, the types (b) and (c) directives are relatively transparent, and the descriptions can be formulated in the very same terms as the part of the signal that describes the action to be done by the addressee. Type (d) is less transparent, in that the signal describes something to be true of the speaker, but the metapragmatic description would have to be in terms of what it is that is demanded of the addressee. And type (e) is less so, since no actual action is described in the directive signal, only some presumably relevant referent being named; and yet, the metapragmatic description would have to say, for example, that "speaker is demanding of the addressee that he or she allow speaker to speak with Dean Lehrer" for (12e). Each type of directive signal, then, has what I suggest is a constantly decreasing metapragmatic transparency in the order given.

Ervin-Tripp reports on two unpublished studies of native speaker evaluations of these different directives, working from actual examples. Subjects were asked to compare various directive forms and rank them essentially in terms of politeness. As might be expected, the subjects ranked the various types in more-or-less the order given here. Now of all the characteristics on our chart, I do not see any that would explain why there is a regular, *linearized* ranking of these different directive types. Clearly, there is no regular orderly formal relationship, like syntactic complexity, or any kind of purely formal politeness machinery in English (unlike, for example, in Javanese, where you can get more and more polite by changing more and more of the vocabulary and syntax, in a kind of regular progression). Nor are any of the other characteristics singly or in combination easily linearized on a single explanatory scale, certainly not the properties called "social features" in our chart (13), which we might expect to be the explanation, since they come from very diverse realms. I propose that it is the scale of metapragmatic transparency of these forms that makes them subject to evaluation and manipulation as most directive like, and hence, in our culture, least "polite," down to least directive like, and hence most "polite." Those directive types which are maximally transparent are much more vividly brought to awareness as directives; which bald fact results in their being termed maximally impolite. And inversely, the tremendous disparity between the form of minimally transparent directives and their metapragmatic descriptions makes them least salient as directives, most veiled in terms of expressing speaker intention in social interaction, and shrouded in so-called politeness, or, if you will allow, in indirection: for "politeness" is essentially the antithesis of giving "directives" in our society, and hence that directive is most polite that is the least directive. This scaling effect deserves much more careful investigation in terms of clarity of responses, salience and scatter of responses, etc., before we can be certain of the interpretation.

In final summary, now, let me turn briefly to two areas in which I think this approach sheds new light, and indicates a means for more intensive research. One such area, harking back to the (alas, misunderstood) work of Benjamin Lee Whorf, seeks understanding of the cognitive bases of the many functions of language. The other area is what methodological lessons might be learned here about the investigation of cultural phenomena in general. I do not have space to develop these implications at any length, and content myself with utterances that you will no doubt take to be overbroad historiography. But I think what follows can be documented in a more elaborate treatment.

Whorf, who developed all the themes of Boasian linguistics to their sharpest formulation, inquired into the classic Boasian problem, the nature of classifications of the cultural universe implicit and explicit in language. In passing, he invented the notion of a "cryptotypic," or, as we now say, "deep" or "underlying" semantic structure that lies behind the overtly segmentable forms of speech. This cryptotypic structure of referential categories constituted the real "rational" classification of the sensory modalities implemented in fully propositional speech, the highest function of language to the Boasian way of thinking. But, the native speaker, faced with tasks that require orientation to an immediate and urgent environment, trying to "think out" a response, or even to "think about" the referential properties of his or her native language in specific situations, is hopelessly at the mercy of so-called "phenotypic," or as we now say "surface" lexicalized forms of the language. The native speaker tends to reason from the misleading surface analogies of forms to which, in piecemeal fashion, he or she attributes true referential effect in segmenting the cultural universe. Whorf is thus contrasting native awareness of the suggestive referential patterns of surface lexical forms, with the linguist's awareness of the cryptotypic semantic structure behind those surface forms, achieved by excruciating analysis in a comparative framework. He claims that insofar as reference is concerned, the native's awareness is focussed on continuously-segmentable ("lexical" in his terms) units, which presuppose the existence of things "out there" that correspond to these units one-to-one on each referential use of speech. Of course, the native is only partially correct, and is generally inaccurate in his or her "awareness." What we have done here is to generalize Whorf's observation for the whole range of functions of speech, reference being just one function that is clearly at the center of the whole ethno-linguistic system. We have claimed that we can best guarantee native speaker awareness for referential, segmental, presupposing functional forms in his or her language. And we can bound the kind of evidence the native speaker can give us in terms of deducible referential propositions about functional forms maximally transparent to description as speech events.

The case is well illustrated by the gradual recognition of non-referential aspects of "meaning" in language within our own tradition of linguistics and related disciplines. Just as we would expect, our Western philosophical theories of language – what I like to call our naive native ethnotheoretical tradition – have traditionally started from word reference, in particular from proper names, which native speakers feel to be concrete, pointing out an absolute reality "out there." Such theories have tried to generalize the notion of how language means from this maximally aware metapragmatic sensibility. With the advent of Frege, and of Saussure, the domain of analysis was broadened to propositional reference, and to structural analysis of referential systems, culminating in the explicit underlying-structure methodology of Chomsky. At the same time, ordinary language philosophy with Austin finally discovered certain lexical items – segmental, referential, presupposing, deducible, maximally transparent forms – called "performatives," that seemed to be a key to the non-referential functions of one's own language. It is not by chance that these performatives, such as *promise, christen, dub,* etc. were discovered first by the linguistically naive native speakers of Oxford; they satisfy all our criteria. But unfortunately, accurate though they may be for certain of our more transparent speech functions in English, they cannot merely be treated as a universal set to be ferreted out by inaccurate translation techniques in the most remote corners of the globe, as some of our colleagues are wont to do. Indeed, they represent only a tiny fraction of the functioning of our language, though a fraction that is easily susceptible of native awareness. The further we get from these kinds of functional elements of language, the less we can guarantee awareness on the part of the native speakers – accurate metapragmatic testimony that can be taken at face value. Hence, for the rest, the more we have to depend upon cross-cultural analysis and the accumulated technical insight based upon this, for native speaker metapragmatic testimony is not going to be necessarily accurate for the general analysis of language.

There is a sense in which our generalization of Whorf's principle, now formulable in terms of limited metapragmatic awareness, has a wider relevance for social anthropology. As many of us are beginning to realize, the linguistic models that have been applied to cultural phenomena have usually been motivated within linguistics itself precisely by the facts of the pure referential system that is unique to language, among all the meaningful social codes. I think, however, that we can show how the other functions of language are always being assimilated to reference in terms of native speaker awareness, and are in fact subject to conscious metapragmatic testimony only to the extent that they *are* assimilable to reference, or "ride along on" referential structure. Thus, how vastly more complicated are the testimonies of native participants in a society, how fraught with danger is our taking at face value any statements by participants about various pragmatically-meaningful action. If we were to generalize from the experience with language reported here, then we would suspect that most of what is of interest to the social anthropologist is beyond native participant testimony as to its "meaning." But, beyond this purely negative statement, we would also expect that, more generally, the limits to pragmatic awareness of social action are also definable, constrained, and semiotically-based.

This, I want to lay before you, is the program for social anthropology, to understand the properties of ideologies and ethnotheories, that seem to guide participants in social systems, as part and parcel of those social systems, which must be seen as meaningful. The salient aspect of the social fact is meaning; the central manifestation of meaning is pragmatic and metapragmatic speech; and the most obvious feature of pragmatic speech is reference. We are now beginning to see the error in trying to investigate the salient by projection from the obvious.

NOTES

[This paper is a transcript of a lecture originally given in 1977. For this reprinting, following the author's request, a few editorial changes have been made and a few references have been added, but the informal tone of the original working paper has not been altered. Ed.]

1 Djirbal: R. M. W. Dixon (1971). A Method of Semantic Description. In D. D. Steinberg and L. A. Jakobovits (eds.), *Semantics: An Interdisciplinary Reader in Philosophy, Linguistics, and Psychology* (pp. 436–71). Cambridge: Cambridge University Press; and R. M. W. Dixon (1967). *The Dyirbal Language of North Queensland.* Ph.D. dissertation, University of London.

2 Kiksht (Wasco-Wishram Chinook): E. Sapir (1911). Diminutive and Augmentative Consonantism in Wishram. In Franz Boas (ed.), *Handbook of American Indian Languages* (pp. 638–45): Bulletin of the Bureau of American Ethnology, Vol. 40, Part 1; and M. Silverstein, field notes, 1966–74. Also M. Silverstein (1978). Deixis and Deducibility in a Wasco-Wishram Passive of Evidence. *Proceedings of the Berkeley Linguistics Society* 4:238–53.

3 American English: Susan Ervin-Tripp (1976). Is Sybil There? The Structure of American English Directives. *Language in Society* 5:25–66.
   Other works cited in this paper: R. Brown and A. Gilman (1960). The Pronouns of Power and Solidarity. In T. A. Sebeok (ed.), *Style in Language* (pp. 253–76). Cambridge, MA: MIT Press; W. E. Lambert, R. C. Hodgson, R. C. Gardner, and S. Fillenbaum (1960). Evaluational Reactions to Spoken Languages. *Journal of Abnormal and Social Psychology* 60:44–51; W. E. Lambert, H. Frankel, and G. R. Tucker (1996). Judging Personality through Speech: A French-Canadian Example. *Journal of Communication* 16:305–21; R. Brown and M. Ford (1961). Address in American English. *Journal of Abnormal and Social Psychology* 62:375–85.

17

Arizona Tewa Kiva Speech as a Manifestation of a Dominant Language Ideology

Paul V. Kroskrity

"What have you learned about the ceremonies?" Back in the summer of 1973, when I first began research on Arizona Tewa, I was often asked this and similar questions by a variety of villagers. I found this strange, even disconcerting, since the questions persisted after I explained my research interest as residing in the language "itself," or in "just the language, not the culture." But my response was very much a managed production. For though my originally formulated object of study was the Arizona Tewa language, even early on in what was to become long-term field research I had become very interested in the tangled relationship of Arizona Tewa language, culture, and society. But despite this interest, I had been coached by my academic advisers and informed by a scholarly tradition of research on Pueblo Indians to recognize the cultural sensitivity of research on religion and the suspicion directed at those who would nevertheless attempt to study it, even in its more esoteric forms. My professional training thus encouraged me to attribute these periodic inquiries to a combination of secrecy and suspicion regarding such culturally sensitive topics as ceremonial language. Yet despite my careful attempts to disclaim any research interest in kiva speech (*te'e hi:li*) and to carefully distinguish between it and the more mundane speech of everyday Arizona Tewa life, I still experienced these occasional interrogations. Did these questions betray a native confusion of the language of the kiva with that of the home and plaza? Was there a connection between these domains of discourse that was apparent to most Tewa villagers, yet hidden from me? In the past few years, after more than two decades of undertaking various studies of Arizona Tewa grammar, sociolinguistic variation, language contact, traditional narratives, codeswitching, and chanted announcements, an underlying pattern of language use has gradually emerged that, via the documentary method of interpretation, has allowed me to attribute a new meaning to these early inquiries.[1] The disparate linguistic and discourse practices of everyday speech, I contend, display a common pattern of influence from *te'e hi:li* "kiva speech." The more explicit rules for language use in ritual performance provide local models for the generation and evaluation of more mundane speech forms and verbal practices.

"Linguistic ideologies," taken in Michael Silverstein's (1979) sense as "sets of beliefs about language articulated by users as a rationalization or justification of perceived language structure and use," provide a useful frame for understanding the Arizona Tewa pattern. By viewing members' reflectivity, or what Giddens (1984) calls "reflexive monitoring," as an irreducible force in language behavior, the notion of linguistic ideology directs attention to cultural actors' rationalization of their own language activity. "The total linguistic fact, the datum for a science of language, is irreducibly dialectic in nature. It is an unstable mutual interaction of meaningful sign forms contextualized to situations of interested human use mediated by the fact of cultural ideology" (Silverstein 1985:220).

Examining the Arizona Tewa culture of language as a site for the investigation of language ideologies is multiply warranted. As a Pueblo Indian group that removed itself from Spanish influence in 1700 by migrating to the easternmost of the Hopi mesas and, since then, has maintained its indigenous Kiowa-Tanoan language, the Arizona Tewa are "twice blessed" with a cultural self-consciousness about language use. First, as Pueblo Indians, they are paragons of what Joel Sherzer (1976) and others have termed "linguistic conservatism" – that celebrated penchant for resistance to linguistic borrowing. But whatever analytical value this concept may have to students of language contact, it has at best only the most tentative footing in terms of its foundations in Arizona Tewa cultural experience. Examination of Arizona Tewa linguistic ideology, I contend, offers an alternative, socioculturally based interpretation – a deconstruction of "linguistic conservatism" into dimensions that are simultaneously more analytically precise and more rooted in Arizona Tewa local knowledge.

A second source of Arizona Tewa cultural emphasis on language is their own remarkable history of language contact and language maintenance. In the diaspora of the Pueblo Revolts of 1680 and 1696, the Arizona Tewa are the only outmigrating group that has retained its language into the present.[2] Maintenance of the Tewa language has served not only to perpetuate an ethnic boundary and to embody a "contrapuntal" linguistic consciousness (Said 1984:171–2) but also to mask a pattern of dramatic cultural change in adapting to the Hopi, the group to whom the ancestors of the Arizona Tewa migrated almost three hundred years ago. This adaptation was quite necessary for physical survival in the harsh western Pueblo environment. The Arizona Tewa saying *Na:-bí hi:li na:-bí wowa:ci na-mu* "My language is my life (history)" reveals the intimate relationships among language, history, and identity that this migration has fostered, as well as the cultural salience of the connection. Thus, the culture-specific history of the Arizona Tewa has enhanced a Pan-Puebloan attention to language that may account for its magnified local significance.

Local Knowledge and Linguistic Ideology

Though the role of native language maintenance in response to their Hopi hosts is somewhat peculiar to the Arizona Tewa, the cultural prominence of kiva speech – the speech performed in religious chambers when sacred ceremonial altars are erected – is common to all Pueblo societies. As a key symbol of Tewa linguistic values, kiva talk embodies four closely related cultural preferences: regulation by convention, indigenous purism, strict compartmentalization, and linguistic indexing of identity. For each of these I briefly sketch: (1) their basis in kiva talk, (2) their cultural salience as manifested in members' awareness, and (3) the "scope" and "force" with which these preferences are manifested in nonritual speech. By "cultural salience" I mean approximate location on a scale of awareness that ranges from practical consciousness/tacit knowledge, on the one hand, to discursive consciousness/explicit knowledge on the other (Giddens 1984). In using "scope" and "force" I follow Geertz's (1968) study of Islamic belief, in which he used the former to refer to the range of contexts in which some value or belief would be manifested and the latter to characterize its intensity.

Regulation by convention

In the kiva, ritual performers rely on fixed prayer and song texts. Innovation is neither desired nor tolerated. Proper ritual performance should replicate past conventions, and, if such repetition is impossible, the ritual should not be performed at all. Thus, in instances where the ceremonial knowledge has not been effectively transmitted from one priest to his apprentice, the ceremony becomes defunct. This concern with regulation by convention is manifested in everyday speech preferences by adherence to greeting formulae, to the extended use of kinship terms in address forms, to rules of hospitality involving kinsmen and visitors, and to avoidance of direct confrontation in interaction with fellow villagers. Culturally valued native genres, involving either histories or traditional stories, must carefully conform to the traditional formal precedents associated with those genres.

In traditional stories, for example, from the Arizona Tewa genre *pé:yu'u*, audience members and performers alike honor a tradition that employs stylized, nonverbal accompaniment and uses familiar storytelling conventions. Foremost among these ways of "speaking the past" is the use of evidential *ba* as a genre marker (Kroskrity 1985a). By disclaiming any novelty on the part of the narrator, this particle and its repeated use provide a continuous and obligatory indexing of "the voice" of the traditional narrator. In example 1, the introductory sentence of the story "Coyote and Bullsnake" (Kroskrity and Healing 1978) exemplifies a pattern of multiple occurrence within each sentence uttered in the voice of the narrator (as opposed to story characters' voices or frame-breaking asides in a personal voice).

(1)	owÉ heyam-ba	long:ago ba	Long ago, so they say
	bayɛna-senó ba	Old Man Coyote ba	Old Man Coyote so
	na-tha.[3]	he lived.	he lived.

Thus a particle that denotes the secondhand nature and traditional character of what is said – similar to our "so they say" – aptly functions as a discourse marker of a genre of traditional stories.

Even when narrators chose to "speak the present" – to contextualize their stories for specific audiences – such innovations should ideally occur in the voice of the narrator (e.g., through episode editing and elaboration, nonverbal audience specification, or the addition of identifying details that might be tied to specific audience members). Narrators who chose such frame-breaking strategies as code-switching and the introduction of a personal voice (unmarked by *ba*) or who merely forgot to clearly delineate the "voice of the traditional narrator" by excluding *ba* were negatively evaluated for their efforts by audience members, who criticized them for not telling it "right," not telling it the "old way."

If innovation, even in the form of contextualization, is to be culturally sanctioned, it must be cloaked in traditional garb. I encountered an interesting and creative use of traditional linguistic form one summer when I heard what sounded like a traditional Tewa public announcement (*tú-khé*). The chanter was clearly using the dramatic rising and falling intonations associated with the "public address" style reserved for crier chiefs to announce upcoming ceremonies or call for volunteers for village projects like cleaning out a spring, replastering the kiva, or for individuals to offer birth announcements or stylized grievance chants (Black 1967). But, while the form was traditional, its content and presenter were not. The chanter was issuing a call for a yard sale and inviting all within earshot to examine items of used clothing and some small appliances that she hoped to sell! An example of this is provided in example 2.

(2) (a) kwiyó: he:wɛ   khe: 'i-kw'ón   wí-t'olo-kánt'ó
        women   some   clothes   they-lie   I/you-tell-will
        Women: I'm telling you there are some clothes lying.

    (b) né'ɛ́   phíní-bí-k'ege   'i:-kú-kwín -ɛ́'ɛ́-mí
        here   Phini-s-house   you:all-buy-look-come-should
        You all should come and shop at Phini's house.

    (c) kinán   dí-tú-'án-dán   wí-t'olo-'án
        this   I/other-say-since   I/you-tell-past
        This is what I was told to tell you.

Though the "commercial" message was hardly traditional, the chanter won general village approval by conforming to the expected intonational and other prosodic patterns, as well as the verbal formulae associated with the genre. Despite the brevity of this "short notice" announcement, its obedience to such generic norms as initial addressee specification and its explicit acknowledgment of the announcer role, as well as its prosodic fidelity to traditional models, prompted all but the most ultra-conservative villagers to overlook the fact that the chanter was a woman (Kroskrity 1992:110–12).[4] Importantly, both the gender of the chanter and the chant's commercial content – both violations in a genre normally performed by men announcing communal activities – were subordinated in public opinion to an approval of its traditional form.

Members' awareness of the value of conventionality is often, as the preceding examples show, quite explicit. While many individuals praise traditionality for its own sake and accept it as a guiding principle, relatively few (with the exception of older members of the ceremonial elite) related this value to the emphasis on replicating past performances or the importance of precedent in calculating ceremonial privilege. One ceremonially well-placed man compared everyday speech to prayers:

You know when we talk to each other it is like when we pray. We look for a way of saying things that has been handed down to us by our grandfathers and grandmothers. We like something old that has lived into the present. It must be strong and powerful to do that. Only difference between prayers and [everyday] talk is that we don't send our prayers to people.

This analogy suggests that ceremonial practitioners' greater experiential familiarity with the realm of kiva speech may provide them with a greater awareness of the intertextuality of kiva and mundane speech than is accessible to those less experienced.

Indigenous purism

Indigenous purism and strict compartmentalization are two dimensions of Arizona Tewa linguistic ideology that, though analytically distinguishable, are intimately joined in most linguistic practices. During ritual performance there is an explicit and enforced proscription against the use of foreign words and/or native vocabulary clearly identified with an equally alien social dialect (such as slang, recently manufactured words lacking any association to prestigious individuals or activities [Newman 1955]). As for enforcement, Frank Hamilton Cushing's experience is exemplary. For uttering a Spanish word in a Zuni kiva he was struck forcefully across the arms by a whipper kachina. After being so purified, he was instructed to say the Zuni equivalent of "Thank you." In his discussion of vocabulary levels of the Zuni, Stanley Newman appears to dismiss purism in passages such as the following:

Likewise obviously borrowed words, such as *melika* "Anglo-American" cannot be used in the kiva. This prohibition against loanwords is obviously not to be equated with traditions of linguistic purism, whereby organizations in many modern national states legislate against foreignisms that threaten to adulterate the native language. It stems rather from the general Zuni injunction against bringing unregulated innovation into ceremonial situations. Using a word like *melika*, as one informant expressed it, would be like bringing a radio into the kiva. (1955:349)

Though Newman has discouraged the interpretation of such kiva practices as strictly analogous to enforced policies of language purism in contemporary nation-states, the kind of purism that Newman is dismissing amounts to an official proscription of linguistic diffusion (e.g., loanwords, grammatical interference) not only in ceremonial speech but in everyday speech as well. But Tewa ceremonial leaders, like those of other pueblos, are not waging a campaign to dictate everyday speech norms. Any purging of foreignisms in everyday speech represents a popular extrapolation, a symbolic "trickle-down" influence of the salient and prestigious model of kiva speech. The primary concern of ceremonial leaders is with maintaining and delimiting a distinctive and appropriate linguistic variety, or vocabulary level, for religious expression, not with minimizing foreign linguistic influence. The strong sanctions against foreign expressions in ceremonial speech, sanctions that involve physical punishment, are motivated not by the linguistic expression of xenophobia or extreme ethnocentrism but by the need for stylistic consistency in a highly conventionalized liturgical speech level. Similarly, the negative evaluation of instances of codemixing in everyday speech by members of the Arizona Tewa speech community reflects not the prevalence of negative attitudes about these other languages but rather the functioning of ceremonial speech as a local model of linguistic prestige. This role should not be too surprising when we observe that the prestige that accrues to "standard languages" in modern nation-states emanates, in part, from the support of and their use by national governments and in part from their association with formal education. Since Pueblo societies are traditionally theocratic, fusing political power and religious authority, and since ceremonial leaders must acquire appropriate knowledge through rigorous verbal instruction, the functional role and cultural associations of ceremonial speech are actually quite analogous to standard languages that derive their prestige from the institutional support of both government and formal education.

Further supporting this claim that the negative evaluation of codemixing, especially prevalent in older speakers (Kroskrity 1978), is attributable more to local models than to xenophobia are two types of telling observations. First, speakers regulate language mixing from languages that they highly value and use proficiently. Certainly, the Arizona Tewa, as I have argued elsewhere (Kroskrity 1993:46–7, 206–10), have many social identities that are performed in the nonethnic languages of their linguistic repertoire: Hopi and English. Hopi is an essential medium of intervillage communication and the appropriate language for relating to Hopi kinsmen. Command of English has permitted the Arizona Tewa to gain significant economic and political advantages over the Hopi in their role as cultural brokers, mediating between Euro-Americans and the more conservative Hopi. Fluency in these languages is necessary for full participation in Arizona Tewa society. Though fluency in these languages is never criticized by the Tewa, language mixing between these languages is routinely and consistently devalued. Second, there is a well-established tradition of "song renewal" from other linguistic traditions (Humphreys 1982). Entire songs, solely encoded in foreign languages, are often performed in Tewa Village and throughout the Pueblos. It is difficult to explain the popularity of this tradition if one wants to argue for a xenophobic interpretation of ideal speech norms against codeswitching.

Though the Arizona Tewa clearly lack the deliberation and institutional enforcement often associated with "purist" movements, Arizona Tewa indigenous purism may not lack other attributes that language planning theorists associate with linguistic purism. Scholars such as Jernudd (1989:4), for example, view such movements in modern nation-states as consisting of a bidirectional process that involves the simultaneous opening of native resources and the closing off of nonnative ones for linguistic change. Manfred Henningsen (1989:31–2) expands on the latter aspect when he says, "the politics of purity . . . originates in a quest for identity and authenticity of a cultural Self that feels threatened by the hegemonic pressure of another culture." Annamalai (1989:225), too, observes that purism is "manifest when there is social change affecting the structure of social control." But while resistance to hegemony and rapid sociocultural change may be the prerequisite of linguistic purism in modern nation-states, these conditions have also prevailed for the Arizona Tewa and their Southern Tewa ancestors since the time of Spanish contact in the sixteenth century. From the repressive colonial program of the Spanish, to post-migration Hopi stigmatization and segregation, to "domestic" colonization by the United States, it is certainly possible to find a consistent pattern of Tewa resistance to hegemonic pressure. But it would be wrong to assume that purism is coincident with such hegemony, that it is largely a component of a "counterlinguistic" response by the Arizona Tewa and their ancestors to a series of oppressions.[5] Data from contact with Apachean languages traceable to the late pre-Spanish contact period shows the same pattern of loanword suppression (Kroskrity 1982, 1985b) and strongly suggests that the practice of indigenous purism was already in place. What has been even more continuous than hegemonic pressure from outside is the prestigious position of the traditional religious leaders – an "internal" hegemonic force – and the speech norms associated with them.

But if Arizona Tewa indigenous purism lacks a social organization dedicated to its systematic enforcement, the Arizona Tewa people themselves are usually quite explicit about its value. In Albert Yava's approximation of a life history known as *Big Falling Snow*, he proudly compares the Arizona Tewa to the Rio Grande Tewa: "We still speak the Tewa language and we speak it in a more pure form than the Rio Grande Tewas do. Over there in New Mexico the Tewa language has been corrupted by other Pueblo languages and Spanish. We also speak Hopi fluently though there are very few Hopi who can converse in Tewa" (1978:1).

Strict compartmentalization

The third value, strict compartmentalization, is also of great importance to the understanding of Arizona Tewa linguistic ideology. Essential to kiva talk is the maintenance of a distinctive linguistic variety that is dedicated to a well-demarcated arena of use. Kiva talk would lose its integrity if it admitted expressions from other languages or from other linguistic levels. Likewise, if kiva talk were to be spoken outside of ceremonial contexts, it would profane this liturgical variety and constitute a flagrant violation. This strict compartmentalization of language forms and use has often been recognized as a conspicuous aspect of the language attitudes of Pueblo cultures (Dozier 1956; Sherzer 1976:244). What is novel here is the recognition that this value, like regulation by convention and indigenous purism, is traceable to the adoption of kiva talk as the local model of linguistic prestige. Just as ceremonial practitioners can neither mix linguistic codes nor use them outside their circum-scribed contexts of use, so – ideally – Tewa people should observe comparable compartmentalization of their various languages and linguistic levels in their every-day speech. The mixing of Tewa with either English or Hopi is explicitly devalued by members of the Tewa speech community, though in unguarded speech some mixing does occur. It is interesting that in the Tewa folk account of speech variation, social categories are ranked in respect to the perceived avoidance of language mixing. Older speakers, for example, are said to approximate this ideal more than younger. Men do so more than women. It should be emphasized that this folk perception can be readily interpreted as a reflection of the different participation of these groups in ceremonial activities, of their differential proximity to the realm of kiva talk.

Examination of both historical linguistic data and more contemporary socio-linguistic studies of the Arizona Tewa confirms the selective influence of indigenous purism and strict compartmentalization. Since I have already extensively reviewed this trend elsewhere (Kroskrity 1993:55–108), it is appropriate to summarize and highlight a pattern of linguistic ideology that shapes the form of linguistic diffusion in three periods of language contact. The pattern features the suppression of linguistic borrowing, especially in the lexicon. In multilingual episodes with Apacheans, the Spanish, and the Hopi lasting 100, 150, and 191 years, respectively, the Arizona Tewa language has admitted two Apachean, seventeen Spanish, and one Hopi loanword (Kroskrity 1982, 1993). Clearly, Arizona Tewa folk linguists have put into practice the indigenous purist and the strict compartmentalization planks of Arizona Tewa linguistic ideology. But there is also clear evidence that folk attention is selective. The approximation of these ideals in actual practice presupposes a folk perception of "alien" linguistic structures, and yet Arizona Tewa linguists, unlike our own, are primarily if not exclusively lexicographers. Abundant evidence suggests that several grammatical structures in Arizona Tewa are the result of linguistic convergence. Thus, as illustrated in example 3, the innovation of a possessive or relational suffix in Tewa appears to be the result of contact with Apachean languages.

(3) TEWA   NAVAJO
     sen-bí ’é:nu   hastiin bi-ye’
     man-’s son   man   ’s[6]-song
     (a) man's son   (a) man's song

     ’é:nu -bí nṵ’ṵ   hastiin bi-ch’ą́ą́h
     boy -’s under   man   ’s-front
     under the boy   in front of the man

These two phrases, in both Arizona Tewa and Navajo, demonstrate both the phonological and the grammatical similarity of the affixes. In both languages, these constituents are used in possessive constructions and with locative postpositions. Significantly, no other Kiowa-Tanoan language has this constituent (Kroskrity 1985b). This strongly suggests grammatical diffusion from Apachean languages as the source for Arizona Tewa -bí.

Similarly, Arizona Tewa has innovated a new passive suffix, which now alternates with an inherited one shared by Rio Grande Tewa. Example 4 illustrates the parallel Arizona Tewa and Hopi constructions.

(4) TEWA   HOPI
     p’o   na-kulu-tí   taawi   yuk-ilti
     water   it-pour-PASSIVE   song   finish-PASSIVE
     The water was poured.   The song was finished.
     (Kalectaca 1978:132)

Though Arizona Tewa has a passive suffix, -n, which it shares with Rio Grande Tewa, the -tí suffix represents a grammatical borrowing from analogous Hopi structures. Again, in an instance of ongoing linguistic change emerging from sociolinguistic variation, younger Arizona Tewa speakers now produce only one of the three structural alternatives for realizing phrasal conjunction that are available for the oldest generation of speakers (Kroskrity 1982). Significantly, it is the one that converges with English structures of the type N and N (i.e., N-ádí N), as represented in example 5:

(5) sen-ná-dí kwiyó-wá-dí
     sen-ná-dí kwiyó
     sen kwiyó-wá-dí
     the man and the woman

There is also evidence that some discourse phenomena join grammar in their location outside the awareness of speakers. In comparative studies of Hopi, Arizona Tewa, and Rio Grande Tewa narratives, I found that, though the Arizona Tewa evidential particle *ba*, as discussed in relation to example 1, was clearly related to a homologous one in Rio Grande Tewa, its pattern of usage more clearly resembled that of the Hopi quotative particle *yaw*, as in Arizona Tewa (example 6) and Hopi (example 7):

(6) 'i-wɛ   ba, di-powa-di ba,   'ó:bé-khwo:li-mak'a-kánt'ó-di
     there-at ba, they-arrive-SUB[7]   they:INV-fly-teach-SUB
     From there so, having arrived so, they were being taught to fly.

(7) noq yaw 'ora:yvi 'atka   ki:tava   yaw piw 'tłpcvo ki'yta
     and yaw Oraibi   below:south from:village yaw also wren   she-live
     And wren also lived below Oraibi, south of the village.
     (from Seumptewa, Voegelin, and Voegelin 1980)

In its frequent and multiple occurrence within sentences, as well as its general service as a genre marker, the Arizona Tewa pattern of use appears to have converged with the Hopi and departed from the norms of other Tewa narrative traditions.

As an ideological preference, "strict compartmentalization" is tangible not only in the practical consciousness of Arizona Tewa speech behavior but also in the "discursive consciousness" of some members. One older man who had recently had primary responsibility for the performance of an important village ceremony offered the following agricultural imagery in his explication of the practice of strict compartmentalization and its ceremonial connections.

This way we keep kiva speech separate from everyday speech reminds me of the way we plant corn. You know those different colors [of corn] just don't happen. If you want blue corn, if you want red corn, you must plant your whole field only in that color. If you plant two together you get only mixed corn. But we need to keep our colors different for the ceremonies. That's why we have so many fields far from one another. Same way our languages. If you mix them they are no longer as good and useful. The corn is a lot like our languages – we work to keep them separate.

This example of native explication demonstrates that strict compartmentalization is not always an unconscious activity but, on occasions and by some individuals, also a discursive strategy that can be both rationalized and naturalized as obedience to ceremonial dictates.

Linguistic indexing of identity

The final dimension of Tewa linguistic ideology concerns itself with the Tewa preference for locating the speaking self in a linguistically well-defined, possibly positional, sociocultural identity and the belief that speech behavior in general expresses important information about the speaker's identity. Related to this is a comment once made to me by Albert Yava regarding the way attention to the speech of others is used to locate them in sociocultural space: "I only have to hear someone talk for a short while before I know who they are and where they have been." In addition to this cultural idea that one's speech is a linguistic biography, the model of ritual speech foregrounds the importance of positional, rather than personal, identities and the use of appropriate role-specific speech.

Outside of kiva talk, we find similar emphases in the more mundane genres of traditional stories and public announcements. In stories, as mentioned earlier, the narrator establishes and maintains his status through adoption of the full range of narrative conventions, including the use of evidential *ba*. These practices permit narrators to adopt the voice of the traditional storyteller in order to "speak the past." Similarly, a conventional component of public announcements is the explicit acknowledgement by the chanter of his mediating status as spokesperson. The scope of this penchant for conveying identity through use of an associated code extends to casual conversation. Among trilingual Tewa men conversing in domestic settings it was not unusual to hear codeswitching deployed for just such expressive purposes. Example 8, extracted from a more detailed study of codeswitching (Kroskrity 1993:193–210) is a brief strip of talk in which a codeswitch signals a reformulation of identity for the speaking selves.

(8)   F: [HOPI] Tutuqayki-t qa-naanawakna.
        "Schools were not wanted."

      G: [TEWA] Wé-dí-t'ókán-k'ege-na'a-di im-bí akhon-i-di.
        "They didn't want a school on their land."

      H: [TEWA] Nɛmbie:yɛ nɛ́lɛ́ɛ-mo díbí-t'o-'am-mí kạ:yị́'i we-di-mu:di.
        "It's better our children go to school right here rather than far away."

Three senior Tewa men have been discussing then recent news about the selection of an on-reservation site for the building of a high school. This topic follows from prior discussion of other building projects on the reservation. As is customary in discussing extravillage reservation matters, the conversation, to which all three men have contributed, has been conducted in Hopi. Speaker F merely notes the opposition to previous efforts to create an on-reservation high school. But speakers G and H switch to Tewa to reformulate their speaking selves as Tewa – members of a group that historically has opposed Hopi obstruction of building plans. G's use of Tewa further distances him from the Hopi "they" who opposed use of "their" tribal lands as school sites. H states what has historically been the Arizona Tewa argument for a reservation high school. Since, in retrospect, most Hopi and Tewa individuals now recognize the disruptive impact on their children over the past few decades of attending boarding schools, H's remark also evaluates the essential correctness of the position promoted by their ethnic group. In both G's and H's remarks, the selection of the "marked" code given the topic reformulates their relevant interactional identity as Arizona Tewa. Thus, the practice of maintaining maximally distinctive codes through strict compartmentalization provides the Tewa with appropriate linguistic resources in order to invoke a variety of corresponding socio-cultural identities in interaction. Awareness (Silverstein 1981) of this aspect of language use on the part of Arizona Tewa speakers is, predictably, selective. Many speakers recognize the resources that their linguistic repertoires provide in permitting them to perform multiple social identities. These speakers often liken their languages and linguistic levels to masks and costumes worn for a specific ceremony.

But it is useful to note that, although the Arizona Tewa openly acknowledge a close association between language and identity, as mentioned earlier, they do not recognize conversational codeswitching as a locus for the expression of identity. This is, no doubt, tied to the fact that most Arizona Tewa trilinguals deny that they codeswitch, even though they routinely engage in this practice. This denial may reflect not only the fact that these behaviors are largely taken for granted but also a popular confusion between culturally devalued "codemixing" and codeswitching. Of much greater cultural salience are members' discourses on language and identity, which either invoke the Tewa practice of multiple names or compare the activity of speaking different languages to wearing different ceremonial masks (Kroskrity 1993:46–7).

Some members view the cultural practice of having many names and acquiring new names as one progresses through the ceremonial system as the most salient connection between language and identity. The discourse involving analogies to impersonation of kachinas is, of course, limited to those men who have "impersonated" kachinas in public ceremonies. The comparisons to such ceremonial performances requires some further commentary, since the dramaturgical imagery of a western view – involving personae, masks, and impersonation – invites a very nonlocal interpretation. For the Arizona Tewa, as for other Pueblo groups, so-called masks are viewed as living "friends" (k'ema), and masking is not a means of hiding one's "real" identity or donning a false one but rather an act of transformation in which the performer becomes the being that is iconically represented by his clan's "friend." When such local meanings are taken into account, it is clear that the imagery of ceremonial performance, even if available only to a restricted group, provides a discourse that recognizes the constitutive role of language in iconically signaling a member's relevant identity.

Conclusions

In this chapter I have explored the potentially fruitful application of the notion of language ideology to the Arizona Tewa speech community. In this section, I attempt to highlight some of the uses of a language ideological approach to the Arizona Tewa data by examining its applicability to two general accounts of Pueblo languages and cultures: the "linguistic conservatism" of the Pueblo Southwest and the relationship of Arizona Tewa language ideology to the political economies of Western Pueblo societies. After this, I return to the issue of members' awareness, or consciousness, as a criterial attribute of language ideologies and suggest that successfully "naturalized" and "contending" language ideologies are routinely associated with different levels of members' awareness.

I start by agreeing with Friedrich (1989:309), who distinguishes several especially valuable senses of "ideology." I employ two of these distinctions in my concluding remarks as a means of assessing both what has been accomplished and what remains to be done. Attending to the "notional" sense of ideology as the basic notions or ideas that members have about a well-demarcated area of a culture, an attention to culturally dominant linguistic ideology greatly improves on the limited "etic" understanding provided by the notion of "linguistic conservatism." Though Pueblo Indian communities are often said to exhibit this trait, scholars have also prematurely reified the notion of linguistic conservatism, treating it as if it were both a self-explanatory and an irreducible analytical account (Kroskrity 1993:213–21). Representative of this approach is Joel Sherzer when he attempts to account for why the indigenous Southwest lacks evidence of linguistic sharing despite its relatively high population density and long-term coresidence of neighboring groups:

The explanation for this situation may be found in a sociolinguistic factor about which we rarely have data – attitude toward language. The Southwest is one area for which many observers have reported attitudes toward one's own language and that of others, perhaps because these attitudes are often very explicit. Southwest Indians are very conservative with respect to language...taking pride in their own language and sometimes refusing to learn that of others. (1976:244)

But language ideology, in this notional sense, permits an account that better captures the cultural unity of otherwise disparate linguistic norms and discourse practices and the guided agency of Tewa speakers in exercising their necessarily selective control over their linguistic resources. In the "pragmatic" (Friedrich 1989:297) or "critical" sense (see Woolard 1998) elaborated here, language ideology provides analytical access to the social processes that construct those practices and attitudes labeled "linguistically conservative" by outside experts. The Arizona Tewa were and continue to be an instructive example of how folk consciousness and rationalization of language structure and use can have a powerful effect on language contact outcomes.

The "pragmatic" sense of ideology – the strategies, practical symbols, and systems of ideas used for promoting, perpetuating, or changing a social or cultural order – directs attention to the role of such local models of language as instruments of power and social control. It is important to remember that Pueblo ceremonial language, like ceremonial behavior in general, is not only the expression of religious belief through the sacred manipulation of cosmic forces but also the implicit justification of rule by a largely hereditary ceremonial elite. Thus, linguistic ideology provides a socially motivated explanation for the sociocultural processes that inform the local beliefs about language and the linguistic products that are labeled merely by the expression "linguistic conservatism." Moreover, linguistic ideology offers an ethnolinguistic account that provides an insightful microcultural complement to recent ethnographic and ethnohistorical efforts to rethink the sociocultural order of "egalitarian" Pueblo societies. Peter Whiteley's (1988) *Deliberate Acts* and Jerrold Levy's *Orayvi Revisited* (1992) have signaled an important turn in a scholarly tradition that had represented the Hopi and other Pueblo groups as if each were an "apolitical, egalitarian society" (Whiteley 1988:64). In Whiteley's analysis of how the Orayvi – the oldest continuously inhabited Hopi village – split as a resolution of factional disputes, he recognizes the importance of local distinctions between *pavansinom* "ruling people" and *sukavuungsinom* "common people." In this ceremonially based system of stratification, ritual privilege – such as ownership and control of group ceremony – symbolizes and rationalizes an indigenous hierarchy that is critical to understanding the accomplishment of order, as well as the occasional disorders that characterize Hopi village societies. Levy's reanalysis of early field research in Orayvi by the anthropologist Mischa Titiev further establishes the stratified nature of Hopi society and also offers an account of why Hopi social inequality was routinely reconfigured in representations by such scholars as Mischa Titiev (1944) and Fred Eggan (1950) as basically egalitarian. Levy reveals a patterned relationship between ceremonial standing and the control of land that indicates that those clans that "owned" the most important ceremonies also had the most and the best land for farming. As Levy (1992:156) observes, "The system of stratification worked to manage scarcity, not abundance." In a subsistence economy in a high desert environment notorious for meager and inconsistent resources, the Hopi religious hierarchy created a stratification, not only of clans but of lineages within clans, that prioritized those most essential to the performance of required village ceremonies. In times of famine, the hierarchy served as a built-in mechanism for instructing low-status clans and lineages to leave the village so as to create the least disruption to the ceremonial order. While Levy's discussion about the management of scarcity is more true of Western Pueblos and their necessary reliance on "dry farming," the notion of an indigenous hierarchy is clearly extendable to Rio Grande Tewa pueblos like San Juan, where Ortiz (1969:16–18) recognizes an opposition between "made people" and "dry food people" that parallels that between "ruling" and "commoner" classes. The Arizona Tewa also recognize a similar opposition between *pa: t'owa* (made people) and *wɛ t'owa* (weed people).[8]

But it is important to emphasize that in Levy's analysis the ceremonial system not only rationalizes a hierarchy but also serves to mask it by offering an alternative ideology of equality and mutual dependence. For village ritual to be successful, it must enjoy the participation not only of sponsoring clans and lineages but also of many others who participate in a variety of ways – from actual ritual performance to the provision of food for performers. In participating in a ritual sponsored by another clan, villagers expected that their efforts would be reciprocated by others when a ceremony sponsored by their own clan was to be performed. The net effect of what Levy calls the "ceremonial ideology" is the erasure of clan ownership and the transformation of a clan-specific ritual into "shared" village ceremony:

Although an ideology emphasizing the importance of all Hopis and all ceremonial activities was probably an essential counterbalance to the divisiveness of social stratification, it is important to recognize that the integrative structural mechanisms were also an important ingredient. Opportunity for participation in the ceremonial life was sufficient to prevent the alienation of the common people under the normal conditions of life. (1992:78)

Thus, in Levy's analysis, the ceremonial system served to integrate Hopi society by providing crosscutting relationships of responsibility across clans and lineages, making Hopi society more than the sum of its otherwise divisively strong kin groups. Coupled with such structural mechanisms as marriage regulation (the requirement that one marry outside both of one's parents' clans) and the extension of kinship relations along ceremonial lines (e.g., ceremonial "mothers" and "fathers"), the importance of the ceremonial system as a means of both erasing clan and class divisions and fostering village and ethnic identities becomes clear (Kroskrity 1994). Thus, the ceremonial system can be viewed as a source of the "ideal" egalitarian society, as well as the "ideal" person (Geertz 1990), often felt and expressed by members who have, in turn, communicated this vision to anthropologists who have, in turn, represented it as an essential feature of Hopi society.[9] Given the importance and power of ritual performance as a rite of unification, it is no wonder that the kiva serves as the "site" of the Arizona Tewa dominant language ideology (Silverstein 1992, 1998). Associated both with the theocratic "authority" of a ruling elite and the promise of a ceremonially based social mobility to commoners, kiva speech provides a model that crosses the boundaries of class and clan. For as Bourdieu (1991:113) observes, "the language of authority never governs without the colla-boration of those it governs, without the help of the social mechanisms capable of producing this complicity."

Although kiva speech is associated with the cultural salience of group ritual, these highly "naturalized" (Bourdieu 1977:164) ritual privileges and events, including kiva speech itself, promote a "taken for grantedness" (Schutz 1967:74) of this language ideological site and a "practical consciousness" (Giddens 1984) of the role of kiva speech as a model for everyday speech. As discussed earlier in this chapter, members have a partial awareness of this system, which occasionally surfaces in members' "discursive consciousness" of selected aspects of their language structure and use. The consistency of Arizona Tewa beliefs about language, their partial awareness of how these beliefs can affect language practices, their selective success in activating this awareness in actual practice, and the capacity of individuals to alter their consciousness of the system depending on their interests and "zones of relevance" (Heeren 1974) all argue for a treatment as "language ideological," despite the general lack of "discursive consciousness."[10] It is perhaps a further commentary on the internal diversity of the language ideology literature noted by Woolard (1998) that as I argue for the expansion and recentering of "language ideology" to be more inclusive, partly by the inclusion of ideologies of practice and practical consciousness, others have called for its elimination. Charles Briggs (1992:400), for example, argues that "ideology" tends to suggest either a "fixed, abstracted, and circumscribed set of beliefs" divorced from their constitution in action or "erroneous and derivative notions that can only provide insight into the means by which Others celebrate their own mystification."

Noting that "beliefs about language are multiple, competing, contradictory and contested," Briggs proposes a Foucault-inspired conceptual shift to "metadiscursive strategies" (Briggs 1992:398–400). But while such a perspective might better capture the more self-conscious reflections of Warao shamans, or of American feminists in their rejection of generic "he" (Silverstein 1985), it is important to observe that ideological contention and discursive consciousness are in a relationship of mutual dependence. Debates and other displays of contention necessarily problematize formerly taken-for-granted language practices, and this self-consciousness of lan-guage is the very condition for rationalizing or challenging conventional practices.

Of course, such an emphasis on strategy and contestation suggests that these are omnipresent in social life and consciousness. But I have already argued that success-fully "naturalized" beliefs and practices, such as the role of Arizona Tewa kiva speech as a "prestige model" for everyday verbal conduct, are not publicly challenged and seldom enter members' discursive consciousness. Any rethinking of language ideology that would exclude naturalized, dominant ideologies and thus analytically segregate beliefs about language according to a criterion of consciousness seems to me to be unwise. Since dominant ideologies can become contended ideologies over time and since members vary, both interindividually and intraindividually, in their degree of consciousness, the creation of a categorical boundary between such language beliefs would falsify their dynamic relationship. But while I can hardly second Briggs's proposed shift to "metadiscursive strategies," I do share his concern to avoid associating language ideology with either the pejorative vision of others' "false consciousness" of their linguistic resources or the valorization of the socio-linguist who can truly and exhaustively comprehend the total system. [...]

Given the connections between ceremonial and more mundane speech delineated here, as well as the partial awareness of it reflected in the rejection of my early claims to diplomatic immunity through appeal to an "autonomous" language, it is no wonder that my early Tewa interrogators found their language so valuable and my linguistic research so controversial.

NOTES

1 By "documentary method of interpretation" I mean the ethnomethodological process that provides that retrospective clarity and revised interpretation in the construction of both commonsense and expert knowledge (Garfinkel 1967:77 ff.).

2 For a more complete discussion of the Pueblo diaspora, interested readers should consult Sando 1992:63–78, Simmons 1979, and Schroeder 1979. In using the term "diaspora" to describe the impact of the Spanish colonial program and the resulting Pueblo Revolts, I am following the more "descriptive" model suggested by Clifford 1994, rather than the prescript-ive model endorsed by Safran 1991 and others. Insofar as the Arizona Tewa are concerned, they certainly qualify as an expatriate minority community, and their history on First Mesa has been characterized by what Said 1984 has described as the "contrapuntal" self-consciousness, the imposed awareness of exile. The Arizona Tewa do not fit models that require that a diasporic group maintain an ongoing memory of the displaced homeland or a desire to return to such an ancestral site. Though this is not the place for an extended discussion on this topic, it is useful to indicate that the Arizona Tewas' lack of nostalgia for their ancestral homeland is importantly connected to their successful multiethnic integration into First Mesa Hopi society and to the fact that their former villages are not ongoing communities but rather defunct pueblos long since abandoned.

3 For ease of presentation to a diverse audience, I have opted to use an orthography that departs from conventional Americanist practices in at least two respects. I have eliminated superscript indications of secondary articulation (e.g., aspiration, palatalization) and have instead repre-sented these with digraphs.

4 Announcements display varying degrees of elaboration, depending on whether they are seen as "advance" or "short" notice. The latter are often viewed as reminders and do not contain the full details.

5 I am using "counterlinguistic" here as an adjectival form of what Marcyliena Morgan 1993 calls "counterlanguage." In this and other works, she successfully demonstrates how indigen-ous discourse preferences, especially those involving indirection, inform African American counterlanguage by creating messages that are simultaneously transparent to members yet opaque to outside oppressors. My point here is that purism appears to predate the Spanish colonial program and therefore is not explainable as a response to Spanish hegemony. It is interesting to speculate that kiva speech may have acquired a connotation of counterlanguage during the early colonial program, when native religion was actively suppressed by the

Spanish. It is doubtful, however, that such a connotation would have extended to the Hopi mesas, where the Spanish were never a formidable military presence, or last into the period of "cultural adjustment" after the second Pueblo Revolt, when the Spanish terminated the policy of religious persecution (Schroeder 1972:59–67). It is also important to observe that African American "counterlanguage" utilizes African speech values that are embodied in everyday speech practices, whereas kiva speech is a sacred lect conventionally set apart from more mundane speech behavior.

6   Though Apachean *bi-* is the source for Tewa *-bí*, Tewa has overgeneralized it as a general possessive morpheme, whereas in the Apachean languages it is limited to the third person.

7   SUB is an abbreviated gloss for subordinator, a grammatical marker for dependent clauses.

8   Ortiz 1969 also recognizes a third class that mediates this opposition between made people and "dry food people" – the *t'owa 'e*, a level of secular government officials that dates at least to the time of Spanish occupation.

9   Levy 1992 also suggests that once prevailing social science notions such as Redfield's "folk society" contributed to an intellectual climate in which ethnographers like Titiev and Eggan would deemphasize Hopi social stratification.

10 Here I follow a phenomenological approach (Schutz 1966; Heeren 1974) in which "zones of relevance" reflect the degree of relevance to an actor's project of a given interaction. Thus, awareness of interactional or symbolic detail may be heightened or altered, depending on the immediacy of that actor's imposed or intrinsic interests. For example, a young Tewa man might become acutely aware of kinship and the practicalities of the rules of clan exogamy when he begins to "date" women from his own village. Yet this same awareness might have been previously regarded as "relatively irrelevant" before that point.

REFERENCES

Annamalai, E. (1989). The Linguistic and Social Dimensions of Purism. In *The Politics of Language Purism*, ed. Björn H. Jernudd and Michael J. Shapiro, pp. 225–31. Berlin: Mouton de Gruyter.

Black, Robert (1967). Hopi Grievance Chants: A Mechanism of Social Control. In *Studies in Southwestern Ethnolinguistics*, ed. Dell H. Hymes and William E. Bittle, pp. 54–67. The Hague: Mouton.

Briggs, Charles L. (1992). Linguistic Ideologies and the Naturalization of Power in Warao Discourse. *Pragmatics* 2:387–404.

Bourdieu, Pierre (1977). *Outline of a Theory of Practice*. Cambridge: Cambridge University Press.

Bourdieu, Pierre (1991). *Language and Symbolic Power*. Cambridge, Mass.: Harvard University Press.

Clifford, James (1986). Introduction: Partial Truths. In *Writing Culture*, ed. James Clifford and George E. Marcus, pp. 1–26. Berkeley: University of California Press.

Clifford, James (1994). Diasporas. *Cultural Anthropology* 9:302–38.

Collins, James (1992). Our Ideologies and Theirs. *Pragmatics* 2:405–16.

Dozier, Edward P. (1956). Two Examples of Linguistic Acculturation: The Yaqui of Sonora and the Tewa of New Mexico. *Language* 32:146–57.

Dozier, Edward P. (1966). Factionalism at Santa Clara Pueblo. *Ethnology* 5:172–85.

Eggan, Fred (1950). *Social Organization of the Western Pueblos*. Chicago: University of Chicago Press.

Friedrich, Paul (1989). Language, Ideology, and Political Economy. *American Anthropologist* 91:295–312.

Garfinkel, Harold (1967). *Studies in Ethnomethodology*. Englewood Cliffs, N.J.: Prentice Hall.

Geertz, Armin W. (1990). Hopi Hermeneutics: Ritual Person Among the Hopi Indians of Arizona. In *Concepts of the Person in Religion and Thought*, ed. H. G. Kippenberg, Y. B. Kuiper, and A. F. Sanders, pp. 309–35. Berlin: Mouton.

Geertz, Clifford (1968). *Islam Observed: Religious Developments in Morocco and Indonesia*. Chicago: University of Chicago Press.

Giddens, Anthony (1984). *The Constitution of Society*. Berkeley: University of California Press.

Heeren, John (1974). Alfred Schutz and the Sociology of Common-sense Knowledge. In *Understanding Everyday Life*, ed. Jack D. Douglas, pp. 45–56. London: Routledge and Kegan Paul.

Henningsen, Manfred (1989). The Politics of Purity and Exclusion. In *The Politics of Language Purism*, ed. Björn H. Jernudd and Michael J. Shapiro, pp. 31–52. Berlin: Mouton de Gruyter.

Hill, Jane H. (1992). "Today There Is No Respect": Nostalgia, "Respect," and Oppositional Discourse in Mexicano (Nahuatl) Language Ideology. *Pragmatics* 2:263–80.

Humphreys, Paul (1982). The Tradition of Song Renewal among the Pueblo Indians of North America. *American Indian Culture and Research Journal* 6:9–24.

Jernudd, Björn H. (1989). The Texture of Language Purism. In *The Politics of Language Purism*, ed. Björn H. Jernudd and Michael J. Shapiro, pp. 1–19. Berlin: Mouton de Gruyter.

Kalectaca, Milo (1978). *Lessons in Hopi*. Tucson: University of Arizona Press.

Kroskrity, Paul V. (1978). Aspects of Syntactic and Semantic Variation in the Arizona Tewa Speech Community. *Anthropological Linguistics* 20:235–58.

Kroskrity, Paul V. (1982). Language Contact and Linguistic Diffusion: The Arizona Tewa Speech Community. In *Bilingualism and Language Contact*, ed. Florence Barkin, Elizabeth A. Brandt, and Jacob Ornstein-Galicia, pp. 51–72. New York: Columbia Teachers College Press.

Kroskrity, Paul V. (1985a). "Growing with Stories": Line, Verse, and Genre in an Arizona Tewa Text. *Journal of Anthropological Research* 41:183–200.

Kroskrity, Paul V. (1985b). Areal Influences on Tewa Possession. *International Journal of American Linguistics* 51:486–9.

Kroskrity, Paul V. (1992). Arizona Tewa Public Announcements: Form, Function, and Language Ideology. *Anthropological Linguistics* 34:104–16.

Kroskrity, Paul V. (1993). *Language, History, and Identity: Ethnolinguistic Studies of the Arizona Tewa*. Tucson: University of Arizona Press.

Kroskrity, Paul V. (1994). Language Ideologies in the Expression and Representation of Arizona Tewa Ethnic Identity. Paper presented at School of American Research Advanced Seminar on Language Ideology. Santa Fe, N.M.

Kroskrity, Paul V., and Dewey Healing (1978). Coyote and Bullsnake. In *Coyote Stories*, ed. William Bright, pp. 162–70. IJAL Native American Texts Series, Monograph No. 1. Ann Arbor: University Microfilms.

Levy, Jerrold E. (1992). *Orayvi Revisited*. Santa Fe, N.M.: School of American Research.

Mertz, Elizabeth (1992). Linguistic Ideology and Praxis in U.S. Law School Classrooms. *Pragmatics* 2:325–34.

Morgan, Marcyliena (1993). The Africanness of Counterlanguage among Afro-Americans. In *Afro-American Language Varieties*, ed. Salikoko Mufwene, pp. 423–35. Athens: University of Georgia Press.

Newman, Stanley (1955). Vocabulary Levels: Zuni Sacred and Slang Usage. *Southwestern Journal of Anthropology* 11:345–54.

Ortiz, Alfonso (1969). *The Tewa World*. Chicago: University of Chicago Press.

Safran, William (1991). Diasporas in Modern Societies: Myth of Homeland and Return. *Diaspora* 1:83–99.

Said, Edward (1984). Reflections of Exile. *Granta* 13:159–72.

Sando, Joe S. (1992). *Pueblo Nations: Eight Centuries of Pueblo Indian History*. Santa Fe, N.M.: Clear Light.

Schroeder, Albert H. (1972). Rio Grande Ethnohistory. In *New Perspectives on the Pueblos*, ed. Alfonso Ortiz, pp. 41–70. Albuquerque: University of New Mexico Press.

Schroeder, Albert H. (1979). Pueblos Abandoned in Historic Times. In *Southwest*. Vol. 9 of *Handbook of North American Indians*, ed. Alfonso Ortiz, pp. 236–54. Washington, D.C.: Smithsonian.

Schutz, Alfred (1966). *Collected Papers*. Vol. 3: *Studies in Phenomenological Philosophy*. The Hague: Martinus Nijhoff.

Schutz, A. ([1932]1967). *The Phenomenology of the Social World*, trans. G. Walsh and F. Lehnert. Evanston, Ill.: Northwestern University Press.

Seumptewa, Evelyn, C. F. Voegelin, and F. M. Voegelin (1980). Wren and Coyote (Hopi). In *Coyote Stories*, Vol. 2, ed. Martha B. Kendall, pp. 104–10. IJAL Native American Texts Series, Monograph No. 6. Ann Arbor: University Microfilms.

Sherzer, Joel (1976). *An Areal-Typological Study of American Indian Languages North of Mexico.* Amsterdam: North-Holland.

Silverstein, Michael (1979). Language Structure and Linguistic Ideology. In *The Elements: A Parasession on Linguistic Units and Levels,* ed. Paul R. Clyne, William F. Hanks, and Carol L. Hofbauer, pp. 193–247. Chicago: Chicago Linguistics Society.

Silverstein, Michael (1981). The Limits of Awareness. Working Papers in Sociolinguistics 84. Austin, Tex.: Southwest Educational Development Library. [Reprinted in this volume.]

Silverstein, Michael (1985). Language and the Culture of Gender: At the Intersection of Structure, Usage, and Ideology. In *Semiotic Mediation,* ed. Elizabeth Mertz and Richard J. Parmentier, pp. 219–39. Orlando, Fla.: Academic Press.

Silverstein, Michael (1992). The Uses and Utility of Ideology: Some Reflections. *Pragmatics* 2:311–24.

Silverstein, M. (1998). The Uses and Utility of Ideology. A Commentary. In *Language Ideologies: Practice and Theory,* ed. B. B. Schieffelin, K. Woolard, and P. Kroskrity, pp. 123–45. New York: Oxford University Press.

Simmons, Marc (1979). History of Pueblo–Spanish Relations to 1821. In *Southwest.* Vol. 9 of *Handbook of North American Indians,* ed. Alfonso Ortiz, pp. 178–93. Washington, D.C.: Smithsonian.

Titiev, Mischa (1944). *Old Oraibi: A Study of the Hopi Indians of Third Mesa.* Papers of the Peabody Museum of American Archaeology and Ethnology, vol. 2, no. 1. Cambridge, Mass.: Harvard University Press.

Whiteley, Peter M. (1988). *Deliberate Acts: Changing Hopi Culture through the Oraibi Split.* Tucson: University of Arizona Press.

Woolard, Kathryn (1989). Sentences in the Language Prison: The Rhetorical Structuring of an American Language Policy Debate. *American Ethnologist* 16:268–78.

Woolard, K. A. (1998). Introduction: Language Ideology as a Field of Inquiry. In *Language Ideologies: Practice and Theory,* ed. B. B. Schieffelin, K. Woolard, and P. Kroskrity, pp. 3–47. New York: Oxford University Press.

Woolard, Kathryn, and Bambi B. Schieffelin (1994). Language Ideology. *Annual Review of Anthropology* 23:55–82.

Yava, Albert (1978). *Big Falling Snow.* New York: Crown.

18

Language, Gender, and Power: An Anthropological Review

Susan Gal

For a number of years now, issues of language have been at the forefront of feminist scholarship. This has been as true in psychology, anthropology, and history as in literary theory and linguistics. Yet, oddly, the studies that result often seem to have little in common. Psychologist Carol Gilligan writes about women's "voices," historian Carol Smith-Rosenberg wants to hear "women's words," anthropologists Shirley Ardener and Kay Warren discuss women's "silence and cultural mutedness," literary critics from Elaine Showalter to Toril Moi explore "women's language and textual strategies." But it is not at all clear that they mean the same thing when they say *voice, words, silence*, and *language* as do the linguists and anthropologists who study women's and men's everyday conversation, who count the occurrence of linguistic variables, analyze slang and euphemisms, or examine the linguistic expression of solidarity in same-sex groups.

To be sure, we share a broad frame of reference, a capacious scholarly discourse that provides a fundamental coherence. First, in all feminist scholarship an initial and often remedial focus on women – their roles and stereotypes – has been replaced by a more sophisticated notion of gender as a system of relationships between women and men (Connell 1987; Gerson & Peiss 1985). As a corollary, gender relations within any social group are seen to be created by a sexual division of labor, a set of symbolic images, and contrasting possibilities of expression for women and men. A second source of coherence within feminist discourse has been the continuing argument about the relative importance of *difference* – between women and men, and among women – as opposed to *dominance* and *power*, in our understanding of gender relations. The contrast between approaches focused on difference and those centered on dominance remains important in orienting debates, and feminist scholars increasingly argue that we need to move beyond such static oppositions (di Leonardo 1987; Scott 1988).

Despite these important commonalities, however, a dilemma remains. On opening a book with a title such as *Language and Gender*, one is likely to find articles on pronouns, pragmatics, and lectal variation jostling unhappily with articles on textual gynesis, Arabic women's poetry, and the politics of gender self-representation. What exactly do such studies have in common? Certainly, a major strength of feminist scholarship is exactly the involvement of many disciplines and their divergent terminologies and interests. But I believe it is important to make some of these very different kinds of scholarship on language and gender speak more cogently to each other.

My aim here is twofold. First, I want to give an example of how two apparently divergent types of research on language and gender can complement each other, indeed must learn from each other. Second, I want to argue that a conceptualization of *power/domination* that is different from our usual, traditional assumptions promises an even broader integration, one that is already under way in much exciting recent work and that allows feminist research to criticize and rethink received notions about power.

Sociolinguistics and Cultural Studies

First then, the two types of research on language and gender that ought to embrace each other: I will call them, for convenience, variationist sociolinguistics and symbolic or cultural studies. Variationist studies of urban communities have provided some powerful insights about the internal and external forces operating in language change, and the central role of gender differences in these processes. But variationists have too often counted linguistic variables, correlated these with sex of speaker, and then merely speculated about why urban Western women usually choose more standard, "prestigious" forms and urban men of all classes evaluate working-class features more positively than women do. Usually, sociolinguists have resorted to universal sexual propensities, or global differences in power, to explain their findings (e.g., Labov 1972; Trudgill 1975). Similarly, other sociolinguists have located and counted moments of silence in female–male talk, or apparent interruptions, and have tried to read off power relations directly from these linguistic asymmetries.

What is missing in such work is the understanding that the categories of *women's speech, men's speech*, and *prestigious* or *powerful speech* are not just indexically derived from the identities of speakers. Indeed, sometimes a speaker's utterances create her or his identity. These categories, along with broader ones such as *feminine* and *masculine*, are culturally constructed within social groups; they change through history and are systematically related to other areas of cultural discourse such as the nature of persons, of power, and of a desirable moral order.

As we know, directness and bluntness are understood in some cultures to be styles appropriate to men, elsewhere to women. In some cultures verbal skills are seen as essential for political power, in others as anathema to it. The links between gender, status, and linguistic practices are not "natural" but culturally constructed (Borker 1980). Indeed, women's forms are sometimes symbolically opposed to men's forms, so that the values enacted by one are denied by the other. A classic case is that of the Malagasy: women's speech is blunt and direct, men's speech veiled and restrained (Keenan [1974] 1989). What "counts" as opposite is culturally defined, and such definitions affect the *form* of the differences between the sexes. In such cases we might even speak of "anti-languages" in Halliday's (1976) sense. Speakers often attribute the differences to the different "natures" of women and men. Nevertheless, historical analysis shows that much ideological work is required to create cultural notions that link forms of talk to social groups in such a way that speakers come to think the relationship is natural.

Silence is a familiar example. The silence of women in public life in the West is generally deplored by feminists. It is taken to be a result and a symbol of passivity and powerlessness; those who are denied speech, it is said, cannot influence the course of their lives or of history. In a telling contrast, however, we also have ethnographic reports of the paradoxical power of silence, especially in certain institutional settings. In religious confession, modern psychotherapy, bureaucratic interviews, oral exams, and police interrogation, the relations of coercion are reversed: where self-exposure is required, it is the silent listener who judges and who thereby exerts power over the one who speaks (Foucault 1979). Silence in American households is often a weapon of masculine power (Sattel 1983). But silence can also be a strategic defense against the powerful, as when Western Apache men use it to baffle, disconcert, and exclude white outsiders (Basso 1979). And this does not exhaust the meanings of silence. For the English Quakers of the seventeenth century, both women and men, the refusal to speak when others expected them to marked an ideological commitment (Bauman 1983). It was the opposite of passivity, indeed a form of political protest. (For other related views on silence, see Lakoff (1995) and Mendoza-Denton (1995).)

Silence, like *r*-dropping, *o*-raising, interrupting, or any other linguistic form, gains different meanings and has different effects within specific institutional and cultural contexts, and within different linguistic ideologies. And these meanings can, of course, be changed. A telling example is the dilemma of elite women during the French Revolution, as described by Dorinda Outram (1987) and Joan Landes (1988). Elite writings during the French Revolution glorified male *vertu* and identified the influence of women with the Old Regime's system of patronage, sexual favors, and corruption in which elite women had actively participated. Revolutionary theorists deliberately committed themselves to an antifeminine logic: political revolution could take place, they argued, only if women and their corrupting influence were excluded from public speaking and from the exercise of power. In part as a result of this new conceptualization, the famous and powerful political participation of upper-class women during the Old Regime was replaced, in the era of the revolution, with vigorous attacks on female political activists. In the new ideology, elite women's public speech and activities brought their sexual virtue into question: for a woman, to be political was to be corrupt. The famous revolutionary calls for universal equality applied only to men. Thus, politically active women such as Jeanne Roland could organize influential forums at which men debated the issues of the day, but her memoirs and letters reveal that this demanded a painful compromise. To retain her dignity she herself had to remain utterly silent.

This example briefly illustrates the contingency of women's silence in Europe, as well as the complex, mediated relationship of women to public speech. It highlights as well the strength of cultural definitions, and that they are not simply the product of nature or some age-old and monolithic male dominance. In this case we can watch them emerge articulately in the writings of the revolutionary theorists and

Enlightenment philosophers who were doing the ideological work of formulating, explaining, justifying, and naturalizing the constraints on women's speech.

Returning now to variationist sociolinguistics, I suggest we take a hint from students of culture. For instance, the well-known affinity of the United States and British urban men for working-class speech variants should be seen within a broader cultural and historical frame. The linguistic evidence is strikingly congruent with a general symbolic structure in which manliness is associated with "toughness" and with working-class culture, not only in language but in other cultural spheres such as dress and entertainment. Femaleness, in contrast, is associated with respectability, gentility, and high culture. Surely, it is not accidental that just these oppositions emerged in literature, popular culture, and scientific discourse on both sides of the Atlantic in the nineteenth century and continue to be one component of current gender images (e.g., Halttunen 1982; Smith-Rosenberg 1985). The enactment of this opposition in linguistic practices strengthens and reproduces it; the encoding in prescriptive grammars and etiquette books institutionalizes it (Kramarae 1980). But it is the broader symbolic opposition itself that makes the linguistic variants meaningful, and allows them to be exploited for ironic play, parody, and ambiguity.

If variationists have neglected such ideological symbolic aspects of talk – the cultural constructions of language, gender, and power that shape women's and men's ideas and ideals about their own linguistic practices – a parallel neglect is apparent on the other side. Some of the anthropologists and others who have found that the women they study are "mute" or "uncommunicative" have often not attended to the contexts of talk, the constraints on the interview situation, and the communicative conventions of the people they study. The situatedness of communication of all kinds is a commonplace for sociolinguists. But it is not so self-evident, for instance, to students of popular culture.

Janice Radway (1984) has shown that if we look only at the content of American pulp romance novels, it is hard to avoid the conclusion that the women who read them are passive consumers masochistically drawn to images of female victimization and male brutality. But Radway examines not just the content of the novels but, inspired by sociolinguistics and the ethnography of speaking, the event of reading itself, its immediate context and meaning for the women who do it. For many romance readers the act of reading, often done in stolen moments of privacy, counts as educational and socially useful, and as something these women do for themselves. It is a way of fighting for a modicum of autonomy and against the usual self-abnegation of their lives. Thus, attention to the immediate performative or receptive context expands the understanding of popular culture, just as attention to the larger symbolic context allows for the interpretation of sociolinguistic variation. Clearly, these kinds of studies should be much more closely integrated with each other.

Although such mutual exchange of analytic strategy is very advantageous, an explicit discussion of what we mean by power promises to be even more so. Traditional views of power emphasize access to resources and participation in decision-making (see Lukes 1974). Certainly, linguistic and interactional factors are often intimately related to such access. But these views of power mask the important relationship between two quite different phenomena, both currently studied under the polysemous rubric of *women's words*.

Unlike linguists and sociolinguists who examine the phonological, semantic, syntactic, and pragmatic details of everyday talk, anthropologists, historians, psychologists, and literary critics often use terms like *voice, speech*, and *words* as a powerful metaphor. This usage has become extraordinarily widespread and influential in social science. Such terms are routinely used not to designate everyday talk but, much more broadly, to denote the public expression of a particular perspective on self and social life, the effort to represent one's own experience rather than accepting the representations of more powerful others. Similarly, *silence* and *mutedness* are used not for inability or reluctance to create utterances in conversational exchange but for failure to produce one's own separate, socially significant discourse. Here, *women's words* are a synecdoche for *gendered consciousness* or for *a positioned perspective*. Thus, although studies of gender differences in everyday talk focus on formal properties of speech or interaction, studies of women's voice have focused more on values and beliefs, asking whether women have cultural conceptions or symbolic systems concerning self, morality, or social reality different from those of men or of some dominant, official discourse.

Power and Domination

It is not only that sociolinguistic studies on the one hand and studies of women's values and beliefs on the other are mutually illuminating, as I argued above. More important, the two are inextricably linked. They both investigate how gender is related to power – with power redefined as *symbolic domination*.

In the familiar, classic cases of symbolic domination, some linguistic strategies, variants, or genres are more highly valued and carry more authority than others (e.g., Bourdieu 1977; Lears 1985). What makes this domination, rather than just a difference in form, is that even those who do not control these authoritative forms consider them more credible or persuasive, more deserving of respect than the forms they do control. As a corollary, people denigrate the very forms they themselves know and identify with. Archetypal examples include standard languages vis-à-vis minority languages or racial/ethnic vernaculars, and ritual speech vis-à-vis everyday talk. But respected, authoritative linguistic practices are not simply forms; they also deliver, or enact, characteristic cultural definitions of social life. When these definitions are embodied in divisions of labor and in social institutions such as schools, they serve the interests of some groups better than others. It is through dominant linguistic practices (such as a standard language, for instance) that speakers within institutions such as schools impose on others their group's definition of events, people, actions. This ability to make others accept and enact one's representation of the world is another, powerful aspect of symbolic domination. Domination and hegemony are matters of expressive form as well as cultural content. Thus, the notion of symbolic domination connects the concerns of linguists and sociolinguists with the broader cultural questions posed by social scientists studying gendered consciousness.

But it is important to remember that domination and power rarely go uncontested. Resistance to a dominant cultural order occurs in two ways: first, when devalued linguistic forms and practices (such as local vernaculars, slang, women's interactional styles or poetry, and minority languages) are practiced and celebrated despite widespread denigration and stigmatization. Second, it occurs because these devalued practices often propose or embody alternate models of the social world. The control of representations of reality occurs in social, verbal interaction, located in institutions. Control of such representations, and control of the means by which they are communicated and reproduced, are equally sources of social power. The reaction to such domination is various: it may be resistance, contestation, conflict, complicity, accommodation, indirection.

This general insight about domination and resistance is articulated in one way or another in the writings of a number of influential social theorists – Gramsci, Bourdieu, Foucault, among others, although they have not always applied it to language. Missing from these theories, however, is a concept of gender as a structure of social relations that is reproduced and sometimes challenged in everyday practice. That is why the emerging work on resistance to gender domination – especially the important work on linguistic resistance – is a powerful critique of social theory.

This returns us to the feminist debate about difference and dominance: if we understand women's everyday talk as well as women's linguistic genres and cultural discourses as forms of resistance, then this implies that difference and dominance are always intertwined. We hear, in any culture, not so much a clear and heretofore neglected "different voice," certainly not separate female and male cultures, but rather linguistic practices that are more ambiguous, often contradictory, differing among women of different classes and ethnic groups and ranging from accommodation to opposition, subversion, rejection, or autonomous reconstruction of reigning cultural definitions. But such practices always occur in the shadow of domination and in response to it. Finding the attempts at resistance will tell us about where and how power is exerted, and knowing how institutions of power work will tell us where to look for possible signs of resistance (Abu-Lughod 1990).

Two examples should clarify these general statements. The first is Carol Edelsky's (1981) intriguing study of different kinds of "floor" in mixed-sex faculty meetings at an American college. Two sets of implicit rules seemed to regulate the length and quality of contributions to the meeting. In episodes characterized by the first kind of floor, speakers took longer and fewer turns, fewer speakers participated overall, they did not overlap much, there were many false starts and hesitations, and speakers used their turns for reporting facts and voicing opinions. The other kind of floor occurred at the same meetings but during different episodes. It was characterized by much overlap and simultaneous talk but little hesitation in speaking, and by more general participation by many speakers who collaboratively constructed a group picture of "what is going on." In the second kind of floor many speakers performed the same communicative functions, such as suggesting an idea, arguing, agreeing, joking, and teasing. It was men who monopolized the first kind of floor by taking longer turns. In the second kind of floor everyone took shorter turns and women and men participated in similar ways in the communicative functions performed. Importantly, the first, more formal kind of floor, in which women participated less, occurred vastly more frequently, at least in this institutional setting. And it was the accepted norm. It is noteworthy that explicit and tacit struggles between speakers about how meetings are to be conducted are not idle; they are conflicts about the control of institutional power, about who will get to speak, and with what effect. Even among status equals, as in this example, the interactional constraints of institutional events such as meetings are not gender-neutral but weighted in favor of male interactional strategies.

I suggest it is useful to reinterpret Edelsky's work within the view of power I have been outlining. As in all the classic cases of symbolic domination, the organization of the meeting masks the fact that speakers are excluded on the basis of gender, while it simultaneously accomplishes that exclusion. But we can also ask about the implicit worldview or value system that is enacted by the different kinds of floors. And then we see the two not as simply different but as mutually dependent, calling on different values within American culture, values conventionally seen as opposed to each other. The kind of floor more congenial for male strategies of interaction depends on images of heroic individuality, competition, and the celebration of planning and hierarchy. The second kind of floor is implicitly a critique of the first because it enacts values of solidarity, simultaneity, and collaborative cooperation. When women constructed the second kind of floor, they were resisting the dominant floor both as form and implicitly as enactment of cultural values. Note that the way in which one set of values is linked to one gender and the other set is associated with the other gender is not explored here. It is an ideological and interactional process that deserves much more attention by social scientists (see Ochs 1992).

My second example draws on the oral lyric poetry performed among intimates by the Bedouin of Egypt's Western Desert. In describing these delicate, brief, and artfully improvised performances, Lila Abu-Lughod (1986) stresses that the dominant ideology, what she calls (metaphorically) the "public language," of the Bedouin is one of honor, autonomy, self-mastery, personal strength, and sexual modesty. The poems directly violate this code of honor and implicitly criticize it by expressing the feelings of dependency, emotional vulnerability, and romantic longing condemned by the official view. The poetry constitutes what Abu-Lughod calls "a dissident or subversive discourse ... most closely associated with youths and women, the disadvantaged dependents who least embody the ideals of Bedouin society and have least to gain from the current social structures. Poetry is the discourse of opposition to the system and of defiance of those who represent it" (251).

But the poetry is anything but a spontaneous outpouring of feeling. Indeed, its formal properties and context of performance enhance its ability to carry subtle messages that run counter to official ideals. It is formulaic, thereby disguising the identities of poet, addressee, and subject. It is fleeting and ambiguous, performed by women and youths among trusted intimates who can decipher it precisely because they already know the reciter well. Yet, this poetry of subversion and defiance is not only tolerated but culturally elaborated and admired because of the paradoxical intertwining of official and dissident discourse. The oral poetry reveals a fundamental tension of Bedouin social and political life that, while valuing and demanding autonomy and equality between families and lineages, demands inequality between the genders and generations within families. This verbal genre of women and youths reveals the contradictions of the ruling ideology.

Conclusion

In sum, I have been arguing that power is more than the chance to participate in decision-making – what early feminist theorists sometimes call *informal* or *micro-*

politics (e.g., Rosaldo 1974). The notions of domination and resistance alert us to the idea that the strongest form of power may well be the ability to define social reality, to impose visions of the world. And such visions are inscribed in language and, most important, enacted in interaction. Although women's everyday talk and women's voice or consciousness have been studied separately, I have argued that both can be understood as strategic responses, often of resistance, to dominant hegemonic cultural forms. Thus, attention to linguistic detail, context of perform-ance, and the nature of the dominant forms is essential to both endeavors. The precise form of questions and turn-taking is crucial in understanding the construc-tion of different floors in American meetings (that is, in everyday talk); the exact formal conventions of intimate Bedouin poetry (expressive genre) are indispensable to understanding how it is suited to the expression of vulnerability and dependence. Although the linguistic materials are quite different, both collaborative floors and intimate poetry locate an opposition or contradiction in dominant conceptions and try to subvert the dominant through rival practices. One undermines the hierarchical form and ideology of meetings that favor men's expertise in competitive talk; the other is seen as the opposite of ordinary talk and undermines the cultural rule of honor, threatening to reveal the illegitimacy of elder men's authority.

This returns us to the cultural constructions about women, men, and language with which I began. These cultural constructions are first of all linguistic ideologies that differentiate the genders with respect to talk. It is only within the frame of such linguistic ideologies that specific linguistic forms such as silence, interruption, or euphemism gain their specific meanings. Like all ideologies, these are linked to social positions, and are themselves sources of power. These ideas are enacted and some-times contested in talk. I believe that the research I have discussed marks a very productive path for future studies of language and gender, one informed by socio-linguistics at least as much as by cultural studies and social theory.

[Many works] explore just this terrain of linguistic ideology, and women's diverse forms of contestation and resistance to dominant definitions of gender categories and of women's speech. For example, Laurel Sutton (1995) and Shigeko Okamoto (1995) remind us that we cannot take for granted the social meanings of individual linguistic forms. Speakers redefine and play with language so that within particular social contexts (and within implicit counterideologies) demeaning lexical items can be recast as terms of solidarity. Similarly, stereotypically or prescriptively "male" forms, when used by women, can index youthfulness, liveliness, and nonconformity. Although socially rather homogeneous, Shigeko Okamoto's sample of Japanese college women nevertheless shows impressive linguistic diversity in the use of forms usually associated with "masculine" speech. This leads Okamoto to question the analytical category of *women's speech*. The fundamental insight is not so much that this analytic category is unduly monolithic but, more important, that it is not an analytical category at all. It also forms part of a larger ideological framework linking language, class, region, and gender, a framework whose historical formation can be located in the Meiji era. As Okamoto shows, it is against the backdrop of this complex ideology that contemporary Japanese women strategically fashion new identities in talk.

The historical construction of identities in talk is also the theme of Anna Livia's (1995) chapter on the fictional representation of butch and femme speech. Here it is obvious that direct correlations between some essentialized category such as *sex of speaker* and the linguistic forms they produce will be of little analytical significance. Livia asks, instead, how *feminine* and *masculine* are constructed in the fictional material she analyzes, and how these images play against, comment upon, contradict, parody, or reinforce ideologies about female/male speech. Livia's work is particularly sensitive to the disjunctures between ideology, representation, and everyday practice. In fictional representations of butch and femme speech, she finds not a simple imitation of everyday talk or even an instantiation of stereotypes but, rather, the use and ironic reuse of earlier literary examples.

In a different vein, Kira Hall (1995) discusses the use of women's language as sexual commodity. As in my examples above, it is not only the sexual content of the talk produced by women in the "adult message industry" that is sex-typed but the forms of conversational exchange as well. Using exactly the stereotyped and stigmatized forms of "women's speech" that many investigators have described, the women on those "fantasy phone lines" owned and operated by women nevertheless see themselves as feminists in control of their work and their lives. What might have seemed at first glance (and according to earlier analyses) to be powerless, sexualized language is economically powerful for these women because it provides a safe, flexible, and relatively lucrative income during hard times. Linguistic forms gain their value, their social meaning and social effect, within specific institutional contexts. As Hall carefully points out, however, this is not some simple reversal in which women unexpectedly gain powerful speech. The women know they must reproduce their clients' negative images of women in the very act of gaining their own relative distance from those stereotypes.

Finally, Bonnie McElhinny's (1995) rich ethnographic description of female police officers in Pittsburgh raises important issues about the local definitions and imbrication of emotions such as sympathy or anger, linguistic strategies such as "facelessness," and the subversion of assumptions about femininity and masculinity. Indeed, contrary to much research on language and gender, McElhinny shows that gender is not always equally relevant; it can be submerged by actors in some institutions and thus can be made variable in its salience in interaction. Because the linkages between linguistic forms or strategies and gender categories are ideologically constructed, female police officers can start to reconstruct femininity and masculinity in their own lives, as they manage their everyday interactions.

As these chapters amply demonstrate, the study of language and gender is significantly enhanced by simultaneous attention to everyday practices on the one hand, and on the other to the ideological understandings about women, men, and language that frame these practices and render them interpretable in particular social contexts, historical periods, and social institutions. These chapters move beyond the notions of "women's and men's speech" or the "difference versus dominance" controversy to analyze the hegemonic power of linguistic ideologies and the ways in which speakers attempt to parody, subvert, resist, contest, or in some way accommodate these positioned and powerful ideological framings.

ACKNOWLEDGMENTS

A somewhat different and much longer version of the argument outlined here appeared in Micaela di Leonardo (ed.) (1991), *Gender at the Crossroads of Knowledge*, Berkeley: University of California Press, 175–203.

REFERENCES

Abu-Lughod, Lila (1986). *Veiled Sentiments*. Berkeley: University of California Press.
Abu-Lughod, Lila (1990). The romance of resistance: Tracing transformations of power through Bedouin women. *American Ethnologist* 17: 41–55.
Basso, Keith (1979). *Portraits of "the Whiteman": Linguistic Play and Cultural Symbols among the Western Apache*. New York: Cambridge University Press.
Bauman, Richard (1983). *Let Your Words Be Few: Symbolism of Speaking and Silence among Seventeenth-century Quakers*. New York: Cambridge University Press.
Borker, Ruth (1980). Anthropology: Social and cultural perspectives. In Sally McConnell-Ginet, Ruth Borker, and Nelly Furman (eds.), *Women and Language in Literature and Society*. New York: Praeger, 25–46.
Bourdieu, Pierre (1977). The economics of linguistic exchanges. *Social Science Information* 16(6): 645–68.
Connell, R. W. (1987). *Gender and Power*. Stanford: Stanford University Press.
di Leonardo, Micaela (1987). The female world of cards and holidays. *Signs* 12(3):440–53.
Edelsky, Carol (1981). Who's got the floor? *Language in Society* 10(3):383–422.
Foucault, Michel (1979). *Discipline and Punish*. New York: Vintage.
Gerson, Judith, and Kathy Peiss (1985). Boundaries, negotiation, consciousness: Reconceptualizing gender relations. *Social Problems* 32(4):317–31.
Hall, Kira (1995). Lip service on the fantasy lines. In K. Hall and M. Bucholtz (eds.), *Gender Articulated: Language and the Socially Constructed Self*. New York: Routledge, 183–216.
Halliday, Michael (1976). Anti-languages. *American Anthropologist* 78:570–84.
Halttunen, Karen (1982). *Confidence Men and Painted Women*. New Haven: Yale University Press.
Keenan, Elinor ([1974] 1989). Norm-makers and norm-breakers: Uses of speech by men and women in a Malagasy community. In Richard Bauman and Joel Sherzer (eds.), *Explorations in the Ethnography of Speaking* (2nd edn.). New York: Cambridge University Press, 125–43.
Kramarae, Cheris (1980). Gender: How she speaks. In E. B. Ryan and Howard Giles (eds.), *Attitudes towards Language Variation*. London: Edward Arnold, 84–98.
Labov, William (1972). *Sociolinguistic Patterns*. Philadelphia: University of Pennsylvania Press.
Lakoff, Robin T. (1995). Cries and whispers: The shattering of silence. In K. Hall and M. Bucholtz (eds.), *Gender Articulated: Language and the Socially Constructed Self*. New York: Routledge, 25–50.
Landes, Joan (1988). *Women and the Public Sphere in the Age of the French Revolution*. Ithaca: Cornell University Press.
Lears, Jackson (1985). The concept of cultural hegemony: Problems and possibilities. *American Historical Review* 90: 567–93.
Livia, Anna (1995). "I ought to throw a Buick at you": Fictional representations of Butch/Femme speech. In K. Hall and M. Bucholtz (eds.), *Gender Articulated: Language and the Socially Constructed Self*. New York: Routledge, 245–78.
Lukes, Steven (1974). *Power: A Radical View*. London: Macmillan.
McElhinny, Bonnie S. (1995). Challenging hegemonic masculinities: Female and male police officers handling domestic violence. In K. Hall and M. Bucholtz (eds.), *Gender Articulated: Language and the Socially Constructed Self*. New York: Routledge, 217–43.

Mendoza-Denton, Norma (1995). Pregnant pauses: Silence and authority in the Anita Hill–Clarence Thomas hearings. In K. Hall and M. Bucholtz (eds.), *Gender Articulated: Language and the Socially Constructed Self*. New York: Routledge, 51–66.

Ochs, Elinor (1992). Indexing gender. In Alessandro Duranti and Charles Goodwin (eds.), *Rethinking Context*. Cambridge: Cambridge University Press, 335–58.

Okamoto, Shigeko (1995). "Tasteless" Japanese: Less "feminine" speech among young Japanese women. In K. Hall and M. Bucholtz (eds.), *Gender Articulated: Language and the Socially Constructed Self*. New York: Routledge.

Outram, Dorinda (1987). Le langage mâle de la vertu: Women and the discourse of the French Revolution. In Peter Burke and Roy Porter (eds.), *The Social History of Language*. New York: Cambridge University Press, 120–35.

Radway, Janice (1984). *Reading the Romance*. Chapel Hill: University of North Carolina Press.

Rosaldo, Michelle (1974). Women, culture, and society: A theoretical overview. In Michelle Rosaldo and Louise Lamphere (eds.), *Woman, Culture, and Society*. Stanford: Stanford University Press, 17–42.

Sattel, Jack W. (1983). Men, inexpressiveness and power. In Barrie Thorne, Cheris Kramarae, and Nancy Henley (eds.), *Language, Gender, and Society*. Rowley, MA: Newbury House, 119–24.

Scott, Joan (1988). *Gender and the Politics of History*. New York: Columbia University Press.

Smith-Rosenberg, Carol (1985). *Disorderly Conduct: Visions of Gender in Victorian America*. New York: Oxford University Press.

Sutton, Laurel A. (1995). Bitches and skankly hobags: The place of women in contemporary slang. In K. Hall and M. Bucholtz (eds.), *Gender Articulated: Language and the Socially Constructed Self*. New York: Routledge, 279–96.

Trudgill, Peter (1975). Sex, covert prestige, and linguistic change in urban British English of Norwich. *Language in Society* 1:179–96.

19

The "Father Knows Best" Dynamic in Dinnertime Narratives

Elinor Ochs and Carolyn Taylor

Historical and sociological studies of gender have pursued the plethora of ways in which cultural concepts of gender impact social life, especially institutions such as the family, the church, the workplace, and the state. Of critical importance to all gender research is the idea that gender ideologies are closely linked to the management of social asymmetries. As Marie Withers Osmond and Barrie Thorne (1993:593) concisely put it, "Gender relations are basically power relations." Notions of patriarchy, male authority, male domination, and gender hierarchy have gained considerable intellectual vitality within feminist argumentation. The import of gender pervades all levels of analysis, from historical and ethnographic studies of gender ideologies, structures, and customs to interactional studies of gendered activities and actions. From a poststructuralist perspective, we need both macro- and microanalyses to illuminate continuity and change in the rights, expectations, and obligations vis-à-vis the conduct, knowledge, understandings, and feelings that constitute the lived experience of being female or male in society.

The present chapter addresses gender asymmetry in middle-class European American families through an examination of a single social activity: narrating a story or a report over family dinner. While recognizing that family interaction is socially and historically enmeshed in the prevailing interests of economic and political institutions (e.g., Hartmann 1981; Stack 1974), we offer a window into how family hierarchies are constituted in day-to-day family life. Our position is that family exchanges do not simply exemplify gender relations otherwise shaped by forces outside the family but, rather, are the primordial means for negotiating, maintaining, transforming, and socializing gender identities. Certainly from the point of view of a child, routine moments of family communication are the earliest and perhaps the most profound medium for constructing gender understandings (Cole & Cole 1989; Dunn 1984; Freud [1921] 1949; Goodwin 1990; Kohlberg 1966; Maccoby & Jacklin 1974; Schieffelin 1990). Awakenings to gender asymmetry may occur from infancy on, for example, in two-parent families, through such everyday activity as watching how mothers and fathers interact with each other and with their daughters and sons.

Our particular attention has been captured by the pervasiveness and importance of collaborative narration, wherein children interact with others in co-narrating, as a locus of socialization (Ochs, Smith, & Taylor 1989; Ochs & Taylor 1992a, b; Ochs, Taylor, Rudolph, & Smith 1992). In the present study, we examine how such narrative practices may instantiate gender-relevant narrator and family-role identities of women and men as mother and father, wife and husband, in white middle-class families in the United States.[1] Indeed, our observations of these households suggest that children are overhearers, recipients, and active contributors to gender-implicative, asymmetrical storytelling exchanges dozens of times in the course of sharing a single meal together.

One of the important tenets of this research is that all social identities, including gender identities, are constituted through actions and demeanors. Individuals come to understand a range of social identities primarily by learning, first in childhood, to recognize and/or display certain behaviors and stances that are permitted or expected by particular community members in particular activity settings. We suggest that, among other routes, children (and adults, taking on new roles as spouses and parents) come to understand family and gender roles through differential modes of acting and expressing feelings in narrative activity.

Another important perspective we propose to be essential to a fuller understanding of gender instantiation concerns the attention we place on family interactions – that is, families as multiparty activity systems (Engeström 1987). In gender research on social interaction, the exchanges analyzed have tended to be dyadic ones, i.e., female–male, female–female, or male–male interactions. This design lends itself to dichotomous comparisons between female and male conduct in these communicative arrangements. While two people may wear many hats within one dyad, which we also recognize, dyadic identity construction seems inherently less complex, less hierarchical than multiparty, and also less representative of the contexts in which most people are socialized into gender notions and roles.

Our study of family narrative-activity interactions examines multiparty two-parent contexts in which participants construct themselves and one another simultaneously as spouse, parent, child, and sibling – as mother and wife, father and husband, daughter and sister, son and brother. Within the variety of dynamics and alignments available, on the one hand, women and men may often work together to inquire about and control their children – and women can be seen as part of a dominating force. On the other hand, these parental alignments may co-occur with sustained internal-dyad exchanges wherein one spouse dominates the other – and women may regularly be part of (and a model for) the dominated.

We argue that the narrative practices of all family members in this study instantiate a form of gender asymmetry that we call a "Father knows best" dynamic. Within this dynamic, the father is typically set up – through his own and others' recurrent narrative practices – to be primary audience, judge, and critic of family members' actions, conditions, thoughts, and feelings as narrative protagonists (actors in the past) or as co-narrators (actors in the present). In our corpus, we are particularly struck by the practices of the women as mothers and wives that contribute to this dynamic, instantiating and modeling in their conduct as narrators a pervasive orientation toward fathers as evaluators. In this chapter, we focus especially on those specific practices.

The "Father knows best" ideology is usually associated with a prefeminist, presumably passé 1950s conceptualization of idyllic domestic order that was popularized and concretized by the television program of the same name. In that situation comedy, the title was often ironic, given that its episodes regularly served to point out that Father did not, in fact, know best but often learned that Mother had been right all along. Yet lip service to a "Father knows best" ideology was often maintained on the surface in that Mother would modestly defer to or indulge Father's ego. In the 1980s, variations on this formula for domestic gender relations included its extension to Black middle-class families, most popularly in *The Bill Cosby Show*. Our appropriation of this title is intended to suggest that the ideology may still be getting daily reinforcement in the everyday narrative practices of postfeminist 1990s American families – with considerable (perhaps unwitting) help from wives and mothers. Indeed, it seems to us that the ideology was instantiated even more strongly in the everyday dinnertime discourse in our study than it was or is in mass-media fictionalized versions of family life – that is, more implicitly and without the irony.

Database

For several years, we have been analyzing discourse practices in twenty middle-class, European American families, focusing especially on dinnertime communication patterns in narrative activity. The present study isolates a subcorpus of these families: seven two-parent families who earned more than $40,000 a year during the 1987–1989 period in which the study was conducted. Each family had a five-year-old child who had at least one older sibling.[2] Two fieldworkers video- and audiotaped each family on two evenings from an hour or so before dinner until the five-year-old went to bed. During the dinner activity, fieldworkers left the camera on a tripod and absented themselves.

The specific database for this study consists of the exactly one hundred past-time narratives (stories and reports) that the seven families told during thirteen dinners where both parents were present. As we elaborate in Ochs and Taylor (1992a, b) and Ochs, Taylor, Rudolph, and Smith (1992), we define a *story* as a problem-centered past-time narrative (e.g., the narrative activity eventually orients toward solving some aspect of the narrated events seen as problematic), whereas a *report* does not entail such a problem-centered or problem-solving orientation.

Narrative Instantiation of Gender Roles in the Family

The narrative roles that we address here as relevant to the construction of gender identities within families are those of *protagonist*, *introducer* (either elicitor or initial teller), *primary recipient*, *problematizer*, and *problematizee* (or *target*). Below we define each of these roles and discuss the extent to which that role was assumed by particular family members in our study.[3]

Protagonist

A *protagonist* is here defined as a leading or principal character in a narrated event. Our examination is limited to those narratives where at least one protagonist in the narrative is present at the dinner table, such as in (1), where the chief protagonist is five-year-old Jodie:

(1) zJodie's TB Shots Report (introductory excerpt)[4]

    Participants:

    Mom
    Dad
    Jodie (female, 5 years)
    Oren (male, 7 years, 5 months)

```
            ┌──────┐ Mom
   Jodie │        │ Dad
         └──────┘
            Oren
```

The following excerpt introduces the first past-time narrative told at this dinner, when the family has just begun eating.

Mom: *((to Jodie))* = oh:: You know what? You wanna tell Daddy what happened to you today? =
Dad: *((looking up and off))* = Tell me everything that happened from the moment you went in – until:
                [
Jodie: I got a sho::t?=
Dad: = <u>EH</u> *((gasping))* what? *((frowning))*
Jodie: I got a sho::t
            [
Dad: <u>no</u>
Jodie: *((nods yes, facing Dad))*
Dad: *((shaking head no))* – Couldn't be
Jodie: (mhm?) *((with upward nod, toward Dad))*
    [
Oren: a TV test? *((to Mom))*
(0.4)
Oren: TV test? Mommy?
Mom: *((nods yes))* – mhm
Jodie: and a sho:t
Dad: *((to Jodie))* (what) Did you go to the uh:: – *((to Mom))* Did you go to the ?animal hospital?
Mom: mhh – <u>no:?.</u>
Dad: (where)
Jodie: I just went to the doctor and I got a shot
Dad: *((shaking head no))* I don't believe it
Jodie: <u>ri:?lly::</u> ...

Protagonist is an important role with respect to the "Father knows best" dynamic in that the protagonist is presented as a topic for comment (e.g., in Jodie's case above, for belief or disbelief) by family members. While being a protagonist puts one's narrative actions, conditions, thoughts, and feelings on the table as a focus of attention, this attention is not always a plus, given that protagonists' actions, thoughts, and feelings are not only open to praise but also exposed to familial scrutiny, irony, challenge, and critique. Furthermore, if there is asymmetric distribution in the allocation of protagonist status, one family member may be more routinely exposed to such evaluation by others than the rest, impacting the degree to which some members' identities are constructed as protagonists more than others. In our corpus, such an asymmetry existed, whereby children were the preferred narrative protagonists, as exemplified in the report of Jodie's activities in (1). Children composed nearly 60 percent of all family-member protagonists; mothers figured as protagonists 23 percent of the time; fathers, 19 percent.[5] Father's being least often in the role of protagonist meant that their past actions, thoughts, and feelings were least often exposed to the scrutiny of others and, in this sense, they were the least vulnerable family members.

Introducer

In light of the vulnerability of protagonists to familial scrutiny, an important factor to consider is the extent to which family members assumed this role through their own initiative as opposed to having this role imposed on them through the elicitations and initiations of other family members. To address this issue, we consider next how narratives about family members were introduced.

The narrative role of *introducer* is here defined as the co-narrator who makes the first move to open a narrative, either by elicitation or by direct initiation. We define these two introducer roles as follows. An *elicitor* is a co-narrator who asks for a narrative to be told. In (1) above, Jodie's mother assumes this role and, in so doing, introduces the narrative. An *initial teller* is a co-narrator who expresses the first declarative proposition about a narrative event. In (1), Jodie assumed this role but, because her mother had elicited her involvement, Jodie was not the narrative introducer per se. In unelicited narratives such as (2), the initial teller (in this case, the mother) is also the narrative introducer.

(2) Broken Chair Story
    Participants:
    Mom
    Dad
    Ronnie (male, 4 years, 11 months)
    Josh (male, 7 years, 10 months)

```
              Josh
            _____
  Ronnie |      | Mom
            _____
              Dad
```

During dinner preparation, as Mom brings Ronnie a spoon to open a can of Nestlé Quik, she scoots Ronnie's chair in to the table. Josh is at his place; Dad is in kitchen area to the right of the table, as shown above.

Mom: Oh This <u>chair?</u> broke – today
                [
                ((microwave? buzzer goes off))
Dad: I? know =
          ((Mom heads back toward kitchen, stops by Josh's chair; Josh begins looking at Ronnie's chair and under table))
Mom: =I- <u>no::</u> I mean it <u>rea:?lly</u> broke today
              [
Dad: <u>I?</u> know (0.2) I know?

Mom: Oh You knew that it was <u>split</u>?
Dad: yeah?,
Mom: the whole wood('s) split?
Dad: yeah,
Mom: Oh Did <u>you</u> do it?
    (0.4)
Dad: I don't know if I <u>did</u>? it but I saw that it <u>wa:?s</u>=
             [
Mom: (oh)
    ((Josh goes under table to inspect chairs; Mom bends over to chair))
    Ron?: (what? where?)
        =[
Mom: yeah I sat <u>down</u>? in it and the whole <u>thing</u> split so I – I tie:d
                                              [
Dad: *((with a somewhat taunting intonation))*   (That's a)
    <u>rea:l si:gn</u>? that you need to go on a <u>di:?</u>et.
Ron?: *((going under table too))* (where)
Mom: hh *((grinning as she rises from stooped position next to Josh's chair))*
Ron?: (where where where)=
Josh: =<u>Mi:ne</u>? broke?
Mom: I fixed it – I tied (it to the-)
           [
Josh: <u>mi:ne</u>? I'm not gonna sit on <u>that</u> chair (if it's broken)
((Josh pushes his chair away and takes Mom's; Mom pushes Josh's chair over to her place, tells the boys to sit down; the subject of the broken chair is dropped))

The role of introducer is one that we see as pivotal in controlling narrative activity. The introducer nominates narrative topics, thus proposing who is to be the focus of attention (i.e., the protagonist), what aspects of their lives are to be narrated, and when. In (1), Jodie's mother directs the family's attention to Jodie at a particular moment in the dinner, suggesting that there is a narrative to be told as well as the tone, focus, and implicit boundaries of that narrative. For that moment, the introducer proposes what is important (to know) about that family member, as a protagonist. In addition, the introducer controls who is to initiate the narrative account itself, either self-selecting, as in (2), or eliciting a co-narrator, as in (1). Finally, introducers also exert control in that they explicitly or implicitly select certain co-narrator(s) to be primary recipients of the narrative (see following section). In both examples above, mother as introducer selected father as primary recipient.

Although the majority of the protagonists in our corpus were the children, the majority of the narrative introducers were the parents (who introduced seventy-one of the one hundred stories and reports), mothers more often than fathers. (Mothers and fathers *elicited* narratives from others almost equally; their difference derives from mothers' greater tendency to introduce by *direct initiation* as well – and often about others rather than about themselves.) All family members were vulnerable to having narratives about themselves introduced by others. Moreover, for parents, there was relative parity in this regard: for mothers and fathers equally, fully half of all narratives in which they figured as protagonists were introduced by themselves – and almost half by someone else.

A striking asymmetry exists, however, between parents and children. Only one-third of the narratives about children were introduced by the child protagonists themselves (for five-year-olds and younger, the figure was only one-quarter).[6] Children became protagonists chiefly because mothers introduced them as such and often by mothers' direct initiation of the narrative account. Thus, mothers were largely responsible for determining which children and which aspects of children's lives were subject to dinnertime narrative examination – and when and how. In light of this finding, we suggest that, for mothers, the role of introducer may be appropriated (at least in some family cultures and contexts within the United States) as a locus of narrative control over children – and, among family members, children may be particularly vulnerable in this sense.

Primary recipient

The narrative role of *primary recipient* is here defined as the co-narrator(s) to whom a narrative is predominantly oriented. This role is a powerful one in that it implicitly entitles the family member who assumes it to evaluate the narrative actions, thoughts, and feelings of family members as protagonists and/or as narrators. Anyone who recurrently occupies this position is instantiated as "family judge." As noted earlier, the introducer is critical to the assignment of primary recipient. In some cases, as in (1) and (2), the introducer designated another family member to be primary recipient; in other cases, as in (3), an introducer may select herself or himself.

(3) Lucy's Swim Team Report (introductory excerpt)

> *Near the end of dinner, Lucy (9 years, 7 months) has been describing her swim class when Dad raises a new, related narrative.*
> Dad: (Your) mother said you were thinking of uh: – getting on the swim team?
> Lucy: *((nods yes once emphatically))*
>   (1.0) *((Mom, who has finished eating, takes plate to nearby counter and returns))*
> Dad: *((nods yes))* – (good) ...

Not surprising but nevertheless striking was the privileging of parents as primary recipients of dinnertime narratives: parents assumed that role 82 percent of the time. Within this privileging of parents as preferred audience, fathers were favored over mothers. Whereas fathers often positioned themselves as primary recipients through their own elicitation of narratives (as in example 3, above), in some families mothers regularly nominated fathers as primary recipients through their narrative introductions, such as in (1): *You wanna tell Daddy what happened to you today?* When we overlay this finding on those discussed above, the overall pattern suggests a fundamental asymmetry in family narrative activity, whereby children's lives were told to parents but, by and large, parents did not narrate their lives to their children.

This preference for fathers as primary recipients is partly accounted for by the fact that the father is often the person at the dinner table who knows least about children's daily lives. Typically, even the women who work outside the home arrived home earlier than their husbands and had more opportunity to hear about the events in their children's days prior to dinner. However, there are several reasons to see that being "unknowing" is an inadequate account for fathers' prominence as primary recipients in these narratives. First, in two of the thirteen dinners studied here, mothers knew less about their children's day that day than did fathers, yet we did not observe fathers nominating mothers as primary recipients of narratives about children (i.e., in this corpus, we did not find fathers saying, "Tell Mommy what you did today"). Second, child initiators oriented more narratives to mothers than to fathers in spite of the mothers' generally greater prior knowledge of children's lives. Third, mothers and children were typically as unknowing about fathers' reportable experiences as fathers were about theirs, yet fathers seldom addressed their lives to mothers or children as preferred recipients. (We also did not find mothers – or fathers – saying to each other the equivalent of "Honey, tell the children what you did today.") These considerations suggest to us that it was not simply being unknowing (about family members' daily activities) that determined primary-recipient selection but, perhaps, a matter of *who* was unknowing.

By considering who the initial teller was for each narrative (i.e., the one who was typically the first to address the primary recipient directly), we determined that it was neither children nor fathers themselves who accounted for fathers' assuming the role of overall preferred recipient. Instead, it was mothers who – in addition to often directing children to orient to fathers through elicitations (e.g., *Tell Daddy about . . .*) – also directly initiated many narratives to fathers as primary recipients. In fact, mothers' direct initiation to fathers was the single greatest factor in accounting for fathers' privileging as preferred recipient. Mothers initiated twice as many narratives oriented to fathers as fathers initiated toward mothers. In light of these findings, we suggest that a gender-socialization factor entered into the nonequation, prompting mothers' elevation of unknowing fathers into primary recipients – and judges – of other family members' lives, unmatched by fathers' similar elevation of unknowing mothers to such status.

We have noted above that narrative introducers exert control by designating primary recipients, but here we emphasize that, at the same time, such designation passes control to the co-narrator who is so designated: the primary recipient is in a position to evaluate, reframe, or otherwise pass judgment on both the tale and how it is told. In our view, the role of primary recipient affords a panopticon-like perspective and power (Bentham 1791; Foucault 1979). The term *panopticon* refers to an all-seeing eye or monitoring gaze that keeps subjects under its constant purview (e.g., a prison guard in a watchtower). Similarly, we suggest that narrative activity exposes protagonists to the surveillance of other co-narrators, especially to the scrutiny of the designated primary recipient (see Ochs & Taylor 1992b). Given that this role was played mainly by the fathers in our data, we further suggest that it is potentially critical to the narrative reconstruction of "Father knows best" because it sets up the father to be the ultimate purveyor and judge of other family members' actions, conditions, thoughts, and feelings.

The family-role preferences we have found with regard to these first three narrative roles – protagonist, introducer, and primary recipient – already present an overall picture of the way in which narrative activity may serve to put women, men, and children into a politics of asymmetry. As noted earlier, in the family context, issues of gender and power cannot be looked at as simply dyadic, i.e., *men* versus *women* as *haves* versus *have-nots*. Rather, in two-parent families, women and men manifest asymmetries of power both dyadically as spouses and triadically as mothers and fathers with children. Although there *are* interesting dyadic observations here regarding women versus men (e.g., women tend to raise narrative topics; men tend to be positioned – often by women – to evaluate them), these apparently gender-based distinctions are part of a *triadic* interaction, or larger picture, wherein children are often the subjects of these narrative moves. Neither women's nor men's control is merely a control over each other but particularly encompasses and impacts children. Furthermore, a narrative role such as that of introducer (seen here to be more aligned with women, at least as initial teller) may have a complex relationship to power, both empowering the holder in terms of agenda-setting, choice of protagonist, and topic, but also disempowering to the degree that the introducer sets up someone else (here more often the man) to be ultimate judge of the narrated actions and protagonists.

Problematizer/problematizee

The narrative role of *problematizer* is here defined as the co-narrator who renders an action, condition, thought, or feeling of a protagonist or a co-narrator problematic, or possibly so. The role of *problematizee* (or *target*) is defined as the co-narrator whose action, condition, thought, or feeling is rendered problematic, or a possible problem. As such, in this study, we consider only problematizing that targeted co-present family members.

An action, condition, thought, or feeling may be problematized on several grounds. For example, it may be treated as untrue, incredible, or doubtful, as when, in (1), the father problematized Jodie's TB shots narrative with mock disbelief (*no*, *couldn't be*, and *I don't believe it*). In other cases, it is problematized because it has or had negative ramifications (e.g., is deemed thoughtless or perilous), as when, in (2), the wife implicitly problematized her husband as thoughtless for not warning her about the broken chair (*Oh You knew that it was split?*).

We also see in (2) how an action, condition, thought, or feeling may be problematized on grounds of incompetence. When the husband indicted his wife for being overweight as the cause of the chair's breaking (*That's a rea:l si:gn? that you need to go on a di:?et.*), we suggest he was implicitly problematizing her for lack of self-control. In (4), the same father again problematizes his wife, this time as too lenient a boss and thus incompetent in her workplace as well:

(4) Mom's Job Story (excerpt)

> *Same family as in (2). At the end of dinner, Mom is at the sink doing dishes as Dad eats an ice cream sundae and seven-year-old Josh does homework at the table opposite Dad. This excerpt comes near the end of a story about Mom's hiring a new assistant at work, which Dad has elicited and already probed considerably.*

Dad: *((eating dessert))* Well – I certainly think that – you're a- you know you're a fair bo?ss – You've been working there how long?
Mom: fifteen years in June *((as she scrapes dishes at kitchen sink))*
Dad: fifteen <u>years</u> – and you got a guy *((turns to look directly at Mom as he continues))* that's been workin there a few <u>weeks?</u> and you do (it what) the way <u>he</u> wants.
Mom: hh *((laughs))*
       (0.6) *((Dad smiles slightly?, then turns back to eating his dessert))*

Mom: It's not a matter of my doin it the way he:wa:nt – It does help in that I'm getting
       more work? done It's just that I'm workin too hard? I don't wanta work so hard
Dad: ((rolls chair around to face Mom halfway)) Well – You're the bo:ss It's up to you to
       set the standards . . .

Further grounds for problematizing were on the basis that an action is out-of-
bounds – e.g., unfair, rude, excessive. In (5), the father problematizes his wife for her
wasteful consumption (e.g., You _had_ a dress right?; Doesn't that sound like a – total:
– w:aste?) and for her lack of consideration toward his mother (e.g., Why did you let
my Mom get you something (that you–); Oh she just _got_ it for you?):

(5) Mom's Dress Story (Round 2 of two-round story)[7]

     Same family as in (1). The children have finished eating and just gone outside to
     play; Dad is helping himself to more meat; Mom had begun a story about her
     new dress, interrupted by a phone call from his mother.

Round 2 ((begins after Mom hangs up phone and sits at table))
Dad: So as you were saying?
Mom: (As I was) saying ((turning abruptly to face Dad)) What was I telling you
Dad: I ?don't? know
Mom: oh about the ?dress?
Dad: (the) dress
       (1.2) ((Mom is drinking water; Dad looks to her, to his plate, then back to her))
Dad: You had a dress right?
Mom: ((nodding yes once)) Your mother bought (me it) – My mother didn't (like) it.
       (0.4) ((Mom tilts head, facing Dad, as if to say "What could I do?"))
Dad: ((shaking head no once)) You're kidding
Mom: no
Dad: You gonna return it?
Mom: No you can't return it – It wasn't too expensive – It was from Loehmann's
       (0.8)
Mom: So what I'll probably do? – is wear it to the dinner the night before – when we go to
       the (Marriott)?
       (1.8) ((Dad turns head away from Mom with a grimace, as if he is debating
       whether he is being conned, then turns and looks off))
Dad: (Doesn't that) sound like a – (total:) – w:aste?
Mom: no?:
Dad: no
Mom: ((with hands out, shaking head no)) It wasn't even that expen?sive
       (1.2)
Mom: ((shaking head no, facing Dad)) even if it were a complete waste
       (0.4) ((Dad looks down at plate, bobs head right and left as if not convinced))
Mom: but it's not. ((looking away from Dad))
       (0.6) ((Mom looks outside, then back to Dad))
Mom: (but the one) my mom got me is gr:ea::t –
                                               [
                                               ((Dad eats from son Oren's plate next to him))
Mom: (Is the ((inaudible)) okay?)
Dad: ((gesturing with palm up, quizzical)) (Well why did) you have –
       Why did you let my mom get you something (that you –)
Mom: Your mo:ther bought it – I hh –

Dad: Oh she just <u>got</u> it for you?

Mom: *((turning away from Dad, nodding yes))* (yeah)

Dad: You weren't there?

Mom: I was <u>there</u> (and your mom) said "No no It's great Let me *buy* it for you" *((turning back to face Dad))* – I didn't <u>ask</u> her to <u>buy</u> it for me?
    (5.0) *((Dad is eating more food from son's plate; Mom looking toward table))*

Dad: So they're <u>fighting</u> over who <u>gets</u> you things?

Mom: *((nods yes slightly))* – *((smiling to Dad))* tch – (cuz I'm) so won?derful
    (9.0) *((no visible reaction from Dad; Mom turns to look outside; the subject of the dress is dropped))*

In the narratives in our corpus, exactly half of them involved someone problematizing a family member at the dinner table. Those fifty narratives generated a total of 229 problematizations of oneself or, much more often, of another family member.[8] Problematizing displays the most significantly asymmetric narrator-role distribution found in this study and reveals a "Father knows best" dynamic in family interaction. Men took on the role of problematizer 45 percent more often than women did and 3.5 times as often as did children. Strikingly, this pattern was mirrored in female and male children's uptake of the problematizer role. Among children, boys did 50 percent more problematizing than girls (even though there were nine girls and eight boys in the corpus who were old enough to co-narrate). With regard to family members' role constitution vis-à-vis narrative problematizing, men were problematizers almost twice as often as they were problematizees; women were as often problematizees as problematizers; and children were predominantly positioned as problematizees.

Examining individual instances to assess who problematized whom (i.e., the preferred target for each family member), we found that the bulk of narrative problematizing occurred between spouses. In 80 percent of the eighty-four instances in which mothers were problematized, the problematizer was the husband. In 63 percent of sixty-seven instances in which fathers were targeted, the problematizer was the wife. Thus, although women also targeted their spouses, men did so 60 percent more often. The targeting of women by their husbands represents the largest allocation of problematizings in our corpus of narratives. The differential in both absolute numbers and percentages of cross-spousal problematizing suggests in more detail the across-the-board nature of men's domination.[9] That is, both women and men vastly outproblematized their children, but men also considerably outproblematized their wives. Examples (1), (2), (4), and (5) above illustrate how men problematized their spouse or their child.

In addition to this overall quantitative difference, there were differences as well in the qualitative nature of women's versus men's problematizations. Notably, there was a distinction in spouses' use of two domains of problematizing: the problematizing of someone's actions, thoughts, or feelings (in the past) as a protagonist versus the problematizing of someone's comments (in the present) as a co-narrator. The latter category includes counterproblematizing in self-defense, as a response to a previous problematizing (here, by the spouse). The distribution of cross-spousal use of these problematizing strategies indicates that husbands criticized their spouse as protagonist far more often than was the case for wives (thirty-six times versus fourteen times).

Many of the husbands' problematizings of wives as protagonists entailed targeting the wife on grounds of incompetence, as exemplified in (4), Mom's Job Story. In contrast, wives did not problematize husbands on the basis of incompetence as protagonists; as noted above, wives relatively infrequently problematized their spouses as protagonists at all. Rather, women most often problematized men as narrators and much of that was of the counterproblematizing type, either in self-defense or in defense of their children. In other words, fathers would target what mothers had done in the reported events and then mothers would refute the fathers' comments as co-narrators. Men's problematizing focused on "You shouldn't have done *x*"; women's problematizing was more a form of resistance – to being problematized. Women were more often saying in essence, "No, that's not the way it happened..."; "Your interpretation is wrong..."; "You don't see the context." Thus, women – to the degree that they are regularly targeted for problematization – may get the impression that they cannot *do* anything right (and wind up defending past actions, as seen in the Mom's Job and Mom's Dress Stories), whereas men – to the degree they are regularly targeted more for their comments as co-narrator – may get the impression that they can't *say* anything right.

Men's preeminence as problematizers is further seen in the fact that they problematized their spouses over a much wider range of narrative topics than did women. Wives' conduct and stance concerning child care, recreation, meal preparation, and even their professional lives were open to husbands' critiques. Narratives about men's workdays, however, were exceedingly rare and were virtually never problematized. This asymmetry, wherein men had or were given "problematizing rights" over a wider domain of their spouses' experiences than were women, further exemplifies how narrative activity at dinner may instantiate and socialize a "Father knows best" worldview, i.e., it is men as fathers and husbands who scrutinize and problematize everything.[10]

Given men's presumption to quantitative and qualitative dominance as problematizers *par excellence* in this corpus, an important issue to raise is the extent to which men's prominence as problematizers was related to their role as preferred primary recipients. There was clearly a strong link between the two roles for them: 86 of men's 116 problematizings occurred when they were primary recipients of the narrative. However, the status of primary recipient does not, in itself, completely account for who assumed the role of problematizer.

Three observations in particular dispute such an interpretation. First, men exploited the primary-recipient role to do problematizing to a far greater extent than other family members did. As primary recipient, fathers problematized a family member, on average, 1.6 times per narrative; women did so only 0.55 times per narrative, and children only 0.05 times per narrative. In both degree and range of problematizing, men used their recipient status distinctively. Second, the whole level of problematizing went up when the father/husband was primary recipient. Of the 229 problematizings in the corpus, 155 occurred when he was primary recipient, averaging 2.8 problematizings per narrative, considerably more than when either women or children were primary recipients (1.6 per narrative and 0.5 per narrative, respectively). As already suggested in the discussion of counterproblematizing, this heightened level of problematization overall occurred largely because men's problematizing of women (as protagonists) triggered women's own counterproblematizing of their husbands. As a result, women became problematizers much more often when men were primary recipients than when the women themselves were primary recipients (54 times versus 22 times). Third, we note that men problematized more than women did even in narratives where the woman was primary recipient (24 times versus 22 times).

For all these reasons, a primary recipient-becomes-problematizer explanation is too simplistic an account. Rather, our corpus suggests conceptualizations of recipientship that differentiate women, men, and children, i.e., differing dispositions and perhaps entitlements to problematize, with men in privileged critical positions. The role of problematizer seems to be a particular prerogative of the family role of father/ husband, manifesting the ideology that "Father knows best," socializing and (re)constituting paternal prerogative and point of view in and through narrative activity.

Because an important issue we are pursuing here is women's role in establishing a "Father knows best" dynamic at the family dinner table and because we have seen that women's most notable narrative role was that of introducer, we examined the introducer-problematizer relationship to discover in particular the extent to which men's problematizings occurred in narratives introduced by women. Our finding is that women's introductions may indeed have triggered men's problematizations. First, when women introduced narratives, problematizing in general was more prevalent than when men or children did the introducing.[11] In narratives introduced by women, family members were problematized, on average, 3.4 times per narrative, considerably more than for narratives introduced by men (2.0 times) or by children (1.1). Second, the majority of men's problematizings (72 out of 116) occurred in narratives introduced by women. Men problematized other family members 1.8 times per narrative in those introduced by women, i.e., an even higher rate than we noted above when the factor of men's status as primary recipients was considered. Furthermore, men problematized more often in narratives introduced by women than in narratives they introduced themselves. This higher number of problematizations in narratives introduced by one's spouse might seem expectable but it was not matched by women, who wound up (counter)problematizing more often in the narratives they themselves introduced.[12] We see in these data an asymmetrical pattern wherein women's raising a topic seems to have promoted men's problematizing but not the reverse.

Women's assumption of the role of introducer co-occurred not only with increased problematization by men but also with increased targeting of women themselves. Women were problematized most often in the very narratives they introduced: 75 percent of all targetings of women occurred in those narratives, an average of 1.6 times per narrative. These figures contrast markedly with those for men: only 33 percent of the problematizings of men occurred in narratives they themselves introduced, an average of only 0.7 times per narrative.

These findings suggest that women were especially vulnerable to exposing themselves to criticism, particularly from their husbands, and thus may have been "shooting themselves in the foot" in bringing up narratives in the first place, as illustrated in (2), the Broken Chair Story, where a woman's designation (i.e., control) of narrative topic and primary recipient boomeranged in an explicit attack on her weight. In (1), Jodie's TB Shots Report, we see an example of how mother-introduced narratives also expose children to problematization by fathers. Reconsidering our earlier observation that women were problematized over a wider range of daily activities, including professional lives, than were men, we can posit that this may have resulted largely from women's introducing themselves as protagonists in a much wider range of contexts to begin with.

One final issue with regard to problematization concerns the extent to which family members self-problematized. In our corpus, women displayed the highest proportion of self-targetings and, in keeping with the findings just discussed, this was also associated with narratives that women themselves raised. Although such targetings account for a relatively small proportion (12 percent) of the targetings of women overall, and they came essentially from only two families, these female self-problematizings are noteworthy in their provoking of a "dumping-on" response. That is, when women did question their own past actions, it seemed to invite considerable additional problematizing by their husbands. As illustrated in (6), a wife problematizes herself as protagonist and her husband elaborates:

(6) Bev Story (excerpt)

> *This family consists of Mom (Marie), Dad (Jon), and four children (who at this point in the dinner have finished eating). Mom runs a day-care center in their home; she has been recounting to Dad how one of her day-care children's mothers, Bev, had given her more money than was owed for day-care services and that she had not accepted the extra money. She then recalled how Bev had not given a required two weeks' notice for withdrawing her daughter from day care, whereupon Dad problematized Mom's nonacceptance of the money as naive (i.e., incompetent).*

Mom: *((head on hand, elbow on table, facing Dad opposite her))* You know – Jon I verbally did tell Bev two weeks' notice Do you think I should've stuck to that? or just done what I did? (0.8) *((The children are standing by their seats, apparently listening))*

Dad: When I say something I stick to it. unless she: -s-brings it up. If I set a policy – and a- – and – they accept that policy – unless they have reason to change it and and say something? I do not change it – I don't automatically assume .h "We:ll it's not the right thing to do" If I were to do that e-I would be saying in the first place I should never have mentioned it I should never have set the policy if I didn't believe in it If I thought it was – a hardship on people I shouldn't a brought it up? – shoulda kept my mouth shut .h If I: say there's two weeks' notice required – .h I automatically charge em for two weeks' noticc without thinking twice? about it I say and i-"If you-you need – Your pay will include till such and such a date because of the two neek-weeks' notice that's required." -I:f THE:Y feel hardship it's on thei:r part – it's – THEIRS to say .h "Marie I really? – you know – I didn't expect this to happen 'n I'm *((softly))* sorry I didn't give you two weeks' notice but it was really un - avoidable" – a:nd you can say "We:ll – okay I'll split the difference with you – it's har- – a one week's notice" – and then they s- then if they push it
                                                                        [
Mom: See? you know in one way wi- in one (instance) *((pointing to Dad))* she owed me that money – but I just didn't feel right? taking it=
                                                                                            [
Dad: well you're – you
Mom: =on that pretense because she (wanted) -she thought she was paying it for some-thing *((twirling her corncob))* that *(she didn't)*
                                                            [

Dad: You: give her the money and
      then you let it <u>bother</u> you then – you – get <u>all</u> ups-set You'll be upset for
      weeks

                                                      [

Mom: No no no – I'm <u>not</u>
                                                      upset – it's just

      (0.4) ((Mom plops corncob down, raps knuckles on table))
Mom: I guess I just wish I would have s:aid – I'm <u>not</u> upset with what happened – I just
      wanted – I think I – <u>would</u> feel better if I had said (something)....

In questioning her own actions as protagonist (*Do you think I should've stuck to that? or just done what I did?*), Marie invites her husband's evaluation and exposes herself to his critical uptake as he problematizes both her past actions (<u>You</u>: *give her the money*) and her present feelings (... *you let it <u>bother</u> you then – you – get <u>all</u> ups-set You'll be upset for weeks*). She is left to backtrack in self-defense, countering his portrayal of her present state and (re)defining her self-problematization on her own terms (... *I just wish I would have* ...), no longer as a question inviting further dumping on.[13]

In our corpus, the uptake on self-problematizing further distinguished women's and men's narrative practices; in contrast to this dumping-on response, women did not further problematize men after the men problematized themselves. When women took the opposite tack and presented themselves as problem-solvers rather than self-problematizers, another asymmetric practice entailed the husband's dismissing his wife's solution and problematizing it until she conceded at least partially. An example of this is seen in (5), Mom's Dress Story, when Mom offers her own solution to the two-dress situation (*So what I'll probably do? – is wear it to the dinner the night before* ...), to which Dad responds, "(Doesn't) that sound like a – (total:) – w:aste?" Mom initially rebuts (*<u>no?:</u>*) but, in the face of Dad's skepticism, concedes " ... even if it were a comp<u>lete</u> waste," thus implicitly problematizing herself by Dad's terms in acknowledging that she might have been wasteful.

Our data also suggest that women's self-problematizing may have socializing effects. This was vividly illustrated in a lengthy story focusing on a mother and her son in a restaurant (the same family as in Jodie's TB Shots Report and Mom's Dress Story). In this narrative, the son, Oren, recalls eating a chili pepper his mother thought was a green bean. Although Oren initially frames the experience as funny, his mother tells him it wasn't funny, that his mouth was burning and hurting. While problematizing his stance as narrator, she also implicates herself as a culprit, thereby self-problematizing as protagonist. In the course of the story, Oren eventually takes on his mother's more serious framing of events, to the point of shouting, "<u>YOUR FAULT – YOUR FAULT</u>." She agrees, nodding her head and saying, "It *was* my fault." While she is saying this, he leans over and pinches her cheeks hard. She gasps and pulls his hands away, saying, "<u>OW</u> That really <u>hurts</u> honey?" As she holds a napkin to her mouth and cheeks, her son comments, "Your fault – I get to do whatever I want to do once – (That was my fee?)," laughs, and adds, "Just like it happened to me it happens to you." Just as husbands piled on to wives' self-targeting, Oren thus follows up on his mother's self-problematizing, extending condemnation and executing punishment for her self-problematized actions. In so doing, he seems to be assuming a dramatic version of what, in this corpus, was a male narrator role.

This discussion calls attention to an appropriate ending caveat to our findings throughout this chapter. Namely, there is family variation even within this sample of seven families of similar socioeconomic status and racial-cultural background. There were men who took up the role of monitor and judge with what seemed almost a vengeance; there were others who displayed much less assertion of the prerogatives of power as primary recipient. Furthermore, we do not wish to fix particular men's (or women's) narrator personae based on two evenings in the lives of these families. Our aim is not to polarize the genders, but, rather, to shed potential new light on some underexplored aspects of gender construction and socialization in everyday narrative activity.

Conclusion

Synthesizing these findings – with the caveats noted above – we construe a common-place scenario of narrative activity at family dinners characterized by a sequence of the following order. First, mothers introduce narratives (about themselves and their children) that set up fathers as primary recipients and implicitly sanction them as evaluators of others' actions, conditions, thoughts, and feelings. Second, fathers turn such opportunities into forums for problematizing, with mothers themselves as their chief targets, very often on grounds of incompetence. And third, mothers respond in defense of themselves and their children via the counterproblematizing of fathers' evaluative, judgmental comments.

In the first stage, we see mothers' narrative locus of power; in the second, however, we see that such exercise of power is ephemeral and may even be self-destructive by giving fathers a platform for monitoring and judging wives and children. In the third stage, we see mothers striving to reclaim control over the narratives they originally put on the table. Given our impression of the recurrence of these preferences and practices, it seems that the struggle of the third stage is not ultimately successful in that the fathers reappear as primary recipients and the cycle of narrative reenactment characterized by this generalized scenario prevails. It may be that all parties obtain a particular type of satisfaction or stasis through this interplay such that it serves underlying needs, self-conceptions, and communicative goals. However, in this generalized scenario, mothers seem to play a pivotal role in enacting and socializing a hegemonic activity system (Engeström 1987; Gramsci 1971) in which fathers are regularly reinstantiated as arbiters of conduct narratively laid before them as in a panopticon.

In the family interactions we observed, when women directed their narratives to their husbands (or when children directed their narratives, voluntarily or not, to their fathers), they disadvantaged themselves by exposing their experiences to male scrutiny and standards of judgment. They performed actions as narrators that rendered them vulnerable to repeated spousal/paternal criticism of them, especially as protagonists. Through such means and with such effects, "Father knows best" – a gender ideology with a deeply rooted politics of asymmetry that has been contested in recent years – is still in reverberating evidence at the two-parent family dinner table, jointly constituted and re-created through everyday narrative practices. In this chapter, we hope to have raised awareness of the degree to which some women as wives and mothers may wittingly or unwittingly contribute to – and even set up – the daily reconstruction of a "Father knows best" ideological dynamic.

ACKNOWLEDGMENTS

This chapter is the result of the equal work of both authors. We are grateful for the support this research has received from the National Institute of Child Health Development (1986–1990: "Discourse Processes in American Families," Principal Investigators Elinor Ochs and Thomas Weisner, Research Assistants Maurine Bernstein, Dina Rudolph, Ruth Smith, and Carolyn Taylor) and from the Spencer Foundation (1990–1993: "Socialization of Scientific Discourse," Principal Investigator Elinor Ochs, Research Assistants Patrick Gonzales, Sally Jacoby, and Carolyn Taylor). We thank Marcelo Diversi for his assistance in editing the final version of this chapter. A preliminary version of this article appeared in the proceedings of the Second Berkeley Women and Language Conference (Ochs & Taylor 1992c).

NOTES

1   Clearly, our findings are implicative for certain family cultures and are not inclusive of the range of linguistic, ethnic, economic, and other forms of group variation within the United States. This study is offered as a basis for possible future studies of family narrative activity as a medium for constituting gender relations in other socioeconomic and cultural settings for which we do not presume to speak here. At the same time, while we suggest a certain resonance in these findings, we recognize the limits of our corpus and do not wish to over-generalize regarding narrative practices even for white middle-class families.

2   This choice of five-year-olds follows from our interest in the roles played by children of an age to be fully capable of collaboration in family talk but still in their earliest, most pivotal years of language socialization (prior to much formal schooling). We also wanted at least one older child in the families so as to capture sibling as well as parent–child interaction.

3   For simplicity, we will often refer to participants by only one family role, e.g., to women as *mothers*, men as *fathers*, and girls and boys as *children*, but we note again, in keeping with our introductory perspectives, that at any one moment each participant may be constructing more than one family identity, e.g., also as spouses, as siblings, as females, as males.

4   All family names are pseudonyms. Transcription procedures are essentially those established by Gail Jefferson (see Atkinson & Heritage 1984:ix–xvi):

[a left-hand bracket indicates the onset of overlapping, simultaneous utterances

=   two equals signs (latches) link utterances either by two speakers where the second jumps in on the end of the first, without any interval, or by the same speaker when lengthy overlap by another speaker requires that a continuous utterance be interrupted on the transcript to show simultaneity with another

(0.4)   indicates length of pause within and between utterances, timed in tenths of a second

a – a   a hyphen with spaces before and after indicates a short pause, less than 0.2 seconds

sa-   a hyphen immediately following a letter indicates an abrupt cutoff in speaking

(())   double parentheses enclose nonverbal and other descriptive information

( )   single parentheses enclose words that are not clearly audible (i.e., best guesses)

you   underlining indicates stress on a syllable or word(s)

CAPS   upper case indicates louder or shouted talk

:   a colon indicates a lengthening of a sound, the more colons, the longer

.   a period indicates falling intonation

,	a comma indicates a continuing intonation
?	a question mark indicates a rising intonation as a syllable or word ends
	Note: bounding question marks (e.g., *Did you go to the ?animal hospital?*) are used (instead of rising arrows) to indicate a higher pitch for enclosed word(s).
h	an *h* indicates an exhalation, the more *h*'s, the longer the exhalation
.h	an *h* with a period before it indicates an inhalation, the more *h*'s, the longer.

5 For tables detailing the quantitative findings of this study, see Ochs and Taylor (1992c).
6 For more detail and elaborated consideration of the roles of children in the narrative activity of this corpus, see Ochs and Taylor (1992b).
7 When a narrative is interrupted or dropped and taken up again after an interval of at least two other turns, we consider the restart to constitute a new "round."
8 Only 10 percent of all problematizations were "self-inflicted," meaning that 90 percent of the problematizations targeted others. The percentage of problematizing directed toward oneself was highest for women, although still only 12 percent. In keeping with our present focus on exploring women's roles in particular, we will discuss and illustrate these self-problematizations in more detail following our examination of cross-spousal problematizing.
9 Accounting for the percentage differential in cross-spousal targeting, the children, albeit infrequent problematizers, did twice as much targeting of fathers as they did of mothers.
10 Perhaps contrary to general expectation, spouses in our corpus did not tend to elicit narratives from each other about their workdays (Mom's Job Story being an exception), so that parental "what-my-day-was-like" narratives, unlike the narratives of children, tended to be directly self-initiated to the spouse without elicitation.
11 Out of the 39 narratives introduced by women, 62 percent included at least one instance of someone's problematizing a family member at the dinner table. In contrast, only 44 percent of the narratives introduced by men and 41 percent of those introduced by children evidenced such problematizing.
12 On average, men problematized in narratives that they introduced themselves only 1.2 times per narrative, i.e., less often than they problematized in narratives introduced by women (1.8 times per narrative). In contrast, women problematized in narratives that they introduced themselves 1.4 times per narrative, i.e., much more often than they problematized in narratives introduced by men (only 0.5 times per narrative).
13 Regarding the roles and implications of problematization or challenges in co-narrators' theories of everyday events, and the potential here for Marie to incorporate her husband's challenge into something of a paradigm shift in her own stance, see Ochs, Smith, and Taylor (1989) and Ochs, Taylor, Rudolph, and Smith (1992).

REFERENCES

Atkinson, J. Maxwell, and John Heritage (eds.) (1984). *Structures of Social Action: Studies in Conversation Analysis.* Cambridge: Cambridge University Press.

Bentham, Jeremy (1791). *Panopticon.* London: T. Payne.

Cole, Michael, and Sheila Cole (1989). *The Development of Children.* New York: Scientific American Books.

Dunn, Judy (1984). *Sisters and Brothers.* Cambridge, MA: Harvard University Press.

Engeström, Yrjö (1987). *Learning by Expanding: An Activity-theoretical Approach to Developmental Research.* Helsinki: Orienta-Konsultit Oy.

Foucault, Michel (1979). *Discipline and Punish: The Birth of the Prison.* Translated by Alan Sheridan. New York: Random House.

Freud, Sigmund ([1921] 1949). *The Standard Edition of the Complete Psychological Works of Sigmund Freud.* London: Hogarth Press.

Goodwin, Marjorie Harness (1990). *He-Said-She-Said: Talk as Social Organization among Black Children.* Bloomington: Indiana University Press.

Gramsci, Antonio (1971). *Selections from the Prison Notebooks of Antonio Gramsci*. Translated and edited by Quintin Hoare and Geoffrey Nowell Smith. New York: International Publishers.

Hartmann, Heidi I. (1981). The family as the locus of gender, class, and political struggle: The example of housework. *Signs* 6(3):366–94.

Kohlberg, Lawrence (1966). *The Development of Sex Differences*. Stanford: Stanford University Press.

Maccoby, Eleanor E., and Carol N. Jacklin (1974). *The Psychology of Sex Differences*. Stanford: Stanford University Press.

Ochs, Elinor, Ruth Smith, and Carolyn Taylor (1989). Detective stories at dinnertime: Problem-solving through co-narration. *Cultural Dynamics* 2(2):238–57.

Ochs, Elinor, and Carolyn Taylor (1992a). Science at dinner. In Claire Kramsch and Sally McConnell-Ginet (eds.), *Text and Context: Cross-disciplinary Perspectives on Language Study*. Lexington, MA: Heath, 29–45.

Ochs, Elinor, and Carolyn Taylor (1992b). Family narrative as political activity. *Discourse & Society* 3(3):301–40.

Ochs, Elinor, and Carolyn Taylor (1992c). Mothers' role in the everyday reconstruction of "Father knows best." In Kira Hall, Mary Bucholtz, and Birch Moonwomon (eds.), *Locating Power: Proceedings of the Second Berkeley Women and Language Conference*. Berkeley: Berkeley Women and Language Group, 447–62.

Ochs, Elinor, Carolyn Taylor, Dina Rudolph, and Ruth Smith (1992). Storytelling as a theory-building activity. *Discourse Processes* 15(1):37–72.

Osmond, Marie Withers, and Barrie Thorne (1993). Feminist theories: The social construction of gender in families and society. In Pauline G. Boss, William J. Doherty, Ralph LaRossa, Walter R. Schumm, and Suzanne K. Steinmetz (eds.), *Sourcebook of Family Theories and Methods: A Contextual Approach*. New York: Plenum Press, 591–623.

Schieffelin, Bambi B. (1990). *The Give and Take of Everyday Life: Language Socialization of Kaluli Children*. Cambridge: Cambridge University Press.

Stack, Carol (1974). *All our Kin: Strategies for Survival in a Black Community*. New York: Harper & Row.

20

Language, Race, and White Public Space

Jane H. Hill

The Study of Racism in Anthropology

Anthropologists share a contradictory heritage: Our intellectual ancestors include both founders of scientific racism and important pioneers of the antiracist movement. After many years in which anthropologists have given far less attention to racism as an object of cultural analysis than have many of our sister disciplines, we are now returning to work that honors and advances our antiracist heritage.

Racism should be as central a question for research in cultural anthropology as "race" has been in biological anthropology. We have always been interested in forms of widely shared apparent irrationality, from divination to the formation of unilineal kin groups to the hyperconsumption of (or abstention from) the flesh of cattle, and racism is precisely this kind of phenomenon. Why, if nearly all scientists concur that human "races" are imaginary, do so many highly educated, cosmopolitan, economically secure people continue to think and act as racists? We know that "apparent irrationalities" seldom turn out to be the result of ignorance or confusion. Instead, they appear locally as quite rational, being rooted in history and tradition, functioning as important organizing principles in relatively enduring political ecologies, and lending coherence and meaning to complex and ambiguous human experiences. Racism is no different: As Smedley (1993:25) has argued, "race ... [is] a worldview, ... a cosmological ordering system structured out of the political, economic, and social realities of peoples who had emerged as expansionist, conquering, dominating nations on a worldwide quest for wealth and power." Racism challenges the most advanced anthropological thinking, because racial formation processes (Omi and Winant 1994) are contested and contradictory, yet global in their scope. At the local level racial practices (Winant 1994) can be very complex. Yet emerging global "racialscapes" (Harrison 1995:49, borrowing from Appadurai 1990) encompass even the most remote populations, as when the Taiap of the backwaters of the Lower Sepik River feel themselves to be "Black" as against "White" (Kulick 1993).

From "All Languages Are Equal" to the Study of Racializing Discourses

Like other anthropologists (and other linguists), linguistic anthropologists have made "education," with its implicit assumption of a confrontation with "ignorance," their central antiracist strategy. Attempts to inoculate students against beliefs in "primitive languages," "linguistic deprivation," or the idea that bilingualism (in certain languages) is inevitably seditious can be found in every introductory text-book in linguistics, and major scholars in the field have tried to spread the message not only as classroom educators, but as public intellectuals in a wide range of functions. And what have we to show for these efforts? "Official English" legislation on the books in many states, and, in the winter of 1996–97, a nationwide "moral panic" (Hall et al. 1978)[1] about whether "Ebonics" might be discussed in the class-rooms of Oakland, California. In the case of the Ebonics panic, the nearly universal reaction among linguists[2] and linguistic anthropologists was "We must redouble our efforts at education! How can we make classroom and textbook units on the equality of all languages, let alone all varieties of English, more effective? How can we place opinion pieces to fight this nonsense?" The problem here, of course, is that such interventions not only neglect the underlying cultural logic of the stigmat-ization of African American English, but also neglect the much deeper problem pointed out by James Baldwin: "It is not the Black child's language which is despised: It is his experience" (Baldwin 1979, cited in Lippi-Green 1997) – and Baldwin might have added, had he not been writing in the *New York Times*, "and his body."

Antiracist education in linguistics and linguistic anthropology has centered on demonstrations of the equality and adequacy of racialized forms of language, ran-ging from Boas's ([1889]1982) demolition of the concept of "alternating sounds" and "primitive languages" to Labov's (1972) canonical essay on "The logic of non-standard English."[3] But until very recently, there has been little research on the "culture of language" of the dominant, "race-making" (Williams 1989) populations. New studies are beginning to appear, such as Fabian (1986), Silverstein (1987), Woolard (1989), and Lippi-Green (1997). Urciuoli's (1996) ethnography of speaking of Spanish and English among Puerto Ricans in New York City is perhaps the first monograph on the talk of a racialized population that foregrounds, and contributes to, contemporary theories of racial formation processes through her analysis of cultural phenomena such as "accent" and "good English."

A central theoretical commitment for many linguistic anthropologists, that "cul-ture is localized in concrete, publicly accessible signs, the most important of which are actually occurring instances of discourse" (Urban 1991:1), prepares us to con-tribute in new ways to the untangling of the complexity of racism. Furthermore, such study is an obvious extension of an active line of research on linguistic ideologies (Woolard and Schieffelin 1994). We can explore questions like: What kinds of signs are made "concrete and publicly accessible" by racializing discourses? What kinds of discourses count, or do not count, as "racist," and by what (and whose) cultural logic? What are the different kinds of racializing discourses, and how are these distributed in speech communities? What discourse processes socialize children as racial subjects?[4] What are the discourses of resistance, and what do they reveal about the forms of racism? What discourse processes relate the racialization of bodies to the racialization of kinds of speech? And all of these questions must, of course, be qualified by the question, in what kinds of contexts?

"Spanish Accents" and "Mock Spanish": Linguistic Order and Disorder in White Public Space

To illustrate a linguistic-anthropological approach to these issues, I build on an analysis by Urciuoli (1996), recentering it from her research on bilingual Puerto Ricans in New York City to a national community of Whites.[5] I have been looking at uses of Spanish by Whites, both through on-the-spot observation of informal talk and through following as wide a range as possible of media and sites of mass reproduction such as advertising fliers, gift coffee cups, souvenir placemats, and greeting cards, for several years. First, I review Urciuoli's analysis of the racialization of Puerto Ricans through attention to their linguistic "disorder."

Puerto Rican linguistic marginalization: disorderly order

Urciuoli argues that her consultants experience language as differentiated into two spheres. In an "inner sphere" of talk among intimates in the household and neighborhood, the boundaries between "Spanish" and "English" are blurred and ambiguous both formally and functionally. Here, speakers exploit linguistic resources with diverse histories with great skill and fluency, achieving extremely subtle interactional effects. But in an "outer sphere" of talk (and engagement with text) with strangers and, especially, with gatekeepers like court officers, social workers, and schoolteachers, the difference between Spanish and English is "sharply objectified" (Urciuoli 1996:2). Boundaries and order are everything. The pressure from interlocutors to keep the two languages "in order" is so severe that people who function as fluent bilinguals in the inner sphere become so anxious about their competence that sometimes they cannot speak at all. Among the most poignant of the intricate ambiguities of this duality are that worries about being "disorderly" are never completely absent from the intimacies of the inner sphere, and people who successfully negotiate outer-sphere order are vulnerable to the accusation that they are "acting White," betraying their friends and relatives.

Urciuoli observes that a (carefully managed) Spanish is licensed in the outer sphere in such contexts as "folk-life festivals," as part of processes of "ethnification" that work to make difference "cultural, neat, and safe" (Urciuoli 1996:9).[6] But Whites hear other public Spanish as impolite and even dangerous. Urciuoli (1996:35) reports that "nearly every Spanish-speaking bilingual I know...has experienced complaints about using Spanish in a public place." Even people who always speak English "in public" worry about their "accents." While "accent" is a cultural dimension of speech and therefore lives largely in the realm of the imaginary, this construct is to some degree anchored in a core of objective phonetic practices that are difficult to monitor, especially when people are nervous and frightened. Furthermore, it is well-known that Whites will hear "accent" even when, objectively, none is present, if they can detect any other signs of a racialized identity.[7] Speakers are anxious about far more than "accent," however: they worry about cursing, using vocabulary items that might seem uncultivated, and even about using too many tokens of "you know." Mediated by cultural notions of "correctness" and "good English," failures of linguistic order, real and imagined, become in the outer sphere signs of race: "difference as inherent, disorderly, and dangerous" (Urciuoli 1996:9).

The main point for my argument is that Puerto Ricans experience the "outer sphere" as an important site of their racialization, since they are always found wanting by this sphere's standards of linguistic orderliness. My research suggests that precisely the opposite is true for Whites. Whites permit themselves a considerable amount of disorder precisely at the language boundary that is a site of discipline for Puerto Ricans (and other members of historically Spanish-speaking populations in the United States) – that is, the boundary between Spanish and English in public discourse. I believe that this contrast, in which White uses of Spanish create a desirable "colloquial" presence for Whites, but uses of Spanish by Puerto Ricans (and members of other historically Spanish-speaking groups in the United States) are "disorderly and dangerous," is one of the ways in which this arena of usage is constituted as a part of what Page and Thomas (1994) have called "White public space": a morally significant set of contexts that are the most important sites of the practices of a racializing hegemony, in which Whites are invisibly normal, and in which racialized populations are visibly marginal and the objects of monitoring ranging from individual judgment to Official English legislation.

White linguistic normalcy: orderly disorder

While Puerto Ricans are extremely self-conscious about their "Spanish" accents in English, heavy English "accents" in Spanish are perfectly acceptable for Whites, even when Spanish speakers experience them as "like a fingernail on the blackboard." Lippi-Green (1997) points out the recent emergence of an industry of accent therapists, who offer their services to clients ranging from White southerners to Japanese executives working at American plant sites. But the most absurd accents are tolerated in Spanish, even in Spanish classes at the graduate level. I have played to a number of audiences a tape of a *Saturday Night Live* skit from several years ago, in which the actors, playing television news writers at a story conference, use absurdly exaggerated "Spanish" accents in names for Mexican food, places, sports teams, and the like. The Latino actor Jimmy Smits appears and urges them to use "normal anglicizations" (Hill 1993a). Academic audiences find the skit hilarious, and one of its points (it permits multiple interpretations) seems to be that it is somehow inappropriate for Whites to try to sound "Spanish."

While Puerto Ricans agonize over whether or not their English is cultivated enough, the public written use of Spanish by Whites is often grossly nonstandard and ungrammatical. Hill (1993a) includes examples ranging from street names, to advertising, to public-health messages. *Wash Your Hands/Lava sus manos*, originally reported by Peñalosa (1980) in San Bernardino County, California, can be found in restrooms all over the southwestern United States. Peñalosa observed that this example is especially remarkable since it has as many grammatical errors as it has words.[8] An excellent case was the reprinting by the *Arizona Daily Star* (August 10, 1997) of an essay by the Colombian Nobelist Gabriel García Márquez that originally appeared in the *New York Times* (August 3, 1997). All of the diacritics on the

Spanish words – and the problem of accent marks had been one of García Márquez's main points – were missing in the *Star* version. Tucson is the home of a major university and has a large Spanish-speaking population, and the audience for the piece (which appeared on the op-ed page of the Sunday edition) no doubt included many people who are literate in Spanish. Clearly, however, the *Star* was not concerned about offering this audience a literate text.

While Puerto Rican code switching is condemned as disorderly, Whites "mix" their English with Spanish in contexts ranging from coffee-shop chat to faculty meetings to the evening network newscasts and the editorial pages of major newspapers. Their "Mock Spanish"[9] incorporates Spanish-language materials into English in order to create a jocular or pejorative "key." The practices of Mock Spanish include, first, semantic pejoration of Spanish loans: the use of positive or neutral Spanish words in humorous or negative senses. Perhaps the most famous example is *macho*, which in everyday Spanish merely means "male." Equally important are Spanish expressions of leave-taking, like *adiós* and *hasta la vista*, used in Mock Spanish as kidding (or as serious) "kiss-offs" (Mock-Spanish "adios" is attested in this sense from the mid-nineteenth century). A second strategy borrows obscene or scatological Spanish words for use as Mock-Spanish euphemisms, as on the handwritten sign "Casa de Pee-Pee" on the door of the women's restroom in the X-ray department of a Tucson clinic, a coffee cup that I purchased in a gift shop near the University of Arizona Main Gate that bears the legend "Caca de Toro," and, of course, the case of *cojones*, exemplified below. In the third strategy, elements of "Spanish" morphology, mainly the suffix -*o*, often accompanied by "Spanish" modifiers like *mucho* or *el*, are borrowed to create jocular and pejorative forms like "el cheap-o," "numero two-o," or "mucho trouble-o." In a recent example, heard on PBS's *Washington Week in Review*, moderator Ken Bode observed that, had the "palace coup" in the House of Representatives in July 1997 not been averted, the Speaker of the House Newt Gingrich would have been "Newt-o Frito." The last major strategy of Mock Spanish is the use of "hyperanglicized" and parodic pronunciations and orthographic representations of Spanish loan words, as with "Grassy-ass," "Hasty lumbago," and "Fleas Navidad" (a picture of a scratching dog usually accompanies this one, which shows up every year on Christmas cards).

Mock Spanish is attested at least from the end of the eighteenth century, and in recent years it has become an important part of the "middling style" (Cmiel 1990), a form of public language that emerged in the nineteenth century as a way for elites to display democratic and egalitarian sensibilities by incorporating colloquial and even slangy speech. Recent relaxations of proscriptions against public vulgarity have made even quite offensive usages within Mock Spanish acceptable at the highest level of public discourse, as when the then-Ambassador to the United Nations Madeleine Albright addressed the Security Council after Cuban aircraft had shot down two spy planes manned by Cuban exiles: Cuban president Fidel Castro, she said, had shown "not *cojones*, but cowardice." Although many Spanish speakers find this particular usage exceptionally offensive,[10] Albright's sally was quoted again and again in admiring biographical pieces in the major English-language news media after she was nominated to be Secretary of State (e.g., Gibbs 1996:33).

The Semiotics of Mock Spanish

In previous work (e.g., Hill 1995), I analyzed Mock Spanish as a "racist discourse." That is, I took its major functions to be the "elevation of whiteness" and the pejorative racialization of members of historically Spanish-speaking populations. Mock Spanish accomplishes the "elevation of whiteness" through what Ochs (1990) has called "direct indexicality": the production of nonreferential meanings or "indexes" that are understood and acknowledged by speakers. Speakers of Mock Spanish say that they use it because they have been exposed to Spanish – that is, they are cosmopolitan.[11] Or, that they use it in order to express their loyalty to, and affiliation with, the Southwest (or California, or Florida) – that is, they have regional "authenticity." Or that they use it because it is funny – that is, they have a sense of humor. In one particularly elaborate example, in the film *Terminator 2: Judgment Day*, Mock Spanish is used to turn Arnold Schwarzenegger, playing a cyborg, into a "real person," a sympathetic hero instead of a ruthless and terrifying machine. When Schwarzenegger, who has just returned from the future, answers a request with a curt Germanic "Affirmative," the young hero of the film, a 12-year-old White boy supposedly raised on the streets of Los Angeles, tells him, "No no no no no. You gotta listen to the way people talk!" He then proceeds to teach Schwarzenegger the Mock Spanish tags "No problemo" and "Hasta la vista, baby" as part of a register that also includes insults like "Dickwad."[12]

Analysis reveals that Mock Spanish projects, in addition to the directly indexed message that the speaker possesses a "congenial persona," another set of messages: profoundly racist images of members of historically Spanish-speaking populations. These messages are the product of what Ochs (1990) calls "indirect indexicality" in that, unlike the positive direct indexes, they are never acknowledged by speakers. In my experience, Whites almost always deny that Mock Spanish could be in any way racist. Yet in order to "make sense of" Mock Spanish, interlocutors require access to very negative racializing representations of Chicanos and Latinos as stupid, politically corrupt, sexually loose, lazy, dirty, and disorderly. It is impossible to "get" Mock Spanish – to find these expressions funny or colloquial or even intelligible – unless one has access to these negative images. An exemplary case is a political cartoon in my collection, showing a picture of Ross Perot pointing to a chart that says, among other things, "Perot for El Presidente." This is funny only if the audience can juxtapose the pompous and absurd Perot with the negative image of a banana-republic dictator, dripping with undeserved medals. It is only possible to "get" "Hasta la vista, baby" if one has access to a representation of Spanish speakers as treacherous. "Mañana" works as a humorous substitute for "later" only in conjunction with an image of Spanish speakers as lazy and procrastinating. My claim that Mock Spanish has a racializing function is supported by the fact that on humorous greeting cards (where it is fairly common) it is often accompanied by grossly racist pictorial representations of "Mexicans."

I have labeled Mock Spanish a "covert racist discourse" because it accomplishes racialization of its subordinate-group targets through indirect indexicality, messages that must be available for comprehension but are never acknowledged by speakers. In this it contrasts with "vulgar racist discourse," which uses the direct referential function in statements like, "Mexicans just don't know how to work," or hate speech ("Lazy greaser!"), which seems to operate through the performative function as a direct verbal "assault" (Matsuda et al. 1993). It is not exactly like the kind of kidding around that most Whites will admit can be interpreted as racist, as when David Letterman joked that the artificial fat olestra, which can cause abdominal pain and diarrhea, was "endorsed by the Mexican Health Department" (*New York Times*, August 24, 1997:F12). It also contrasts with the "elite racist discourse" identified by van Dijk (1993). Van Dijk pointed out that like Mock Spanish this type has as one function the presentation by the speaker of a desirable persona. Since "being a racist" is an undesirable quality, tokens often begin with qualifications like "I'm not a racist, but . . ." and then continue with a racializing argument like "I really resent it that all these Mexicans come up here to have babies so that American taxpayers will support them." Such qualifications do not make sense with Mock Spanish: One cannot say, "I'm not a racist, but no problemo," or "I'm not a racist, but comprende?," or "I'm not a racist, but adios, sucker." The reason this frame does not work is because Mock Spanish racializes its objects only covertly, through indirect indexicality.

Mock Spanish sometimes is used to constitute hate speech (as in posters saying "Adios, Jose" held by demonstrators supporting anti-immigration laws in California), and co-occurs with racist joking and with vulgar and elite racist discourses as well. It is sometimes used to address apparent Spanish speakers; many of my consultants report being addressed as "amigo," and Vélez-Ibáñez (1996:86) reports an offensive use of "comprende?" (pronounced [kəmprɛndiy]). However, it is found very widely in everyday talk and text on topics that have nothing to do with race at all. Because of its covert and indirect properties, Mock Spanish may be an exceptionally powerful site for the reproduction of White racist attitudes. In order to be "one of the group" among other Whites, collusion in the production of Mock Spanish is frequently unavoidable.

In my previous work, reviewed above, I have assumed that the "elevation of whiteness" and the constitution of a valued White persona was accomplished in Mock Spanish entirely through direct indexicality. However, in the light of Urciuoli's new work on the imposition of "order" on Puerto Ricans, I now believe that Mock Spanish accomplishes the "elevation of whiteness" in two ways: first, through directly indexing valuable and congenial personal qualities of speakers, but, importantly, also by the same type of indirect indexicality that is the source of its negative and racializing messages. It is through indirect indexicality that using Mock Spanish constructs "White public space," an arena in which linguistic disorder on the part of Whites is rendered invisible and normative, while the linguistic behavior of members of historically Spanish-speaking populations is highly visible and the object of constant monitoring.

Research on "whiteness" (e.g., Frankenberg 1993) has shown that Whites practice not only the construction of the domain of "color" and the exclusion from resources of those racialized as "colored," but also the constitution of "whiteness" as an invisible and unmarked "norm."[13] Like all such norms, this one is built as bricolage, from the bits and pieces of history, but in a special way, as what Williams (1989), borrowing from Gramsci, calls a "transformist hegemony": "its construction results in a national process aimed at homogenizing heterogeneity fashioned around assimilating elements of heterogeneity through appropriations that devalue and deny their link to the marginalized others' contribution to the patrimony" (Williams 1989:435).[14]

Bits and pieces of language are important "elements of heterogeneity" in this work. Urciuoli (1996) has shown that precisely this kind of "heterogeneity" is not permitted to Puerto Ricans. What I have tried to show above is that linguistic heterogeneity and even explicit "disorder" is not only permitted to Whites, it is an essential element of a desirable White public persona. To be White is to collude in these practices, or to risk censure as "having no sense of humor" or being "politically correct." But White practice is invisible to the monitoring of linguistic disorder. It is not understood by Whites as disorder – after all, they are not, literally, "speaking Spanish" (and indeed the phenomena of public ungrammaticality, orthographical absurdity, and parodic mispronunciations of Spanish are evidence that they go to some lengths to distance themselves from such an interpretation of their behavior [Hill 1993a]). Instead, they are simply being "natural": funny, relaxed, coloquial, authentic.

I have collected some evidence that members of historically Spanish-speaking populations do not share Whites' understanding of Mock Spanish. For instance, the sociologist Clara Rodríguez (1997:78) reports that she was "puzzled … with regard to [the] relevance" of the Mock Spanish in *Terminator 2: Judgment Day*. Literate Spanish speakers in the United States are often committed linguistic purists, and Mock Spanish is offensive to them because it contains so many grammatical errors and because it sometimes uses rude words. They focus on this concern, but of course they have little power to change White usage.[15] It is clear that many Spanish speakers do hear the racist message of Mock Spanish. In an interview,[16] a Spanish-speaking Chicano high school counselor in Tucson said, "You know, I've noticed that most of the teachers never use any Spanish around here unless it's something negative." A Spanish-speaking Chicano businesswoman said, "When you first hear that stuff, you think, that's nice, they're trying, but then you hear more and more and you realize that there's something nasty underneath." In lecturing on Mock Spanish, I have found that Chicano and Latino people in my audiences strongly concur with the main outlines of my analysis, and often bring me additional examples. Chicano scholars, especially Fernando Peñalosa (cf. 1980), have long pointed out the racist implications of disorderly Spanish usage by Whites. Thus, for thoughtful Spanish speakers, the fact that disorderly Spanish and "Mock Spanish" constitute a "White public space" is not news. One of the dimensions of this space is that disorder on the part of Whites (including not only Mock Spanish, but also cursing and a variety of locutionary sins of the "you know" type) is largely invisible, while disorder on the part of racialized populations is hypervisible to the point of being the object of expensive political campaigns and nationwide "moral panics."

More Sources for Homogeneous Heterogeneity

The "incorporation"[17] of linguistic elements into the linguistic "homogeneous heterogeneity" of White public space draws on many sources. Perhaps the most important is what Smitherman (1994) calls the "crossover" of forms from African American

English (AAE).[18] Gubar (1997) builds on the work of Morrison (1992) and others in a richly detailed study of very widespread and pervasive incorporative processes in the usage of White artists and writers. However, AAE and White English are so thoroughly entangled in the United States that crossover is extremely difficult to study. While obvious "wiggerisms" like "Word to your Mother"[19] or moth-eaten tokens of minstrelsy like "Sho' nuff, Mistah Bones" are easy to spot, many other usages are curiously indeterminate.[20] Even where an AAE source is recognizable to an etymologist, it is often impossible to know whether the usage indexes any "blackness" to its user or audience. One way of understanding this indeterminacy might be to see it as a triumph of White racial practice. New tokens of White "hipness," often retrievable as Black in origin only by the most dogged scholarship (although often visible to Blacks), are constantly created out of AAE materials.

An example of indeterminate crossover appeared in the "For Better or for Worse" comic strip published in the *Arizona Daily Star* (August 22, 1997). Two White Canadian lads discuss how Lawrence should deal with his partner's departure to study music in Paris. Bobby, who is straight, tries to reassure Lawrence, who is gay,[21] that falling in love is always worth it, even knowing the risk of loss. Lawrence jokes, "Let it be known that this speech comes from a guy who's in a 'happening' relationship." "Happening" in this sense comes from AAE "happenin," but it seems unlikely that here it is intended to convey anything more than the strip creator's alertness to "the speech of today's young people" (although the quotation marks around the form do suggest that she regards this register as not part of her own repertoire). Yet similar usages can be highly salient for Blacks: Lippi-Green (1997:196) quotes an audience member on an episode of Oprah Winfrey: "This is a fact. White America use black dialect on commercials every day. Be observant, people. Don't let nobody tell you that you are ignorant and that you don't speak right. Be observant. They started off Channel 7 Eyewitness news a few years ago with one word: whashappenin. So what's happening, America?"

Now, contrast the episode of "For Better or for Worse" described above with another episode, published a couple of years ago. Here the young people are on a ski slope, and one boy, Gordon, "hits on" (I am sure Smitherman [1994] is correct that this is AAE, but in my own usage it feels merely slangy) a pretty girl with our now-familiar token, "What's happening?" She "puts him down" (probably also AAE, but not in Smitherman 1994)[22] with "With you? Nada." While probably few White readers of this strip sense "blackness" in "What's happening?", most will immediately detect "Nada" as "Spanish." That is, while the "Black" indexicality of "What's happening" is easily suppressed, it is virtually impossible to suppress the "Spanish" indexicality of "Nada," which has in "Mock Spanish" the semantically pejorated sense "absolutely nothing, less than zero." It seems likely that there are tokens that originate in Mock Spanish where the original indexicality is suppressable (the word *peon*, pronounced [piyan], which appeared in English by the seventeenth century, may be an example of this type), but in general tokens of this practice are relatively easy to spot and interpret.

Because of this relative transparency of Mock Spanish, it is a good choice for linguistic-anthropological research. However, precisely because it is narrower in its range of opacity and transparency than is AAE "crossover," it must function somewhat differently in White public space, an issue that needs investigation.

Furthermore, African Americans themselves apparently use Mock Spanish; Terry McMillan's 1996 novel, *How Stella Got Her Groove Back*, is rich in attestations in the speech of Stella, a beautiful and successful African American professional woman from California. In contrast, as far as I know no members of historically Spanish-speaking populations use Mock Spanish, at least not in anything like the routine way that Whites do.[23]

The same question, of differential functions of such linguistic incorporations into White "homogeneous heterogeneity," occurs with borrowings from other languages. For instance, tokens of "Mock French" like "Mercy buckets" and "bow-koo" do occur, but they are relatively rare, especially in comparison with the very extensive use of French in advertising, especially in the fashion industry, to convey luxury and exclusivity. "Mock Italian" seems to have been relatively important in the 1940s and 1950s but is apparently on the way out; I have found very few examples of it. "Mock Yiddish" is common but is used by members of historically Yiddish-speaking groups as well as by outsiders. "Mock Japanese" "sayonara" is perfectly parallel to Mock Spanish "adios," but may be the only widely used token of this type.[24] In summary, "Mock" forms vary widely in relative productivity and in the kinds of contexts in which they appear. By far the richest examples of linguistic incorporations are Mock Spanish and AAE crossover.

Can Mock Forms Subvert the Order of Racial Practices?

A number of authors, including Hewitt (1986), Gubar (1997) and Butler (1997), have argued that usages that in some contexts are grossly racist seem to contain an important parodic potential that can be turned to the antiracist deconstruction of racist categorical essentializing. Hewitt studied Black–White friendships among young teenagers in south London and found a "productive dialogue of youth" (1986:99) in which he identifies antiracist potential. Especially notable were occasions where Black children would tease White friends as "nigger," and the White teens would reply with "honky" or "snowflake." Hewitt comments, "This practice … turns racism into a kind of effigy, to be burned up in an interactive ritual which seeks to acknowledge and deal with its undeniable presence whilst acting out the negation of its effects" (1986:238). Gubar (1997) suggests that posters by the artist Iké Udé (such as a famous image of Marilyn Monroe, but in "blackface," and a transformation of Robert Mapplethorpe's infamous "Man in a Polyester Suit" with white skin and a circumcised penis) may use the symbolic repertoire of racism as "a crucial aesthetic means of comprehending racial distinction without entrenching or denying it" (Gubar 1997:256). An example in the case of Spanish might be the performance art of Guillermo Gómez Peña,[25] who creates frenzied mixtures of English and multiple registers and dialects of Spanish (and even Nahuatl). Butler (1997), writing in opposition to the proscription of racist vocabulary by anti-hate speech legislation, argues that gays and lesbians have been able to subvert the power of "queer," and that other "hate words" may have similar potential. The kinds of games reported by Hewitt, however, remain reserved to childhood, unable to break through the dominant voices of racism; Hewitt found that the kind of interracial friendship that permitted teasing with racist epithets essentially vanished from the lives of his subjects by the time they reached the age of 16. In the light of the analysis that I have suggested above, the "subversions" noted by Gubar and Butler can also be seen simply as one more example of "orderly" disorder that is reserved to elites in White public space, rather than as carnivalesque inversions. Or, perhaps we should say that carnivalesque inversions can be a "weapon of the strong" as well as a "weapon of the weak."[26] The art of a Gómez Peña, to the degree that it is acceptable to White audiences, may precisely "whiten" this performer and others like him.

An important possible exception is the phenomenon of "crossing," discussed by British sociolinguist Ben Rampton (1995), who reports extensive use of out-group linguistic tokens among British adolescents of a variety of ethnic origins, including strongly racialized populations like West Indians and South Asians as well as Whites. "Crossings," while they retain some potential to give offense, often seem simply to acknowledge what is useful and desirable in the space of urban diversity. Thus, working-class White girls learn the Panjabi lyrics to "bhangra" songs, and Bengali kids speak Jamaican creole (which seems to have emerged in general as a prestigious language among British youth, parallel to the transracial "hip-hop" phenomenon in the United States). Early reports by Shirley Brice Heath of new work with American adolescents has identified similar "crossing" phenomena.[27] However, only slightly more than a decade ago Hewitt (1986) found that such crossings did not survive the adolescent years. We cannot be sure that these phenomena are genuinely outside the linguistic order of racism until we understand dimensions of that order – within which age-graded cohorts may have a relatively enduring place. I have tried above to show how linguistic-anthropological attention to the history, forms, and uses of White language mixing can help us toward such an understanding.

NOTES

Acknowledgements. I would especially like to thank María Rodríguez, Bambi Schieffelin, and Kathryn Woolard, who have provided me with valuable material on Mock Spanish.

1 Hall et al. (1978) borrow the notion of "moral panic" from Cohen (1972).
2 In a survey of 34 entries, encompassing about 100 messages, under the heading "Ebonics" on Linguist, the list that probably reaches the largest number of linguists, I found only one explicit mention of "racism" by an author who used the expression "institutional racism." It is, perhaps, appropriate for linguists to focus on their special areas of scholarly expertise, and it is certainly the case that there may be a linguistic dimension to the educational problems confronted by many African American children, but the neglect of racism on the list was quite striking. It was sometimes addressed obliquely and euphemistically, as with one author's proposal of the "special" situation of African Americans in the United States.
3 The "all languages are equal" argument continues in spite of a warning by Dell Hymes (1973) that this claim is technically incorrect in many subtle ways.
4 Hirschfeld (1996) documents the very early association between raced categories and an essentialized understanding of "human kinds" for young children in the United States.
5 I am mindful of Hartigan's (1997) argument that "Whites" are by no means a homogeneous population. Indeed, in other work (Hill 1995) I have suggested that working-class speakers are less likely to use "Mock Spanish" than are other Whites. Much of my material comes from mass media that are part of the homogenizing project of "whiteness," and there is no question that different "Whites" experience this project in different ways. I use "Whites" here (perhaps injudiciously) as a sort of shorthand required first by lack of space and second because the data required to precisely characterize the population I have in mind are not available. Certainly it includes White elites such as screenwriters and nationally syndicated columnists.

6   Urciuoli (1996:16) points out that it is essential to use Spanish in the folklife festival context because to translate songs, the names of foods, and the like into English would render them less "authentic," this property being essential to claims on "ethnicity" that are one way to resist racialization.

7   Here the canonical study is the matched-guise test conducted by Rubin (1992). Sixty-two undergraduate native speakers of English listened to a brief lecture (on either a science or humanities topic) recorded by a native speaker of English from central Ohio. While they listened, one group of students saw a slide of a White woman lecturer. The other half saw a slide of an Asian woman in the same setting and pose (and even of the same size, and with the same hair style, as the White woman). Students who heard the lecture under the "Asian slide" condition often reported that the lecturer had an Asian accent and, even more interestingly, scored lower on tests of comprehension of the lecture.

8   It should be *Lavarse las manos*, the usual directive for public places being the infinitive (e.g., *No fumar* "No Smoking," *No estacionarse* "No Parking"), the verb being reflexive, and body parts are not labeled by the possessive pronoun *su* unless they are detached from the body of their owner.

9   In earlier publications (e.g., Hill 1993b), I referred to these practices as "Junk Spanish." I think James Fernandez for the expression "Mock Spanish" and for convincing me that "Junk Spanish" was a bad nomenclatural idea, and the source of some of the problems I was having getting people to understand what I was working on (many people, including linguists and anthropologists, assumed that by "Junk Spanish" I meant something like the "Border Spanish" of native speakers of Spanish, rather than jocular and parodic uses of Spanish by English speakers). The most extensive discussion of Mock Spanish available is Hill (1995).

10 I am indebted to Professor Raúl Fernández of the University of California-Irvine for a copy of a letter he wrote to the *Los Angeles Times* protesting the appearance of *cojones* in a film review. Ernest Hemingway is probably to blame for the widespread knowledge of this word among monolingual speakers of English.

11 While some Whites who use Mock Spanish have a classroom competence in that language (I was a case in point), most of the speakers I have queried say that they do not "speak Spanish."

12 An anonymous referee for the *American Anthropologist* argues that this analysis, suggesting that the "elevation of whiteness" is accomplished through direct indexicality, is not exactly correct. Instead, the direct indexicality of Mock Spanish elevates the individual, conveying "I am a nice/easy-going/funny/locally-rooted/cosmopolitan person." The elevation of "whiteness" is then accomplished indirectly when combined with the indirectly indexed message "I am White." This is an interesting suggestion, but I think the *Terminator 2: Judgment Day* sequence argues that the indexicality is direct: Mock Spanish is precisely "the way people talk" – and "people" can only be that group that is unmarked and thereby "White." Thus positive individual qualities and "whiteness" are simultaneously indexed. (A direct version of this, perhaps mercifully obsolete, is the expression that applauds some act of good fellowship with "That's mighty White of you.")

13 As Harrison (1995) points out, a more explicit construction of whiteness often appears among marginalized Whites, as in the current far-right "White pride" movement. She notes that this "undermines whatever incipient class consciousness exists among poor Whites" (Harrison 1995:63). Thus we can see such movements as part of the very large cultural formation wherein "race" may be the single most important organizer of relationships, determinant of identity, and mediator of meaning (Winant 1994).

14 Williams focuses her analysis on the "national process," the creation of what she calls the race/class/nation conflation, but the construction of whiteness is probably a project of global scope, and in fact Mock Spanish seems to be widespread in the English-speaking world. Bertie, a character in the Barrytown novels (*The Commitments, The Snapper, The Van*, which depict life in working-class Dublin) by the Irish author Roddy Doyle, often uses Mock Spanish. For another example from outside the United States, I am indebted to Dick Bauman for a headline from the gardening section of a Glasgow newspaper, inviting the reader to "Hosta la vista, baby!" (that is, to plant members of the genus *Hosta* for their decorative foliage).

15 I have discovered only one case of apparent concern about Spanish-speaking opinion in reference to the use of Spanish in mass media. Chon Noriega (1997:88) reports that when the film *Giant* was presented for review to the Production Code Administration in 1955, Geoffrey Shurlock, the head of the PCA, requested that the ungrammatical Spanish in the film (in which Spanish appears without subtitles) be corrected, apparently for fear of offending the government of Mexico, then seen as a "good neighbor."

16 Dan Goldstein and I have begun a project of interviewing members of historically Spanish-speaking populations about Mock Spanish. We have compiled a scrapbook of examples, and subjects are audiotaped as they leaf through these and comment on them.

17 I borrow this term from Raymond Williams (1977).

18 I do not include "Vernacular" (many scholars refer to "African American Vernacular English" or AAVE), because AAE has a full range of register ranging from street argot through middle-class conversational usage to formal oratory and *belles lettres*. Scholars like Smitherman (1988) and Morgan (1994) have criticized sociolinguists for typifying AAE only through attestations of street registers.

19 Smitherman (1994:237) defines *wigger* as "literally, a white NIGGER, an emerging positive term for White youth who identify with HIP HOP, RAP, and other aspects of African American Culture." She gives the proper form of the affirmation as "Word to the Mother," but I first heard it (from a young White woman) in the form given.

20 In the lexicon of AAE provided by Smitherman (1994) I recognized many forms in my own usage that she does not mark as "crossovers" (to give only one example, "beauty shop" for a hair-and-nails salon was the only term I knew for such establishments as I was growing up, and it was universally used by my grandmothers, aunts, and mother, all White ladies who would never have dreamed of essaying any "Dis and Dat" [Gubar's (1997) term for the adoption of AAE forms by White writers]). My grandfather, an egregious racist who grew up in south-eastern Missouri, was very fond of "copacetic," which Smitherman attributes to the speech of "older blacks" and does not recognize as ever having "crossed over."

21 A number of U.S. newspapers refused to publish the series of episodes in which Lawrence mourns his partner's departure.

22 The *American Heritage Dictionary of the English Language* (Third Edition) lists "put down" as "slang." Unsurprisingly, their sentence of attestation comes from the work of Dr. Alvin Poussaint, an African American.

23 Some Spanish speakers find some of the greeting cards in my sample funny. One woman said that she might send a "Moochos Smoochos" card (illustrating hyperanglicized parody and the use of Spanish morphology to be funny) to her husband; she said, "That one's kinda cute."

24 "Honcho," from Japanese *han* "Squad" and *chō* "chief" (*American Heritage Dictionary of the English Language*, Third Edition) seems to be etymologically inaccessible as Japanese except to specialists; many Whites probably think that it is Spanish.

25 See, for instance, his *Warrior for Gringostroika* (1993). However, Gómez Peña uses so much Spanish that one must be bilingual to understand him; his art seems to me to be addressed mainly to multilingual Spanish-speaking audiences. Woolard's (1988) study of a comic in 1970s Barcelona, who entertained audiences with jokes that code switched between Castilian and Catalan during a period of extreme linguistic conflict and purism, provides another example of this type of subversion.

26 "Weapon of the weak" comes, of course, from Scott (1985). Work on discourses of resistance by scholars like Scott (see also 1990) and Bhabha (1994) often seems to imply that parody and humor are primarily strategies of resistance. However, it is obvious that humor is an important part of racist discourse, and the accusation that antiracists "have no sense of humor" is an important weapon of racists.

27 In a colloquium presented to the Department of Anthropology, University of Arizona, Tucson, January 27, 1997.

REFERENCES

Appadurai, Arjun (1990). Disjuncture and Difference in the Global Cultural Economy. *Public Culture* 2:1–24.

Bhabha, Homi K. (1994). *The Location of Culture*. New York: Routledge.

Boas, Franz ([1889] 1982). On Alternating Sounds. In *The Shaping of American Anthropology, 1883–1911: A Franz Boas Reader*, George W. Stocking (ed.), pp. 72–6. Chicago: University of Chicago Press.

Butler, Judith (1997). *Excitable Speech*. New York: Routledge.

Cmiel, Kenneth (1990). *Democratic Eloquence*. New York: William Morrow.

Cohen, Stan (1972). *Folk Devils and Moral Panics: The Creation of the Mods and the Rockers*. London: MacGibbon and Kee.

Fabian, Johannes (1986). *Language and Colonial Power: The Appropriation of Swahili in the Former Belgian Congo, 1880–1938*. Cambridge: Cambridge University Press.

Frankenberg, Ruth (1993). *White Women, Race Matters: The Social Construction of Whiteness*. Minneapolis: University of Minnesota Press.

Gibbs, Nancy (1996). An American Voice. *Time* 149(1):32–3.

Gómez Peña, Guillermo (1993). *Warrior for Gringostroika*. St. Paul, MN: Graywolf Press.

Gubar, Susan (1997). *Racechanges: White Skins, Black Face in American Culture*. Oxford: Oxford University Press.

Hall, Stuart, Chas Critcher, Tony Jefferson, John Clarke, and Brian Roberts (1978). *Policing the Crisis*. London: The Macmillan Press Ltd.

Harrison, Faye V. (1995). The Persistent Power of "Race" in the Cultural and Political Economy of Racism. *Annual Review of Anthropology* 24:47–74.

Hartigan, John, Jr. (1997). Establishing the Fact of Whiteness. *American Anthropologist* 99:495–505.

Hewitt, Roger (1986). *White Talk Black Talk: Inter-Racial Friendship and Communication among Adolescents*. Cambridge: Cambridge University Press.

Hill, Jane H. (1993a). Hasta La Vista, Baby: Anglo Spanish in the American Southwest. *Critique of Anthropology* 13:145–76.

Hill, Jane H. (1993b). Is It Really "No Problemo"? In *SALSA I: Proceedings of the First Annual Symposium about Language and Society – Austin*, Robin Queen and Rusty Barrett (eds.), *Texas Linguistic Forum* 33:1–12.

Hill, Jane H. (1995). *Mock Spanish: A Site for the Indexical Reproduction of Racism in American English*. Electronic document. University of Chicago Lang-cult Site. http://www.cs.uchicago.edu/discussions/l-c.

Hirschfeld, Lawrence A. (1996). *Race in the Making*. Cambridge, MA: MIT Press/Bradford Books.

Hymes, Dell H. (1973). Language and Speech: On the Origins and Foundations of Inequality among Speakers. In *Language as a Human Problem*, Einar Haugen and Morton Bloomfield (eds.), pp. 45–72. New York: W. W. Norton and Co.

Kulick, Don (1993). *Language Shift and Cultural Reproduction*. Cambridge: Cambridge University Press.

Labov, William (1972). *Language in the Inner City*. Philadelphia: University of Pennsylvania Press.

Lippi-Green, Rosina (1997). *English with an Accent: Language, Ideology, and Discrimination in the United States*. London: Routledge.

Matsuda, Mari J., Charles R. Lawrence III, Richard Delgado, and Kimberlé Williams Crenshaw (eds.) (1993). *Words that Wound: Critical Race Theory, Assaultive Speech, and the First Amendment*. Boulder, CO: Westview Press.

McMillan, Terry (1996). *How Stella Got Her Groove Back*. New York: Viking.

Morgan, Marcyliena (1994). The African-American Speech Community: Reality and Sociolinguists. In *Language and the Social Construction of Identity in Creole Situations*, Marcyliena Morgan (ed.), pp. 121–50. Los Angeles: UCLA Center for Afro-American Studies.

Morrison, Toni (1992). *Playing in the Dark: Whiteness and the Literary Imagination*. Cambridge, MA: Harvard University Press.

Noriega, Chon (1997). Citizen Chicano: The Trials and Titillations of Ethnicity in the American Cinema, 1935–1962. In *Latin Looks*, Clara E. Rodríguez (ed.), pp. 85–103. Boulder, CO: Westview.

Ochs, Elinor (1990). Indexicality and Socialization. In *Cultural Psychology*, James Stigler, Richard A. Shweder, and Gilbert Herdt (eds.), pp. 287–308. Cambridge: Cambridge University Press.

Omi, Michael, and Howard Winant (1994). *Racial Formation in the United States* (2nd edn.). New York: Routledge.

Page, Helán E., and Brooke Thomas (1994). White Public Space and the Construction of White Privilege in U.S. Health Care: Fresh Concepts and a New Model of Analysis. *Medical Anthropology Quarterly* 8:109–16.

Peñalosa, Fernando (1980). *Chicano Sociolinguistics*. Rowley, MA: Newbury House Press.

Rampton, Ben (1995). *Crossing: Language and Ethnicity among Adolescents*. London: Longman.

Rodríguez, Clara E. (1997). The Silver Screen: Stories and Stereotypes. In *Latin Looks*, Clara E. Rodríguez (ed.), pp. 73–9. Boulder, CO: Westview Press.

Rubin, D. L. (1992). Nonlanguage Factors Affecting Undergraduates' Judgments of Nonnative English-Speaking Teaching Assistants. *Research in Higher Education* 33:511–31.

Scott, James C. (1985). *Weapons of the Weak: Everyday Forms of Peasant Resistance*. New Haven, CT: Yale University Press.

Scott, James C. (1990). *Domination and the Arts of Resistance: Hidden Transcripts*. New Haven, CT: Yale University Press.

Silverstein, Michael (1987). *Monoglot "Standard" in America*. Working Papers of the Center for Psychosocial Studies, 13. Chicago: Center for Psychosocial Studies.

Smedley, Audrey (1993). *Race in North America: Origin and Evolution of a Worldview*. Boulder, CO: Westview Press.

Smitherman, Geneva (1994). *Black Talk: Words and Phrases from the Hood to the Amen Corner*. Boston: Houghton Mifflin Company.

Smitherman-Donaldson, Geneva (1988). Discriminatory Discourse on Afro-American Speech. In *Discourse and Discrimination*, Geneva Smitherman-Donaldson and Teun van Dijk (eds.), pp. 144–75. Detroit: Wayne State University Press.

Urban, Greg (1991). *A Discourse-Centered Approach to Culture*. Austin: University of Texas Press.

Urciuoli, Bonnie (1996). *Exposing Prejudice: Puerto Rican Experiences of Language, Race, and Class*. Boulder, CO: Westview Press.

Van Dijk, Teun A. (1993). *Elite Discourse and Racism*. Newbury Park, CA: Sage Publications.

Vélez-Ibáñez, Carlos G. (1996). *Border Visions: Mexican Cultures of the Southwest United States*. Tucson: University of Arizona Press.

Williams, Brackette (1989). A Class Act: Anthropology and the Race to Nation across Ethnic Terrain. *Annual Review of Anthropology* 18:401–44.

Williams, Raymond (1977). *Marxism and Literature*. Oxford: Oxford University Press.

Winant, Howard (1994). *Racial Conditions: Politics, Theory, Comparisons*. Minneapolis: University of Minnesota Press.

Woolard, Kathryn A. (1988). Codeswitching and Comedy in Catalonia. In *Codeswitching: Anthropological and Sociolinguistic Perspectives*, Monica Heller (ed.), pp. 53–70. Berlin: Mouton de Gruyter.

Woolard, Kathryn A. (1989). Sentences in the Language Prison. *American Ethnologist* 16:268–78.

Woolard, Kathryn A., and Bambi Schieffelin (1994). Language Ideology. *Annual Review of Anthropology* 23:55–82.

References

to "Linguistic, Anthropology: History, Ideas, and Issues"

Agha, A. (1994). Honorification. *Annual Review of Anthropology, 23*, 277–302.

Agha, A. (1997). "Concept" and "communication" in evolutionary terms. *Semiotica, 116*(2–4), 189–215.

Anzaldúa, G. (1987). *Borderlands / La Frontiera: The New Mestiza*. San Francisco: Spinsters/Aunt Lute.

Anzaldúa, G. (1990). How to Tame a Wild Tongue. In R. M. Ferguson, T. Trinh Minh-ha Geve, & C. West (eds.), *Out There: Marginalization and Contemporary Cultures* (pp. 203–11). New York: The New Museum of Contemporary Art/MIT Press.

Austin, J. L. (1962). *How to Do Things with Words*. Oxford: Oxford University Press.

Austin, J. L. (1975). *How to Do Things with Words* (2nd edn.), J. O. Urmson and Marina Sbisà, editors. Cambridge, MA: Harvard University Press.

Bailey, B. (1997). Communication of Respect in Interethnic Service Encounters. *Language in Society, 26*(3), 327–56.

Bailey, B. (2000). Communicative Behavior and Conflict between African-American Customers and Korean Immigrant Retailers in Los Angeles. *Discourse & Society, 11*(1), 87–108.

Bakhtin, M. M. (1981). *The Dialogic Imagination: Four Essays*. Edited by M. Holquist, translated by C. Emerson & M. Holquist. Austin: University of Texas Press.

Bakhtin, M. M. (1984). *Problems of Dostoevsky's Poetics*. Edited and translated by C. Emerson. Introduction by Wayne C. Booth. Minneapolis: University of Minnesota Press.

Bakhtin, M. M. (1986). *Speech Genres & Other Late Essays*. Translated by Vern W. McGee. Austin: University of Texas Press.

Bamberg, M. (ed.) (1997). Oral Versions of Personal Experience: Three Decades of Narrative Analysis. *Journal of Narrative and Life History, 7*(1–4) (Special Issue).

Barwise, J., & Perry, J. (1983). *Situations and Attitudes*. Cambridge, MA: MIT Press.

Baugh, J. (1999). *Out of the Mouths of Slaves. African American Language and Educational Malpractice*. Austin: University of Texas Press.

Bauman, R. (1975). Verbal Art as Performance. *American Anthropologist, 77*, 290–311. [Reprinted in this volume.]

Bauman, R. (1977). *Verbal Art as Performance*. Rowley, MA: Newbury House.

Bauman, R., & Sherzer, J. (eds.) (1975). The Ethnography of Speaking. *Annual Reviews, 4*, 95–119.

Beeman, W. O. (1993). The Anthropology of Theater and Spectacle. *Annual Review of Anthropology, 22*, 369–93.

Berlin, B., & Kay, P. (1969). *Basic Color Terms: Their Universality and Evolution.* Berkeley: University of California Press.

Besnier, N. (1995). *Literacy, Emotion, and Authority: Reading and Writing on a Polynesian Atoll.* Cambridge: Cambridge University Press.

Biber, D. (1988). *Variation Across Speech and Writing.* Cambridge: Cambridge University Press.

Biber, D., & Finegan, E. (eds.) (1994). *Sociolinguistic Perspectives on Register.* New York: Oxford University Press.

Bloch, M. (1975a). Introduction. In M. Bloch (ed.), *Political Language and Oratory in Traditional Society* (pp. 1–28). London: Academic Press.

Bloch, M. (1975b). *Political Language and Oratory in Traditional Society.* London: Academic Press.

Blom, J.-P., & Gumperz, J. J. (1972). Social Meaning in Linguistic Structures: Code-Switching in Norway. In J. J. Gumperz & D. Hymes (eds.), *Directions in Sociolinguistics: The Ethnography of Communication* (pp. 407–34). New York: Holt, Rinehart, and Winston.

Bloomfield, L. (1935). *Language.* London: Allen & Unwin.

Blount, B. G. (1995). Parental Speech and Language Acquisition: An Anthropological Perspective. In B. G. Blount (ed.), *Language, Culture, and Society. A Book of Readings* (pp. 551–66). Prospect Heights, IL: Waveland.

Boas, F. (1889). On Alternating Sounds. *American Anthropologist, 2 (o.s.),* 47–53.

Boas, F. (1900). Sketch of the Kwakiutl Language. *American Anthropologist,* 2(4), 708–21.

Boas, F. (1911). Introduction. In F. Boas (ed.), *Handbook of American Indian Languages* (Vol. BAE-B 40, Part I). Washington, D.C.: Smithsonian Institution and Bureau of American Ethnology.

Boas, F. (1925). Stylistic Aspects of Primitive Literature. *Journal of American Folk-Lore, 38,* 329–39.

Boas, F. (1940). *Race, Language, and Culture.* New York: The Free Press.

Bourdieu, P. (1982). *Ce que parler veut dire.* Paris: Fayard.

Bourdieu, P. (1985). *Distinction: A Social Critique of the Judgement of Taste.* Cambridge, MA: Harvard University Press.

Brenneis, D. L., & Myers, F. (eds.) (1984). *Dangerous Words: Language and Politics in the Pacific.* New York: New York University Press.

Briggs, C. L. (1986). *Learning How to Ask: A Sociolinguistic Appraisal of the Role of the Interview in Social Science Research.* Cambridge: Cambridge University Press.

Briggs, C. L., & Bauman, R. (1992). Genre, Intertextuality, and Social Power. *Journal of Linguistic Anthropology,* 2(2), 131–72.

Bright, W. (ed.) (1966). *Sociolinguistics: Proceedings of the UCLA Sociolinguistics Conference, 1964.* The Hague: Mouton & Co.

Brown, G., & Yule, G. (1983). *Discourse Analysis.* Cambridge: Cambridge University Press.

Brown, P. (1993). Gender, Politeness, and Confrontation in Tenejapa. In D. Tannen (ed.), *Gender and Conversational Interaction* (pp. 144–62). New York: Oxford University Press.

Brown, P., & Levinson, S. C. (1978). Universals in Language Usage: Politeness Phenomena. In E. N. Goody (ed.), *Questions and Politeness Strategies in Social Interaction* (pp. 56–311). Cambridge: Cambridge University Press.

Brown, P., & Levinson, S. C. (1987). *Politeness: Some Universals in Language Usage.* Cambridge: Cambridge University Press.

Bucholtz, M. (1999). Bad Examples: Transgression and Progress in Language and Gender Studies. In M. Bucholtz, A. C. Liang, & L. A. Sutton (eds.), *Reinventing Identities: The Gendered Self in Discourse* (pp. 3–24). New York: Oxford University Press.

Bucholtz, M., Liang, A. C., & Sutton, L. A. (eds.) (1999). *Reinventing Identities: The Gendered Self in Discourse.* New York: Oxford University Press.

Capps, L., & Ochs, E. (1995). *Constructing Panic: The Discourse of Agoraphobia.* Cambridge, MA: Harvard University Press.

Cardona, G. R. (1976). *Introduzione all'etnolinguistica.* Bologna: Il Mulino.

Carroll, J. B. (1956). Introduction. In J. B. Carroll (ed.), *Language, Thought, and Reality: Selected Writings of Benjamin Lee Whorf* (pp. 1–34). Cambridge, MA: MIT Press.

Caton, S. C. (1990). *"Peaks of Yemen I summon": Poetry as Cultural Practice in a North Yemeni Tribe.* Berkeley: University of California Press.

Cazden, C. B., John, V. P., & Hymes, D. (eds.) (1972). *The Functions of Language in the Classroom.* New York: Teachers College Press.

Chomsky, N. (1959). Review of *Verbal Behavior* by B. F. Skinner. *Language, 35*, 26–58.

Chomsky, N. (1965). *Aspects of the Theory of Syntax*. Cambridge, MA: MIT Press.

Chomsky, N. (1966). *Cartesian Linguistics*. New York: Harper & Row.

Chomsky, N. (1973). Introduction to Adam Schaff's *Language and Cognition*. New York: McGraw-Hill.

Chomsky, N. (1982). *Lectures on Government and Binding: The Pisa Lectures* (2nd edn.). Dordrecht: Foris.

Chomsky, N. (1986). *Knowledge of Language: Its Nature, Origin and Use*. New York: Praeger.

Chomsky, N. (1995). *The Minimalist Program*. Cambridge, MA: MIT Press.

Chomsky, N., Halle, M., & Lukoff, F. (1956). On Accent and Juncture in English. In M. Halle, H. Lunt, & H. MacLean (eds.), *For Roman Jakobson: Essays on the Occasion of His Sixtieth Birthday* (pp. 65–80). The Hague: Mouton.

Collins, J. (1995). Literacy and Literacies. *Annual Review of Anthropology, 24*, 75–93.

Conklin, H. C. (1962). Lexicographical Treatment of Folk Taxonomies. In F. W. Household & S. Saporta (eds.), *Problems in Lexicography*. Bloomington: Indiana University Research Center in Anthropology, Folklore, and Linguistics.

Cook-Gumperz, J. (ed.) (1986). *The Social Construction of Literacy*. Cambridge: Cambridge University Press.

Crystal, D. (1997). *A Dictionary of Linguistics and Phonetics* (4th edn.). Oxford: Blackwell.

Darnell, R. (1990). *Edward Sapir: Linguist, Anthropologist, Humanist*. Berkeley: University of California Press.

Darnell, R. (1998a). *And Along Came Boas: Continuity and Revolution in Americanist Anthropology*. Amsterdam/Philadelphia: John Benjamins.

Darnell, R. (1998b). Camelot at Yale: The Construction and Dismantling of the Sapirian Synthesis, 1931–39. *American Anthropologist, 100*(2), 361–72.

Darnell, R. (1998c). Toward a History of Canadian Departments of Anthropology: Retrospect, Prospect and Common Cause. *Anthropologica, 40*, 153–68.

Dixon, R. M. W. (1972). *The Dyirbal Language of North Queensland*. Cambridge: Cambridge University Press.

Dixon, R. M. W. (1977). *A Grammar of Yidin*. Cambridge: Cambridge University Press.

Dixon, R. M. W., & Aikhenvald, A. Y. (eds.) (1999). *The Amazonian Languages*. Cambridge: Cambridge University Press.

Dorian, N. (1993). A Response to Ladefoged's Other View of Endangered Language. *Language, 69*(3), 575–9.

Dorian, N. C. (1994). Purism vs. Compromise in Language Revitalization and Language Revival. *Language in Society, 23*(4), 479–94.

Drechsel, E. J. (1988). Wilhelm von Humboldt and Edward Sapir: Analogies and Homologies in Their Linguistic Thoughts. In W. Shipley (ed.), *In Honor of Mary Haas: From the Haas Festival Conference on Native American Linguistics* (pp. 225–64). Berlin: Mouton de Gruyter.

Drew, P., & Heritage, J. (eds.) (1992). *Talk at Work*. Cambridge: Cambridge University Press.

Du Bois, J. (1986). Self-Evidence and Ritual Speech. In W. Chafe & J. Nichols (eds.), *Evidentiality: The Linguistic Coding of Epistemology* (pp. 313–36). Norwood, NJ: Ablex.

Du Bois, J. W. (1993). Meaning Without Intention: Lessons from Divination. In J. Hill & J. Irvine (eds.), *Responsibility and Evidence in Oral Discourse* (pp. 48–71). Cambridge: Cambridge University Press.

Duranti, A. (1981). *The Samoan Fono: A Sociolinguistic Study*. Pacific Linguistics Monographs, Series B. Vol. 80. Canberra: Australian National University, Department of Linguistics, Research School of Pacific Studies.

Duranti, A. (1988). Intentions, Language and Social Action in a Samoan Context. *Journal of Pragmatics, 12*, 13–33.

Duranti, A. (1992a). Language and Bodies in Social Space: Samoan Ceremonial Greetings. *American Anthropologist, 94*, 657–91.

Duranti, A. (1992b). Language in Context and Language as Context: The Samoan Respect Vocabulary. In A. Duranti & C. Goodwin (eds.), *Rethinking Context: Language as an Interactive Phenomenon* (pp. 77–99). Cambridge: Cambridge University Press.

Duranti, A. (1993). Intentionality and Truth: An Ethnographic Critique. *Cultural Anthropology*, 8, 214–45.

Duranti, A. (1994). *From Grammar to Politics: Linguistic Anthropology in a Western Samoan Village*. Berkeley and Los Angeles: University of California Press.

Duranti, A. (1997a). Indexical Speech Across Samoan Communities. *American Anthropologist*, 99(2), 342–54.

Duranti, A. (1997b). *Linguistic Anthropology*. Cambridge: Cambridge University Press.

Duranti, A., & Brenneis, D. (1986). The Audience as Co-Author. Special Issue of *Text* (6–3): 239–347.

Duranti, A., & Goodwin, C. (eds.) (1992). *Rethinking Context: Language as an Interactive Phenomenon*. Cambridge: Cambridge University Press.

Duranti, A., & Ochs, E. (1997). Syncretic Literacy in a Samoan American Family. In L. Resnick, R. Säljö, C. Pontecorvo, & B. Burge (eds.), *Discourse, Tools, and Reasoning: Situated Cognition and Technologically Supported Environments* (pp. 169–202). Heidelberg: Springer-Verlag.

Eckert, P., & McConnell-Ginet, S. (1992a). Think Practically and Look Locally: Language and Gender as Community-Based Practice. *Annual Review of Anthropology*, 21, 461–90.

Eckert, P., & McConnell-Ginet, S. (1992b). Communities of Practice: Where Language, Gender, and Power All Live. In K. Hall, M. Bucholtz, & B. Moonwomon (eds.), *Locating Power. Proceedings of the Second Berkeley Women and Language Conference* (Vol. 1, pp. 89–99). Berkeley: Berkeley Women and Language Group, University of California.

Eckert, P., & McConnell-Ginet, S. (1999). New Generalizations and Explanations in Language and Gender Research. *Language in Society*, 28, 185–201.

Errington, J. J. (1998). *Shifting Languages: Interaction and Identity in Javanese Indonesia*. Cambridge: Cambridge University Press.

Ervin-Tripp, S. (1972a). On Sociolinguistic Rules: Alternation and Co-occurrence. In J. J. Gumperz & D. Hymes (eds.), *Directions in Sociolinguistics: The Ethnography of Communication* (pp. 213–50). New York: Holt, Rinehart, and Winston.

Ervin-Tripp, S. (1972b). Sociolinguistic Rules of Address. In J. B. Pride & J. Holmes (eds.), *Sociolinguistics* (pp. 225–40). Harmondsworth: Penguin Books.

Fasold, R. (1990). *The Sociolinguistics of Language*. Oxford: Oxford University Press.

Feld, S. (1982). *Sound and Sentiment: Birds, Weeping, Poetics, and Song in Kaluli Expression*. Philadelphia: University of Pennsylvania Press.

Ferguson, C. (1964). Baby Talk in Six Languages. *American Anthropologist*, 66(6), 103–14.

Ferguson, C. A. (1978). Talking to Children: A Search for Universals. In J. H. Greenberg (ed.), *Universals of Human Language* (pp. 205–24). Stanford: Stanford University Press.

Ferguson, C. A., & Gumperz, J. J. (eds.) (1960). *Linguistic Diversity in South Asia: Studies in Regional, Social and Functional Variation* (Vol. 26). Indiana University Research Center in Anthropology, Folklore, and Linguistics: International Journal of American Linguistics.

Fletcher, P., & MacWhinney, B. (eds.) (1995). *The Handbook of Child Language*. Oxford: Blackwell.

Foley, W. (1986). *The Papuan Languages of New Guinea*. New York: Cambridge University Press.

Foley, W. A. (1997). *Anthropological Linguistics: An Introduction*. Malden, MA: Blackwell.

Ford, C. (1993). *Grammar in Interaction: Adverbial Clauses in American English Conversations*. Cambridge: Cambridge University Press.

Foucault, M. (1979). *Discipline and Punish: The Birth of the Prison*. New York: Random House.

Foucault, M. (1980). *Power/Knowledge: Selected Interviews & Other Writings 1972–1977*. Edited by Colin Gordon; translated by Colin Gordon, Leo Marshall, John Mepham, and Kate Soper. New York: Pantheon.

Foucault, M. (1984). The Birth of the Asylum. In P. Rabinow (ed.), *The Foucault Reader* (pp. 141–68). New York: Pantheon Books.

Frake, C. O. (1969). The Ethnographic Study of Cognitive Systems. In S. A. Tyler (ed.), *Cognitive Anthropology* (pp. 28–41). New York: Holt, Rinehart, and Winston.

Frake, C. O. (1972). "Struck by Speech": The Yakan Concept of Litigation. In J. J. Gumperz & D. Hymes (eds.), *Directions in Sociolinguistics: The Ethnography of Communication* (pp. 106–29). New York: Holt, Rinehart, and Winston.

Friedrich, P. (1966). Structural Implications of Russian Pronominal Usage. In W. Bright (ed.), *Sociolinguistics: Proceedings of the UCLA Sociolinguistics Conference, 1964* (pp. 214–59). The Hague: Mouton & Co.

Friedrich, P. (1986). *The Language Parallax: Linguistic Relativism and Poetic Indeterminacy.* Austin: University of Texas Press.

Gadamer, H.-G. (1976). *Philosophical Hermeneutics.* Translated by David E. Linge. Berkeley: University of California Press.

Gal, S. (1978). Peasant Men Can't Get Wives: Language Change and Sex Roles in a Bilingual Community. *Language in Society,* 7, 1–16.

Gal, S. (1979). *Language Shift. Social Determinants of Linguistic Change in Bilingual Austria.* New York: Academic Press.

Gal, S. (1989). Language and Political Economy. *Annual Review of Anthropology,* 18, 345–67.

Gal, S. (1992). Language, Gender, and Power: An Anthropological Perspective. In K. Hall, M. Bucholtz, & B. Moonwomon (eds.), *Locating Power. Proceedings of the Second Berkeley Women and Language Conference* (Vol. 1, pp. 153–61). Berkeley: Berkeley Women and Language Group, University of California.

Gal, S. (1995). Language, Gender, and Power. An Anthropological Review. In K. Hall & M. Bucholtz (eds.), *Gender Articulated: Language and the Socially Constructed Self* (pp. 169–82). New York: Routledge. [Reprinted in this volume.]

Garfinkel, H. (1972). Remarks on Ethnomethodology. In J. J. Gumperz & D. Hymes (eds.), *Directions in Sociolinguistics: The Ethnography of Communication* (pp. 301–24). New York: Holt, Rinehart, and Winston.

Garvin, P. L., & Riesenberg, S. H. (1952). Respect Behavior in Ponape: An Ethnolinguistic Study. *American Anthropologist,* 54, 201–20.

Gatschet, A. S. (1899). "Real," "True," or "Genuine," in Indian Languages. *American Anthropologist,* 1, 155–61.

Givón, T. (ed.) (1979). *Syntax and Semantics,* Vol. 12, *Discourse and Syntax.* New York: Academic Press.

Givón, T. (1989). *Mind, Code, and Context: Essays in Pragmatics.* Hillsdale, NJ: Lawrence Erlbaum Associates.

Goffman, E. (1959). *The Presentation of Self in Everyday Life.* Garden City, NY: Doubleday.

Goffman, E. (1963). *Behavior in Public Places: Notes on the Social Organization of Gathering.* New York: Free Press.

Goffman, E. (1971). *Relations in Public: Microstudies of the Public Order.* New York: Harper & Row.

Goffman, E. (1981). *Forms of Talk.* Philadelphia: University of Pennsylvania Press.

Goodenough, W. H. (1956). Componential Analysis and the Study of Meaning. *Language,* 32, 195–216.

Goodenough, W. H. (1965). Rethinking "Status" and "Role": Toward a General Model of the Cultural Organization of Social Relationships. In M. Banton (ed.), *The Relevance of Models for Social Anthropology* (pp. 1–24). London: Tavistock.

Goodwin, C. (1979). The Interactive Construction of a Sentence in Natural Conversation. In G. Psathas (ed.), *Everyday Language: Studies in Ethnomethodology* (pp. 97–121). New York: Irvington Publishers.

Goodwin, C. (1981). *Conversational Organization: Interaction Between Speakers and Hearers.* New York: Academic Press.

Goodwin, C. (1986). Audience Diversity, Participation and Interpretation. *Text,* 6(3), 283–316.

Goodwin, C. (1994). Professional Vision. *American Anthropologist,* 96(3), 606–33.

Goodwin, C. (1995). Seeing in Depth. *Social Studies of Science,* 25, 237–74.

Goodwin, C. (1996a). Practices of Color Classification. *Ninchi Kagaku (Cognitive Studies: Bulletin of the Japanese Cognitive Science Society),* 3(2), 62–81.

Goodwin, C. (1996b). Transparent Vision. In E. Ochs, E. A. Schegloff, & S. A. Thompson (eds.), *Interaction and Grammar* (pp. 370–404). Cambridge: Cambridge University Press.

Goodwin, C. (1997). The Blackness of Black: Color Categories as Situated Practice. In L. Resnick, R. Säljö, C. Pontecorvo, & B. Burge (eds.), *Discourse, Tools, and Reasoning: Situated Cognition and Technologically Supported Environments* (pp. 111–40). Heidelberg: Springer-Verlag.

Goodwin, C., & Duranti, A. (1992). Rethinking Context: An Introduction. In A. Duranti & C. Goodwin (eds.), *Rethinking Context: Language as an Interactive Phenomenon* (pp. 1–42). Cambridge: Cambridge University Press.

Goodwin, C., & Goodwin, M. H. (1992). Assessments and the Construction of Context. In A. Duranti & C. Goodwin (eds.), *Rethinking Context: Language as an Interactive Phenomenon* (pp. 147–89). Cambridge: Cambridge University Press.

Goodwin, C., & Heritage, J. (1990). Conversation Analysis. *Annual Reviews of Anthropology, 19*, 283–307.

Goodwin, M. H. (1990a). Byplay: Participant Structure and the Framing of Collaborative Collusion. In B. Conein, M. D. Fornel, & L. Quéré (eds.), *Les Formes de La Conversation* (Vol. 2, pp. 155–80). Paris: CNET.

Goodwin, M. H. (1990b). *He-Said-She-Said: Talk as Social Organization among Black Children.* Bloomington, IN: Indiana University Press.

Goodwin, M. H. (1995). Co-Construction of Girls' Hopscotch. *Research on Language and Social Interaction, 28*, 261–82.

Goodwin, M. H. (1998). Games of Stance: Conflict and Footing in Hopscotch. In S. Hoyle & C. T. Adger (eds.), *Language Practices of Older Children* (pp. 23–46). New York: Oxford University Press.

Goodwin, M. H. (1999). Constructing Opposition within Girls' Games. In M. Bucholtz, A. C. Liang, & L. A. Sutton (eds.), *Reinventing Identities: The Gendered Self in Discourse* (pp. 388–409). New York: Oxford University Press.

Goodwin, M. H., & Goodwin, C. (1987). Children's Arguing. In S. Philips, S. Steele, & C. Tanz (eds.), *Language, Gender, and Sex in Comparative Perspective* (pp. 200–48). Cambridge: Cambridge University Press.

Goodwin, M. H., & Goodwin, C. (2000). Emotion within Situated Activity. In N. Budwig, I. C. Uzgirls, & J. V. Wertsch (eds.), *Communication: An Arena of Development* (pp. 33–53). Stamford, CT: Ablex. [Reprinted in this volume.]

Goody, E. (1972). "Greeting", "begging", and the Presentation of Respect. In J. S. La Fontaine (ed.), *The Interpretation of Ritual* (pp. 39–71). London: Tavistock.

Goody, J., & Watt, I. (1962). The Consequences of Literacy. *Comparative Studies in Society and History, 5*, 304–26.

Goody, J., & Watt, I. (1968). The Consequences of Literacy. In J. Goody (ed.), *Literacy in Traditional Society* (pp. 27–68). Cambridge: Cambridge University Press.

Gopnik, A., Meltzoff, A. N., & Kuhl, P. K. (1999). *The Scientist in the Crib: Minds, Brains, and How Children Learn.* New York: William Morrow.

Graham, L. R. (1995). *Performing Dreams: Discourses of Immortality among the Xavante of Central Brazil.* Austin: University of Texas Press.

Gramsci, A. (1971). *Selections from the Prison Notebooks.* Edited and translated by Quintin Hoare and Geoffrey Nowell Smith. New York: International Publishers.

Gramsci, A. (1975). *Gli intellettuali e l'organizzazione della cultura.* Roma: Editori Riuniti.

Greenberg, J. H. (1968). *Anthropological Linguistics: An Introduction.* New York: Random House.

Grenoble, L. A., & Whaley, L. J. (eds.) (1998). *Endangered Languages: Current Issues and Future Prospects.* Cambridge: Cambridge University Press.

Gumperz, J. J. (1958). Dialect Differences and Social Stratification in a North Indian Village. *American Anthropologist, 60*, 668–82.

Gumperz, J. J. (1964). Linguistic and Social Interaction in Two Communities. *American Anthropologist, 66*(6), 137–53.

Gumperz, J. J. (1968a). The Speech Community. *International Encyclopedia of the Social Sciences* (pp. 381–6). New York: Macmillan. [Reprinted in this volume.]

Gumperz, J. J. (1968b). Types of Linguistic Communities. In J. A. Fishman (ed.), *Readings in the Sociology of Language* (pp. 460–72). The Hague: Mouton.

Gumperz, J. J. (1977). Sociocultural Knowledge in Conversational Inference. In M. Saville-Troike (ed.), *Georgetown University Round Table on Languages and Linguistics 1977.* Washington, D.C.: Georgetown University Press.

Gumperz, J. J. (1982a). *Discourse Strategies.* Cambridge: Cambridge University Press.

Gumperz, J. J. (ed.) (1982b). *Language and Social Identity.* Cambridge: Cambridge University Press.

Gumperz, J. J. (1992). Contextualization and Understanding. In A. Duranti & C. Goodwin (eds.), *Rethinking Context: Language as an Interactive Phenomenon* (pp. 229–52). Cambridge: Cambridge University Press.

Gumperz, J. J., & Hymes, D. (1964). The Ethnography of Communication. *American Anthropologist, 66, 6, part II.*

Gumperz, J. J., & Hymes, D. (1972). *Directions in Sociolinguistics: The Ethnography of Communication.* New York: Holt, Rinehart, and Winston.

Gumperz, J. J., & Levinson, S. (1991). Rethinking Linguistic Relativity. *Current Anthropology, 32,* 613–23.

Gumperz, J. J., & Levinson, S. C. (eds.) (1996). *Rethinking Linguistic Relativity.* Cambridge: Cambridge University Press.

Haas, M. (1953). Sapir and the Training of Anthropological Linguistics. *American Anthropologist, 55,* 447–9.

Haas, M. R. (1977). Anthropological Linguistics: History. In A. F. C. Wallace (ed.), *Perspectives in Anthropology 1976* (pp. 33–47): A Special Publication of the American Anthropological Association.

Haas, M. R. (1978a). The Study of American Indian Languages: A Brief Historical Sketch. In *Language, Culture, and History: Essays by Mary R. Haas.* Selected and Introduced by Anwar S. Dil (pp. 110–29). Stanford, CA: Stanford University Press.

Haas, M. R. (1978b). Boas, Sapir, and Bloomfield: Their Contribution to American Indian Linguistics. In *Language, Culture, and History: Essays by Mary R. Haas.* Selected and Introduced by Anwar S. Dil (pp. 194–206). Stanford, CA: Stanford University Press.

Hale, K., Krauss, M., Watahomigie, L. J., Yamamoto, A. Y., Craig, C., Jeanne, L. M., & England, N. C. (1992). Endangered Languages. *Language, 68*(1), 1–62.

Hall, K., & Bucholtz, M. (eds.) (1995). *Gender Articulated: Language and the Socially Constructed Self.* New York: Routledge.

Hall, K., Bucholtz, M., & Moonwomon, B. (eds.) (1992). *Locating Power. Proceedings of the Second Berkeley Women and Language Conference.* Berkeley: Berkeley Women and Language Group, University of California.

Halliday, M. A. K. (1973). *Explorations in the Functions of Language.* London: Arnold.

Halliday, M. A. K. (1978). *Language and Social Semiotic: The Social Interaction of Language and Meaning.* Baltimore, MA: University Park Press.

Hanks, W. F. (1986). Authenticity and Ambivalence in the Text: A Colonial Maya Case. *American Ethnologist, 13*(4), 721–44.

Hanks, W. F. (1987). Discourse Genres in a Theory of Practice. *American Ethnologist, 14(4),* 668–92.

Hanks, W. F. (1990). *Referential Practice: Language and Lived Space Among the Maya.* Chicago: University of Chicago Press.

Hanks, W. F. (1993). Notes on Semantics in Linguistic Practice. In C. Calhoun, E. LiPuma, & M. Postone (eds.), *Bourdieu: Critical Perspectives* (pp. 139–55). Cambridge: Polity Press.

Hanks, W. F. (1996). *Language and Communicative Practices.* Boulder, CO: Westview.

Haviland, J. B. (1996). Projections, Transpositions, and Relativity. In J. J. Gumperz & S. C. Levinson (eds.), *Rethinking Linguistic Relativity* (pp. 271–323). Cambridge: Cambridge University Press.

Heath, S. B. (1983). *Ways with Words: Language, Life and Work in Communities and Classrooms.* Cambridge: Cambridge University Press.

Henson, H. (1974). *British Social Anthropologists and Language: History of Separate Development.* Oxford: Clarendon Press.

Heritage, J. (1990/91). Intention, Meaning and Strategy: Observations on Constraints on Interaction Analysis. *Research on Language and Social Interaction, 24,* 311–32.

Hill, A. A. (1964). A Note on Primitive Languages. In D. Hymes (ed.), *Language in Culture and Society: A Reader in Linguistic Anthropology* (pp. 86–9). New York: Harper & Row.

Hill, J. H. (1998). Language, Race, and White Public Space. *American Anthropologist, 100,* 680–9. [Reprinted in this volume.]

Hill, J. H., & Hill, K. C. (1986). *Speaking Mexicano: Dynamics of a Syncretic Language in Central Mexico.* Tucson: University of Arizona Press.

Hill, J. H., & Irvine, J. T. (eds.) (1993). *Responsibility and Evidence in Oral Discourse*. Cambridge: Cambridge University Press.

Hill, J. H., & Mannheim, B. (1992). Language and World View. *Annual Review of Anthropology*, *21*, 381–406.

Hoijer, H. (1961). Anthropological Linguistics. In C. Mohrmann, A. Sommerfelt, & J. Whatmough (eds.), *Trends in European and American Linguistics 1930–1960* (pp. 110–25). Utrecht and Antwerp: Spectrum Publishers.

Hopper, P. J., & Thompson, S. A. (1980). Transitivity in Grammar and Discourse. *Language, 56*, 251–99.

Hopper, P. J., & Traugott, E. C. (1993). *Grammaticalization*. Cambridge: Cambridge University Press.

Hudson, R. A. (1980). *Sociolinguistics*. Cambridge: Cambridge University Press.

Hymes, D. (1962). The Ethnography of Speaking. In T. Gladwin & W. C. Sturtevant (eds.), *Anthropology and Human Behavior* (pp. 13–53). Washington, D.C.: Anthropological Society of Washington. (Reprinted in J. A. Fishman (ed.), *Readings in the Sociology of Language*, pp. 99–138. The Hague: Mouton, 1968.)

Hymes, D. (1964a). General Introduction. In D. Hymes (ed.), *Language in Culture and Society: A Reader in Linguistics and Anthropology* (pp. xxi–xxxii). New York: Harper & Row.

Hymes, D. (1964b). Introduction to Part I. In D. Hymes (ed.), *Language in Culture and Society: A Reader in Linguistic Anthropology* (pp. 3–14). New York: Harper & Row.

Hymes, D. (1964c). Introduction: Toward Ethnographies of Communication. In J. J. Gumperz & D. Hymes (eds.), *The Ethnography of Communication* (pp. 1–34). Washington, D.C.: American Anthropologist (Special Issue).

Hymes, D. (ed.) (1964d). *Language in Culture and Society: A Reader in Linguistic Anthropology*. New York: Harper & Row.

Hymes, D. (1966). Two Types of Linguistic Relativity. In W. Bright (ed.), *Sociolinguistics* (pp. 114–67). The Hague: Mouton.

Hymes, D. (ed.) (1971a). *Pidginization and Creolization of Languages*. Cambridge: Cambridge University Press.

Hymes, D. (1971b). Sociolinguistics and the Ethnography of Speaking. In E. Ardener (ed.), *Social Anthropology and Language* (pp. 47–93). London: Tavistock.

Hymes, D. (1972a). Models of the Interaction of Language and Social Life. In J. J. Gumperz & D. Hymes (eds.), *Directions in Sociolinguistics: The Ethnography of Communication* (pp. 35–71). New York: Holt, Rinehart, and Winston.

Hymes, D. (1972b). On Communicative Competence. In J. B. Pride & J. Holmes (eds.), *Sociolinguistics* (pp. 269–93). Harmondsworth: Penguin. [Reprinted in this volume.]

Hymes, D. (1974a). *Foundations in Sociolinguistics: An Ethnographic Approach*. Philadelphia: University of Pennsylvania Press.

Hymes, D. (1974b). Ways of Speaking. In R. Bauman & J. Sherzer (eds.), *Explorations in the Ethnography of Speaking* (pp. 433–51). Cambridge: Cambridge University Press.

Hymes, D. (1975). Breakthrough into Performance. In D. Ben-Amos & K. S. Goldstein (eds.), *Folklore: Performance and Communication* (pp. 11–74). The Hague: Mouton.

Hymes, D. (1981). *"In Vain I Tried to Tell You": Essays in Native American Ethnopoetics*. Philadelphia: University of Pennsylvania Press.

Hymes, D. (1996). *Ethnography, Linguistics, Narrative Inequality*. Bristol, PA: Taylor & Francis.

Hymes, D. (1999). Boas on the Threshold of Ethnopoetics. In L. P. Valentine & R. Darnell (eds.), *Theorizing the Americanist Tradition* (pp. 84–107). Toronto: University of Toronto Press.

Irvine, J. T. (1974). Strategies of Status Manipulation in Wolof Greeting. In R. Bauman & J. Sherzer (eds.), *Explorations in the Ethnography of Speaking* (pp. 167–91). Cambridge: Cambridge University Press.

Irvine, J. T. (1979). Formality and Informality in Communicative Events. *American Anthropologist*, *81*(4), 773–90. [Reprinted in this volume.]

Jakobson, R. (1944). Franz Boas' Approach to Language. *International Journal of American Linguistics*, *10*, 188–95.

Johnstone, B. (1996). *The Linguistic Individual: Self-Expression in Language and Linguistics*. New York: Oxford University Press.

Jupp, T. C., Roberts, C., & Cook-Gumperz, J. (1982). Language and the Disadvantage: The Hidden Process. In J. J. Gumperz (ed.), *Language and Social Identity* (pp. 232–56). Cambridge: Cambridge University Press.

Kay, P., & Maffi, L. (2000). Color Appearance and the Emergence and Evolution of Basic Color Lexicons. *American Anthropologist, 101*, 743–60.

Keane, W. (1997). *Signs of Recognition: Powers and Hazards of Representation in an Indonesian Society.* Berkeley: University of California Press.

Keating, E. (1998). *Power Sharing: Language, Rank, Gender and Social Space in Pohnpei, Micronesia.* Oxford: Oxford University Press.

Keenan, E. O. (1974). Conversation and Oratory in Vaninankaratra Madagascar. Unpublished Ph.D. dissertation, University of Pennsylvania.

Keil, C., & Feld, S. (1994). *Music Grooves.* Chicago: University of Chicago Press.

Kingten, E. R., Kroll, B. M., & Rose, M. (eds.) (1988). *Perspectives on Literacy.* Carbondale and Edwardsville: Southern Illinois University Press.

Kirch, P. V. (1984). *The Evolution of Polynesian Chiefdoms.* Cambridge: Cambridge University Press.

Koerner, E. F. K. (1992). The Sapir–Whorf Hypothesis: A Preliminary History and a Bibliographical Essay. *Journal of Linguistic Anthropology, 2*(2), 173–98.

Kroeber, A. L. (1905). Systematic Nomenclature in Ethnology. *American Anthropologist, 7*, 579–93.

Kroskrity, P. V. (1993). *Language, History, and Identity: Ethnolinguistic Studies of the Arizona Tewa.* Tucson: University of Arizona Press.

Kroskrity, P. V. (1998). Arizona Tewa Kiva Speech as a Manifestation of a Dominant Language Ideology. In B. B. Schieffelin, K. Woolard, & P. Kroskrity (eds.), *Language Ideologies* (pp. 103–22). New York: Oxford University Press.

Kroskrity, P. V. (2000a). Regimenting Languages: Language Ideological Perspectives. In P. V. Kroskrity (ed.), *Regimes of Language: Ideologies, Politics and Identities* (pp. 1–34). Santa Fe, NM: School of American Research Press.

Kroskrity, P. V. (ed.) (2000b). *Regimes of Language: Ideologies, Politics and Identities.* Santa Fe, NM: School of American Research Press.

Kuipers, J. C. (1990). *Power in Performance: The Creation of Textual Authority in Weyewa Ritual Speech.* Philadelphia: University of Pennsylvania Press.

Kuipers, J. C. (1998). *Language, Identity, and Marginality in Indonesia: The Changing Nature of Ritual Speech on the Island of Sumba.* Cambridge: Cambridge University Press.

Kulick, D. (1992). *Language Shift and Cultural Reproduction: Socialization, Self, and Syncretism in a Papua New Guinean Village.* Cambridge: Cambridge University Press.

Labov, W. (1966a). Hypercorrection by the Lower Middle Class as a Factor in Linguistic Change. In W. Bright (ed.), *Sociolinguistics* (pp. 84–113). The Hague: Mouton.

Labov, W. (1966b). *The Social Stratification of English in New York City.* Arlington: Center for Applied Linguistics.

Labov, W. (1969). The Logic of Nonstandard English. In J. Alatis (ed.), *Georgetown Monographs on Language and Linguistics* (Vol. 22, pp. 1–44). Washington, D.C.: Georgetown University Press.

Labov, W. (1970). *The Study of Nonstandard English.* Champaign, IL: National Council of Teachers.

Labov, W. (1972a). *Language in the Inner City: Studies in the Black English Vernacular.* Philadelphia: University of Pennsylvania Press.

Labov, W. (1972b). On Mechanism of Linguistic Change. In J. J. Gumperz & D. Hymes (eds.), *Directions in Sociolinguistics: The Ethnography of Communication* (pp. 512–38). New York: Holt, Rinehart, and Winston.

Labov, W. (1972c). *Sociolinguistic Patterns.* Philadelphia: University of Pennsylvania Press.

Labov, W., & Waletzky, J. (1966). Narrative Analysis: Oral Version of Personal Experience. In J. Helm (ed.), *Essays on the Verbal and Visual Arts: Proceedings of the 1996 Annual Spring Meeting of the American Ethnological Society* (pp. 12–44). Seattle: University of Washington Press.

Lakoff, G. (1987). *Women, Fire, and Dangerous Things: What Categories Reveal About the Mind.* Chicago: Chicago University Press.

Lakoff, G., & Johnson, M. (1980). *Metaphors We Live By*. Chicago: Chicago University Press.

Lakoff, R. (1973). Language and Women's Place. *Language in Society*, 2, 45–80.

Lave, J. (1988). *Cognition in Practice*. Cambridge: Cambridge University Press.

Lave, J. (1990). The Culture of Acquisition and the Practice of Understanding. In J. W. Stigler, R. A. Shweder, & G. Herdt (eds.), *Cultural Psychology: Essays on Comparative Human Development* (pp. 309–27). Cambridge: Cambridge University Press.

Lave, J., & Wenger, E. (1991). *Situated Learning: Legitimate Peripheral Participation*. Cambridge: Cambridge University Press.

Lee, B. (1997). *Talking Heads: Language, Metalanguage, and the Semiotics of Subjectivity*. Durham, NC: Duke University Press.

Lee, D. (1944). Linguistic Reflection of Wintu Thought. *International Journal of American Linguistics*, 10, 181–7.

Lee, P. (1991). Whorf's Hopi Tensors: Subtle Articulation in the Language/Thought Nexus? *Cognitive Linguistics*, 2(2), 123–47.

Lee, P. (1996). *The Whorf Theory Complex: A Critical Reconstruction*. Amsterdam: John Benjamins.

Lévi-Strauss, C. (1966). *The Savage Mind*. Chicago: Chicago University Press.

Levinson, S. C. (1983). *Pragmatics*. Cambridge: Cambridge University Press.

Levinson, S. C. (1992). Primer for the Field Investigation of Spatial Description and Conception. *Pragmatics*, 2(1), 5–47.

Levinson, S. C. (1996). Relativity in Spatial Conception and Description. In J. J. Gumperz & S. C. Levinson (eds.), *Rethinking Linguistic Relativity* (pp. 177–202). Cambridge: Cambridge University Press.

Levinson, S. C. (1997). Language and Cognition: The Cognitive Consequences of Spatial Description in Guugu Yimithirr. *Journal of Linguistic Anthropology*, 7(1), 98–131.

Levinson, S. C. (2000). Yelî Dnye and the Theory of Basic Color Terms. *Journal of Linguistic Anthropology*, 10(1).

Lounsbury, F. G. (1969). The Structural Analysis of Kinship Semantics. In S. A. Tyler (ed.), *Cognitive Anthropology* (pp. 193–212). New York: Holt, Rinehart, and Winston.

Lucy, J. A. (1992a). *Grammatical Categories and Cognition: A Case Study of the Linguistic Relativity Hypothesis*. Cambridge: Cambridge University Press.

Lucy, J. A. (1992b). *Language Diversity and Cognitive Development: A Reformulation of the Linguistic Relativity Hypothesis*. Cambridge: Cambridge University Press.

Lucy, J. A. (ed.) (1993). *Reflexive Language: Reported Speech and Metapragmatics*. New York: Cambridge University Press.

Lucy, J. A., & Shweder, R. A. (1979). Whorf and His Critics: Linguistic and Nonlinguistic Influences on Color Memory. *American Anthropologist*, 81, 581–615.

Malinowski, B. (1920). Classificatory Particles in the Language of Kiriwina. *Bulletin of the School of Oriental and African Studies*, 1, 33–78.

Malotki, E. (1983). *Hopi Time: A Linguistic Analysis of the Temporal Concepts in the Hopi Language*. Berlin: Mouton.

Maltz, D. N., & Borker, R. A. (1982). A Cultural Approach to Male-Female Miscommunication. In J. J. Gumperz (ed.), *Language and Social Identity* (pp. 196–216). Cambridge: Cambridge University Press.

Mandelbaum, J. (1987a). Couples Sharing Stories. *Communication Quarterly*, 35(4), 144–71.

Mandelbaum, J. (1987b). Recipient-driven Storytelling in Conversation. Unpublished Ph.D. dissertation, The University of Texas at Austin.

Mandelbaum, J. (1989). Interpersonal Activities in Conversational Storytelling. *Western Journal of Speech Communication*, 53(2), 114–26.

Mannheim, B. (1991). *The Language of the Inka since the European Invasion*. Austin: University of Texas Press.

Martin, L. (1986). Eskimo Words for Snow: A Case Study in the Genesis and Decay of an Anthropological Example. *American Anthropologist*, 88, 418–23.

Mason, O. T. (1900). The Linguistic Families of Mexico. *American Anthropologist*, 2, 63–5.

McConvell, P., & Evans, N. (eds.) (1997). *Archaeology and Linguistics: Aboriginal Australia and Global Perspective*. Melbourne: Oxford University Press.

McTear, M. (1985). *Children's Conversation*. Oxford: Basil Blackwell.

Mendoza-Denton, N. (1996). "Muy Macha": Gender and Ideology in Gang-Girls' Discourse about Makeup. *Ethnos, 1–2*, 47–63.

Mendoza-Denton, N. (1999). Sociolinguistics and Linguistic Anthropology. *Annual Review of Anthropology, 28*, 375–95.

Merlan, F., & Rumsay, A. (1991). *Ku Waru: Language and Segmentary Politics in the Western Nebilyer Valley, Papua New Guinea*. Cambridge: Cambridge University Press.

Mertz, E. (1996). Consensus and Dissent in U.S. Legal Opinions: Narrative Structure and Social Voices. In C. L. Briggs (ed.), *Disorderly Discourse: Narrative, Conflict, and Inequality* (pp. 135–57). New York: Oxford University Press.

Milroy, L. (1987). *Language and Social Networks* (2nd edn.). Oxford: Blackwell.

Milroy, L., & Milroy, J. (1992). Social Network and Social Class: Toward an Integrated Sociolinguistic Model. *Language in Society, 21*, 1–26.

Moerman, M. M. (1988). *Talking Culture: Ethnography and Conversation Analysis*. Philadelphia: University of Pennsylvania Press.

Morgan, M. M. (1994a). The African-American Speech Community: Reality and Sociolinguists. In M. M. Morgan (ed.), *Language and the Social Construction of Identity in Creole Situations* (pp. 121–48). Los Angeles: Center for Afro-American Studies, UCLA. [Reprinted in this volume.]

Morgan, M. M. (1994b). Theories and Politics in African American English. *Annual Review of Anthropology, 23*, 325–45.

Murray, S. O. (1993). *Theory Groups and the Study of Language in North America*. Amsterdam and Philadelphia: John Benjamins.

Murray, S. O. (1998). *American Sociolinguistics: Theorists and Theory Groups*. Amsterdam and Philadelphia: John Benjamins.

Newmeyer, F. J. (1980). *Linguistic Theory in America: The First Quarter Century of Transformational Generative Grammar*. New York: Academic Press.

Newmeyer, F. J. (1986). Has There Been a "Chomskian Revolution" in Linguistics? *Language, 62*(1), 1–18.

Newport, E. (1976). Motherese: The Speech of Mothers to Young Children. In N. J. Castellan, D. B. Pisoni, & G. R. Potts (eds.), *Cognitive Theory* (Vol. 2). Hillsdale, NJ: Lawrence Erlbaum.

Nichols, J. (1992). *Linguistic Diversity in Space and Time*. Chicago: University of Chicago Press.

Nichols, J. (1995a). Diachronically Stable Structural Features. In H. Anderson (ed.), *Historical Linguistics 1993: Selected Papers from the 11th International Congress of Historical Linguists, Los Angeles, 16–20 August, 1993* (pp. 337–55). Amsterdam: John Benjamins.

Nichols, J. (1995b). The Spread of Language around the Pacific Rim. *Evolutionary Anthropology, 3*, 206–15.

Nichols, J., & Peterson, D. A. (1996). The Amerind Personal Pronouns. *Language, 72*(2), 336–71.

Nuckolls, J. B. (1996). *Sounds like Life: Sound-symbolic Grammar, Performance, and Cognition in Pastaza Quechua*. Oxford: Oxford University Press.

Ochs, E. (1988). *Culture and Language Development: Language Acquisition and Language Socialization in a Samoan Village*. Cambridge: Cambridge University Press.

Ochs, E. (1992). Indexing Gender. In A. Duranti & C. Goodwin (eds.), *Rethinking Context: Language as an Interactive Phenomenon* (pp. 335–58). Cambridge: Cambridge University Press.

Ochs, E. (1996). Linguistic Resources for Socializing Humanity. In J. J. Gumperz & S. C. Levinson (eds.), *Rethinking Linguistic Relativity* (pp. 407–37). Cambridge: Cambridge University Press.

Ochs, E. (1997). Narrative. In T. van Dijk (ed.), *Discourse as Structure and Process* (pp. 185–207). London: Sage.

Ochs, E., & Capps, L. (1996). Narrating the Self. *Annual Review of Anthropology, 25*, 19–43.

Ochs, E., Gonzales, P., & Jacoby, S. (1996). "When I Come Down I'm in the Domain State": Grammar and Graphic Representation in the Interpretive Activity of Physicists. In E. Ochs, E. A. Schegloff, & S. A. Thompson (eds.), *Interaction and Grammar* (pp. 328–69). Cambridge: Cambridge University Press.

Ochs, E., Jacoby, S., & Gonzales, P. (1994). Interpretive Journeys: How Physicists Talk and Travel through Graphic Space. *Configurations, 2*(1), 151–71.

Ochs, E., Schegloff, E. A., & Thompson, S. A. (eds.) (1996). *Interaction and Grammar*. Cambridge: Cambridge University Press.

Ochs, E., & Schieffelin, B. B. (1979). *Developmental Pragmatics*. New York: Academic Press.

Ochs, E., & Schieffelin, B. B. (1983). *Acquiring Conversational Competence*. Boston: Routledge & Kegan Paul.

Ochs, E., & Schieffelin, B. B. (1984). Language Acquisition and Socialization: Three Developmental Stories and Their Implications. In R. A. Shweder & R. A. LeVine (eds.), *Culture Theory: Essays on Mind, Self, and Emotion* (pp. 276–320). Cambridge: Cambridge University Press. [Reprinted in this volume.]

Ochs, E., & Schieffelin, B. B. (1995). The Impact of Language Socialization on Grammatical Development. In P. Fletcher & B. MacWhinney (eds.), *The Handbook of Child Language* (pp. 73–94). Oxford: Blackwell.

Olson, D. R., & Torrance, N. (eds.) (1991). *Literacy and Orality*. Cambridge: Cambridge University Press.

Palmer, G. B. (1996). *Toward a Theory of Cultural Linguistics*. Austin: University of Texas Press.

Palmer, G. B., & Jankowiak, W. R. (1996). Performance and Imagination: Toward an Anthropology of the Spectacular and the Mundane. *Cultural Anthropology*, 11(2), 225–58.

Philips, S. U. (1998). Language Ideologies in Institutions of Power. In B. B. Schieffelin, K. Woolard, & P. Kroskrity (eds.), *Language Ideologies* (pp. 211–25). New York: Oxford University Press.

Platt, M. (1982). Social and Semantic Dimensions of Deictic Verbs and Particles in Samoan Child Language. University of Southern California, unpublished Ph.D. dissertation.

Powell, J. W. (1880). *Introduction to the Study of Indian Languages, 2nd edition*. Washington, D.C.

Rampton, B. (1995a). *Crossing: Language and Ethnicity among Adolescents*. London: Longman.

Rampton, B. (1995b). Language Crossing and the Problematisation of Ethnicity and Socialisation. *Pragmatics*, 5(4), 485–515.

Rickford, J. R. (1997). Unequal Partnership: Sociolinguistics and the African American Speech Community. *Language in Society*, 26(2), 161–98.

Rickford, J. R. (1999). *African American Vernacular English*. Malden, MA: Blackwell.

Ricoeur, P. (1981). *Hermeneutics and the Human Sciences*. Cambridge: Cambridge University Press.

Rogoff, B. (1990). *Apprenticeship in Thinking*. New York: Oxford University Press.

Rogoff, B., & Lave, J. (1984). *Everyday Cognition: Its Development in Social Context*. Cambridge, MA: Harvard University Press.

Romaine, S. (1982). *Sociolinguistic Variation in Speech Communities*. New York: Edward Arnold.

Romaine, S. (1995). *Bilingualism* (2nd edn.). Oxford: Blackwell.

Rosen, L. (ed.) (1995). *Other Intentions*. Santa Fe, NM: School of American Research.

Salmon, V. (1986). Effort and Achievement in Seventeenth-Century British Linguistics. In T. Bynon & F. R. Palmer (eds.), *Studies in the History of Western Linguistics* (pp. 69–95). Cambridge: Cambridge University Press.

Salzmann, Z. (1993). *Language, Culture, and Society: An Introduction to Linguistic Anthropology*. Boulder, CO: Westview.

Sankoff, G. (1980). *The Social Life of Language*. Philadelphia: University of Pennsylvania Press.

Sapir, D. (1985). Introducing Edward Sapir. *Language in Society*, 14(3), 289–97.

Sapir, E. (1921). *Language*. New York: Harcourt, Brace & World.

Sapir, E. (1927). The Unconscious Patterning of Behavior in Society. In E. S. Dummer (ed.), *The Unconscious: A Symposium* (pp. 114–42). New York: Knopf.

Sapir, E. (1929). Male and Female Forms of Speech in Yana. In S. W. J. Teeuwen (ed.), *Donum Natalicium Schrijnen* (pp. 79–85). Nijmegen-Utrecht.

Sapir, E. (1933). Language. *Encyclopaedia of the Social Sciences* (pp. 155–69). New York: Macmillan.

Sapir, E. (1949a). Language. In D. G. Mandelbaum (ed.), *Selected Writings of Edward Sapir in Language, Culture and Personality* (pp. 7–32). Berkeley and Los Angeles: University of California Press.

Sapir, E. (1949b). The Unconscious Patterning of Behavior in Society. In D. G. Mandelbaum (ed.), *Selected Writings of Edward Sapir in Language, Culture and Personality* (pp. 544–59). Berkeley and Los Angeles: University of California Press.

Sapir, E. (1964). Conceptual Categories in Primitive Languages. In D. Hymes (ed.), *Language in Culture and Society* (p. 128). New York: Harper & Row.

Sapir, E. (1994). *The Psychology of Culture: A Course of Lectures*. Reconstructed and edited by Judith T. Irvine. Berlin: Mouton de Gruyter.

Sapir, J. D., & Crocker, J. C. (eds.) (1977). *The Social Uses of Metaphor*. Philadelphia: University of Pennsylvania Press.

Schaff, A. (1973). *Language and Cognition*. Translated by Olgierd Wojtasiewicz. New York: McGraw-Hill.

Schegloff, E. A. (1972). Sequencing in Conversational Openings. In J. J. Gumperz & D. Hymes (eds.), *Directions in Sociolinguistics: The Ethnography of Communication* (pp. 346–80). New York: Holt, Rinehart, and Winston.

Schegloff, E. A. (1986). The Routine as Achievement. *Human Studies*, *9*, 111–51.

Schieffelin, B. B. (1979a). Getting It Together: An Ethnographic Approach to the Study of the Development of Communicative Competence. In E. Ochs & B. B. Schieffelin (eds.), *Developmental Pragmatics* (pp. 73–110). New York: Academic Press.

Schieffelin, B. B. (1979b). How Kaluli Children Learn What to Say, What to Do, and How to Feel: An Ethnographic Study of the Development of Communcative Competence. Unpublished Ph.D. dissertation, Columbia University.

Schieffelin, B. B. (1990). *The Give and Take of Everyday Life: Language Socialization of Kaluli Children*. Cambridge: Cambridge University Press.

Schieffelin, B. B., & Ochs, E. (1986). Language Socialization. In B. J. Siegel, A. R. Beals, & S. A. Tyler (eds.), *Annual Review of Anthropology* (pp. 163–246). Palo Alto: Annual Reviews, Inc.

Schieffelin, B. B., Woolard, K., & Kroskrity, P. (eds.) (1998). *Language Ideologies: Practice and Theory*. New York: Oxford University Press.

Schiffrin, D. (1987). *Discourse Markers*. Cambridge: Cambridge University Press.

Schiffrin, D. (1994). *Approaches to Discourse*. Oxford: Blackwell.

Schlegel, J. (1998). Finding Words, Finding Meanings: Collaborative Learning and Distributed Cognition. In S. M. Hoyle & C. T. Adger (eds.), *Kids Talk: Strategic Language Use in Later Childhood* (pp. 187–204). New York: Oxford University Press.

Scribner, S. (1984). Studying Working Intelligence. In B. Rogoff & J. Lave (eds.), *Everyday Cognition: Its Development in Social Context* (pp. 9–40). Cambridge, MA: Harvard University Press.

Scribner, S., & Cole, M. (1981). *Psychology of Literacy*. Cambridge, MA: Harvard University Press.

Searle, J. R. (1965). What is a Speech Act? In M. Black (ed.), *Philosophy in America* (pp. 221–39). London: George Allen & Unwin.

Searle, J. R. (1969). *Speech Acts: An Essay in the Philosophy of Language*. Cambridge: Cambridge University Press.

Sherzer, J. (1983). *Kuna Ways of Speaking: An Ethnographic Perspective*. Austin: University of Texas Press.

Sherzer, J. (1990). *Verbal Art in San Blas: Kuna Culture through its Discourse*. Cambridge: Cambridge University Press.

Sherzer, J., & Darnell, R. (1972). Outline Guide for the Ethnographic Study of Speech Use. In J. J. Gumperz & D. Hymes (eds.), *Directions in Sociolinguistics: The Ethnography of Communication* (pp. 548–54). New York: Holt, Rinehart, and Winston.

Sidnell, J. (1997). Organizing Social and Spatial Location: Elicitations in Indo-Guyanese Village Talk. *Journal of Linguistic Anthropology*, *7*(2), 143–65.

Silverstein, M. (1976). Shifters, Linguistic Categories, and Cultural Description. In K. H. Basso & H. A. Selby (eds.), *Meaning in Anthropology* (pp. 11–56). Albuquerque: University of New Mexico Press.

Silverstein, M. (1977). Cultural Prerequisites to Grammatical Analysis. In M. Saville-Troike (ed.), *Linguistics and Anthropology: Georgetown University Round Table on Languages and Linguistics 1977* (pp. 139–51). Washington, D.C.: Georgetown University Press.

Silverstein, M. (1979). Language Structure and Linguistic Ideology. In P. R. Clyne, W. F. Hanks, & C. L. Hofbauer (eds.), *The Elements: A Parasession on Linguistic Units and Levels* (pp. 193–247). Chicago: Chicago Linguistic Society.

Silverstein, M. (1981). *The Limits of Awareness. Sociolinguistic Working Paper No. 84.* Austin: Southwest Educational Development Laboratory. [Reprinted in this volume.]

Silverstein, M. (1984). On the Pragmatic "Poetry" of Prose: Parallelism, Repetition, and Cohesive Structure in the Time Course of Dyadic Conversation. In D. Schiffrin (ed.), *Meaning, Form, and Use in Context: Linguistic Applications* (pp. 181–99). Washington, D.C.: Georgetown University Press.

Silverstein, M. (1996a). Encountering Language and Languages of Encounter in North American Ethnohistory. *Journal of Linguistic Anthropology, 6*(2), 126–44.

Silverstein, M. (1996b). Monoglot "Standard" in America: Standardization and Metaphors of Linguistic Hegemony. In D. Brenneis & R. H. S. Macaulay (eds.), *The Matrix of Language: Contemporary Linguistic Anthropology* (pp. 284–306). Boulder, CO: Westview.

Silverstein, M. (1997). The Improvisational Performance of Culture in Realtime Discursive Practice. In R. K. Sawyer (ed.), *Creativity in Performance* (pp. 265–312). Greenwich, CT: Ablex.

Silverstein, M., & Urban, G. (eds.) (1996). *Natural Histories of Discourse.* Chicago: University of Chicago Press.

Slobin, D. I. (ed.) (1967). *A Field Manual for Cross-Cultural Study of the Acquisition of Communicative Competence.* Berkeley: Language Behavior Research Laboratory, University of California.

Slobin, D. I. (1973). Cognitive Prerequisites for the Development of Grammar. In C. A. Ferguson & D. I. Slobin (eds.), *Studies of Child Language Development* (pp. 175–208). New York: Holt, Rinehart, and Winston.

Slobin, D. I. (1982). Universal and Particular in the Acquisition of Language. In W. Deutsch (ed.), *Language Acquisition: The State of the Art* (pp. 128–72). Cambridge: Cambridge University Press.

Slobin, D. I. (1985a). The Crosslinguistic Evidence for the Language-making Capacity. In D. I. Slobin (ed.), *The Crosslinguistic Study of Language Acquisition,* Vol. 2: *Theoretical Issues* (pp. 1157–256). Hillsdale, NJ: Lawrence Erlbaum.

Slobin, D. I. (ed.) (1985b). *The Crosslinguistic Study of Language Acquisition* (Vol. 1). Hillsdale, NJ: Lawrence Erlbaum.

Spears, A. K. (ed.) (1999). *Race and Ideology: Language, Symbolism, and Popular Culture.* Detroit: Wayne State University Press.

Spitulnik, D. (1998a). Anthropology and Mass Media. *Annual Review of Anthropology, 22,* 293–315.

Spitulnik, D. (1998b). The Language of the City: Town Bemba as Urban Hybridity. *Journal of Linguistic Anthropology, 8*(1), 30–59.

Spitulnik, D. (1999). Mediated Modernities: Encounters with the Electronic in Zambia. *Visual Anthropology Review, 14*(2), 63–84.

Stocking, G. W. (1974). The Boas Plan for the Study of American Indian Languages. In D. Hymes (ed.), *Studies in the History of Linguistics: Traditions and Paradigms* (pp. 454–83). Bloomington: Indiana University Press.

Streeck, J. (1980). Speech Acts in Interaction: A Critique of Searle. *Discourse Processes, 3,* 133–54.

Streeck, J. (1994). Gesture as Communication II: The Audience as Co-author. *Research on Language and Social Interaction, 27,* 239–67.

Streeck, J., & Hartge, U. (1992). Previews: Gestures at the Transition Place. In P. Auer & A. di Luzio (eds.), *Contextualization of Language* (pp. 135–58). Amsterdam: John Benjamins.

Street, B. V. (1984). *Literacy in Theory and Practice.* Cambridge: Cambridge University Press.

Street, B. V. (ed.) (1993). *Cross-Cultural Approaches to Literacy.* Cambridge: Cambridge University Press.

Street, B. V., & Besnier, N. (1994). Aspects of Literacy. In T. Ingold (ed.), *Companion Encyclopedia of Anthropology: Humanity, Culture, and Social Life* (pp. 527–62). London: Routledge.

Stubbs, M. (1983). *Discourse Analysis.* Oxford: Blackwell.

Swanton, J. R. (1900). Morphology of the Chinook Verb. *American Anthropologist, 2*(2), 199–237.

Tannen, D. (ed.) (1982). *Spoken and Written Language: Exploring Orality and Literacy.* Norwood, NJ: Ablex.

Tannen, D. (1989). *Talking Voices: Repetition, Dialogue, and Imagery in Conversational Discourse.* Cambridge: Cambridge University Press.

Tannen, D. (1990). *You Just Don't Understand: Women and Men in Conversation*. New York: William Morrow and Co.

Tedlock, D. (1983). *The Spoken Word and the Work of Interpretation*. Philadelphia: University of Pennsylvania Press.

Teeter, K. V. (1964). "Anthropological Linguistics" and Linguistic Anthropology. *American Anthropologist*, 66, 878–9.

Trudgill, P. (1986). *Dialects in Contact*. Oxford: Blackwell.

Tyler, S. A. (1972). Context and Alternation in Koya Kinship Terminology. In J. J. Gumperz & D. Hymes (eds.), *Directions in Sociolinguistics: The Ethnography of Communication* (pp. 251–69). New York: Holt, Rinehart, and Winston.

Urciuoli, B. (1991). *Exposing Prejudice: Puerto Rican Experiences of Language, Race, and Class*. Boulder, CO: Westview.

Voegelin, C. F. (1952). The Boas Plan for the Presentation of American Indian Languages. *Proceedings of the American Philosophical Society*, 96, 439–51.

Voegelin, C. F., & Harris, Z. S. (1945). Linguistics in Ethnology. *Southwestern Journal of Anthropology*, 1, 455–65.

Voegelin, C. F., & Harris, Z. S. (1952). Training in Anthropological Linguistics. *American Anthropologist*, 54, 322–7.

Vološinov, V. N. (1973). *Marxism and the Philosophy of Language*. Translated by Ladislav Matejka and I. R. Titunik. New York: Seminar Press. (First published 1929 and 1930.)

von Humboldt, W. ([1836] 1971). *Linguistic Variability and Intellectual Development*. Translated by George C. Buck and Frithjof A. Raven. Philadelphia: University of Pennsylvania Press.

Wardhaugh, R. (1986). *An Introduction to Sociolinguistics*. Oxford: Blackwell.

West, C., & Zimmerman, D. H. (1983). Small Insults: A Study of Interruptions in Cross-Sex Conversation between Unacquainted Persons. In B. Thorne, C. Kramarae, & N. Henley (eds.), *Language, Gender and Society* (pp. 102–17). Rowley, MA: Newbury House.

Whorf, B. L. (1938). Some Verbal Categories of Hopi. *Language*, 14, 275–86.

Whorf, B. L. (1941). The Relation of Habitual Thought and Behavior in Language. In L. Spier, A. I. Hallowell, & S. S. Newman (eds.), *Language, Culture, and Personality: Essays in Honor of Edward Sapir* (pp. 75–93). Menasha, WI: Sapir Memorial Publication.

Whorf, B. L. (1956a). Grammatical Categories. In J. B. Carroll (ed.), *Language, Thought, and Reality: Selected Writings of Benjamin Lee Whorf* (pp. 87–101). Cambridge, MA: MIT Press.

Whorf, B. L. (1956b). Linguistics as an Exact Science. In J. B. Carroll (ed.), *Language, Thought, and Reality: Selected Writings of Benjamin Lee Whorf* (pp. 220–32). Cambridge, MA: MIT Press.

Whorf, B. L. (1956c). The Relation of Habitual Thought and Behavior to Language. In J. B. Carroll (ed.), *Language, Thought, and Reality: Selected Writings of Benjamin Lee Whorf* (pp. 134–59). Cambridge, MA: MIT Press.

Wilce, J. M. (1998). *Eloquence in Trouble: The Poetics and Politics of Complaint in Rural Bangladesh*. New York: Oxford University Press.

Williams, R. (1977). *Marxism and Literature*. Oxford: Oxford University Press.

Wodak, R., & Reisigl, M. (1999). Discourse and Racism: European Perspectives. *Annual Review of Anthropology*, 28, 175–99.

Woolard, K. A. (1985). Language Variation and Cultural Hegemony: Toward an Integration of Sociolinguistic and Social Theory. *American Ethnologist*, 12, 738–48.

Woolard, K. A. (1989). *Double Talk: Bilingualism and the Politics of Ethnicity in Catalonia*. Stanford, CA: Stanford University Press.

Woolard, K. A. (1998). Simultaneity and Bivalency as Strategies in Bilingualism. *Journal of Linguistic Anthropology*, 8(1), 3–29.

Woolard, K. A. & Schieffelin, B. B. (1994). Language Ideology. *Annual Review of Anthropology*, 23, 55–82.

Yankah, K. (1995). *Speaking for the Chief: Okeyame and the Politics of Akan Royal Oratory*. Bloomington: Indiana University Press.

Zack, N., Shrage, L., & Sartwell, C. (eds.) (1998). *Race, Class, Gender, and Sexuality: The Big Questions*. Malden, MA: Blackwell.

Zentella, A. C. (1997). *Growing Up Bilingual: Puerto Rican Children in New York*. Oxford: Blackwell.

Index